8137

P9-EEL-713

36: *British Novelists, 1890-1929: Modernists,* edited by Thomas F. Staley (1985)

37: *American Writers of the Early Republic,* edited by Emory Elliott (1985)

38: *Afro-American Writers After 1955: Dramatists and Prose Writers,* edited by Thadious M. Davis and Trudier Harris (1985)

39: *British Novelists, 1660-1800,* 2 parts, edited by Martin C. Battestin (1985)

40: *Poets of Great Britain and Ireland Since 1960,* 2 parts, edited by Vincent B. Sherry, Jr. (1985)

41: *Afro-American Poets Since 1955,* edited by Trudier Harris and Thadious M. Davis (1985)

42: *American Writers for Children Before 1900,* edited by Glenn E. Estes (1985)

43: *American Newspaper Journalists, 1690-1872,* edited by Perry J. Ashley (1986)

44: *American Screenwriters,* Second Series, edited by Randall Clark, Robert E. Morsberger, and Stephen O. Lesser (1986)

45: *American Poets, 1880-1945,* First Series, edited by Peter Quartermain (1986)

46: *American Literary Publishing Houses, 1900-1980: Trade and Paperback,* edited by Peter Dzwonkoski (1986)

47: *American Historians, 1866-1912,* edited by Clyde N. Wilson (1986)

48: *American Poets, 1880-1945,* Second Series, edited by Peter Quartermain (1986)

49: *American Literary Publishing Houses, 1638-1899,* 2 parts, edited by Peter Dzwonkoski (1986)

50: *Afro-American Writers Before the Harlem Renaissance,* edited by Trudier Harris (1986)

51: *Afro-American Writers from the Harlem Renaissance to 1940,* edited by Trudier Harris (1987)

52: *American Writers for Children Since 1960: Fiction,* edited by Glenn E. Estes (1986)

53: *Canadian Writers Since 1960,* First Series, edited by W. H. New (1986)

54: *American Poets, 1880-1945,* Third Series, 2 parts, edited by Peter Quartermain (1987)

55: *Victorian Prose Writers Before 1867,* edited by William B. Thesing (1987)

56: *German Fiction Writers, 1914-1945,* edited by James Hardin (1987)

57: *Victorian Prose Writers After 1867,* edited by William B. Thesing (1987)

58: *Jacobean and Caroline Dramatists,* edited by Fredson Bowers (1987)

59: *American Literary Critics and Scholars, 1800-1850,* edited by John W. Rathbun and Monica M. Grecu (1987)

60: *Canadian Writers Since 1960,* Second Series, edited by W. H. New (1987)

61: *American Writers for Children Since 1960: Poets, Illustrators, and Nonfiction Authors,* edited by Glenn E. Estes (1987)

62: *Elizabethan Dramatists,* edited by Fredson Bowers (1987)

63: *Modern American Critics, 1920-1955,* edited by Gregory S. Jay (1988)

64: *American Literary Critics and Scholars, 1850-1880,* edited by John W. Rathbun and Monica M. Grecu (1988)

65: *French Novelists, 1900-1930,* edited by Catharine Savage Brosman (1988)

66: *German Fiction Writers, 1885-1913,* 2 parts, edited by James Hardin (1988)

67: *Modern American Critics Since 1955,* edited by Gregory S. Jay (1988)

68: *Canadian Writers, 1920-1959,* First Series, edited by W. H. New (1988)

69: *Contemporary German Fiction Writers,* First Series, edited by Wolfgang D. Elfe and James Hardin (1988)

70: *British Mystery Writers, 1860-1919,* edited by Bernard Benstock and Thomas F. Staley (1988)

LIBRARY
ST. MICHAEL'S PREP SCHOOL
1042 STAR RT. - ORANGE, CA. 92667

(Continued on back endsheets)

Dictionary of Literary Biography • Volume Eighty-eight

Canadian Writers, 1920-1959
Second Series

Dictionary of Literary Biography • Volume Eighty-eight

Canadian Writers, 1920-1959 Second Series

8137

Edited by
W. H. New
University of British Columbia

A Bruccoli Clark Layman Book
Gale Research Inc.
Detroit, New York, Fort Lauderdale, London

Advisory Board for
DICTIONARY OF LITERARY BIOGRAPHY

Louis S. Auchincloss
John Baker
William Cagle
Jane Christensen
Patrick O'Connor
Peter S. Prescott

Matthew J. Bruccoli and Richard Layman, *Editorial Directors*
C. E. Frazer Clark, Jr., *Managing Editor*

Manufactured by Braun-Brumfield
Ann Arbor, Michigan
Printed in the United States of America

"Now That The Dark Sunburn," p. 338, reprinted
from *The Collected Poems of George Whalley,*
edited by George Johnston, with
the permission of Quarry Press,
Kingston, Ontario, Canada.

Copyright © 1989
Gale Research Inc.
835 Penobscot Bldg.
Detroit, MI 48226-4094

Library of Congress Cataloging-in-Publication Data

Canadian writers, 1920-1959 second series/edited by
W. H. New.
    p. cm. – (Dictionary of literary biography; v. 88)
    "A Bruccoli Clark Layman book."
    ISBN 0-8103-4566-8
    1. Canadian literature–20th century–Dictionaries. 2. Canadian literature–20th century–Bio-bibliography. 3. Authors, Canadian–20th century–Biography–Dictionaries. 4. French-Canadian literature–20th century–Dictionaries. 5. French-Canadian literature–20th century–Bio-bibliography. 6. Authors, French-Canadian–20th century–Biography–Dictionaries. I. New, William H. II. Series.
PR9186.2.C36 1989
810.9'971–dc20
[B]
                                                89-12065
                                                CIP

Contents

Plan of the Series

. . . Almost the most prodigious asset of a country, and perhaps its most precious possession, is its native literary product—when that product is fine and noble and enduring.

Mark Twain*

The advisory board, the editors, and the publisher of the *Dictionary of Literary Biography* are joined in endorsing Mark Twain's declaration. The literature of a nation provides an inexhaustible resource of permanent worth. We intend to make literature and its creators better understood and more accessible to students and the reading public, while satisfying the standards of teachers and scholars.

To meet these requirements, *literary biography* has been construed in terms of the author's achievement. The most important thing about a writer is his writing. Accordingly, the entries in *DLB* are career biographies, tracing the development of the author's canon and the evolution of his reputation.

The purpose of *DLB* is not only to provide reliable information in a convenient format but also to place the figures in the larger perspective of literary history and to offer appraisals of their accomplishments by qualified scholars.

The publication plan for *DLB* resulted from two years of preparation. The project was proposed to Bruccoli Clark by Frederick G. Ruffner, president of the Gale Research Company, in November 1975. After specimen entries were prepared and typeset, an advisory board was formed to refine the entry format and develop the series rationale. In meetings held during 1976, the publisher, series editors, and advisory board approved the scheme for a comprehensive biographical dictionary of persons who contributed to North American literature. Editorial work on the first volume began in January 1977, and it was published in 1978. In order to make *DLB* more than a reference tool and to compile volumes that individually have claim to status as literary history, it was decided to organize volumes by topic, period, or genre. Each of these freestanding volumes provides a biographical-bibliographical guide and overview for a particular area of literature. We are convinced that this organization—as opposed to a single alphabet method—constitutes a valuable innovation in the presentation of reference material. The volume plan necessarily requires many decisions for the placement and treatment of authors who might properly be included in two or three volumes. In some instances a major figure will be included in separate volumes, but with different entries emphasizing the aspect of his career appropriate to each volume. Ernest Hemingway, for example, is represented in *American Writers in Paris, 1920-1939* by an entry focusing on his expatriate apprenticeship; he is also in *American Novelists, 1910-1945* with an entry surveying his entire career. Each volume includes a cumulative index of subject authors and articles. Comprehensive indexes to the entire series are planned.

With volume ten in 1982 it was decided to enlarge the scope of *DLB*. By the end of 1986 twenty-one volumes treating British literature had been published, and volumes for Commonwealth and Modern European literature were in progress. The series has been further augmented by the *DLB Yearbooks* (since 1981) which update published entries and add new entries to keep the *DLB* current with contemporary activity. There have also been *DLB Documentary Series* volumes which provide biographical and critical source materials for figures whose work is judged to have particular interest for students. One of these companion volumes is entirely devoted to Tennessee Williams.

We define literature as the *intellectual commerce of a nation:* not merely as belles lettres but as that ample and complex process by which ideas are generated, shaped, and transmitted. *DLB* entries are not limited to "creative writers" but extend to other figures who in their time and in their way influenced the mind of a people. Thus the series encompasses historians, journalists, publishers, and screenwriters. By this means readers of *DLB* may be aided to perceive litera-

*From an unpublished section of Mark Twain's autobiography, copyright © by the Mark Twain Company.

ture not as cult scripture in the keeping of intellectual high priests but firmly positioned at the center of a nation's life.

DLB includes the major writers appropriate to each volume and those standing in the ranks immediately behind them. Scholarly and critical counsel has been sought in deciding which minor figures to include and how full their entries should be. Wherever possible, useful references are made to figures who do not warrant separate entries.

Each *DLB* volume has a volume editor responsible for planning the volume, selecting the figures for inclusion, and assigning the entries. Volume editors are also responsible for preparing, where appropriate, appendices surveying the major periodicals and literary and intellectual movements for their volumes, as well as lists of further readings. Work on the series as a whole is coordinated at the Bruccoli Clark Layman editorial center in Columbia, South Carolina, where the editorial staff is responsible for accuracy of the published volumes.

One feature that distinguishes *DLB* is the illustration policy–its concern with the iconography of literature. Just as an author is influenced by his surroundings, so is the reader's understanding of the author enhanced by a knowledge of his environment. Therefore *DLB* volumes include not only drawings, paintings, and photographs of authors, often depicting them at various stages in their careers, but also illustrations of their families and places where they lived. Title pages are regularly reproduced in facsimile along with dust jackets for modern authors. The dust jackets are a special feature of *DLB* because they often document better than anything else the way in which an author's work was perceived in its own time. Specimens of the writers' manuscripts are included when feasible.

Samuel Johnson rightly decreed that "The chief glory of every people arises from its authors." The purpose of the *Dictionary of Literary Biography* is to compile literary history in the surest way available to us–by accurate and comprehensive treatment of the lives and work of those who contributed to it.

The *DLB* Advisory Board

Foreword

DLB 88: Canadian Writers, 1920-1959, Second Series is the fourth of six DLB volumes devoted to the writers of Canada who use English or French as their main language of artistic expression. (Canada is officially bilingual, but a large number of writers publish in languages other than these two.)

The first two published volumes, Canadian Writers Since 1960, first and second series, include authors whose careers were effectively established during the decades of the 1960s and 1970s. This volume is a companion to DLB 68. Together volumes 68 and 88 cover the preceding decades, beginning with the 1920s. Each comprises essays on novelists and short-story writers, poets, dramatists, and other literary figures, although in DLB 68 there is a concentration of entries on important fiction writers of the period (including Morley Callaghan, Anne Hébert, Hugh MacLennan, and Gabrielle Roy), while DLB 88 brings together entries (Earle Birney, Louis Dudek, Hector de Saint-Denys Garneau, Gilles Hénault, Irving Layton, Al Purdy, F. R. Scott, A. J. M. Smith, and others) on a noteworthy series of poets who changed the shape of Canadian literature.

Between World War I and 1959 Canadian literature went through several evolutionary changes. These had to do with the nature of image and the power of image to "represent" national experience; the relation of class, economics, and social change; voice and the articulation of the "marginal" experience of women, regions, and ethnic minorities; and the abstraction of language and the rejection of "representative" presumptions about art and society.

Like other nations in 1918, Canada was deeply affected by the realities of the war in which it had just fought, and in the wake of the Treaty of Paris it considered itself at last a recognizably independent nation. But World War I did not usher in a golden age; it stimulated change instead: industrialization, urbanization, alterations in the status quo. Some people began to celebrate the new national identity; some went so far as to turn literature into cultural boosterism. Oth-

ers articulated antinationalist sentiments; John Glassco, for example, turned his back on his establishment Montreal family and followed the "lost generation" to Paris. While some writers attempted to preserve an illusion of tradition and order, most resisted any hint of sentimentalism, and often sentimentalism and tradition seemed indissolubly connected. Those who questioned the validity of convention did so in part by upsetting the conventions of formal style—by using vernacular speech as a literary norm, condemning war and social hypocrisy, and attacking the very institutions (church, state) upon which civilization was presumed to rest, but which were now equated with social and moral decay. Albert Laberge's La Scouine, for example, denounced in 1918 for anticlericalism and immorality, was a critique of a system of values that did not take into account its own involvement in civil disarray.

One of the most striking agents of attitudinal change in the 1920s was the art of painting. In the late 1920s and early 1930s such writers as Robert Choquette (in Metropolitan Museum, 1931) and Alfred DesRochers were drawing on analogues in American art for symbols of change in society; A. J. M. Smith and F. R. Scott (who as students founded the influential McGill Fortnightly Review in 1925) responded to the imagists, to T. S. Eliot, and to the Toronto-based painters known as the Group of Seven. The Group of Seven, formally founded in 1920, included such painters as Lawren Harris, Arthur Lismer, Frederick Varley, and J. E. H. MacDonald. Associated with them were Tom Thomson and (on the west coast) Emily Carr. Carr looked to the art of the native Indians for a different "art-spirit," one that would break Canadian art free from European models. Harris was a theosophist abstractionist. For all their differences, the Group of Seven, using bolder colors and stronger lines than Canadian landscape painters before them, substantially shaped Canadian taste in art for several decades to come. Their influence on literature was significant, too: just as the Seven wanted to "see" place more accurately, so did the poets they influenced (Smith, Scott) want to "sing" place by means of an authentically local speech.

Whereas Smith and others went on to celebrate the "objectivity" of image, Scott involved himself more directly in the social arena. Liberal reformer, he made no apology for subjective engagement. Lawyer, teacher, social activist, he used his poetic gifts to satirize the emptiness of the "social register" and the passing fad. Scott was, moreover, by the 1930s, at the forefront of legal challenges to the restrictive Quebec laws enacted by Premier Maurice Duplessis and to the national legislation that still limited the rights of women.

By the 1930s, in response to depression, drought, sporadic civil unrest, and other forces, Canadian governments were instituting legislation to deal with social problems. For many, however, the efforts were not enough. There were calls from the Theatre of Action and other left-wing groups (and journals: *New Frontier, Masses*) for more attention to the homeless and the jobless; at the same time there were literary calls from the radical right for exclusion of non-Europeans from Canada and for a revolution to bring a Catholic autocracy into power. By far the majority of writers was left-leaning in the 1930s—though not all were as partisan as Dorothy Livesay and Earle Birney. Winnipeg-born George Woodcock, poet, critic, man of letters, strove to be apolitical; he was a pacifist, intellectual anarchist, and civil libertarian, one of a group of intellectuals in England (associated with George Orwell and others), who after his return to Canada in 1948 had a substantial effect on the course of criticism and social commentary.

In fiction, by the 1930s, social realism was in fashion, displacing the attachment to the wilderness romance. Many writers focused on the grimmer realities of rural life, disputing the clichés of bucolic arcadia and habitant peasant happiness. In the scenes they portrayed, women had to resist becoming victims of men and power; immigrants had to assess their real position in the social hierarchy. Raymond Knister, in his landmark 1928 anthology, *Canadian Short Stories,* drew attention to the changes that were taking place in prose style as well. While sympathetic and influential critics were quick to recognize what was going on in the new fiction but slow to appreciate it, English prose style in Canada after Knister and Morley Callaghan would not ever be quite the same again.

One of the other developments of the 1930s was the establishment of a national broadcasting system, the CBC (with a French counterpart called Radio-Canada). Rapidly the medium became a forum for the discussion of ideas, for the communication of values and perspectives from region to region, as well as an opportunity for literary artists. While at first the CBC was an arbiter of received standards (anglophone actors adopted a "mid-Atlantic" accent), the ordinary Canadian speaking voice quickly won out as the norm. Radio drama developed as an art form in its own right, Andrew Allan, Gratien Gélinas, Roger Lemelin, W. O. Mitchell, and Earle Birney being among the many writers to adapt the medium to their own purposes. Radio drama was, to many critics, even more interesting than contemporary writing for the stage. With Robert Weaver's involvement in the CBC, another genre found a home in radio. Weaver set up such programs as *CBC Wednesday Night* and *Canadian Short Stories.* Weaver actively encouraged writers to write short fiction (in many respects he can claim to have "discovered" Alice Munro and others), and he arranged to have their works read on the air. The revolution that Callaghan began, marrying speech rhythm with fictional form, acquired further momentum in this new medium.

Film, too, had an impact on literature. The National Film Board's well-earned reputation for documentary perhaps clarifies the character of the writing that attracted critical attention over the next ten years. Documentary (in that it fastened on empirical problems), this writing was also acutely subjective, shaped, as it were, by the cinematic lens, concerned with the perceiving eye. Many of the most important poets to emerge at this time used observation—with a perceiving "I" as persona or narrator—to invite readers to participate in a social dialogue.

Such poetry was also a vehicle for criticizing the status quo. Another war brought new discontent in tow. "Dieppe" became a watchword for social resentment of Britain's imperial presumptions. Quebeckers resisted conscription once again. P. K. Page created verbal portraits of psychological case studies. Raymond Souster, influenced by W. W. E. Ross, observed poverty with dispassionate judgment. Dorothy Livesay drew attention to discrimination, A. M. Klein to anti-Semitism and the limits of provinciality. Ralph Gustafson, Louis Dudek, James Reaney: all devised separate systems (involving myth, music, mechanical media, drawing on the critical and historical theories of Northrop Frye, Harold Adams Innis, Lionel Groulx, and Marshall McLuhan) to separate art from society or to claim the connection between the two.

The dominant English-language voice in poetry was that of Irving Layton—passionate, proud, idiosyncratic, ironic, iconoclastic, bawdy, shrewd, tender, wry. All these adjectives apply. Consciously setting himself apart from the provinciality he perceived in both anglophone and francophone traditions in Canada (the one, in his terms, angloprotestant and life-denying, the other Jansenist and infatuated with martyrdom), he celebrated his own Jewishness, his links with a separate tradition, as the agency of vitality that could transform the present age. A critic of the status quo, he courted conventional displeasure. Masks were Layton's métier. Coming to recognize the self was what he demanded of his readers; hence his poetry issued challenges, with which many were unwilling to comply.

In francophone Quebec the dominant voices were those of Hector de Saint-Denys Garneau and his cousin Anne Hébert. Acutely private, highly symbolic, they represent the very kind of self-preoccupation Layton found limiting, though (after Saint-Denys Garneau's death) Hébert embarked on a much more critical engagement with words, celebrating her female freedom from male norms of language and the conventional shapes of Quebec history.

In anglophone Canada the literary status quo to which Layton objected consisted of imitative forms: the historical romances of E. J. Pratt, the "realistic" allegories of Hugh MacLennan, the ironies of Robertson Davies, the historical conservatism of Donald Creighton, the now-established lyricism of Scott, Smith, and Douglas LePan. Theirs was an angloprotestant, centralist version of Canada, nudging toward biculturalism. (MacLennan's 1945 novel *Two Solitudes* gave this vision of Canada a name.) But while these changes were under way, Quebec was moving toward the separatism that was to occupy the 1960s and 1970s; the ethnic minorities in Canada were starting to preempt biculturalism (announcing the reality of multiculturalism instead); and writers were beginning to declare the separation of art from a direct, mimetic relation with society altogether.

Joyce Marshall, Adele Wiseman, Sinclair Ross, Henry Kreisel: in the works of these writers there was still a strong sense of the empirical bases of art. Their art was "about" people in time and place. But in every case the angle of representation was as important to the reader's connection with the work of art as was the fact of representation itself. Ross manipulated first-person narrative in *As For Me and My House* (1941), for example, to contrive an ambivalent portrait of resentment and desire.

While these years did see the publication of comedic satires, fantasies, rhythmic experiments (including the expressionist writings of Herman Voaden and the vorticist works of Bertram Brooker), and symbolic stories (such as those of Ernest Buckler and the part-Montagnais narrative artist Yves Thériault), "mythic departures" from realism went largely unnoticed until later decades. It was, for example, not until the 1970s that there was a substantial readership sympathetic to Howard O'Hagan's *Tay John* (1939). Even less was there in English Canada a readership ready for the stream-of-consciousness of Elizabeth Smart or for the Joycean play of A. M. Klein's fiction. And the Birney that was appreciated at the time was the early lyrical poet, reminiscent of Robert Frost; the later Birney, anarchist of literary form, was yet to be heard from.

The year 1959 constitutes a terminus for this volume, as well as for its companion, because it was a year in which several changes are, with hindsight, clearly observable. The Canada Council (formed in 1958 on a recommendation by the Massey Commission) was beginning its mandate to assist in financing artistic composition, publication, performance, and research. New journals came into existence in 1959–*Canadian Literature, Liberté, Prism*–serving the academic study of Canadian literature as a discipline. Fiction was beginning to change subject and form, with a new generation coming into print.

It must also be added that 1959 is a more appropriate terminus date for anglophone than it is for francophone writing. In Quebec the "significant moments of change" that hindsight recognizes occurred in 1948, 1953, and 1960. As in 1920, one of the major changes in the cultural climate derived from painting, when in 1948 the painters Emile Borduas and Jean-Paul Riopelle, along with the absurdist dramatist Claude Gauvreau, issued their *Refus global*. Basically an attack on Duplessis's Quebec, their pamphlet was a claim for freedom from political and imaginative enclosure. But as freedom did not exist in the conventionally structured political world, the only way of claiming it was, the authors said, to utter a "collective refusal" of convention: to embrace abstraction, to embrace surrealism (as did Gilles

Hénault and others), to reject the possibility of "representation" in art or "meaning" in language (a position that would influence Paul-Marie Lapointe directly, and through him several contemporary poets and dramatists), and therefore to compose by means of "automatisme."

In 1953 another rebel against the status quo, Gaston Miron, established a new press, Editions de l'Héxagone. It was an important agency for making these revolutionary voices heard–publishing Lapointe, for instance, and (sporadically, for he long opted for silence rather than speech, in resistance to the linguistic status quo) Miron himself. Héxagone also became the center for a writer's group; it was there that poets would gather–Jean-Guy Pilon, Gilbert Langevin, Roland Giguère, Gilles Hénault, Fernand Ouellette. It was there that Juan Garcia would meet Miron and befriend Langevin, there that the revolutionary spirit of one generation was being handed on to another. In 1959 Duplessis died. When Jean Lesage took over as premier of Quebec in 1960, and won reelection in 1962 under the slogan "maîtres chez nous" (masters in our own house), the so-called Quiet Revolution was underway. In the decades to follow it would have a profound effect both on the political assumptions Canadians had of themselves and on the literary structures and strategies they chose to employ.

–W. H. New

Acknowledgments

This book was produced by Bruccoli Clark Layman, Inc. Karen L. Rood is senior editor for the *Dictionary of Literary Biography* series. Margaret A. Van Antwerp was the in-house editor.

Production coordinator is James W. Hipp. Systems manager is Charles D. Brower. Photography supervisor is Susan Todd. Layout and graphics supervisor is Penney L. Haughton. Copyediting supervisor is Joan M. Prince. Typesetting supervisor is Kathleen M. Flanagan. William Adams, Laura Ingram, and Michael D. Senecal are editorial associates. The production staff includes Rowena Betts, Anne L. M. Bowman, Nancy Brevard-Bracey, Joseph M. Bruccoli, Teresa Chaney, Patricia Coate, Allison Deal, Holly Deal, Sarah A. Estes, Willie M. Gore, Cynthia Hallman, Susan C. Heath, Mary Long, David Marshall James, Kathy S. Merlette, Laura Garren Moore, Philip R. Moore, Sheri Beckett Neal, and Jack Turner. Jean W. Ross is permissions editor.

Walter W. Ross and Jennifer Toth did the library research with the assistance of the reference staff at the Thomas Cooper Library of the University of South Carolina: Lisa Antley, Daniel Boice, Faye Chadwell, Cathy Eckman, Gary Geer, Cathie Gottlieb, David L. Haggard, Jens Holley, Jackie Kinder, Marcia Martin, Jean Rhyne, Beverly Steele, Ellen Tillett, Carol Tobin, and Virginia Weathers.

The editor expresses special thanks to Joe Jones of the University of British Columbia Library (Humanities Division), to Robin Van Heck, and to Beverly Westbrook. Nicky Drumbolis of Letters, Steven Temple of Steven Temple Books, and Kenneth Landry of the *Dictionnaire des œuvres littéraires du Québec* have provided valuable assistance in securing illustrative materials.

Canadian Writers, 1920-1959
Second Series

Dictionary of Literary Biography

Andrew Allan
(11 August 1907-15 January 1974)

Jerry Wasserman
University of British Columbia

BOOK: *Andrew Allan: A Self-Portrait* (Toronto: Macmillan, 1974).

PLAY PRODUCTION: *Narrow Passage*, Toronto, Museum Theatre, 13 January 1950.

SELECTED RADIO: *Mistress Nell, Radio Drama*, CBC, 13 October 1936;
Palatine Hill, Within These Walls, CBC, 28 November 1937;
Mary Queen of Scots, CBC, 7 December 1939;
It Must Be Simple, Theatre Time, CBC, 10 January 1940;
The Devil's Receipt, Theatre Time, CBC, 17 January 1940;
Catherine the Great, Theatre Time, CBC, 31 January 1940;
Dead Man's Business, Theatre Time, CBC, 21 February 1940;
Sir Guy Proposes, Theatre Time, CBC, 27 March 1940;
The Thing That Walked, Theatre Time, CBC, 10 December 1940;
The Mystery Play of the Nativity, adaptation, CBC, 24 December 1940;
Proud Procession, Drama, CBC, 23 April 1941;
All the Bright Company, Theatre Time, CBC, 4 August 1942;
The Oracles Are Dumb, by Allan and John Bethune, *Pacific Playhouse*, CBC, 23 December 1942;
Peace in Our Time, by Allan and Bethune, *Pacific Playhouse*, CBC, 30 December 1942;
Summer in Paradise, by Allan and Bethune, *Pacific Playhouse*, CBC, 20 January 1943;

Andrew Allan (photograph by Herb Nott & Co. Ltd., courtesy of the Canadian Broadcasting Corporation)

My Bonnie Boy, Stage, CBC, 11 June 1944;
Henry V, adapted from Shakespeare's play, *Readings from Shakespeare*, CBC, 30 November 1944;
Give Us Back Our Miracle, Stage, CBC, 13 May 1945;

There Are Very Few of Us Left, Stage, CBC, 17 February 1946;

Uncertain Glory, Stage, CBC, 21 April 1946;

The Snow Queen, adapted from Hans Christian Andersen's story, *Stage,* CBC, 22 December 1946;

The Zeal of Thy House, adapted from Dorothy Sayers's novel, *Stage,* CBC, 28 March 1948;

For the Time Being, adapted from W. H. Auden's book of poems, *Wednesday Night,* CBC, 15 December 1948;

Heart of Darkness, adapted from Joseph Conrad's novel, *Stage,* CBC, 23 January 1949;

The Way of the World, adapted from William Congreve's play, *Wednesday Night,* CBC, 15 June 1949;

The Fifth Column, adapted from Ernest Hemingway's play, *Stage,* CBC, 2 October 1949;

Salome, adapted from Oscar Wilde's play, *Stage,* CBC, 16 October 1949;

Kidnapped, adapted from Robert Louis Stevenson's novel, *Stage,* CBC, 27 November 1949;

Camille, adapted from Alexandre Dumas *fil's* play *La Dame aux camélias, Stage,* CBC, 26 March 1950;

The Lady Knows Too Much, Curtain Time, CBC, 19 April 1950;

A Sense of Sin, Stage, CBC, 11 January 1953;

The Liars, adapted from Henry Arthur Jones's play, *Stage,* CBC, 22 March 1953;

The York Passion Play, adaptation, *Stage,* CBC, 18 April 1954;

The Tempest, adapted from Shakespeare's play, *Wednesday Night,* CBC, 20 April 1955;

Volpone, adapted from Ben Jonson's play, *Wednesday Night,* CBC, 2 November 1955;

The Rivals, adapted from Richard Brinsley Sheridan's play, *Wednesday Night,* CBC, 18 January 1956;

Becket, adapted from Alfred Tennyson's play, *Wednesday Night,* CBC, 28 November 1956;

The Trojan Women, adapted from Euripides' play, *Stage,* CBC, 3 March 1957;

Youth, adapted from Joseph Conrad's story, *Wednesday Night,* CBC, 12 June 1957;

Venus Observed, adapted from Christopher Fry's play, *Wednesday Night,* CBC, 26 November 1958.

OTHER: William Allan, *Memories of Blinkbonnie,* edited, with a memoir, by Andrew Allan (Toronto: Nelson, 1939);

All the Bright Company: Radio Drama Produced by Andrew Allan, edited by Howard Fink and John Jackson (Kingston, Ont.: Quarry / Toronto: CBC Enterprises, 1987).

Andrew Allan's name is synonymous with the Golden Age of Radio in Canada. From 1943 to 1955 when he was supervisor of drama for CBC and producer of its *Stage* series, the stable of Canadian writers and actors he assembled–"far and away the most exciting repertory group that can be heard," according to a *New York Times* article in 1946–was Canada's equivalent of a national theater. Although Allan was also well respected as an actor, writer, and director for theater and television, he is best remembered for the consistently high quality of his award-winning radio productions.

Andrew Edward Fairbairn Allan was born in Arbroath, Scotland, the son of William Allan, a Presbyterian minister, and Agnes Hannah Fairbairn Allan. His family immigrated to Australia, then moved to New York and Boston before settling in Peterborough, Ontario, in 1925. Allan attended the University of Toronto from 1927 to 1930 but left without graduating: "I cannot afford to go through life with the stigma of a university degree," he would later say. In 1931 he got a job with CFRB radio in Toronto, working on and off through 1937, acting, announcing, producing, and writing the first Canadian soap opera, *The Family Doctor.*

After almost two years with the BBC in London, Allan returned to Canada in 1939 to go to work for the fledgling Canadian Broadcasting Corporation in Vancouver. There, serious Canadian radio drama had its real beginnings as Allan developed his production techniques and began gathering the nucleus of what, for the next two decades, would be his "company," including John Drainie, Lister Sinclair, Fletcher Markle, Tommy Tweed, Len Peterson, and Lucio Agostini. His production of Markle's *Baker's Dozen* (1942) series gained Allan national recognition, and in 1943 he returned to Toronto as the CBC's supervisor of drama.

Stage went on the air on 23 January 1944. During the first twelve years of the series Allan produced and directed more than four hundred programs, the majority original Canadian scripts. He also produced many of the shows on *CBC Wednesday Night,* the long-running drama series that began in 1947, featuring mostly adaptations. He said he encouraged his *Stage* writers to "write what they wanted ... and in the way they wanted," and on the whole they did, tackling a wide range of subjects and attitudes previously considered taboo for radio drama. The result was a consistently bold, imaginative writers' theater of the air. Allan himself wrote more than thirty original dramas and another fifty adaptations of works by a wide range of writers, from Euripides and Shakespeare to Conrad and Hemingway. His radio plays, such as *The Oracles Are Dumb* (a 1942 collaboration with John Bethune), *My Bonnie Boy* (1944), and *Uncertain Glory* (1946), received mixed reviews. His stage play, *Narrow Passage*, produced in Toronto in 1950, was called "unmitigated claptrap" by critic Nathan Cohen.

During the 1950s Allan moved into television production but was never the success he was in radio. After two failed marriages (to Dianne Foster in 1951 and Linda Trenholme Ballantyne in 1955), he left the CBC in 1962 to become the first artistic director of the Shaw Festival at Niagara-on-the-Lake, Ontario. In 1965 he returned to radio where he worked as an actor and commentator until his death in 1974. Published posthumously was *Andrew Allan: A Self-Portrait* (1974), half autobiography and half selected essays, all originally broadcast by Allan over the radio.

As a producer Andrew Allan was not always personally liked; he had a reputation for cold authoritarianism and "could be a bully . . . and a holy terror," according to radio historian Sandy Stewart. But the quality of his productions was unimpeachable, and they were without a doubt a major contribution to the development of Canadian culture in the postwar years. When *Stage* won the first of its many American radio-drama awards in 1945, it was cited for "originality, emotional appeal, and intellectual integrity," characteristics typical of Allan's best work and that of the writers and actors he cultivated throughout the "golden age" of his CBC stewardship.

Bibliography:
Howard Fink, with Brian Morrison, *Canadian Na-tional Theatre on the Air, 1925-1961: CBC-CRBC-CNR Radio Drama in English, A Descriptive Bibliography and Union List* (Toronto: University of Toronto Press, 1983).

References:
Fred Davis, "Andrew Allan Says!," *Performing Arts in Canada*, 2 (Summer 1963): 4-6, 33-34, 48-51;

Bronwyn Drainie, *Living the Part: John Drainie and the Dilemma of Canadian Stardom* (Toronto: Macmillan, 1988), pp. 53-122;

N. Alice Frick, *Image in the Mind: CBC Radio Drama, 1944 to 1954* (Toronto: Canadian Stage and Arts Publications, 1987);

Roger Lee Jackson, "An Historical and Analytical Study of the Origin, Development and Impact of the Dramatic Programs Produced for the English Language Network of the Canadian Broadcasting Corporation," Ph.D. dissertation, Wayne State University, 1966, pp. 52-55, 62-84;

Eric Koch, "Andrew Allan Founds New Radio Technique," *Saturday Night*, 60 (14 October 1944): 24-25;

Thelma LeCocq, "On Stage with Allan," *Maclean's*, 60 (1 February 1947): 21-24;

Leonard Peterson, "With Freedom in Their Eye. . . ," *Canadian Theatre Review*, 36 (Fall 1982): 23-29;

Lister Sinclair, "Andrew Allan," *Canadian Forum*, 30 (May 1950): 35.

Papers:
Andrew Allan's signed original production scripts for the complete *Stage* series and for most of his other productions are housed at the CBC Radio Drama Archives, Centre for Broadcasting Studies, Concordia University, Montreal.

Pierre Baillargeon
(10 September 1916-15 August 1967)

Jane Koustas
Redeemer College

BOOKS: *Hasard et moi* (Montreal: Beauchemin, 1940);

Eglogues (Montreal: Amérique Française, 1943);

Les Médisances de Claude Perrin (Montreal: Lucien Parizeau, 1945);

Commerce (Montreal: Editions Variétés, 1947);

La Neige et le feu (Montreal: Editions Variétés, 1948);

Le Scandale est nécessaire (Montreal: Editions du Jour, 1962);

Madame Homère (Montreal: Editions du Lys, 1964);

Le Choix: Essais, edited by Robert Bernier (Montreal: HMH, 1969).

PLAY PRODUCTION: *Madame Homère*, Montreal, Ecole Normale Jacques-Cartier, 13 December 1963.

Essayist, novelist, literary critic, and poet, Pierre Baillargeon was part of a group of young writers who set out to change the Quebec literary scene. Often shocking the public and critics with his bold criticism of Quebec, Baillargeon was praised for his pure and concise style, "son français impeccable, . . . soigneux, méticuleux autant qu'Asselin" (his impeccable French, . . . as polished and meticulous as that of [Olivar] Asselin). Referred to sometimes as a moralist rather than an essayist, a fabulist rather than a novelist, Baillargeon published more than 420 poems, stories, and essays, occasionally using the pseudonym "Henri Brulard," as well as eight book-length works. He is now recognized as an important Canadian writer of the 1940s and 1950s. His condemnation of the Roman Catholic Church, the Quebec education system, and literary critics frequently earned him harsh criticism in the early part of his career, but he was later recognized as a "prophet" and forerunner of the Quiet Revolution, though he did not take an active part in this movement. His last published essay, *Le Scandale est nécessaire* (Scandal Is Necessary, 1962), is considered a classic.

Pierre Baillargeon

Born in Montreal on 10 September 1916 to Oliva Baillargeon, a political organizer, and Alphonsine Mercier Baillargeon, Baillargeon completed his elementary education at the Ecole Querbes d'Outremont and his *études classiques* at the Collège Jean-de-Brébeuf. He earned his *baccalauréat* in 1938 and left for France, where he began to study medicine. There he met Jacqueline Mabit, whom he married in July 1939. They later had four children.

Forced to return to Canada because of ill health and the German invasion of France at the beginning of World War II, Baillargeon worked as a translator for the Royal Canadian Air Force and began writing for the journal *La Relève*. In 1941, on the advice of François Hertel, he founded a literary review, *Amérique Française*, which he directed until 1944. In 1945 Baillargeon began working as a journalist for *La Patrie*. He returned to France in 1948 but spent the summer of 1949 in Quebec, where he worked for *La Presse*. Back in France, he continued to write for *La Patrie* (1948-1960) and *Le Petit Journal* (1950-1951) while pursuing his own studies and teaching Latin and French at Vézelay and at the Ecole de Roches in Normandy. He worked as well as translator for Editions Robert Laffont (1956) and as a literary consultant for *Sélection du Reader's Digest*.

During the 1950s Baillargeon wrote primarily articles for Montreal newspapers, mostly for *La Patrie* and *Le Petit Journal*. Many of these articles were based on his own travels as well as on interviews with numerous artists and writers. A study of the essay in Quebec from 1940 to 1959 suggests that Baillargeon, like Guy Sylvestre and Rex Desmarchais, did not produce any major works during this period because of the strict censorship imposed by church officials and the Quebec government, as outlined in the "Loi concernant les publications et la morale publique" (Law Concerning Publications and the Public Morale) passed by the government of Maurice Duplessis in 1950. In 1957 Baillargeon was appointed secretary to the Canadian ambassador in Paris. Upon his return to Canada in 1959, he worked as an editor at Bell Canada (1960-1962) and a translator at Canadien National (1962-1966). Awarded the Silver Medal of the Académie Française in 1938, a Canada Council Senior Arts Fellowship for 1959-1960, and elected to the Royal Society of Canada in 1963, Baillargeon also served as president of the Société des Ecrivains Canadiens. He died on 15 August 1967 in Rochester, Minnesota, where he was undergoing heart surgery at the Mayo Clinic.

His first book, *Hasard et moi* (Chance and I, 1940), is a short work that has characteristics of the novel, essay, and diary forms. Written in the third person and dedicated "Aux impersonnels" (to impersonals), the book is described in the subtitle as a tract "dirigé contre le culte de moi" (directed against the "me" cult). *Hasard et moi* is an obscure, hermetic work which explores the thoughts of Pierre, the vague central character. In Baillargeon's words, Pierre "entre en lui-même et il en sort. Il entre dans sa chambre; il sort" (enters himself and leaves. He enters his room; he leaves). For the central character, as well as for the author, as Claude-Henri Grignon stated in his review of the work (*Pamphlets de Valdombre*, July 1940), "il n'y a qu'une vie: celle des mots" (there is only one life: that of words). Critics praised Baillargeon's style and saw in this work traces of Paul Valéry, Maurice Blanchot, Francis Ponge, and Claude Gauvreau.

Eglogues (1943) is a collection of three poems by Baillargeon, "Printemps," "Regards," and "Ombres," set to music by Jean Papineau-Couture and illustrated by Jacques de Tonnancour. Certain critics found the intellectual, conservative poetry written in measured verse too academic, claiming that Baillargeon did not explore images but concentrated on conveying a meaning. However, as André Gaulin has pointed out in an essay for the *Dictionnaire des Œuvres littéraires du Québec*, *Eglogues*, dedicated to the French conductor and musician Nadia Boulanger, is important as a collective work of some of the best talents of the period.

The publication of Baillargeon's *Les Médisances de Claude Perrin* (Claude Perrin's Slander, 1945) was heralded as a literary event. The main character, Claude Perrin, largely autobiographical, reappears later in Baillargeon's *Commerce* (1947) and *La Neige et le feu* (Snow and Fire, 1948), as well as in his unpublished play "Autour d'un gros bonhomme" (About a Stout Fellow). Concise, ironic, often scathing, *Les Médisances de Claude Perrin* is a harsh look at Quebec society through the eyes of a critically ill author who has retreated to the fictitious village of Saint-Larron (the village of the repentant thief) to write his spiritual testament. Rather than a novel, the work is a series of reflections on Claude's family, school and married life, and seemingly pointless existence. Perrin, his daughter who accompanies him to Saint-Larron, the village priest who cannot understand Perrin's desire to write, and a doctor who cannot cure his illness are the only characters who appear in the present. The other characters exist in Perrin's memory.

Dividing his work into two distinct parts, "Testament" and "Portrait," Perrin claims initially to be writing for himself but ends up trying to put his ideas in order for a potential reader. By reliving his past, Perrin reveals his present condition, that of a man who, disappointed in his per-

Frontispiece by Jacques de Tonnancour for Baillargeon's 1943 poetry collection, Eglogues

sonal and professional life, is driven by the need to write. Perrin reflects on his failure and on the fate of writers in Quebec. The account becomes a bitter condemnation of Quebec society, particularly of its educational and religious institutions. In the "Testament" Perrin sets forth some ideals for Quebec writers, urging them to remain true to themselves, rather than to conform and respond to critics' expectations and literary trends. Reviewers praised Baillargeon's concise language and his cruel but humorous irony but noted the fact that Perrin blamed others, especially literary critics, for his own failure.

In *Commerce* Claude Perrin owns a bookshop which displays the slogan "Lire, c'est élire" (To read is to elect). Perrin's chief interest is not the exchange of books for dollars but rather the exchange of conversation.

His shop is a meeting place where all subjects are discussed, particularly those not freely mentioned in Quebec–the church, for example, and its control of education. The patrons of the bookshop, as the critics pointed out, are doubles of the author. The narrator is a student who visits the shop regularly.

The book is divided into four parts. The first part includes a prologue and texts, some of

which were previously published in *Le Quartier Latin*. The second and third parts comprise epigrams, maxims, and morals. These concise comments, which became the author's trademark, are written in a conversational tone. The narrator quotes Perrin's views on various topics, including writing and life: "la vie du roman c'est la tienne que tu perds à le lire" (the life of a novel is your own that you waste reading it); "la littérature, c'est la vie intérieure qui devient la vie" (literature is inner life that becomes life). Perrin comments as well on literary criticism, and the narrator remarks: "J'aime bien la prose nue, toute spirituelle de Claude Perrin. Elle est sèche, mais sèche comme la poudre, et fait explosion à la moindre étincelle d'intelligence du lecteur" (I like Claude Perrin's naked, spiritual prose. It is dry like powder and explodes at the slightest spark of intelligence in the reader). Reviewers saw this statement as a direct reply to one critic's negative comment on the dryness of Baillargeon's work. The final section of *Commerce* is a letter of advice to the narrator on the art of reading, an art dependent on liberty "à l'égard des mots, à force de les manipuler" (with respect to words by manipulating them). This section ends with a poem, "La Fin d'un homme de lettres."

While some critics were annoyed by this repeat of Claude Perrin's bitter criticism, others, such as Dostaler O'Leary (*La Revue Populaire*, February 1948) and René Garneau (*Le Canada*, 14 July 1947), praised Baillargeon's talent. Jérôme Séverin (in several editions of *Le Clarion* for August 1947) lauded his style and added that the critics' negative comments were a result of their inability to remain objective when confronted by Baillargeon's stern criticism.

In *La Neige et le feu* Baillargeon combines his literary and philosophical views with a "roman de moeurs" (novel of manners). The main character, Philippe Boureil, who bears the same initials as the author, has an outlook like that of Claude Perrin. Abandoned by his wife. Boureil takes up lodgings in Westmount where he has limited contact with his fellow boarders, one of whom is a journalist. Having refused an offer to direct an anticlerical newspaper, Boureil leaves for France, where he discovers the cultural and intellectual stimulation of Paris. In the second part of the novel he meets fellow expatriates who have come to study, as well as Simone Audigny, an intellectual with whom he falls in love. Boureil is particularly excited by the conversations he has with Simone's father, Ambroise, a philologist. The third part of the novel recounts Boureil's return to Canada at the request of his wife, who is pregnant. When the child dies, she again leaves Boureil, who must work for his former newspaper acquaintances to survive. In describing Boureil's return home, his boredom and disillusionment, his difficulty in thinking freely in such an intolerant and stifling environment, Baillargeon attacks the social climate of Quebec: "Ce n'est pas que les gens ne pensaient qu'à l'argent et au confort; mais sur tout le reste, religion, morale, métaphysique, art, littérature, ils avaient à peu près les mêmes idées; l'école avait façonné leurs esprits sur le même plan" (It was not because people thought only about money and comfort but because they all had almost identical ideas about everything else, religion, morals, metaphysics, art, literature; school had formed all their minds according to the same plan).

Seeing themselves as a target of Baillargeon's criticism, clerical reviewers described the novel as mediocre. Father Paul Gay (*Lectures*, November 1948) called *La Neige et le feu* the work of an author of no humility, and Father Emile Bégin (*L'Enseignement Secondaire au Canada*, March/April 1949) charged that Baillargeon lacked the courage to "sortir de soi-même" (come out of himself). Most critics saw Boureil as a self-centered failure too quick to blame others for his own mistakes. However, Jean Dufresne (writing as Marcel Valois in *La Presse*, 22 May 1948) and Guy Jasmin (*Le Canada*, 17 May 1948) congratulated Baillargeon on his accurate description of life "au pied de le pente amère" (at the foot of the bitter slope).

Baillargeon's next book, *Le Scandale est nécessaire*, was published in 1962, ending a fourteen-year period during which the author had devoted himself almost entirely to journalistic and editorial pursuits. Believing that readers must be shocked into thinking for themselves, in this book Baillargeon again bombards his public with controversial maxims designed to stimulate reflection on society's mediocrity, hypocrisy, and materialism. The volume, which also includes prose texts, is divided into eight chapters. Four of these comprise the maxims. In "Epigrammes" Baillargeon's sayings express his skepticism concerning the real effects of the Quiet Revolution, which was taking place in Quebec during the 1960s; in "Littérature" the focus is on the refined reader; the maxims of "Réflexions" reveal Baillargeon's talent as a critical though humorous moralist; and those of "Journal d'Alceste" expose a somewhat paradoxical view of social history. The four chapters devoted to longer texts are entitled "Le Scandale est nécessaire," "Influences," "Portraits," and "Voisins" (Neighbors). In the first two Baillargeon again attacks conformism, Canada's stifling intellectual climate, and the education system. The final two are sketches of artists who influenced Baillargeon: Alfred Laliberté, Paul Morin, Berthelot Brunet, Ringuet, Maurice de Vlaminck, and Jean de La Varende. *Le Scandale est nécessaire* was Baillargeon's first work to be received with unqualified praise, a fact which indicates, as André Gaulin has pointed out, that the Quiet Revolution was indeed changing Quebec.

Madame Homère (1964) is Baillargeon's only published play. Rewritten many times, the play, the fictitious story of the poet Homer's wife, whom Baillargeon calls Agathe, was a dismal failure when it was produced on 13 December 1963 in the auditorium of Montreal's Ecole Normale Jacques-Cartier. In his review of the play for *La Presse* (16 December 1963) Jean O'Neil spoke of "complaintes et frénésie" (complaints and frenzy); Roger Duhamel, in *Le Droit* (25 January 1964), described Baillargeon as "un écrivain en marge" (a marginal writer). The play was completely out of touch with the social and cultural concerns of the Quiet Revolution.

After Baillargeon's death in 1967, Robert Bernier, a Jesuit, former teacher at Jean-de-Brébeuf, and longtime friend of Baillargeon, edited a collection of both previously published and unpublished essays by Baillargeon under the title *Le Choix* (Choice, 1969). Bernier states that though the texts are from various periods, they all illustrate "la rigueur de pensée et de style qui est la marque de l'auteur" (the rigorous thought and style that are the author's trademark). Although critics of Baillargeon's time largely ignored his contribution to Quebec literature, he is now considered, in the words of one, "la mauvaise conscience" (the guilty conscience) of his era.

References:

Madeleine Ducrocq-Poirier, "Les Méfaits de la subjectivité littéraire ou les vrais mérites de Pierre Baillargeon," *Voix et Images du Pays*, 8 (1974): 127-132;

André Gaulin, "Claude Perrin, un prophète mal-aimé sous 'la grande noirceur,'" *Livres et Auteurs Québécois* (1973): 325-336;

Gaulin, "La Neige et le feu ou L'Image critique d'un intellectuel sous la societe duplessiste," *L'Action nationale* (January 1976): 339-351;

Gaulin, "Pierre Baillargeon intime," *Voix et Images*, 1 (September 1975): 57-71;

Paul Toupin, "Pierre Baillargeon," *Cahiers de l'Académie Canadienne Française*, second series, no. 14 (1972): 120-130; republished in his *Au commencement était le souvenir* (Montreal: Fides, 1973), pp. 183-192.

Constance Beresford-Howe
(10 November 1922-   )

Barbara Pell
Trinity Western University

BOOKS: *The Unreasoning Heart* (New York: Dodd, Mead, 1946; London: Hammond, 1948; Toronto: Macmillan, 1978);

Of This Day's Journey (New York: Dodd, Mead, 1947; London: Hammond, 1949);

The Invisible Gate (New York: Dodd, Mead, 1949; London: Hammond, 1952);

My Lady Greensleeves (New York: Ballantine, 1955);

The Book of Eve (Toronto: Macmillan 1973; Boston: Little, Brown, 1974);

A Population of One (Toronto: Macmillan, 1977; New York: St. Martin's, 1978);

The Marriage Bed (Toronto: Macmillan, 1981; New York: St. Martin's, 1981; London: New English Library, 1982);

Night Studies (Toronto: Macmillan, 1985);

Prospero's Daughter (Toronto: Macmillan, 1988).

TELEVISION: *The Cuckoo Bird*, CBC, 1981.

OTHER: "Stages in an Education," in *A Fair Shake: Autobiographical Essays by McGill Women*, edited by Margaret Gillett and Kay Sibbald (Montreal: Eden, 1984), pp. 30-39.

PERIODICAL PUBLICATIONS: "Martha and God and the Bright Blue Marble on a Dusty Road," *Saturday Night* (13 January 1945): 27;

"One Plus One," *Maclean's* (1 December 1947): 10-11, 35-36, 41;

"Character and Incident," *Writer*, 68 (August 1955): 264-267;

"The Second Mrs. Lindsay," *Chatelaine*, 52 (November 1979): 64-65, 93, 96, 98, 101, 105-106, 108.

Constance Beresford-Howe is a successful popular writer who has also achieved critical acclaim by portraying the realistic lives of contemporary women in their struggle for freedom against popular expectations–both sexist and feminist. Constance Elizabeth Beresford-Howe was born in Montreal, the only daughter of Russell and Marjory Mary Moore Beresford-Howe. Her father was an insurance salesman, her mother a housewife and aspiring author. She grew up in Notre Dame de Grace during the Depression, living with her parents and brother in a succession of low-rent flats. An attack of rheumatic fever at age eleven, which confined her to bed for months, strengthened her inclination to introspection, reading, and writing, and by the time she was fourteen she was planning an epic novel about Napoleon. Encouraged by her English teachers at West Hill High School, she entered the second year of the Honours English course at McGill University in 1942 (on a bursary loan), intending to become a high-school teacher. There she excelled, graduating in 1945 with the Shakespeare Gold Medal for highest standing in English and the Peterson Prize for Creative Writing.

At McGill, the inspiration of her creative-writing professor, Harold G. Files, led to her first

photograph by Peter Patterson, courtesy of Macmillan of Canada

Constance Beresford-Howe

story publications and her first full-length novel, *The Unreasoning Heart*, which won the Dodd, Mead Intercollegiate Literary Fellowship for North America in 1945, the year before it was published. Files also supervised her master of arts (completed in 1946), helped her win a provincial scholarship for Ph.D. studies at Brown University, and, after her two years of residence there, offered her a lectureship at McGill. She received her Ph.D. from Brown in 1950 and taught at McGill–as lecturer, assistant professor, and associate professor–from 1948 to 1969.

During her student years Beresford-Howe wrote three apprenticeship novels. *The Unreasoning Heart* is the story of an orphaned adolescent girl who is befriended by the matriarch of a prosperous Montreal family. In a rather melodramatic plot, the pampered son is pushed to suicide by his social-climbing wife and his domineering mother, who must then be nursed back to life and hope by the orphan. Meanwhile, this young heroine has fallen in love with the older and wiser son, who eventually reciprocates

her affections. Beresford-Howe's use of the sixteen-year-old orphan as the center of consciousness in this novel makes the narration seem too contrived and inconsistent to validate the characters' experiences. Anne Wilkinson dismissed the book as overambitious "hammock fiction" (*Canadian Forum*, June 1946).

Of This Day's Journey (1947) traces the doomed romance between a passionate young lecturer, who has just arrived from Montreal to teach at a small American college, and the college president, who is encumbered with a crippled wife. Although the characters and situations are mostly romantic clichés, the tripartite narrative structure, which tells the slight story in flashbacks through three different narrators, adds complexity and saves the ending from sentimentality. But the "similarity of tone" of each section cannot redeem the "faded material" of the book, according to Claude Bissell in "Letters in Canada: 1947" (*University of Toronto Quarterly*, July 1948).

The Invisible Gate (1949), set in Montreal after World War II, portrays the cynical exploita-

Dust jacket for Beresford-Howe's most recent novel

tion of two sisters by a returned serviceman. Eventually, the high-spirited and responsible heroine saves herself and her naive sister from the charming, amoral villain and returns to her childhood sweetheart. While the critics indicted this novel, like its predecessors, for a tendency to "cardboard figures" and "melodramatic" plots, Bissell noted the development of Beresford-Howe's "lively talent" and especially the "easy fluency" of prose style that has come to distinguish her writing ("Letters in Canada: 1949").

In the 1950s Beresford-Howe was part of a lively academic and cultural community at McGill, a colleague of Louis Dudek and Hugh MacLennan, and a president of the local branch of the Canadian Authors' Association. During these first years of teaching she wrote her only historical romance, *My Lady Greensleeves* (1955), based on an authentic Elizabethan love triangle and lawsuit. Although the historical documentation gives her characters and plot more substance and her prose style is rich and skillful, critics still

faulted her intellectual and emotional themes as facile.

In 1960 Beresford-Howe married Christopher W. Pressnell, a high-school teacher; they had a son, Jeremy W. Howe, in 1967. By 1969 the student unrest at McGill and the political turmoil in Montreal persuaded Beresford-Howe and her husband reluctantly to leave Quebec. They moved to Toronto, where they now live. She became a professor of English at Ryerson Polytechnical Institute in 1971 and taught English and creative writing there until her retirement in 1988. Since then she has been a writer in residence at the North York Public Library.

The eighteen years between *My Lady Greensleeves* and *The Book of Eve* (1973) were filled with academic and domestic responsibilities for Beresford-Howe. It was not until the interval between her departure from McGill and her employment at Ryerson that she found the leisure to write the book which demonstrated her maturation as a writer and won her best-seller status, critical praise, and the Canadian Booksellers Award. *The Book of Eve* tells the story of Eva, who at sixty-five suddenly leaves her husband of forty years and the bourgeois wilderness of Notre Dame de Grace to descend into a tenement flat and an eccentric existence as a scavenger. But, in her freedom from convention and materialism, she finds an independent identity, strength for survival, new values, fellowship, and even love. In an inversion of the original fall from grace, she is reborn. Eva is a triumph of realistic characterization and convincing narrative voice, although her redemptive romance seems too contrived. *The Book of Eve* was adapted for the stage by Larry Fineberg and performed at the Stratford Festival in Ontario in 1976.

A Population of One (1977) and *The Marriage Bed* (1981) completed the trilogy "The Voices of Eve," about women who redefine modern conventions to find their own fulfillment. In the former, a thirty-year-old Ph.D. comes to Montreal with a dual "project": to teach college English and to lose her virginity. She succeeds in attaining her first goal (despite the student revolution) but fails in the second, learning instead to reject her contemporaries' casual sex and accept her very Canadian isolation with dignity. In *The Marriage Bed* the heroine, pregnant, with two small children, and abandoned by her lawyer husband, is trapped in domestic drudgery. The thematic inversion is that she refuses all offers to be liberated and wins back her husband by delivering their baby on the floor of his mistress's communal rooming house. These two novels confounded the feminist following of *The Book of Eve*, but they are sensitive, moving, and often very comic portrayals of modern women, although the death that ends *A Population of One* and the birth that concludes the later novel are too arbitrary. Andrea O'Reilly, in an analysis published in *Canadian Women's Studies* (1987), concludes: "though the trilogy is feminist in its consideration of female freedom, it ultimately expresses through the textual ambiguities and theoretical contradictions and authorial voice uncomfortable with and unsure about feminism in both its theory and praxis."

Night Studies (1985) is an innovative collage of character studies unified in the narrative framework of three evenings of classes at a Toronto community college. The complex interrelationships and the bleak vision of contemporary society behind them are deftly developed with irony and compassion but also humor and suspense. The two central characters, in the end, convincingly demonstrate the human potential to transcend tragedy. The more than fifteen other characters are merely cameos, Louise Longo maintains, "who are dangerously close to cliché" (*Books in Canada*, October 1985).

In *Prospero's Daughter* (1988) Beresford-Howe deconstructs the literary myth so that Prospero's autocratic and abortive matchmaking results in Miranda's escape with Caliban, Prospero's

broken decline in a nursing home, and Ariel's retirement to a suburban bedsitter. The Shakespearean themes of illusion and reality (played out in the characters of a wealthy novelist, his family and friends) are complex and intriguing. But the idealized English country-house setting, the ritualistic round of parties, and the stereotyped characters undermine any profound possibilities. Carefully crafted and impeccably written like all of Beresford-Howe's mature novels, it nevertheless suffers from her weakness for romantic resolutions. Jane Kulyk Keefer's assessment of *Prospero's Daughter* (*Books in Canada*, April 1988), that "Beresford-Howe has mastered the craft of novel-writing, but the art of fiction is something else," generally represents critical opinion of this author: she is a competent and popular, but not profound, novelist.

Reference:

Andrea O'Reilly, "Feminizing Feminism: Constance Beresford-Howe and the Quest for Female Freedom," *Canadian Woman Studies/ Les Cahiers de la Femme*, 8, no. 3 (1987): 69-72.

Papers:

The manuscript for *The Unreasoning Heart* is at the McGill University Library. The rest of Beresford-Howe's papers are at the University of Calgary Library.

Earle Birney
(13 May 1904-   )

Paul Matthew St. Pierre
Simon Fraser University

BOOKS: *David and Other Poems* (Toronto: Ryerson, 1942);

Now Is Time (Toronto: Ryerson, 1945);

Canada Calling (Montreal: CBC International Service, 1946);

The Strait of Anian: Selected Poems (Toronto: Ryerson, 1948);

Turvey: A Military Picaresque (Toronto: McClelland & Stewart, 1949); republished as *Turvey: A Picaresque Novel* (London: Abelard-Schuman, 1958); republished as *The Kootenay Highlander* (London: Landsborough, 1960); revised and unexpurgated edition published as *Turvey: A Picaresque Novel* (Toronto: McClelland & Stewart, 1976);

Trial of a City and Other Verse (Toronto: Ryerson, 1952); *Trial of a City* revised as *The Damnation of Vancouver* (Toronto: McClelland & Stewart, 1977);

Down the Long Table (Toronto: McClelland & Stewart, 1955; London: Abelard-Schuman, 1959);

Ice Cod Bell or Stone: A Collection of New Poems (Toronto: McClelland & Stewart, 1962);

Near False Creek Mouth: New Poems (Toronto: McClelland & Stewart, 1964);

The Creative Writer (Toronto: CBC Publications, 1966);

Selected Poems, 1940-1966 (Toronto: McClelland & Stewart, 1966);

Memory No Servant (Trumansburg, N.Y.: New Books, 1968);

The Poems of Earle Birney (Toronto: McClelland & Stewart, 1969);

pnomes jukollages & other stunzas, Gronk, fourth series, no. 3 (Toronto: Ganglia, 1969);

Rag & Bone Shop (Toronto: McClelland & Stewart, 1971);

Responses (London: National Book League / Poetry Society, 1971);

The Cow Jumped Over the Moon: The Writing and Reading of Poetry (Toronto: Holt, Rinehart & Winston, 1972);

Four Parts Sand, by Birney, Bill Bissett, Judith Copithorne, and Andrew Suknaski (Ottawa: Oberon, 1972);

The Bear on the Delhi Road: Selected Poems (London: Chatto & Windus, 1973);

what's so big about GREEN? (Toronto: McClelland & Stewart, 1973);

The Collected Poems of Earle Birney, 2 volumes (Toronto: McClelland & Stewart, 1975);

Alphabeings & Other Seasyours (London, Ont.: Pikadilly, 1976);

The Rugging and the Moving Times: Poems New and Uncollected (Coatsworth, Ont.: Black Moss, 1976);

Ghost in the Wheels: Selected Poems (Toronto: McClelland & Stewart, 1977);

Fall by Fury & Other Makings (Toronto: McClelland & Stewart, 1978);

Big Bird in the Bush: Selected Stories and Sketches (Oakville, Ont.: Mosaic Valley Editions, 1978);

Spreading Time: Remarks on Canadian Writing and Writers: Book I, 1904-1949 (Montreal: Véhicule, 1980);

The Mammoth Corridors (Okemos, Mich.: Stone, 1980);

Essays on Chaucerian Irony, edited by Beryl Rowland (Toronto & Buffalo: University of Toronto Press, 1985);

Words on Waves: The Selected Radio Plays of Earle Birney (Kingston, Ont.: Quarry / Toronto: CBC Enterprises, 1985);

The Copernican Fix (Toronto: ECW, 1985).

RADIO: *Johnny Dunn and the Wolves*, International Service, British Section, CBC-International, December 1945;

Court-Martial, Vancouver Theatre, CBC, 3 October 1946;

David, Wednesday Night, CBC, 28 January 1948;

November Eleven 1948, CBC, 11 November 1948;

Sir Gawain and the Green Knight, adaptation by Birney, *Wednesday Night*, CBC, 3 January 1950;

Earle Birney (courtesy of the National Film Board of Canada)

Beowulf, adaptation by Birney, *Producer's Workshop*, CBC, 17 April 1950;

The Griffin and the Minor Canon, adapted from Frank R. Stockton's story, *Fall Fare*, CBC, 29 September 1950;

The Murder in the Pawnshop, adapted from Robert Louis Stevenson's story "Markheim," *Four to the Queen*, CBC, 7 November 1950;

A Party at the Undertaker's, adapted from Alexander Pushkin's story, *Four to the Queen*, CBC, 14 November 1950;

The Case of Dr. Trifon, adapted from Ivan Turgenev's story, *Four to the Queen*, CBC, 21 November 1950;

The Queen of Spades, adapted from Pushkin's story, *Four to the Queen*, CBC, 28 November 1950;

The Duel, adapted from Joseph Conrad's novella, *Wednesday Night*, CBC, 30 January 1952;

The Damnation of Vancouver, *Wednesday Night*, CBC, 8 October 1952;

Piers Plowman, adaptation by Birney, *Stage*, CBC, 26 May 1957.

OTHER: "Aldous Huxley," in *The Art of the Novel*, edited by Pelham Edgar (New York: Macmillan, 1933), pp. 280-290;

Twentieth-Century Canadian Poetry: An Anthology, edited, with an introduction, by Birney (Toronto: Ryerson, 1953);

Record of Service in the Second World War, a supplement to the University of British Columbia War Memorial Manuscript Record, edited by Birney (Vancouver: University of British Columbia, 1955);

New Voices: Canadian University Writing of 1956, edited by Birney, Ira Dilworth, Desmond Pacey, Jean-Charles Bonenfant, and Roger Duhamel (Toronto: Dent, 1956);

"E. J. Pratt and His Critics," in *Our Living Tradition*, second and third series, edited by Robert L. McDougall (Ottawa: Carlton University Press / Toronto: University of Toronto Press, 1959), pp. 123-147;

Selected Poems of Malcolm Lowry, edited, with an introduction, by Birney (San Francisco: City Lights, 1962);

Malcolm Lowry, *Lunar Caustic*, edited by Birney and Margerie Bonner Lowry (London: Cape, 1968).

PERIODICAL PUBLICATIONS: "Proletarian Literature: Theory and Practice," review of *Novel and the People*, by Ralph Fox, *Canadian Forum*, 17 (May 1937): 58-60;

"The Two William Faulkners," review of Faulkner's *The Unvanquished*, *Canadian Forum*, 18 (June 1938): 84-85;

"War and the English Intellectuals," *Canadian Forum*, 21 (July 1941): 110-114;

"The Two Worlds of Geoffrey Chaucer," *Manitoba Arts Review*, 2 (Winter 1941): 3-16;

"On Being a Canadian Author," *Canadian Library Association Bulletin*, 9 (November 1952): 77-79;

"The Writer and the H-Bomb: Why Create?," *Queen's Quarterly*, 62 (Spring 1955): 37-44;

"The Poet and the University," *Bulletin of the Humanities Association of Canada*, 20 (January 1957): 6-7;

"Random Remarks on a Random World," *Humanities Association Bulletin*, 29 (January 1960): 10-11, 18-20;

"Glimpses into the Life of Malcolm Lowry," *Tamarack Review*, 19 (Spring 1961): 35-41;

"Poems by Malcolm Lowry," *Canadian Literature*, 8 (Spring 1961): 17-19; republished in *Malcolm Lowry: The Man and His Work*, edited by George Woodcock (Vancouver: University of British Columbia Press, 1971), pp. 91-93;

"The Unknown Poetry of Malcolm Lowry," *British Columbia Library Quarterly*, 24 (April 1961): 33-40;

"Struggle Against the Old Guard: Editing the *Canadian Poetry Magazine*," *Essays on Canadian Writing*, 21 (Spring 1981): 9-31;

"Child Addict in Alberta," *Canadian Literature*, 90 (Autumn 1981): 6-12;

"Meeting George Lamming in Jamaica," *Canadian Literature*, 95 (Winter 1982): 16-28.

Since the 1920s, Alfred Earle Birney has become a venerated literary figure. Throughout his career Birney has done more than most writers to legitimize and consolidate what is often considered a mésalliance between Canadian academic life and literary life, mainly because he has allowed his own academic and literary lives to complement each other and because he has prevented them from compromising one another. (*New Voices: Canadian University Writing of 1956*, edited by Birney and others, attests to his dedication to the academic tradition of Canadian literature.) Although his academic interests in Anglo-Saxon and Middle English and his scholarly articles on Chaucer may help to explain the at once antiquated, anachronistic, and avant-garde metrics of some of his poetry, they remain quite distinct from his poetic interests and his various and numerous collections of verse. Birney has consistently written poetry—as well as fiction, criticism, and drama—with a popular appeal, partly a result of his fascination with people and his interest in his own personality, and partly a result of his extensive travels and personal worldview.

His equally extensive poetic subject matter has shadowed his odysseys throughout North America and to Europe, the Caribbean, South America, Asia, and Australia, and to some of the internal settings of his own character. Birney's decision to arrange the contents of his *Collected Poems* (1975) not only chronologically but also geographically is an acknowledgment of the importance of place in his life and poetics. Although unimportant in themselves, places assume significance for Birney when they are inhabited, when they are entered, when they are quitted: when they are peopled and depopulated. For this reason, the act and process of journeying have been sources of fascination to him. Even Birney's predominantly technical concern with matters ranging from the intricate meters and cadences of Old English to the minimalist typographies of concrete poetry have to do with the relations between space and time and with the desire of the human being bound by mortality to transcend his place, to reconcile space and time by staying in motion, remaining moved by life.

To appreciate the role that place occupies in Birney's life and art, one must first consider the site of his birth, Calgary, in the foothills of Alberta (on 13 May 1904, when Alberta was still part of the Northwest Territories), and his childhood in Erikson, in the Kootenay Valley of mountainous eastern British Columbia. Birney is a kind of literary equivalent of the British sculptor Henry Moore, carving and caressing the monoliths of language, polishing shape until it becomes sound, polishing sound until it becomes visible, dedicating himself as much to pure form as to the particularities of function and meaning. To Birney language is an endless mountain range of massive stone blocks, some jagged, others rounded, each containing a letter, a word, a phrase, or a sound, some clue to the great mystery of the living alphabet. That in recent years he has preferred to call his poems simply "makings" and "alphabeings" suggests that he regards them as entities in which to discover the human mystery and human expressions of the mysterious.

Just as the setting of Birney's early childhood may have been the initial source of his interest in the shape of language, so his parents and their backgrounds may have been ultimately responsible for his attraction to sound and rhythm and for his concern with motion and physical absence. William George Birney, his father, was a painter and a decorator who often had to be away from home to earn a living for his family; and Earle Birney learned early to discern his father's presence in absence and to accept the paradox of the missing personality. He was able to discover the natural curiosity of his mother's accents when he accompanied Martha Stout Birney (née Robertson) on a trip to her birthplace in the Shetland Islands, an adventure (the first of his many odysseys) that Birney described in "Child Addict in Alberta" (*Canadian Literature*, Autumn 1981) as "just the thing to hatch a bookworm into a boy."

His interest in Walter Scott, however, was less ancestral than intellectual: his reading was as eclectic as could be expected for a boy in the Canadian wilderness: Robert Louis Stevenson, H. Rider Haggard, Daniel Defoe, John Bunyan, Alexandre Dumas, Mark Twain, Jack London, and O. Henry, and even a few living Canadian writers–Bliss Carman, Pauline Johnson, Charles G. D. Roberts–whom Birney discovered in the *Oxford Book of Canadian Verse*. Years later, as the editor of the *Canadian Poetry Magazine* and a twice-published poet himself, Birney was to recognize in the *Oxford Book of Australian Verse* certain qualities he thought were missing from Canadian poetry, notably "colourful and original popular speech," a vernacular he discovered again when he made an extended reading tour of Australia in the late 1960s.

Throughout his childhood, but also later while he was an honours English undergraduate and the editor of the student newspaper, the *Ubyssey*, at the University of British Columbia, a University of Toronto master's student working on Old and Middle English, and a doctoral candidate at Toronto examining Chaucer's irony, Birney was essentially an explorer of the landscape of language, gradually and carefully charting the territory of his artistic and academic vocation, his calling to originate, to color, and to popularize the speech and the speech acts we all have in common.

After a long graduate student's tenure made uncertain by the political and societal vicissitudes of the Depression, including moves from the University of Toronto (where he was a Leonard Fellow) to the University of Utah and from the University of London back to the University of Toronto, partly to raise funds for the Trotskyites by taking on instructorships and lectureships, Birney began to discover personal security and the beginnings of intellectual maturity. In 1933 he had married Sylvia Johnstone; they separated almost immediately, and the marriage was annulled in 1936. From 1936 to 1941 he was a lecturer in English at University College, University of Toronto, and from 1941 to 1942 he served as assistant professor.

With the outbreak of World War II and the concomitant suppression of Communist propaganda, Birney sought a new and more acceptable outlet for his burgeoning ideas and principles, especially since the *Canadian Forum*, which had been his political soapbox since 1936, released him from his editorial duties in 1940. By this time also, Birney's attitude to the war changed dramatically, his focus turning from opposing the capitalist military push to acknowledging the more pressing need to close ranks in stopping Hitler. His wife Esther Bull, whom he married on 6 March 1940, was Jewish; some members of her family were put to death in concentration camps in Poland. Birney felt strongly about fighting on behalf of their son, William, who he knew would have been considered a Jew in Hitler's Germany. He made his first commitment to the war effort by joining the Canadian Officers Training Corps (COTC), serving as a lieutenant from 1940 to 1942.

Birney continued to contribute to the *Canadian Forum* until 1941, but in effect he had already turned from political and social journalism to discover his poetic voice. He collected some of the verse he had written while editing the *Forum* and composed the other poems that would make up his first, and in some ways still his most important, volume, *David and Other Poems* (1942), which won a Governor General's Award for Poetry. Throughout the collection there is a paradoxical tension between the poet's philosophic doubt and insecurity and his clear vision and confident expression. In the title poem the mountain peaks of his youth reappear as poetic images. This poignant parable about a young man lying paralyzed on a mountain ledge after a climbing accident, begging his companion to push him off and thus save him from the life of a cripple in a wheelchair, is as much an expression of a society choosing between the paralysis of war and death and the rebirth of moral disfigurement as it is an expression of a culture whose historical imperfections are so great that it actually depends on them for its continued imperfect existence.

David's choice–"If I could move.... Or die...."–is essentially the choice Birney considers in his own life and the choice with which he confronts his readers through his poetics of place and motion. The popularity of this frequently anthologized poem suggests the poet's own enduring success and his ability to identify a place common to all readers and to move them through it safely. The theme of "David," a kind of secular ascent of Mt. Sinai, has become an essential part of the Canadian poetic tradition. But for Birney himself the poem offered a way to come to terms with his past: "there were too many mountains in my memory," he wrote in 1972, in *The Cow Jumped Over the Moon: The Writing and Reading of Poetry.* For Birney, "David" also represented a means of establishing the terms of his future: "there was still an immediate decision to be made about shape before I could stop swimming in chaos." But before he could continue to assign poetic shapes to memory, he would have to do his part toward shaping the immediate chaos that faced his generation in the form of global war.

After castigating Canadian poets for not responding to the war, in a *Canadian Forum* article, "To Arms with Canadian Poetry" (January 1940; collected in *Spreading Time*, 1980), Birney went on to make a more physical response, leaving the COTC reserve and enrolling in the Canadian Active Army, where he served from 1942 to 1945. While awaiting overseas infantry duty, he declined offers (prompted by the success of *David and Other Poems*) to compose more verse, but as an officer with the Infantry Personnel Selection Service in England, Birney endeavored to maintain contact with literature, acting as an unofficial spokesman for Canadian literature and contributing to English journals for the first time. His contacts over the next two years included Cyril Connolly, John Lehmann, and the Canadian novelist Sinclair Ross, serving in London with the Ordnance Corps; he also was in touch with a host of Canadian writers at home, in a correspondence dedicated to supplanting the conservative Canadian Authors Association. After spending the last

months of the war on the Continent as a major in charge of reallocating Canadian troops in the North-West Theater (Holland and Belgium), he was invalided back to Canada, where, after a brief period of recovery in a hospital, he was ready to start his academic and artistic pursuits again, full of what were really his first uncloistered, nonacademic experiences of the world. His response to the conflict and to his somewhat official and bureaucratic involvement in it was generally positive and fruitful.

Now Is Time, his second volume of verse, published in 1945, was composed during the war, when Birney was not involved with interviewing and assessing soldiers, yet it employs some of the psychoanalytical skills he had developed with Personnel Selection. The volume is based on a poetic consideration of time, the poet juggling "Tomorrow," "Yesterday," and "Today" (as the three sections of the book are called) in order to decide which one the postwar generation should regard as its own, letting the others drop into historical oblivion. Several selections republished from *David and Other Poems*, including "Vancouver Lights" ("We are a spark beleaguered/by darkness this twinkle we make in a corner of emptiness"), "Anglosaxon Street" ("Sit after supper on smeared doorsteps/not humbly swearing hatedeeds on Huns/profiteers politicians pacifists Jews"), and "War Winter" ("lodgers on this/your slantwhirling lackey life-crusted satellite/this your one wrynecked woedealing/world"), suggest Birney's emphasis on the human and realist reaction to a world turned inhuman and fantastic. With the end and the aftermath of the war and with the vision of a fragile future, the poet anxiously moves away from destruction and despair toward at least the possibility of rebirth and hope. He at once celebrates the impermanence of war, entertains the possibility of a permanent peace, and anticipates a historical transition to the transitory itself. In "Lines for a Peace" Birney contemplates a peace that in 1943 he can only anticipate, yet his ideas are hopeful and to a certain extent prophetic:

> The hours flash below the sun
> and space is now and now is time
> to bed the beast and with the pain
> of love shock him to the brain–
> then certify the future sane

A complementary poem, "Death of a War," announces that "Somewhere the leaven of reason is poised / to splinter the stone of our sky," an idea that, by apparently defying logic, defies the illogical course of man in history. Like *David and Other Poems* before it, *Now Is Time* was immensely popular and critically successful, winning its author a Governor General's Award for 1945. In the years immediately following the war, Birney gained entrance into various salons of respectability that before the war the radical in him would have wished defaced or destroyed.

In 1945 he accepted a position as a supervisor of European foreign-language broadcasts with the International Shortwave Service of the Canadian Broadcasting Corporation. Although he welcomed the position as a natural extension of his work during the war, by 1946 he considered the job too physically and emotionally demanding, especially in the severe climate of Montreal. That same year he accepted an offer from University of British Columbia president Norman MacKenzie to teach Anglo-Saxon and Medieval English literature at the institution where he had been a successful undergraduate. Birney would spend the next nineteen years at UBC. Before taking up his fist major academic appointment, he joined the Canadian Authors Association, the very group that during the war he had sought to undermine, and he accepted an offer from William Arthur Deacon, president of the CAA, to become editor of the Association's *Canadian Poetry Magazine*. Birney held the post from 1946 until 1948, moving the magazine's offices from Toronto to Vancouver, editing and contributing to the journal faithfully, and taking it in some new and vivifying aesthetic directions.

As early as his first editorial, Birney unveiled his change in policy, very much an expression of his personal views on Canadian poetry and periodicals, and he announced the introduction of uniform payment rates for the magazine's contributors, emphasizing a movement toward eclecticism and excellence. In addition to announcing the appointment of former *Canadian Poetry Magazine* editor and "our greatest living poet" E. J. Pratt to a newly formed editorial board, Birney praised the credentials of some of his contributors, including Roy Daniells. Moved by the encouragement of Pratt, Birney gave the journal a modern, innovative appearance, despite occasional interference from the Canadian Authors Association. His first issue of the magazine was received encouragingly by his peers, by Pratt, A. M. Klein, Raymond Souster, Dorothy Livesay, Ralph Gustafson, Louis Dudek, and others, but Birney soon began to realize the enormous strug-

Dust jacket for the 1976 edition of Birney's first novel, winner of the 1949 Leacock Medal for Humour

gle ahead of him even if he were merely to fulfill his own editorial promises and "transform *CPM* from a feeble house-organ to Establishment poetasters into that national outlet for contemporary work and criticism every good young poet in Canada still wanted." He continued to assert his editorial and aesthetic principles for two years. Among his important accomplishments during his editorship were his representation (the first for the *Canadian Poetry Magazine*) of some of Canada's most highly regarded poets, his introduction of Canadian poetry (through radio broadcasts and university reading tours) to the western United States, and his endorsement of Malcolm Lowry's poetry (which he was later to edit) and of Paul Hiebert's satire on editing Canadian poetry, *Sarah Binks* (1947), which Birney himself reviewed, citing it as "required reading" for the Canadian Authors Association.

Throughout his life Birney has been able to draw something positive from negative experiences: all his positive contributions to Canadian literature seem to have arisen ultimately from his wartime experiences and the brilliant poetry it helped him to produce. Through his series of editorial disputes and struggles came another development. During the summer of 1947, in the middle of his tenure at the *Canadian Poetry Magazine*, Birney made an outline of what was to become his first novel, *Turvey: A Military Picaresque* (1949). As he began the novel, he was finishing work on his third volume of poems, *The Strait of Anian* (1948). For Birney, *Turvey* was a new venture generically, but its subject matter was wholly familiar, since he drew heavily on his military experience to produce a Canadian version of Henry Fielding's "comic Epic-Poem in Prose," *Joseph Andrews* (1742). Over the next year, making use of a friend's cabin on Bowen Island and (briefly) of Lowry's squatter's shack at Dollarton (both places near Vancouver), Birney completed his preparatory notes and began writing a book that was not unlike Hiebert's mock heroic *Sarah Binks*. Completing a rough draft of *Turvey* that summer, he spent the following academic year revising it.

Birney, in "Creativity Through Fiction" (collected in *The Creative Writer*, 1966), describes *Turvey* as "a picaresque, a succession of incidents half-farcical, half-serious proceeding from his [Turvey's] enlistment to his discharge." As the name of the eponymous character suggests, the novel is a topsy-turvy picaresque in which Birney inverts and reverses the roles of the most famous picaresque heroes, Don Quixote and Sancho Panza. Semi-autobiographical, too, *Turvey* is the story of an ordinary odd-man-out whose adventure starts in 1942 when he joins the chaotic world of the Canadian army. Throughout his training in Canada, England, and Europe, Turvey attempts to win a transfer into the legendary Kootenay Highlanders regiment, in which his old friend Mac (his quixotic counterpart) is serving. Thwarting his efforts each step of the way is a Selection of Personnel Officer whose sole duty in the army seems to be to give Turvey aptitude tests at any cost. After suffering the effects of several personal rebellions and debaucheries, Turvey finds himself in the hospital, suffering from diphtheria and pursuing his love for a girl to whom he has become engaged and who promises to follow him to Canada.

Turvey's experiences are in the main (and with the proper amount of literary embellishment and exaggeration) Birney's own; the novel is an attempt, like his other literary works immediately after the war, to reconcile, as he put it in "Creativity Through Fiction," "a complex unit of my life completed, forever finished with—except in my mind, which demanded that it be assessed, and emotionally contained." *Turvey* was not as immediately well received as Birney's poetry had been. Yet it did enjoy some success, "by Canadian standards—all of seven thousand copies sold." Since its initial publication the novel has enjoyed several revivals, especially among audiences interested in Birney as a precursor of other writers (notably the Black Mountain poets) who explore the boundaries of language and who consider any kind of discourse appropriate to literary expression. The profanity in *Turvey* led to its ban in several Ontario libraries, even though the 1949 edition had been much revised and bowdlerized prior to publication. In 1960 a pirated edition, *The Kootenay Highlander*, appeared in England; a revised and unexpurgated edition was published in 1976. *Turvey* won the 1949 Leacock Medal for Humour.

While he was writing *Turvey* Birney was active in many other literary and academic areas, notably as a UBC English professor who was laying the groundwork for what would eventually become an independent creative-writing program. He was also acting as a spokesman for Canadian writing, much as he had done in England during the war, trying to make the literature more universally known, as in October 1947, when he read on radio a script entitled "The Representative Canadian Poet Today" (subsequently collected in *Spreading Time*). Just as he had tried to reach an American audience in his *Canadian Poetry Magazine* days through radio broadcasts and university reading tours, so now he attempted to address a British audience by reading over the International Service of the Canadian Broadcasting Corporation.

In characterizing the Canadian poet, he referred to a person who "has turned to sprung rhythms, jazz dissonances, half-rhymes, etc., not because he personally felt the need of them but because in England and America they are now the thing." He saw Canadian poetry at a halfway point, and possibly he saw himself as the poet who could lead it the other half of the way, to the point where current traditions and conventions (and the absences of both) would be recognized as particular characteristics of Canadian verse.

Ironically, while Birney was encouraging his fellow poets not to conform blindly to English and American styles, he was having to conform to the more immediate demands of his academic life at UBC. Both *Turvey* and his third volume of poems, *The Strait of Anian*, were composed during summer terms. *The Strait of Anian* contains several poems republished from his previous volume, *Now Is Time*, but within a new context of Canadian concern quite distinct from the contexts of his earlier war-inspired poems and even of his war novel. Birney makes a poetic pilgrimage across the country (mirroring his own migration to the West Coast) in poems ranging from "Atlantic Door," in which he calls for a turning away from the preoccupation with the war ("think no more than you must / of the simple unhuman truth of this emptiness / that down deep below the lowest pulsing / of primal cell / tar-dark and dead / lie the bleak and forever capacious tombs of the sea"), to "Pacific Door," in which he reveals that "there is no clear Strait of Anian" (referring to the voyage of Sir Francis Drake in search of the Northwest passage) and effectively repeats the "think no more" refrain of the companion poem, suggesting the necessity of finding as much a rite of passage as a geographic passage for contemporary cultures.

For the next few summers, Birney worked on a verse play for radio and a related group of poems, all of which he published in 1952 as *Trial of a City and Other Verse*. The volume was a departure for Birney in its concerns with the associations and disassociations of urban life and with the self-contained and self-containing urban setting. The play is an attractive modernistic phantasmagoria about a contemporary city (Vancouver) put on trial. The prosecutor has the enviable power—his name is Gabriel Powers—to conjure witnesses from the past, from explorer Captain George Vancouver to medieval poet William Langland. The defense counsel—her name is Mrs. Anyone, even though she lacks the power to call anyone to the stand—actually manages, through a series of well-handled philosophical arguments, to win an indefinitely suspended judgment for the city and indeed for Western culture. The carefully guarded optimism of *Trial of a City* is recurrent in Birney's writing from this point on.

The poems accompanying the verse drama are more varied in subject matter than anything Birney had written so far, suggesting a new dimen-

sion to his poetic abilities. "The Monarch of the Id," for example, shows Birney treating a serious subject in a comic manner: that of official government censorship, the kind that D. H. Lawrence, William Faulkner, and James Joyce have all suffered in Canada, and the sort that Birney himself endured with *Turvey*.

Since beginning his academic career at the University of British Columbia, Birney had become increasingly conscious of some obstacles to the further evolution of Canadian literature. While working on *Trial of a City*, he realized that if widely recognized authors were not commonly known and their works not readily available in Canada, then Canadian authors stood very little chance of permanent recognition. He found himself, as he wrote in one of the essays collected in *Spreading Time*, having "to beg the university library to buy contemporary poets" when he discovered that the stacks contained no works by such important poets as Stephen Spender and A. M. Klein, among others.

Even though he often directed his dissatisfaction with Canadian academic and literary life into his poems, as in the satirical *Strait of Anian*, Birney endeavored to better the situation by teaching creative writing, by offering poetry readings, by working with various media, and by setting an impressive and challenging example with his own work. In an effort to reach the widest possible audience, Birney turned to radio, certainly the most powerful of the media at the time. From 1946 to 1957, he wrote numerous radio plays for the Canadian Broadcasting Corporation Drama Department in Vancouver and Toronto, the best of which have been collected in *Words on Waves: The Selected Radio Plays of Earle Birney* (1985).

In these undertakings for radio Birney revealed two new skills: his sensitive ear for dialogue suited to broadcast over the radio, and his deft hand at adapting classic works of literature. These dramas are increasingly regarded as among Birney's major works, because of their originality (his plays are as different from conventional radio drama as they are from traditional broadcast poetry) and because of their ambitiousness and their sheer bulk (they range in length from four thousand to twenty-five thousand words).

Some of the plays are imaginative adaptations of Birney's own works, including "David" and *Trial of a City* (revised as *The Damnation of Vancouver*, broadcast in 1952 and published in a trade edition in 1977), and of the works of oth-

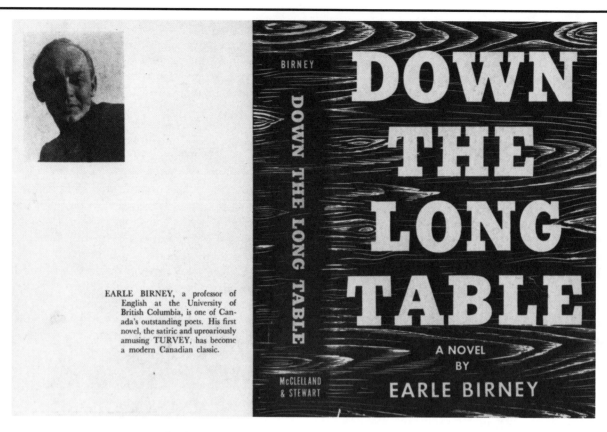

EARLE BIRNEY, a professor of English at the University of British Columbia, is one of Canada's outstanding poets. His first novel, the satiric and uproariously amusing TURVEY, has become a modern Canadian classic.

McCLELLAND & STEWART

Dust jacket for Birney's second novel, written in France in the early 1950s

ers, including stories by Pushkin, Turgenev, and Conrad; other plays are dramatic translations and recastings of *Beowulf, Piers Plowman,* and *Sir Gawain and the Green Knight;* still others are pieces written exclusively for broadcast by CBC-Radio. The peak of Birney's career in radio drama came in 1950, when he contributed seven radio plays to the CBC, matching his interest in early English poetry with his dedication to reaching a wide audience through innovative literary forms and methods. His apparent decrease in activity between the publication of *Turvey* in 1949 and of *Ice Cod Bell or Stone* in 1962, during which Birney published only one volume of poetry and one novel (his second, *Down the Long Table,* 1955), is attributable mainly to his dedication to radio drama, a form that, partly through his efforts, survives on the CBC to this day.

At the time Birney was honored by the Royal Society of Canada with the 1952 Lorne Pierce Medal, an award granted to the Canadian writer who best succeeds in articulating his culture to his compatriots, he was devoting his time to fiction once again. In 1953, on leave from the university on a Canadian government fellowship, he went to France, where he worked on *Down the*

Long Table. Like his earlier novel, much of this work is autobiographical. In this case the source, Birney's academic and Communist activities in the United States and Canada, predates World War II. The story is about Gordon Saunders, a university English instructor who becomes involved with organizing Trotskyist groups and meetings in Vancouver. After a police informer is found murdered, Saunders is forced to flee to the United States, where he pursues a respectable academic life until, as the book closes, he falls victim to a committee charged with investigating leftist activities.

Technically the novel is an exploration of the possibilities of poetic language in a politically prosaic story. Birney builds upon the picaresque form of his earlier novel and makes effective use of the dramatic voice of his poems and radio plays, combining them with various modern fictional and narrative techniques to create a curiously personal work with historical authenticity and insight. Evidence of the uninterrupted time that he was able to devote to his writing while he was in France, the novel is a concentrated, concentrating effort that suggests a new direction and an even more authoritative voice for the writer.

In "Creativity Through Fiction" Birney has expressed his admiration for *Down the Long Table* (even at the expense of *Turvey*), describing it as "a longer and more serious and (I still think) much better one, which took three times as long to write, and was generally damned, and eventually remaindered at seventy cents a copy." Critics have generally come to agree with Birney, remarking that the later novel's technique and stylistic subtlety are of enduring value.

Possibly Birney was able to comprehend one of his novel's main themes of loneliness and exile because he himself was finally away from the country with which he had been preoccupied since the end of World War II. In both his novels Birney was looking for financial as much as for artistic success, hoping for a regular income that would free him from academic work and enable him to devote himself to writing full-time. Ironically it was his long association with universities that would eventually give him his share of financial independence and artistic freedom. Even though in "Creativity Through Fiction" he alludes to a third novel that he feels "compelled to write," it has yet to appear in any form.

His tenure at the University of British Columbia was not simply a time of security but also a time of exploration, geographical as well as intellectual and intuitive, during which Birney tried to form a harmonious relationship between academia and travel, allowing each to inform and to inspire the other. It was on a second major leave from the university, 1958-1959, as a Nuffield fellow studying Chaucer at the British Museum, that he composed some of his best poetry to date, collected in *Ice Cod Bell or Stone: A Collection of New Poems*. A subsequent and more adventurous trip in 1962-1963, as a Canada Council fellow on a reading tour in the Caribbean and Latin America, gave Birney the impetus and the detachment he needed to write another volume of verse, *Near False Creek Mouth: New Poems* (1964), in which he allows his reader to accompany him on a poetically inspired tour not just through the Caribbean and South America but also through Europe and finally through Canada to False Creek Mouth, the center of Vancouver.

In *Ice Cod Bell or Stone*, Birney begins to recognize himself as a Canadian poet with international interests and universal concerns. Here, as in *Near False Creek Mouth*, the theme is travel and exploration, the poet inspired by settings as diverse as Japan and Spain, Mexico and northern Canada. Birney contrasts the historical explorers James Cook and Vitus Bering, who sought to populate the Earth's empty spaces, with existentialist or imaginative explorers who seek to contemplate the empty spaces that still remain because only explorers have bothered to pass through them. The profound reflection of "Ellesmereland" (one of the Queen Elizabeth Islands in the Canadian Arctic, featuring the northernmost point in North America) suggests the thematic and technical direction his work would begin to take during the 1960s: "No man is settled on that coast / The harebells are alone / Nor is there talk of making man / from ice cod bell or stone." In a 1965 sequel called "Ellesmereland II," Birney satirically refers to the hazards of a rapidly increasing population and of an expanding town in a contracting wilderness.

It was during the 1960s that Birney learned what for him is the true relation between the poet and his land: the poet's work is important not because it captures the absolute meaning of a setting but because it records an impermanent response to a setting whose meaning is constantly changing. In *Ice Cod Bell or Stone* he explores the complex relations between space and time and between space-time and man, whose paradoxes he tried to capture in the 1970s through concrete poetry. That as a Nuffield research fellow he should have traveled to England via Japan, Hong Kong, Southeast Asia, and the subcontinent (instead of on the customary transatlantic route) indicates the importance he placed on reaching his ultimate destination in a creative, informing manner, but not at the expense of the fascinating destinations along the way.

Near False Creek Mouth, his second volume of travel poems, is a series of new poems recording the itinerant musings of a well-traveled poetic explorer who sometimes assumes the persona of an impressionable tourist. "November Walk Near False Creek Mouth," for example, is about a man's mystical journey through a metaphysical landscape whose meaning is overwhelming in its elusiveness. The metaphor of exploration is similar to that of "David," except that here the reflections are of a man who has reached a plateau of middle age and who wonders how he will venture over the cliff and down into the unfathomable mysteries of old age. As Birney puts it in the conclusion to the poem:

> But still on the highest shelf of ever
> washed by the curve of timeless returnings
> lies the unreached unreachable nothing

"This book contains the longest non-dramatic poem I have ever written. Its setting is Vancouver but its theme is our precarious universe. Most of the poems involve people and places thousands of miles away from False Creek, near whose mouth I live, but they are all close to us now, not only in time-space, but in the sharing of needs and hopes — and premonitions of disaster."

EARLE BIRNEY

Earle Birney's reputation as a poet was firmly established by *David and Other Poems* (1942) and *Now is Time* (1945), both winners of the Governor-General's Award for Poetry. These were followed by *Strait of Anian* (1948), *Trial of a City* (1952) and *Ice Cod Bell or Stone* (1962). He has won numerous awards for single poems, including the Lorne Pierce gold medal for literature and the President's Medal of the University of Western Ontario. His poems have appeared in magazines throughout the Commonwealth and the United States and have been included in more than twenty Canadian and American anthologies. He is also the author of the hilarious novel *Turvey*, which won the Leacock Medal for Humour in 1950, and a second novel, *Down the Long Table*, which appeared in 1955.

He has been a professor of English at the University of British Columbia since 1946 and in 1963 was appointed Head of the Department of Writing there.

MCCLELLAND AND STEWART LIMITED

Covers for the first paperback edition of Birney's 1964 poetry collection, inspired by his travels in Canada, South America, and the Caribbean

whose winds wash down to the human shores
and slip shoving

into each thought nudging my footsteps now
as I turn to my brief night's ledge.

Throughout these poems, and especially in those with Mexican and South American settings and subjects, Birney considers the possibility that while the order of the poet and the disorder of the traveler might create a beautiful paradox, the order of the academic and the order of the poet who is also a traveler might create only an existential and vocational contradiction. When Birney entered his sixties, he decided to give his life yet another new direction, without denying any of the old ones.

While on his travels to England and through Latin America and in between these journeys, when he worked on the Lowry manuscripts at the University of British Columbia, Birney rea-

lized that although he still enjoyed academic work and profited from his association with a university, he no longer wished his work or his association to be as formal as they had been in the past. After serving as editor in chief of *Prism International* from summer 1964 to autumn 1965, Birney resigned from the university to pursue a series of more ephemeral academic postings. He initially accepted groundbreaking positions as writer in residence at Scarborough and Massey Colleges, the University of Toronto (1965-1967), at the University of Waterloo (1967-1968), and a Regents Professorship at the University of California, Irvine, from April to June 1968. Later he went on to writer-in-residence positions at the University of Western Ontario (1981-1982) and at the University of Alaska, Fairbanks (1984). His new academic career allowed Birney to commit himself to writing to an extent that he had not been able to do before. In this way Birney showed Canadians in particular that although the academic and literary lives were often incompatible, they could be pursued in such a way that they would lend support to each other.

In this new phase Birney began to reflect upon his career and to document it retrospectively for the first time, a practice that he has continued to the present day. He produced two important books in 1966, the year after his resignation from UBC: *Selected Poems, 1940-1966* and *The Creative Writer*. The first brought before the public some of Birney's best poems, incorporating revisions so extensive as to transform old Birney standards into wholly new poems. Several express Birney's dissatisfaction with academic life and especially with its political disputes, a discontent that would continue through his various writer-in-residence positions and that would eventually lead to his resignation from teaching and from the formal academic life altogether. Senior arts fellowships from the Canada Council (1968, 1974, and 1978-1981) helped Birney achieve his artistic independence. On one of these fellowships, Birney spent a year (beginning in July 1968) on a reading and writing tour of Australia and New Zealand, further exploring the poetic and cultural possibilities of the English language.

Birney's second other important publication of 1966, *The Creative Writer*, comprises transcripts of a series of talks he gave on CBC-Radio; they have to do with his personal (and at times quite idiosyncratic) views on poetry, fiction, education, writing, and on experimentation in these fields. Just as Birney had consistently combined his roles as poet, editor, novelist, traveler, and academic, so now he began to meld his roles as critic and autobiographer, an association he was to fortify in *The Cow Jumped Over the Moon* (1972) and in the first volume of his memoirs, *Spreading Time: Remarks on Canadian Writing and Writers: Book I, 1904-1949* (1980). In *The Creative Writer* Birney plays the professional teacher, expounding upon theories that he has practiced both as an instructor of creative writing and as a constantly creating writer himself. Each of the agreeably didactic chapters, in its articulate garrulousness and reserved gregariousness, belies its origin as an informal half-hour radio talk, the work of a kind of literary celebrity. Looking back critically on his career, Birney comments on what he regards as important aspects of his life and art, offering some elucidating remarks on experimental poetry (ranging from Black Mountain to Pop to the libretti of Gian-Carlo Menotti), which help to explain his own growing interest, especially during the 1970s, in concrete poetry and other nontraditional poetic forms.

In a succession of publications beginning with *Memory No Servant* in 1968, Birney made increasingly personal experiments with typography and language, including some that only he could fully understand, which was probably his aesthetic intention. Under the influence of B. P. Nichol and other experimental Canadian poets, he composed and compiled *pnomes jukollages & other stunzas* (1969), literally an envelope of poetic oddities and bits of verbal witticism, including found poems and concrete poems, as well as a few more traditional pieces. At the same time that he was writing his most peculiar verse, Birney was coediting, with Margerie Bonner Lowry, Malcolm Lowry's posthumously published novel *Lunar Caustic* (1968); his editorial work was, in part, a heartfelt reply to the favorable review of *Turvey* that Lowry wrote for *Thunderbird* in 1949. In 1962, with Mrs. Lowry's assistance, he had also edited *Selected Poems of Malcolm Lowry*.

In some of his first works of the 1970s Birney showed the poetic extremes that he joyously cultivated. *Rag & Bone Shop* (1971) comprises a variety of poems about time, particularly the contrast between the past, now stationary because of its distance and detachment, and the present, uncomfortably close in its withering energy. Notable is "The Mammoth Corridors" because of its contrast between the flat, choral voice of a travel brochure, describing how tourists can retrace the paths of Indians and European explorers of Canada's West Coast, with the poet's account of his own experiences exploring through his imagination periods and regions that transcend Western concepts of time and space yet remain eerily attached to the present: "A morning drunk is spattering curses / over a halfbreed girl in a blotched doorway." At another extreme, *what's so big about GREEN?* (1973), appearing soon after Birney's textbook on criticism, *The Cow Jumped Over the Moon*, comprises poems that are pessimistic and even cynical and that seem less celebrations of poetic life than poetic denunciations of life altogether. In "I Accuse Us," the text of a speech he gave at a 1967 protest in Toronto against the Vietnam War, Birney is angrier than anywhere else in his poetry, an angry old man attempting to infuriate the young people of his country, guilty of complicity in an immoral war:

I accuse Us
of celebrations without cause
of standing not moving
in passionate urgency
towards the *real* civilization
there may just be time
to glimpse before our species
crawls off to join the dinosaurs.

Yet, characteristically, Birney leaves himself open to positive responses to even the worst situations and conditions.

During the 1970s Birney continued to publish with regularity. Under the title *The Bear on the Delhi Road* (1973), the English publisher Chatto and Windus brought out an edition of some of Birney's previously published poems; in 1975, the year before the unexpurgated version of *Turvey* was published, *The Collected Poems of Earle Birney* appeared. During this period Birney received his most sustained critical acclaim since the publication of his first two volumes of poetry. In 1976, the year preceding his divorce from Esther Bull, he produced *Alphabeings & Other Seasyours*, a collection of concrete poems whose visual elements almost totally overshadow their verbal elements. "Jukiliage No. 5: The Song I Sing," for example, consists of a found list of jukebox entries, arranged in alphabetical order. *Ghost in the Wheels* (1977) is Birney's own selection of his poems mainly for students and teachers.

With the publication of the collected edition of his verse in 1975 and *The Rugging and the Moving Times: Poems New and Uncollected* (1976), which serves as a kind of afterword, Birney began to slow down. *Fall by Fury & Other Makings* (1978) contains several mature, dense poems that Birney wrote in the 1970s, as if to balance his concrete and minimalist experiments, including a poem titled simply "Birthday," in which he celebrates his seventy-third birthday:

Some nine hundred fifty circlings of my moon
i doubt i'll see a thousand
my face lunar now too
strings of the limbs unravelled
trunk weak at the core   like an elm's.

Here and elsewhere his reflections on old age and on his own history are among his most poignant and permanent contributions to Canadian literature, almost as though Birney were trying now to prepare his own oeuvre, to fashion his own memory, and identify his place in Canadian literary history. Through his publication of a selection of his stories and sketches called *Big Bird in the Bush* (1978), Birney drew to attention a neglected part of his art: his short-story writing and, by implication, his extensive and varied contributions of reviews, essays, and articles to little magazines of all sorts throughout Canada and in the United States and England. With the publication of the first volume of his memoirs, *Spreading Time*, and with the promise of a second volume covering the years 1950-1980, Birney has begun to put his life into a comprehensive literary order for his readers' and critics' benefits, for himself, and for posterity.

Birney has two more ambitious projects in the works, both reminiscences. One focuses on his experiences as a Royal Society of Canada research fellow at the University of London and as a political activist in London's Trotskyist circles. In 1934 Birney traveled to Norway to conduct a one-week interview with Trotsky, just two years before Trotsky went into his final exile in Mexico. The interview has aged for over half a century, but there are plans to publish it as a three-volume work titled "Conversations with Trotsky." The other reminiscence examines Birney's friendships with Dylan Thomas and Malcolm Lowry. Birney corresponded with Thomas and played host to him when he stopped in Vancouver on two North American reading tours. Birney knew Lowry during the last decade of his life (when Lowry lived mainly at Dollarton, near Vancouver), from the publication of *Under the Volcano* in 1947 (of which Birney claims proudly, "I read it. The first edition.") to Lowry's death in England in 1954. Birney has compiled a collection of essays on the two British writers, tentatively titled "Dylan Thomas and Malcolm Lowry in Vancouver." He is also working on other projects, mainly poetry but also some autobiographical works.

His two most recent volumes of poems, *The Mammoth Corridors* (1980) and *The Copernican Fix* (1985), are both limited-edition retrospectives, featuring some of Birney's most accomplished versifying and some of his most perfect poems. *The Mammoth Corridors* collects poems from the past forty years, culled from literary periodicals and little magazines from around the world. The material is vintage Birney. By allowing some of his poems to stand unrevised ("The Bear on the Delhi Road," for example), Birney seems to challenge them to stand the test of time. In *The Copernican Fix*, however, Birney tinkers with his verse. "Ellesmereland I" and "Ellesmereland II" appear

Covers for Birney's collection of concrete poems, published in 1976

intact but assume fresh associations when juxtaposed with a new poem, "Ellesmereland III." Birney's celebration of virgin arctic territory and his lamentation on man's upsetting the arctic harmony now become a kind of imagistic manifesto on the politics of arctic sovereignty: "The 'land beyond the human eye' / the Inuit call it still . . . / Under the blinding midnight sky / subs and missiles wait our will." Other poems, such as "buoy off Juan de Fuca" (1934), "Still life near Bangalore" (1974), and "my love is young" (1973), receive subtle touchings-up. Still other poems point to the continuity of Birney's poetic output: "looking UP (for Wailan on her 29th)" clearly recalls "She Is (for wai-lan, on her 24th birthday)" in *The Mammoth Corridors*. The title poem is one of Birney's latest. In "Copernican Fix" (1983) Birney achieves a perfect simplicity: "the sun never sets / it's we who rise / & think / to shine." "Copernican Fix" is one of sixty-two poems recorded in 1982 on three albums titled *Nexus and*

Earle Birney, on which Birney reads his poems to the improvised musical accompaniment of the Canadian jazz group Nexus.

In recent years Birney has continued to publish a variety of material in Canadian literary periodicals and little magazines, ranging from a series of poems dedicated to his friend and companion Wai-lan Low to a brief diary that he kept while he was eleven years old. Recently, declining health has interrupted Birney's retrospective on his life and letters and on Canadian literary history, but even this imposed silence has its place in the meter of the poet's recollective utterance, like caesurae in the Anglo-Saxon verse Birney loves. *Essays on Chaucerian Irony* (1985), edited by Beryl Rowland, is a compilation of his major articles on Geoffrey Chaucer. The articles first appeared from 1937 to 1960 but stand up well today, acknowledging Birney's substantial contribution to medieval studies and Canadian academic life over the course of three decades.

Over the years Birney has emerged in Canadian literature and literary life as principally what one might call a humorist, a writer who identifies and analyzes the complex, delicate, elusive humors of human nature. Despite his reputation as a late-starter–he published his first poems at the age of thirty-eight–he has been for nearly half a century the definitive living Canadian poet. On 20 March 1987 Earle Birney had a heart attack and was hospitalized. He recovered well enough to be able to accept an honorary doctor of letters degree from the University of British Columbia on 28 May 1987, but by the end of the month he suffered a stroke. Birney continues to make his home in Toronto.

Bibliography:

Peter Noel-Bentley, "Earle Birney: An Annotated Bibliography," in *The Annotated Bibliography of Canada's Major Authors*, volume 4, edited by Robert Lecker and Jack David (Downsview, Ont.: ECW, 1983), pp. 13-128.

References:

Peter Aichinger, *Earle Birney* (Boston: Twayne, 1979);

Aichinger, *Earle Birney and His Works* (Toronto: ECW, 1984); republished in *Canadian Writers and Their Works: Poetry Series*, volume 5, edited by Robert Lecker, Jack David, and Ellen Quigley (Toronto: ECW, 1985), pp. 27-91;

Frank Davey, "Black Days on Black Mountain," *Tamarack Review*, 36 (Spring 1965): 62-71;

Davey, *Earle Birney* (Toronto: Copp Clark, 1971);

Sandra Djwa, "A Developing Tradition," *Essays on Canadian Writing*, 21 (Spring 1981): 32-52;

D. J. Dooley, "The Satiric Novel in Canada Today," *Queen's Quarterly*, 64 (Winter 1957-1958): 576-590;

Earle Birney, edited by Bruce Nesbitt (Toronto & New York: McGraw-Hill Ryerson, 1974);

L. R. Early, "Birney and Purdy: An Intertextual Instance," *Canadian Poetry*, 23 (Fall-Winter 1988): 1-13;

Essays on Canadian Writing, special issue on Birney, 21 (Spring 1981); republished as *Perspectives on Earle Birney* (Downsview, Ont.: ECW, 1981);

Howard Fink, "Earle Birney's Radio Dramas," *Essays on Canadian Writing*, 21 (Spring 1981): 53-72; revised as "A Critical Introduction: Earle Birney's Radio Dramas," in *Words on Waves: Selected Radio Plays of Earle Birney* (Kingston, Ont.: Quarry / Toronto: CBC Enterprises, 1985), pp. xv-xxviii;

Lynn E. Jakes, "Old English Influences in Earle Birney's 'Anglosaxon Street' and 'Mappemounde,'" *Journal of Canadian Poetry*, 2 (Winter 1979): 67-75;

David Latham, "From the Hazel Bough of Yeats: Birney's Masterpiece," *Canadian Poetry*, 21 (Fall-Winter 1987): 52-58;

Louis K. MacKendrick, "Gleewords and Old Discretions: Birney's Benefictions," *Essays on Canadian Writing*, 21 (Spring 1981): 158-173;

Bruce Nesbitt, "The Political Prose of Earle Birney: Trotsky and the 1930s," *Essays on Canadian Writing*, 21 (Spring 1981): 174-183;

W. H. New, "Prisoner of Dreams: The Poetry of Earle Birney," *Canadian Forum*, 52 (September 1972): 29-32; revised as "Maker of Order, Prisoner of Dreams: The Poetry of Earle Birney," in his *Articulating West: Essays on Purpose and Form in Modern Canadian Literature* (Toronto: New Press, 1972), pp. 259-269;

Desmond Pacey, "Earle Birney," in his *Ten Canadian Poets: A Group of Biographical and Critical Essays* (Toronto: Ryerson, 1958), pp. 293-326;

Arthur L. Phelps, "Two Poets: Klein and Birney," in his *Canadian Writers* (Toronto: McClelland & Stewart), pp. 111-119;

Zailig Pollock, "Earle Birney," in *Profiles in Canadian Literature*, volume 1, edited by Jeffrey M. Heath (Toronto: Dundurn, 1980): 89-96;

Richard Robillard, *Earle Birney* (Toronto: McClelland & Stewart, 1971);

Beryl Rowland, "Earle Birney and Chaucer," *Essays on Canadian Writing*, 21 (Spring 1981): 73-84;

Laurence Steven, "Purging the Fearful Ghosts of Separateness: A Study of Earle Birney's Revisions," *Canadian Poetry*, 9 (Fall-Winter 1981): 1-15;

George Woodcock, "The Wanderer: Notes on Earle Birney," in his *The World of Canadian Writing: Critiques and Recollections* (Vancouver: Douglas & McIntyre, 1980), pp. 284-302; revised in *Essays on Canadian Writing*, 21 (Spring 1981): 85-103;

J. B. Zenchuk, "Earle Birney's Concrete Poetry," *Essays on Canadian Writing*, 21 (Spring 1981): 104-129.

Papers:

Most of Earle Birney's papers are in the Birney Collection at the Thomas Fisher Rare Book Library, University of Toronto. His major radio scripts are in the Concordia University Radio Archives. Other Birney manuscripts are held at the Main Library, University of British Columbia; Douglas Library, Queen's University; University Library, University of Calgary; Peter Whyte Foundation, Archives of the Canadian Rockies, Banff; the Harry Ransom Humanities Research Center, University of Texas, Austin; Lockwood Memorial Library, State University of New York at Buffalo; Alderman Library, University of Virginia.

Patricia Blondal

(12 December 1926-4 November 1959)

Laurie Ricou
University of British Columbia

BOOKS: *A Candle to Light the Sun* (Toronto: McClelland & Stewart, 1960; New York: Appleton-Century-Crofts, 1961);

From Heaven with a Shout (Toronto: McClelland & Stewart, 1963; London: Barrie & Rockliff, 1963).

Patricia Blondal's reputation rests on a single frenzied yet lyrically perceptive novel, and on the stark irony of her death. She is reported to have written *A Candle to Light the Sun* (1960) in three months, driven to complete the novel before cancer could kill her. She died in November 1959, two months after McClelland and Stewart agreed to publish the novel but several months before the novel appeared. The novel was greeted with an unusual amount of publicity and praise, but, probably because of the reviewers' emphasis on the novels that would never be written, *A Candle to Light the Sun* was soon forgotten. Even its 1976 republication in the New Canadian Library, when a commentator for *Books in Canada* called it "dazzlingly brilliant," did little to renew interest.

A Candle to Light the Sun makes an intricate study of the society of Mouse Bluffs, a small prairie town. As the name suggests, the fictional town draws heavily on Souris (*souris* is the French word for mouse), Manitoba, where Blondal was born to Nathaniel Jenkins and Nora Urilla Pearl Wark in 1926. Much of the novel, whose central story follows David Newman's journey from Mouse Bluffs to college in Winnipeg and his growth as artist and man, obviously incorporates the pattern of Blondal's own early life. When her father, a railroad engineer, was transferred, the family moved to Winnipeg in 1936. In 1944 Blondal began attending United College, receiving a B.A. in 1947.

At United Blondal met Margaret Laurence, who recalls their talks in the Jenkins apartment and at Tony's, the college café: "We showed each other our writing a good deal. . . . I don't think either of us had the slightest doubt we would be writers–it was the only work either of us wanted to do."

In a 1958 autobiographical note, Blondal remembers these years as "the poetry phase" devoted to "verse so free it might have been called abandoned, as indeed it should have been, and has been." In 1946 she married Harold Blondal, a medical doctor who became a cancer researcher. After graduation she wrote and broadcast for CBC-Radio in Winnipeg and worked in public relations. In 1951 she traveled to England. In 1952 her daughter, Stephanie, was born, and later a son, John.

Throughout the 1950s Blondal was writing, agonizingly and obsessively, and increasingly frantically. She is said to have destroyed two novels; another, "Good Friday," a documentary fiction based on the murder trial of a Winnipeg taxi driver, exists in manuscript. By 1956-1957 Blondal was circulating, unsuccessfully, at least thirteen short stories and one playlet (about

461

"Would you like to see the parade?" David asked

Gavin and the old man wrote; No. dancing tonight save xix self.

David nodded andhelped him to the bed.

"If you want me, pull the cord." Gavin nodded and

closed his eyes. Downstairs David saw Cassie and Billy leaving

for the parade and went to find Christine, as he did so he

heard a car drive up.

"It seemed like a good excuse," Roselee smiled. She

wore a pink cotton suit and was fuller in the hips, her face

tanned and her hair longer than she had worn it.

"Do you need excuses?"

"For mother I do."

"W..y doesn't she come to see him?"

"Because he was against her, he wouldn't help her

save Darcy."

"He was right."

"But," she threw her hat down, "he was her son and

it's been hell for her. You know, all her friends being so

damned good and not mentioning it; I think she'd rather they

were mean. She hardly goes anywhere."

"What about your father?"

"There's a-- He never got over Darcy pulling that--

gag?--and wrecking the appeal. I think he feels worse about

Marvin Green than about Darcy."

"Do you want to go up and see the doctor."

"Not yet. I want to see you. You're looking better."

She came very close to him, waited. All the curious lack of

embarrassment they had shared during the bad time was gone.

her nearness had a quality.

She blushed, kissed him on the cheek. "Have you seen her?"

she turned away and lighted a cigaret.

Page from a draft for Blondal's A Candle to Light the Sun *(Special Collections, University of British Columbia Library; by permission of Stephanie Blondal)*

Dust jacket for Blondal's first published novel, which appeared several months after her death

Louis Riel) among North American magazines and agents. Finally "Strangers in Love," a serialized version of her second published novel, *From Heaven with a Shout* (1963), was published in *Chatelaine*. In the last two months of her life "Strangers in Love" appeared, Simon and Schuster took an option on it, McClelland and Stewart accepted *A Candle to Light the Sun,* and rumors of movies flourished. But Blondal did not live to see her obsession with writing justified by the novel's reception.

Margaret Laurence began her review of the novel in the Vancouver *Sun* (21 January 1961)–she and Blondal had lost touch after Blondal's marriage–by stating: "this novel's treatment of a Canadian prairie town is the best I have ever read." If Blondal writes sensitive and rhythmically powerful description, she also creates, through a carefully planned structure of paired characters, a fascinating study of a slowly maturing observer coming to recognize his own solitude and his own need to write. The novel certainly has the breathlessness and crowded detail of a work written with compulsive haste, yet within its gothic complexities is continually revealed the concern for language of a fine writer.

From Heaven with a Shout, although it was published later, is an earlier and weaker novel than *A Candle to Light the Sun*. Through a classified advertisement wealthy Alex Lamond finds a wife, Arden Calcott, and takes her from London to his home on Vancouver Island. The story describes their mutual attempts to transcend the misunderstandings inherent in such strange beginnings. Arden must try to understand both Alex and his twin brother, George, a "duality in one man." But the plot is too bizarre to be convincing without much more fully developed characterizations than Blondal manages. As one reviewer summed it up: "The story moves ahead in a series of mechanical manoeuvres and many of the chapters, in structure and in tone, resemble incidents in a soap opera."

If this judgment is as just as it is typical, then *A Candle to Light the Sun,* as prairie novel, as portrait of a small town, as bildungsroman, as a work of distinctive narrative style, must carry the great bulk of Blondal's claim to a place in the history of Canadian fiction.

References:
Laurence Ricou, Introduction to Blondal's *A Candle to Light the Sun,* New Canadian Library

edition (Toronto: McClelland & Stewart, 1976), pp. vii-xi;

Ricou, "Twin Misunderstandings: The Structure of Patricia Blondal's *A Candle to Light the Sun*," *Canadian Literature*, 84 (Spring 1980): 58-71.

Papers:

Special Collections at the University of British Columbia Library, Vancouver, has notebooks, some correspondence, typescripts for *A Candle to Light the Sun*, the typescript for an unpublished novel, and a few unpublished short stories. An inventory of the papers, "Patricia Blondal 1926-1959: An Inventory of Her Papers in the Library of the University of British Columbia," was compiled by Tracy Westell for the Special Collections division in 1979.

Bertram Brooker

(31 March 1888-21 March 1955)

Paul Matthew St. Pierre
Simon Fraser University

BOOKS: *Subconscious Selling*, as Richard Surrey (Toronto: Privately printed, 1923);

Layout Technique in Advertising, as Surrey (New York: McGraw-Hill, 1929);

Copy Technique in Advertising, Including a System of Copy Synthesis, a Classification of Copy Sources, and a Section on Copy Construction, as Surrey (New York: McGraw-Hill, 1930);

Elijah (New York: William Edwin Rudge, 1930);

Think of the Earth (London: Cape, 1936; Toronto: Thomas Nelson, 1936);

The Tangled Miracle: A Mortimer Hood Mystery, as Huxley Herne (Toronto: Thomas Nelson, 1936);

The Robber: A Tale of the Time of the Herods (Toronto: Collins, 1949; New York: Duell, Sloan & Pearce, 1949);

Sounds Assembling: The Poetry of Bertram Brooker, edited by Birk Sproxton (Winnipeg: Turnstone, 1980).

OTHER: *Yearbook of the Arts in Canada*, for 1928-1929 and 1936, edited, with contributions, by Brooker (Toronto: Macmillan, 1929, 1936).

Bertram Brooker (Department of Archives and Special Collections, University of Manitoba)

Very much an inaugural figure in the history of twentieth-century Canadian literature and in the development of contemporary Canadian culture, Bertram Brooker assumes his lasting historical and cultural significance through association with Canadian literature's various comings of age and especially with its merging with other media forms. That Brooker should have received formal recognition both from Lord Tweedsmuir for his contributions to the literary field and from *Who's Who* for his contributions to the field of advertising is not at all incongruous in a career characterized by fervent participation in journalistic, critical, technical, and creative writing, and in the commercial and fine arts. As the first recipient of the Governor General's Award for Fiction (1936), Brooker heads the list (temporally if not qualitatively) of Canada's most prestigious writers. As an advertising executive whose literary pursuits conformed to the principles of business and communication, he anticipated the typographical and typological interests of Marshall McLuhan, nearing the end of his life precisely as McLuhan was beginning his career in such works as *The Mechanical Bride* (1951) and in the journal *Explorations*. As an artist who expressed himself through a variety of forms, he acted as a precursor of multimedia investigation, interdisciplinary and comparative studies, and multigeneric professions. Even his personal British background and his dedication to the Canadian foreground of art, culture, and society are representative of Canada's literary evolution in the twentieth century.

Born 31 March 1888 in Croydon, England, to Richard and Mary Ann Skinner Brooker, Bertram Brooker received his primary and secondary schooling in Croydon before his family immigrated to Portage la Prairie, Manitoba, in 1905. At the age of seventeen he worked on the Grand Trunk Pacific Railway during that railway's last push to complete a trans-Canada line to compete with Canadian Pacific's. He stayed with the railway about six years, working at first with his father as a laborer and afterward as a clerk. Later he and a brother bought and managed a movie theater in Neepawa, Manitoba, which would prove to be his first venture in the vanguard of the new media. Inspired by this project, Brooker managed to sell some movie scripts he had written to the American film company Vitagraph. He first became involved in journalism in 1914, in Portage la Prairie, as editor of the *Review*, but his budding career was interrupted by World War I, during which Brooker served in the Royal Canadian Engineers. After the war he worked as a journalist in Winnipeg, for the *Telegram* and the *Free Press*, and in Regina, where he also got his start in advertising. His most promising journalistic work was his drama and music criticism for the *Free Press*.

In 1921 Brooker made a career move to Toronto, where he became editor of the advertising trade journal *Marketing*, which he went on to purchase in 1924, only to sell it two years later. He began to devote his journalistic talents to the advertising profession and to a growing interest in illustration and painting that came from his work as an advertising executive. He drew much of his inspiration from the Group of Seven, in particular Lawren Harris, whose article "Revelation of Art in Canada" (*Canadian Theosophist*, 15 July 1926), along with the aesthetic writings of Wassily Kandinsky, awakened Brooker to the spiritual dimension of the making of art. He often traveled to New York, a special place of inspiration to him.

During the 1920s he began to emerge as an important figure in business, literature, and art alike. He is sometimes credited with producing the first truly abstract paintings in Canada. He had his first exhibition in 1927, only a year after he began painting. The following year he exhibited with the Group of Seven. He also edited two volumes of *Yearbook of the Arts in Canada*, in 1929 and 1936. These compilations of essays by artists on their own works–literature, drama, music, painting, and sculpture–were very much Brooker's own: he compiled and edited them, designed them, and contributed essays to them.

In 1930 Brooker joined the advertising firm of J. J. Gibbons, mainly because after the stock-market crash of 1929 he wanted to provide the kind of security for his family that he was unable to offer with his free-lance writing and painting. He had married Mary Aurilla Porter in 1913, and they had three children (Victor, Doreen, and Phyllis). Under the pseudonym Richard Surrey he published three cogent advertising handbooks: *Subconscious Selling* (1923), *Layout Technique in Advertising* (1929), and *Copy Technique in Advertising* (1930). He took his advertising skills in a slightly different direction when he published his first artistic book, *Elijah* (1930), a collection of pen-and-ink drawings inspired by the Book of Kings and especially by Mendelssohn's oratorio, and based on Brooker's contributions to the 1929 exhibition of the Ontario Society of Artists.

These commitments to design and publication helped Brooker to establish himself as an abstract painter during the 1920s and as a realist painter during the 1930s, working in both oils and watercolors. He was elected to the Ontario Society of Artists in 1936. Just as Brooker experimented with expressionistic and representational

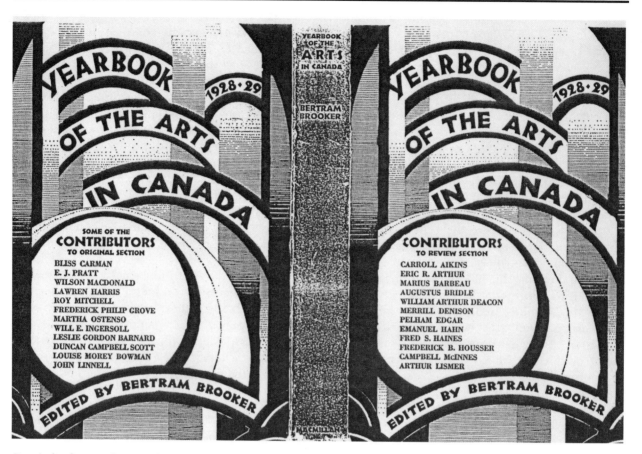

Dust jacket for one of two yearbooks Brooker edited for Macmillan. According to a publisher's blurb, the purpose of Macmillan's series was twofold: "to chronicle the chief . . . artistic events and achievements of each year; and . . . to reprint and reproduce a careful selection of the outstanding works produced in Canada during the year."

modes in his painting, so he explored romantic and realistic modes in his fiction. Although he was critically acclaimed as a painter, he has also received lasting recognition through the publication of his first and third novels.

Think of the Earth (1936), for which he won his Governor General's Award, is a philosophical tale about the experience of a wanderer in a Manitoba town. The personification of ambivalence, the protagonist seems destined to perform an absolute act of evil but persists in believing that even a supremely evil act can be salvific. Rather than endorsing the Judeo-Christian concept of good overcoming evil or even arising out of evil, Brooker entertains the modernist premise that good and evil are often indistinguishable. In *The Tangled Miracle: A Mortimer Hood Mystery* (1936), published under the pseudonym Huxley Herne, Brooker offers a more conventional morality; it is a slighter story whose religious overtones are in the mystery vein rather than in the philosophical mode.

Brooker's descriptive strengths in *Think of the Earth* are surpassed by the imaginative fortitude of his third, and last, novel, *The Robber: A Tale of the Time of the Herods* (1949), which focuses on the biblical narrative of Barabbas. Here Barabbas responds to his liberation from prison and the state of sin by allowing himself to undergo a spiritual transformation in the crucifical shadow of Christ the Redeemer. The idea of the salvific act assumes full moral significance: the good man Christ overcomes evil through sacrifice; the evil man Barabbas saves himself at the expense of Christ but becomes Christ-like himself in the end. This reexamination of Christian values in the person of Barabbas anticipates Morley Callaghan's similar treatment of the figure of Judas in his novel *A Time for Judas* (1983).

The value of Brooker's novels to Canadian literature is more historical than thematic and aesthetic, partly because the novels represent an evolving literature in mid century, but mainly because they represent an inaugural literary and media figure in mid career. Although he is best

Two.

noise issued now and again. It was a restive horse champing at its bit. Sometimes a raised hoof thudded in the grass. A horse and rider were concealed in the gloom under rose trees. The motionless figure was sitting side-saddle. The skirt of her ~~nut-colored~~ riding-habit was drawn tightly about her knees, which in turn gripped the flanks of her mount with nervous urgency. She had just reined him in. He was breathing hard, and the vapour rising from his neck and sides enveloped the girl in a cloud of ~~floating~~ gossamer. She was leaning back in the saddle, her head on one side, her chin lowered, listening.

A distant rumble startled her. She had expected hoof-falls behind; but this was ahead.

Page from the manuscript for Brooker's short story "Javelin" (Department of Archives and Special Collections, University of Manitoba) known in Canada, Brooker did establish some reputation in the United States through the New York publication of *The Robber* and through numerous articles on art and literature in American journals.

Although he published only three poems during his life, all in the *Canadian Forum* in 1930, Brooker was quite a gifted poet. His verse, posthumously published in *Sounds Assembling: The Poetry of Bertram Brooker*, edited by Birk Sproxton (1980), shows him to have been very much in the forefront of the modernist movement in Canada. Among his best poems is "An Artist," which captures much of the geometric kinesis of his paintings:

energy leaping from him always
pulsing in his temples
thrusting outward
in the twin prominences over his eyes
striking forward
in the shooting of his lips
springing from his fingertips
as they move
resolutely
in or out
or up or down[.]

Here is a poet celebrating language as a futurist extension of human being. By the time of his death in Toronto in 1955 Brooker had earned a kind of fourfold professional respectability: as a mediaphile, novelist, illustrator, and painter.

References: Jean-C. Dumont, "Bertram Brooker: Peindre des verbes," *Vie des Arts*, 20 (Summer 1975): 28-29;

D. M. LeBourdais, "Protean," *Saturday Night*, 65 (2 May 1950): 20;

Thomas R. Lee, "Bertram Brooker: 1888-1955," *Canadian Art*, 13 (Spring 1956): 286-291;

Jennifer Oille-Sinclair, ed., *Bertram Brooker: An Emergent Modernism*, Provincial Essays, volume 7 (Toronto: Provincial Essays, 1989);

Dennis Reid, *Bertram Brooker, 1888-1955* (Ottawa: National Gallery of Canada, 1973);

Jehanne Bietry Salinger, "The Work of Bertram Brooker," *Canadian Forum*, 10 (June 1930): 331-332;

Joyce Zemans, "The Art and Weltanschauung of Bertram Brooker," *Artscanada*, 30 (February-March 1973): 65-68.

Papers:
Some of Bertram Brooker's papers are at the University of Manitoba library.

Donat Coste
(Daniel Boudreau)

(12 January 1912-25 April 1957)

Hans R. Runte
Dalhousie University

BOOK: *L'Enfant noir* (Montreal: Chantecler, 1950).

PERIODICAL PUBLICATIONS: "Conte de No-ël," *Almanach du Peuple*, 63 (1932): 362-368; "Rapt," *Almanach du Peuple*, 71 (1940): 185-190; "Le Père de l'*Enfant noir* nous écrit," *Le Devoir*, 4 November 1950, p. 9; "En rupture de file," *Le Canada*, 2 December 1950, p. 5; "A la mémoire d'Eddy Boudreau: Elégie," *L'Evangéline*, 27 April 1954, p. 4.

Donat Coste was born Daniel Boudreau on 12 January 1912, in Petit-Rocher, New Brunswick, to Joseph and Marie Roy Boudreau, who had moved there from Lamèque, New Brunswick. He was the grandnephew of Jérôme Boudreau, the first French-speaking schoolteacher in the province, and one of the three brothers of Eddy Boudreau, a well-known journalist with *L'Evangéline*, the Acadian newspaper, and author of *La Vie en croix* (Life on the Cross, 1948) and *Vers le triomphe* (Toward Triumph, 1950).

The Boudreau children were orphaned in 1917, and Daniel was adopted by the French industrialist J.-Edouard Coste, from the islands of Saint-Pierre et Miquelon. He received his early schooling in Saint-Pierre (1918-1927) and in Montreal (with the Frères des Ecoles Chrétiennes and the Abbé Adolphe Poisson, 1927-1929), where the Coste family had settled. Having been awarded a scholarship to study at the Sorbonne, he was about to leave for Paris when he was struck by paraplegia and confined to a wheelchair. He spent the next thirteen years with the Frères Saint-Jean de Dieu, at the Hôpital de la Merci in Montreal, where he worked for *La Voix de la Charité*, the in-house hospital magazine. He replaced Louis Dantin as author of the literary column "La Tribune de Mentor" at Jean-Charles Harvey's Montreal newspaper, *Le Jour*. In 1943

Donat Coste (Centre d'Etudes Acadiennes, Université de Moncton)

he married Mariana Tardif, a nurse with the Université de Montréal. The couple moved to Laval-des-Rapides, across the Rivière des Prairies north of downtown Montreal; in 1944, their son, Alain, was born.

Daniel Boudreau, who signed all of his works with the name Donat Coste, had written and then destroyed his first novel in 1928. He was first published in 1932 when a Christmas story that Eugène Issalis of the Beauchemin publishing house had purchased from him in 1931 appeared in the *Almanach du Peuple*. Donat Coste's early experience with writing and his debut in the world of publishing established a pattern that marked his entire literary career: he was unable, with one exception, to place his novels, and was reduced to seeing only his shorter pieces, of which he wrote many, appear in newspapers and magazines. In an interview for *Le Petit Journal* of Montreal, republished on 21 July 1949 in *L'Evangéline*, these circumstances were ascribed to his physical inability to promote his major literary efforts actively; critical responses to his published novel suggest in addition that his skills as a writer may not have been sufficiently honed.

By 1956 Coste would seem to have completed at least eight major works: "J'ai deux amours" (I Have Two Loves); "Le Désaxé" (The Unbalanced One); "L'Etoile en or" (The Golden Star); "L'Onde opaque" (The Opaque Wave); a novel on the reintegration into society of returning war veterans; a novel on the role of doctors and nurses in the colonization of the Abitibi region of Quebec; "L'Ile aux sortilèges" (The Charmed Island); and "Le Dauphin." On 5 November 1956 he wrote to Father René Baudry: "J'ai dans mes tiroirs . . . un roman sur l'Anticosti, un roman sur Montréal. . . . J'ai soumis aux Editions du Bien Public un roman dont l'action se passe en Nouvelle-France, . . . premier roman du genre" (I have in my drawers . . . a novel about Anticosti [Island; "L'ile aux sortilèges"], [and] a novel about Montreal. . . . I have submitted to the Editions du Bien Public a novel set in New France, . . . the first novel of its kind ["Le Dauphin"]; in the interview, "L'Etoile en or" is described as a "roman paysan" (peasant novel).

In a letter to Coste dated 22 October 1956, Father Baudry called Coste's only published novel, *L'Enfant noir* (The Black Child, 1950), "absolument invendable dans nos milieux dévots" (absolutely unsellable in our devout milieus), to which the author replied, on 5 November 1956: "Mon grand tort . . . a été de ne pas écrire pour les couventines" (My great misfortune . . . has been not to write for convent girls). Even secular assessments tended to echo Baudry's view, finding Coste's book badly structured and badly written. Contemporary reviews characterized much of it as "nasty" and "silly," and more recent commentary has taken it as a Francophone example of "racist mentality in Canada."

L'Enfant noir tells the story of Madeleine Chaloute, maid in the household of millionaire businessman Gratien Pindus and his wife, Juliette de Lairy-Pindus, of Sainte-Exupérance, southwest of Lévis, Quebec. Madeleine is expecting a child by her lover, the estate's Senegalese gardener Gilles Gélos, who is dismissed by Gratien and drowns himself in the Saumonée River. Madeleine, saved by Juliette from committing suicide herself, returns to live with her aunt, Mrs. Maticotte, who arranges a hasty marriage with Fabien Lalancette. To prepare Fabien for the eventuality that his wife may give birth to a black child, Mrs. Maticotte has Norée Pelquier, her Métis servant, take on the appearance of a black and frighten Madeleine so thoroughly that little Jules's dark skin may be attributed to the shock his mother received during pregnancy. Fabien accepts the explanation, and to make the couple's situation even better, Mrs. Maticotte's prayers to the Virgin are heard and Jules dies in infancy.

The provocative themes (Juliette's frigidity, Madeleine's religious upbringing, cross-racial and premarital social and sexual intercourse, suicide) and the implausible plot of *L'Enfant noir* have confined to almost total neglect Coste's literary accomplishments, few as they may be. His best quality is probably the richness of his vocabulary, including an abundance of specifically Quebec turns of expression, which stands him in good stead when it comes to describing poignantly the social milieu of his characters or the potent feelings aroused by passion and despair. Yet he would perhaps have been more successful had he applied his talents to a less unlikely first novel.

References:

"L'Odyssée étrange d'une jeune écrivain acadien," interview, *L'Evangéline*, 21 July 1949, p. 4;

Peter Igboneku Okeh, "Donat Coste's *L'Enfant noir*, A Literary Projection of the Francophone Example of Racist Mentality in Canada," in *Black Presence in Multi-Ethnic Canada*, edited by Vincent D'Oyley (Vancouver: Centre for the Study of Curriculum and Instruction, Faculty of Education, University of British Columbia / Toronto: Ontario Institute for Studies in Education, 1978), pp. 317-340.

Papers:

Donat Coste's papers are at the Centre d'Etudes Acadiennes, Université de Moncton.

Donald Creighton

(15 July 1902-19 December 1979)

George Woodcock

SELECTED BOOKS: *The Commercial Empire of the St. Lawrence, 1760-1850* (Toronto: Ryerson / New Haven: Yale University Press, 1937); republished as *The Empire of the St. Lawrence* (Toronto: Macmillan, 1956; Boston: Houghton Mifflin, 1958);

Dominion of the North: A History of Canada (Toronto: Macmillan, 1944; London: Hale, 1947); revised and enlarged as *A History of Canada: Dominion of the North* (Boston: Houghton Mifflin, 1958; London: Macmillan, 1958);

John A. Macdonald, 2 volumes (Toronto: Macmillan, 1952, 1955; Boston: Houghton Mifflin, 1953, 1956);

Harold Adams Innis: Portrait of a Scholar (Toronto: University of Toronto Press, 1957);

The Story of Canada (Toronto: Macmillan, 1959; London: Faber & Faber, 1959; Boston: Houghton Mifflin, 1960; revised, Toronto: Macmillan, 1971; London: Faber & Faber, 1971);

The Road to Confederation: The Emergence of Canada, 1863-1867 (Toronto: Macmillan, 1964; Boston: Houghton Mifflin, 1965);

Canada's First Century, 1867-1967 (Toronto: Macmillan, 1970; New York: St. Martin's, 1970);

Towards the Discovery of Canada: Selected Essays (Toronto: Macmillan, 1972);

Canada: The Heroic Beginnings (Toronto: Macmillan, 1974);

The Forked Road: Canada 1939-1957 (Toronto: McClelland & Stewart, 1976);

Takeover (Toronto: McClelland & Stewart, 1978);

The Passionate Observer: Selected Essays (Toronto: McClelland & Stewart, 1980).

Donald Creighton (photograph copyright © by Ashley-Crippen; University Archives, Thomas Fisher Rare Book Library, University of Toronto)

Donald Creighton is Canada's best-known and most influential historian, and much of his influence lies in the fact that he always considered history—and biography, in which he has also excelled—to be among the literary arts. Facts are their material, but in both kinds of writing, as Creighton saw them, the imagination must play over the facts and transform them in such a way that the outlines of a country's history or a man's life emerge as clearly as the theme of a novel or the composition of a painting. This attitude has made Creighton at once influential and controversial, since he dealt, essentially, in national myths.

Donald Grant Creighton, the son of William Black Creighton, an editor, and Laura Harvie Creighton, was born in Toronto in 1902, and Upper Canada shaped the attitudes and values he expressed throughout the rest of his life. Suspicious of Quebec's desire for autonomy, he asserted an anglocentric version of Canadian history and destiny; as this was an Ontario-centered vision as well, he attached little importance to the regional differences that divided central from western Canada. Except for a short period at Balliol College, Oxford, from which he returned in 1926 (his degrees, B.A. and M.A., were granted in 1927 and 1929), he never lived away from Toronto or its vicinity for long. He was educated at the University of Toronto (Victoria College, B.A., 1925), and he returned to teach in the Department of History in 1927; he remained there even after he retired as University Professor in 1970, for he ended his life as a Fellow of Massey College. Creighton never lost his zest for teaching, and in spite of his great tasks of writing, he was also an active member of the academic community. He was head of the Department of History for five years (1954-1959) and active in the Royal Society of Canada, which awarded him the Tyrrell Medal in 1951; he was president of the Canadian Historical Association from 1956 to 1957. He was garlanded with medals and the hoods of honorary doctorates, and he was a winner of the Molson Prize in 1963, the first year it was awarded.

But Creighton was never simply an academic historian. His writing was always opinionated and strongly colored by his conservative political attitudes. He disputed readily with the liberal historians who in his younger days represented the dominant trend among Canadian historians. He thought daringly and designed his books on a dramatic scale. He wrote a fluent and craftsmanlike prose and set out to make his books accessible to readers outside the universities.

Undoubtedly Creighton was helped if not influenced in this course by the fact that at the beginning of his career, when he returned from Oxford, he married Luella Sanders Bruce, a fellow Ontarian, who shared his interest in both history and literature. In her own right Luella Creighton was a well-known popular writer, all of whose books were historical in orientation; they included children's fiction, two historical novels, *High Bright Buggy Wheels* (1951) and *Turn East, Turn West* (1954), and a book about manners in the Confederation era, *The Elegant Canadians* (1967). Sometimes a married couple who share the same interest become rivals, and the rivalry inhibits one or the other. This was not the case with the Creightons. There is no doubt Luella Creighton's deep involvement in Canadian history encouraged and stimulated her husband throughout a marriage that lasted more than half a century.

More directly—and more fundamentally—the influence that helped form Creighton's economic vision of political history was the work of Harold Adams Innis (to whom Creighton paid tribute in a 1957 biography). An economist, and author of such influential books as *The Fur Trade in Canada* (1930) and *The Cod Fisheries* (1940), Innis had argued that Canada's development derived from the way in which certain staple products—furs, fish—had been exploited and distributed. The patterns of trade, said Innis, determined the structure of economic relationships and therefore the paradigms of political power. Adopting and adapting Innis's ideas, Creighton expressed himself more lucidly than Innis did. He transformed what in Innis was obscure into an elegant thesis drawing cultural conclusions from historical events, and his first book—*The Commercial Empire of the St. Lawrence, 1760-1850* (1937; republished in 1956 as *The Empire of the St. Lawrence*)—focused on the fur-trading system of the St. Lawrence and the Great Lakes. Showing how this system developed in Canada in an east-west pattern involving transportation and settlement, Creighton went on to argue that this configuration became a potent historical and cultural counter to the natural geographical lines of the continent, which run north-south.

Because Creighton saw the process of Canadian historical development during the century before Confederation in terms of a single urge—the fur trade and the exploration that accompanied the desire for furs—his view of nationhood emphasized a central power, institutional authority, and cultural unity. Neither a regionalist, impressed by the historical differences that distinguish various parts of the country, nor a continentalist, expecting some inevitable form of coalescence with the United States, Creighton from the beginning was a nationalist. His nationalism became abundantly evident in his second major work, *Dominion of the North: A History of Canada* (1944). As its title suggests, this book was based on Creighton's conviction that Canada has its own manifest destiny and that even to think of union with the United States constitutes a kind of treason to the real nature of Canada. In Creighton's rendering of history, the highways and railways built during the post-Confederation years reproduced the patterns of the old trade routes from Montreal to the Pacific. An exacting research supports the arguments presented in *Dominion of the North*. Admir-

Dust jacket for Creighton's only work of fiction, about the American takeover of a family-owned distillery in Toronto

ably written, the book polemically designs a myth about Canadian history, on the grand scale.

The idea of Canada as a nation emerged in the movement toward Confederation that followed the dwindling of the fur trade, and Creighton saw its personification in Sir John A. Macdonald, Canada's first prime minister. He wrote the earliest adequate biography of Macdonald. The first volume, *The Young Politician*, reaching to the year of Confederation (1867), appeared in 1952; the second and final volume, *The Old Chieftain*, came out in 1955. For both books he won Governor General's awards. Creighton avoids a common fault of political biographies—to make the background of events dwarf the man—and he presents a vital, if heroic, portrait of Macdonald, which reinforced the mythic version of Canadian nationalism.

Creighton concentrated on a key period in the life of Macdonald and his country in *The*

Road to Confederation: The Emergence of Canada, 1863-1867 (1964). The book reiterates the earlier thesis in a new way. British North Americans from Nova Scotia to Upper Canada, Creighton argued, realized not only that unity would best serve their common economic interests but also that it might be the only way they could avert the political threat that the United States newly posed when it emerged from the Civil War.

As he grew older, Creighton increasingly became aware of the dangers that threatened Canada. The north-south pull, he realized, was stronger than he had thought; the historical east-west ties within Canada were harder to maintain than he had anticipated, and they were constantly under pressure from American economic and cultural invasion. He was so much a nationalist that he could read the rise of Quebec separatism (and the general trend toward provincial autonomy in various economic and legislative matters) only as a weakening of the Canadian political structure. And he was so convinced a centralist, he could not admit the possibility that a new kind of federalism, more adapted to the modern world, might be based on stronger regions. The result was a deepening pessimism about the fate of his country that clouded the last years of his life.

Over the next fifteen years, until he died in 1979 in Brooklin, Ontario, he continued to write pessimistically and sometimes even intemperately about Canada's future. *The Forked Road: Canada 1939-1957* (1976) casts Prime Minister Mackenzie King in the villain's role—in contrast to the heroic role accorded Macdonald earlier and hinted at again in a 1974 pictorial history entitled *Canada: The Heroic Beginnings*. The Liberals, Creighton argued, gave Canada to American continentalism, a theme picked up in *Takeover* (1978), Creighton's only venture into fiction. Ambiguous in its conclusions, this novel suggests that the myth of Canada, for which he had so vigorously argued, was slowly dying. Here, and in his essays, Creighton continued to argue during the 1970s for conservative solutions to contemporary problems. Separatism seemed to strike him as a personal affront, and in one essay he reacted almost punitively: if Quebec secedes, he argued, only the original boundaries of Quebec should stand, and the northern part of the province, ceded to Quebec in 1895, should return to Canada.

While *The Forked Road* drew some attention, it had nothing like the effect of the earlier books. The historiographer Carl Berger remarked laconically that Creighton never did adequately demonstrate, for all his persuasive power, that there *was* another fork in the road. Yet Creighton continued to influence many, by means of the "Laurentian Thesis" he had constructed in *The Empire of the St. Lawrence*; though other historians, including the westerner W. L. Morton, were to attack its premises, it deeply marked the national presumptions of such writers as Hugh MacLennan and Margaret Atwood. Creighton's essays, too, continue to be read. *Towards the Discovery of Canada* (1972) provides a sampling of essays and memoirs. A minor work in the Creighton canon, it nonetheless illustrates the historian's continuing stylistic force. Though his conclusions are in dispute, he remains one of the most potent, imaginative designers of one version of a Canadian national character.

References:

Carl Berger, *The Writing of Canadian History* (Toronto: Oxford University Press, 1976);

J. S. Moir, ed., *Character and Circumstance: Essays in Honour of Donald Grant Creighton* (Toronto: University of Toronto Press, 1970);

George Woodcock, "The Servants of Clio: Notes on Creighton and Groulx," *Canadian Literature*, 83 (Winter 1979): 131-141.

Gwladys Downes

(22 April 1915-)

Jeanette Lynes
Mount Allison University

BOOKS: *Lost Diver* (Fredericton: Fiddlehead, 1955);

When We Lie Together: Poems from Quebec and Poems by G. V. Downes (Vancouver: Klanak, 1973);

Out of the Violent Dark: Poems and Translations (Victoria, B.C.: Sono Nis, 1978).

OTHER: "W. B. Yeats and the Tarot," in *The World of W. B. Yeats: Essays in Perspective*, edited by Robin Skelton and Ann Saddlemyer (Seattle: University of Washington Press, 1965), pp. 67-69;

John Glassco, ed., *The Poetry of French Canada in Translation*, includes translations by Downes (Toronto: Oxford University Press, 1970);

Dorothy Livesay and Seymour Mayne, eds., *40 Women Poets of Canada*, includes poems by Downes (Montreal: Ingluvin, 1971);

Robert Sward, Tim Groves, and Mario M. Martinelli, eds., *Vancouver Island Poems*, includes poems by Downes (Victoria, B.C.: Soft Press, 1973);

Livesay, ed., *Woman's Eye: 12 B.C. Poets*, includes poems by Downes (Vancouver: Air, 1978);

"Contrasts in Psychic Space," in *In the Feminine*, edited by Ann Margaret Dybikowski (Vancouver: Longspoon, 1985), pp. 114-121;

Gwladys Downes (photograph by Tivoli Studios)

Rosemary Sullivan, ed., *Poetry by Canadian Women*, includes poems by Downes (Toronto & Oxford: Oxford University Press, 1989).

PERIODICAL PUBLICATIONS: "Aunt Di," *Malahat Review*, 50 (April 1979): 245-257; "Women Poets in Quebec Society," *Malahat Review*, 63 (October 1982): 100-110; "Robert Finch and the Temptation of Form," *Canadian Literature*, 97 (Summer 1983): 26-33.

Gwladys Downes has worked in three areas: original poetry, translations, and criticism. The daughter of Gordon Downes and Doris Gwendoline Bywater-Jones Downes, she was born in Victoria, British Columbia, on 22 April 1915. After receiving her elementary and secondary education in Oak Bay and studying for one year at Victoria College (now University of Victoria), Downes received a B.A. from the University of British Columbia in 1934 and an M.A. in 1940. During the 1930s she also earned teaching diplomas from the University of British Columbia and the Sorbonne in Paris. In 1953 Downes was granted a doctoral degree from the Sorbonne, writing her dissertation on Paul Valéry.

As well as teaching at Duncan High School in British Columbia from 1936 to 1939, Downes has served on the faculties of the English and French departments at the University of British Columbia (1940-1941; 1946-1949) and the University of Victoria (1951-1978). She has also taught creative writing and participated in numerous poetry and translation seminars. Downes has been a member of various literary organizations, including the League of Canadian Poets and the Association for Canadian and Quebec Literature. In 1969 she was a recipient of a Canada Council Senior Arts Award.

Downes has produced three books–*Lost Diver* (1955), *When We Lie Together* (1973), and *Out of the Violent Dark* (1978)–and her poems and translations have appeared in numerous periodicals, including *Malahat Review, Canadian Literature, Event, Prism, Canadian Forum, Tamarack Review, Alphabet*, and the *Fiddlehead*. Her work has also been broadcast by the CBC. Downes resides in Victoria, where she continues to write poetry and criticism; she also works as an archivist at the Art Gallery of Greater Victoria.

Downes's poetry is influenced by the "marvellous ghosts" she cites as strong presences behind the writing of Rina Lasnier, Michèle Lalonde, and Anne Hébert. The ghosts, as she enumerates them in "Women Poets and Quebec Society," a 1982 article for *Malahat Review*, are the French poets André Breton, Paul Eluard, Paul Valéry, St. Jean Perse, Charles Baudelaire, and the symbolists. Her first book of poems, *Lost Diver*, published by Fiddlehead, exhibits their influences as well as that of poets of the English tradition, including Shakespeare and T. S. Eliot. The sixteen poems in *Lost Diver*, written in a symbolist mode, primarily explore private, internalized landscapes and tend to be oriented toward mythic oppositions: innocence and experience, exile / underworld and garden. The descent into an underworld, sometimes associated with death and sometimes with the subconscious, is a prevalent theme, and the diver or swimmer a central figure.

Downes's penchant for form, revealed also in her 1983 critical study in *Canadian Literature*, "Robert Finch and the Temptation of Form," is readily apparent in the *Lost Diver* poems. Many of these lyrics use quatrains and couplets, and "An Arrow for Mr. Eliot" is a Shakespearean sonnet. Although Downes often adopts a first-person speaker, the tone of the poems tends to be formal, resulting from a self-consciously rhetorical approach to poetics and, more specifically, from the poet's frequent questioning and her use of allusion, figurative language, and, occasionally, archaic diction. Although, as a reviewer of *Lost Diver* noted in the *Fiddlehead*, the speaker of Downes's final poem in the collection laments the writer's entrapment in a stultifying world of "these symbols" and "memory"–in short, the world of tradition and form–abstracted from the phenomenal present, the *Lost Diver* poems ultimately celebrate the world of artistic form as a refuge from corporeal decay and the chaotic shapelessness of a darker, more subterranean level of consciousness.

The title of Downes's 1973 collection, *When We Lie Together*, is taken from "Words," her translation of a French poem by André Major included in the volume. *When We Lie Together* contains four of Downes's own poems prefaced by ten translations of poems by Paul-Marie Lapointe, Roland Giguère, Yves Préfontaine, Rina Lasnier, Alain Grandbois, Pierre Trottier, and André Major. The central themes of descent and innocence and experience, as well as the figure of the swimmer / diver of her first collection, continue to preoccupy Downes. The juxtaposition of her original poems and her translations is an interesting one because of the strong parallels that emerge between the two. For example, the white

Dust jacket for the 1978 collection in which Downes alternates her own poetry with translations of French-Canadian verse by Hector de Saint-Denys Garneau, Anne Hébert, and others

birds of Lapointe's "Poem for Winter" reflect a kind of inner space which resembles that represented by the "soft birds" "dying / in the long room" of Downes's "Mirror, Mirror." Similarly, the "shadowy places" and "uneasy pools of memory" in Giguère's "Looking Is Enough" and the dark / light images of Grandbois's "Ambiguous Dawn" evoke Downes's own ambiguous world of the subconscious.

The "dreams in the violent dark" of Downes's poem "The Other Room" are echoed in *Out of the Violent Dark*, the title of her most recent book of poems and translations. The structure of *Out of the Violent Dark* differs from that of *When We Lie Together;* the later volume includes seventy-one of Downes's poems and twenty-seven translations, and the two alternate throughout the book. As well as the poets previously translated by Downes in *When We Lie Together*, the most recent collection includes translations of Anne Hébert, Hector de Saint-Denys Garneau, Gustave Lamarche, Jean-Guy Pilon, and Fernand Ouellette. The sections of the book presenting Downes's poems include new work and poems from her two earlier collections. Her new poems remain private in scope and retain the motifs of descent, drowning, and exile, but they also demonstrate a less rigid approach to form and make use of effective new images, such as the "delicate networks / of waiting / neurones," to convey the poet's inner experience. The continued influence of the symbolists combined with a less remote and formal persona than that of previous poems results in several strong, original lyrics.

As a critic, Downes draws on an extensive knowledge of art, music, and French and English literature. In her article on Robert Finch she presents a convincing argument illustrating parallels between the concerns of Canadian modernist poets and the aesthetic theories of Renaissance and eighteenth-century French art as they intersect in Finch's work. Downes's criticism reveals as well an awareness of feminist writing and recent intellectual trends in Europe and North America. In "Women Poets in Quebec Society" she traces a line of development, since 1945, of Quebec women poets including Rina Lasnier, Anne Hébert, and Nicole Brossard. Downes's interest in language–both French and English–and her skills as poet and translator demonstrate an admirable range of abilities, and her bringing francophone poetry to anglophone readers represents a noteworthy contribution to Canadian letters.

Louis Dudek
(6 February 1918-   )

Frank Davey
York University

BOOKS: *East of the City* (Toronto: Ryerson, 1946);

The Searching Image (Toronto: Ryerson, 1952);

Cerberus, by Dudek, Irving Layton, and Raymond Souster (Toronto: Contact, 1952);

Twenty-four Poems (Toronto: Contact, 1952);

Europe (Toronto: Laocoön / Contact, 1954);

The Transparent Sea (Toronto: Contact, 1956);

En México (Toronto: Contact, 1958);

Laughing Stalks (Toronto: Contact, 1958);

Literature and the Press: A History of Printing, Printed Media, and Their Relation to Literature (Toronto: Ryerson, 1960);

Atlantis (Montreal: Delta, 1967);

The First Person in Literature (Toronto: CBC Publications, 1967);

Collected Poetry (Montreal: Delta, 1971);

Epigrams (Montreal: DC Books, 1975);

Selected Essays and Criticism (Ottawa: Tecumseh Press, 1978);

Selected Poems (Ottawa: Golden Dog Press, 1979);

Technology and Culture: Six Lectures (Ottawa: Golden Dog Press, 1979);

Poems from Atlantis (Ottawa: Golden Dog Press, 1980);

Cross-section: Poems 1940-1980 (Toronto: Coach House Press, 1980);

Texts and Essays, Open Letter, fourth series, nos. 8-9 (Spring/Summer 1981);

Continuation I (Montreal: Véhicule, 1981);

Ideas for Poetry (Montreal: Véhicule, 1983);

Zembla's Rocks (Montreal: Véhicule, 1986);

In Defence of Art: Critical Essays and Reviews, edited by Aileen Collins (Kingston, Ont.: Quarry, 1988);

Infinite Worlds: The Poetry of Louis Dudek, edited by Robin Blaser (Montreal: Véhicule, 1988).

OTHER: Ronald Hambleton, ed., *Unit of Five*, includes poems by Dudek (Toronto: Ryerson, 1944);

Canadian Poems, 1850-1952, edited by Dudek and Irving Layton (Toronto: Contact, 1952; revised and enlarged, 1953);

photograph by Gregory Dudek

Poetry of Our Time: An Introduction to Twentieth-Century Poetry Including Modern Canadian Poetry, edited by Dudek (Toronto: Macmillan, 1966);

The Making of Modern Poetry in Canada: Essential Articles on Contemporary Canadian Poetry in English, edited by Dudek and Michael Gnarowski (Toronto: Ryerson, 1967);

All Kinds of Everything: Worlds of Poetry, edited by Dudek (Toronto: Clarke, Irwin, 1973);

DK–Some Letters of Ezra Pound, edited, with notes, by Dudek (Montreal: DC Books, 1974).

Louis Dudek has been a pioneer in Canadian small-press publishing and a major influence on the development of the Canadian long poem. He was born in Montreal on 6 February 1918 to parents (Vincent and Stanislawa Rozynska Dudek) who had emigrated the previous year from Poland. He entered McGill University in 1936 and received a B.A. in English and history in 1939. He had begun writing poetry while in grade school, and during a year of unemployment following graduation from McGill "reading H. D., Richard Aldington, Sandburg, and Masters . . . branched off into an experimental free verse" with "not the least idea of publishing." During this period he also began writing advertising copy free-lance, and in 1940 he obtained a salaried job with the Canadian Advertising Agency in Montreal.

In 1943 he became associated with John Sutherland's newly founded little magazine *First Statement* and together with Irving Layton moved it toward an iconoclastic, antiestablishment, anti-British orientation. Through *First Statement* he met not only the young Toronto poet Raymond Souster, with whom he would later enjoy a long and fruitful editorial collaboration, but also Stephanie Zuperko, whom he married later that year and with whom he lived until their divorce in 1965. Unhappy with his advertising work and with the commercialism which he saw stifling the writers of his generation, he moved to New York that fall and began graduate work at Columbia University in the sociology of literature. His master's thesis was entitled "Thackeray and the Profession of Letters" and studied a writer who had, much like John Sutherland, attempted to combine serious writing with the editing of periodicals. In his doctoral dissertation (completed in 1955 and published in 1960 as *Literature and the Press: A History of Printing, Printed Media, and Their Relation to Literature*) he argued that commercialism and technology have progressively debased mass literary standards to the point where significant literature can be supported only by fugitive publication.

While at Columbia, Dudek was strongly influenced by the elitist cultural criticism of Lionel Trilling and later by that of Ezra Pound, whom he volunteered to assist during the latter's confinement at St. Elizabeths Hospital. Through Pound he became acquainted with numerous American writ-

Dust jacket for the published version of Dudek's doctoral dissertation

ers, and in 1950 he launched a "poetry mailbag," an envelope of poems to which writers on a predetermined postal route contributed both poems and criticism of the envelope's contents. The mailbag circulated among approximately thirty writers, including Pound, Charles Olson, William Carlos Williams, Harold Norse, and Paul Blackburn. Dudek's own poetry in this period included imagist-influenced lyrics and brief attacks on social injustice, some of which were collected in *Unit of Five*, edited by Ronald Hambleton for Ryerson Press in 1944, and in Dudek's first book, *East of the City*, published by Ryerson in 1946. Dudek's later years in New York were extremely busy; in addition to his other activities, from 1946 to 1951 he held a full-time job as instructor of English at City College.

Dudek returned to Canada in 1951 to a professorship at Montreal's McGill University. Almost immediately he started a Canadian version of his poetry mailbag and began a monthly exchange of letters with Souster, whom he appears to have recognized as his natural ally in Canadian literature. Disappointed by both the new conservatism of John Sutherland, whose *First Statement* had in late 1945 merged with *Preview* to become the country's major literary journal, *Northern Review*, and with the abridgment by Ryerson Press of the manuscript for his collection *The Searching Image* (1952), he, in 1951, encouraged Souster in his founding of the mimeograph periodical *Contact*. In 1952 he joined Souster and Layton in the founding of Contact Press, and in 1953 he became with Layton a shadow editor of Aileen Collins's magazine *CIV / n*. Contact Press's first book was *Cerberus* (1952), poems and prose statements by the press's three editors. In the next fifteen years Contact, largely under the direction of Dudek and Souster, became the major Canadian publisher of poetry; its lists came to include a remarkable array of first major collections by almost every important new poet of the late 1950s and early 1960s. For Dudek, Contact provided an immediate outlet for the ever-lengthening "experimental free verse" he had thought unpublishable in 1940. His present experiment of this kind, the long meditative poem *Europe*, he published through Contact in 1954; he published a retrospective collection of lyrics and shorter meditations, *The Transparent Sea*, in 1956.

In 1957 Dudek began his own little magazine, *Delta*, which he printed himself on hand-set type in his basement. This was a major step for Dudek, who had returned to Canada eager to change Canadian poetry from within and interested therefore in collaborative projects such as the poetry mailbag, *CIV / n*, and Contact Press. His chief motive for beginning *Delta* seems to have been his dissatisfaction with Souster's *Contact* and its successor *Combustion*, which he had argued from the beginning were too open to international writing and too patronizing to Canadian writing. Dudek published twenty-six issues of *Delta* ("Delta for Dudek," he announced in a letter to Souster) between 1957 and 1966. It was an esoteric magazine, with ninety percent Canadian content, much of it poetry by young writers, and punctuated with paragraphs from Dudek's personal readings in sociology and psychology. The implicit message of such juxtapositions was that literature must occur in society and have an effect on human action. In *Delta* Dudek published his two major statements on prosody, "A Note on Metrics" (October 1958) and "Functional Poetry"

(July 1959). "A Note on Metrics" proposed that the "essential music" of a poem was sound fitted to its "content"; "Functional Poetry" continued this emphasis on content by looking toward a "poetry of exposition and discourse" that had become art by "having the shape of clouds."

Dudek's conviction that poetry must have a cultural role, that it must participate effectively in the intellectual and cultural issues of its time, also became dominant in his poetry and criticism from the 1950s onward. In numerous essays he attacked various theories of literature which discounted its role in influencing mankind to action—aestheticism, surrealism, romanticism, and particularly Northrop Frye's mythopoeic theories. To Dudek such theories separated art from life, encouraged the study of the surface properties of art at the expense of its content, and led to the most revolutionary work being read merely as artistic commodity. In long poems such as *Europe* (1954), *En México* (1958), and *Atlantis* (1967) he set out to prevent aestheticist admiration of his writing by employing few of the conventional characteristics of poetry and by making its dominant element denotative meaning. This choice has made his work difficult to anthologize and caused it to be ignored by major critical surveys.

The flourishing in the mid 1960s of new small presses and of young poets whose work Dudek considered disorganized and incoherent brought abrupt changes in Dudek's publishing activities. He began to work more closely with tradition-oriented Montreal writers, such as R. G. Everson, Peter van Toorn, Glen Siebrasse, Michael Gnarowski, and John Glassco, and to become critical of Souster's proposals to publish through Contact Press work by Margaret Atwood, Gwendolyn MacEwen, Victor Coleman, and Richard Clarke. In 1966 Dudek terminated *Delta* and founded the press Delta Canada with Siebrasse and Gnarowski. In 1967, discouraged by Souster's publishing of the Contact Press anthology *New Wave Canada*, he agreed to Contact's dissolution. In 1970, when Siebrasse and Gnarowski moved on to other publishing activities, Dudek founded, with his new wife, Aileen Collins, DC Books, which they still operate.

The 1950s and 1960s have been the two most productive decades of Dudek's career. In addition to his writing and his work with little magazines and small presses, he financed and operated the McGill Poetry Series (whose first volume was Leonard Cohen's first book, *Let Us Compare Mythologies*), edited two high-school poetry antholo-

*Cover for Dudek's 1986 poetry collection, dedicated to
R. G. Everson*

gies, and contributed weekly columns to the *Montreal Gazette*. He also coedited with Gnarowski *The Making of Modern Poetry in Canada* (1967), an anthology of theoretical writings by Canadian poets and critics that is still the standard work on the emergence of modernism in Canadian poetry.

Dudek's long poems, *Europe*, *En México*, and *Atlantis*, are landmarks in the development of the Canadian long poem, comparable to Basil Bunting's *Briggflatts* (1966) in English poetry and to William Carlos Williams's *Paterson* (1946-1958) and Charles Olson's *The Maximus Poems* (1960-1975) in American. They are the first Canadian long poems to abandon narrative sequence and to attempt open form. Although they are in a sense narratives of Dudek's visits to Europe and Central America, they are more than mere travel poems because each challenges its materials to reveal pattern, coherence, and meaning. The journey provides only a context in which the search through language for primitive energies of life can be conducted.

Each of these long poems is a chronicle and a record of its own composition. Because each challenges the commonplace to reveal meaning, each takes the risk of presenting the uninspired moment and the banal reflection. Readers proceed through the ordinary to the remarkable, to the powerful "Epilogue" of *Atlantis* and to "After the thirteenth century," section 55 of *Europe*. Perhaps Dudek's greatest innovation in these poems is to present his ideas as experiences, so that it is not the idea itself that the reader encounters but the process of Dudek experiencing the idea. Dudek achieves this effect by using the subtleties of rhythm and rhyme he wrote about in "Functional Poetry" to capture the actual rhythm, the phenomenology of thought.

Just as the articles and reviews that Aileen Collins edited in 1988 under the title *In Defence of Art* testify to Dudek's ongoing commitment to tradition–a mainstream notion of "culture" is his alternative to "chaos"–so do the shorter poems reveal his faith in order, as two meditative lyrics in *Zembla's Rocks* (1986) illustrate. "Atlantis" counters the suggestion that life is nothing, without meaning, by asserting: "It appears in fragments, / or whole, at certain moments– / real in every detail, / itself, or a false shine / of the real thing." "The Word-Meccano" reflects again on alternatives to order, and finds that it is, ironically, language that frequently (and deceptively) constructs chaos: "We torture the world with words, / turn it into a madhouse or a funfest, / gabble, confuse, scramble the atoms of being– / only to return to sunlight and sand, / the playground of our existence, where everything is real and in place." These lines indicate Dudek's control over cadence. Yet it is through his long poems that he has most deeply altered the textures of Canadian literature.

Despite being little known in academic circles Dudek has been a major influence on the work of other writers. He had close contact with the writers of the *Tish* group; his work with the long poem had a direct effect on George Bowering's *Rocky Mountain Foot* (1968) and *Sitting in Mexico* (1969), Frank Davey's *The Scarred Hull* (1966), and an indirect one on Fred Wah's *Mountain* (1967) and Daphne Marlatt's *Rings* (1971), *Vancouver Poems* (1972), and *Steveston* (1974). He is currently active in encouraging the publication of poetry, especially with Montreal's Véhicule group of poets, including Ken Norris, Stephen Morrissey, and John MacAulay.

References:

Douglas Barbour, "Poet as Philosopher," *Canadian Literature*, 53 (Summer 1972): 18-19;

Robin Blaser, Introduction to Dudek's *Infinite Worlds: The Poetry of Louis Dudek*, edited by Blaser (Montreal: Véhicule, 1988);

Michael Darling, "Redeeming Reality," *Canadian Literature*, 94 (Autumn 1984): 114-117;

Frank Davey, *Louis Dudek and Raymond Souster* (Vancouver: Douglas & McIntyre, 1980);

Wynne Francis, "A Critic of Life: Louis Dudek as a Man of Letters," *Canadian Literature*, 22 (Autumn 1964): 5-23;

Terry Goldie, *Louis Dudek* (Toronto: ECW, 1985);

Dorothy Livesay, "The Sculpture of Poetry," *Canadian Literature*, 30 (Autumn 1966): 26-35;

Susan Stromberg-Stein, *Louis Dudek: A Biographical Introduction to his Poetry* (Ottawa: Golden Dog Press, 1983).

Robert Elie

(5 April 1915-19 January 1973)

Grazia Merler
Simon Fraser University

BOOKS: *Borduas* (Montreal: L'Arbre, 1943);

La Fin des songes (Montreal: Beauchemin, 1950); translated by Irene Coffin as *Farewell My Dreams* (Toronto: Ryerson, 1954; New York: Bouregy & Curl, 1955);

Il suffit d'un jour (Montreal: Beauchemin, 1957);

Œuvres, edited by Paul Beaulieu (Cité de LaSalle, Que.: Hurtubise / HMH, 1979).

OTHER: Hector de Saint-Denys Garneau, *Poésies complètes: Regards et jeux dans l'espace; Les Solitudes*, edited by Elie and Jean Le Moyne, introduction by Elie (Montreal: Fides, 1949);

Garneau, *Journal*, edited, with a foreword, by Elie and Le Moyne (Montreal: Beauchemin, 1954);

Garneau, *Lettres à ses amis*, edited, with a foreword, by Elie, Le Moyne, and Claude Hurtubise (Montreal: HMH, 1967).

Robert Elie is best known for two novels: *La Fin des songes* (1950; translated as *Farewell My Dreams*, 1954) and *Il suffit d'un jour* (It Only Takes a Day, 1957). Together with other young Quebec writers and intellectuals, he began in the 1940s to portray with a critical eye the moral and psychological dilemmas of his people, confronted by the need to find answers to fundamental existential questions. If the criticism of a whole generation in his fictional work is bitter, throughout his public life Elie showed generosity and understanding

Robert Elie (courtesy of Kenneth Landry)

for his fellow Quebeckers. He served as a cultural ambassador for Quebec both in Canada and abroad.

Born to Emile and Maria Dubois Elie in Montreal's working-class neighborhood of Pointe Saint-Charles, he pursued his classical studies at Collège Sainte-Marie. In 1933, at eighteen, he met and became the friend of the poet Hector de Saint-Denys Garneau, whose work Elie championed until his own death in 1973. They both joined forces with the group that came to be associated with the journal *La Relève,* and, on several occasions, they met with the philosopher Jacques Maritain, who influenced Elie's particular vision of the human condition. Other members of the group were Jean Le Moyne, Claude Hurtubise, Robert Charbonneau, and Paul Beaulieu, the last of whom edited Elie's *Œuvres* in 1979.

Elie continued his education at the Faculté des Lettres of the Université de Montréal (1935-1936) and at McGill University (1939-1940), where he studied English literature and history. About 1937 he met the painter Paul-Emile Borduas, who in 1948 was a signatory, with Claude Gauvreau and Jean-Paul Riopelle, of *Refus global (Total Refusal),* the influential manifesto attacking Quebec premier Maurice Duplessis's entente with business and the Catholic church. Borduas, and the relation between art and the state, were to become recurrent themes in the articles and essays Elie contributed from 1935 to 1973 to such journals and papers as *Cité Libre, La Relève, La Presse,* and *La Revue Dominicaine.* A complete list of Elie's periodical publications and prefaces is included in the *Œuvres,* in which most of his nonfiction is collected.

At the age of twenty-five Elie began his public life: at first as a reporter and art critic with the newspapers *Le Canada* and *La Presse* and then with the news service at Radio-Canada. In 1943 he published a monograph on the work and socio-aesthetic ideas of Borduas. He extended his career as an art critic when, in 1947, he became principal founder and chief editor of the journal *Architecture, Bâtiment, Construction.* In 1948 he became assistant director of the news service at Radio-Canada.

It was during the 1950s that Elie did most of his writing, producing a play, poems, and his two novels. In 1958 he became the director of the Ecole des Beaux-Arts in Montreal, and in 1961 he was charged with overseeing all of the art schools in the province of Quebec. In 1962 he continued his public career as cultural attaché at the Délégation du Québec in Paris; two more plays were published in 1964; and in 1966 he became assistant director to the Secretariat Spécial du Bilinguisme. In 1970 he was named associate director of the Canada Council, a position he occupied until his death at the age of fifty-seven. He

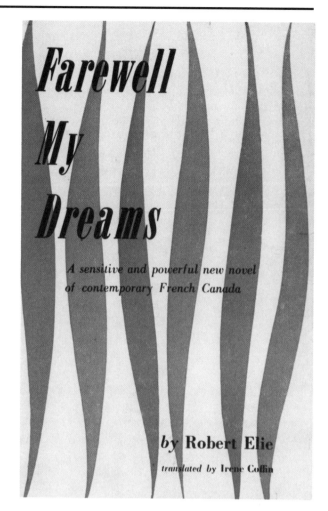

Dust jacket for the 1954 translation of Elie's first novel, La Fin des songes

was survived by his wife, Marie-Marthe Huot, whom he had married in Montreal on 22 April 1944.

Elie's first novel, *La Fin des songes,* winner of the Prix David, is an introspective work relating the efforts of Marcel Larocque to dissipate the anguish he feels when he is forced to face the vanishing dreams of adolescence. Neither his faithful friend, Bernard Guérin, nor Marcel's wife, Jeanne, nor his sister-in-law, Louise, with whom he has a brief affair, can divert him from his suicide. The novel is an adventure in a "dead zone," Elie observed in "Réflexions sur le dialogue," a 1951 essay collected in *Œuvres.* Using both journal form (for Marcel) and indirect narration, Elie opposes two ways of living in the novel. Bernard is the survivor, the fighter; Marcel is incapable of overcoming his existential despair and chooses suicide. It has been suggested that Marcel's spiritual crisis resembles that experienced by the poet Garneau.

Il suffit d'un jour, Elie's second novel, covers a twenty-four-hour span in the life of the sleepy village of Saint-Théodore. Village life is menaced by the arrival of an American canning company, and on the personal level, the lives of individuals are threatened by the sudden arrival of a stranger who leads them to question life, love, human relationships. The novel has been criticized for sketching in too short a time span too many characters and plots. The moral themes Elie develops in *Il suffit d'un jour*, especially through the character of the adolescent Elisabeth, make it clear that this is a novel with a spiritual message.

The outcome of Elie's desire to unmask and denounce mediocrity in his fictional works often borders on caricature. His condemnation of a fatalism that leads to stagnation is bitter. Some characters lose themselves in their own introspection (*La Fin des songes*) or, because of their bigoted egoism (Charlie Lafont and Jeanne in *Il suffit d'un jour*), never reach existential lucidity. The more plausible characters in *Il suffit d'un jour*, Pierre, the priest, and Elisabeth, live according to a standard of Christian charity, humanism, and free will.

Individual freedom and rejoicing, however, are always obtained at the expense of someone else, be it on a personal level, as in the play *L'Etrangère* (published in *Ecrits du Canada Français* in 1954 and collected in *Œuvres*), or on a collective level, as in the plays *Le Silence de la ville* and *La Place publique* (both published in *ECF* in 1964 and collected in *Œuvres*). The intensity of one's happiness is proportional to the innocence and purity of the victim. As the characters strive toward some type of communication with other human beings, they are irrevocably confronted with the realization of their solitude; juxtaposed to their emotional isolation are death and violence.

A substantial collection of Elie's poetry appeared, under the title *Poèmes*, in *Ecrits du Canada Français* (1961; collected in *Œuvres*). Here the solitude of man is more metaphysical. Even beyond the visible world, in the realm of fantasy and in the face of eternity, man is confronted with his limitations. Elie's nonfiction presents a more optimis-

tic side of his humanism. His articles and essays cover subjects as varied as writers, painters, poetry, philosophical questions, society, ideologies, and the work ethic. His aesthetic preoccupations are linked to a world of Christian ethics. Living, for Elie, is an act of faith; it is man's responsibility to search for truth, no matter how risky the existential experience may prove to be. In his search dialogue is essential, and when it is undertaken in a spirit of love, it never leads to defeat. At the opposite pole of this good faith lies the realization, however, that even gestures of brotherly love are only declarations of intentions. What seems to be central to his ethics is the infinite hope of the continuous renewal of these intentions. Hence Elie reiterates the notion that man is in a state of perpetual becoming; each moment is important; present movement, especially, is crucial. It is in man's creativity, notably in art and poetry, that one finds proof of his capacity to renew his questioning and his quest for answers to existential questions.

It can be said of Robert Elie throughout his literary and public life that he remained faithful to the precepts of his early writings: openness, generosity, intellectual honesty, and the need for dialogue among men. The articulation of these beliefs is perhaps the greatest contribution Elie made to Quebec culture.

References:

Paul Beaulieu, "Re-découvrir Robert Elie," introduction to Elie's *Œuvres* (Cité de LaSalle, Que.: Hurtubise / HMH, 1979), pp. ii-v;

Marc Gagnon, *Robert Elie* (Montreal: Fides, 1968);

France Ouellet, with Michel Biron, *Inventaire sommaire du fonds Robert Elie* (Montreal: Ministère des Affaires Culturelles, Bibliothèque Nationale du Québec, 1988);

Jeanette Urbas, "Reflêt et révelation. La Technique du miroir dans le roman canadien-français moderne," *Revue de l'Université d'Ottawa* (October / December 1973): 573-586.

Papers:

Robert Elie's papers are at the Bibliothèque Nationale du Québec.

R. G. Everson

(18 November 1903-   )

Ralph Gustafson
and
W. H. New
University of British Columbia

BOOKS: *Of this and that*, by Everson, J. C. Johnston, and J. L. Charlesworth (Montreal: Privately printed, 1940);

Three Dozen Poems, drawings by Colin Haworth (Montreal: Cambridge Press, 1957);

A Lattice for Momos, drawings by Haworth (Toronto: Contact, 1958);

Blind Man's Holiday, drawings by Haworth (Toronto: Ryerson, 1963);

Four Poems (Norwich, Vt.: American Letters Press, 1963);

Wrestle with an Angel, drawings by Haworth (Montreal: Delta, 1965);

Incident on Côte des Neiges, and Other Poems (Amherst, Mass.: Green Knight Press, 1966);

Raby Head, and Other Poems (Amherst, Mass.: Green Knight Press, 1967);

The Dark Is Not So Dark, drawings by Haworth (Montreal: Delta, 1969);

Selected Poems; 1920-1970, drawings by Haworth (Montreal: Delta, 1970);

Indian Summer (Ottawa: Oberon, 1976);

Carnival (Ottawa: Oberon, 1978);

Everson at Eighty, edited by Al Purdy (Ottawa: Oberon, 1983).

R. G. Everson (courtesy of the author)

The publication of *Everson at Eighty* in 1983 honored a man whose fifty-year contribution to Canadian letters has been quiet, constant, and without fanfare. Edited by Al Purdy, selecting from Everson's earlier volumes and also introducing some new poems, *Everson at Eighty* reveals the poet's conservative Ontario morality, his mature creativity, and his continuing passion for poetry. Traditional in syntax and in some ways old-fashioned in vocabulary, writing what Purdy calls "almost a guideline to a never-never world of the future," Everson still remains relevant and contemporary. In these introductory statements are some of the central paradoxes of Everson's life. For fanfare (as in his career in public relations) is precisely what he has unobtrusively brought to others, avoiding it for himself; and the passion of his poetry takes the formal shape of metaphor and muted observation.

Insufficiently acknowledged in his native land, though praised by the American poet James Dickey in the *Sewanee Review* for the volumes that appeared in 1958 and 1963, Everson withdraws from a high public profile. He prefers to publish with little presses, whose efforts to re-

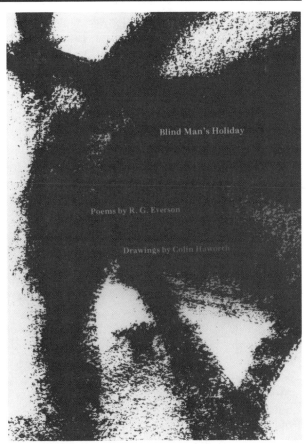

Front cover and dust jacket for two of Everson's six poetry collections illustrated by Colin Haworth

shape the arts he has long encouraged. Sometimes in his poetry sparks fly, as in "When I'm Going Well" (in *A Lattice for Momos*, 1958):

> When I'm going well
> as now at Westmount Glen and CPR
> in wet October dusk, the winds
> taste firecrackery. Loud sparks
> jump up laughing like a Breughel bride.
> Crayoned in phosphorus, the station agent
> vibrates. He's electrocuted.

Westmount Glen, on the Canadian Pacific Railway line near Montreal, is close to where Everson has lived for many years; but though his business and literary careers have been centered in Montreal, his background and training stem from Ontario. A seventh-generation Canadian of Norse, English, and Scottish stock, Everson was born in Oshawa, Ontario, on 18 November 1903 to Thomas Henry and Mary Elizabeth Farwell Everson; he was one of seven children. Living on a farm at the edge of town, he attended public schools in Oshawa till 1919 and Toronto schools till 1923, working on the General Motors assem-

bly line in Oshawa during summer holidays. Moving on to the University of Toronto, he enrolled in an arts course, began to work on his poetry, and edited *Acta Victoriana*, the school journal. Graduating with a B.A. in economics in 1927, he went on to legal training at the prestigious Osgoode Hall Law School in Toronto, paying his fees by writing pulp fiction–westerns, detective stories–for the U.S. firm of Street and Smith. He was called to the Ontario bar in 1930, but he has never practiced as a lawyer. In 1930 he also published three poems in *Poetry* (Chicago).

Everson married Lorna Jean Austin (of Niagara-on-the-Lake) on 15 April 1931, and they moved to a cabin in the woods near Muskoka. Until 1936 he continued to write pulp fiction; he also began to send poems to other journals. *Canadian Forum* was one periodical that accepted his work; and although Macmillan rejected a book-length manuscript, a literary career seemed under way. A family illness intervened, and a declining market for pulp fiction meant he had to seek funds in other ways. The Eversons left the Lake Ontario region and moved to Montreal.

There Everson began his long career with the public-relations firm of Johnston, Everson and Charlesworth. He was president by 1938, and with his partners he wrote his first published book, *Of this and that,* a collection of essays and opinions privately printed in 1940. During World War II Everson worked with Sir William Stephenson in intelligence gathering, but he remained centered in Montreal. His public-relations career continued unimpeded till his retirement in 1963. He was for many years copublisher of Canada's often-quoted monthly journal of opinion, the *Printed Word.* In 1964 Everson was listed as chairman of Communications 6, Inc., of Montreal; this position was, he told Purdy, primarily an honorary one that allowed him to retain an office in which to continue his writing.

Though at the University of Toronto Everson had studied under that great Canadian narrative poet E. J. Pratt, his own poems are uniformly lyric. The several small volumes from *Three Dozen Poems* in 1957 to *Everson at Eighty* in 1983 are much of a piece. *Wrestle with an Angel* (1965) focuses on other Canadian literary figures—Louis Dudek, Earle Birney, Desmond Pacey, Fred Cogswell—and on their symbolic function in the contemporary literary scene. *A Lattice for Momos* focuses on Montreal districts. But the techniques are similar. Like the 1957 and 1965 volumes, *A Lattice for Momos* has drawings by Colin Haworth, not illustrations but parallel artistic explorations of mood, and the emphasis on mood reveals the way in which a typical poem by Everson is an exercise in responding. It attempts, with terse, hard images and colloquial adjectives, to evoke in the reader a response equivalent to the poet's own reaction to an observed event.

A Lattice for Momos includes some of Everson's clearest expressions of gaiety and love in the face of terrible events and bleak darkness. The title allusion—to Momos, the son of Night, who said that human beings should have been made with latticework in their chests so that their emotions would be revealed—suggests both the poet's concern for lucidity and his (sometimes wry) awareness of human duplicity. This duality appears throughout *A Lattice for Momos*. The recurrent image of children, for example, is a reminder of missed opportunities, trained responses, and still-possible hopes. " 'Squeezed the Slave Out of Himself' "—the title a quotation from Chekhov—opens the volume with the poetic persona painfully, slowly "squeezing the slave from my ego," seeking to "recapture / original sin /

of childhood rapture." And the volume closes with "Christening," a charm to "name mysterious fissures in the ground / and unseen mists where stars grow. / Name your child." Between these two are poems about social unrest, thwarted sexuality, literary theory. In "Report for Northrop Frye" Everson wonders aloud: "if, 'Poetry can only be made out of other poems' / —in new space, to what may I refer? / We bring our own light to a dark place. / Crowbar, sledge hammer, pick / pound Labrador granite. / / We make sounds from Arctic silence." Laughter and good sense are Everson's answer to many of life's problems; he is on the side of affirmation and moral possibility—but not naively. In "Child with Shell" the poet observes sagely:

> The child scrapes scrapes away
>   at the shell—
> always the same swirling colour shown;
>   it won't come off.
> A waste of time, child. It's in the bone,
>   like tides and love.

If, Everson seems to be saying, like Canute, we cannot command the tide, at least we can love one another.

The later volumes extend this stance. *Blind Man's Holiday,* which appeared under the Ryerson Press imprint in 1963, brought him the attention an established publisher attracts, but with several other publications, including *Wrestle with an Angel,* he returned to small and coterie presses, both in Canada and in the United States. He never won more than a small but faithful following, though he is respected by other writers; yet the wide appeal of his work is testified to by the fact that he has published verse (and some stories) in journals ranging from *Adam* (London), *Saturday Review, Poetry,* and the *New York Times* to *Atlantic Advocate, Atlantic Monthly, Canadian Forum, Fiddlehead, Queen's Quarterly,* and *Tamarack Review.* Later volumes—titled *Indian Summer* (1976) and *Carnival* (1978)—continue to celebrate late summertime and joy; but these volumes are also filled with acerbic contrasts. *Indian Summer* emerges from the poet's travels and comments on politics and social mores in Norway, Mexico, and South Africa. "The Midnight Watch" works on the mordant distinction between the poet's enthusiasm for an Arctic flower he sees and his realization that the flower is really a piece of discarded tissue paper:

> My Norse forebears' sagas (set down
>   in Iceland) tell of this headland as lonely

Front cover for Everson's 1976 poetry collection, inspired by his travels

a fit place for their fierce gods.
I look about in the warm midnight sunlight

and count hundreds of tents, trailers and autos
Over two thousand people are taking photos
of each other, throwing down candy wrappers,
not looking at the Arctic Ocean or Barents Sea
trying to climb the wire fence at the cliff edge
and crowding the knick-knack store for picture
    postcards
of the celebrated North Cape and Midnight Sun[.]

While the liveliness and immediacy of Everson's poetry constitute its strengths, these characteris-

tics perhaps also explain why his name–despite Purdy's warm endorsement in 1983–has so strikingly disappeared from contemporary critical commentary. In an age when surface complexities are praised, Everson's apparent simplicities go unappreciated.

In the foreword he wrote for *A Lattice for Momos,* Louis Dudek contrasts "Laprairie Hunger Strike" with "L'Abbé Lemaître's Universe" as representative of the two poles of Everson's imagination; the first poem is serious; the second, "dominated by the lighter tone, within which the seriousness is concealed," is "written in a style that seems to be the exact keynote for poetry in this decade [the 1950s]: Baroque, the perfect oval containing its tensions." Everson's delight at being alive frequently takes this ironic tone, as when, in "Laurentian Motel," the poet sardonically observes a young Breton chambermaid kicking about the "enigmatic bed" of a departed honeymoon couple and cautions, "Be calm, sweet child: you'll learn / how awesome love checks in, and out." More problematic still is his ironic aside in "Cold-Weather Love": "Remember the rape outside Drumheller / at fifty below? Canadians are hardy." Politics and wit seem to be in tension. At the same time, laughter, for Everson, remains the self's commonsense answer to most problems; in "June 21" the poet observes: "No things but in emotions. Seasons turn / cartwheels. I laugh while huge reality, / A mindless lout, summersaults for my pleasure."

Praising Everson's urbane wisdom, his "sense of lived reality, and of emotional elasticity in living," Dudek links Everson with such poets as Goodridge MacDonald and W. W. E. Ross. While Everson's "stiff adaptation . . . to the new ways of doing things"–betrayed "in a euphemistic approach to language"–somewhat limits his appeal, he is still, says Dudek, "a poet of craftsmanlike integrity, of true humility, and of touching humanity." This comment, made in 1958, remains a valid tribute to a poet whose entire career has been spent asserting the capacity of love and nature and creativity to triumph over horror, power, and ranging vanity.

Robert Finch

(14 May 1900-   )

Susan Gingell
University of Saskatchewan

BOOKS: *Poems* (Toronto: Oxford University Press, 1946);

The Strength of the Hills (Toronto: McClelland & Stewart, 1948);

A Century Has Roots: A Masque (Toronto: University of Toronto Press, 1953);

Acis in Oxford, and Other Poems (Oxford: Privately printed, 1959; Toronto: University of Toronto Press, 1961);

Dover Beach Revisited, and Other Poems (Toronto: Macmillan, 1961);

The Sixth Sense: Individualism in French Poetry, 1686-1760 (Toronto: University of Toronto Press, 1966);

Silverthorn Bush and Other Poems (Toronto: Macmillan, 1966);

Variations and Theme: Poems (Erin, Ont.: Porcupine's Quill, 1980);

Has and Is: Poems (Erin, Ont.: Porcupine's Quill, 1981);

Twelve for Christmas (Erin, Ont.: Porcupine's Quill, 1982);

The Grand Duke of Moscow's Favourite Solo (Erin, Ont.: Porcupine's Quill, 1983);

Double Tuning (Erin, Ont.: Porcupine's Quill, 1984);

For the Back of a Likeness (Erin, Ont.: Porcupine's Quill, 1986);

Sail-boat and Lake (Erin, Ont.: Porcupine's Quill, 1988).

PLAY PRODUCTION: *A Century Has Roots: A Masque*, Toronto, Hart House Theatre, 1953.

OTHER: *New Provinces: Poems of Several Authors*, edited by F. R. Scott and A. J. M. Smith, includes poems by Finch (Toronto: Macmillan, 1936);

Chateaubriand, *René*, edited by Finch and C. R. Parsons (Toronto: University of Toronto Press, 1957);

French Individualist Poetry, 1686-1760: An Anthology, edited by Finch and Eugène Joliat (Toronto: University of Toronto Press, 1971);

"The Paris Years," chapter four in *Douglas Duncan: A Memorial Portrait*, edited by Alan Jarvis (Toronto: University of Toronto Press, 1974);

Saint-Evremond, *Sir Politik Would-be*, edited by Finch and Joliat (Paris & Geneva: Droz, 1978);

"War and Peace," chapter 4 in *The Enduring Word: a Centennial History of Wycliffe College*, edited by Arnold Edinborough (Toronto: University of Toronto Press, 1978);

Saint-Evremond, *Les Opéra*, edited by Finch and Joliat (Geneva: Droz, 1979).

Twice the winner of a Governor General's Award, for *Poems* (1946) and *Acis in Oxford, and Other Poems* (1959), Robert Finch was in the early years of his publishing career a controversial figure in Canadian poetry; his later books have sparked limited though generally positive critical response. A paraphrase of a line from the early credo "Beauty My Fond Fine Care" may offer at least a partial explanation of the controversy his work aroused in the socially and politically aware 1940s intellectual world, for, as that poem has it, Finch's verse does aim to seduce an erudite company. Undeniably conservative in outlook, serene, and secure in his Christian faith, Finch is a disciplined user of and experimenter with established forms and rhythms, the tailored structures of the sonnet and the quatrain, and use of the iambic pentameter line being characteristic of his work. Finch's poems exhibit an almost total lack of political awareness–of war, terrorism, poverty, the human struggle to survive–so that they lack a contemporary feel, for all their occasional references to computers, hang gliders, daycare, and rock and roll. Furthermore, these poems are infrequently grounded in the Canadian experience, Finch being surely the most European of the modern Canadian poets. Mountains, oceans, woods,

ACIS IN OXFORD

Acis in Oxford and other poems by Robert Finch

University of Toronto Press

Dust jacket for the first Canadian edition of the book that earned Finch his second Governor General's Award

and gardens, along with flowers, fountains, statues, and urns are typical settings and furnishings of his poems, blending as they do the two realms of nature and art. Individuals in society are seldom the focus of his vision, but private friendships and intimate relationships more frequently find expression.

Robert Duer Claydon Finch, the son of Edward and Ada Finch, was born in Freeport, Long Island, and grew up in a highly cultivated atmosphere. By the age of four he could read both English and French and would be read daily the work of the major English poets and required to commit to memory a passage of Scripture. At the family home at Morris Point the young Finch learned to share his father's passion for gardens and was impressed by his partially French moth-

er's maintenance of her European connections. A typical Saturday in the boy's fourth, fifth, and sixth years would find him listening to his godfather, John King Duer of the wealthy Duer Du Pont Breck family, describing either the history of pictures and objets d'art in the Breck family mansion, or the most recently imported antique Japanese miniature gardens which Duer sold from a posh Madison Avenue shop. The young Finch's early summers were spent largely outdoors on the beaches and dunes of Fire Island, a landscape that recurs frequently in his oeuvre.

While still in the United States, Finch attended a variety of public and private institutions, but when the family moved in 1906 to a ranch in the foothills of the Canadian Rockies, his mother gave the children their daily lessons, which Finch supplemented by reading his way through several abandoned barrels of the complete works of well-known Victorian writers. He went on to attend the University of Toronto in 1919, where he won the Jardine Memorial Prize in 1924 for a poem, "Rain" (unpublished), graduating (B.A., Honour Moderns in French and German) and winning the Governor General's proficiency medal in 1925. His studies had been interrupted for two years when he took up a post at Ridley College, a private boys' school in St. Catharines, Ontario. The headmaster of the lower school, H. G. Williams, had a vast knowledge of and love for verse and gave the young poet the encouragement of a regular and informed criticism.

After postgraduate studies at the Sorbonne (1926-1928), Finch accepted a post as lecturer in the Department of French, University College, University of Toronto, where he spent his entire academic career, though he also had an office at Massey College from the time of its founding. The two books for which he won the highest scholarly acclaim are *The Sixth Sense: Individualism in French Poetry, 1686-1760* (1966) and its companion anthology, *French Individualist Poetry, 1686-1760* (1971), coedited by Finch's close friend and colleague Eugène Joliat.

Finch is an avid North American and European traveler, but when he is home his interests are also wide ranging. There have been more than a dozen public exhibitions of his paintings, and his work is represented in many collections. He also has long-standing interests in music history, composing, and instrumental and vocal performance, particularly of baroque period pieces. His work with both English- and French-language theater as performer, producer, and director is also noteworthy. Finch has been frequently honored for his contributions to the cultural life of Canada: election to the Royal Society of Canada (1963), the Lorne Pierce Gold Medal (1968), and honorary degrees from the University of Toronto and York University (1973 and 1976) are among his accolades.

The first major selection of Finch's poems appeared in the landmark anthology *New Provinces: Poems of Several Authors* (1936). Art and the artistic process are his most prevalent themes here; the imagist influence is often felt, and the literary allusions and color symbolism that are typical of the texture of a Finch poem are already much in evidence. Seven of the eleven pieces by Finch in *New Provinces* were republished, all but one unrevised, in either *Poems* or *The Strength of the Hills* (1948).

Poems is divided into four thematically determined sections. The verse of the first, entitled "The Statue," depicts scenes from nature and the human sphere with the visual artist's eye for detail and arrangement; art as an imposition of a frame of order on transient experience is ever the superior state, though Finch expresses an awareness of the fallibility of even the creative man's perceptions. The poems of the section entitled "Livery" are satiric portraits, for the most part, of a complacent Canadian bourgeoisie; those of "The Captive" explore the relationships between friends or lovers, though there is nothing of physical passion expressed, while those from "The Reticent Phrase" discuss poetry and the nature of man in highly figurative language.

The quatrain is the dominant stanza form, and diction, rhythm, and rhyme are used for a variety of effects. In "Vézelay," for example, they reinforce the satiric intentions, while "The Statue," a poem that juxtaposes the disorder and triviality of human occurrences with the order and timelessness of art, marries sound, form, and sense to create an elegant and harmonious effect: "Stone that endured the chisel's cutting chillness / Is tolerant of the stone at its foot of stone / And the pigeon sitting awry on its carved curls." Sometimes, however, Finch's delight in sound play betrays his larger purpose ("Your treason is my reason / My poison is your raisin"), and his rhythms can become mechanical or awkward, as they do in the last six lines of "The Five."

When the presentation of the Governor General's Award for *Poems* was made at the annual Canadian Authors' Association convention, Finch was not present to receive it because the C.A.A. had not advised Finch that he had won the award. Earle Birney, who, in his capacity as editor of the *Canadian Poetry Magazine*, had given *Poems* a most favorable review, praising Finch for his maturity, honesty, sensitivity, and courteous independence, was pressed into an extemporaneous rebuttal of the attack launched on the book at the presentation ceremony, but the controversy over the volume's merits was just beginning. John Sutherland, the editor of *Northern Review*, used that magazine to berate Finch's work for its intellectual bathos and moral sententiousness, and to arraign the Awards Committee, suggesting a series of reasons why Finch had won out over poets whose cause Sutherland championed. The intemperate review led to the resignations of five members of the editorial board, including A. M. Klein, F. R. Scott, and A. J. M. Smith, and of two regional editors, P. K. Page and Ralph Gustafson, but Finch's critical reputation suffered badly, and his reception has continued to be extremely varied.

Finch's European-influenced sensibility was a primary shaping force in his next book, *The Strength of the Hills*. Though the poet had firsthand experience of the Rockies from his youth, the mountain sonnets that form the opening section of the book reflect more of a mind steeped in the literature of Christian Europe than they do a Canadian experience of nature. A Christian ethic stands behind many of the poems of this collection, though their theology is rather commonplace. Finch is more successful when he uses Bible stories as his source of image or analogy as he uses the Joseph of Egypt story in "The Five Kine," a poem about a creative famine that results from the failure to get the poetic harvest in.

Music is an important source of figurative language in *The Strength of the Hills* while poetry and painting are recurrent subjects, and there is a synaesthetic quality in many of the descriptions involving artistic forms. Finch speaks of the snow as a harp "Chasing the theme / Of winter's dream / In fugues for eyes / To memorize / Till ears catch flight / Of sound through sight." The metamorphic qualities of nature are reflected in an acute seasonal awareness, and the metamorphic qualities of man's perceptions, their richness as well as their limitations, are all repeatedly explored. Poems growing out of Finch's professorial experiences and several variations on the theme of snow—a natural phenomenon that frequently serves as thematic inspiration and as source of image and metaphor in the Finch canon–constitute further noteworthy groups of poems. The poems of *The Strength of the Hills* are predominantly meditative or speculative in tone, tetrameter or pentameter rhyming couplets or alternating rhyme being the most frequently used structural units, though tercets are also employed with some virtuosity. The repetition of a word, often used with different grammatical values, emerges forcefully as a hallmark of the Finch style. The last four lines of "The Messenger," one of the snow poems, typify his particular brand of wordplay: "Waiting, a comforter uncomforted, / Till its potential manna melt from sight / Even more softly than sight felt it fall, / So the green snow of spring may spring to heaven."

"Acis in Oxford," the title poem of the third book-length collection, is written in predominantly iambic *abba* quatrains, though the meter is often irregular. Part one of the poem describes the context and effects of an Oxford performance of Handel's secular choral work *Acis and Galatea* and introduces the three principal characters of the classical story. The latter two parts of the poem examine other contemporary reincarnations of the trio: a statue of a nymph in a secluded grotto by a river (Acis was turned into a river after being crushed by a rock hurled by his rival Polyphemus) and boats (bearing the names of the three characters) lying at anchor in a nearby harbor.

The remaining poems are primarily meditations on often proverbial views of subjects such as absence, alienation, love, unrecognized beauty, the real, and the remembered. Seasons of nature and the heart are represented, principally elegiacally, in sonnet form and in a diction that frequently recalls an earlier age. Words such as "hark," "athwart," "thither," and "thence" are typical. Most of the poems lack a particularized sense of place or character, generalized concepts and traits taking precedence over individuality.

The literary allusiveness of Finch's verse is exemplified by the title poem of *Dover Beach Revisited, and Other Poems* (1961). "Eleven Revisit the Poem," the first of two parts, is a series of monologues in which successive characters react to the philosophical, moral, or emotional premises of Matthew Arnold's well-known poem. The Mariner, for example, objects to Arnold's speaker ascribing emotion to the indifferent sea. Other monologues–"The Philosopher," for example– have remarkably little to do with the original poem, an observation that can also be made

about the second part of Finch's poem, "The Place Revisited." Here, Arnold's "darkling plain . . ./Where ignorant armies clash by night" is given a specific historical reference because the allied troops were lifted off to Dover after the evacuation of Dunkirk in World War II. Lacking as it does a controlling imaginative vision, Finch's cadenced retelling of the heroic rescue suffers by comparison to E. J. Pratt's earlier *Dunkirk* (1941).

Many of the verses that fill out the book use the sea, its waves, tides, and beaches as metaphors for the human condition. The interests that led Finch to become a member of the Council of Wycliffe College, an Anglican theological institution, and a trustee of the Toronto School of Theology influence the diction, form, and substance of several poems, and the results of his yearly travels in France and knowledge of French cultural history are fruitfully exploited. The five sonnets that comprise the poem "After Breughel" represent Finch's response to the Flemish painter's *Landscape with the Fall of Icarus*, a response perhaps influenced by W. H. Auden's "Musée des Beaux Arts," for both poets view the Icarian flight as a type of artistic daring and courage that goes unrecognized by society at large.

In *Silverthorn Bush and Other Poems* (1966) Finch adds to his usual repertoire of forms many lighthearted and satirical anecdotal poems which experiment with free verse and an unmannered contemporary diction. The satirical vein is particularly strong, though the arts, particularized nature, and generalized man are still the focal points of Finch's work. Flowers, shrubs, and trees, especially those characterized by fragility and delicacy, recur as symbols of a transitory earthly beauty that can be held forever in the mind or in art. The following lines from "Mimosa" are typical of the blending of images, ideas, and musical sounds found in the best Finch poems: "The confidences of a clavichord / Are not discreeter than the muted word /Mimosa turns to music for the sight." The final section of *Silverthorn Bush* is given over to occasional pieces. "The Corner-stone of University College Speaks . . ." reworks much of the material from Finch's 1953 masque *A Century Has Roots*, and the four-hundredth anniversary of Shakespeare's birth is commemorated by three sonnets and an acrostic.

Four major scholarly works appeared in the fourteen-year interval between *Silverthorn Bush* and *Variations and Theme* (1980), the first of the flood of books of poems that followed Finch's retirement from the University of Toronto. The vol-

Front cover for Finch's eleventh poetry collection

umes of the 1980s show Finch still working intensively with established forms and rhythms, and his themes, while often exploring territory similar to that of the earlier books, have expanded in range. *Variations and Theme* contains poems addressing subjects varying from art to race relations to birds; other poems offer wry commentary on the Olympic games, the Tutankhamen Exhibition, and a society that values its antiques but not its aged; while still others, such as "Well-Tempered Clavier" and "On the Same Rose Bush," are more rarefied but nonetheless beautifully crafted. The Finch who delights in both gardened and wild nature, France and her culture, and artistic beauties of all kinds speaks again in these poems, though music replaces the visual and verbal arts as the most prevalent subject and source of rhetorical figures.

The most impressively realized of these music poems, "Moments Musicaux," uses the rondeau form to create its music, a form that is increasingly present in subsequent volumes. The

fourteen variations and concluding theme which comprise the final section of the book are formally similar but thematically diverse poems whose common ground is the life of the imagination and senses. The sets of thirteen couplets point numerologically to patterns of death and rebirth, and the "Theme" section of the poem suggests a reading of "Variations" as records of "Points of arrival and departure" in the poet's life. The sequence opens with a return to the beaches of Fire Island and then makes its way through the gardens, woods, playing fields, retreats, homes, and musical and public occasions that have been part of Finch's experience.

The seven sections of *Has and Is* (1981) offer a blend of aesthetic, moral, social, and spiritual commentary, simultaneously exploiting the potential and pushing the limits of various forms. One indication of how carefully the individual parts are organized is the balance between the opening title poem, which argues the supremacy of human soul over human body in a tightly constructed sonnet, and the concluding poem of the initial part, which argues the dependence of word on act in a similarly constructed sonnet. The other parts offer further evidence. Part two has a decidedly epigrammatic quality that unites it. Section three examines the interplay of art, nature, and life; past and present; old and new. Part four, while grounded in the here and now of Canadian life–exemplified by the witty vision of the University of Toronto Robarts Library: "What is this out-size mastodonic nook? / A classic hippie sit-in for the Book"–can nonetheless be appreciated in the larger context of contemporary life in the Western world. The fifth part is given over to persons loved, lost, or loathed. The sixth reflects the vistas of Finch's widely traveled experience, and the seventh has a spiritual focus that is broad enough to encompass aspects of the poetic life.

Twelve for Christmas (1982) was published as a gift or collector's item. Finch's mastery of the technically demanding rondeau form in the book's "Twelve Christmas Rondeaus on Poets" is interestingly complemented by a speculative but scholarly essay on the well-known carol "The Twelve Days of Christmas."

The Grand Duke of Moscow's Favourite Solo (1983) is dedicated to two musical friends of the poet, and the poems of the first section have the feel of occasional works. The learned, esoteric, and occasionally witty poems of which it is comprised are often marred by forced or awkward rhymes, and the flute composition referred to in the book's title poem proves too frail a foundation for so extended a suite of poems. The interest of the next two sections is broader, and, with a return to the sonnet form Finch had abandoned for all but one poem of the opening section, his formal expertise reasserts itself. He effects an appropriate marriage of English words to the French rondeau form in "Two Rounds for Canada," for example, creating a pair of sonnets that reverses the initial refrain of an expatriate visitor "There is nothing here" to the forceful assertion "Here there is everything." Equally accomplished is Finch's use of the sonnet form in "Announcement" where he uses the octave to display his amusement at the naive claims of an alien religion that it will enrich the lives of Torontonians, reserving the sestet for his more complex ironic response. The poignancy of "Way Out," a poem about the unexpected pleasure of hearing the masterful execution of a tune by an old, blind subway violinist, makes the sonnet a vehicle of sincere, humble admiration, while "Doubles" uses a predominantly envelope rhyming pattern to analyze the ambiguous unities of each individual in a pair of lovers and of the pair itself. The irregular rhyme and stanzas of "Double Assignment"; a pair of acrostics celebrating the accomplishments of Ludwig van Beethoven and Charles Dickens; "Three Epigrammatic Sonnets and Four Epigrammes"; and a rondeau, "The Greeting," give further indication of Finch's formal range in the middle sections of the book. Following a well-established pattern, *The Grand Duke of Moscow's Favourite Solo* ends with poems on spiritual themes, poems that are most remarkable for the security with which they rest on a Waspish Christian foundation, easily dismissing existentialism as decidedly uncomfortable and firmly rejecting the veneration of Christian symbols in favor of the true veneration of Christ.

That Finch warmly embraced French culture has left its mark on all volumes of his poetry, but nowhere is this embrace as strongly felt as in the collection *Double Tuning* (1984). Titles of individual poems as well as the grouping of poems in part three under the rubric "Faits Divers" are the most superficial aspects of the French presence. French landscapes, French history, and the distortion in modern productions of the work of the classic French playwright Molière serve as thematic focuses. Part four announces in its title, "Epigrammes," the use it makes of a French form, and its first poem questions the validity and ramifications of the well-known French statement about autobiographical assertion, "Je est un Autre," formulated by Arthur Rimbaud but taken up in a critical study by Phillipe Lejeune. Furthermore, although Finch has never published poems in French, in *Double Tuning* he does use French vocabulary in his English texts, employing it to answer the demands of his rhyme scheme in the poems "The Island," "Supernumerary," "The Stand," and "Epigramme 6: The road of excess leads to the palace of wisdom."

In most respects *Double Tuning* is a confirmation of the thematic interests and technical achievements of earlier volumes rather than a groundbreaking work. Once more the sonnet form predominates, the sequence "A Concise History of Correspondence" forming an entire section of the book; the poems are based on art (especially poetry, music, and painting), on the humane condition, on nature, and on matter of the human spirit (the last section of the book is again given over to religious poems); and Finch's propensity for playing with, undermining, or revivifying clichés is again in evidence, most notably here in "Mindsight," which rhetorically questions the maxim "Out of sight, out of mind" in order to arrive at the conclusion "Never out of mind is never out of sight." The title poem, which records the way in which a harpsichord tuner also attunes the poet's mind to flight, may well be the volume's most memorable piece, thanks, in part, to Finch's witty choice of the sonnet length but couplet form as a complement to the poem's theme.

Double Tuning also invites a remarkably modest approach to the Finch canon in its two-sonnet "Manifesto." The first explains:

> I see and feel. Whatever the consequence,
> My verses, good or bad, come as they come.
> I complain in them, if I have cause to complain,
> I confide in them my secrets and my joy,
> They are the secretaries of my heart,
> Combing or curling them would make them vain,
> All I can call my lines, and not be coy,
> Is random note and comment without art.

The second maintains: "What I intend at most is to dispose / My bent in prosy rhyme or rhymy prose." Too literal an application of these characterizations would undoubtedly lead to an undervaluing of Finch's achievement: rarely, if ever, is a Finch poem "without art," and while some of the weaker poems might match the descriptions "prosy rhyme or rhymy prose," many do not. Nonetheless, the core of the manifesto seems just. Finch's poems appear indeed to be the "secretaries of [his] heart."

In recent years Porcupine's Quill has published two additional collections of Finch's verse, *For the Back of a Likeness* (1986) and *Sail-boat and Lake* (1988), both of which testify to the poet's continuing faith in traditional form.

Critical attention to Finch's work has been limited, though admiration for and hostility to it have come in almost equal measure. Earle Birney, an early champion of Finch's verse, records in his memoirs, *Spreading Time* (1980), the opinion that Finch's sonnets are finely crafted but that the form itself has cramped the poetic vision. Harsher criticism has come from Frank Davey, who, in *From There to Here* (1974), claims that most new Canadian poets who are aware of Finch's poetry regard it as "the epitome of the controlled, self-conscious artistry they seek to avoid." There have been voices that are ready to appreciate the strengths of his poetics. George Woodcock, in *Canadian Literature* (Summer 1962), has noted the urbanity of Finch's style, and the English critic William Walsh, writing in the *Bulletin of Canadian Studies* (April 1978) of Finch's sensibility as one which "aspires to make explicit . . . the [continental] Europeanism latent in the Canadian spirit," offers this praise: "Robert Finch has a beautifully coherent and single sensibility, subject and detail, thought and feeling, tone and language issuing without manipulation from a single, organic response." G. V. Downes, in *Canadian Literature* (Summer 1983), comments admiringly on Finch's work in "that infinitely tricky medium facing thought in one direction and music in another" and offers an intelligent approach to the understanding of Finch's use of form, hazarding the idea that "metrical form helps in the process of listening to one's truths." The verse Finch writes seems unlikely to gain wide popularity with the contemporary reading audience, but those who find pleasure in a sophisticated, elegant, and refined vision of the world will continue to read and enjoy his poems.

References:

Earle Birney, "The Poetry of Robert Finch," *Canadian Poetry Magazine*, 10 (March 1974): 6-8;

Frank Davey, "Robert Finch," in his *From There to Here: A Guide to English-Canadian Literature Since 1960* (Erin, Ont.: Press Porcépic, 1974), pp. 103-105;

G. V. Downes, "Robert Finch and the Temptation of Form," *Canadian Literature*, 97 (Summer 1983): 26-33;

Susan Gingell-Beckmann, "Against an Anabasis of Grace: A Retrospective Review of the Poems of Robert Finch," *Essays on Canadian Writing*, 23 (Spring 1982): 157-162;

Kay Mathers, "The Triumvirate of Robert Finch as Poet, Painter, and Pianist," *Saturday Night*, 63 (20 September 1947): 16;

John Sutherland, Review of *Poems* by Robert Finch, *Northern Review*, 1 (August-September 1947): 38-40;

William Walsh, "The Poetry of Robert Finch," *Bulletin of Canadian Studies*, 2 (April 1978): 1-15;

George Woodcock, "The Virtues of Urbanity," *Canadian Literature*, 13 (Summer 1962): 71-72.

R. A. D. Ford

(8 January 1915-   )

Peter Stevens
University of Windsor

BOOKS: *A Window on the North* (Toronto: Ryerson, 1956);
The Solitary City: Poems and Translations (Toronto: McClelland & Stewart, 1969);
Holes in Space (Toronto: Hounslow, 1979);
Needle in the Eye: Poems New and Old (Oakville, Ont.: Mosaic, 1983);
Doors, Words and Silence (Oakville, Ont.: Mosaic, 1985);
Dostoyevsky and Other Poems (Oakville, Ont.: Mosaic, 1989);
Our Man in Moscow: A Diplomat's Reflections on the Soviet Union (Toronto: University of Toronto Press, 1989).

OTHER: *Russian Poetry: A Personal Anthology*, edited and translated by Ford (Oakville, Ont.: Mosaic, 1984).

Robert Arthur Douglas Ford has had a distinguished career in the Canadian diplomatic service to which his poetic career has been secondary. His long absences from Canada have caused him to remain outside contemporary trends and movements in Canadian poetry, so that his poetry is more international in flavor than much written by Canadian poets, particularly as he has shown a wide-ranging interest in the poetry of the countries in which he has worked in Canadian embassies.

Ford, the son of Arthur Rutherford Ford, a journalist, and May Lavinia Scott Ford, was born in Ottawa and educated in London, Ontario, at the University of Western Ontario, where he studied English literature and history, receiving a B.A. in 1937. His postgraduate work in history (M.A., 1939) was undertaken at Cornell University and from 1938 to 1940 he taught in Cornell's history department. In 1946 he married Maria Thereza Gomes. In the preface to Ford's 1983 volume of selected poems, *Needle in the Eye*, his friend Ralph Gustafson tells of the Fords' swift romance: "I repeat here the delightful story that *Time* magazine told of Robert Ford attending

R. A. D. Ford (photograph by Wiktor Ruikowitsch, Fotocorrespondent, Moscow; courtesy of the author)

the United Nations Assembly's first meeting in London in 1946. 'There, one engaging day, he listened with amusement as a pretty young Brazilian delegate gossiped aloud, in Portuguese, about the other delegates. Leaning down from his 6 ft. 3 in., Ford quietly informed her: "It's about time you Brazilians realized that Portuguese is not a secret language." They were married a few weeks later.' The pretty delegate was Thereza Gomes from Rio de Janeiro. I had met Thereza even before–any litterateur could guess where: in New York at Frances Steloff's Gotham Book Mart on West 47th Street, the mecca of international writers. Later, in New York, with my wife, the four of us dined; still later the four of us dined in Moscow. How much of the vitality of Robert's poetry

63

is Thereza? It must be a formidable quantity. The vivacity!"

Ford joined the Department of External Affairs, Ottawa, in 1940, and from that time he has held a variety of positions with a succession of ambassadorial posts in Colombia (1957-1958), Yugoslavia (1959-1961), Egypt and, concurrently, the Sudan (1961-1964). From 1964 to 1980 he was the Canadian ambassador to the Soviet Union; from 1972 to 1980 he served as dean of the diplomatic corps in Moscow. From 1974 to 1980 he was also ambassador to Mongolia. In 1980 Ford became special adviser to the Canadian government on East-West relations (a position he held until 1984), as well as a member of the Palme Independent Commission on Disarmament and Security Issues. For his services to his country and to literature, in 1971 he was made a Companion of the Order of Canada. A recipient of honorary degrees from the University of Western Ontario (1965) and the University of Toronto (1987), he currently lives in France. Ford's travel and experience in foreign countries, his immersion in political life, and his openness to other cultures and languages are all apparent in his first book of poems, *A Window on the North* (1956), which won a Governor General's Award in 1957.

As the title suggests, these poems look into the vast northern reaches of the earth, a landscape both Canadian and Russian; "the arctic ends of the earth" are the words used in the title poem, and such physical environments become metaphors for "our true sadness, the gripping melancholy" in the same poem. The violence and extremes of such places, both real and figurative, surface in many of the poems in images associated with creatures of the north, such as the wolf and the lynx, as well as in poems concerned with hunting and hunters. The pervasive bleakness of tone is broken occasionally by hints of the warmth of human love and memories of summer and greenness.

These polarities are further emphasized in the Portuguese and Russian poems which Ford translated and included in this volume. He was one of the first to focus on the poetry of Boris Pasternak and Anna Akhmatova, together with that of the earlier Russian poet, Sergei Yessenin. In a note at the end of the volume, Ford claims that these three should "take their place among the great lyric poets of the twentieth century."

This same note explains Ford's approach to translation: "to make of each adaptation as fine or even finer a poem in his (the translator's) own

Front cover for Ford's 1983 collection, comprising poems written from 1940 to 1979

language." This view seems to be an early attempt at what became known, in Robert Lowell's term, as "imitations," for Ford admits to taking "considerable liberties with the verse form and rhyme in order to transmit the spirit of the original."

The northern Russian poems in this volume are offset to some extent by Ford's translations from modern Brazilian poetry. Translations from Russian and Brazilian Portuguese, as well as from Serbo-Croatian and French, make up one half of the next volume of poetry, *The Solitary City* (1969). There is the same bleak feeling in Ford's own poems, even though the landscapes have changed. The verse in this volume for the most part comes out of his experience in South America and the Middle East, but the scenes are still filled with a sense of loss and regret, of oppression and cruelty, of wastes and deserts. The poetry remains mostly formal in metric and stanzaic ar-

Doors, Words and Silence

R.A.D. Ford

Front cover for the 1985 volume which includes poems by Ford and his translations of Latin-American verse

rangement, though Ford shows an awareness of looser forms, particularly in the translations of the Russian poets Semyon Kirsanov, Zinovi Rozhdestvenski, and Andrei Voznesensky, as well as in some translations of Brazilian poets.

There is little difference, either thematically or technically, between the poetry in Ford's first volume and that in his 1979 collection, *Holes in Space*. If anything, the forms and language have become set so that this later volume in general is not as lively as the other two. Even the translations here, this time from Russian, French, and German, are less adventurous, and that heavy bleakness remains in place. The violence and cruelty he fixed on in his first two books are often metamorphosed into the raging force of the seasons and the rush of time. Although the poet seems to want to reduce his language to accommodate a bare and more direct style, the resulting poems lose much of the metaphoric thrust and res-

onant descriptions of his earlier poems. In the poet's melancholy vision there is little to redeem the world so that all his poetry seems to hammer away at one note.

In the early 1980s there appeared two books of original verse: *Needle in the Eye* (1983) and *Doors, Words and Silence* (1985). The first of these two volumes–subtitled *Poems New and Old*–samples the work Ford published from 1940 to 1979 and adds to it an initial section containing twenty-one new poems, some of them reprinted from *Malahat Review, Canadian Literature,* and other journals. The new poems reiterate themes, forms, and attitudes familiar to readers of Ford's earlier volumes. The opening poem, "Sleeplessness of Our Time," sets the tone:

> This is a decade of insomnia
> The nights white with fear
> Every dawn is a sigh every day
> Seems to greet another year
>
> Maybe there is a pill to take
> Against this century
> But I think our conscience is too bad
> For any remedy.

"Recollecting" speaks of the "frozen forests of memory." In other poems "distance" and "anonymous space" reinforce the separation between human beings–despite their desire to love–and "Winter in Ungava turns the hard / Man into a blind guide in the excess / of night." In the northern woods people are solitary wanderers, and, as the title poem has it,

> The logic of our times
> Breaks like a thread, and my
> Fingers are not firm enough
> To bring it back again through
> The eye of the needle.

"Old Geography" declares that "The barrenness of the desert land" is "Already in our suburbs." "Gestures" speaks of "The vacuity of words, / The emptiness of promise." Yet despite these solemnities, Ford sees hope in the very contrariness of human beings' blind belief in their own infallibility:

> We have a fault line all
> Our own, and the experts confidently
> Predict catastrophe.
> But no true seismist knows
> When the continents will close.

The deceptiveness of words, the desire for truce, the power of disbelief, the improbability of love: these recur as motifs in *Doors, Words and Silence*, too. In this later volume, Ford also returns to memories of South America and to translations from Spanish and Brazilian lyricists.

In another volume from these years, he once again comes back to the Russian poets he has long admired; *Russian Poetry: A Personal Anthology* (1984) is a collection of poems he has edited and translated, the scope of which is indicated by Marya Fiamengo's appreciative review in *Canadian Literature* (Spring 1987):

> Himself a poet of distinction whose work has not received the acknowledgement it deserves, Ford distills here the essence of the originals and brilliantly recreates them. . . .
>
> A number of the more luminous Ikons of the Russian poetic pantheon are assembled in Ford's pages: the lyrical Akhmatova and the confessional, rebellious Akhmadulina, the brilliant, erratic Essenin, the delicate Tsvetayeva, the towering Mandelshtam and Mayakovsky, the contemporary controversial Evtushenko and Voznesensky. . . .
>
> Characteristics of Ford's personal poetic style, imaginative subtlety, and precise nuances of language do much to extract and convey the particular essence of each poet–especially so in the case of Pasternak, who is (like Pushkin) a difficult poet to capture in translation. . . .
>
> Ford's Russian poets forcibly remind us that while poetry of itself may not change social and political realities, it does reveal those realities, as the lesser known Bulat Okudzhava observes,

> the poems remain
> And their outrage at the world goes on,
> asking no indulgence.

The 1989 publication of *Dostoyevsky and Other Poems* and *Our Man in Moscow: A Diplomat's Reflections on the Soviet Union* drew attention to the close connection between Ford's life and poetry. As Ann Munton observed, in a review for *Canadian Literature* (Spring 1989), the new works reveal a continuing "dialectic" between "I" and "Other." Taking one shape in his translations, another in his tribute to Russian writers, a third in his diplomatic memoirs, this dialectic shows in yet another way his distance from contemporary Canada. Resident so long abroad, he lives now in retirement, in central France. He finds Canada, "the land, the lake, while ours, / . . .alien" ("a Temporary Destination"). The formal restraint of the verse in *Dostoyevsky and Other Poems* is matched by the caution of the memoirs; commenting on artistry and politics in the Soviet Union, Ford urges that assessments of individuals not be divorced from history. Such measured awareness of the other, though it often results in conclusions which seem bleak, leads Ford ultimately toward a measured sense of the self.

Reference:

Ralph Gustafson, "The World of R. A. D. Ford," in Ford's *The Needle in the Eye* (Oakville, Ont.: Mosaic, 1983), pp. 11-15.

Hector de Saint-Denys Garneau

(13 June 1912-24 October 1943)

John E. Hare
University of Ottawa

BOOKS: *Regards et jeux dans l'espace* (Montreal, 1937);

Poésies complètes: Regards et jeux dans l'espace; Les Solitudes, edited by Robert Elie and Jean Le Moyne (Montreal: Fides, 1949); translated in part by F. R. Scott in *St.-Denys Garneau & Anne Hébert: Translations / Traductions* (Vancouver: Klanak, 1962); translated by John Glassco as *Complete Poems of Saint-Denys Garneau* (Ottawa: Oberon, 1975);

Journal, edited, with a foreword, by Elie and Le Moyne (Montreal: Beauchemin, 1954); translated by Glassco as *The Journal of Saint-Denys Garneau* (Toronto: McClelland & Stewart, 1962);

Saint-Denys Garneau: Œuvres, edited and annotated by Jacques Brault and Benoît Lacroix (Montreal: Presses de l'Université de Montréal, 1971).

PERIODICAL PUBLICATIONS: "L'Art spiritualiste," *La Relève*, first series, cahier 3 (May 1934): 39-43;

"Monologue fantaisiste sur le mot," *La Relève*, third series, cahier 3 (January-February 1937): 71-73.

Hector de Saint-Denys Garneau

Hector de Saint-Denys Garneau is remembered as the most important Quebecois poet of the first half of the twentieth century. Often considered to be Quebec's first modern poet, his influence only became apparent after the publication of his *Poésies complètes* in 1949. Since that time the number of studies on his life and work has multiplied considerably. Portions of the *Poésies complètes* were translated into English in 1962, and the entire volume was translated, as *Complete Poems of Saint-Denys Garneau*, in 1975. Perhaps only Emile Nelligan has been the object of so much critical attention.

Born into a family with aristocratic roots, he was given the names Hector in honor of his godfather and de Saint-Denys in honor of his maternal uncle, a descendant of Nicolas Juchereau de Saint-Denys, one of the heroes of New France. Through his father he was descended from the historian Francois-Xavier Garneau and the poet Alfred Garneau (his grandfather); his cousin is the poet and novelist Anne Hébert. The poet signed his name either de Saint-Denys or more usually Saint-Denys Garneau. At the time of his birth his father, Paul Garneau, was in the banking business in Montreal. His mother was Hermine Prévost Garneau. From 1916 to 1922 the family lived in Sainte-Catherine de Fossambault (Portneuf), in the seigneurial manor of his ancestors, about twenty-five miles north of Quebec City. He would often return to this quiet spot, and it is here that he spent his final years. In 1922 the family moved to Quebec City, and he studied in the Couvent du Bon-Pasteur. The following year they moved to Montreal where he undertook his classical studies with the Jesuits, for the first year at Collège Sainte-Marie and from 1924 at Collège Loyola. He also went for a short time to Collège Brébeuf.

From 1924 to 1927 Saint-Denys Garneau attended classes in painting at the Ecole des Beaux-Arts, and later he took part in a few exhibitions. However, he had to abandon his studies of painting in 1927 because of his heavy scholastic load. His literary debut occurred in 1926, when he won the first prize in a competition for young people organized by the Henry Morgan department store; his entry, a thirteen-stanza poem, was entitled "Dinosaurus." In 1928 he won the prize from the poetry group of the Canadian Authors Association with "Automne." His first essays on art and his first poems were published in 1927 in *La Revue Scientifique et Artistique*.

In 1934 he was forced to abandon his formal education on account of a heart condition. Garneau now had the leisure to attend concerts and art exhibitions. However, he was immediately confronted with the ever-present possibility of death. That same year some of his paintings were exhibited at the Montreal Art Gallery. He spent much time with a group of young intellectuals (Robert Charbonneau, Robert Elie, and Paul Beaulieu) who in 1934 started *La Relève*, a monthly literary review devoted to literature, philosophy, and religion. This group was particularly influenced by Jacques Maritain and his Catholic humanism. From 1934 to 1937 Saint-Denys Garneau published many critical articles and poems in this journal, as well as in *Idées, Le Canada*, and *L'Action Nationale*.

In spite of these activities the state of his health led to a deepening feeling of melancholy and to periods of depression. He had abandoned his studies without any hope of resuming them; outside activities only served to remind him of the futility of his existence. It was during this period that he discovered his poetical voice and developed the free-verse form that characterizes his mature work; some of the poems that would be incorporated into his *Regards et jeux dans l'espace* (Glimpses and Games in Space, 1937)–"Maison fermée" (Closed House), "Ma Maison" (My House), "Tu croyais tout tranquille" (You Thought All was Tranquil)–were composed in 1934. His personal diary in which he transcribed his poems as well as his reflections on life and religion took on great importance. His time was spent in a feverish search for the religious certainty and the poetic truth that had become an obsession. Periods of intense activity, however, would give way to periods of solitude.

Outwardly the years 1934 to 1937 were marked by a whirl of activity. Although he had periods of doubt, as can be seen in his journal, he felt that at last he was becoming the poet who had only been a dream a few years earlier. This serenity can be measured by the poem "Esquisses en plein air" (Painting in the Open Air), written in the summer of 1935. This period of intense work resulted in at least seven long articles completed from November 1935 to June 1936. And he spent much time on his first volume of verse, *Regards et jeux dans l'espace*. This elegant volume of seventy-five pages appeared in March 1937, in an edition of one thousand copies. However, the literary establishment was not prepared to accept this new poetical voice, and many of the critical comments were quite harsh.

In spite of the enthusiasm of his friends and of the younger poets, Saint-Denys Garneau was shaken by the strident comments of such reviewers as Claude-Henri Grignon, Albert Pelletier, and Camille Roy. Roy, the official historian and guardian of traditional literary values, wrote, in *Manuel de la littérature canadienne* (1942): "Il y a dans ces poèmes un effort certain, combien laborieux, soit d'introspection, soit d'interprétation des choses extérieures. Mais cet effort aboutit le plus souvent à l'inintelligible. Pour d'aucuns, l'hermétisme est du sublime. Le sublime est ici trop voilé. L'esprit français ne s'accommodera jamais d'une pensée qu'il ne peut apercevoir, le poète l'ayant cachée sous le boisseau d'un symbole trop obscur. M. Garneau, par surcroît, écrit sans point ni virgules" (In these poems there is undoubtedly an attempt, however labored, either at introspection or at the interpretation of the external. But this attempt all too often results in unintelligibility. For some readers, the hermetic partakes of the sublime. Here, the sublime is too closely veiled. *L'esprit français* will never lend itself to a thought that it cannot perceive–the poet having hidden it under the bushel of an overly obscure symbolism. Moreover, Monsieur Garneau writes without periods or commas).

Within three weeks the volume had been taken out of circulation by the young poet. The preparation of this volume had taken its toll; in a letter to his friend André Laurendeau dated 18 March 1937, he states: "Ce livre est bien moi" (This book is me), but he mentions also that he is in the throes of a "dépression nerveuse." He became convinced that he had exposed himself in a manner so much at variance with his natural reserve. He had, as he wrote in his journal, the sensation of having actually violated and soiled himself; his neurosis transformed the publication of his volume of verse into an act of self-betrayal.

In July 1937 he went to Paris with Jean Le Moyne, a close friend, hoping to find some respite. However, after only a few days his poor health and growing depression forced him to return to Montreal. The last period of his life, from 1937 to 1943, is marked by a slow withdrawal into a world of solitude and silence. He kept up his personal diary and his correspondence with a few of his close friends at least until 1939. The few other texts from this period are difficult to date. He still wrote poems, but there was never any thought of publishing them. There was no attempt to communicate them even to his friends.

From 1940 he spent most of his time at Sainte-Catherine de Fossambault; during the winters of 1939-1940 and 1940-1941 he lived there alone. From 1941 until his death his parents lived with him. On Sunday, 24 October 1943 he went out on the lake for a paddle and did not come back. The next day his body was found on shore; it seems probable that he had a heart seizure. After a funeral mass on 28 October he was buried in the local cemetery.

In December 1944 his friends brought out a special issue of *La Nouvelle Relève* (the successor to *La Relève*) in his honor. It included three critical studies, several unpublished poems, and tributes from Anne Hébert, his cousin, and from Raissa Maritain, who ranked him with the French poet Paul Eluard. Apart from his friends, however, Saint-Denys Garneau was little known until the publication of *Poésies complètes*. Five years later, in 1954, portions of his journal were published; they appeared in translation in 1962, under the title *The Journal of Saint-Denys Garneau*. In 1967 a selection of his letters appeared, followed in 1971 by a critical edition of all his extant texts. The diversity and the richness of this work, written by Saint-Denys Garneau in a few short years before he reached the age of thirty, have made him the best-known Quebec poet of his generation.

Saint-Denys Garneau's journal as we know it consists of eight notebooks and many loose sheets in five folders, about eight hundred manuscript pages. This strange mass of documents, made up of expense accounts, lists of books read or lent, fragments of poems as well as intimate meditations, chronicles his existence from December 1927 to 22 February 1939. (It is possible that other notebooks exist for the period up to the autumn of 1941.) All the documents known at the time were included in the critical edition of the poet's works published in 1971.

The extracts published in 1954 by his friends Robert Elie and Jean Le Moyne represent about one-half of the whole. They concentrate on the years from 1935 to 1939, the most fruitful: the preparation of his volume of verse, his participation in *La Relève*, and his intense interest in art. The journal chronicles also the moments of euphoria as Saint-Denys Garneau discovers the magic of words and the powers of images and symbols. Much of the interest in the *Journal* has been for the light it sheds on psychological and religious matters rather than on literary ones. This document gives unusual insight into the spiritual itinerary of a young Quebecois intellectual in the 1930s. In the beginning he was nourished by his ambition for a great spiritual revolution under the aegis of Art, "l'expression suprême de son âme et de sa volonté" (the supreme expression of the human soul and will). However, he came to realize that there is no salvation in Art; a few months after the publication of his volume of verse he had abandoned all hope of self-realization through poetry.

At the beginning of 1935 he wrote a few intense pages on a spiritual crisis involving both a sense of exhaustion and a moral revelation: "J'ai, la semaine dernière été mis en face du dilemme du bien et du mal.... J'ai connu une expérience intérieure de délassement, d'humiliation, de solitude" (Last week, I was confronted with the dilemma of Good and Evil.... I had an interior experience of fatigue, of humiliation, of solitude). By 1937 the obsessive character of his sense of solitude is evident: "Je suis traqué. Je me sens traqué comme un criminel. Depuis long temps. Mais cela devient vraiment insupportable" (I feel hunted. I feel myself hunted like a criminal. For a long time. But this begins to be overwhelming). He tries desperately to strengthen his spiritual intention, to seek the path to God, but he feels himself to be "broken." He clings to his journal as a means of stabilizing his universe, and he records with a certain satisfaction brief moods of serenity, of communication with Jesus Christ. But disillusionment always follows, and in January 1938 he feels submerged by the weight of despair with no hope and no awareness. The introspective character of the entries for these years leads the reader into the very soul of the poet. Also the movement of the fragments, from the moments of intensity to the periods of silence, gives the measure of the rhythm of his life. It is the ever-present "I" that gives the meaning to this singular document. In the end he sees himself as a lifeless hulk, amputated and meaningless, like a tree with its branches lopped off.

The 1971 critical edition of Saint-Denys Garneau's writings includes the texts of ten short stories, eleven essays, and fifty or so fragments. It also adds 154 letters to the selection of 242 published as *Lettres à ses amis* in 1967. Saint-Denys Garneau's correspondence, close to 500 letters in all, played a significant role in the creative process. In fact, for him it was even more important than his journal. Many of the most important texts in the *Journal* are extracts from the correspondence. At times he added to one letter passages from another, and he sometimes asked one of his correspondents to contact another in order to read an important letter. Paradoxically, in spite of at times being unable to support contact with the outside world, the poet kept up a vast correspondence.

The critical edition presents the texts of 257 poems or fragments of poems. The juvenilia (1925-1933) include 157 works, of which 10 were published. From his period of maturity (1934-1939) there are 102 poems, of which 29 were published during Saint-Denys Garneau's lifetime. The most important series from this period comprises the 28 pieces published in *Regards et jeux dans l'espace*. This poetical suite in seven parts is a spiritual itinerary, a tragic voyage of discovery that leads the poet from the exalted desire to create a new world to the understanding of his incapacity to overcome the anguish of solitude and death. Even in the moments of intense euphoria, however, he is haunted by an underlying darkness of the soul and death.

In the beginning there is play, "Jeux," a metaphor for the activity of the poet. The five poems of this section touch on the poet's ability to construct new worlds. (The English translations are by John Glassco.)

Ne me dérangez pas je suis profondément occupé

Un enfant est en train de bâtir un village
C'est une ville, un comté
Et qui sait
    Tantôt l'univers.

(Do not interrupt me I am completely preoccupied

A child is building a village
It is a city, a county
And who knows
    Soon the universe.)

This section is followed by two poems on the theme of children, "Enfants," for they represent the poetical spirit which is free as air.

As the title of the volume suggests, poetic creation is seen as a combination of the artist's insight ("le regard") and his representation of the reality he perceives ("les jeux dans l'espace"). It is by this combination that the poet seeks to take possession of reality and to overcome the walls that are built around, to overcome the feeling of being attached to the ground:

Mes enfants vous dansez mal
Il faut dire qu'il est difficile de danser ici
Dans ce manque d'air
Ici sans espace qui est toute la danse.

(My children you dance badly
True, it is difficult to dance here
In this airless place
Here without space which is the heart of the dance.)

The poet withdraws into his own mind, to a place of pure and free vision, symbolized by the insight of a child:

Tout le monde peut voir une piastre de papier vert
Mais qui peut voir au travers
    si ce n'est un enfant
Qui peut comme lui voir au travers et tout liberté.

(Everyone can see a green paper dollar
But who can see through it
    if not a child
Who can like him see wholly through it.)

"Esquisses en plein air," the third section, represents the moment of serenity when the poet feels that he can capture the essence of life and its colors. The seven poems have a musical quality and convey feelings of summer and light. However, the landscape begins to darken. In "Deux paysages" (Two Landscapes) the poet meets up with the underside of life and light, death and darkness.

Then, in "De gris en plus noir" (From Gray to Ever More Black), the fifth section, the feeling of desolation, of the absurdity of all hope, be-

First page of the manuscript for an untitled poem first published in Garneau's Poésies complètes *(1949)*

comes ever stronger. There is no refuge from the fire that destroys everything, home and hearth as well as poetry and the poet himself. "Faction," with its three poems, represents the crisis of identity, the eternal beginning ("Commencement perpétuel"). The destiny of man seems to lead nowhere; yet, the poet wishes to find a new sense to life, to the poetical search. Just at the moment when he understands that there is a certain hope in accepting his lot, death comes again in the next section, "Sans titre" (Without Title). Finally, in the epilogue, "Accompagnement" (Escort), the poet feels the hot breath of another being walking beside him:

> Je marche à côté d'une joie
> D'une joie qui n'est pas à moi
> D'une joie à moi que je ne puis prendre[.]

> (I walk beside a joy
> A joy that is not mine
> A joy of mine that I cannot enjoy.)

Regards et jeux dans l'espace is the first great modern poetical work in Quebecois literature. The intensity of Saint-Denys Garneau's quest and the multiple levels of meaning make this book an enduring one, open to many interpretations, as can be seen in the abundant critical literature. However, what remains finally is the truth of the poet's adventure.

Perhaps only forty or so of Saint-Denys Garneau's poems were finished in the conventional sense. Most of his work that has been collected in the critical edition consists of unrehearsed fragments, sometimes little more than jottings. However, John Glassco, his translator, feels that these texts are, "both actually and potentially, superior to the work published during his lifetime."

For the generations that followed Saint-Denys Garneau, his tormented, inward-looking poetry sometimes seems outmoded, almost "impertinent," to quote Glassco. "He knew his limitations; ... he was looking always inward, forging his style out of his *entrailles*, pushing back his own horizon, always exploiting his originality, to which was tragically joined the sense of his solitude."

Paul Wyczynski wrote in *Poésie et symbole* (1965), concerning the symbolic vision of Saint-Denys Garneau: "[Il] tend, et de toutes ses forces, à la possession non pas des simples apparences, mais bien plus à celle de la plénitude, de la vérité absolue, à ce que Baudelaire appelle, dans les *Fusées*, 'l'expression infaillible de l'âme.' Avec une rare intuition le poète inquiet découvre dans la sensation reçue un miroitement qui fait entrevoir un paradis d'enfance perdu ... (He strains with all his being to the possession not just of simple appearances, but even more to that of plenitude, of absolute truth, of that which Baudelaire calls in *Fusées*, "the infallible expression of the soul." With a rare intuition, the poet in his anguish, discovers through the sensations received a reflection that gives him the vision of a lost paradise ...).

Here is how Eva Kushner, in *Saint-Denys Garneau* (1965), sums up the message of the poet: "Dans sa retraite, il espérait par l'ascétisme religieux concilier enfin son besoin d'amour. [La poésie] deviendra l'expression unifiée d'un moi enfin réel qui se connaîtrait lucidement et s'offrirait à autrui dépouillé de ses masques" (In his retreat, he hoped through asceticism to conciliate his need for sincerity and his need for love. Poetry thus becomes the unified expression of a real being, of the "I," who will discover the other without any masks). And David Hayne states, in "A Forest of Symbols" (*Canadian Literature*, Winter 1960): "Despite the undoubted fascination of his spiritual adventure, it is probably for his poetic theories and achievements that Saint-Denys Garneau will retain a place in the history of French-Canadian letters. In poetic theory, he belongs to the long tradition of Symbolism in the widest sense, a tradition that links Baudelaire and Mallarmé, Claudel and Valéry." While more recent commentary has focused on Garneau's linguistic patterns and paradigms, these judgments have not fundamentally questioned his position as the foremost poet in the literary history of Quebec in the first half of the twentieth century.

Letters:

Lettres à ses amis, edited, with a foreword, by Robert Elie, Jean Le Moyne, and Claude Hurtubise (Montreal: HMH, 1967).

References:

Jacques Blais, "Documents pour servir à la bibliographie critique de l'œuvre de Saint-Denys Garneau," *La Revue de l'Université Laval*, 18 (January 1964): 428-438;

Blais, *Saint-Denys Garneau et le mythe d'Icare* (Sherbrooke, Que.: Editions Cosmos, 1973);

Roland Borneuf, *Saint-Denys Garneau et ses lectures européennes* (Quebec: Presses de l'Université Laval, 1969);

Nicole Durand-Lutzy, *Saint-Denys Garneau, la couleur de Dieu* (Montreal: Fides, 1981);

Marie-Blanche Ellis, *De Saint-Denys Garneau: Art et réalisme* (Montreal: Chanteclerc, 1949);

David Hayne, "A Forest of Symbols: An Introduction to Saint-Denys Garneau," *Canadian Literature*, 3 (Winter 1960): 5-16;

Eva Kushner, *Saint-Denys Garneau* (Paris: Seghers, 1965);

Romain Légaré, *L'Aventure poétique et spirituelle de Saint-Denys Garneau* (Paris: Fides, 1957);

Jean Louis Major, *Le Jeu en étile: Etudes et essais* (Ottawa: University of Ottawa Press, 1978);

Georges Risers, *Conjonction et disjonction dans la poésie de Saint-Denys Garneau. Etude du fonctionnement des phénomènes de cohésion et de rupture dans des textes poétiques* (Ottawa: Editions de l'Université d'Ottawa, 1984);

Robert Vigneault, *Saint-Denys Garneau à travers "Regards et jeux dans l'espace"* (Montreal: Presses de l'Université de Montréal, 1973);

Paul Wyczynski, *Poésie et symbole* (Montreal: Déom, 1965), pp. 109-146.

Papers:

The National Archives of Canada and the Bibliothèque Nationale du Québec hold some of Garneau's papers.

Claude Gauvreau
(19 August 1925-9 July 1971)

Roger Chamberland
Université Laval

BOOKS: *Sur fil métamorphose* (Montreal: Erta, 1956); translated in part in *Entrails* (1981);
Brochuges (Montreal: Editions Feu-Antonin, 1957);
Etal mixte (Montreal: Editions d'Orphée, 1968);
Œuvres créatrices complètes (Montreal: Parti Pris, 1977); section 1 translated in *Entrails* (1981);
Entrails, translated by Ray Ellenwood (Toronto: Coach House Press, 1981).

PLAY PRODUCTIONS: *Bien-être*, produced with *Une Pièce sans titre*, by T. J. Maeckens (Jean Mercier), as *Théâtre Moderne*, Montreal Repertory Theatre, 20 May 1947;
La Jeune Fille et la lune, Montreal, Ecole des Beaux-Arts, 1959;
Les Grappes lucides, Montreal, Ecole des Beaux-Arts, 1959;
La Charge de l'orignal épormyable, Montreal, La groupe "Zéro" at the Théâtre du Gesù, 2 May 1970;
Les Oranges sont vertes, Montreal, Théâtre du Nouveau Monde at the Comédie-Canadienne, January 1972.

PERIODICAL PUBLICATIONS: *Le Coureur de Marathon*, by Gauvreau and Muriel Guilbault, *Ecrits du Canada Français*, 4 (1958): 195-219;
"Ma Conception du théâtre," *La Barre du Jour*, 1, nos. 3-5 (1965): 71-73;
"L'Epopée automatiste vue par un cyclope," *La Barre du Jour*, nos. 17-20 (January-August 1969): 48-96;
"Lettres à Jean-Isidore Cleuffeu," *Etudes Françaises*, 7, no. 4 (1971): 373-388.

Claude Gauvreau (courtesy of Pierre Gauvreau)

It was not until the 1977 publication of *Œuvres créatrices complètes* (Collected Creative Works), a text that Claude Gauvreau had prepared before his death, that the author's extraordinarily fertile and innovative imagination began to be recognized. This volume is impressive as much for the diversity of its themes as for the variety of techniques used to express them. It is not, however, a work that has been appreciated by the public. Several of the "dramatic objects" collected in it–the word *plays* does not exactly describe them–are practically unproducible because the complexity of the settings requires almost unmanageable techniques of representation. Several of the plays use what Gauvreau has called "langage exploréen" (exploratory language): a language that is rich in sound, but private, making arduous demands on vocal skills. Gauvreau's originality also makes his work difficult to comprehend. He wanted to cross traditional literary boundaries. The terms he used to refer to his own writings–much of them still unpublished when he died in 1971–suggest his efforts to break down old categories: "paroles radiophoniques," "fantaisie fantastique," "futurisme en un acte," "roman moniste," "fiction dramatique," "télé-théâtre cosmique," "treize textes à quatre voix," "prose radiophonique" (radio speech, fantastic fantasy, futurism in one act, monist novel, dramatic fiction, cosmic television drama, thirteen texts in four voices, radio prose). His work was not warmly welcomed by critics when he was alive; always it was the subject of controversy and of fascination.

For several commentators, Gauvreau's work is indivisible from his life, biographical details serving as interpretive keys. Born on 19 August 1925 in Montreal, the younger of two boys, he was raised by a single mother in a financially strapped home. His mother encouraged the artistic interests of her sons; Gauvreau's brother, Pierre, later became a student at the Ecole des Beaux-Arts and a frequent visitor at the studio of the painter Paul-Emile Borduas. In an interview with Axel Maugey published in 1971, Gauvreau said he decided at the age of fifteen to be a writer; but it was at the age of nine, after he and Pierre had taken part in a performance organized by the theatrical troupe of Thérèse Bouthillier, that Claude Gauvreau wrote his first play, "Ma Vocation" (My Vocation). After elementary school, he attended the Collège Sainte-Marie, a Jesuit institution in Montreal, and there published several articles in the student paper, the *Journal de Sainte-Marie*. Expelled because he had circulated some of his own stories and drawings which the school considered obscene, he continued studies with a tutor, Hermas Bastien, and he was readmitted to the school, as Ray Ellenwood notes in the introduction to *Entrails*, his 1981 translation of Gauvreau's work, only long enough "to win a speaker's prize and be expelled again for writing a paper on the absurdity of the notion of Hell." Later Gauvreau pursued a degree in philosophy at the Université de Montréal. It was during these years, in the early 1940s, that his life and work changed in important ways.

Through his brother, in 1942 he met Borduas and several other artists and writers with whom he became close friends. They were interested in revolutionary artistic techniques and in social reform; among them were Marcel Barbeau, Jean-Paul Mousseau (who illustrated Gauvreau's 1957 collection of poems, *Brochuges*),

Fernand Leduc, Thérèse Renaud, and Jean-Paul Riopelle. During 1943, 1944, and 1945 Gauvreau became involved with Leduc working on the art pages of the Université de Montréal student newspaper, *Quartier Latin*, and in February 1945 he contributed to the paper a sharply worded essay on the artist as the absolute visionary, victimized by society. It was the first of many such essays, and it employed an image ("of the creative person opening his breast to let the light shine forth," in Ellenwood's phrase) that suggests something of the sensibility Gauvreau brought to artistic expression and something of the identity which he took on for himself.

Along with Borduas and others, he signed the influential *automatiste* manifesto *Refus Global (Total Refusal)* in 1948; *Bien-être* (translated as *The Good Life*, in *Entrails*), performed in Montreal the preceding year, with Gauvreau and Muriel Guilbault in leading roles, was published with this manifesto, and Gauvreau became a leading spokesman for the values and principles of the autonomist group. He defended freedom of artistic and ideological expression; he denounced the general control which the clergy held over culture and education; and as an ardent voice for *automatisme* he wrote polemically for such papers as *Notre Temps, Le Canada, Le Petit Journal*, and *L'Autorité*. Gauvreau organized several showings of the *automatiste* school; in March 1950 an exhibition entitled *Exposition des Rebelles* was an open protest against the conservative policies of the Montreal Museum of Art and against the Quebec art establishment generally. In 1953 Borduas left for the United States, and Gauvreau became, in Jacques Ferron's word, the "soul" of the group that remained. A traveling exhibition called *La Matière Chante*, arranged in 1954, was the automatistes' last public showing before the group effectively dissolved. But Gauvreau remained true to the cause, and in April 1970, in "Réflexions d'un dramaturge débutant" (translated as "Reflections of a Young Dramatist," in *Entrails*), he was still expounding its principles, attacking social realism and Jansenist Pauline Christianity, and asserting (to quote Ellenwood's translation) that "the avant-garde must begin in the non-figurative and go beyond," that "living art is a plunge into the unknown" in order to regenerate the emotion that "can in turn engender a new civilization."

From 1952 to 1969 Gauvreau wrote several dramatic radio scripts, among them *L'Oreille de Van Gogh* (Van Gogh's Ear), a meditation on the anguish of the artist, expressed through symbols of the ear, mirrors, and mutilation, but the lesser quality of these writings is indicated in part by the fact that they are mostly omitted from the *Œuvres créatrices complètes*. A more conventional radio play, *Le Coureur de Marathon* (The Marathon Runner), written with Guilbault and broadcast in 1954, won the Canadian Radio Award for that year. The 1952 suicide of Guilbault, with whom Gauvreau had very strong personal and professional ties, profoundly marked his personal life and led to the preoccupation with suicide in the writings of his later years.

As though to carry himself through his personal crisis, he wrote at this time his only novel, "Beauté baroque" (Baroque Beauty), a poignant work describing Guilbault's life; but despite his efforts, this exercise had little effect. Over the next decade and a half, his life was interrupted by a series of confinements in Saint-Jean-de-Dieu psychiatric hospital. And over the course of the same years, he continued to write. Besides the novel, he wrote plays, radio and television scripts, and especially poetry. Two of the plays were those that have since become his most celebrated: *Les Oranges sont vertes* (The Oranges are Green), written between 1958 and 1970 and staged in 1972, and *La Charge de l'orignal épormyable* (The Charge of the Pneumoparsable Moose), written in 1956, given a public reading at the Centre d'Essai des Auteurs Dramatiques in Montreal in 1968, and staged in 1970. Some of the textual difficulty of this latter work can be gauged from the fact that it closed on the fourth night, when some of the actors refused to continue. Gauvreau had by this time begun to experiment in neologism and nonreferential syllable clusters.

Such experimentation also marked his poetry, which acquired a certain notoriety. Although Gauvreau saw only two collections actually appear during his lifetime–*Brochuges* (1957) and *Etal mixte* (1968)–he read several other poems at public recitals. It was in these poems that he showed the degree to which all his work was devoted to a kind of exacerbated lyricism, an excessive rushing which completely overturned language, sometimes reducing words to the letters alone, rich with sound, like echoes. The titles suggest some of the density of language he used. *Brochuges* is a portmanteau word, suggesting *brochure*, *brochette*, and *brocade:* these are poems that at once ornament, skewer, and assert their commitment to *automatiste* principles. *Etal mixte* suggests a mixed table or perhaps mixed feast, but *étal*, re-

Drawing by Gauvreau for Etal mixte, *his 1968 poetry collection (by permission of Pierre Gauvreau)*

ferring to a butcher's block, implies the abrupt or violent measures that the poetry will serve.

In his "Lettres à Jean-Isidore Cleuffeu," in *Etudes Françaises* (1971), as well as in his numerous essays, and in a correspondence still largely unpublished, Gauvreau indicated the degree to which he had become the insistent theoretician of pure sound poetry. Ellenwood explains as follows the four kinds of images Gauvreau isolated: "the *image rythmique* (rhythmic image), which is basic to the sound of poetry, involving both onomatopoeia and stress; the *image mémorante* (reflective image), which is the standard metaphor or comparison between similar elements; the *image transfigurante* (transformational image) which involves a strained comparison actually transforming its elements, creating a new compound, but whose elements are still traceable (this applies to most surrealist images); and the *image exploréenne* (explorational image). . . . Here the basic elements are completely modified and can no longer be easily traced by analysis." As Gauvreau expressed it, "La poésie, c'est la syllabe qui tonne. C'est le mot qui chahute, c'est la lettre qui explose. Tout ce qui bout à l'intérieur est projeté dans les évidence du rythme. Les syllables amalgamées et vociférantes sont des trous de serrurues qui divulguent la vie intérieure la plus fondamentale" (In poetry it's the syllable that thunders, the word that kicks up a row, the letter that explodes. Everything that is bottled up inside is thrown outward through rhythm. Syllables, merging and clamoring, are the keyholes that reveal the most fundamental inner life).

At least from 1949 on, he had been reading French surrealism, the works of André Breton, Antonin Artaud, and Tristan Tzara. His later works especially show these influences. In *Les Oranges sont vertes*, for example–to the degree to which it can be summarized–a writer and art critic named Yvirnig goes mad after his lover commits suicide, while other writers, jealous of his talents, kick him to death; the text proceeds through hallucinatory associations, erotic asides, and denunciations of censorship. Shortly before the play was produced on stage, Gauvreau committed suicide, on 9 July 1971.

His work constitutes the interior drama of the disintegration of a sensibility, fallen prey to psychotic delirium, as in these lines from his last poems, "Jappements à la lune" (Yapping at the Moon), written a few months before his death: "beûlokdokbloughezoum achia chichenéchiné chachouann aduppt étréoflagonta amu mimaulomaromurméfléjauglionairaretel lincz. . . ." Gauvreau's creative works, along with numerous articles and lectures, demonstrate his commitment to an art totally free from social and ideological limitations and from artistic conservatism. His entire creative effort was directed toward a poetry that, shifting toward other genres, made use of its full potential. Close to dadaism, Gauvreau was not, however, unappreciative of social contexts. He knew how to relate his writing practice to a Quebec particularly characterized by political and religious constraints. His major themes stress love and eroticism (a quest for love that is never satisfied, an eroticism that is hidden) and the social function of the artist and writer. One way or another, he transformed his own inner life into art, or took it as an exemplary condition, especially in his plays and his novel. According to Jacques Marchand, who, in his *Claude Gauvreau, poète et mythocrate* (1979), attempts to demystify Gauvreau's life and writings, Gauvreau forged a myth of a damned-poet-in-exile for whom suicide was the only possible way to give legitimacy to a fragmentary body of work. Despite Marchand's argument, one cannot ignore the contribution such writings made to the field of Quebec literature, or their influence, especially apparent in the works of Raoul Duguay and other sound poets of the 1970s, upon a subsequent generation.

Interviews:

Axel Maugey, "La Parole vivante et unique de Claude Gauvreau," *L'Information Médicale et Paramédicale* (19 October 1971): 65-66;

Raoul Duguay and Richard Giguère, "Poetry is Yrteop: Interview / Conversation," *Ellipse*, 17 (1975): 80-97.

References:

Marcel Bélanger, "La Lettre contre l'esprit, ou quelques points de repère sur la poésie de Gauvreau," *Etudes Littéraires*, 3 (December 1972): 481-497;

André G. Bourassa, "Gauvreau," in his *Surréalisme et littérature québécoise* (Montreal: Etincelle, 1977), pp. 126-158;

Bourassa, "The Poetic Design of Claude Gauvreau," translated by Christine Von Aesch, *Essays on Canadian Writing*, 9 (Winter 1977-1978): 70-82;

Roger Chamberland, *Claude Gauvreau: La Libération du regard* (Quebec: Presses de l'Université Laval, 1986);

Jean-Marcel Duciaume, "Le Théâtre de Gauvreau: Une Approche," *Livres et Auteurs Québécois* (1972): 327-340;

Ray Ellenwood, "Introduction and Translator's Note," in Gauvreau's *Entrails* (Toronto: Coach House Press, 1981), pp. 7-18;

Ellenwood, "Traduire le non-traduisible: Faisant front à Claude Gauvreau," in *La Traduction: L'Universitaire et le praticien*, edited by Arlette Thomas and Jacques Flamand (Ottawa: University of Ottawa Press, 1984), pp. 173-178;

Jacques Ferron, "Claude Gauvreau," translated by Ellenwood, *Exile*, 1, no. 2 (1972): 32-52;

Jacques Marchand, *Claude Gauvreau, poète et mythocrate* (Montreal: VLB, 1979);

Janou Saint-Denis, *Claude Gauvreau, le cygne* (Montreal: Université du Québec / Noroît, 1978).

Gratien Gélinas
(8 December 1909-   )

John Ripley
McGill University

BOOKS: *Tit-Coq* (Montreal: Beauchemin, 1950); translated by Kenneth Johnstone, with Gélinas (Toronto: Clarke, Irwin, 1967);

Bousille et les justes (Quebec: Institut Littéraire du Québec, 1960); translated by Johnstone and Joffre Miville-Dechêne as *Bousille and the Just* (Toronto: Clarke, Irwin, 1961);

Yesterday the Children Were Dancing, translated by Mavor Moore (Toronto & Vancouver: Clarke, Irwin, 1967); original French version published as *Hier, les enfants dansaient* (Montreal: Leméac, 1968);

Les Fridolinades, 1945 et 1946 (Montreal: Quinze, 1980);

Les Fridolinades, 1943 et 1944 (Montreal: Quinze, 1981);

Les Fridolinades, 1941 et 1942 (Montreal: Quinze, 1981);

La Passion de Narcisse Mondoux (Ottawa: Leméac, 1987);

Les Fridolinades, 1938, 1939, 1940 (Ottawa: Leméac, 1988).

PLAY PRODUCTIONS: *Fridolinons*, 9 revues, Montreal, Monument National, 1938-1946;

Tit-Coq, Montreal, Monument National, 22 May 1948;

Bousille et les justes, Montreal, Comédie-Canadienne, 17 August 1959;

Hier, les enfants dansaient, Montreal, Comédie-Canadienne, 11 April 1966;

La Passion de Narcisse Mondoux, Toronto, Théâtre du p'tit Bonheur, 2 October 1986; Montreal, Théâtre du Rideau Vert, 14 January 1987.

PERIODICAL PUBLICATIONS: "Pour une littérature théâtrale," *La Nouvelle Relève*, 6 (December 1947): 17-22;

"Pour un théâtre national et populaire," *Amérique Française*, 7 (March 1949): 32-42;

"Why Broadway Turned Me Down," *Saturday Night*, 66 (6 March 1951): 8, 12;

"Discrimination and Canada's Future," *Labour Gazette*, 55 (March 1955): 288-289;

"Réponse de M. Gratien Gélinas, M.S.R.C.," *Présentation* (Royal Society of Canada, French Section), no. 13 (1958-1959): 119-127;

"Credo of the Comédie-Canadienne," *Queen's Quarterly*, 66 (Spring 1959): 18-25;

"Jeune Auteur, mon camarade," *La Revue dominicaine*, 65 (November 1960): 216-225;

"Le Crédo professional d'un homme de théâtre," *University of Toronto Quarterly*, 50 (Fall 1980): 81-89.

Gratien Gélinas, playwright, actor, and director, may accurately be called a founding father of the contemporary French-Canadian theater. His lovable gamin, Fridolin, was the first authentically Quebecois dramatic character; his 1948 play, *Tit-Coq*, was the first literary work to limn the urban, as distinct from the rural, Quebec environment; and his *Bousille et les justes* (1959) first used the Quebec stage as a forum for social criticism. In 1957 he founded the Comédie-Canadienne, a Montreal playhouse dedicated to the production of native drama, where a generation of fledgling Quebecois playwrights found inspiration, support, and a showcase for their talents. Gélinas's commitment to Quebec culture, however, has never vitiated his robust Canadianism. Through extensive tours of his plays in English translations, stage and film roles in both languages, and service to national cultural organizations (including as president of the Canadian Theatre Centre and chairman of the Canadian Film Development Corporation), he has continuously and sensitively interpreted each major linguistic group to the other.

Born in Saint-Tite, Quebec, on 8 December 1909, the son of Mathias Gélinas and the former Genève Davidson, Gélinas moved to Montreal in infancy when his father, a harness maker, was forced by the advent of the automobile to turn insurance agent. His graduation from the Collège de Montréal in 1929 coincided with the onset of

Gratien Gélinas (photograph by Kèro)

the Depression, and dreams of a law degree were abruptly scuttled in favor of a post in the accounting department of La Sauvegarde Insurance Company. While at La Sauvegarde, Gélinas's dramatic flair, earlier noted and nourished by his teachers, assumed the dimensions of a passion. Every free evening and weekend found him on local French and English amateur stages, where in time his talents caught the attention of radio-drama producers. In 1932 a string of successful minor radio parts earned him a principal role in the weekday serial *Le Curé de village* and launched his professional career. About the same time he made his debut as a stage monologist in a revue titled *Télévise-moi-ça*. "Le Bon Petit Garçon et Le Méchant Petit Garçon," a sketch written and performed by Gélinas, was an instant hit; and over the next few years his monologues enjoyed top billing at cabarets, charitable functions, and social events throughout the city.

In 1937 CKAC, a local radio station, offered him seventy-five dollars weekly to write and perform a half-hour comedy program broadcast each Friday. With the blessing of his wife, Simone Lalonde, whom he had married in 1935, Gélinas quit the insurance office for a full-time entertainment career. The premiere of the show (first titled *Le Carrousel de la gaîte* and later *Le Train de plaisir*) on 23 September 1937 introduced Montrealers to a new kind of hero, an undersized, adolescent urchin from the city's East End slums. Each week Fridolin, played by Gélinas, encountered a new fact of urban adult life. Despite poverty, illegitimacy, and the pangs of despised love, Fridolin maintained a Chaplinesque resilience, a thrill of adventure at every turn of a corner. When reality crowded him too closely, he sought refuge in daydreams; and much of the humor of the series derived from his repeated discovery that fact and fancy make uncomfortable bedfellows. To his listeners' surprise and delight, Fridolin spoke colloquial Quebec French unashamedly—the first time a dramatic character had done so.

Fridolin's success was both immediate and prolonged. His jaunty self-confidence, perpetual *joie de vivre,* and rejection of cynicism and despair mirrored Quebecois society's image of itself. Throughout almost a decade of Fridolin's street-smart, yet sensitive, companionship, Francophone audiences learned to articulate, share, and mitigate through laughter anxieties born of urbanization, cultural alienation, World War II, and federal-provincial political strife.

Within a year of his advent, Fridolin's thriving celebrity persuaded his creator to feature him in a stage revue. *Fridolinons,* starring Gélinas as a scrawny adolescent in short trousers, a tricolor hockey sweater, and droopy knee socks, ran for twenty-five performances at the Monument National in 1938; and its successors (titled *Fridolinons '39, Fridolinons '40,* and so forth), packed the playhouse for weeks each year until 1946. In the theater Fridolin's idiom was coarser, his satirical bite sharper, and his adventures richer textured than they had been on the radio program, which Gélinas abandoned in 1941. At first the revue comprised only Fridolin's sallies and the gambols of a lavishly costumed dance troupe; but within a year or two Gélinas added domestic playlets, written and directed by himself and performed by local actors. These sketches, brief situation comedies featuring stock characters (harassed father, dominant mother, morose maiden aunt, and a variety of young people), exploited communication failures, marital conflicts, moral paradoxes, and social absurdities. "I contend," Gélinas argued in "Credo of the Comédie-Canadienne" (*Queen's Quarterly,* Spring 1959), "that a play of Canadian inspiration and expression will always grip our public more strongly than the greatest masterpieces of the foreign theatre, past or present, however incomparable their dramatic value." The unprecedented popularity of his homegrown satire and domestic buffoonery amply vindicated his claim. In 1946, for example, the revue ran for a total of seventy performances in Montreal and Quebec City, was seen by more than one hundred thousand people, and grossed in the neighborhood of $150,000. Four volumes of the *Fridolinons* have been published, in 1980, 1981, and 1988.

Well before the final *Fridolinons* performance in 1946, it was apparent that Gélinas's art was chafing under the rigidity of the revue format; and the premiere of *Tit-Coq* (Little Rooster), his first full-length play, on 22 May 1948 occasioned more enthusiasm than surprise. The drama, a dark comedy with the playwright in the title role, ran, over a two-year period, for some three hundred performances at the Monument National and Gésu theaters. In 1950 Gélinas produced and starred in an English version which concluded a Montreal season and a cross-Canada tour with two hundred presentations to its credit. The play was published in French in 1950 and in English translation in 1967.

Tit-Coq, a cocky, pugnacious army recruit, was born a bastard, grew up unloved, and longs one day to find legitimacy, security, and affection through marriage into a large family. While in training camp, he is invited by a friend, Jean-Paul Désilets, to come home with him for a country Christmas. The Désilets clan, numerous and warmhearted, is precisely the stuff of Tit-Coq's dreams. He promptly falls in love with Marie-Ange, Jean-Paul's sister, and finds his ardor returned; but their engagement is scarcely arranged when Tit-Coq is shipped overseas. During his absence Marie-Ange pines for social life while her lover seeks companionship by looking at the Désilets family photograph album. At war's end, Tit-Coq returns to find his fiancée married to a family friend. During a stormy reunion Marie-Ange repents her faithlessness and resolves to leave her husband. An opportune intervention by Tit-Coq's chaplain, however, convinces the lovers that their relationship has no future. Marie-Ange realizes that Tit-Coq loves her family and the sense of identity it offers, almost as much as he loves her. To live together in adultery (divorce being out of the question in Quebec) would irrevocably alienate the Désilets household and rob Tit-Coq of the kinship he craves. Tit-Coq, in his turn, ruefully recognizes that the children of the union would be, like himself, illegitimate. To subject them to such a fate is unthinkable. Reluctantly the couple part.

The play, predictably, owes much to the *Fridolinons* revues. Tit-Coq is an older version of Fridolin, while the Désilets family—adoring mother, jolly father, loyal brother, dour spinster aunt—clearly derive from the domestic sketches. The tone of *Tit-Coq,* however, is not satirical, nor is the humor broad. The piece is clearly an attempt at sociological realism, although Gélinas's portraits of the army padre and Désilets family life are somewhat idealized. The bulk of the action, whether staged, narrated, or recollected, evokes wartime Montreal—its working-class apartments, factories, bars, and dance halls. The characters are recognizably Quebecois and speak local

*Gélinas in the title role and Muriel Guilbault as Marie-Ange
in the first production of* Tit-Coq *(photo by Henri Paul)*

*Dust jacket for the published version of Gélinas's first full-
length play*

French in all its colloquial crudity. For the first
time in a full-length drama, urban Quebec audiences recognized their own faces and heard the
sound of their own voices. As if in a mirror,
French-Canadian society was permitted to scruti-
nize its traditional attitudes toward religion, love,
marriage and divorce, the family, and, indirectly,
sex. Gélinas all the while was less disposed to
judge than to hold the mirror steady. Tit-Coq,
like Fridolin, was an overnight folk hero. In both
figures French-Canada discovered symbols of its
alienation and, simultaneously, a celebration of
its determination to survive and to love.

The advent of television attracted Gélinas
briefly. In 1954 he created a weekly comedy series, *Les Quat' fers en l'air* (Anything Goes),
around a gossipy East End barber, Exubert
Lajoie, whom Gélinas played. The experiment
lasted only one season. In 1956 he returned to
the stage with a nostalgic reprise of *Fridolinons*
and a few months later starred at the Stratford,
Ontario, Shakespeare Festival in *Henry V* and *The
Merry Wives of Windsor*.

While he dabbled in television and Shakespeare, his mind was preoccupied with the sorry
state of the contemporary Canadian theater. Was
public indifference to the stage perhaps
prompted by a lack of Canadian content? "Did
our public really see itself in the theatre?," he
asked in "Credo of the Comédie-Canadienne." "Instead of its own reflection, wasn't it rather being offered the portrait of another? Its own cousin, no
doubt; well painted, and framed in the best of
taste–but still, another." Gélinas's practical response was to purchase and renovate (with financial help from governments and a brewery) a mid-
town vaudeville house, which he rechristened La
Comédie-Canadienne and dedicated to the creation of Canadian plays. "Without ceasing to
write for the stage," he announced in his
"Credo," "I intend in the future to place at the dis-
posal of my colleagues in the world of the theatre the material organization which I have at
hand and the experience I have acquired, to produce their plays . . . with the same care and devotion with which I would produce my own plays."

From the opening of the theater in 1958 to its close in 1972, Gélinas abundantly honored his pledge; from 1958 to 1969, for example, thirty-one out of thirty-six of the theater's premieres featured Canadian works. Unfortunately the caliber of the scripts failed to justify Gélinas's faith, and his production expertise was frequently wasted on inferior material. Yet the project was far from a failure. No theater before or since has done as much to make the drama of each major language group accessible to the other: productions from other parts of Canada were generously showcased; plays were staged in both French and English; and audiences were provided with simultaneous translation services. La Comédie-Canadienne remains the most efficient and successful bilingual playhouse Canada has yet seen. Even more important, perhaps, was Gélinas's championship of the Canadian playwright. Although he discovered few significant scripts, the seriousness with which he conducted his search inspired other Canadian artistic directors to give higher priority to the nurture of native dramatists. The impact of that decision on the Francophone theaters of the mid 1960s and their Anglophone counterparts of the early 1970s is well-nigh incalculable. In the short term, however, the only major hits of the Comédie-Canadienne were Gélinas's own dramas *Bousille et les justes* (1959; published in 1960 and translated as *Bousille and the Just*, 1961) and *Hier, les enfants dansaient* (1966; published as *Yesterday the Children Were Dancing* in 1967 and in French, 1968).

Bousille et les justes, a tragicomedy which premiered 17 August 1959, revealed Gélinas in an unwontedly somber mood. *Tit-Coq*'s soft-focused portrayal of traditional Quebec values under urban stress now gave way to a savage exposé of pharisaism in a rural family. Set in a Montreal hotel suite, *Bousille et les justes* charts the antics of the Grenon clan over a forty-eight-hour period as they await the outcome of the trial of the youngest son, Aimé, on a charge of murder. The family, pillars of society in the village of Saint-Tite, are determined at all costs to have Aimé declared innocent, not out of concern for the welfare of that violent, drunken thug, but because a criminal record in the family would lower their social status among their neighbors. When the young religious Brother Nolasque promises to "continuer de prier pour que justice se fasse" (keep praying that justice be done), Mother Grenon insists, with a fine disdain of such irrelevancy, "Prie pour

qu'on gagne: c'est tout ce que je te demande!" (Pray that we win: that's all I ask!).

The only witness who can prove that Aimé's murder of Bruno Maltais was premeditated, and so dash the family's hopes, is Bousille, a deeply devout, simpleminded cousin. Bousille's determination to tell the whole truth, born of his terror of God's displeasure, must somehow be undermined. When bribery and flattery fail, Henri, Aimé's older brother, physically tortures Bousille until he agrees to commit perjury. While the family rejoices in its freshly purged honor, Bousille, devastated by the betrayal of his convictions, returns home and hangs himself.

The play derives much of its moral and dramatic thrust from the juxtaposition of Bousille's straightforward Christian integrity with the hypocrisy of the rest of the family. Mother Grenon compulsively orders her life around pious ritual but lacks the humane sensibility which should inform it. Her son Henri accepts religious observance as a fact of life but never lets it inhibit his brutal quest for power. Aurore, his sister, clings to church attendance as a social rite, even though her moral sense has long since atrophied. Aurore's husband, Phil Vezeau, a drunken, spineless cynic, makes no pretense to religious devotion but happily reaps the material benefits of the family's sanctimony.

Gélinas's portrayal of French-Canadian religiosity was not pleasant, despite his hilarious caricature of Madame Grenon's self-centered piety, Phil's cynical asides, and Bousille's unconscious double entendres. Nevertheless the public flocked to the production. With the playwright in the title role, it enjoyed lengthy French and English runs in Montreal, followed by a national tour of twenty-six cities. Performances totaled about three hundred in all. Today *Bousille et les justes* constitutes a landmark in Canadian stage history. Gélinas's assault on false piety on the eve of the Quiet Revolution signaled the Quebec theater's acceptance of its role as a vehicle of social criticism; and few socially conscious dramatists of the past three decades have owed nothing to his inspiration.

Gélinas's third play, *Hier, les enfants dansaient*, premiered at the Comédie-Canadienne 11 April 1966, a year before the hundredth anniversary of Canadian confederation. Against the backdrop of mounting political pressure for Quebec's independence and random acts of violence which culminated four years later in the October Crisis, Gélinas marshals with remarkable evenhandedness the arguments for and against separatism. Far from being a mere exercise in polemic, however, the play is a compassionate object lesson, a reminder that politics are ultimately made by people and that public choices are often inseparable from private pain.

The plot of the drama is unpretentious and straightforward. Pierre Gravel, a prominent Montreal lawyer and longtime Liberal, decides to run for the seat of the federal minister of justice who has just died. If he wins the election he is promised the same cabinet post as his predecessor. He is about to file his nomination papers when he learns that his elder son, André, a recent law-school graduate, is leader of a terrorist organization dedicated to Quebec separatism. Within the next hour or two he will blow up a local monument and surrender to the police as an act of political protest. The latter half of the play is devoted to the attempts of André's parents and uncle to dissuade him from simultaneously wrecking his own future and that of his father. The argument begins as a political debate but quickly transforms itself into a classical intergenerational conflict. Pierre Gravel is determined to preserve a political structure he inherited and helped entrench. André insists on creating, through revolution if necessary, a new world for his children. Both are men of integrity; and each is convinced that to betray his principles is to destroy himself. What was once a warm father-son relationship degenerates by degrees into mutual disrespect and, finally, physical violence. Meanwhile the bomb is detonated, on André's orders, by Gravel's younger son, Larry. As André goes off to surrender to the police, his father is left to contemplate a lackluster future and a shattered family. In the play's concluding moments Gravel reminds the rest of Canada that Quebec's political conflicts are not a provincial but a national calamity: "ma maison divisée ne saurait périr," he warns, "sans ébranler la vôtre dans ses fondations mêmes" (my divided house will not go down without shaking yours to its very foundations).

Hier, les enfants dansaient was only moderately successful in Quebec. Francophone critics found the subject relevant but felt the federalist-separatist debate was undramatic, simplistic, even wearisome at times. The English-language premiere of the play (with Gélinas as Pierre Gravel) at the Charlottetown Festival took place on 5 July 1967. For the first time newspaper headlines dealing with French-Canadian nationalism assumed a human dimension for non-Quebeckers. "*Yesterday the Children Were Dancing,*" wrote Nathan Cohen, "is the most jolting play in the experience of the Canadian theatre. Words are spoken in this drama, emotions made naked and vulnerable, conflicts defined and pinpointed that must strike terror into most people's hearts" (*Toronto Star*, 6 July 1967). The production did not, unfortunately, make a national tour, and Cohen's enlightenment was shared by relatively few of his compatriots.

The father of six children, and a widower since 1967, Gélinas married the actress Huguette Oligny in 1973. In 1969 he was named chairman of the Canadian Film Development Corporation, a position he filled with distinction until his retirement in 1978.

After eight years of relative inactivity, Gélinas returned to the theater in 1988 in *La Passion de Narcisse Mondoux* (Narcisse Mondoux's Passion), a two-character script he created for himself and his wife. A romantic comedy, laced with sharp but good-natured comment on municipal and sexual politics, *La Passion de Narcisse Mondoux* limns the struggles of a retired plumber to woo his lifelong love, the feminist widow Laurencienne Robichaud. The play premiered in Toronto at the Théâtre du p'tit Bonheur on 2 October 1986 and transferred to Montreal's Théâtre du Rideau Vert on 14 January 1987. Both the script and the Gélinas-Oligny interpretation were acclaimed in both cities, and subsequent performances elsewhere, in both French and English, have brought similar success. From 9 January to 7 February 1987, the National Arts Centre staged a fetching reprise of excerpts from the *Fridolinons*.

The contemporary relevance of *La Passion de Narcisse Mondoux* apart, Gélinas's major plays must today be judged period pieces. The very topicality which ensured their initial success has been their undoing. Easy divorce and sexual permissiveness now render Tit-Coq's plight implausible; the churchgoer, so central a figure in *Bousille et les justes*, is almost an endangered species; and without the sophisticated packaging provided by the Parti Québécois and Liberal propaganda machines, the federalist-separatist arguments of *Hier, les enfants dansaient* seem somewhat drab, and even naive. Gélinas's place among the pioneers of contemporary Canadian theater is, nevertheless, assured and has been impressively recognized by a Fellowship in the Royal Society of Canada (1959), several honorary degrees, the Medal of the Order of Canada (1967), and several cultural prizes.

References:

Léo Bonneville, "Rencontre avec Gratien Gélinas," *Séquences*, 107 (January 1982): 4-8;

Gratien Gélinas: Dossiers de presse, 1940-1980 (Sherbrooke, Que.: Séminaire de Sherbrooke, Bibliothèque, 1981);

Jean-Paul Gélinas, "*Bousille et les justes* (1959-1969)," *Culture*, 30 (September 1969): 217-226;

Arthur Laurendeau, "Pour la 150ᵉ de *Tit-Coq*," *L'Action Nationale*, 33 (March-April 1949): 173-182;

Edouard Laurent, "Tit-Coq, un conscrit qui passera à l'histoire," *Culture,* 9 (December 1948): 378-383;

Mavor Moore, *Four Canadian Playwrights: Robertson Davies, Gratien Gélinas, James Reaney, George Ryga* (Toronto: Holt, Rinehart & Winston, 1973), pp. 32-51;

Marguerite A. Primeau, "Gratien Gélinas et le théâtre populaire au Canada français," in *Dramatists in Canada,* edited by W. H. New (Vancouver: University of British Columbia Press, 1972), pp. 105-113;

Donald Smith, "Gratien Gélinas, rénovateur du théâtre québécois," *Lettres Québécoises,* 36 (Winter 1984-1985): 48-55;

Renate Usmiani, *Gratien Gélinas* (Toronto: Gage, 1977).

Phyllis Gotlieb

(25 May 1926-)

D. J. Dooley
St. Michael's College, University of Toronto
and
W. H. New
University of British Columbia

BOOKS: *Within the Zodiac* (Toronto: McClelland & Stewart, 1964);

Sunburst (Greenwich, Conn.: Fawcett Publications, 1964; Toronto: Fitzhenry & Whiteside, 1977);

Ordinary, Moving (Toronto: Oxford University Press, 1969);

Why Should I Have All the Grief ? (Toronto: Macmillan, 1969);

Dr. Umlaut's Earthly Kingdom (Toronto: Calliope Press, 1974);

O Master Caliban! (New York: Harper & Row, 1976);

The Works: Collected Poems (New York: Calliope Press, 1978);

A Judgment of Dragons (New York: Berkley, 1980);

Emperor, Swords, Pentacles (New York: Ace, 1982);

Son of the Morning and Other Stories (New York: Ace, 1983);

The Kingdom of the Cats (New York: Ace, 1985);

Heart of Red Iron (New York: St. Martin's, 1989).

RADIO: *Dr. Umlaut's Earthly Kingdom, Anthology,* CBC, February-March 1970;

The Military Hospital, Anthology, CBC, 2 October 1971;

Silent Movie Days, CBC, 1971;

The Contract, CBC, 1972;

Garden Varieties, Tuesday Night, CBC, 3 April 1973;

God on Trial before Rabbi Ovadia, Best Seat in the House, CBC, 18 April 1976.

OTHER: *Dr. Umlaut's Earthly Kingdom,* in *Poems for Voices,* edited by Robert Weaver (Toronto: Canadian Broadcasting Corporation, 1970), pp. 40-65;

"Score / Score," in *Visions 2020,* edited by Stephen Clarkson (Edmonton: Hurtig, 1970), pp. 211-221;

"Planetoid Idiot," in *To the Stars: Eight Stories of Science Fiction,* edited by Robert Silverberg (New York: Hawthorn Books, 1971), pp. 147-202;

Phyllis Gotlieb (courtesy of the author)

"Hasidic Influences in the Work of A. M. Klein," in *The A. M. Klein Symposium*, edited by Seymour Mayne (Ottawa: University of Ottawa Press, 1975), pp. 47-64;

"The King's Dogs," in *The Edge of Space: Three Original Novellas of Science Fiction*, edited by Silverberg (New York: Elsevier / Nelson Books, 1979);

Tesseracts², edited by Gotlieb and Douglas Barbour (Victoria, B.C.: Press Porcépic, 1987).

PERIODICAL PUBLICATIONS: "Item: One Bed, Two Cups Sack," *Canadian Life*, 1 (Spring 1950): 24;

"No End of Time," *Fantastic Stories*, 9 (June 1960);

"A Bone to Pick," *Fantastic Stories*, 9 (October 1960): 48-71;

"Valedictory," *Amazing Stories*, 38 (August 1964): 46-52;

"Rogue's Gambit," *If* (January 1968);

"The Dirty Old Men of Maxsec," *Galaxy* (November 1969);

"Yeshua X," *Jewish Dialog*, Hanukkah 1972, pp. 4-5;

"Mother Lode," *Fantasy and Science Fiction* (November 1973);

"The Newest Profession," *Speculations* (1982): 167-190.

Phyllis Gotlieb is known as poet, verse dramatist, and author of short stories and novels. As a poet, one might say, she is in need of rescue– from critics and other Canadian poets. Fred Cogswell, in a generally favorable review in *Canadian Literature* (1965), labeled her verse almost exclusively cerebral, while other reviewers have found her writing overly clever and trivial. She has been accused of playing dictionary games and of writing detached intellectual poetry with a touch of snobbery; her verse, one reviewer asserted, is not likely to affect the course of contemporary composition. A few, however, notably Douglas Barbour (in *Tamarack Review*, Winter 1979) and Louis L. Martz (in *Yale Review*, June 1970), have recognized Gotlieb's originality and skill.

The daughter of Leo and Mary Kates Bloom, she was born in Toronto on 25 May 1926 and has lived there virtually all her life. Her family owned and managed several movie theaters, and she often exploits this aspect of her background for humorous effect in her writing, as in the dramatic poem, "Silent Movie Days," commissioned by Anne Gibson for CBC-Radio broadcast in 1971.

At the University of Toronto, Gotlieb studied English literature, receiving a B.A. in 1948 and an M.A. in 1950. In the intervening year (on 12 June 1949) she married Calvin Carl Gotlieb, who was to become a University of Toronto professor in the field of computer science. They have three children, a son and two daughters.

By Gotlieb's own account, she started writing verse at the age of eleven. In 1950 she turned to science fiction, returning to poetry toward the end of the decade. She has had many works published in such magazines as *Fantastic Stories*, *Amazing Stories*, and *Galaxy*, and her novella *Son of the Morning* was shortlisted for a Nebula Award (given by the Science Fiction Writers of America) in 1972. Several of these stories, including "Gingerbread Boy," "A Grain of Manhood," "The Military Hospital," and "Phantom Foot," all much anthologized, have been collected in *Son of the Morning and Other Stories* (1983).

Gotlieb's reputation in the field long rested primarily on her first novel, *Sunburst* (1964). It deals with the effects of radiation from an explo-

Dust jacket for the 1964 collection that includes Gotlieb's poem "A Bestiary of the Garden for Children Who Should Know Better"

sion at a nuclear plant in the United States; a group of mutant children with preternatural powers breaks out of the sanctuary in which they have been confined and threatens to destroy a computer bank which controls half the world. In his introduction to the 1977 school edition of the novel, Andrew Machaiski says that *Sunburst* "is about the effects gadgets have on people," but this is only one theme. The central character, a thirteen-year-old girl named Shandy, differs from the other children because she has a moral sense which gives her a resistance to the mind-controls of others. In such a sense is the promise Gotlieb sees for small advances in civilization.

Order and justice win out in the end in *Sunburst*, as they do in *O Master Caliban!* (1976), a novel set on Barrazan V, a violent stormy planet constantly in turmoil, on which a scientist named Edvard Dahlgren has set up laboratories for genetic exploration. His machines, called ergs, take over the planet and threaten to create a replica

of him which will enable them to take over the universe. Good wins out, but ambivalently; there are subtleties and complexities here which anticipate the novel's sequel, *Heart of Red Iron* (1989).

Gotlieb's one novel not in the science-fiction mode, *Why Should I Have All the Grief?* (1969), effectively dramatizes the interior world of an Auschwitz survivor, Heinz Dorfman, who has come to Canada. As Anne Montagnes perceptively shows in a review for *Saturday Night* (May 1969), the novel is not about Heinz's experience in the concentration camp; rather, it concerns Jewish poverty and miserliness in a Jewish village, ceremonials, love and hate between fathers and sons, and the tension between a religion of money and one of tradition. As Heinz faces the past he has been trying to evade, his wife, Sara, starts her own investigation of the reasons for his hatred of himself and others. Atmosphere and feeling in the novel are genuine, but the expected twist in the plot which begins a new phase in Heinz's life is not subtly handled.

Reviewers who called *Within the Zodiac* (1964), Gotlieb's first collection of poems, too cerebral and academic were probably responding to the elaborately metaphysical and overly ingenious imagery. Mercator's map is like a tangle of embryos, the grasshopper has a "mobled thorax," someone's "dirty hand snapfingers / taut english to conjure." There are poems on Breughel, Hokusai, and suburbia, but the realities of human behavior are not sentimentalized. Reviewers should have noticed the movement within the collection from the remote to the immediate and personal. Often Gotlieb achieves a light touch, as in her amusing poem "A Bestiary of the Garden for Children Who Should Know Better," somewhat in the manner of Hilaire Belloc's *Bad Child's Book of Beasts*. The conclusion of the bestiary refutes any charge of unmitigated black humor: "& there is nothing more to ask / of daybreak than the gift of being / alive under the wing of evening." Gotlieb has said, "Humanity is my department"; the joy of being alive—and of observing people and things—is strong in her work. The personal note enters into poems such as "This One's on Me," in which the speaker contemplates a faded snapshot of herself—"O child of the thirties / of stonewarm porches and spiraea snowfalls / in print cotton dress with matching panties hanging well down." With the increasing emphasis on person and family, this collection also focuses more and more on the nature and sustenance of Jewish ceremony.

Dust jacket for Gotlieb's second science-fiction novel, set on the planet Barrazan V, where machines called ergs plot to take over the universe

Gotlieb's next poetry collection, *Ordinary, Moving* (1969), represents a technical advance. In one amusing poem the speaker tries to clear her head of her grandmother's telephone number and all the old Toronto numbers she remembers. In "Stamp" the poet's desire for immortality is compared to bird tracks in cement. But the most memorable pieces are relatively long ones—a moving elegy on the death of a child, "For John Andrew Reaney"; an anatomy lesson entitled "A Discourse," which is a tour de force; and the title poem, in which children's games and rhymes take on several levels of meaning. In this poem Gotlieb invokes other lands and languages and times to suggest the universal experience of children; the tone becomes increasingly sober with the mention of a woolpicker and a chimneysweep, a black child born into slavery, a victim of Belsen, and the children buried under slag at Aberfan in Wales. As Louis Martz stated, the poem is a celebration and a lament for all the

world's children and transforms the ordinary into the extraordinary.

Dr. Umlaut's Earthly Kingdom (1974) comprises several short poems and three verse dramas commissioned by the CBC. *Silent Movie Days* draws on popular Western film format, and *Garden Varieties* draws on miracle-play tradition, combining the story of the biblical Flood with the techniques of music-hall entertainment. The title play, which gives further indication of Gotlieb's continuing interest in fantasy, was published in its full radio version in the 1970 anthology *Poems for Voices*.

Gotlieb's 1978 volume, *The Works: Collected Poems*, which adds a fourth verse drama, *The Contact*, to the three published in *Dr. Umlaut's Earthly Kingdom*, provides an opportunity to evaluate her poetic achievement, which is substantial. Although her use of the vernacular sometimes descends to slapstick, she commands a wide variety of tones. She is both eclectic and individual, strongly influenced by the Montreal poet A. M. Klein (about whom she has written), and indebted to many others. Far from dealing with life in a remote and intellectual way, she is concerned with the effect of ancestral and personal memories (especially Jewish experiences and rituals) upon her own sensibility. Whether *The Works* represents a poetic terminus or a phase in her literary career remains to be seen; by itself it ought to give her a higher standing than that enjoyed by many Canadian poets of more established reputation.

Gotlieb began to publish much more speculative fiction during the 1980s and to achieve greater attention for her popular prose. Several of her short stories were collected. A trilogy appeared—*A Judgment of Dragons* (1980), *Emperor, Swords, Pentacles* (1982), and *The Kingdom of the Cats* (1985)—following the adventures of a pair of cats as they discover the warmth and the limitations of human behavior. As with much of Gotlieb's fiction, the author narrates history as much to probe the future's potential as to chart the past. In 1982 she won the Canadian Science Fiction and Fantasy Award; the anthology of Canadian short science fiction *Tesseracts²*, edited by Gotlieb and Douglas Barbour, was published in 1987.

The concerns of *Heart of Red Iron* indicate not only her development as a writer of fantasy but also her ongoing fascination with the links between generations. The novel recounts the main plotline of *O Master Caliban!* but focuses on

Dahlgren's son Sven, who has been born a mutant (with four arms) when the renegade machine ergs tampered with his genetic structure. Rather than foil the human father and son, however, the interference leads to greater love between them, resulting ultimately in human survival and machine defeat. This sequel to *O Master Caliban!* opens with Sven (now married and a father) returning to Barrazan V on a mission to attempt to settle new communities of alien beings there. Carefully plotted and sometimes poetically phrased, the novel focuses on the parent-child paradigm and the character of love. Not only are Sven's relationships with his father and son tested, so is a parallel series of connections: among them Sven's newly discovered brother's link with his adoptive father; a doctor's responsibility to a patient; a pregnant female's reaction to a miscarriage; and the relation between a sentient crystalline structure and her created but thankless "daughters." Behind the human relationships lies the continuing threat–or at least presence–of the ergs, underpinning Gotlieb's meditation on "generations" of machine intelligence, on bionics and genetic experiments, and on the character of "love" between human and machine.

Throughout, *Heart of Red Iron* draws on Gotlieb's reading of other writers. (A defiant passage reads like a narrative gloss on E. J. Pratt's poem "The Truant"; a sensitivity to poetry is also repeatedly ascribed as a sign of humane behavior.) The concern for the plurality of cultures and the naturalness of difference marks the book's social and cultural context. But that the novel should end not with a simple triumph but with a quietly ironic revelation of the way myth-making distorts all stories of creation, generation, conquest, and survival suggests something of the tone and stance of most of Gotlieb's writing. Aspiring to greater freedoms for a civilization in the midst of technological advances, Gotlieb is conscious always of the moral paradigms of history and the persistent limits of human behavior.

Gwethalyn Graham
(Gwethalyn Graham Erichsen-Brown)

(18 January 1913-25 November 1965)

Barbara Opala
Concordia University

BOOKS: *Swiss Sonata* (London: Cape, 1938; New York: Scribners, 1938);

Earth and High Heaven (London: Cape, 1944; Philadelphia & New York: Lippincott, 1944);

Dear Enemies: A Dialogue on French and English Canada, by Graham and Solange Chaput-Rolland (Toronto: Macmillan, 1963); French version published as *Chers ennemis* (Montreal: Editions du Jour, 1963); English version republished (New York: Devin-Adair, 1965).

PERIODICAL PUBLICATIONS: "Refugees: The Human Aspect," *Saturday Night,* 54 (12 November 1938): 8-9;

"Economics of Refugees," *Saturday Night,* 54 (19 November 1938): 10-11;

"Germans' Revolt Will Not Be Towards Stalinism," *Saturday Night,* 55 (30 December 1939): 3;

"The Church of St. Mary Magdalene," *Saturday Night,* 55 (18 May 1940): 16-17;

"Our Newest Radio Program," *Saturday Night,* 56 (7 June 1941): 4;

"Earth and High Heaven," *Wings* (October 1944): 5-9;

"Appraisal of Canada's Political Trends and Parties," *Chicago Daily News,* 6 December 1944, C3;

"Let's Have Immigrants And Not All Farmers," *Saturday Night,* 60 (30 December 1944): 6;

"We Are A Self-Satisfied Nation," *Chatelaine,* 18 (August 1946): 10-11; 58, 62, 72;

"Why Books Cost Too Much," *Maclean's,* 60 (15 September 1947): 22, 39, 40;

"What's Wrong With Work?," *Maclean's,* 61 (1 May 1948): 52-56;

"Women, Are They Human?," *Canadian Forum,* 16 (December 1963): 21-23;

"Freedom Under Fire," *Canadian Author and Bookman,* 40 (Summer 1965): 6.

Gwethalyn Graham in the 1940s

Gwethalyn Graham's two published novels, *Swiss Sonata* (1938) and *Earth and High Heaven* (1944), both won awards in Canada. But it is the spectacular critical and popular success of her second novel which established her as an internationally known writer, and it is for this novel that she is best remembered.

Graham was one of the harbingers of a new spirit in Canadian literature; she belongs to that

88

group of Canadian novelists, which includes such writers as Frederick Philip Grove, Hugh MacLennan, and Gabrielle Roy, who were the first to deal seriously and realistically with the problems of contemporary Canada. Central to her work is an abiding concern for the rights of the individual in society, and there are strong indications in her family background that the experience of her early childhood and adolescence shaped her vision as a writer to a considerable degree.

Graham was born Gwethalyn Graham Erichsen-Brown in Toronto on 18 January 1913. Her family had for generations been active supporters of civil liberties and human rights. Graham's father, Frank Erichsen-Brown, was a lawyer and amateur painter; her mother, Isabel Russell MacCurdy Erichsen-Brown, was a leader in the Canadian woman suffrage movement. Graham enjoyed meeting visitors in the home of her parents, but the greatest impact upon her youthful sensibilities was made by her much-admired maternal grandfather, James F. MacCurdy, a noted Orientalist at the University of Toronto. Of him, she said: "He was an individualist in the finest sense of the word and I remember that he would not tolerate the use of any of the derogatory slang words which label national or religious groups on this continent. . . ."

Later Graham frequently expressed her appreciation for the intellectual stimulus provided by these early relationships and contacts and the liberal ambiance. However, according to accounts of friends and family and the evidence in "West Wind," her thinly veiled autobiographical novel which has never been published, there was as well much unhappiness in her life. Her power to convey in her novels the pain of an outcast's existence had in some measure been honed by her own experience as a lonely adolescent outsider, out of step with her peers because of her unusual height and size for her age. Although a brilliant student, life at a Toronto private school was an agony for the painfully self-conscious Graham. Nor did the emotional tenor of her situation improve markedly at a finishing school in Lausanne, Switzerland, which she entered in the fall of 1929. She did, nevertheless, form some lasting friendships there with girls of different nationalities; these relationships later formed the basis for *Swiss Sonata*.

Smith College in Massachusetts, to which she was admitted in the fall of 1931, was a happier and more successful experience. Her formal studies, however, were ended abruptly when, at

the beginning of her second year at Smith, at age nineteen, she eloped with John McNaught, the son of C. B. McNaught, a prominent Canadian financier. John McNaught formed a liaison with another woman shortly after his marriage to Graham; divorce proceedings were begun before their son, Anthony, was a year old. In the latter part of 1934 Graham and her son moved to Montreal, a city she loved, and she started to work on *Swiss Sonata* and "West Wind." Following her divorce Graham lived on a fixed allowance, and beginning in 1937 she sporadically supplemented her income by buying and selling books for her British publisher, Jonathan Cape.

Swiss Sonata was published in Great Britain and the United States in early 1938, went through two British editions, won a Governor General's Award in Canada, and is reported to have been banned in Nazi Germany. The very good press it received established its author as a promising young writer. The setting of *Swiss Sonata* is a Swiss *pensionnat*, or boarding school, for girls; the time is January 1935, the politically ominous and tense period in Europe just before the Saar plebiscite; and the story is a reflection of the racial conflicts and alienation developing in the world in the years before World War II. Jew-baiting and factionalism among the students from many nations threatens the headmistress's cherished goal to "inculcate the international idea in minds which are not yet too set, too limited by prejudice, too mired in conventional patriotism."

A passionate argument for international cooperation forms one movement of Graham's "sonata." Also important is the existential theme of commitment to something larger than one's self as an antidote to the loneliness and vacuity of life. The novel is marred by an unwieldy cast of twenty-seven characters, the superintricacy of its plot, and the implausibility of the events taking place in a single day. But its notable achievements more than offset these failings, for the witty and often humorous dialogues ring true, and most of the characterizations are vivid and powerful. Reviews in Great Britain, the United States, and Canada were generally favorable.

Following the publication of *Swiss Sonata*, Graham spent some six months in mid 1938 in Europe, where she witnessed and was deeply moved by the plight of the homeless victims of Hitler's *Anschluss*. When she returned to Canada, it was to Toronto, the center of the Canadian publishing trade as well as her family home. In Toronto in the fall of 1938, she wrote two well-documented

Graham (center) with Dorothy Duncan and Hugh MacLennan,
Montreal, 1946 (courtesy of Hugh MacLennan)

articles for *Saturday Night,* arguing for the admission of refugees into Canada, and she gathered petitions and made speeches on the refugees' behalf. In the course of these activities she met and became emotionally involved with a Jewish-Canadian lawyer whom her father declined to meet. The relationship came to an end, and Graham returned to Montreal, where she wrote *Earth and High Heaven.*

Earth and High Heaven, set against the background of World War II, concerns two young people who meet by chance, fall in love, and attempt to transcend the racial prejudice all around them. The girl is Erica Drake of the prominent Drakes in Montreal's upper-class WASP establishment; the man is Marc Reiser, a lawyer and an army captain waiting to be sent overseas. He is also the first-generation son of immigrant Jews from a small Ontario town. Erica is shocked to discover that her father, Charles Drake, a cultivated and enlightened man of professedly liberal views, will not countenance the marriage of his daughter to a Jew. The narrative is shaped by the struggle between Erica and her father. Charles Drake's grim psychological maneuverings to de-

stroy his daughter's attachment are the focus of study of a man harboring within himself conflicting values and unexamined emotions toward his daughter. He finally attains self-awareness under the double onslaught of losing a son in the war and almost losing his daughter. His sudden reversal provides the novel's "happy" ending with the two lovers about to be married. In the father-daughter conflict anti-Semitism stands revealed in its baneful effects upon Jew and Gentile alike. Prejudice engulfs Charles Drake's humane instincts and judgment to the point that he accepts and repeats the false generalizations and cheap innuendoes circulating in his milieu about "Jews." In contrast, sensitive Marc Reiser accepts the mortmain of traditional bias and sinks into a state of hopelessness.

Earth and High Heaven, written with a compelling intensity of conviction, won the acclaim of critics and captured the imagination of the public when it was published in 1944. The novel won a Governor General's Award in Canada and the Anisfield-Wolf Award (for a book on race relations) in the United States; it was translated into nine languages and topped best-seller lists in

1945. It eventually sold 1,250,000 copies and remains a perceptive and powerful examination of anti-Semitism and a classic of its kind in Canadian literature.

Graham wrote no other novels, and biographical evidence suggests that the phenomenal success of *Earth and High Heaven* was for her a mixed blessing. A compulsive overachiever, she was paralyzed by the prospect of failing to gain, with another work, the reception accorded to *Earth and High Heaven.* In 1947 she married David C. Yalden-Thomson. From 1950 to 1958 she and her husband lived in the United States, where he was a professor of philosophy at the University of Virginia. It was not until she returned to Montreal from Virginia in 1958, after the failure of her marriage, that she began writing scripts for CBC television. One of these, an adaptation of André Laurendeau's play *Deux Femmes terribles*, was broadcast in March 1965 under the title *Two Terrible Women.*

In 1963 she published *Dear Enemies,* a book on French-English relations written in collaboration with Solange Chaput-Rolland, a Quebecois critic and broadcaster. Written in the form of an exchange of letters, *Dear Enemies* is a witty and urbane but forthright airing of long-standing grievances and tensions between Canada's two founding nations. The book was published in French as *Chers ennemis,* also in 1963. Graham was at work on a novel about English-Canadian and Quebecois relations when illness overtook her. She died in Montreal of cancer of the brain on 25 November 1965; she was fifty-two.

Reference:

Eli Mandel, Introduction to Graham's *Earth and High Heaven* (Toronto: McClelland & Stewart, 1960).

George Grant

(13 November 1918-27 September 1988)

Susan Jackel
University of Alberta

BOOKS: *Canada: An Introduction to a Nation* (Toronto: Canadian Institute of International Affairs, 1943);

The Empire: Yes or No? (Toronto: Ryerson, 1945);

Philosophy in the Mass Age (Vancouver: Copp Clark, 1959; New York: Hill & Wang, 1960);

Lament for a Nation: The Defeat of Canadian Nationalism (Toronto: McClelland & Stewart, 1965; Princeton, N.J.: Van Nostrand, 1965);

Technology and Empire: Perspectives on North America (Toronto: Anansi, 1969);

Time as History (Toronto: Canadian Broadcasting Corporation, 1969);

English-Speaking Justice (Sackville, N.B.: Mount Allison University, 1974; revised edition, Notre Dame, Ind.: University of Notre Dame Press, 1985);

Technology and Justice (Toronto: Anansi, 1986).

OTHER: "Philosophy," in *Royal Commission Studies* (The Massey Report) (Ottawa: King's Printer, 1951), pp. 119-135;

"Philosophy and Religion," in *The Great Ideas Today*, edited by Robert M. Hutchins and Mortimer J. Adler (Chicago: Encyclopaedia Britannica, 1961), pp. 337-376;

"An Ethic of Community," in *Social Purpose for Canada*, edited by Michael Oliver (Toronto: University of Toronto Press, 1961), pp. 3-36;

" 'The computer does not impose on us the ways it should be used,' " in *Beyond Industrial Growth*, edited by Abraham Rotstein (Toronto: University of Toronto Press, 1976), pp. 117-131;

"Abortion and Rights," by Grant and Sheila Grant, in *The Right to Birth: Some Christian Views on Abortion*, edited by Eugene Fairweather and Ian Gentles (Toronto: Anglican Book Centre, 1976), pp. 1-12.

PERIODICAL PUBLICATIONS: "The Uses of Freedom—A Word in Our World," *Queen's Quarterly*, 60 (Winter 1956): 515-527;

"Canadian Fate and Imperialism," *Canadian Dimension*, 4 (1973): 21-25;

"Faith and the Multiversity," *Compass*, no. 4 (Autumn 1978): 3-14.

Although more absorbed with questions of philosophy, religion, and politics than with literature, George Grant has had a considerable and continuing impact on literary and cultural nationalists in English-speaking Canada. It is necessary to insist on the adjective *English-speaking*, for it is one that Grant himself is careful to use, in recognition of the fact that developments in Quebec lie largely outside his domain. The result is that Grant's writing is either unknown or mistrusted by the majority of contemporary Francophone writers and critics, while even among Anglophone Canadians Grant's elegant and lucid conservatism provokes wide extremes of respect and scorn. Therefore no discussion of Grant's place in Canadian letters can be free of controversy.

George Parkin Grant, the son of William Lawson and Maude Parkin Grant, was born and raised in Toronto. He spent his undergraduate years at Queen's University (B.A., 1939) and then went to Oxford. There he read history, politics, and law. After World War II he studied philosophy at Oxford, which granted him a doctoral degree. In 1947 Grant married; he and his wife, Sheila, had six children. From 1947 to 1960 Grant taught philosophy at Dalhousie University in Halifax, moving next to McMaster University in Hamilton, where he became head of the department of religion. In 1980 he returned to Dalhousie, with teaching privileges in the departments of classics, religion, and political science.

Grant's grandfathers were the late-nineteenth-century minister and educator George Munro Grant, longtime principal of Queen's, and Sir George Parkin, strong supporter of Imperial Federation and head of the Rhodes Trust. His father was for a time professor of colonial history at Oxford and then headmaster of Upper Canada College, a prestigious preparatory school for

George Grant (photograph by Carlos, courtesy of the Public Relations Office, Dalhousie University)

boys in Toronto. To the extent that Canadians can boast of an intellectual aristocracy, the Grants are at its center, and George Parkin Grant's sensitive working out of his own heritage is a major strand in his appeal to younger Canadian scholars and writers.

Occasionally Grant's lineage is held against him, as when unsympathetic critics interpret his defense of tradition and of loyalist ideals as the peevish complaint of a justly displaced oligarchic remnant. But despite the title of Grant's best-known book, *Lament for a Nation: The Defeat of Canadian Nationalism*, the tone of his writing is neither plaintive nor noisily protesting. Indeed, it is of some concern to those most open to Grant's argument that he insists all too philosophically on the nobility of loving and embracing fate–even the fate of one's own irrelevance and futility, if one is conservative-minded, in the modern world.

Grant's shift from the secular liberalism of his upbringing to the religious conservatism of his mature thought turned on an experience of religious conversion during his war service in England. All his writing has therefore gone forward within the framework of Christian theology, superimposed on the long Western tradition of moral philosophy from Plato to Heidegger.

Grant the philosopher and religious thinker is not always understood, or even read, by students of Canadian literature. His most ardent followers in the arts have responded to the particular critique employed by Grant in considering Canada's relation to the United States, first in *Lament for a Nation* and then in essays collected under the title *Technology and Empire: Perspectives on North America*. Published in 1965 and 1969, respectively, these two slim volumes at once focused and spurred the contemporaneous debate over how (or even whether) Canadians might withstand the increasingly pervasive influence of America in Canadian affairs. If Canadians of the 1960s could not avoid the acceptance of nuclear warheads for Bomarc missiles, or complicity in the production of napalm for American forces in Vietnam, how could they expect to stand outside the homogenizing culture, much less the integrated economy, that made all North Americans one in beliefs, customs, interests, and imaginings? What place, then, for a distinctively Canadian art or literature? And if none, what hope–indeed, what point–in Canadian persistence with the charade of a separate political identity?

These questions, and similar related ones, Grant posed in their moral and political dimensions. Other writers, notably those associated with the nationalist House of Anansi press of Toronto, extrapolated from the political to the cultural sphere. That *Technology and Empire* was published by Anansi was only one small measure of the close and fruitful exchange of ideas that developed between Grant and such important writers and editors as Dave Godfrey, Margaret Atwood, and, especially, Dennis Lee. Both *Technology and Empire* and the later *English-Speaking Justice*, the Josiah Wood Lectures delivered by Grant in 1974, contain dedications to Lee; Lee's *Civil Elegies* (1968; enlarged edition, 1972) uses Grant's thought as the departure point for poetry. Atwood's controversial critical survey of Canadian writing, *Survival* (1972), includes four epigraphs from Grant.

Grant's ruminations on the persistence of an alternative American society in the northern half of the continent were only a part, although an integral part, of a more broadly conceived meditation on freedom, necessity, and tyranny. After *Technology and Empire* these philosophical explorations have turned increasingly to the theme of justice in the modern state.

His last book, *Technology and Justice* (1986), comprises six essays which pursue the ramifications of his ideas vis-à-vis contemporary definitions of "rights." He attacks euthanasia, for example, and abortion and criticizes the role of technology in disputing values or "traditions"; technology, by making some things possible, makes them seem right–an equation Grant resists.

Grant was the recipient of several honorary degrees, from Trent (1970), Mount Allison (1972), Dalhousie (1974), and the University of Calgary (1978). Whether his impact on Canadian letters is drawing to a close, or merely entering a new phase, cannot safely be predicted. On grounds of cogency and expressiveness alone, however, Grant's essays hold a secure place in English-language prose, a place that will probably grow as readers outside Canada become better acquainted with his work.

References:

Eugene Combs, ed., *Modernity and Responsibility: Essays for George Grant* (Toronto: University of Toronto Press, 1983);

Arthur Kroker, *Technology and the Canadian Mind* (Montreal: New World Perspectives, 1984);

Eli Mandel, "George Grant: Language, Nation, the Silence of God," *Canadian Literature*, 83 (Winter 1979): 163-175;

Joan E. O'Donovan, *George Grant and the Twilight of Justice* (Toronto: University of Toronto Press, 1984);

Larry Schmidt, ed., *George Grant in Process: Essays and Conversations* (Toronto: Anansi, 1978);

Charles Taylor, *Radical Tories: The Conservative Tradition in Canada* (Toronto: Anansi, 1982), pp. 127-157.

Eldon Grier
(13 April 1917-   )

Barbara Pell
Trinity Western University

BOOKS: *A Morning from Scraps* (Montreal: Privately printed, 1955);
Poems (Montreal: Privately printed, 1956);
The Ring of Ice (Montreal: Cambridge Press, 1957);
Manzanillo and Other Poems (Montreal: Privately printed, 1958);
A Friction of Lights (Toronto: Contact, 1963);
Pictures on the Skin (Montreal: Delta, 1967);
Selected Poems 1955-1970 (Montreal: Delta, 1971);
The Assassination of Colour (Fredericton: Fiddlehead, 1978).

RADIO: *Fitzgerald and My Father*, CBC, 1978.

As a painter turned poet in mid life, Eldon Grier demonstrates strong visual elements of both imagism and surrealism in his poetry. His work has also been influenced, in its sophistication and humanity, by his extensive travels. He is a poet who is well regarded by critics but has not achieved wide popularity.

Grier was born in 1917, in London, England, to Canadian parents, Charles Brockwill Grier (a captain in the Canadian army) and Kathleen Phyllis Black Grier. The family returned to Montreal in 1918, where his father became a stockbroker, and Grier grew up, in his words, in "a rather isolated ghetto of wealth" and was educated at private schools in Montreal, Ottawa, and Toronto. He left home to become a painter at the age of seventeen and struggled to make a living in the bohemian art world of the 1930s and 1940s, studying with Goodridge Roberts and John Lyman in Montreal, and in 1945 with the muralists Alfredo Zalce and Diego Rivera in Mexico. He returned to teach at the Montreal Museum of Fine Arts under Arthur Lismer but contracted tuberculosis in 1950 and was hospitalized for two and a half years.

His marriage in 1944 to Elizabeth Temple Jamieson, which had produced a daughter, Sharon, in 1948, ended in 1952. In 1954 he married the painter Sylvia Tait and began a new ca-reer as a poet. The Griers traveled widely in Europe and Mexico until 1968 when they settled in West Vancouver. They have two children, Brock (born in 1956) and Alexa (born in 1960).

Grier's first four books (three of them privately printed) had a small circulation, but *A Friction of Lights* (1963), which included a selection of his earlier work, was widely and favorably reviewed. A blurb on the dust jacket helps explain Grier's movement from painting to poetry: "in its present state painting is rather functional and pas-

Dust jacket and front cover for two of Grier's volumes of verse. A Friction of Lights *(1963) is a collection of imagist poems, many from Grier's earlier books;* Selected Poems 1955-1970 *(1971) includes surrealistic and experimental later poems.*

sive: it can only make the most general nod in the direction of meaning. Poetry on the other hand can never hope to escape the onus of meaning, and meaning arrived at through feeling is one of its distinctive revelations." The imagism in these poems deftly combines strong painterly images with intense personal feeling to probe "the moral and psychological dilemmas of his time." The meanings that emerge are direct but not didactic, the voice already mature and relaxed, though sometimes uneven. His long twenty-part poem "An Ecstasy" (actually numbered to 21 but with part 11 missing) reflects a dominant Grier theme in its ambivalent attitude to the inevitable transition from the old world to the new, mingling nostalgic regret with courageous optimism: "Let us speak the dignified language of man. / Let us bring back from bitter exile, / the colours of our exaltation." Also characteristic of Grier's interests are the numerous poems about artists and artworks in which he transposes color and design into words and meaning.

The poems in *Pictures on the Skin* (1967) are interleaved with photographs by Grier and collages and drawings by Sylvia Tait. Negatives, silhouettes, and stark, dramatic colors and shapes among the illustrations reinforce the surrealistic juxtaposition of images in these poems, as in "Giacometti": "his intention / was like a table / without graffiti / or mythic hair / like the ragged lighting / in bottles." The illogical succession of image fragments attempts to break through rationality into a dream-nightmare world of acute insight, but too often the result is vague abstraction.

Selected Poems 1955-1970 (1971) comprises fifty-eight unrevised poems from Grier's earlier books and twenty-eight new ones. The volume illustrates his development from the relaxed lyricism and direct imagism of his earlier books to the surrealistic complexity and technical experimentation of his later work. The constants are his thoughtful intelligence, his urbanity and sensitivity, his colloquial voice, and his painter's eye. These virtues are evident in his most frequent poetic portraits–of places and people–in which he captures the quintessential qualities of his subject, often in an anecdotal moment, as in the poem "Climate":

> this could be a poem
> about cold or death or sensuality
> or contradiction
> the place is a delicatessen the
> month November the principal actor
> whatever he wanted to say said
> "I'm sixty-seven and I'm going to die[.]"

The language may be tougher than in earlier poems, but the tone is still more ironic than sardonic. Grier balances modern disillusionment and skepticism with a compassionate humanism, nurtured by his travels in foreign societies such as rural Mexico which, in his words, "greatly expanded my outlook and my love of people."

His latest book, *The Assassination of Colour* (1978), begins with a series of vivid memories of Mexico, followed by reminiscences and tributes to painters and paintings, occasional verses, letters to friends, and meditations on a variety of topical interests, many evoked by life in Vancouver. It is a rich retrospective, with some experiments in stanzaic forms; the subjects are not always important but usually interesting. The most moving pieces, again, are informed by Grier's visual imagery and compassion. This makes the petulant sarcasm of "Doctor David Suzuki" and "Gary Snyder" an aberration.

Judging from the eighty-four poems in *The Assassination of Colour*, Grier did not decrease in energy during the 1970s. He is now working on a collection of short poems as well as a volume of collected poetry.

Ralph Gustafson

(16 August 1909-   )

Wendy Robbins
University of New Brunswick

BOOKS: *The Golden Chalice* (London: Nicholson & Watson, 1935);

Alfred the Great (London: Joseph, 1937);

Epithalamium in Time of War (New York: Privately printed, 1941);

Lyrics Unromantic (New York: Privately printed, 1942);

Flight into Darkness (New York: Pantheon, 1944);

Poetry and Canada: A Guide to Reading (Ottawa: Canadian Legion Educational Series, 1945);

Rivers among Rocks (Toronto: McClelland & Stewart, 1960);

Rocky Mountain Poems (Vancouver: Klanak, 1960);

Sift in an Hourglass (Toronto: McClelland & Stewart, 1966);

Ixion's Wheel (Toronto: McClelland & Stewart, 1969);

Selected Poems (Toronto: McClelland & Stewart, 1972);

Theme and Variations for Sounding Brass (Sherbrooke, Que.: Privately printed, 1972);

The Brazen Tower (Tillsonburg, Ont.: Ascham Press, 1974);

Fire on Stone (Toronto: McClelland & Stewart, 1974);

Corners in the Glass (Toronto: McClelland & Stewart, 1977);

Soviet Poems, Sept. 13 to Oct. 5, 1976 (Winnipeg: Turnstone, 1978);

Sequences (Windsor, Ont.: Black Moss Press, 1979);

Landscape with Rain (Toronto: McClelland & Stewart, 1980);

Nine Poems (Toronto: League of Canadian Poets, 1980);

The Vivid Air: Collected Stories (Victoria, B.C.: Sono Nis, 1980);

Conflicts of Spring (Toronto: McClelland & Stewart, 1981);

Dentelle/Indented (Colorado Springs: The Press at Colorado College, 1982);

Gradations of Grandeur (Victoria, B.C.: Sono Nis, 1982);

The Moment Is All: Selected Poems, 1944-1983 (Toronto: McClelland & Stewart, 1983);

Solidarność: Prelude (Sherbrooke, Que.: Progressive Publications, 1983);

At the Ocean's Verge: Selected Poems, edited by John Walsh (Redding Ridge, Conn.: Black Swan, 1984);

Directives of Autumn (Toronto: McClelland & Stewart, 1984);

Impromptus (Lantzville, B.C.: Oolichan, 1984);

Twelve Landscapes (Toronto: Shaw Street Press, 1985);

Manipulations on Greek Themes (Tillsonburg, Ont.: Ascham Press, 1986);

Collected Poems (Victoria, B.C.: Sono Nis, 1987);

Plummets and Other Partialities (Victoria, B.C.: Sono Nis, 1987);

Winter Prophecies (Toronto: McClelland & Stewart, 1987).

OTHER: *Anthology of Canadian Poetry (English)*, edited by Gustafson (Harmondsworth, U.K. & New York: Penguin, 1942);

A Little Anthology of Canadian Poets, edited by Gustafson (Norfolk, Conn.: New Directions, 1943);

Canadian Accent: A Collection of Stories and Poems by Contemporary Writers from Canada, edited by Gustafson (Harmondsworth, U.K. & New York: Penguin, 1944);

The Penguin Book of Canadian Verse, edited by Gustafson (Harmondsworth, U.K. & Baltimore: Penguin, 1958; revised, 1967, 1975, 1984).

Early in his career Ralph Gustafson won international attention as an anthologist of Canadian literature. His short stories have appeared in Canadian and American periodicals and anthologies, and since 1960 he has enjoyed a national audience as a music critic for CBC-Radio. But he is best known for his poetry–learned, densely allusive, and stylistically sophisticated.

Ralph Gustafson (courtesy of the author)

The son of Carl Otto Gustafson, a photographer, and Gertrude Barker Gustafson, Ralph Barker Gustafson was born in 1909 in Lime Ridge and raised in nearby Sherbrooke, Quebec. Gustafson entered Bishop's University, Lennoxville, in 1926, graduating at the head of his class in 1929 with a B.A., first class honors in English and history. During these years his increasing commitment to literature was fostered by Frank Oliver Call and W. O. Raymond, who taught courses on modern poetry and Browning, respectively. But, "Alas, no one told me," he recalled in a 1972 letter, "that Pound, Yeats, Eliot, were alive!"

He worked as music master at Bishop's College School while completing an M.A. at the university in 1930, writing a thesis on Shelley and Keats, and, in fact, striving to be "another Johnny Keats without the Consumption." The influence of the English romantics is pervasive in the poems of *The Golden Chalice* (1935), which he began at Bishop's. This volume won Gustafson the Prix David. At Keble College, Oxford, he took a second B.A. (1933) and M.A. (awarded

much later, when he resumed his academic career, in 1963).

His travels around England and reading of Anglo-Saxon literature while at Oxford provided the inspiration for *Alfred the Great* (1937), a blank-verse history play set in ninth-century England. Written in the 1930s as Europe headed toward war, it focuses on war, peace, love, and the safeguarding of Western civilization. The main action follows the battles and truces of the Saxons under Alfred and the Danes under the unscrupulous Guthrum, while a subplot traces the tragic paths of two young lovers.

Gustafson spent 1933-1934 teaching at Saint Alban's School for Boys in Brockville, Ontario, but deeply missed England's rich cultural life. The following year he settled in England, working as a tutor and free-lance writer. The poems composed at this period show a modernist influence, for, when *New Verse* editor Geoffrey Grigson rejected some of his work in 1932 as static and conventional, Gustafson set about reading D. H. Lawrence, T. S. Eliot, William Butler Yeats, W. H. Auden, Stephen Spender, and Louis Mac-

Neice to bring himself up to date. Several poems published in *Sewanee Review* (April 1940), *Epithalamium in Time of War* (1941), and *Lyrics Unromantic* (1942) are all experimental amalgamations of old and new models.

In 1939 Gustafson moved to New York. There he prepared *Anthology of Canadian Poetry (English)*, which had been commissioned by Allen Lane of Penguin Books for distribution among Canadian soldiers abroad during the war. The nature of this assignment did not influence Gustafson's selections, which were made in the light of a fresh and discriminating evaluation of Canadian tradition. Canadian publishers who were suspicious of the new paperback market made copyright negotiations a protracted and costly matter. Gustafson incurred a personal debt of one thousand dollars to clear permissions, but his uncompromising standards were rewarded: the anthology, published in 1942, sold fifty thousand copies and was warmly received by an appreciative international audience. (Further volumes under Gustafson's editorship, *A Little Anthology of Canadian Poets* [1943], *Canadian Accent* [1944], and *The Penguin Book of Canadian Verse* [1958; revised, 1967, 1975, 1984], were published over the next three decades.)

Flight into Darkness (1944) collects poems written from 1936 to 1943–a period of dislocation and change in Gustafson's life. His faith in the goodness of nature and the harmony of the human, natural, and divine was eroded by his exposure to the Depression and the war, and by the premature death of his mother after a protracted battle with cancer. His poetry expands to encompass themes of disillusionment, uncertainty, and flux. Several poems, such as the frequently anthologized "On the Struma Massacre," are marked by increased social consciousness. The collection as a whole shows substantial integration of modernist techniques and was praised by reviewers for accurately reflecting the temper of the times.

From 1942 to 1946 Gustafson worked for British Information Services in New York, preparing digests of American newspapers and radio broadcasts (and in one instance receiving the personal compliments of Winston Churchill). At the end of the war he left in order to have more time for writing. He wrote record liners and musical monographs, contributed some "New York Letters" to *First Statement* and *Northern Review*, and published more than a dozen short stories during the period from 1946 to 1959.

Probing domestic conflicts and revealing a vivid consciousness of violence and psychological trauma, Gustafson's stories were published by such journals as *Atlantic Monthly, Story, Canadian Forum,* and *Queen's Quarterly* and were anthologized in Martha Foley's *The Best American Short Stories* for 1948 and 1950. The main characters tend to be sensitive children, artists, or lovers who run up against a puritanical, philistine society. His best-known story is "The Pigeon," which focuses on the terrifying guilt of a ten-year-old girl over the accidental killing of a bird that she was trying to set free. Like his poems, the stories celebrate a healthy instinct for life, but they do so indirectly by probing the human suffering caused when passion is blocked or stunted. The stories were not collected until *The Brazen Tower* (1974) and were not widely available until the paperback publication of *The Vivid Air: Collected Stories* in 1980. (An autobiographical regional novel also dates to the 1950s but remains unpublished.)

In the mid 1950s, Gustafson met Elisabeth (Betty) Renninger, an American nurse who shared his love for music. Many of his finest love poems were written during their courtship. In 1958 they married and in 1959 traveled together across Canada and through the Rockies. The most productive and interesting phase of Gustafson's career as a poet begins at this period, and his inspiration can be summed up, he states, in one word: Betty.

Rivers among Rocks (1960), illustrated by Frank Newfeld, collects poems written from 1944 to 1959. They center on ephemerality, nature, art, and love. It is notable that the nature poems, set in Canada, employ a concise, elemental style, while the art poems, based on European tradition, utilize a densely allusive, elliptical technique. Gustafson quarries two separate sources of imagery and speaks with two quite distinct poetic voices. The poems are disputatious, anti-Keatsian ("Unheard music is not sweeter"), and critical of Christian dogma. Showing the diverse influences of Gerard Manley Hopkins and Ezra Pound, the poems celebrate beauty in all its temporal, sensuous manifestations (moving one critic to call Gustafson a "married Hopkins").

Rocky Mountain Poems (1960), composed on location in the fall of 1959, is a collection of eighteen descriptive and speculative nature poems. Written in a spare, chiseled style, they present Canada as "a country without myths," a place without a long history, where "all is a beginning." Deeply compelling poems such as "At Moraine Lake"

Dust jacket for Gustafson's 1969 book of poetry, inspired by travels in Great Britain, Italy, Greece, Turkey, and Egypt

and "In the Yukon" are structured on the polarity between the wilderness (Canada) and civilization (Europe)–a theme pursued in subsequent books. *Rocky Mountain Poems* won the Borestone Mountain Poetry Award in 1961.

In 1963 Gustafson took up teaching again, joining the Department of English at his alma mater, Bishop's University, and settling in the village of North Hatley on the shores of Lake Massawippi–a locale which is featured prominently in his later work. *Sift in an Hourglass* (1966) is preoccupied with the cycles of birth and death. Yet love and art, which seem to transcend death, are praised as he articulates his defiant affirmation of life. Poems such as "Aspects of Some Forsythia Branches" and "A Row of Geraniums" explore the image of the garden / grave as a paradigm for life, while the long poem "Ariobarzanes" sums up many of his concerns. A trip to Europe in the summer of 1962 provided the subject matter for the travel poems included in the final "Year of Voyages" section. The book was favorably reviewed, Gustafson being praised

as a stylist and "poet's poet." In 1966 he was appointed poet in residence at Bishop's.

Travels through Great Britain, Italy, Greece, Turkey, and Egypt inspired the new poems of *Ixion's Wheel* (1969). The main themes again are love, death, and art, and Greek mythology figures importantly. His exploration of European museums and the ruins of ancient civilizations was intended as an Odyssean voyage through the underworld of history and myth, yet some of these travel poems lack intensity. Critical reaction was mixed, several reviewers dismissing Gustafson as a "superior tourist," but Michael Hornyansky in the *University of Toronto Quarterly* (July 1970) praised him as "the heir of civilized centuries." The collection's finest poems, such as "Agamemnon's Mask: Archeological Museum, Athens" and "At the Pinakothek Ruins: Munich," are clearly among Gustafson's best; in a direct and compassionate way, they focus on the cycles of birth, copulation, and death, their dominant tone being that of tragic gaiety.

In 1969 Gustafson traveled to Eastern Europe and was moved to write the protest poem "Nocturne: Prague 1968." *Theme and Variations for Sounding Brass* (1972) includes this and four other committed, topical poems which were the product of a deliberate decision to deal with the political realities of the Vietnam era, including the F.L.Q. (Front de Libération du Québec) crisis. The main theme is love, broadened to a conception of compassion for victims of violence all over the world. "I got sick of hearing that I'm a romantic who writes about the head of Nefertiti," he explained in 1975. The poems were researched in contemporary news sources, and the style is simple, even prosaic. Two of the poems were commissioned by the CBC and broadcast nationally over radio and television.

Gustafson published his *Selected Poems* in 1972, including material from *Flight into Darkness* through *Ixion's Wheel*. By the mid 1970s critical neglect of his work ended, and he won a Governor General's Award for *Fire on Stone* (1974), a book which celebrates individual moments of beauty and personal happiness, fleeting as these may be. This book marks a sharp departure from public poetry and a return to a personal lyric mode. Some of the poems were written during a lengthy hospitalization in the winter of 1973; several focus on the local landscape or on homely, domestic routines such as gardening. Typically they explore dualities–stone and fire, debris and miracle. Showing the ongoing influence of his musical training, they structure experience in counterpoint.

Corners in the Glass (1977) similarly presents impassioned meditations on life, and again Gustafson stresses the here and now. He writes in a pithy, direct style about concrete objects and sensual delight. His best poems on the carpe diem theme include "An Instant of Grosbeaks," "The Moment Is Not Only Itself," and "The Overwhelming Green." These, along with poems bearing such homespun titles as "Wednesday at North Hatley," "The Philosophy of Cutting Petunias," "In Dispraise of Great Happenings," and "Of Green Steps and Laundry," are among the best he has written and suggest how Gustafson, sharply criticized for being a Grand Tour poet in the 1960s, has become increasingly a regional poet, picking up a thread worked much earlier in the nature poems of *Rivers among Rocks* and *Rocky Mountain Poems*. In *Corners in the Glass* there is a simultaneous clarification of style and repatriation of theme.

His reading tour of the U.S.S.R. in the mid 1970s resulted in the slim volume *Soviet Poems, Sept. 13 to Oct. 5, 1976* (1978), which reads like a travel diary. In 1977 he retired from university teaching, though he remains active as poet in residence, gives readings in Canada and abroad, and continues to publish new work almost every year. *Sequences* (1979) republishes *Rocky Mountain Poems, Theme and Variations for Sounding Brass, Soviet Poems*, and portions of other books. The limited amount of new material in the sections entitled "Winter Sequence" and "Country Walking" centers on the Canadian winter, an analogue for old age and death, which sets a boundary to love but also brings fulfillment. In this work, Canada serves as a microcosm, containing both good and evil, creation and destruction.

Landscape with Rain (1980) is set primarily in North Hatley, though a short sequence of poems involves Iran and Greece. Gustafson speaks in one poem of "the advantage of being yourself," and his themes and simplified style reflect this virtue. He notices in the world, finally, a balance between beauty and love and violence and death. His own aging and approach to death are the subjects of the wrenching "Walking Through Thick Snow"; yet he nonetheless chooses to celebrate light, sun, flowers, birds, landscape, woman, love, music, art, and architecture. He writes in "April" that "The heart aches with the shortness of life," but he records to the last "All the joy."

The 1980s have been yet another productive decade for Gustafson. From 1981 to 1987 he produced more than a dozen books reiterating his passions for place and love, for music and classical grace, for friendship and social justice. *Gradations of Grandeur* (1982) is a somewhat austere, intellectual poem, intended as a magnum opus to sum up the philosophy arrived at over a lifetime of study and travel. It offers praise for nature's beauty, instinct, sexual intimacy, and love between man and woman, as well as for art, ceremony, poetry, music, and the great monuments and works of civilization. Its affirmative attitude recalls Wallace Stevens, while its stress on love echoes Ezra Pound: "Not *cogito: amo ergo sum.*"

Always supportive of small presses committed to artistry, Gustafson published his collections *Nine Poems* (1980), *Dentelle/Indented* (1982), *Impromptus* (1984), and *Twelve Landscapes* (1985) with the League of Canadian Poets, The Press at Colorado College, Oolichan Books, and Shaw Street Press, respectively. *Solidarność: Prelude*, published in 1983, furthers his interest in East European politics and the shapes of violence. *Manipulations on Greek Themes* (1986) demonstrates his continuing facility with musical form. *The Moment Is All* (1983) is another volume of selected poems, drawing on work from 1944 onward. The following year another volume of selected poems, *At the Ocean's Verge*, appeared in the United States. It is organized by theme by the editor, John Walsh, who also made the selections. Poems that employ landscape motifs lead into poems with a seasonal focus and then to those that stem from travel and the classics and from reflections on great and local events. The volume closes with verses on love, music, and the art of poetry itself.

Gustafson provides something of a credo of his own beliefs about poetry and its relation to life in "The Saving Grace," an essay published in *Canadian Literature* (Summer 1983). Poetry is, he writes, "the enlightenment of fact, the worth of experience, the attainment of sensibility, the establishment of compassion." His new poems of the 1980s primarily appear in *Conflicts of Spring* (1981), *Directives of Autumn* (1984), and *Winter Prophecies* (1987). The lyrics of *Directives of Autumn* are characteristic of this decade's voice. The poet's passionate engagement with others (as in "To Simon Wiesenthal" or in any of Gustafson's love poems to his wife) is only slightly tempered by the metaphoric nearness of winter. "Your love is constant though cold death is in it," the poet ob-

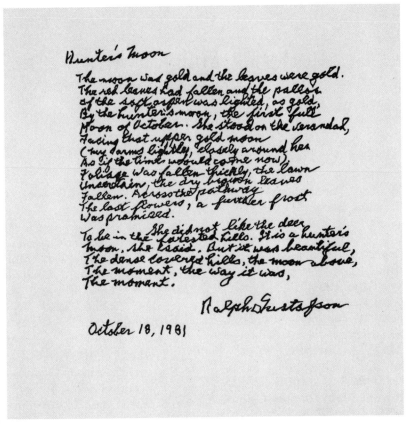

Fair copy of a poem collected in Gustafson's 1983 volume, The Moment Is All *(by permission of the author)*

serves in "Through Clear Crystal"; "Nothing shall harm it, not years and oppositions, / Not seasons and their dispositions. Nothing will." And "The Fall of Snow," which opens with a warning–"The world in this dusk is again blue"–closes with affirmation: "The slightest wind, tomorrow / Will bring down the world where it / Exists in the dusk, / the reflection of the fire gone, / At the window the / Gold intercession."

Ralph Gustafson's development as a poet provides a miniature history of Canadian literature, moving from outdated imitation of romantic nature poets, through a transitional phase of dependency on the early modernists, to a more fully independent yet still richly eclectic style, his late work riveted unselfconsciously on Canadian experience and on the universal cycles of life and death which Canada's four sharply defined seasons seem to magnify. Valuing both the life of the senses and the heritage of the arts, and writing at his best so as to fuse intellect with passion, Gustafson has justly been singled out as "one of the most complete Canadian poets." His unified but constantly evolving vision, articulated with im-

peccable artistry, has staked for him a valid and enduring claim among the foremost ranks of contemporary Canadian poets.

Letters:

A Literary Friendship: The Correspondence of Ralph Gustafson and W. W. E. Ross, edited by Bruce Whiteman (Toronto: ECW, 1984).

Reference:

Wendy Robbins Keitner, *Ralph Gustafson* (Boston: G. K. Hall, 1979).

Papers:

The Lockwood Memorial Library, State University of New York at Buffalo, has the manuscript for the "Sequence to War" section of *Flight into Darkness.* The Murray Memorial Library, University of Saskatchewan, Saskatoon, holds other early manuscript material and correspondence pertaining to Gustafson's early anthologies. Queen's University Archives, Kingston, houses the manuscripts of his most important works–those from 1960 on.

Roderick Haig-Brown

(21 February 1908-9 October 1976)

T. D. MacLulich

SELECTED BOOKS: *Silver: The Life Story of an Atlantic Salmon* (London: Black, 1931);

Pool and Rapid: The Story of a River (London: Black, 1932);

Ki-Yu: A Story of Panthers (Boston & New York: Houghton Mifflin, 1934); also published as *Panther* (London: Cape, 1934);

The Western Angler: An Account of Pacific Salmon and Western Trout (2 volumes, New York: Derrydale Press, 1939; abridged edition, 1 volume, New York: Morrow, 1947; Toronto: Collins, 1947);

Return to the River: The Story of the Chinook Run (New York: Morrow, 1941; London: Collins, 1942; Toronto: McClelland & Stewart, 1946);

Timber: A Novel of Pacific Coast Loggers (New York: Morrow, 1942; Toronto: Collins, 1946); republished as *The Tall Trees Fall* (London: Collins, 1943);

Starbuck Valley Winter (New York: Morrow, 1943; London: Collins, 1944; Toronto: Collins, 1946);

A River Never Sleeps (New York: Morrow, 1946; Toronto: Collins, 1946; London: Collins, 1948);

Saltwater Summer (New York: Morrow, 1948; Toronto: Collins, 1948; London: Collins, 1949);

On the Highest Hill (New York: Morrow, 1949; Toronto: Collins, 1949; London: Collins, 1950);

Measure of the Year (New York: Morrow, 1950; Toronto: Collins, 1950);

Fisherman's Spring (New York: Morrow, 1951; Toronto: Collins, 1951);

Fisherman's Winter (New York: Morrow, 1954; Toronto: Collins, 1955);

Mounted Police Patrol (New York: Morrow, 1954; London: Collins, 1954; Toronto: Collins, 1954);

Captain of the Discovery: The Story of Captain George Vancouver (Toronto: Macmillan, 1956);

Fisherman's Summer (New York: Morrow, 1959; Toronto: Collins, 1959);

The Farthest Shores (Toronto: Longmans, Green, 1960);

The Living Land: An Account of the Natural Resources of British Columbia (Toronto: Macmillan, 1961; New York: Morrow, 1961);

Fur and Gold (Toronto: Longmans, 1962);

The Whale People (Toronto: Collins, 1962; London: Collins, 1962; New York: Morrow, 1963);

Fisherman's Fall (New York: Morrow, 1964; Toronto: Collins, 1964);

A Primer of Fly-Fishing (New York: Morrow, 1964; Toronto: Collins, 1965);

The Salmon (Ottawa: Environment Canada, Fisheries & Marine Services, 1974);

Bright Waters, Bright Fish: An Examination of Angling in Canada (Vancouver: Douglas & McIntyre / Portland: Timber Press, 1980);

Alison's Fishing Birds (Vancouver: Colophon Books, 1980);

Woods and River Tales: From the World of Roderick Haig-Brown, edited by Valerie Haig-Brown (Toronto: McClelland & Stewart, 1980);

The Master and His Fish: From the World of Roderick Haig-Brown, edited by Valerie Haig-Brown (Toronto: McClelland & Stewart, 1981; Seattle: University of Washington Press, 1981);

Writings and Reflections: From the World of Roderick Haig-Brown, edited by Valerie Haig-Brown (Toronto: McClelland & Stewart, 1982; Seattle: University of Washington Press, 1982).

RADIO: *The Land Is Bright*, CBC, May-June 1958.

OTHER: "With Its Face to the West," in *The Face of Canada* (Toronto: Clarke, Irwin, 1959);

"British Columbia," in *The Pacific Northwest*, edited by Anthony Netboy (Garden City, N.Y.: Doubleday, 1963);

"The Land's Wealth," in *The Canadians, 1867-1967*, edited by J. M. S. Careless and R. Craig Brown (Toronto: Macmillan, 1967).

Roderick Haig-Brown (photograph copyright © 1989 by Mary Randlett)

PERIODICAL PUBLICATIONS: "Canada's Pacific Salmon," *Canadian Geographical Journal*, 44 (March 1952): 109-127;

"Hardy's Dorset," *Tamarack Review*, 1 (Winter 1957): 46-54;

"The Writer in Isolation: A Surprised Exploration of a Given Subject," *Canadian Literature*, 1 (Summer 1959): 5-12;

"The Fraser Watershed and the Moran Proposal," *Nature Canada*, 1 (April/June 1972): 2-10.

Roderick Langmere Haig-Brown was one of Canada's most versatile men of letters. He wrote novels, prizewinning juvenile fiction, several works on British Columbia's history and geography, and a series of internationally acclaimed books on angling. Through all his work, however, there runs a unifying thread: the message that man must respect the natural world of which he is an integral part.

Haig-Brown was born in Lancing, Sussex, England. His parents were Lt. Col. Alan R. Haig-

Brown and Violet Mary Haig-Brown (née Pope). As a boy, Haig-Brown was encouraged by his father to learn to hunt and fish. After his father's death in 1918, his sporting education was continued by his uncles and by the redoubtable H. M. Greenhill. Emulating his father, who had written on sporting topics, Haig-Brown published his first article in *Fishing Gazette* at age sixteen. In 1925 a youthful escapade led to his abrupt departure from Charterhouse School, where his grandfather had formerly served as headmaster. Finding he was too young to enter the Colonial Civil Service, he studied history with a tutor, until a family friend's invitation took him to Washington state in 1926. There he worked in a logging camp before moving north early in 1927 to work in the woods around the Nimpkish River on Vancouver Island.

Haig-Brown kept a promise to his mother by returning to England in 1930; however, when he found that the civil service now required a university degree, he turned to the literary career he really preferred. In his Chelsea flat he wrote the children's book *Silver: The Life Story of an Atlantic*

Salmon (1931). His experiences on the Nimpkish River prompted *Pool and Rapid: The Story of a River* (1932), whose theme was the fascination a river exercised over successive generations of Indians and settlers. This same fascination drew Haig-Brown back to Vancouver Island late in 1931, and the next winter he hunted cougars with Cecil Smith, the government predator-control officer, acquiring knowledge that went into *Ki-Yu: A Story of Panthers* (1934), an animal biography in the tradition of Charles G. D. Roberts and Ernest Thompson Seton.

In 1934 Haig-Brown married Ann Elmore of Seattle (with whom he eventually had four children), and they settled on a riverside farm near the village of Campbell River on Vancouver Island. He now considered himself a full-time writer and continued to produce stories and articles based on his experiences as a logger, trapper, guide, and fisherman. With the help of the biologist Charles Mottley, he also began the four years of research and writing that led to *The Western Angler: An Account of the Pacific Salmon and Western Trout* (1939). This book effectively combines scientific data with angler's lore and personal experiences and shows the complexity of the relationship between fish and their environment. When it was republished in a less expensive, slightly condensed form in 1947, the book was (in the words of a reviewer for the Toronto *Globe and Mail*) already considered by many sportsmen "the finest book ever written on Western salmon and trout."

Haig-Brown used his extensive knowledge of fish and their habits to write *Return to the River: The Story of the Chinook Run* (1941). Concerned with the life cycle of the Columbia River salmon, the book is strongly didactic. It urges the necessity of preserving the rivers on which the salmon runs depend and reveals the impact on the salmon of the newly completed Bonneville dam. Logging and trapping provide the backgrounds for the novel *Timber* (1942), which deals with the working conditions and the mentality of loggers, and for *Starbuck Valley Winter* (1943), an appealing boy's story about how young Don Morgan achieves maturity during a winter spent running his own wilderness trapline.

In 1942 Haig-Brown became a magistrate in Campbell River. Shortly afterward, while waiting to be called for military service, he began a different kind of fishing book, more anecdotal and personal than *The Western Angler*. In 1943 he entered the Canadian army as a personnel officer, and sub-

sequently he was seconded to the RCMP for a year, an experience he later drew on for the background of *Mounted Police Patrol* (1954), for a juvenile audience. While in the army, he did little writing beyond completing the fishing book *A River Never Sleeps* (1946). This work is a thoroughly engaging mixture of boyhood reminiscences and North American fishing adventures; it presents angling not as a war between man and fish but as a highly civilized activity having its own time-honored customs and code of ethics.

After his discharge from the army in 1946, Haig-Brown wrote a juvenile novel, *Saltwater Summer* (1948), in which Don Morgan continues his initiation into adult life by running his own commercial fishing boat. Haig-Brown's next book treated the initiation theme quite differently. Colin Ensley, the protagonist of the adult novel *On the Highest Hill* (1949), recoils from the cruelty and violence of an imperfect civilization. When society intrudes into Colin's wilderness retreat, he reacts with unthinking violence, then dies in the embrace of the wilderness he prefers to the civilized world. *On the Highest Hill* is Haig-Brown's most ambitious novel. Clearly, he wanted to show how society demoralizes an essentially good man. But Colin's repugnance at the world's inevitable flaws seems disproportionate to any real harm or pain he suffers.

The favorable reception of *A River Never Sleeps* encouraged Haig-Brown to attempt other books of familiar essays. In *Measure of the Year* (1950) he affectionately describes his own rural life, in which farm chores alternate with writing, fishing, and hearing legal arguments. *Fisherman's Spring* (1951) is the first of four books that detail the fishing experiences associated with particular seasons. Although deservedly popular with sportsmen, these later fishing books do not have the richness of character and incident that makes *A River Never Sleeps* appealing even to nonanglers.

During the 1950s Haig-Brown began to study and write about the history of his adopted homeland, first in *Captain of the Discovery: The Story of Captain George Vancouver* (1956), an account of the British explorer for young readers. His research also led to other projects, including *The Land Is Bright*, a series of CBC-Radio broadcasts on West Coast history, part of which were subsequently published as *The Farthest Shores* (1960) and *Fur and Gold* (1962). Haig-Brown's interests in conservation and in Western history converged when he wrote *The Living Land: An Account of the Natural Resources of British Columbia* (1961). His ad-

Haig-Brown fishing in the Campbell River, Vancouver Island, May 1965 (photograph copyright © 1989 by Mary Randlett)

miration for the region's natives prompted *The Whale People* (1962), a sympathetic fictional portrayal of a boy's development to manhood in a coastal fishing and whaling tribe.

An appointment as a full-time judge in 1964 left Haig-Brown with less time for writing. But the last two books he wrote, as well as his nomination in 1970 to the International Pacific Salmon Fisheries Commission, confirmed his role as a semi-official spokesman for the Canadian natural environment. *The Salmon* (1974) is a handsomely illustrated monograph published by the Canadian government to coincide with the third United Nations Conference on the Law of the Sea, and *Bright Waters, Bright Fish: An Examination of Angling in Canada* (1980) is an informal survey covering sport fisheries management in Canada.

Throughout his career, Haig-Brown's most characteristic writing has dealt with fish and angling. He is, as George Woodcock remarked in an editorial in *Canadian Literature* (Winter 1976), a "true heir of Isaak Walton." Like Walton's *The Compleat Angler*, Haig-Brown's writing transcends its ostensible subject. His graceful style, attractively opinionated personality, and sensitive descriptions of the natural world give his best books a universal appeal.

Interviews:
"Roderick Haig-Brown Talks with Joan Heiberg," *British Columbia Library Quarterly*, 35 (April 1972): 5-13;

Glenys Stow, "A Conversation with Roderick Haig-Brown," *Canadian Children's Literature*, 1 (Summer 1975): 9-22.

References:
Jim Casada, "Roderick Haig-Brown: An Angler for All Seasons," *Fly Fisher* (Spring 1988): 14-15;

Russell Chatham, "Roderick Haig-Brown: Observation, Ethics and a Real Good Time," in his *Dark Waters* (Livingston, Mont.: Clark City Press, 1988);

Paul Grescoe, "The Complete Canadian," *Canadian* (7 July 1977): 14-15;

W. J. Keith, "Roderick Haig-Brown," *Canadian Literature*, 71 (Winter 1976): 7-20;

Alex Lucas, "Haig-Brown's Animal Biographies," *Canadian Children's Literature*, 11 (1978): 21-38;

Al Purdy, "Cougar Hunter," in his *No Other Country* (Toronto: McClelland & Stewart, 1977);

Anthony Robertson, *Above Tide: Reflections on Roderick Haig-Brown* (Madeira Park, British Columbia: Harbour, 1984);

George Woodcock, "Remembering Roderick Haig-Brown," in his *The World of Canadian Writing* (Vancouver: Douglas & McIntyre / Seattle: University of Washington Press, 1980).

Papers:

An extensive collection of letters, notes, manuscripts, and clippings covering Haig-Brown's career is available at the Special Collections Division, University of British Columbia Library.

Arthur Hailey

(5 April 1920-   )

Russell Brown
University of Toronto, Scarborough Campus

See also the Hailey entry in *DLB Yearbook: 1982.*

BOOKS: *The Final Diagnosis* (Garden City, N.Y.: Doubleday, 1959; London: Joseph / Souvenir Press, 1960);

Close-up on Writing for Television (Garden City, N.Y.: Doubleday, 1960);

In High Places (Garden City, N.Y.: Doubleday, 1962; London: Joseph / Souvenir Press, 1962);

Hotel (Garden City, N.Y.: Doubleday, 1965; London: Joseph / Souvenir Press, 1965);

Airport (Garden City, N.Y.: Doubleday, 1968; London: Joseph / Souvenir Press, 1968);

Wheels (Garden City, N.Y.: Doubleday, 1971; London: Joseph / Souvenir Press, 1971);

The Moneychangers (Garden City, N.Y.: Doubleday, 1975; London: Joseph / Souvenir Press, 1975);

Overload (Garden City, N.Y.: Doubleday, 1979; London: Joseph / Souvenir Press, 1979);

Strong Medicine (Garden City, N.Y.: Doubleday, 1984; London: Joseph / Souvenir Press, 1984);

The Evening News (Garden City, N.Y.: Doubleday, forthcoming 1990).

MOTION PICTURE: *Zero Hour,* screen story by Hailey, screenplay by Hailey, Hall Bartlett, and John Champion, adapted from Hailey's television play *Flight into Danger,* Paramount, 1958.

Arthur Hailey (courtesy of the author)

OTHER: *Flight into Danger,* in *Four Plays for Our Time,* edited by Herman Voaden (Toronto: Macmillan, 1960).

After a brief career as a television writer, Arthur Hailey turned to writing novels and created a string of best-sellers which became pop staples and made him Canada's most financially successful author: his books have been translated into thirty-five languages and turned into films and television miniseries. His 1968 novel, *Airport,* gave rise to two film sequels, and eventually to two parodies; *Hotel* (1965) provided the basis for a television series. In novels such as *Airport* Hailey perfected what became one of the most successful formulas for the 1960s and 1970s best-seller by depicting a crisis taking place within a large institution in a plot that was constructed episodically and that maintained several separate lines of action. His first two novels are not as formulaic as those that followed, and although they were not as popular, they remain his best. His use of an intrusive and discursive narrator throughout his fiction makes his books seem old-fashioned and often heavy-handed in their presentation, and his fiction has been criticized for its shallow characters, mechanical plotting, and naively optimistic infatuation with technology and progress. In spite of these weaknesses—and in spite of his novels' dependence on coincidence and contrivance—Hailey has obviously provided the mass-market audience with what they sought for more than twenty years.

Born in Luton, England, of working-class parents, George and Elsie Wright Hailey, Hailey left school when he was fourteen. Although he had demonstrated a love of reading and an interest in writing that had been encouraged by one of his teachers, he was unable to pursue further studies because of financial need. During World War II Hailey served as an airman in the RAF. A tendency to airsickness hampered him, but he achieved the rank of sergeant-pilot and was commissioned shortly after being transferred to Canada in 1943. He received the RAF Air Efficiency Award and ended his military career as an Air Ministry Staff officer. In 1944 he married Joan Fishwick; they had three children before they were divorced in 1950. While Hailey was still flying for the air force, he sold his first story, a brief tale of an English pilot's self-sacrificing heroism; his continuing fascination with aviation is evident in his later writing.

After the war Hailey returned to Canada to live, becoming a citizen in 1953. (He also retains his British citizenship.) In 1947 he took an editorial position at Maclean-Hunter Publishing Company in Toronto; there he met Sheila Dunlop, the woman who became his second wife in 1951. (They have two daughters and one son.) In 1953 Hailey left editing to become sales promotion manager for a trailer firm; when he grew dissatisfied after two years, he consulted an industrial psychologist, who prepared a psychological profile that concluded: "The subject is a strongly work-oriented individual. . . . He has a great deal of creativity which seeks expression. . . . He would do well as a writer and may be wasted in industry. He really should switch to a field of straight creative endeavour." Soon after, encouraged by this assessment, Hailey began to think about the dramatic possibilities of a mid-air crisis while he was on a trans-Canada flight; within days he completed a television script in which a pilot and co-pilot are incapacitated by food poisoning. CBC produced the script two months later (April 1956) as *Flight into Danger*; and the play was given a second live production later that year, this time on NBC. Twelve of Hailey's television plays were aired during the late 1950s, making him one of the important contributors to the heyday of live television drama.

Hailey moved from television to fiction partly by chance. He turned down a request from a British publisher, Ernest Hecht, to write a novel based on *Flight into Danger,* but allowed Ronald Payne and John Garrod (writing under the pseudonym John Castle) to do the job. The book, which included Hailey's name on the title page, appeared in Great Britain in 1958 (it was published in the United States two years later as *Runway Zero-Eight*). Hailey was so encouraged by its success that he decided to follow their example and converted his two-part television play *No Deadly Medicine* (for which he had won an Emmy) into *The Final Diagnosis* (1959).

Set in a large hospital, *The Final Diagnosis* shows the need for Joe Pearson, the aging head of pathology, to acknowledge that he is no longer able to cope with the rapid developments of medical technology, nor can he any longer deal with the size and complexity of the institution he serves. Pearson is portrayed as a tragic figure, destroyed by his own inflexibility, but he also is the prototype of a character that recurs throughout Hailey's fiction: the loner struggling to maintain integrity within a large corporate structure, the man who seeks to preserve meaning in a period characterized by change.

Hailey next wrote *In High Places* (1962)—his first novel not drawn from material written for television and the only book in which he deals with a Canadian topic or uses a Canadian locale. The novel tells the story of a debate over whether Canada and the United States ought to accept complete economic and military union. As the crucial vote in Parliament for such a union approaches, the Canadian prime minister has to deal not only with political dissension in his party but also with two distracting issues: an old political scandal threatens to emerge and ruin him and a trivial immigration problem has become a public-relations disaster. *In High Places* is unusual for Hailey in that its conclusion does not resolve all its questions: the novel closes–"not knowing what the future held"–as the deciding vote is about to begin.

With *In High Places* Hailey established the pattern of composition he followed thereafter: one year of intensive research and travel followed by six months of planning and composing a detailed outline, then a year and a half of writing. Although these first two novels sold well, it was with *Hotel* that Hailey's name became associated with phenomenal popular success. Hailey's third novel appeared on the *New York Times* bestseller list not long after publication and stayed there a full year, selling eighty-two thousand hardcover copies. Its popularity may have resulted partly from Hailey's increased use of melodramatic events–especially of a kind that resonates with readers' anxieties (fears of hotel-room break-ins, or entrapment in a falling elevator)–but it is evident that his audience also enjoyed the sense of a privileged look at the complexity beneath the surface of a large contemporary institution. In this novel, as in *Airport* and *Wheels* (1971), Hailey works to convey the sense that his readers are privy to inside knowledge that will make them more competent (revealing such information as how hotel valets attempt to double their tips, how to get free drinks on economy flights, and why not to buy a car built on Monday or Friday), and he underlines his revelations with lines such as "Only the naive or uninformed believed wait lists and reservations were operated with unwavering impartiality."

The hardcover sales of *Airport* (more than 260,000 copies) and of *Wheels* (more than 200,000) indicate the popular appeal of his research-heavy fiction, and *Airport* even had the effect of initiating public discussion of the psychological burdens of air-traffic controllers. With its slowly building suspense over whether a mad bomber will succeed in destroying a plane in mid-flight, *Airport* remains Hailey's most conventionally constructed thriller.

Dust jacket for Hailey's second best-seller

In *Wheels* the kind of concern that moved Hailey to write about the air-traffic controllers led him to deal with such social issues in the auto industry as race relations (also a feature of *Hotel*) and the monotony faced by workers on assembly lines. Although *Wheels* evinces the soap-opera emotions present in most of Hailey's fiction, it does not depend on suspense to the degree that Hailey's first four novels did; no potential cataclysm is in the offing as the plot follows a corporation-wide effort to ready a new-model car. *Wheels* deals instead–as do the novels that come after it–with a large industry responding to a big problem.

While researching *Airport*, Hailey spent time in northern California's Napa Valley; in 1965 he moved there from Canada. While working on *Wheels*, he left California in 1969 and moved (partly for tax reasons) to the Bahamas. There he completed *Wheels* and later in the decade wrote *The Moneychangers* (1975) and *Overload*

(1979). In these later novels Hailey's increasing concern with social problems resulted in a further shift away from single, anomalous events to plots that focus on preventing the social distortions that would result if major institutions (giant banking corporations, power companies) should fail. However, unlike the disaster novels that became popular after *Airport,* the tragedies that threaten in Hailey's fiction are always averted. Both *Overload* and *The Moneychangers* end reassuringly, with strong but compassionate men taking charge to check the slide toward chaos.

The Moneychangers does, however, deviate in one way from Hailey's usual fashion. In it Hailey adopted a tougher kind of story telling, one that recalls the style of Joseph Wambaugh or George V. Higgins. Going beyond the vaguely erotic scenes that were an occasional feature of his earlier fiction, Hailey included in *The Moneychangers* a homosexual gang rape, scatological language, and more explicit violence. Some readers were disturbed by this departure from the usually conservative sensibility, and in his two most recently published novels Hailey has not made further use of such material.

Overload suffers most from a weakness that marks all of Hailey's fiction: a tendency to lecture the reader, either in the author's own voice or through the agency of his characters. (About one of his characters he writes, without irony, "He spoke in the manner of a schoolmaster addressing a class.") Moreover in both *Overload* and *The Moneychangers,* Hailey's ability to respond to the temper of his times–which has surely been one of the reasons for his success–results only in a confusing and contradictory mixture of ideas: these books combine sympathetic presentation of the most right-wing attitudes of their day– forecasts of a coming financial crash in which only the strong and the hoarders of gold will survive–with those of the left: advocacy of corporate responsibility and attacks on the failure of big business to serve the people. There have always been unresolved contradictions in Hailey's fiction (which permitted *Wheels,* for example, to be read both as an attack on the Big Three automakers and as a defense of them), but in these books the irresolution is particularly disturbing.

Although still a popular writer, Hailey's command of the best-seller market was no longer so complete as it had been, and he announced his retirement after *Overload.* However, the experience of a complicated quadruple-bypass operation at the Texas Heart Institute moved him to write an-

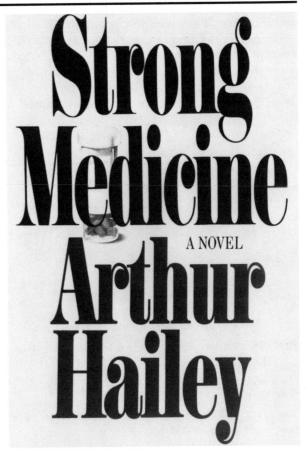

*Dust jacket for Hailey's novel about the
pharmaceutical industry*

other novel. The result, *Strong Medicine* (1984), is an inside look at the pharmaceutical industry that largely follows the pattern he had used since *Wheels.* Its one difference is that the plot of *Strong Medicine*–a story of social upheaval brought about by the marketing of a memory drug that seems to increase the libido and also act as a perfect diet pill–moves more in the direction of science fiction than Hailey's work had previously. Despite the sensational quality of the events it describes, this novel is somewhat subdued in tone and functions mainly as a screed on the dangers of the American drug industry and the difficulties of regulating it. Although lacking the drama of *Airport* or the glossy attractions of *Hotel,* this latest novel by Hailey remained on the *New York Times* best-seller list for twenty weeks. Hailey has recently completed another novel, *The Evening News,* dealing with television news and terrorism and scheduled for publication on 5 April 1990, Hailey's seventieth birthday.

It may ultimately be as irrelevant to criticize Hailey for his plotting as it is to fault him for stylistic blunders. The most important thing to observe about the body of work he has created is that, in a time when literary and popular writing were far apart, Arthur Hailey, perhaps more than any other writer of his generation, gave a large general audience the stories they wanted to hear and told those stories in the way that audiences wanted to hear them.

Reference:

Sheila Hailey, *I Married a Best Seller* (Garden City, N.Y.: Doubleday, 1978).

Christie Harris
(21 November 1907-)

J. Kieran Kealy
University of British Columbia

BOOKS: *Cariboo Trail* (Toronto & New York: Longmans, Green, 1957);

Once upon a Totem (New York: Atheneum, 1963; Toronto: McClelland & Stewart, 1973);

You Have to Draw the Line Somewhere (New York: Atheneum, 1964);

West with the White Chiefs (New York: Atheneum, 1965);

Raven's Cry (Toronto: McClelland & Stewart, 1966; New York: Atheneum, 1966);

Confessions of a Toe Hanger (New York: Atheneum, 1967);

Forbidden Frontier (New York: Atheneum, 1968);

Let X Be Excitement (Toronto: McClelland & Stewart, 1968; New York: Atheneum, 1969);

Figleafing through History: The Dynamics of Dress, by Harris and Moira Johnston (New York: Atheneum, 1971);

Secret in the Stlalakum Wild (Toronto: McClelland & Stewart, 1972; New York: Atheneum, 1972);

Mule Lib, by Harris and Thomas Arthur Harris (Toronto: McClelland & Stewart, 1972);

Once More upon a Totem (Toronto: McClelland & Stewart, 1973; New York: Atheneum, 1973);

Sky Man on the Totem Pole? (Toronto: McClelland & Stewart, 1975; New York: Atheneum, 1975);

Mouse Woman and the Vanished Princesses (Toronto: McClelland & Stewart, 1976; New York: Atheneum, 1976);

Christie Harris (Vancouver Sun photo)

Mouse Woman and the Mischief-Makers (Toronto: McClelland & Stewart, 1977; New York: Atheneum, 1977; London: Macmillan, 1978);

Mystery at the Edge of Two Worlds (Toronto: McClelland & Stewart, 1978; New York: Atheneum, 1978);

Mouse Woman and the Muddleheads (Toronto: McClelland & Stewart, 1979; New York: Atheneum, 1979; London: Macmillan, 1980);

The Trouble with Princesses (Toronto: McClelland & Stewart, 1980; New York: Atheneum, 1980);

The Trouble with Adventurers (Toronto: McClelland & Stewart, 1982; New York: Atheneum, 1982).

PERIODICAL PUBLICATIONS: "In Tune with Tomorrow," *Canadian Literature*, 78 (Autumn 1978): 26-30;
"The Shift from Feasthouse to Book," *Canadian Children's Literature*, 31 / 32 (1983): 9-11.

Like Mouse Woman, her most celebrated creation, Christie Harris has spent a lifetime teaching the young, telling story after story about what she has learned from her own experiences, from the history of the early Canadian West, and, most significant, from the legends of the Northwest Coast Indians.

Born in Newark, New Jersey, in 1907, she immigrated to Canada in 1908, settling with her Irish parents, Edward and Matilda Christie Irwin, in a log-cabin homestead in British Columbia's Lower Fraser Valley. She began her literary career as a high-school student, submitting news and children's items to various local newspapers. Though her marriage to Thomas Arthur Harris in February 1932 concluded her brief career as a schoolteacher, she continued to write, contributing, for more than twenty-five years, hundreds of radio scripts to the CBC, often using the domestic crises of her five children as her subject matter. In 1957 she converted one of her radio serials into fictional form and published, at the age of fifty, her first book, *Cariboo Trail*, the story of the adventures faced by a young girl, Maeve Hawthorne, and her family during their westward trek to Cariboo gold.

This particular period of Canadian history also dominates two later historical novels, *West with the White Chiefs* (1965), a fictionalized account of the crossing of the Rockies in 1863 by Viscount Milton and Dr. W. B. Cheadle, and *Forbidden Frontier* (1968), a sympathetic exploration of the inevitable conflict between white gold-seekers and the half-Indian, half-white world they invaded. Harris focuses specifically on the effect this conflict has on two children: Alison Steward, a rebellious girl who refuses to deny her Indian heritage, and a white child, Megan Scully.

Dust jacket for the first American edition of Harris's second collection of "recreated" Indian legends associated with figures carved on totem poles

Harris's historical narratives are complemented, in a sense, by her fictional biographies of her own children, *You Have to Draw the Line Somewhere* (1964), *Confessions of a Toe Hanger* (1967), and *Let X Be Excitement* (1968). The best of these is the first, an episodic description of her oldest daughter's quest to become a fashion artist. Though Harris's historical fictions are often criticized because of their lack of believable characters, these stories do contain a humor and vitality that clearly differentiate them from traditional children's stories of this type.

Unarguably, Harris's most successful historical fiction is *Raven's Cry* (1966). The result of years of research, it rages against the white man's consistently unfeeling treatment of the people and culture of the Haida Nation. Specifically, Harris presents a fictionalized biography of the last three great Haida chieftains, describing their hopeless battle to preserve their culture against the white man's liquor, laws, and God. Though some have criticized her history as unnecessarily one-sided, one cannot deny the impact of the final scenes, in which Bill Reid suddenly, through the intervention of his dead great-uncle, Charles Edenshaw, rediscovers his past and begins to carve totem poles, thus resurrecting a culture precariously close to extinction.

Harris's fascination with the culture of the Northwest Coast Indians is also evident in her collections of "recreated" Indian legends. *Once upon a Totem* (1963) and *Once More upon a Totem* (1973), for example, collect tales traditionally associated with figures found on totem poles, each legend including a brief historical introduction that explores the culture of the people who told the stories, reminding the reader that "each figure on a totem pole was a potent image, as meaningful and inspiring to the one who owned it as was a coat-of-arms to a knight."

Similarly, her three extremely successful collections, *Mouse Woman and the Vanished Princesses* (1976), *Mouse Woman and the Mischief-Makers* (1977), and *Mouse Woman and the Muddleheads* (1979), tell of that time long ago when "supernatural beings roamed the seas and the vast green wilderness of the Northwest Coast." One of these beings is Mouse Woman, whose delightfully enigmatic presence unifies the somewhat disparate individual legends. *Mouse Woman and the Mischief-Makers* won Harris her second Book of the Year for Children Medal from the Canadian Association of Children's Librarians. She had received her first medal in 1967 for *Raven's Cry*.

The Trouble with Princesses (1980) is the third of Harris's books to win a national book-of-the-year award, in this case the Children's Literature Prize from the Canada Council. This work focuses not on Mouse Woman, but on the problems faced by various New World princesses, problems which, Harris asserts, are often quite similar to those faced by heroines in the European fairy-tale tradition.

Harris's interest in the culture of the Northwest Coast Indians also influences three texts that might generally be categorized as fantasies. *Sky Man on the Totem Pole?* (1975), one of Harris's least critically successful books, considers the possibility that the Man-from-the-Sky of an ancient Indian legend is an extraterrestrial creature. *Secret in the Stlalakum Wild* (1972), in contrast, does not relate individual legends but simply includes the Indian world as part of a traditional maturation novel, telling the story of Morgan Fenn's journey to the mountains of Northern British Columbia

Dust jacket for the first American edition of the second of Harris's three books of tales about Mouse Woman, a supernatural being celebrated in Northwest Indian lore

where, through the assistance of Siem, one of the Stlalakum spirits, she both comes to a better understanding of her own importance and learns that the true treasure of this mysterious place is not its hidden gold, but its natural beauty.

Though the title of *Mystery at the Edge of Two Worlds* (1978) promises a story similar to *Secret in the Stlalakum Wild*, it is actually little more than a traditional girl's adventure story, concluding with a conventional confrontation with a gang of smugglers. And yet this title does suggest what is probably Harris's most significant accomplishment for, through her sympathetic portraits of the Indian and his culture, she has helped her audience understand the mysteries that lie just at the edge of the white man's world. As Susan Wood says of Harris in a 1980 article for *Canadian Children's Literature:* "her gift is to make us regard our own world through Indians' eyes, and with, perhaps, something of their reverence." Harris's most recent collection of Indian tales, *The Trouble with Adventurers*, was published in 1982 and acts as a companion piece to *The Trouble with Princesses*.

Christie Harris was made a member of the Order of Canada in 1981. She is working on a text that she simply says is completely different from anything she has done before. Quite clearly, Canada's honored and prolific storyteller has more tales to tell.

References:

Sheila Egoff, *The Republic of Childhood* (Toronto: Oxford, 1975), pp. 24-27, 73-75;

Gwyneth Evans, "Mouse Woman and Mrs. Harris," *Canadian Children's Literature*, no. 31 / 32 (1983): 53-62;

Kenneth Radu, "Canadian Fantasy," *Canadian Children's Literature*, 1, no. 2 (Summer 1975): 73-79;

Susan Wood, "Stories and Stlalakums: Christie Harris and the Supernatural World," *Canadian Children's Literature*, no. 15 / 16 (1980): 47-56.

Papers:

Manuscripts and notes by Harris are at the University of Calgary Library.

Jean-Charles Harvey

(10 November 1891-3 January 1967)

Paul Matthew St. Pierre
Simon Fraser University

BOOKS: *La Chasse aux millions: L'Avenir industriel du Canada-français* (Quebec: Crédit Industriel, 1921);

Marcel Faure (Montmagny, Que.: Imprimerie de Montmagny, 1922);

Pages de critique sur quelques aspects de la littérature française au Canada (Quebec: Le Soleil, 1926);

L'Homme qui va . . . : Contes et nouvelles (Quebec: Le Soleil, 1929);

Les Demi-Civilisés (Montreal: Totem, 1934); translated by Lukin Barette as *Sackcloth for Banner* (Toronto: Macmillan, 1938);

Sébastien Pierre: Nouvelles (Lévis, Que.: Editions du Quotidien, 1935);

Jeunesse (Quebec: Editions de Vivre, 1935);

Art et combat (Montreal: Action Canadienne-Française, 1937);

French Canada at War (Toronto: Macmillan, 1941);

Les Grenouilles demandent un roi (Montreal: Editions du Jour, 1943); translated by Harvey as *The Eternal Struggle: The Truceless Conflict Between the Rights of the Individual and the Forces of Despotism* (Toronto: Forward, 1943);

L'U.R.S.S.: Paradis des dupes (Montreal: La Patrie, 1945); translated as *U.S.S.R.: A Fool's Paradise* (Montreal: La Patrie, 1947);

Les Armes du mensonge (Montreal: La Patrie, 1945); translated as *The Weapons of Falsehood* (Montreal: La Patrie, 1945?);

L'Epidémie des grèves (Montreal: La Patrie, 1945);

Les Paradis de sable (Quebec: Institut Littéraire du Québec, 1953);

La Fille du silence (Montreal: Editions d'Orphée, 1958);

Pourquoi je suis antiséparatiste (Montreal: Editions de l'Homme, 1962);

Visages du Québec (Montreal: Cercle du Livre de France, 1964); translated by Alta Lind Cook as *The Many Faces of Quebec* (Toronto: Macmillan, 1966);

Des bois, des champs, des bêtes (Montreal: Editions de l'Homme, 1965).

Jean-Charles Harvey, drawing by J.-Arthur Le May for Le May's book Milles Têtes

PERIODICAL PUBLICATIONS: "Rénovation de l'art religieux," *Le Canada*, 16 June 1936, p. 2;

"L'Ile enchantée," *Le Canada*, 4 August 1936, p. 2;

"Opinion canadienne sur le roman," *Liberté*, 6 (November-December 1964): 441-451.

Jean-Charles Harvey, who exploited his articles and stories to mainly political, nonliterary ends, has assumed a special historical significance among francophone and, increasingly, among anglophone Canadians because of his anticipation of three important themes in Quebecois life during the 1960s, 1970s, and 1980s: economic independence, moral and spiritual liberation, and separatist debate. A prophet of the still-emerging modern Quebec, he recognized the inseparability of socioeconomic and political ethics and realized that idealistic fiction and practical journalism could serve both didactic and provocative ends. His literary reputation rests largely on three novels, but it was informed by his sometimes stormy tenures with a succession of newspapers, echoing Quebec's own restlessness which culminated in the outburst of the 1960s Quiet Revolution of Premier Jean Lesage. That Harvey's reputation could not rest entirely comfortably in René Lévesque's separatist Quebec (1976-1985) suggests something of his ideological shortsightedness and his cultural anachronism, but also the surprising influence that his ideas continue to have on *la francophonie du Québec*, an influence that may one day bring his work back into sharp focus and clear synchronization within Quebec's postreferendum cultural evolution.

Jean-Charles Harvey was born 10 November 1891 at La Malbaie (Murray Bay), Quebec, to John Harvey, a carpenter, and Mina Trudel Harvey. His early years were marked by a family sojourn in Massachusetts (1894-1896), the premature death of his father (1897), and his enrollment in the minor seminary at Chicoutimi, where he received his secondary schooling from 1905 to 1908. When the Harvey family moved to Montreal in 1908, Jean-Charles continued his priestly studies for the next six years with the Jesuits, studying the classical humanities, receiving his baccalaureate, and finally making his simple vows as a Jesuit in 1910. Eventually, however, Harvey became disenchanted with his vocation. He left the Society of Jesus in 1915, and, after two months of intellectual soul-searching at the Université Laval in Quebec City, he pursued two wholly new vocations: journalism and marriage. He joined the staff of *La Patrie* as a reporter, moving to *La Presse* the following year. Also in 1916 he married Marie-Anne Dufour, who bore him three daughters before her death in 1921. With his second wife, Germaine Miville-Deschênes, whom he married in 1922, he had four sons, thus achieving in his life a kind of biological duality to complement his earlier spiritual one. Even professionally his life had a dual nature: in 1922

he moved from his job as an information officer with the Machine Agricole Nationale (National Farm Machinery Company) of Montmagny, Quebec, to an editorial position with the Montreal newspaper *Le Soleil*. It was the collapse of National Farm Machinery that inspired Harvey to write his first novel, *Marcel Faure* (1922). Ironically, this misfortune launched the most fruitful of his endeavors as a man of ideas and inaugurated the most controversial of all his careers.

Whereas Harvey enjoyed the publicity surrounding *Marcel Faure*, with its innovative theme of economic independence for Quebec, the publication of *Les Demi-Civilisés* (1934; translated as *Sackcloth for Banner*, 1938), with its provocative theme of moral liberation from church authority and tradition, initially brought him only misfortune. Just twenty days after the novel's appearance, the Roman Catholic church printed an official condemnation of *Les Demi-Civilisés*; Cardinal Jean-Marie-Rodrigue Villeneuve placed it on the index of forbidden books on 26 April 1934. In the aftermath of this scandal, *Le Soleil* fired Harvey from the position as editor in chief, which he had assumed in 1927. In contrast to the passionate reception of his first two novels, the appearance of two fine volumes of short stories, *L'Homme qui va* (The Man Who Goes, 1929) and *Sébastien Pierre* (1935), drew considerably less attention, although the former earned Harvey the Prix David. If to be anti-imperialist in *Marcel Faure* was challenging and to be anticlerical in *Les Demi-Civilisés* was heterodox, to be antiseparatist, as Harvey was in his next novel, *Les Paradis de sable* (Paradise of Sand, 1953), had a certain historical appropriateness, anticipating as it did the rise and the fall of the Parti Québécois.

Harvey maintained his staunch antiseparatist position throughout his life: in his journalistic career as editor of *Le Jour* (which he founded in 1937 and edited until 1946), as a news commentator with Radio-Canada (1946-1953), and as a technical director with *Le Petit Journal* and *Le Photo Journal* (1953-1966); and in his literary career, in several collections of articles and commentary: *Les Grenouilles demandent un roi* (1943; translated as *The Eternal Struggle: The Truceless Conflict Between the Rights of the Individual and the Forces of Despotism*, 1943), *L'U.R.S.S.: Paradis des dupes* (1945; translated as *U.S.S.R.: A Fool's Paradise*, 1947), *Les Armes du mensonge* (1945; translated as *The Weapons of Falsehood*, 1945?), and most notably *Pourquoi je suis antiséparatiste* (Why I Am Antiseparatist, 1962).

Front covers for Harvey's two story collections. L'Homme qui va . . . *earned the author the 1929 Prix David.*

In 1965 Harvey, separated from his second wife since the late 1930s, married Evangéline Pelland. That same year, when he published his third short-story collection, *Des bois, des champs, des bêtes* (Woods, Fields, Beasts), he in effect consolidated his contribution to the "conte" tradition of Quebecois storytelling, somewhat in the manner associated with Jacques Ferron. But he articulated his attitudes to francophone narrative modes and to the politics of art even more clearly in two relatively early works: *Pages de critique sur quelques aspects de la littérature française au Canada* (Critical Pages on Some Aspects of French Literature in Canada, 1926) and *Art et combat* (1937). Here one finds Harvey's manifesto on the art of Quebecois culture. By the time of his death in 1967, Jean-Charles Harvey had won official recognition both in French-speaking and in English-speaking Canada for *Les Demi-Civilisés* and thus reconciled his patrimony with his spirituality and sense of posterity. In 1982 *Fear's Folly*, a new translation by John Glassco of Harvey's best-known work, was pub-

lished by Carleton University Press. In 1988 Les Presses de l'Université de Montréal published a critical edition of *Les Demi-Civilisés*, edited by Guildo Rousseau.

Letters:
La Correspondance étrangère de Jean-Charles Harvey, 1932-1966: Edition critique, edited by Sylvianne Savard Boulanger (Sherbrooke, Que.: Naaman, 1984).

References:
Pierre Chalout, "Jean-Charles Harvey qui fut grand-père de la révolution tranquille," *La Patrie*, 18 February 1956, p. 6;
Roland-M. Charland, "Jean-Charles Harvey," *Lectures*, 12 (September 1965): 3-7;
Luc Dufresne, "Québec chez Harvey et Lemelin," *Parti-Pris*, 2 (May 1965): 31-36;
Marcel-Aimé Gagnon, *Jean-Charles Harvey: Précurseur de la révolution tranquille* (Montreal: Beauchemin, 1970);

Claude-Henri Grignon, "Jean-Charles Harvey sous son vrai jour," *Pamphlets de Valdombre*, 2 (July 1938): 331-375;

Helen Marsh, "Semi-Civilization in Quebec," *Canadian Forum*, 18 (February 1939): 348-349;

John O'Connor, Introduction to Harvey's *Fear's Folly* (*Les Demi-Civilisés*), translated by John Glassco, edited by O'Connor (Ottawa: Carleton University Press, 1982), pp. 1-24;

Guildo Rousseau, Introduction to Harvey's *Les Demi-Civilisés*, edited by Rousseau (Montreal: Presses de l'Université de Montréal, 1988), pp. 7-52;

Rousseau, *Jean-Charles Harvey et son Œuvre romanesque* (Montreal: Centre Educatif et Culturel, 1969);

Jacques Tardif, "Les Demi-Civilisés ou le procès d'une génération," *Le Quartier Latin*, 44 (27 February 1962): 13, 15;

J. S. Will, "Canadian Courage," *Canadian Bookman*, 20 (February-March 1939): 65.

Papers:

Most of Jean-Charles Harvey's manuscripts are held at the Université de Sherbrooke, Quebec.

Gilles Hénault
(1 August 1920-)

Richard Giguère
Université de Sherbrooke

BOOKS: *Théâtre en plein air* (Montreal: Cahiers de la File Indienne, 1946);

Totems, illustrated by Albert Dumouchel (Montreal: Erta, 1953); translated in part in *Seven Poems . . .* (1955);

Voyage au pays de mémoire, illustrated by Marcelle Ferron (Montreal: Erta, 1959);

Sémaphore, suivi de Voyage au pays de mémoire (Montreal: Editions de l'Hexagone, 1962);

Signaux pour les voyants: Poèmes 1941-1962 (Montreal: Editions de l'Hexagone, 1972); selections republished, with English translations, *Ellipse*, 18 (1976): 8-61;

A l'inconnue nue (Montreal: Parti Pris, 1984).

OTHER: "La Poésie et la vie," in *La Poésie et nous*, by Hénault, Michel van Schendel, Jacques Brault, Wilfrid Lemoine, and Yves Préfontaine (Montreal: Editions de l'Hexagone, 1958), pp. 29-41;

"Tu m'exorcises," in *Un Siècle de littérature canadienne/A Century of Canadian Literature*, edited by Guy Sylvestre and H. Gordon Green (Montreal: HMH / Toronto: Ryerson, 1967), pp. 540-541;

"La Poésie est mot de passe," in *Littérature du Québec: Poésie actuelle*, revised and enlarged edition, edited by Guy Robert (Montreal: Déom, 1970), pp. 71-81;

John Glassco, ed., *The Poetry of French Canada in Translation*, includes poems by Hénault (Toronto: Oxford University Press, 1970);

David Fennano, *Without a Parachute*, translated by Hénault as *Sans parachute* (Montreal: Parti Pris, 1977);

Darko Survin, *Pour une poétique de la Science-fiction: Etudes en théorie et en histoire d'une genre littéraire*, translated by Hénault (Montreal: Presses de l'Université du Québec, 1977);

Emile Nelligan après cent ans, 1879-1979, includes a contribution by Hénault (Montreal: Grainier, 1979);

Roland Giguère, *A l'orée de l'œil*, introductory text by Hénault (Montreal: Noroît, 1981).

The importance of Gilles Hénault and his role as a pioneer of the surreal in Quebec literature no longer need to be demonstrated. Along with Claude Gauvreau, Paul-Marie Lapointe, and Roland Giguère, he was one of the first to introduce automatic writing and the surrealist aes-

Gilles Hénault (photograph by Kèro)

thetic into French-Canadian poetry during the 1940s; he was also among the first to signal the direction that contemporary Quebec poets were to follow. Hénault wrote works of protest and demands for social justice, poems of dissent which influenced not only the generation of Hexagone writers during the 1950s, but the poets of the 1960s and 1970s as well. He set the example of a poet who did not confine himself to writing in a vacuum but who ventured into the world.

Joseph-Paul-Gilles-Robert Hénault, the son of Octavien and Edouardine Joyal Hénault, was born in Saint-Majorique, a village in Drummond County, one hundred kilometers east of Montreal, in 1920. While he was still very young his family moved to Montreal, where he lived in the very modest circumstances of a working-class household. Upon completing his primary and secondary educations, in which he achieved notable success in the sciences, he was awarded a scholarship to the Collège Mont-Saint-Louis, but the financial difficulties which beset his family during

the Depression forced him to give up his studies, although eventually he took courses in the social sciences at the Université de Montréal. For a few years he was unemployed or held a variety of small jobs, but he eventually learned the trade of newspaperman while working on Jean-Charles Harvey's daily *Le Jour* in the late 1930s. Journalism would henceforth occupy a substantial part of his life, at *Le Canada* and at *La Presse*, and eventually as a news writer for Radio-Canada and for station CKAC. Married, he and his wife have two children, sons born in 1943 and 1950.

Hénault had become persona non grata in Quebec because of his union activities and his political commitment. He worked in turn at half a dozen unions in the Montreal area, but it was particularly as a member of the Canadian Communist party from 1946 to 1950 that he attracted suspicion. He spent the years 1949 to 1956 in Sudbury and Blind River in northern Ontario, where he took several jobs working for the miners' unions. Upon returning to Montreal in 1957 he worked for different periodicals as critic of the arts, chiefly painting but also theater, cinema, and television. Beginning in 1959 he acted as literary and art editor of *Le Devoir*, finally becoming foreign-policy columnist for *Le Nouveau Journal* in 1961.

It was Hénault's intellectual preoccupations as well as his concerns as a militant unionist which inspired his first writings. Toward the end of the 1930s, the period which saw the publication of his first poems in *Le Jour*, he spent his periods of unemployment at the Montreal City Library. At the age of eighteen he was reading Rimbaud, Verhaeren, Maeterlinck, and later he turned to Mallarmé, Saint-John Perse, and especially Valéry, who was the inspiration for his ambitious poem "L'Invention de la roue" (The Invention of the Wheel), written in 1941, published in *La Nouvelle Relève* in October of that year, and collected in *Signaux pour les voyants* (Signals for Seers, 1972). From the outset Hénault's poetry aimed at an objective from which he was never to swerve: the attempt to reconcile knowledge which has its source in the domain of science with that which is acquired through the eyes of the poet.

During World War II Hénault became increasingly active in contributing to reviews such as *La Nouvelle Relève*, *Amérique Française*, *Gants du ciel*, in which he published poems, feature articles, and regular columns. It was during this time that two events conspired to give a decisive orientation to his poetry. First, he discovered the poetry of Guillaume Apollinaire, Paul Eluard, and Louis Aragon and the theoretical writings of André Breton and Jean-Paul Sartre; he then met the intellectual leader, painter, and essayist Paul-Emile Borduas and Borduas's disciples, known as the automatist painters (Leduc, Mousseau, and Riopelle, among others), as well as the art critics Robert Elie and Guy Viau. It was then that he first experimented with the technique of automatic writing, but no one was willing to publish the work he submitted, so in 1946, along with Eloi de Grandmont, he founded Les Cahiers de la File Indienne, which published the first collection of his works.

The reason for the impact of *Théâtre en plein air* (Open-air Theater, 1946) on Quebec poetry of the immediate postwar period is that in this collection Hénault experimented in two areas which had been known in France since the advent of the surrealists but which were new to Quebec: automatic writing and increasing attention to

dreams and to the role of the unconscious in the language of poetry. In the matter of the structure and wording of his poems, he declared during a 1977 interview with Hugues Corriveau (published in *Gilles Hénault: Lecture de "Sémaphore,"* 1978): "je pensais d'abord au thème, ainsi qu'aux premiers vers, au rythme et j'intuitionnais probablement la fin. Je ne les corrigeais pas non plus. Je ne les ai jamais corrigés. . . . Mais en général, j'écrivais un poème sous une dictée impérieuse . . ." (first of all, I thought of the theme, the first few verses, the rhythm, and I probably knew intuitively what the ending would be. I didn't correct my work. . . . But in general, I wrote a poem under an overmastering compulsion . . .). As for content, Hénault rejected a decadent world and proclaimed the birth of a new humanity and a new era, all the while crying out in anger and rebellion, as did Paul-Marie Lapointe in *Le Vierge incendié* (The Virgin Burned, 1948) and Roland Giguère in *Faire naître* (Bringing to Birth, 1949) and *Yeux fixes* (Fixed Stare, 1951). This new age, this "âge de la parole" or word, this search for the unsullied and the primitive were in large part inspired by the primal and invigorating sensations that characterized the surrealist venture. This attempt to return to a basic harmony between man and nature, between the intuitive or instinctive and the reasoned, between the primitive and the civilized constitutes the main purpose not only of *Théâtre en plein air* but of Hénault's entire poetic output as well.

Hénault's cries of revolt became even more insistent with "Dix poèmes de dissidence" (Ten Poems of Dissent), written during the years 1945-1949 and 1959-1963 and collected in *Signaux pour les voyants*. In these he repudiates the nostalgia and the traditional resistance to change that for him characterize the Quebec heart; he calls for rejection of the image of the French-Canadian as Catholic, obedient, and submissive; and he appeals, as in the poem "Bordeaux-sur bagne," to the coming of " . . . l'homme international surgi du miroir ardent /d'un prolétaire soudé à la terre, au marteau, à la mine" (the international man, sprung from the fiery mirror / of a proletarian bound to the land, to the hammer, to the mine). The poet proclaims, in "Camarades," solidarity with the Communist guerrillas in Greece and with the comrades in China to sing of the "marche immense," "la montée, la marée," "la terre ébranlée" (the great leap forward, the ascent, the rising tide, the shaken earth), in a word, the revolution. This period in Hénault's life was

 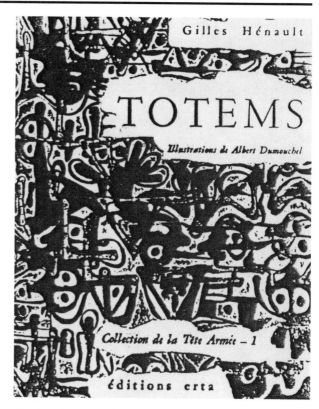

Front covers for Hénault's first two poetry collections (courtesy of Kenneth Landry)

that of his militant unionism in Montreal, of his first reading of the *Communist Manifesto,* and of his joining the Canadian Communist Party. It likewise saw the publication of the manifesto *Refus global* (*Total Refusal,* 1948), by Borduas and his friends, attacking the role of capitalism and the Catholic Church in assuring the submission of Quebec.

In an interview with Philippe Haeck, Jean-Marc Piotte, and Patrick Straram (*Chroniques,* January 1975), Hénault declared that it was with the publication of *Totems,* his second collection, in 1953 that he gave further scope to problems. With *Totems* the task of the writer and the purpose of writing become more precise. The writer's task consists of arousing the consciences of others in order to stimulate change. The purpose of writing is to prolong awareness, what Mayakovski called the "social imperative." Irony stands at the center of *Totems* and is especially important for Hénault because it destroys from within and serves as the basis for a kind of subversive poetry.

Hénault's *Voyage au pays de mémoire* (Journey to the Land of Memory), which appeared in 1959, explores more deeply the themes of dreams, of the possible, of utopia. The images of

underground exploration and interior exploration impart strength to poems such as "No Man's Land," "Bestiaire" (Bestiary), "Fusée" (Rocket), and "Le Jeu de l'amour" (The Game of Love), coupling intuition with scientific knowledge and validating again the power of dreams. In 1962 *Sémaphore* was published in an edition that also included *Voyage au pays de mémoire.* Hugues Corriveau in 1978 called the long poem "Sémaphore" a "texte particulièrement propice à notre pénétration du langage et du monde de Hénault" (work particularly apt to help us penetrate Hénault's language and poetic world). Here, in fact, Hénault comes closest to his poetic ideal, as he expressed it in 1977: poetry that is "très simple et directe, un peu comme la parole courante.... Je voudrais que mes poèmes deviennent des clichés, qu'ils soient faits comme des clichés, qu'ils offrent cette simplicité et cette organisation complexe de la parole, comme image, comme métaphore" (very simple and direct, something like the spoken word.... I want my poems to be clichés, to be made like clichés, to offer that simplicity and the complex organization that comes from language, as image, as metaphor).

Sémaphore won the Prix du Grand Jury des Lettres and second prize in the Concours Littéraires du Québec. In 1966 Hénault was named director of the Montreal Museum of Contemporary Art, and in 1971 he was appointed museum adviser with the Department of Cultural Affairs. In 1972 he published *Signaux pour les voyants*, a retrospective including poems written from 1941 to 1962, which earned him a Governor General's Award. His 1984 volume, *A l'inconnue nue* (To the Unknown Naked Woman), indicates his continuing preoccupation with the power of the word and its independence from referentiality. Hénault was writer in residence at the Université d'Ottawa in 1974-1975; he has also directed writers' workshops at the Université du Québec à Montréal and served as a member of the editorial board for the magazine *Possible*.

If Hénault wrote a type of poetry which was too innovative to obtain favorable reviews during the latter half of the 1940s, he nevertheless won the ear of the young poets of the 1950s. Those young poets were Roland Giguère, who published two of Hénault's books, *Totems* and *Voyage au pays de mémoire*, at his Editions Erta, and Louis Portugais and Gaston Miron of the Editions de l'Hexagone, who published Hénault's essay "La Poésie et la vie" (in *La Poésie et nous*, 1958), as well as *Signaux pour les voyants* and *Sémaphore*. In the 1960s, as the Quiet Revolution in Quebec gathered force, Michel Van Schendel and Gilles Marcotte praised Hénault's poetry, and in 1969, in a special issue of *La Barre du Jour*, Hénault was classified among Les Automatistes.

During the 1970s, after the publication of his award-winning collected poems, university reviews recognized his works. The 1975 interview by Haeck, Piotte, and Straram confirmed the importance of Hénault as a writer not only for his own generation but also for the next generation of poets–the moving spirits behind such magazines as *La Nouvelle Barre du Jour*, *Les Herbes Rouges*, and *Chroniques*–who formed the literary and intellectual avant-garde during the 1970s in Quebec. In 1981 he collaborated with Ronald Giguère in producing *A l'orée de l'œil* (On the Edge of the Eye). He currently lives in Montreal.

References:

Hugues Corriveau, *Gilles Hénault: Lecture de "Sémaphore"* (Montreal: Presses de l'Université de Montréal, 1978);

Jean Fisette, "Gilles Hénault: Between Simplification and Analogy," *Ellipse*, 18 (1976): 62-71;

Philippe Haeck, Jean-Marc Piotte, and Patrick Straram, "Entretien avec Gilles Hénault– 30 ans après le *Refus Global*," *Chroniques*, 1 (January 1975): 12-26;

Laurent Mailhot, "La Poésie de Gilles Hénault," *Voix et Images du Pays*, 8 (1974): 149-161;

Gilles Marcotte, "Gilles Hénault," in his *Le Temps des poètes: Description critique de la poésie actuelle au Canada français* (Montreal: HMH, 1969), pp. 85-89;

Michel Van Schendel, "Poésie québécoise 1960-1965," *Livres et Auteurs Canadiens, 1965* (Montreal: Jumonville, 1966), 13-22.

Harold Adams Innis

(5 November 1894-8 November 1952)

William Christian
University of Guelph

BOOKS: *A History of the Canadian Pacific Railway* (London: King / Toronto: McClelland & Stewart, 1923);

The Fur-Trade of Canada (Toronto: University of Toronto Library, 1927);

The Fur Trade in Canada: An Introduction to Canadian Economic History (New Haven: Yale University Press / London: Oxford University Press, 1930);

Peter Pond: Fur Trader and Adventurer (Toronto: Irwin & Gordon, 1930);

Problems of Staple Production in Canada (Toronto: Ryerson, 1933);

Settlement and the Mining Frontier (Toronto: Macmillan, 1936);

The Cod Fisheries: The History of an International Economy (New Haven: Yale University Press / Toronto: Ryerson, 1940);

Political Economy and the Modern State (Toronto: Ryerson, 1946);

Engineering and Society, part 1 by C. R. Young, part 2 by Innis and J. E. Dales (Toronto: University of Toronto Press, 1946);

Empire and Communications (Oxford: Clarendon Press, 1950);

The Bias of Communication (Toronto: University of Toronto Press, 1951);

Changing Concepts of Time (Toronto: University of Toronto Press, 1952);

Essays in Canadian Economic History, edited by M. Q. Innis (Toronto: University of Toronto Press, 1956);

The Idea File of Harold Adams Innis, edited by William Christian (Toronto & Buffalo: University of Toronto Press, 1980);

Innis on Russia: The Russian Diary and Other Writings, edited by William Christian (Toronto: Harold Innis Foundation, 1981).

OTHER: Henry Laurys, *The Foreign Trade of Canada,* translated by Innis and Alexander H. Smith (Toronto: Macmillan, 1929);

Harold Adams Innis

Select Documents in Canadian Economic History, 1497-1783, edited by Innis (Toronto: University of Toronto Press, 1929);

Select Documents in Canadian Economic History, 1783-1885, edited by Innis and A. R. M. Lower (Toronto: University of Toronto Press, 1933);

The Canadian Economy and Its Problems: Papers and Proceedings of Study Groups of Members of the Canadian Institute of International Affairs, 1933-1934, edited by Innis and A. F. W.

Plumptre (Toronto: Canadian Institute of International Affairs, 1934);

J. A. Ruddick, W. M. Drummond, R. E. English, and J. E. Lattimer, *The Dairy Industry in Canada*, edited by Innis (Toronto: Ryerson /New Haven: Yale University Press, 1937);

Labor in Canadian-American Relations: The History of Labor Interactions, by Norman J. Ware; Labor Costs and Labor Standards, by H. A. Logan, edited by Innis (Toronto: Ryerson / New Haven: Yale University Press, 1937);

Essays in Political Economy in Honour of E. J. Urwick, edited by Innis (Toronto: University of Toronto Press, 1938);

The Japanese Canadians, by Charles H. Young and Helen R. Y. Reid, with a Second Part on Oriental Standards of Living by W. A. Carrothers, edited by Innis (Toronto: University of Toronto Press, 1938);

The Diary of Alexander James McPhail, edited by Innis (Toronto: University of Toronto Press, 1940);

Essays in Transportation in Honour of W. T. Jackman, edited by Innis (Toronto: University of Toronto Press, 1941);

The Diary of Simeon Perkins, 1766-1780, edited, with an introduction and notes, by Innis (Toronto: Champlain Society, 1948).

During the last decade or so of his life, Harold Innis was undoubtedly the single most influential academic figure in Canada. Trained as an economic historian, he became interested in economic geography and during the later years of his life in the study of communications as a tool for understanding political stability and cultural creativity. Aside from his publications Innis exerted tremendous influence through his position as head of the University of Toronto's Department of Political Economy; later he was also dean of the graduate school.

Although Innis eventually made a reputation which placed him in the forefront of his contemporary economic historians and made him welcome in such diverse centers of learning as Chicago, Oxford, and Moscow, the atmosphere in which he was raised was more rustic than sophisticated. Innis was born on 5 November 1894 on a farm near Otterville, Ontario. Both his mother, Mary Adams, and his father, William Innis, were strict Baptists, but Harold Innis, even as a child, did not believe in belief. Although he felt no need for organized religion he had an intense faith in the supreme importance of the individ-

ual and personal responsibility. He inherited from his parents a Scottish respect for education and hard work, and his mother, who was an amateur painter, brought a touch of delicacy into his rural youth. A feature of farm life that probably influenced Innis's later career was his immediate awareness of the struggle to produce commodities from nature. His first major work would be about trapping and trading and his next about the fisheries.

The province of Ontario provided, under the circumstances, reasonably good education. He first attended a small local school and then spent two years at Otterville High School. Then he transferred to Woodstock High School, in spite of the fact that he had to walk two miles to catch the train for the five-cent eighteen-mile ride each morning. Innis was a good and conscientious student, and after a brief experience teaching school, he decided to pursue his education at McMaster University, a Baptist University then in Toronto, in the same building where his Department of Political Economy was later housed.

He was, at first, lonely and miserable, away from home and far from adequately provided with funds. However, it did not take long for him to demonstrate his talents, and he graduated in May 1916 with a double honors degree in political economy and philosophy. Although he hoped to become a lawyer, he was at graduation a young man whose country was in the midst of a great military conflict. Other of his contemporaries had interrupted their schooling to enlist, and Innis felt that he, too, had a moral duty to fight against German aggression.

His World War I experience affected him profoundly. His leg was severely wounded by shrapnel at Vimy Ridge, and he spent a year in the hospital. He never lost his intellectual and psychological conviction that war made no sense. While recuperating he started his M.A. thesis for McMaster on the subject of the returned soldier. He received the M.A. in 1918. Although still interested in a legal and perhaps a political career, Innis decided to rectify what he considered to be gaps in his knowledge of economics, and he chose another institution with a Baptist heritage, the University of Chicago.

At Chicago, Innis acquired much. First, he earned his Ph.D. degree in 1920, writing his dissertation (which was published in 1923) on the topic of the history of the Canadian Pacific Railway. He had asked his superviser for a Canadian topic, and this choice was to prove of great significance for the future economic history of his native land. The second important influence of the University of Chicago was more general. There he made the acquaintance of F. H. Knight who, with other Chicago theoreticians, would contribute to an intellectual framework which, although Innis's own, would always bear the traces of their thought.

Just as important, it was also at Chicago that Innis met and courted Mary Emma Quayle, an American whom he married on 10 May 1921. The marriage gave Innis an opportunity to pursue his career, though it meant that Mary Innis postponed her own literary ambitions while she looked after their four children, two girls, Mary and Anne, and two boys, Hugh and Donald. At the same time as he was settling his private life he was also making important decisions about his professional career. In 1920 he had accepted a position with the University of Toronto in its political economy department. This was to be his academic home for the rest of his life.

The department he joined included not only economics and political science but commerce, geography, sociology, and anthropology as well. This diversity proved fortunate since it allowed Innis's thoughts to range widely without running into institutional disciplinary boundaries. Although he began work on several important minor projects, such as an assessment of the work of Thorstein Veblen, his major task of the 1920s was an economic history of the fur trade. The main text was itself complex and difficult. Innis followed his train of thought wherever it led, and this forced him to speculate about biology (for example, the beaver's breeding habits), geography (the effect of the Canadian Shield and its rivers on transportation), anthropology (European settlement's effects on Indian culture), technology (the invention of steel traps and boats capable of navigating the rivers that flowed into Hudson's Bay), as well as political and economic factors in both Europe and North America.

The Fur Trade in Canada: An Introduction to Canadian Economic History (1930) was a major development of *The Fur-Trade of Canada* (1927), in which Innis had been mainly concerned with assembling primary documents. It marked the creation and application to Canada of what came to be called the staple theory of economic development. This theory was not treated dogmatically by Innis but in his hands served as a tool for analyzing the distinctive character of Canada's development. Innis had been generally concerned that theories imported from advanced and diversified economies such as the British and the American yielded inadequate results when applied to a qualitatively different sort of economy such as Canada's.

Canada had been settled by Europeans whose main concern was to trade with the native Indians for beaver fur which would then be shipped to Europe where it would be felted, mainly for use in the manufacture of hats. A beaver pelt had certain characteristics (it was, for example, relatively light in weight compared to its value) which, given the other prevailing circumstances, permitted the trade to develop in a certain pattern. Innis summarized his approach in the brilliant conclusion to *The Fur Trade in Canada* in which he pointed out that the economic history of Canada had involved a shift from one staple to another, fish, fur, timber, wheat, minerals, and metals, and each one of these shifts had important though unintended consequences which affected a whole range of economic, political, and cultural matters.

However, Innis's argument in this seminal work was more than merely academic. Against the prevailing economic orthodoxy of the 1920s which claimed that Canada was an economic irrationality, Innis countered with the claim that: "Canada emerged as a political entity with boundaries largely determined by the fur trade. These boundaries included a vast north temperate land area extending from the Atlantic to the Pacific and dominated by the Canadian Shield. The present Dominion emerged not in spite of geography but because of it. The significance of the fur trade consisted in its determination of the geographic framework. Later economic developments in Canada were profoundly influenced by this background." It was this argument and others like it that made Innis the hero of the Canadian academic nationalists of the 1960s and 1970s, even among those neo-Marxists who had little sympathy for the moral and political individualism which was such a powerful leitmotiv running through almost everything he wrote.

The decade of the 1930s brought economic depression and misery to many countries and not least of all to Canada, dependent on staple products and having a heavy, fixed capital investment in transportation which became a crushing burden when the volume of goods declined. For Innis, this crisis also posed a serious threat to the universities. Innis revered education and considered it the highest duty of a scholar to pursue his

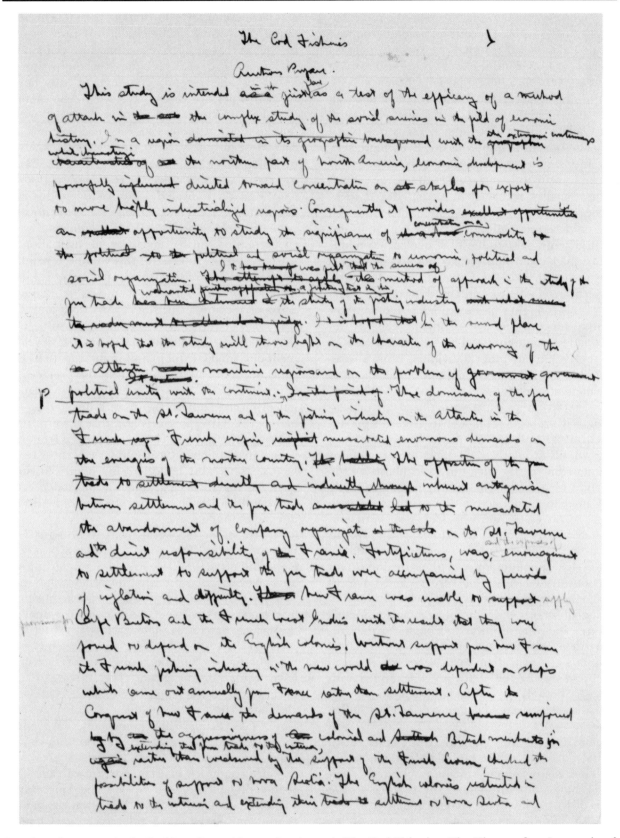

Page from the manuscript for Innis's preface to his second major work, The Cod Fisheries: The History of an International
Economy *(University of Toronto Archives)*

chosen investigation to whatever end the subject itself dictated, without concern for academic boundaries let alone such external pressures as political interference or blandishments from business. Yet Innis saw his colleagues, especially those who supported the newly created social democratic Cooperative Commonwealth Federation (CCF), all too ready to speak out publicly on issues which they had not studied thoroughly. Even more serious, they let their political worries influence their research activities and concentrated on short-term remedies rather than taking the time to probe more deeply. During this time Innis led both by example and by his direct criticisms and chastisements. His studies of Canadian economic history had given him certain important insights into the nature of the Canadian economy, and on such matters he was prepared to speak. Otherwise Innis thought that no academic should allow political concerns, no matter how pressing, to deflect him from the course of his scholarship. Probably more than any other individual, Innis was responsible for the relative political detachment of Canadian academics.

In 1937 he was chosen to head his department, having been promoted to associate professor in 1929 and to full professor in 1936. In spite of his scholarly reputation his promotions did not come easily since Innis's emphasis on the creation of a distinctive paradigm for the study of Canadian economic life did not sit easily with many of his colleagues who had been born and trained in the United Kingdom or the United States. Although he was not by nature an administrator, his appointment was to prove important for both the University of Toronto and for Canada's intellectual development. Innis was the first Canadian scholar to attain international academic stature, and this distinction brought further respect to his department. He was instrumental in founding the Canadian Political Science Association, and during the 1930s he collaborated with James Shotwell as Canadian editor of the Canadian-American relations series. His influence also spread in this period because he was often associated with grant-awarding bodies such as the Carnegie and Rockefeller foundations; in addition, many young academics were dispatched to teaching posts throughout the country on the basis of Innis's favorable recommendation.

During this period Innis was at work on his second influential work in economic history, *The Cod Fisheries*, which appeared in 1940, somewhat delayed as his publisher tried to render Innis's complex writing style into a more palatable presentation. This work solidly established Innis as one of the world's leading economic historians, and his status was quickly recognized when he was selected as the second president of the newly formed American Economic History Association.

From many points of view, this work was a development of themes in *The Fur Trade in Canada*. Most obviously, it continued Innis's analysis of staple products, this time the codfish. Yet it was more, as its subtitle, *The History of an International Economy*, indicated. Innis had begun his conclusion to *The Fur Trade in Canada* with the uncompromising observation that: "Fundamentally the civilization of North America is the civilization of Europe and the interest of this volume is primarily in the effects of a vast new land area on European civilization." Canada, then, was defined as a European country in North America, and *The Cod Fisheries* pursued that analysis to show that the discovery, settlement, and economic development of Canada tied it in important ways to its European origins. As Innis put it in the preface: "It is not too much to say that European civilization left its impress on North America through its demands for staple products and that these in turn affected the success of empires projected from Europe." In addition to the grand scale of these treatments, Innis also indicated his points in such works as his 1930 biography of fur trader Peter Pond and his 1940 edition of the diary of Alexander James McPhail.

The onset of World War II brought him new problems. The most celebrated was the Underhill affair of 1940. Frank H. Underhill was a University of Toronto historian who had strongly anti-British views, and he spoke out publicly against extensive Canadian involvement in the British war effort. These views were not well received by the politicians, and pressure was brought to bear on the university president to have Underhill dismissed. The threat to Underhill and to academic freedom was real, and although Innis thoroughly disapproved of Underhill's actions and viewpoint, he rallied forces within the university and in the United States to defend him.

He continued his close contact with the University of Chicago, and toward the end of the war Chicago tried to hire him away from Toronto. Innis seriously considered the very generous offer but declined for two reasons. First, he felt loyal to the University of Toronto which had supported his research. Second, and probably more emotionally compelling, he remembered that when he had returned after World War I the universities were completely unprepared for the wave of veterans. Innis felt that he and his comrades had been shabbily treated, and he was determined as a debt of honor that he would as best he could make sure that the returned soldiers of World War II would find the universities prepared. Indeed Innis had fought vigorously to prevent drastic cuts in the budgets of Canadian universities which were threatened on the grounds that they contributed little of value to the war effort. It would have been a cruel irony, Innis thought, if a country fighting in the name of civilization narrow-mindedly destroyed one of its central institutions. As part of his war effort, he assembled a collection of his essays, *Political Economy and the Modern State*, and contributed essays to *Engineering and Society*. Both of these works were published in 1946 and meant to serve as textbooks for the returned soldiers.

After V-E Day but before the war against Japan ended, Innis was invited as part of a three-man Canadian delegation to visit the Soviet Union to celebrate the 220th anniversary of the Russian Academy of Sciences. His Russian diary, unpublished until 1981 when it appeared in *Innis on Russia*, shows Innis's brilliant powers of observation and his capacity for creative and fertile speculation. More important, though, it shows a mind that was coming with increasing intensity to wrestle with the crisis he believed Western civilization faced.

As a humanist who admired ancient Greece, Innis thought that it was an urgent matter for Western thinkers to come to terms with Russia. Russia, Innis suggested, had inherited a different strand of classical civilization, and in order to regain the whole of the Greek inheritance it was necessary for the West to acquire an intellectual and emotional understanding of Russia in spite of the great barriers that lay in the way of this undertaking.

It was at this time that Innis began to undertake his most innovative work, the research that leads many to credit him with founding the field of communication studies. First presented in his classes at the University of Toronto, the ideas Innis presented were refined in the Beit lectures delivered at Oxford and subsequently published as *Empire and Communications* (1950). Two essay collections on related matters, *The Bias of Communication* and *Changing Concepts of Time*, appeared in 1951 and 1952. Although the Oxford invitation

was to speak about economic history, Innis justified his change of topic by suggesting "that the subject of communication offers possibilities in that it occupies a crucial position in the organization and administration of government and in turn of empires and Western civilization." Indeed it was the latter that was his real subject. "Civilizations can survive only through a concern with their limitations and in turn through a concern with the limitations of their institutions, including empires."

This topic was to absorb him until his death in 1952. He had been strongly influenced by Charles Cochrane, a colleague in Classics who was the author of *Christianity and Classical Culture* (1940), a work which Innis had been instrumental in getting published. Cochrane's general argument was that the decline in Imperial Rome stemmed in large part from the philosophical inadequacies which had gone into the Augustan settlement. Only with Saint Augustine's synthesis of classical idealism and Christianity was the West provided with a new intellectual framework adequate to sustain a high civilization.

Innis was among those who thought that the philosophic supports of the modern West had increasingly rotted away. Like many others, he had lived through World War I and the economic and social crises of the Depression. He had also witnessed the rise of Bolshevism, National Socialism, and fascism. His fears were not imaginary.

There continues to be controversy about whether Innis's communications studies represented a continuation or a radical departure in his thought. There was certainly a link in that Innis had looked at the staple products of pulp and paper in his studies in economic history and had followed these products from the supply of newsprint in Canada to the demand for them in the United States.

However, this represented only one connection between his early and later work. From his earliest works in the 1920s Innis had infused a moral sense throughout his writings. In *The Fur Trade in Canada* he rejoiced at the failures of the trading monopolies to exert their control, and he particularly admired the fierce independence of the coureurs de bois. As he noted laconically: "Regulations were difficult to enforce under conditions of competition." *The Cod Fisheries* also treated the struggle between individuals and oppressive institutions. A key element in Innis's analysis of the fishing industry off Newfoundland was an appreciation of the ability of fishermen in the West Country of England to raise the small amounts of capital required for fishing boats and to evade the regulations imposed by Parliament and the government.

A key theme that was first explicitly introduced into his work in the 1930s was what he called bias. He had been interested in economic history in the way in which, for example, the fur trade had expanded along the river routes. In this Innis was not suggesting any sort of geographic determinism because he readily recognized that many other forces could be at work affecting the eventual outcome: the character of the staple, political decisions, economic developments, even religious changes. Military factors could also prove decisive. Battles or skirmishes between French and English could be lost or won by luck or a superior military organization whose excellence had little to do with the fur trade. More important, creative human thought could invent new ways of doing things that would substantially alter a balance of forces. Mere human caprice could have a devastating effect, as it did when changes in European fashion undermined the demand for beaver pelts.

The idea of bias became the central concern of his work in the last decade of his life. His concern, though, was now more general. He hoped to analyze the factors present in the media of communication which altered human consciousness and social reality subtly and imperceptibly. His 1947 presidential address to the Royal Society of Canada, "Minerva's Owl" (collected in *The Bias of Communication*), little understood at the time, set the theme of his later works. "I have attempted to suggest that Western civilization has been profoundly influenced by communication and that marked changes in communication have had important implications," he stated.

The study of communication was important because it could have an unfortunate effect on those who were unconscious of its power. As he said in his lecture "The Bias of Communication," which became the 1951 collection's title piece: "We can perhaps assume that the use of a medium of communication over a long period will to some extent determine the character of knowledge to be communicated and suggest that its pervasive influence will eventually create a civilization in which life and flexibility will become exceedingly difficult to maintain and that the advantages of a new medium will become such as to lead to the emergence of a new civilization."

Casting his reflections over all the major civilizations from ancient Egypt to his contemporary world, Innis advanced the hypothesis that the various media of communication influenced the territorial extent and the duration of political organizations. Some media–papyrus, for example–were relatively inexpensive and easy to transport, and these factors facilitated the administration of a far-flung empire. Others, such as the stone tablet or the parchment book, were more expensive, more durable, and more difficult to transport, though these made the transmission of thought through time easier.

Two societies had succeeded in avoiding the domination of one or the other bias, that encouraging control over territory or that facilitating continuity. The only civilization which successfully balanced the two forces was the Byzantine Empire, but this accomplishment did not arise from any sort of social science. Rather it had resulted from an accidental balancing of two media of communication. Eventually even it failed, and its destruction, like the end of any empire, was attended with human misery on a vast scale.

Even in his study of the fur trade Innis had noted the unintended consequences of social change. The lives of the North American Indians had been irrevocably affected by the opportunities afforded by contact with an industrial society. Muskets and metal pots, technologically superior as they were to bows and arrows and clay vessels, were quickly adopted by the Indians. However, they developed a dependency on these products of industrialized Europe, and when the demand for their products disappeared, their resources proved inadequate to sustain them at their new standard or even at the level they had attained before the arrival of the Europeans.

Such consequences always followed in the wake of major cultural disturbances, and those which introduced a new medium of communication were generally the most severe. The general, though not invariable, pattern was as follows. In any mature society there was usually one dominant medium of communication, and control over that medium would be in the hands of some important social group, such as priests, warriors, or merchants. The dominant group would use its monopoly over the means of communication to support its own privileged position, but eventually it would succumb to biases inherent in the medium and would become increasingly rigid and unable to respond to new circumstances.

As this rigidification stifled creativity at the center, the opportunity would present itself to those who were marginal to the civilization to challenge for supremacy. Their confrontation could be military, commercial, religious, or in some other form. But those at the margins, Innis expected, would have a creativity and energy that those at the center lacked. However, no success could be promised or predicted absolutely because, for Innis, human beings were ultimately undetermined.

What Innis thought he had discovered in communications was a factor of human consciousness which had previously been unnoticed. Because it had not been understood, those who had previously escaped its influence had done so more from good luck than anything else. It was now open to human beings for the first time to acknowledge and study the biases of communication and then to take the steps necessary to preserve as large a measure of free consciousness as possible. By becoming aware of the forces that affected consciousness, mankind could strive to create a political organization which would be responsive to the territorial as well as the temporal aspects of its existence. Future societies, aware of the conditions which stimulate creativity, could ensure that they allowed the full development of their citizens. Because they would also be aware of the consequences of changes in the media of communications, they could take the steps necessary to mitigate undesirable consequences.

Innis's work along these lines continued from the end of World War II until his death from cancer at the age of fifty-eight. While developing his analysis of the interpenetration of culture and communications, he continued to be honored for his work in economic history with honorary degrees from the University of Glasgow and four Canadian universities, the University of New Brunswick (1944), McMaster University (1945), Université Laval and the University of Manitoba (1947). He also had added administrative responsibilities; in 1947 he became dean of the University of Toronto's graduate school, and later he served on the Federal Government Royal Commission on Transportation. Visited regularly by friends almost to the end of his life, he worked on his address for the American Economics Association, of which he had been elected the first non-American president.

It is difficult to make an accurate assessment of Innis's influence because his legacy was so varied. Although not without its critics, his sta-ple theory was widely influential during his lifetime and continues to exert an appeal in Canada to the present. Innis is also generally credited as a major figure in the establishment of the field of communication studies, although outside Canada it is his younger University of Toronto colleague Marshall McLuhan who is the better known. Although Innis was undoubtedly a significant influence on McLuhan, the two thinkers differed extensively both in their approaches and in their conclusions. During the late 1960s and 1970s Innis was important to many young Canadian academics who were anti-American and who favored a neo-Marxist interpretation of Canadian politics and economics. They sought in Innis a figure who could legitimate their position within the Canadian intellectual context, but in doing so they were forced either to ignore or to accept Innis's powerful individualism, his fierce hatred of dogma, and his scathing remarks on the baneful effects of nationalism. Their calls for the increasing politicization of the universities also ran directly counter to Innis's view of academia as a haven of detachment from commerce, religion, and politics. It was in Innis's view the only institution in contemporary society which could possibly provide the needed counterbalance to the obsession with the present, a view of time that increasingly threatened to undermine contemporary civilization. "The university must play its major role in the rehabilitation of civilization which we have witnessed in this century by recognizing that western civilization has collapsed."

Few have attempted to match the range and depth of Innis's speculations, as revealed in his collection of reading notes, travel observations, and aphorisms, posthumously published in 1980 as *The Idea File of Harold Adams Innis*. This is not an inappropriate legacy for a man who once observed that it was the search for truth, not truth itself, that sets one free.

Biography:
Donald Creighton, *Harold Adams Innis: Portrait of a Scholar* (Toronto: University of Toronto Press, 1957).

References:
Eric A. Havelock, *Harold A. Innis: A Memoir* (Toronto: Harold Innis Foundation, 1982);
Arthur Kroker, *Technology and the Canadian Mind* (Montreal: New World Perspectives, 1982);

William H. Melody, Liora Salter, and Paul Weyer, eds., *Culture, Communication, and Dependency: The Tradition of H. A. Innis* (Norwood, N.J.: Ablex, 1981);

Robin Neill, *A New Theory of Value* (Toronto & Buffalo: University of Toronto Press, 1972);

Graeme Patterson, "Harold Innis and the Writing of History," *Canadian Literature*, 83 (Winter 1979): 118-130;

John Watson, "Marginal Man: Harold Innis' Communication Works in Context," Ph.D. dissertation, University of Toronto, 1981.

Papers:

The University of Toronto Archives holds Innis's papers.

Mary Quayle Innis

(13 April 1899-10 January 1972)

Barbara Pell
Trinity Western University

BOOKS: *An Economic History of Canada* (Toronto: Ryerson, 1935; revised and enlarged, 1943);

Stand on a Rainbow (Toronto: Collins, 1943; New York: Duell, Sloan & Pearce, 1944);

Unfold the Years: A History of the Young Women's Christian Association in Canada (Toronto: McClelland & Stewart, 1949);

Changing Canada, 2 volumes (Toronto: Clarke, Irwin, 1951-1952);

Living in Canada, by Innis, Alex A. Cameron, and Arnold Boggs (Toronto: Clarke, Irwin, 1954);

Travellers West (Toronto: Clarke, Irwin, 1956).

OTHER: Harold A. Innis, *The Cod Fisheries: The History of an International Economy*, revised, with a preface, by Mary Quayle Innis, S. D. Clark, and W. T. Easterbrook (Toronto: University of Toronto Press, 1954);

Innis, *The Fur Trade in Canada: An Introduction to Canadian Economic History*, revised, with a preface, by Mary Quayle Innis, Clark, and Easterbrook (Toronto: University of Toronto Press, 1956);

Innis, *Essays in Canadian Economic History*, edited by Mary Quayle Innis (Toronto: University of Toronto Press, 1956);

Elizabeth Simcoe, *Mrs. Simcoe's Diary*, edited, with an introduction, by Innis (Toronto: Macmillan / New York: St. Martin's, 1965);

The Clear Spirit: Twenty Canadian Women and Their Times, edited, with an introduction, by Innis (Toronto: University of Toronto Press for the Canadian Federation of University Women, 1966);

Nursing Education in a Changing Society, edited by Innis (Toronto: University of Toronto Press, 1970);

Harold A. Innis, *Empire and Communications*, revised by Mary Quayle Innis (Toronto: University of Toronto Press, 1972).

Although she spent much of her life in the shadow of her celebrated husband, Mary Quayle Innis was an intelligent and capable writer, editor, and academic administrator. She was born Mary Emma Quayle in St. Mary's, Ohio, to Frederick R. Quayle, an installer of telephone units, and his wife, Effie Lloyd Quayle, a homemaker. She grew up in a series of small towns in the United States and finished her secondary schooling in New Trier High School in Winnetka, Illinois. From 1915 to 1919 she attended the University of Chicago, graduating with a Ph.B. in English. During her final year she met a young Canadian economics instructor, Harold Adams Innis, who was beginning a Ph.D. at Chicago; they were engaged when he graduated in the summer of 1920. After their marriage on 10 May 1921, she joined him in Toronto where he had

Mary Quayle Innis as a young woman (University of Toronto Archives)

just finished his first year of teaching in the political economy department at the University of Toronto, where he remained for the rest of his life.

Even before their marriage, Quayle had helped Innis with his dissertation, *A History of the Canadian Pacific Railway* (published in 1923). She continued to accompany him on research tours to Great Britain and Europe in the summer of 1922, and to Kingston, Montreal, and British Columbia in the summer of 1923, as he began work on his best-known book, *The Fur Trade in Canada* (1930). Only the birth of their son Donald Quayle, on 21 April 1924, prevented her from exploring the Mackenzie River basin with her husband that summer. The Innises had three more children in the next nine years: Mary Ellan (born 5 September 1927), Hugh Roderick (born 17 November 1930), and Anne Christine (born 25 January 1933).

During the years in which she was at home raising a growing family, Innis continued the creative writing she had begun in a course at university and produced a variety of stories, most of them published in the *Canadian Forum*. She also wrote, with some assistance from her husband, *An Economic History of Canada* (1935; revised and enlarged, 1943) which became a standard university text. It surveyed the economic and industrial growth of Canada in clear, accessible prose for the student and general reader (a contrast to her husband's elliptical style). This book was followed by two other informative and interesting history texts for use in the schools: *Changing Canada* (2 volumes, *Fish, Fur and Exploration* and *New France and the Loyalists*, 1951-1952) and *Living in Canada* (1954), written in collaboration with Alex A. Cameron and Arnold Boggs.

In the 1940s Innis continued to write short stories, mainly about middle-class family life; most of her publications were in *Saturday Night* (forty-five stories between 1938 and 1947). Several of these were rewritten for inclusion in *Stand on a Rainbow* (1943). This autobiographical "novel" in twenty-four self-contained episodes tells the story of a young mother, three children, and mostly absentee father during one year of daily rites and seasonal rituals, beginning and ending with a joyous retreat to their summer cottage (modeled on the Innises' annually rented cottage on Lake Joseph, Ontario). The action is deliberately mundane, and the sexist stereotypes are uncomfortably dated now. But, as one contemporary reviewer noted, this book was "really a wartime gift to thousands of mothers": a skillful blend of psychological realism and romantic nostalgia, of humorous domesticity and charming idealism. For ten years Innis was editor of the *YWCA Quarterly,* and in 1949 she wrote a history of that organization, *Unfold the Years.* It is a careful, clear survey of the growth of the Young Women's Christian Association in Canada from its inception in 1873 as the Boarding House for Young Women in Toronto to its complex national and international services after World War II.

From 1943 to 1956 the four Innis children successively entered, and graduated from, University College at the University of Toronto. Innis was again able to accompany her husband on his travels. In 1948 they spent a summer in Oxford from which she gathered materials for five articles and a story in *Saturday Night.* Harold Innis died of cancer, after a year-long illness, in November 1952 at the age of fifty-eight.

Dust jacket for Innis's 1966 volume assembling biographical essays on twenty Canadian women

After her husband's death Mary Innis emerged into a more public life of her own. In 1955 she became dean of women at University College, where she served for nine years. She was a Canadian delegate to the Commonwealth Conference on Education held in Oxford in 1959. After her retirement she became vice-chairman of the Committee on Religious Education in the Public Schools of the Province of Ontario. For her literary and academic achievements, Innis was honored with LL.D.'s from Queen's University in 1958 and the University of Waterloo in 1965.

During these busy years, Innis continued to write and also worked as an editor. In *Travellers West* (1956) she re-created three epic journeys westward in the nineteenth century: the Earl of Southesk's hunting trip from the Red River to the Rockies in 1859-1860; Viscount Milton and

Dr. W. B. Cheadle's "party of pleasure" from Atlantic to Pacific in 1862-1863; and Sandford Fleming and George Munro Grant's railway exploration from Lake Superior to the Pacific in 1872. Editing, paraphrasing, and quoting from their published journals, she popularized rather than analyzed these classic travelers' tales. In the same year she also published a selection of her husband's articles and addresses, *Essays in Canadian Economic History*. While a University of Toronto committee was largely responsible for the selection, she did the editing.

In *Mrs. Simcoe's Diary* (1965) Innis transcribed "exactly and completely" the original record which the wife of the lieutenant-governor kept of her experiences in Upper Canada from 1791 to 1796. This fascinating picture of the social life of the young colony is presented with a sympathetic introduction and a sensible minimum of explanatory notes. Innis also worked with two university groups to edit commemorative anthologies. *The Clear Spirit* (1966), the centennial project of the Canadian Federation of University Women, assembles biographies of twenty famous Canadian women by fifteen women authors. Innis's introduction highlights the impressive thematic unity of the volume. For *Nursing Education in a Changing Society* (1970), Innis edited a collection of fourteen specialists' analyses of Canadian nursing education for the fiftieth anniversary of the founding of the School of Nursing at the University of Toronto.

Mary Quayle Innis died suddenly of a stroke on 10 January 1972, the day before her final editorial labor appeared. She had previously helped S. D. Clark and W. T. Easterbrook of the University of Toronto to add Harold Innis's marginalia and corrections to the revised editions of *The Cod Fisheries* (1954) and *The Fur Trade in Canada* (1956). In 1972 the revised edition of his *Empire and Communications* included her painstaking incorporation of manuscript material left by him twenty years before. During the final years of her life she continued to write stories, many of which were published in the *United Church Observer*.

Papers:
Mary Quayle Innis's papers are at the University of Toronto Archives.

George Johnston

(7 October 1913-   )

Elizabeth Waterston
University of Guelph

BOOKS: *The Cruising Auk* (Toronto: Oxford University Press, 1959);
Home Free (Toronto: Oxford University Press, 1966);
Happy Enough: Poems, 1935-1972 (Toronto: Oxford University Press, 1972);
Taking a Grip: Poems, 1972-1978 (Ottawa: Golden Dog, 1978);
Auk Redivivus: Selected Poems (Ottawa: Golden Dog, 1981);
Ask Again (Moonbeam, Ont.: Penumbra, 1984);
Carl: Portrait of a Painter: Carl Schaefer (Moonbeam, Ont.: Penumbra, 1986).

OTHER: *The Collected Poems of George Whalley*, edited, with an introduction, by Johnston (Kingston, Ont.: Quarry, 1986).

TRANSLATIONS: *Gisla saga Súrssonar*, translated as *The Saga of Gisli* (Toronto & Buffalo: University of Toronto Press, 1963; London: Dent, 1973);
Færeyinga saga, translated, with an introduction and notes, as *The Faroe Islanders' Saga* (Ottawa: Oberon, 1975);
Grænlendinga þáttr, translated, with an introduction and notes, as *The Greenlanders' Saga* (Ottawa: Oberon, 1976);
Rocky Shores: Modern Faroese Poems, translated, with an introduction and notes (Paisley, U.K.: Wilfion, 1981);
Knut Odegaard, *Vind gjennom Romsdal*, translated as *Wind Over Romsdal* (Moonbeam, Ont.: Penumbra, 1981);
Olafur Johann Sigurdsson, *Pastor Bødvar Brev*, translated as *Pastor Bodvar's Letter* (Moonbeam, Ont.: Penumbra, 1985);
Odegaard, *Bie Surr, Lakesprang*, translated as *Bee-Buzz, Salmon-Leap* (Kapuskasing, Ont.: Penumbra, 1988);
Christian Matras, *Ur sjon og ur minni*, translated as *Seeing and Remembering* (Torshavn, Faroe Islands: Foroya Frodskaparseteur, 1988; Kapuskasing, Ont.: Penumbra, 1988).

George Johnston (courtesy of the author)

"My why and how are me," George Johnston wrote in an early poem. Unusual qualities in the way he maneuvers words into verse and puzzles about the motivations for these maneuvers have kept interest in Johnston's poems high over the past thirty years.

George Benson Johnston was born in 1913 into an "urban scene" in Hamilton, Ontario, son of an Irish father, Benson Edward Johnston, and a fourth-generation-Canadian mother, Margaret Black Johnston. He has one sister; a younger brother died in infancy. The family moved to the Toronto outskirts in 1923. Visits to Peterborough

Elsewhere the crucifixion
has been cooling off; we do not think about it
crossing these fields where Quebec
marches with the State of New York.

· We are going on a walk across the fields
after tea, between Good Friday & Easter
in gray weather, unseasonably warm,
soft, overhead soft, soft underfoot.

The fields seem shut away
by a spell; elm, hardhack, wild apple
and the many different kinds of thorn bush
enchant their edges; here and there

an asymmetrical runt tree,
cobwebbed with vines, lifts, as I say,
meaning to sound witty,
beseeching arms. We are all three

witty. The walk is going well.
On to the ruined work-shop under the willow
with its gambrel roof and its hoard
of oak plugs, maple scantlings, butternut shells.

We peer into the farm living-room
at the doll, still on the floor beside the hole.
The house is subsiding ~~in~~ among raspberry canes,
& box elders. The frame barn has at last caved in.

Hazy with new green & pink the woods
offer no sous-bois yet, only beneath stands
of hemlock in Fred's pasture or on the way
back to the brook. We have a goal

which is to look at a black cherry tree that Andrew
knows about. An hour and there it is
in a field fence ~~line~~ beside a glade,
a strand of barbed wire running through it,

old black wire at the heart of an old black tree,
whose bark scrolls & whose hard branches reach out
every way. We take our knives
to some lopped pieces to try them for the ~~darkness of the wood~~

                                          grain
dark~~ness~~ of the wood. In this standstill
harmlessness becomes imaginable;
yet who can believe himself harmless or herself
even for a moment? We have come

roundabout & are now on our way home.
Gin & dry vermouth await us there
to ease the pain; a good dinner & good company:
Sydney & Betty, ~~will be there~~ & ~~our own~~ us all.

But in this warm early dusk reluctance
to move sets in. What if it could stay like this?
no ~~A~~to mutability, ~~any more~~ no ties of love,
no ~~A~~to Good Friday yesterday, no Easter tomorrow?

We are on a walk through fields
where Quebec marches with New York State
after tea, between Good Friday and Easter;
a warm late afternoon, overcast.

· The fields seem shut away
by a spell, elm, hardhack, wild apple
and the many kinds of thorn bush
                cluster
enchant their edges; here & there

an asymmetrical runt tree
cobwebbed with vines, lifts, as I say
in my Saturday afternoon vein,
~~meaning to sound witty,~~
beseeching arms; we are all three

witty. The walk is going well.
On to the ruined workshop under the willow
with its gambrel roof and its clutter
                              ~~hoard~~
of oak plugs, maple scantlings, butternut shells.

We peer into the farm living-room
                            where the stove was
at the doll, still on the floor ~~beside the hole.~~
The house is subsiding ~~among~~ raspberry canes
and box elders. The frame barn has at last caved in.

Hazy with new green & pink the woods
offer no sous-bois ~~as~~ yet, only beneath stands
of hemlock in Fred's pasture or on the way
back to the brook. We have a goal

---

which is to look at a black cherry tree that
Andrew knows. An hour and there it is
in a field fence beside a glade
a strand of barbed wire running through it:

old black wire at the heart of an old black tree
                    furls
whose bark scrolls & whose hard branches reach out
                     take
every way. We ~~try~~ our knives
to some lopped pieces to try them for the

dark grain of the wood. In this standstill
harmlessness becomes imaginable:
yet who can believe himself harmless or herself
even for a moment? We have come

roundabout and are now on our way home
where gin & dry vermouth await us
to ease the pain, a good dinner & good company,
Sydney & Betty & us all.

But in this warm early dusk reluctance
          return
to ~~move~~ sets in. What if it could stay like this?
no mutability any more, no ties ~~of love~~,
no crucified yesterday, no risen tomorrow?

The rest of the way is upstream:
when we come in sight Mark runs, he diminishes
before our pace from which hurry
has been lifted.

Two drafts for Johnston's poem "Between" (by permission of the author)

136

We are on a walk through fields
where Québec marches with New York
after tea, between Good Friday and Easter;
a warm late afternoon, overcast.

The fields seem shut away
by a spell; elm, hardhack, wild apple
and the many kinds of thorn
bind their edges; here and there

an a-symmetrical runt tree,
cobwebbed with vines, lifts, as I say
in my Saturday afternoon vein,
beseeching arms. We are all three

witty. The walk is going well.
On to the ruined workshop under the willows
with its gambrel roof and its clutter
of oak plugs, maple scantlings, butternut shells.

We peer into the farm living room
at the doll, still on the floor where the stove was.
The house is subsiding among raspberry canes
and box elders. The barn has at last caved in.

Fair copy for the version of "Between" published in Johnston's 1978 collection, Taking a Grip *(by permission of the author)*

and Stoney Lake strengthened an influential friendship with Gordon Roper, later a professor of Canadian literature and critic; before finishing high school Johnston knew that he wanted to be a writer.

At Victoria College, University of Toronto, Johnston entered, in 1932, a heady atmosphere; under the guidance of E. J. Pratt and Pelham Edgar, he read T. S. Eliot, the early William Butler Yeats, James Joyce, Ezra Pound, and added Alexander Pope as a personal favorite. As an undergraduate Johnston published, in *Acta Victoriana* in 1935, two poems, "The Life in August" and "Annabelle," sufficiently polished to be included in *The Cruising Auk* (1959) and later in his *Happy Enough: Poems, 1935-1972* (1972).

In 1936 Johnston earned his B.A. and traveled to Europe. He cycled through Germany, then stayed in England, writing. A story appeared in *London Mercury* in 1937. Returned to Canada, he sent his work to British publishers, Canadian outlets being negligible. When World War II erupted Johnston started a four-and-one-half-

year stint with the RCAF, as reconnaissance pilot in the United Kingdom, Canada, and West Africa. Near the war's end, in 1944, he married Jeanne McRae and returned to the University of Toronto.

Northrop Frye directed Johnston's master's thesis. The M.A. completed in one year, Johnston began work toward a Ph.D., but moved in 1947 to an assistant professorship at Mount Allison University in Sackville, New Brunswick. He was publishing now in *Northern Review* and *Contemporary Verse*. There were three children in the family by 1950, when the Johnstons moved to Ottawa, where Johnston had accepted a job as a lecturer at Carleton College (now Carleton University). Two more children were born between 1952 and 1959; the Johnstons adopted their sixth child, in 1964.

In the 1950s Johnston composed laconic lyrics that appeared in such publications as the *New Yorker*, *Atlantic Monthly*, and *Canadian Forum*. From family and neighborhood experience, a cast of characters had emerged: Mrs. McGonigle,

Mr. Murple–and a persona named Edward, amorous, unheroic, doomed to drown. (As a child Johnston had experienced a near-drowning; Northrop Frye, in the annual "Letters in Canada" survey for 1959 [*University of Toronto Quarterly*, July 1960], noted an archetypal use of the death-by-drowning motif in Johnston's poetry.) By 1959 there were enough poems to make up Johnston's first volume, *The Cruising Auk*. Meanwhile Johnston had commenced a second line of writing. He had learned Old Norse from Peter Foote of the University of London and in 1957 began translating Norse sagas. International events–the Suez crisis, the Hungarian revolution– distressed the now-pacifist poet; the sagas' fierce economy of language offered distraction. Johnston's first translation, *The Saga of Gisli*, appeared, with an introduction and notes by Foote, in 1963. Published ten years later by Dent as an Everyman University Paperback, Johnston's *Saga of Gisli* remains in print. Seven poems from this volume were included in *The Oxford Book of Verse in English Translation*, edited by Charles Tomlinson.

Johnston's poetry collection *The Cruising Auk* was favorably reviewed by Eric Nicol in the first issue of *Canadian Literature* (1959) and analyzed by Northrop Frye in "Letters in Canada" for 1959. These "pellucid lyrics," according to Frye, modulate from innocence to anxiety, and from intimate glimpses of childhood to a sense of dauntless energy even in a disconsolate world. *The Cruising Auk* was also reviewed in *Alphabet*, which became, along with *Poetry* (Chicago) and *Tamarack Review*, an outlet for Johnston's work.

From 1963 new images reflected the Quebec farm where the Johnstons now summered. Political winters in Ottawa seemed darker; a group of poems commissioned by Robert Weaver for the CBC included the somber "Remembrance Day." The new poems were in tune with the Canadian commitment to national identification in the 1960s.

Johnston's second volume of verse, *Home Free* (1966), is framed by two long poems, "Under the Tree," a poem about the effects of capital punishment that was used on a poster by Gerald Trottier as a plea for the abolition of the death penalty, and "Love in High Places," a satire of politics and family life that gives a final turn to characters, including Mrs. McGonigle and Edward, who had appeared in the poems of *The Cruising Auk*. *Home Free* was reviewed by George Whalley in *Canadian Literature* (Winter 1968). Whalley noted "a

new manner and a wider ambience" but also heard "a touch of weary disgust" and "ironic regret" in poems whose "colloquial fluency was generally admirable." In 1971 Queen's University signaled its admiration for Johnston with an honorary LL.D.

New poems in the 1972 volume *Happy Enough* are more private, in a tightly controlled form, and they speak of the real tensions of modern living. For they are poems about death, winter, butchering, and wrecking; yet they come from a time of "happy enough" home life.

In 1974 the Johnstons visited Iceland, and the next year saw publication of Johnston's translation *The Faroe Islanders' Saga*. *The Greenlanders' Saga* appeared in 1976. The steady force of the saga lines contrasts with the quick rushes of rhythm in the Canadian poems; yet themes and language show comparable tensions balancing the stretch or reach of imagination against the control of wit and containing form. Johnston's next volume, *Taking a Grip: Poems, 1972-1978* (1978), instances the values of containment: it celebrates talk, stove-fire, fine calligraphy, old-fashioned party fun, friendly affection, food and drink. Increasingly, domesticity and old friendships have occupied his life and become the subjects of his poetry.

Carleton University awarded Johnston an honorary degree in 1979, and in 1980, the year of his own retirement, Johnston contributed a poem to a testimonial dinner for his former mentor Northrop Frye. Johnston's witty poems from these occasions, "Convocation Address" and "A Celebration," are collected in *Ask Again* (1984) and in many ways characterize his most recent verse. Also collected here are a poem recalling a visit to Venice with fellow academic William Blissett; a retirement poem for another colleague, Albert Trueman, long involved in the Canada Council; a tribute to a younger poet, George Bowering; an acrostic for George Whalley whose collected poems he had edited; poems to celebrate marriages; elegies; and other occasional verse. His forms, as Frank Davey described them in *From There to Here* (1974), remain deft, his tone genial and unpretentious. In 1986 Johnston produced *Carl: Portrait of a Painter*, a personal memoir of his friend Carl Schaefer.

George Johnston continues to write occasional verse. He has recently produced two new translations. He has toured Britain on a reading tour with Susan Musgrave and Bill Bissett. Friends find him, tall, spare, bearded, at Athelstan, Quebec, in his orderly farmhouse at the American border, but still in a small corner of Canada.

References:
Frank Davey, *From There to Here* (Erin, Ont.: Press Porcépic, 1974), pp. 142-144;

D. G. Jones, "George Johnston," *Canadian Literature*, 59 (Winter 1974): 81-87;

Malahat Review, special issue on Johnston, 78 (March 1987);

George Whalley, "George Johnston," *Canadian Literature*, 35 (Winter 1968): 85-90.

Patricia Joudry

(18 October 1921-)

Chris Johnson
University of Manitoba

BOOKS: *Teach Me How to Cry* (New York: Dramatists Play Service, 1955);

The Song of Louise in the Morning (New York: Dramatists Play Service, 1960);

The Dweller on the Threshold (Toronto: McClelland & Stewart, 1973);

And the Children Played (Montreal & Plattsburgh, N.Y.: Tundra, 1975);

Spirit River to Angels' Roost: Religions I Have Loved and Left (Montreal & Plattsburgh, N.Y.: Tundra, 1977);

The Selena Tree (Toronto: McClelland & Stewart, 1980);

The Sand Castle (Toronto: Playwrights Canada, 1981);

Sound Therapy for the Walk Man (St. Denis, Sask.: Steele & Steele, 1982);

A Very Modest Orgy (Toronto: Playwrights Canada, 1982).

PLAY PRODUCTIONS: *The Stranger in My House*, Toronto, early 1950s;

Teach Me How to Cry, New York, Theatre de Lys, 5 April 1955; produced again as *Noon Has No Shadows*, London, England, Arts Theatre Club, 16 July 1958;

The Sand Castle, Dallas, Margo Jones Theatre, 1955;

Three Rings for Michelle, Toronto, Avenue Theatre, 15 November 1956;

Semi-Detached, Wilmington, Del., 10 February 1960; New York, Martin Beck Theatre, 10 March 1960;

Walk Alone Together, London, England, Duke of York's Theatre, June 1960;

Valerie, London, England, 1961;

The Man With the Perfect Wife, Palm Beach, Fla., Royal Poinciana Playhouse, 22 March 1965;

A Very Modest Orgy, Saskatoon, Sask., Twenty-fifth Street House Theatre, 1 October 1981.

RADIO: *Penny's Diary*, CBC, 1940-1943;

The Aldrich Family (coauthor), NBC, 1945-1949;

Forsaking All Others, Curtain Time, CBC, 3 May 1950;

The Luckiest Guy, Summer Stage, CBC, 4 June 1950;

Listen, He's Proposing, Curtain Time, CBC, 7 June 1950;

By Any Other Name, Winnipeg Drama, CBC, 17 August 1950;

The Storm, Winnipeg Drama, CBC, 21 September 1950;

An Inspector Calls, adapted from J. B. Priestley's play, Ford Theatre, CBC, 6 October 1950;

Intermission, Stage, CBC, 18 January 1951;

The Apple Tree, adapted from John Galsworthy's story, Ford Theatre, CBC, 30 March 1951;

Eve Does Her Durndest, Summer Fallow, CBC, 18 June 1951;

The Examiner, Vancouver Theatre, CBC, 6 July 1951;

Affectionately, Jenny, CBC, 1951, 1952;

The Monster, Vancouver Theatre, CBC, 31 August 1951;

Winter Fallow, Summer Fallow, CBC, 8 October 1951;

No Highway, adapted from Neville Shute's novel, *Ford Theatre*, CBC, 28 March 1952;

The Land is Your Inheritance, Summer Fallow, CBC, 28 April 1952;

Visit to the City, Summer Fare, CBC, 5 September 1952;

Pig in the Parlor, adapted from H. Gordon Green, *Summer Fallow*, CBC, 29 September 1952;

The Auction Sale, Summer Fallow, CBC, 13 October 1952;

Mother Is Watching, Stage, CBC, 23 November 1952;

Lace on Her Petticoat, adapted from Aimee Stuart's play, *Ford Theatre*, CBC, 12 December 1952;

Happy is the Day, Stage, CBC, 14 December 1952;

Anne of Green Gables, adapted from Lucy Maud Montgomery's novel, CBC, 2 January-8 January, 1953;

Thatcher Place, Stage, CBC, 29 March 1953;

Teach Me How to Cry, Stage, CBC, 19 April 1953;

Taking Stock, Summer Fallow, CBC, 19 April 1954;

The Landrace Lands Again, Summer Fallow, CBC, 24 May 1954;

Corrida, Vancouver Theatre, CBC, 10 September 1954;

Anne of Avonlea, adapted from Montgomery's *Anne of Avonlea*, CBC, 24 September-24 December 1954;

The Hermit, Summer Fallow, CBC, 25 October 1954;

Child of the Cliffs, Stage, CBC, 15 January 1956;

The Arrival of Anne, adapted from Montgomery's *Anne of Green Gables, Wednesday Night*, CBC, 12 June 1957;

Bitter Gold, Drama in Sound, CBC, 10 June 1958.

TELEVISION: *Teach Me How To Cry, Television Theatre*, CBC, 15 October 1953;

The Sand Castle, General Motors Presents, CBC, 12 April 1955;

The Painted Blind, General Motors Presents, CBC, 14 February 1956;

A Woman's Point of View, On Camera, CBC, 8 July 1957;

The Song of Louise in the Morning, CBS, *Television Workshop*, 1960;

Gift of Truth, CBC, May 1961;

Something Old, Something New, General Motors Presents, CBC, 11 June 1961;

Valerie, Playdate, CBC, 18 October 1961;

Bitter Gold, Shoestring Theatre, CBC, 21 November 1965.

OTHER: *Mother Is Watching*, in *All the Bright Company: Radio Drama Produced by Andrew Allan*, edited by Howard Fink and John Jackson (Kingston, Ont.: Quarry Press, 1987), pp. 171-202.

PERIODICAL PUBLICATIONS: *Think Again, Canadian Theatre Review*, 23 (Summer 1979): 49-98;

"Woman As Artist," *Canadian Theatre Review*, 29 (Winter 1981): 129-134.

Patricia Joudry is the author of *Teach Me How to Cry*, one of the most commercially successful Canadian plays ever written. The play was first produced at the Theatre de Lys, New York, 5 April 1955, and under the title *Noon Has No Shadows* became the first Canadian play mounted by an all-Canadian cast in London, opening at the Arts Theatre Club, 16 July 1958. A film version of the play, *The Restless Years*, was released by Universal Studios in 1959. Adaptations of the work have been broadcast and televised.

Born 18 October 1921 in Spirit River, Alberta, in 1925 Joudry moved to Montreal with her parents, Clifford G. Joudry, a magazine editor, and Beth Gilbart Joudry, a potter. In Montreal she appeared as a child performer with Dorothy Davis's Children's Theatre, and as a teenager she performed in radio for the Canadian Broadcasting Corporation. After moving to Toronto in 1940, she began to write scripts for the CBC. From 1940 to 1943 she wrote scripts for and played the title role in *Penny's Diary*, a situation comedy. From 1945 to 1949 she lived in New York, where she was coauthor of NBC's well-known radio series, *The Aldrich Family*. After returning to Toronto in 1949, she continued to work for CBC-Radio, writing and starring in the series *Affectionately, Jenny* in 1951 and 1952 and writing several individual radio and television plays, among them *Mother Is Watching*, an attack on conformity and middle-class values of the day, included in *All the Bright Company*, an anthology of radio plays published in 1987. During this period she began to write for the stage; her first stage work was *The Stranger in My House*, a one-act piece produced in Toronto, and her second

Dust jacket for Joudry's first novel, written at the MacDowell Colony in Peterborough, Vermont

was the highly successful *Teach Me How to Cry*.

Melinda Grant and Will Henderson, the protagonists of *Teach Me How to Cry*, are "star-crossed" teenage lovers, a motif emphasized by Melinda's being cast as Juliet in a school production of *Romeo and Juliet*. Both adolescents are isolated: Melinda by her mother's peculiarities and Will by his family's frequent moves. During Will's brief sojourn in the small town where Melinda lives, love between the two grows, and he successfully persuades Melinda to face life honestly. Although the lovers are parted at the end, it is implied that they will choose life over death as a solution to their problems, in contrast to their classic predecessors. Although the characters are somewhat two-dimensional and the play is heavily dependent on sentiment, the effects are carefully and expertly calculated. The Toronto Alumnai Dramatic Club's production of the play at Hart House Theatre in Toronto, 13 and 14 March 1956, was eligible for entry in the

Dominion Drama Festival competition that year, and *Teach Me How to Cry* won the festival's award for best Canadian play.

Several plays followed in quick succession. *The Sand Castle*, first produced at the Margo Jones Theatre in Dallas, Texas, in 1955, published in 1981, is a comedy in which a distinguished, middle-aged psychiatrist is forced to reassess his values after falling in love with and marrying a free-spirited, childlike young woman. *Three Rings for Michelle*, a three-act drama in which an orphan girl brings meaning and love to the life of the family who adopts her, was first produced at the Avenue Theatre, Toronto, 15 November 1956. In 1957 Joudry shared the Woman of the Year Award in Literature and Art with novelist Gabrielle Roy. That same year Joudry moved to England with her second husband, John Steele (she was divorced from her first husband, Delmar Dinsdale, in 1952), and, pressed for money, continued to write commercially oriented plays at a rapid pace. *Semi-Detached*, a three-act drama about English-Canadian prejudice against French-Canadians, opened at the Martin Beck Theatre in New York in March 1960 after a month-long out-of-town-tour beginning in Wilmington, Delaware, and *Walk Alone Together*, a comedy, was produced in London shortly after, but both closed after disappointingly short runs.

The Song of Louise in the Morning (published in 1960 and given many amateur productions since) is a long one-act domestic drama. Stanley, jealous of the child his wife Louise looks after, attempts to control Louise's life; his manipulation leads to her death in a suspicious accident. Despite some intrusive plot devices, the play communicates the tension of domestic strife, and Joudry expertly portrays the neurotic Stanley, alternating endearing and manipulative characteristics so that the audience's response mirrors Louise's mixed reactions to her husband.

While in England, exposed to a variety of spiritualist persuasions and suffering from what she later described as "religious delusion," Joudry became convinced that Bernard Shaw was "transmitting" plays through her. While some of the many "Shavian" plays aroused interest, none was produced or published, in part because Joudry refused to rewrite and because she insisted on Shaw being given credit. Later, restored to health, Joudry wrote a witty account of this part of her life in the autobiographical *Spirit River to Angels' Roost: Religions I Have Loved and Left*, published in 1977.

Joudry completed her first novel, *The Dweller on the Threshold*, while on a fellowship at the MacDowell Colony in Vermont, and the book was published after her return to Canada in 1973. The male narrator encounters a disturbing female, his cousin Cecilia, twice in his life, in childhood and in late adolescence. The novel is marred by overly lush and extensive description and by vagueness which leaves the reader as well as the protagonist groping for significance.

Joudry then wrote her two autobiographical books. She and her second husband, whom she divorced in 1975, educated their five daughters (two from Joudry's first marriage) outside the public school system. *And the Children Played* (1975) is an engaging account and lively defense of "unstructured learning." After *Spirit River to Angels' Roost*, Joudry returned to the novel with *The Selena Tree* (1980).

As in *The Dweller on the Threshold*, in this work a woman attempts to communicate the insights of a rich inner life to a spiritually impoverished environment. Stranded in a small prairie town by the collapse of a touring opera company, Sophia da Silva marries the local storekeeper but yearns for the cultural riches of the East. As the dream dies, she transfers her longing to her daughter, but there is no fulfillment until, after Sophia's death, her granddaughter Selena leaves for Ontario to study music. While marred by vagueness and overblown rhetoric, *The Selena Tree* has scale and a tangible sense of place. A play based on the novel, "O Listen!," has never been published or given a full production, but it was workshopped at the Banff Playwrights' Colony in the summer of 1983.

Joudry continues to write sporadically for the stage. *Think Again* is a three-act comedy which was published in a 1979 issue of *Canadian Theatre Review*. The play's protagonist is, in effect, a bishop's brain, transplanted to a baboon and eventually to another bishop. Joudry substitutes skulls for the multiple doors of traditional farce and in the process scores satirical hits against medical science, religion, animal lovers, marriage, and humanity in general. *A Very Modest Orgy*, first produced by the Twenty-fifth Street House Theatre, Saskatoon, 1 October 1981, and published the following year, is also an elaboration on the conventions of farce: a middle-aged couple contemplates "swinging" as an antidote to their boredom, but their plans are thwarted by a sequence of farcical misadventures and by their discovery of unexpected qualities in each other and in their unorthodox family.

Joudry has expressed her disillusionment with the prospects for original work on Canadian stages, so it seems likely that she will continue to devote most of her energy to prose and to her research in educational methods. It also seems likely that she will continue to be preoccupied with the development of a personal, spiritual "map" of cosmic order and inner life.

References:

Anton Wagner, "Biographical Checklist: Patricia Joudry," *Canadian Theatre Review*, 23 (Summer 1979): 45-48;

Wagner, ed., *Canada's Lost Plays*, volume 2, *Women Pioneers* (Toronto: Canadian Theatre Review Publications, 1979), pp. 4-19, 206-207.

Leo Kennedy
(22 August 1907-   )

Lee Briscoe Thompson
University of Vermont

BOOK: *The Shrouding* (Toronto: Macmillan, 1933); republished, with a foreword by Kennedy (Ottawa: Golden Dog Press, 1975).

SELECTED PERIODICAL PUBLICATIONS:
FICTION

"Preoccupation of a Puppet," *Canadian Mercury* (December 1928): 13;

"Portion of Your Breath," *Canadian Forum*, 10 (January 1930): 123-125;

"We All Got to Die," *Canadian Forum*, 11 (December 1930): 99-100;

"The Joy Ride," *Canadian Forum*, 12 (August 1932): 418-419;

"A Priest in the Family," *Canadian Forum*, 13 (April 1933): 258, 260-262.

NONFICTION

"The Future of Canadian Literature," *Canadian Mercury*, nos. 5-6 (April/May 1929): 99-100;

Review of *Twenty-Seven Poems, McGilliad* (February/ March 1931): 87;

"Canadian Writers of Today: IX Raymond Knister," *Canadian Forum*, 12 (September 1932): 459-461;

"Archibald Lampman," *Canadian Forum*, 13 (May 1933): 301, 303;

"Direction for Canadian Poets," *New Frontier*, 1 (June 1936): 21-24;

"Streamlining the Epitaph," *Saturday Night*, 58 (31 October 1942): 41;

"A Poet's Memoirs," review of *Journal of Canadian Fiction*, 4, no. 2 (1975), special issue on Raymond Knister, *CV/II* (May 1976): 23-24.

POETRY

"Seasons," *McGilliad* (November 1930): 5;

"Bigot," *McGilliad* (November 1930): 7;

"Christian Burial," *McGilliad* (December 1930): 11;

"The Bough Broken," as Wm. Crowl, *McGilliad* (December 1930): 16;

"Intimations of Immortality," *McGilliad* (April 1931): 94;

"Exile," *Dalhousie Review*, 11 (1931-1932): 520;

Leo Kennedy in his seventies (photograph by Patricia Morley)

"Cursed Be Ghouls," *Canadian Forum*, 15 (October 1934): 10;

"Loser Take All," *Canadian Forum*, 15 (August 1935): 323;

"Summons for this Generation," *New Frontier*, 1 (April 1936): 15;

"Michael David," *Saturday Night*, 53 (August 1936);

"New Comrade," as Arthur Beaton, *New Frontier*, 1 (September 1936): 1;

"Revolutionary Greeting," as Beaton, *New Frontier*, 1 (November 1936): 5;

"You, Spanish Comrade," as Beaton, *New Frontier*, 1 (November 1936): 23;

"Memorial to the Defenders (for Bess and Ben),"
as Leonard Bullen, *New Frontier*, 1 (February 1937): 15;

"Advice To a Young Poet," as Beaton, *New Frontier*, 1 (April 1937): 26;

"Calling Eagles," *New Frontier*, 2 (June 1937): 14;

"Poem," *Canadian Bookman*, 21 (October / November 1938): 5;

"Carol For Two Swans," *Contemporary Verse*, 1 (September 1941): 8-9;

"Elegy in a Suburban Churchyard," *Canadian Forum*, 21 (January 1942): 313;

"Continuous Performance," *Contemporary Verse*, 36 (Fall 1951): 15;

"New, Old Movie," *CV/II*, 2 (August 1976): 5.

Leo Kennedy is valued perhaps less for any of his publications–a single volume of verse, a handful of short stories, a few dozen essays–than he is for his central role in the Montreal Group as midwife to modernism and cosmopolitanism in Canadian poetry of the 1920s and to the use of social themes in Canadian literature of the 1930s.

Inheritor of an Irish gift for words, John Leo Kennedy was born in Liverpool, England, on 22 August 1907, and at the age of five he was brought to Canada by his parents, John A. and Lillian Bullen Kennedy. His early education in Montreal's St. Patrick's Academy ended after grade six, and at thirteen Kennedy went to work as a shipping clerk and bookkeeper for his father's ship-chandling business. Although he returned to school only briefly–two years of night schooling as an extension student at the University of Montreal–Kennedy estimates that, by his late adolescence and first encounter with what came to be known as the Montreal Group or McGill Movement, he had the self-taught equivalent of a bachelor of arts.

Leon Edel, involved with fellow students A. J. M. Smith and F. R. Scott in the running of the *McGill Fortnightly Review* (1925-1927), tells of Kennedy's catching the group's attention by publishing "soulful letters and mocking verses" under the first of his pseudonyms, Helen Laurence, in the lonely hearts column of the *Montreal Star*. In December 1928, when the short-lived *Canadian Mercury* stepped into the gap created by the demise of the *McGill Fortnightly Review*, Kennedy was a founding member of the editorial board. He made an immediate critical mark with his article "The Future of Canadian Literature" (April/May 1929), in which he vigorously at-

tacked the Victorianism of most of Canada's poets, the asininity of the Canadian Authors Association, and the "infantile paralysis" of Canadian letters generally. He concluded, however, with a vision of hope that a frank and idealistic young generation would come to express "a spirit and a consciousness distinctively Canadian." The article, apart from identifying Kennedy as of one mind with his modernist McGill associates, demonstrates the candor, wit, and reformist energy which occur in all of his youthful critical writing.

Shortly after the demise of the *Canadian Mercury*, Kennedy and his bride, Miriam Carpin, moved to New York City, where he hoped to make his mark in journalism. Newspaper reporting, book reviewing, and bookkeeping were insufficient to support the Kennedys, whose return to Montreal after the crash of the stock market was to last until late in the Great Depression.

The mixed social and literary group that had helped bring an intellectual Catholic boy to an even wider awareness of literature nationally and internationally continued to stimulate Kennedy in the 1930s. A recognized member of the Montreal Group, Kennedy eked out a living in a variety of odd jobs and regularly contributed poetry, short fiction, and literary criticism to a range of journals from the *Canadian Forum*, the *Dalhousie Review*, and the *McGilliad* to *Saturday Night* and the *Canadian Bookman*. On occasion he adopted such pseudonyms as Wm. Crowl, Leonard Bullen, and Arthur Beaton.

These were also years of savoring relationships with other writers, including Raymond Knister, E. J. Pratt, Dorothy Livesay, A. M. Klein, Robert Finch, A. J. M. Smith, F. R. Scott, and Leon Edel. The jocular camaraderie of this circle may be gauged by a literary hoax in which Kennedy elaborately reviewed for the *McGilliad* a nonexistent book entitled *Twenty-Seven Poems* and attributed to Smith. Smith retaliated with an equally tongue-in-cheek review of Kennedy's fictitious collection *Cerberus and the Mole*, published by Huntley and Palmer–a biscuit company. Of these times Kennedy has written nostalgically, "We who wrote poetry in the bleak late 20's and early 30's throve on friendships as warm as a Quebec Heater and the conviction that we would somehow survive to 40 years, the age limit for any working poet."

The Great Depression delayed the customary progression of young poets from having their works published in periodicals to seeing them appear in book form. Given that Klein, Scott, and

Smith were all so impeded, the publication in 1933 of Kennedy's *The Shrouding* was a remarkable accomplishment. Published by Macmillan at the suggestion of E. J. Pratt, the slim black-and-white book gathered together new poetry and verse published not only in the journals noted above but also in the prestigious American reviews *Poetry,* the *Dial,* and the *Commonweal.*

Dedicated to drowned Canadian writer Raymond Knister, *The Shrouding* is divided into four sections: "Weapons Against Death," "Spade Thrusts," "Cloth for Cerements," and "Outcry on the Time." The influences of the early poetry of T. S. Eliot and of Sir James George Frazer's *The Golden Bough,* of A. J. M. Smith and seventeenth-century metaphysical verse are immediately evident in the themes, diction, and imagery of virtually all thirty-nine poems. There are cycles of life, fertility, death, burial, rebirth, and resurrection; litanies of lament and rejoicing, despair and ecstasy; ritual sacrifice linked both with Christ and with pagan rites; a strong element of the morbid and the macabre; prolonged images of decay and reminders of grim mortality; considerable irony and powerful paradox; classical and ecclesiastical vocabulary. The forms and versification are traditional: blank verse, quatrains, sonnets, couplets, slant rhyme. Their execution is modern: condensed lyricism, musical but unsentimental resonances, crisply polished cadences. The critics praised his achievement, admired his ability to fuse emotional impact with controlled craftsmanship, and were impressed by the music of his lines. "Words for a Resurrection," "Mad Boy's Song," and the sardonic "Self Epitaph to Be Carved in Salt" were considered among the volume's best poems. At the time of the republication of *The Shrouding* more than four decades later, in 1975, critics continued to remark approvingly upon these qualities but tended to concentrate more upon the author as an important figure in the development of modern Canadian poetry.

Early in the 1930s plans had been hatched by Kennedy, Smith, and Scott to bring out a small anthology of contemporary Canadian verse. The intention was to verify the existence in Canadian poetry of a new and vital modernist direction, and to bring to public attention a body of verse which departed clearly from conventional form and romantic sentiment. That volume, *New Provinces,* did not appear until 1936, despite constant attention from its initiators, joined by E. J. Pratt. By that time Kennedy, for one, re-

garded his contributions to the anthology as dated and important primarily as indications of a stage in his development. His mythologizing and preoccupation with classical themes had come to seem to him irrelevant in the face of an urgent social imperative.

To Canadian writers of the Depression committed to social change and the role of literature in that transformation, the need for a new journal was apparent. *Masses* (1932-1934) had often sacrificed aesthetics to political goals, and the *Canadian Forum* had sometimes done the reverse; in founding the leftist periodical *New Frontier* in April 1936, Kennedy and others hoped for a finer balance of literary and social criteria. In the June 1936 issue of *New Frontier,* Kennedy published a fiery milestone essay, "Direction for Canadian Poets," which in characteristically lively style indicted those "ivory tower" artists who, in an era of great suffering, could "blithely comb their wooly wits for stanzas to clarify intimate subjective reactions to Love, Beauty, the First Crocus, Snow in April and similar graceful but immediately irrelevant bubbles." Arguing that "the function of poetry is to interpret the contemporary scene faithfully, is to interpret especially the progressive forces in modern life which alone stand for cultural survival," Kennedy was honestly obliged to condemn his own verse as "lack[ing] contact with a larger reality," in spite of the section in *The Shrouding* entitled "Outcry on the Time." It was the dilemma of the poet caught between the creative and the social impulses, in danger of gratifying neither. Convinced that each artist must turn to "the teeming life-stuff all around him that is also the stuff of great poetry," Kennedy resolutely rejected his self-confessed "preoccupation with abstractions of death and rebirth." In an appeal to the modern writer to join the social struggle, entitled "Calling Eagles" (*New Frontier,* June 1937), he simultaneously argued his case and presented a poetic model, concluding:

> You are part of this turmoil, Eagles, knit to its
> glory.
> There is work for your strong beaks and thundering wings
> For the clean flight of the mind and the sharp perception.
>
> There is only a glacial death on the lonely crags.

Of a lesser note than his poetry or critical prose have been Kennedy's short stories, a half dozen of which appeared in such periodicals as the *Canadian Forum* and *Saturday Night*. (According to Kennedy a literary sleuth could locate several other stories in now-defunct, obscure New York City periodicals.) This short fiction divides into primarily two types, with some stories a combination of the two: 1) stories of social realism, sketches of lower-class lives, variously exhibiting stoicism, tedium, frustration, piety, limitation, delusion, usually recounted by an omniscient but highly colloquial narrator ("We All Got to Die," for example); 2) streetwise tales in the style of Damon Runyon or parts of Morley Callaghan, heavy-laden with gangsterisms and other slang ("The Joy Ride"). Edward O'Brien's *Best Short Stories* series singled out a couple of Kennedy's stories for their high quality: "Preoccupation of a Puppet" in 1929 and "We All Got to Die" in 1931. One story in particular, "A Priest in the Family," has received substantial critical approval and several republications. Focusing on an earthy, amusing, and eventually violent rivalry between an Irish-Canadian and an Italian-Canadian charwoman, this story avoids the stilted or artificial dialogue that sometimes mars Kennedy's narratives. The vividness of characterization and the authenticity of action are strong and satisfying. In their popular diction and everyday themes, if not in the somber social vision which underlies this very modern fiction, Kennedy's stories anticipated the bread-and-butter writing that would become his main endeavor from 1937 on.

Financial considerations finally forced Kennedy to draw on U.S.-affiliated Toronto advertising connections to seek employment once again in the States. Accepting a position in Chicago by 1940 as a commercial writer, Kennedy produced over the next forty years only the occasional poem, usually concerned with an ironic perspective on a poet in love, and pseudonymous (as Edgar Main, Leonard Bullen, Peter Quinn) book reviews and light verse for the *Chicago Sun* and later *Sun-Times*. The man to whom we owe the Maxwell House coffee slogan "The jar with the stars on top," Kennedy poured into jingles the lyricism and the humor that had distinguished much of his literary writings, and he testifies candidly to having thoroughly enjoyed these labors.

Kennedy's marriage, which produced a son Stephen, had broken down in the early 1930s. He subsequently married an American, Esther Nichamin, and they devoted their energies to the rearing of a family (Peter and Deborah) in Chicago and then Connecticut and gradually lost touch with most of the Canadian literary circle.

Correspondence from these expatriate decades is marked above all by a delightful sense of humor, modest deprecation of his importance in Canadian literature, and sincere admiration for the continuing activity and accomplishments of old friends.

After retirement in the late 1970s from copywriting for Reader's Digest, Kennedy renewed some of those links and resettled in Montreal. He began to aid in the assembling of retrospective materials, to write anecdotal literary criticism and literary/social history about Montreal of the 1920s and 1930s, and to offer his recollections as a resource for understanding of the interwar period in Canada. He also wrote poetry for children, satiric verse, and other poems, which regrettably were lost before they could be published. He hoped to embark on a volume of memoirs, to be called "The Unexpurgated Anecdotes of Leo Kennedy," but illness interfered, and Kennedy has now returned to the United States, living in a residential hotel in Pasadena, California.

The republication in 1975 of *The Shrouding* and of W. E. Collin's essay on Kennedy in *The White Savannahs* has combined with the renewed accessibility of Kennedy's poetry and prose in such anthologies as Louis Dudek and Michael Gnarowski's *The Making of Modern Poetry in Canada* (1967), Peter Stevens's *The McGill Movement* (1969), and *New Provinces* (included in the Literature of Canada reprint series, 1976) to make a new generation aware of the poet Collin dubbed "This Man of April." Unquestionably a secondary poet, Leo Kennedy has nevertheless played a considerable part in the evolution of modern Canadian verse, both in his theory and in his practice. The hope, the melancholy, the wit, the music, the heart of the man may be glimpsed in the concluding lines of his "Self Epitaph": "He wrote of dying / As though life mattered."

References:

W. E. Collin, "Leo Kennedy and the Resurrection of Canadian Poetry," *Canadian Forum*, 14 (October 1933): 24-27;

Collin, "This Man of April," in *The White Savannahs* (Toronto: Macmillan, 1936; republished, Toronto & Buffalo: University of Toronto Press, 1975);

Leon Edel, "When McGill Modernized Canadian Literature," in *The McGill You Knew: An Anthology of Memoirs 1930-1960*, edited by Edgar Collard (Don Mills, Ont.: Longmans, 1975);

Lorraine McMullen, "Leo Kennedy," *Le Chien d'Or/The Golden Dog,* no. 1 (January 1972): 46-62;

Patricia Morley, "The Young Turks: A Biographer's Comment," *Canadian Poetry: Studies/ Documents/Reviews,* 11 (Fall/Winter 1982): 67-72.

Papers:
The Leo Kennedy Collection, which includes correspondence, manuscript and typescript material, and galleys, is at the Public Archives of Canada, Ottawa.

Henry Kreisel
(5 June 1922-)

Neil Besner
University of Winnipeg

BOOKS: *The Rich Man* (Toronto: McClelland & Stewart, 1948; London, Heinemann, 1952);

The Betrayal (Toronto: McClelland & Stewart, 1964);

The Almost Meeting and Other Stories (Edmonton: NeWest, 1981);

Another Country: Writings by and about Henry Kreisel, edited by Shirley Neuman (Edmonton: NeWest, 1985).

TELEVISION: *The Betrayal,* CBC, December 1965.

RADIO: *He Who Sells His Shadow: A Fable for Radio, Wednesday Night,* CBC, 1956.

OTHER: John Heath, *Aphrodite and Other Poems,* edited, with an introduction, by Kreisel (Toronto: Ryerson, 1959).

PERIODICAL PUBLICATIONS: "Joseph Conrad and the Dilemma of the Uprooted Man," *Tamarack Review,* 7 (Spring 1958): 78-85;

"The Prairie: A State of Mind," *Transactions of the Royal Society of Canada,* series 4, 6 (June 1968): 171-180.

Henry Kreisel (photograph by W. Rauschning, University of Alberta Photo Service)

The title of Henry Kreisel's best short story, "The Broken Globe," is an apt metaphor for the world–and worldview–of many of his fictional characters. For Kreisel's immigrant (and for those he leaves behind), the journey to the New World opens up fissures between European and North American experience. Looking across the Atlantic, vision is blurred by New World innocence and nostalgic delusion or by Old World dreams of freedom and fabled prosperity. The two worlds are further separated from each other by war and the aftermath of the Holocaust. What is left is a broken globe: Kreisel's novels and many of his short stories document what he calls the "double experience" of the immigrant struggling to bridge (or widen) the temporal, spiritual, and psychological gulfs between European background and Canadian foreground. The immigrant must learn the contours of both landscapes; he can only fully realize his present by waking up to the nightmare of his all-too-recent past. To dissociate himself from either world, or to misperceive it, diminishes his humanity.

Kreisel was born on 5 June 1922 in Vienna, where he lived until he was sixteen. Fleeing the Nazis in 1938, he went with his parents, David Leo and Helen Schreier Kreisel, to England and worked as an apprentice cutter in a clothing factory in Leeds. In May 1940 he and his father were interned as "enemy aliens" by the British government; in July they were shipped to Canada, where they were confined in Camp B in New Brunswick and then in Camp I on the Ile aux Noix, Quebec. Kreisel was one of the first to be released in Canada in late 1941. By that time he was determined to be a writer and had decided to write in English, adopting Joseph Conrad as "a kind of patron saint." His immediate impressions of camp life are recorded in the journal he kept, published as "Diary of an Internment" (*White Pelican*, Summer 1974) and collected in *Another Country: Writings by and about Henry Kreisel* (1985). The entries reveal a precociously literary adolescent's resentment and bewilderment at being detained in England and then sent to a country, Kreisel writes, "that I barely knew by name and that was only a large red stretch on the school maps we had used in Vienna in our geography lessons." Looking back thirty-five years later, Kreisel attests to the importance of the camps to his life: "In many ways the internment camp experience is central to my own development. Suspended in a kind of no man's land for more than eighteen months, I could look back at the horrendous events of the 1930's and see them in some kind of perspective, and I could prepare myself intellectually for the tasks I wanted to undertake in the future."

The diary is an important document both for its vivid account of day-to-day life in the camps and for the insight it provides into the genesis of Kreisel's fictional world. The impact of a

forced and radical immigration, with all its attendant anxiety and feelings of displacement, is captured in the entry for "i.I.1941": "New-Year. A rather sad New-Year. Is it our New-Year at all? Should Jews celebrate New-Year twice a year? There are discussions in our group about it. In the afternoon I signed a refusal paper to go back to England. Reason: Immigration to the United States. I hope it will be possible. Our future is like a dark, impenetrable wall. I said I should give something if I knew where I will be next year at the same time. 1938 Vienna, 1939-1940 England, 1941 Canada. 1942–where?"

As it turned out, 1942 found him enrolled in the University of Toronto to study language and literature. He received his B.A. in 1946, winning several scholarships along the way. The following year he married Esther Lazerson. They have one son, Philip. After finishing his M.A. at Toronto, also in 1947, he took a position with the English department at the University of Alberta, where he taught until 1952. His first novel, *The Rich Man*, was published in 1948, dedicated to his parents and to Omama Toni Mendel, a member of the Toronto family who sponsored his release from camp and his university studies. Kreisel had begun to "sketch" *The Rich Man* in Toronto in 1944, reading parts of it to the Modern Letters Club, founded by Kreisel and Robert Weaver, among others; James Reaney was a member, and Hugh Kenner came to meetings to read his work on G. K. Chesterton and Hilaire Belloc.

The plot of *The Rich Man* is straightforward: in 1935 Jacob Grossman returns to Europe for a six-week visit with his family after working for thirty-three years as a presser in a Toronto clothing factory. To his widowed mother and his married sisters in Vienna, he styles himself a prosperous clothes designer, fulfilling their Old World dreams of his New World success. To Tassigny, a French artist he meets on shipboard, he becomes a patron of the arts, buying (but ironically not understanding) Tassigny's *L'Entrepreneur*, a picture of an Orwellian demagogue blaring hollow New World promises from a megaphone. The painting accrues symbolic force on several levels as the story develops, until Jacob flings the picture out of a train window at the very end of the novel, in dim and baffled recognition of his own deception. Dressed up in a rich man's white alpaca suit, Jacob returns to Europe seeking his Hollywood-inspired nostalgic delusion–an elegant and carefree Vienna dancing to the stately rhythms of "The Blue Danube." In-

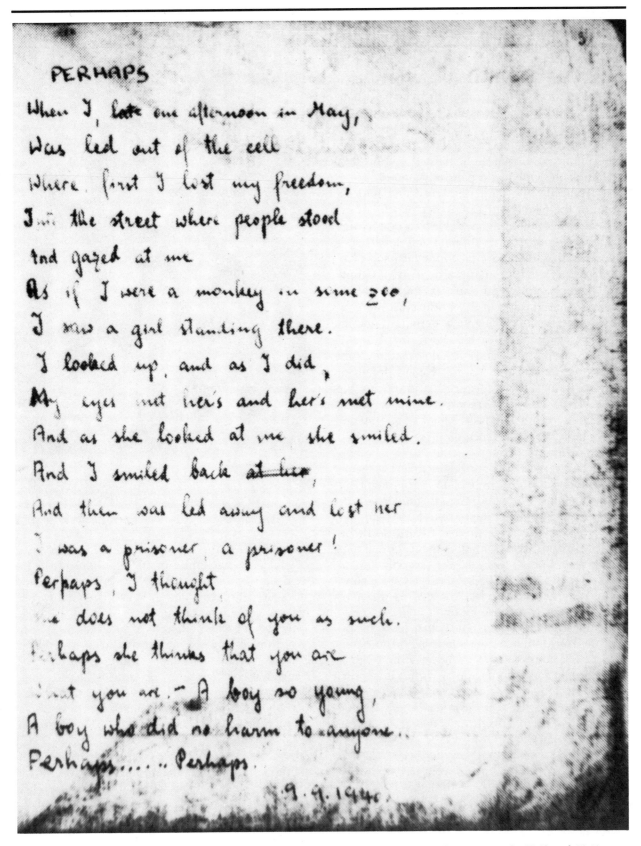

PERHAPS

When I, late one afternoon in May,
Was led out of the cell
Where first I lost my freedom,
Into the street where people stood
And gazed at me
As if I were a monkey in some zoo,
I saw a girl standing there.
I looked up, and as I did,
My eyes met hers and hers met mine.
And as she looked at me she smiled.
And I smiled back at her,
And then was led away and lost her
I was a prisoner, a prisoner!
Perhaps, I thought
she does not think of you as such.
Perhaps she thinks that you are
what you are – A boy so young,
A boy who did no harm to anyone..
Perhaps...... Perhaps.

9.9.1940.

Page from one of the seven notebooks Kreisel kept during his internment by the British government in 1940 and 1941 (by permission of the author)

149

stead, he finds Vienna waiting for Hitler to march, anti-Semitism on the rise, his family struggling to survive, and tens of thousands out of work. When his sister Shaendl's husband is killed, she turns in desperation to Jacob for financial help, and his facade is shattered: he must reveal, to his family's disbelief, that he is poor like them. He begins his return to Canada shaken and humiliated, his image of himself and his perception of the Old World painfully altered.

Ironically, the most clear-eyed and hopeful vision in the novel is that of Robert Koch, an ex-journalist masquerading as a clown to escape official persecution. At once flippant and deadly serious, he is able to chastise Jacob for his pose: "No, to enjoy himself thoroughly a man should come [to Vienna] alone and have a great deal of money. What goes on in the world must not concern him. He must be selfish—definitely not his brother's keeper." When his clown's mask is off, Koch's compassion and insight counterpoint Jacob's obtuseness and naïveté; Koch's dream of a more humane "world-spirit" rising from the ashes of the Holocaust relieves the utter gloom of Jacob's brother-in-law Albert's apocalyptic vision—man's descent, sanctioned by law, into bestial depravity.

The strength of the novel lies in Kreisel's sensitive and carefully controlled exploration of Jacob's failings. With understated compassion, he shows how Jacob, an immigrant Everyman, remolds his experience in the New World to fit his family's dreams, returning to present himself as a fifty-two-year-old prodigal, the incarnation of their hopes. With Europe collapsing around them, they look to Jacob's "success" as proof of possible salvation in the cities and open spaces of a fabulous new continent. But when Jacob's radical New World innocence is shattered by his exposure to his family's harsh experience in Vienna, his rich man's pseudometaphysic is left in shreds. He will no longer be able to sentimentalize family blood-ties or his real European legacy by disguising himself in an alpaca suit and humming "The Blue Danube."

In 1952 Kreisel was awarded a Royal Society of Canada Fellowship and went to the University of London, where he completed a Ph.D. in 1954. His dissertation, "The Problem of Exile and Alienation in Modern Literature," focused on Conrad, D. H. Lawrence, James Joyce, and Virginia Woolf. In a 1974 interview with Felix Cherniavsky (excerpted in *Another Country*) Kreisel commented on his academic work: "I've

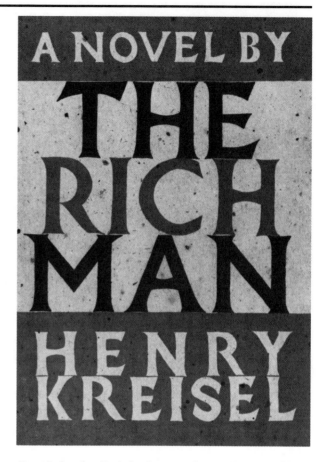

Dust jacket for Kreisel's first novel. In The Rich Man, *Kreisel explained in a 1974 interview, "I tried to relate the Canadian experience to the European experience by taking an immigrant back to Europe and thus gaining a double view."*

never been a dispassionate scholar. . . . I focused on subjects that would be of some interest to me as a person and as a writer. . . . I wanted to look at exile and alienation because. . . . that would tell me something about myself. I mean I was, in one way, an exile. I had lived in Austria, . . . and was then in a sense banished during the Hitler time. I became an exile, a refugee and so, because I was an outsider, certain of the alienating features of modern society were clear to me."

Kreisel resumed his teaching position in Edmonton in 1954, becoming a full professor in 1959 and department head from 1961 to 1967, when he was appointed a senior associate dean of the Faculty of Graduate Studies. He was acting dean of faculty from 1969 to 1970; he then served as academic vice-president of the university until 1975, when he was named University Professor. In 1988 he became an Officer of the Order of Canada. *The Betrayal*, his second novel, appeared in 1964. In the interview with Cherniavsky, Kreisel explains that in *The Rich*

Man he "tried to relate the Canadian experience to the European experience by taking an immigrant back to Europe and thus gaining a double view"; in *The Betrayal* he "brought a European to this country and particularly to Edmonton. In one sense, I . . . saw in *The Betrayal* the European experience of the war through Canadian eyes."

The Betrayal is more ambitious, more complex, more technically accomplished, and more explicitly a literary novel than *The Rich Man*. It is more literary in its deliberate, repeated allusions to and echoes of Conrad, Eliot, Auden, Yeats, Wordsworth, Shakespeare, and Dante; more technically accomplished both in its elaborate Conradian narrative structure and in its intricate meshing of realistic with symbolic settings, characters, and relationships; more ambitious in its moral scope; and more complex (and ambiguous) in its elusive, many-edged ironies.

Mark Lerner, the first-person narrator, is a young professor of history at the University of Alberta. Objective, dispassionate, pedantic, he lectures his naive Canadian undergraduates on the French Revolution. He is attracted to one of his students, Katherine Held, who brings him into contact with Theodore Stappler. Stappler is the lone survivor of a group of Austrian refugees betrayed twelve years earlier by Joseph Held, Katherine's father. Held had been paid to get them safely to France from Vienna, but he had handed them over to the Nazis to save his own family. Stappler has come to Canada seeking revenge on Held, but he is haunted by the feeling that he, too, betrayed the group (and himself); forewarned by a few minutes, he could not bring himself to act in time to save the others (including his mother) from being led away. Stappler chooses Lerner to be the secret sharer of his burden; as Lerner listens, he is drawn out of his detached professorial stance and forced to look history in the face and judge both men's actions. Are they, were they wholly responsible for what they did, as Stappler claims? Is Lerner, by hearing the story, also implicated? By extension, are we all? Stappler's unforeseen attraction to Katherine complicates his plans for revenge, and his long-awaited confrontation with Held is anticlimactic. Finally he leaves Edmonton and Katherine, his quest for justice and revenge unfulfilled. In a "postscript" Lerner describes Stappler's last years as a doctor in the far North, which end with his disappearance on a dangerous rescue mission. Lerner is left to ponder the meaning of Stappler's odyssey; his retelling of

Stappler's story makes him, the "learner," the novel's central figure.

The Betrayal is an inquiry on several levels into the nature of men's responsibility to one another and for their own actions. Lerner, unwilling as he is to judge, is inclined to see both Held's and Stappler's acts as determined by the press of extraordinarily trying circumstances. But Lerner's Olympian objectivity constitutes a betrayal of his own subjective response; his austere and safely detached pose becomes an indictment of Canadian complacency toward recent history. Kreisel's academic narrator learns through Stappler's impassioned pleading that history is a living presence; by setting what one critic calls his "morality play" in Edmonton and Vienna, Kreisel again brings the citizens of his broken globe into a charged confrontation. Lerner's version of Stappler's story is shaped as much by the history of actual places and events as by the literary tradition on which Kreisel draws to identify both characters' common inheritance: romantics, ironists, self-conscious hollow men in a wasteland, secret sharers of "the horror, the horror" of a postwar moral desert, each disturbs the universe with his tentative groping toward fuller vision.

Kreisel's short fiction is collected in *The Almost Meeting and Other Stories* (1981). Six of the eight stories, which first appeared in such journals as the *Literary Review*, *Prism*, *Queen's Quarterly*, and *Tamarack Review*, are republished without revision. The title story is published for the first time, and "Homecoming," first published in the anthology *Klanak Islands* (1959), is expanded from nine to fifty pages and subtitled "A Memory of Europe After the Holocaust." In these two stories, and in "Chassidic Song," "Two Sisters in Geneva," and "The Broken Globe" (which has been dramatized and translated into several languages), Kreisel continues to explore the ruptures, discontinuities, and "almost meetings" between Old and New World characters and visions.

In 1985 *Another Country: Writings by and about Henry Kreisel*, edited by Shirley Neuman, was published in Edmonton by NeWest Press. This collection is indispensable for readers of Kreisel's work. It comprises previously unpublished letters; selections from Kreisel's writings during his internment; various previously uncollected works; a selection of critical essays on Kreisel, including important studies by Michael Greenstein ("The Language of the Holocaust in *The Rich Man*," "Perspectives on the Holocaust in

Henry Kreisel's *The Betrayal*"), Robert Lecker ("States of Mind: Henry Kreisel's Novels"), and Thomas Tavsky ("Under Western Canadian Eyes: Conrad and *The Betrayal*"); and both the fullest interview with Kreisel and the most current bibliography of his work, by Neuman. Kreisel has said that A. M. Klein showed him the possibility of setting his whole experience in a Canadian context; Kreisel sees himself as "one of the first people . . . to bring to modern Canadian literature the experience of the immigrant." Canadian literature is the richer for his work.

References:

Neil Besner, "Kreisel's Broken Globes," *Canadian Literature*, 107 (Winter 1985): 103-111;

Shirley Neuman, ed., *Another Country: Writings by and about Henry Kreisel* (Edmonton: NeWest, 1985);

John Stedmond, Introduction to Kreisel's *The Rich Man* (Toronto: McClelland & Stewart, 1961);

S. Warhaft, Introduction to Kreisel's *The Betrayal* (Toronto: McClelland & Stewart, 1971).

Papers:

In the fall of 1989 Kreisel's papers became part of the archives and special collections at the University of Manitoba Libraries.

Gatien Lapointe

(18 December 1931-15? September 1983)

Alexandre L. Amprimoz
Brock University

BOOKS: *Jour malaisé* (Montreal, 1953);

Otages de la joie (Montreal: Editions du Muy, 1955);

Le Temps premier (Paris: Grassin, 1962);

Ode au Saint-Laurent, précédé de J'appartiens à la terre (Montreal: Editions du Jour, 1963);

Le Premier Mot, précédé de Le Pari de ne pas mourir (Montreal: Editions du Jour, 1967);

Confrontation, English version of "Face à face" from *Le Premier Mot*, translated by Fred Cogswell (Fredericton: Fiddlehead, 1973);

Arbre-radar (Montreal: Editions de l'Hexagone, 1980);

Barbare inouï (Trois-Rivières, Que.: Ecrits des Forges, 1981);

Corps et graphie (Trois-Rivières, Que.: Editions du Sextant, 1981);

Corps transistor (Trois-Rivières, Que.: Editions du Sextant, 1981);

Le Premier Passage, by Lapointe, drawings by Christine Lemire (Trois-Rivières, Que.: Ecrits des Forges, 1983).

OTHER: Mia and Klaus Matthes, *Quebec*, text by Lapointe (Montreal: Libre Expression, 1981).

Mainly known for his *Ode au Saint-Laurent* (Ode to the Saint Lawrence, 1963), Gatien Lapointe is representative of the *Hexagone* poets, a group of writers who gave Quebec literature a new spirit of independence and a distinct postcolonial voice. A sign of his lasting influence is the society Les Amis de Gatien Lapointe, founded and directed by the Quebec poet Cécile Cloutier.

Joseph-Gatien-Fernand Lapointe was born on 18 December 1931 in Sainte-Justine-de-Dorchester, a small town in the Etchemain valley, seventy miles south of Quebec and three miles from the United States border. His parents, Evangéliste and Elisa Lessard Lapointe, worked the family farm. According to the poet, this land–where "tout est excessif et lointain" (everything is

Gatien Lapointe (photograph by Adrien Thério, courtesy of Editions Québec/Amérique, Montreal)

excessive and distant)–provided the raw material of his poetry.

In 1937 he was enrolled in the local grade school, and in 1943 his father died, a personal tragedy for Lapointe which left its mark in the courageous pessimism of his later writing. In the fall of 1944 he was sent to Quebec City, where he studied at the Petit Séminaire until 1950. Some of the poems included in Lapointe's first two collections date to this period. He wrote them at the age of seventeen and, later in life, humbly referred to them as "des brouillons," or rough drafts, of poems.

In the fall of 1950 Lapointe moved to Montreal where he studied at the Ecole des Arts Graphiques. This period was one of hesitation during which he tried his hand at music, painting, and theater. His great discovery of those years was the work of the French surrealist poet Paul Eluard. In 1952 Lapointe left the Ecole des Arts Graphiques to study literature at the Université de Montréal; he graduated in 1955 with a B.A. and in 1956 with an M.A.

A fellowship from the Royal Society of Canada (1956-1958) allowed him to go to Paris and begin doctoral studies, focusing on Eluard. Lapointe traveled throughout Europe until 1962. It was in January 1961, in Paris (and not in Montreal as has sometimes been reported), that the poet wrote *Ode au Saint-Laurent*–a detail that recalls James Joyce's notion of the necessity of exile for a powerful insight into the life of one's native land.

Back in Quebec in 1962, Lapointe began contributing to French-Canadian periodicals, including *Le Soleil*, *Le Devoir*, *L'Action*, *Liberté*, *Hobo-Québec*, and *Estuaire*. In the fall of the same year he took a position teaching French and French-Canadian literature at the Collège Militaire de Saint-Jean. The publication of *Ode au Saint-Laurent* in 1963 brought the poet three literary prizes: the Prix du Club des Poètes, the Prix Du Maurier, and a Governor General's Award. Lapointe was visiting professor at McGill University (1963-1964) and at Carleton University (1965). In 1967 he received the Prix de la Province de Québec for *Le Premier Mot* (The First Word), and in 1969 he accepted a position teaching creative writing at the Université du Québec à Trois-Rivières. There, two years later, he founded and became director of the publishing house Ecrits des Forges, dedicated to producing works by young and unknown poets. In the early 1980s Lapointe produced three experimental poetry collections. He was found dead at his home in Trois-Rivières in September 1983.

Jour malaisé (Difficult Day, 1953), the first of Lapointe's books, concerns the pain of growing up, both on an individual level and for the whole of a Quebec society striving for cultural maturity. Thus, from the start, the lyrical and ideological dimensions of Lapointe's poetry are inseparable. *Jour malaisé* is composed of sixty-four short (eleven- to fourteen-line) poems divided into five sections: "Musique painte" (Painted Music), "A-

quarelle d'automne" (Autumn Watercolor), "Chiffons de lumière" (Rags of Light), "Etoiles mortes" (Dead Stars), and "Murailles du soir" (Evening Walls). Joseph Bonenfant, in *Livres et Auteurs Québécois* (1970), sees the symbolic structure of *Jour malaisé* in the poet's effort to part day from night and links this verbal chiaroscuro effect to Jacques Ferron's *L'Amelanchier* (*The Juneberry Tree*, 1970), in that both use natural dualities to comment on Quebec's social condition. Cécile Cloutier-Wojciechowska's analysis in *Poetics of the Elements in the Human Condition* (1985) further emphasizes how the dualities of Lapointe's poetry reveal the essence of Quebecois aesthetics.

Otages de la joie (Hostages of Joy, 1955), like *Jour malaisé*, with its themes of love and human solidarity, with its focus on the image of the child, continues to demonstrate the influence of Eluard, to whom Lapointe dedicates the last of the twenty-seven poems in this collection. The intensity of the poetry in this volume is summarized by Wilfrid Lemoine in a notice for *La Revue Dominicaine* (July-August 1955): "Elle traduit un être sensible, ardent, qui vous donne un peu le vertige et qui vous surprend" (It reveals a sensitive and passionate human being; it makes you a little dizzy, and it startles you).

Lapointe's work culminates with *Ode au Saint-Laurent*. The following lines from the opening section indicate how the river is made to be the speech of the Quebecois, the center of consciousness and self-knowledge:

> Ma langue est d'Amérique
> Je suis né de ce paysage
> J'ai pris souffle dans le limon du fleuve
> Je suis la terre et je suis la parole
> ....
> Mon enfance est celle d'un arbre
> Neiges et pluies pénètrent mes épaules
> Humus et germes montent dans mes veines
> Je suis mémoire je suis avenir
> J'ai arraché au ciel la clarté de mes yeux
> J'ai ouvert mes paumes aux quatre vents
> Je prends règne sur les saisons
> Mes sens sont des lampes perçant la nuit
> ....
> J'ai allumé un feu sur la haute clairière
> Je suis descendu dans l'aine des sources
> Le parfum du sol me frappe au visage
> La femme aux hanches brillantes d'aurore
> L'homme à genoux inventant Dieu
> Je suivrai la marche du fleuve
> Je connais ensemble hier et demain
> Et c'est aujourd'hui qu'il me faut construire

Front cover for the collection that includes Lapointe's best-known poem, an ode to the Saint Lawrence River (courtesy of Kenneth Landry). The volume won a Governor General's Award for 1963.

(My speech is from America
I was born of this landscape
I drew my first breath from the silt of the river
I am the earth and I am the word
....
My childhood is that of a tree
Snows and rains penetrate my shoulders
Humus and seeds rise in my veins
I am memory I am the future
I tore from the sky the light in my eyes
I opened my palms to the four winds
I rule over the seasons
My senses are lamps piercing the night.
....
I lit a fire in the clearing high above
I went down to the groin of the sources
The fragrance of the ground strikes me in the face
Woman's hips gleaming in the morning light
Man kneeling inventing God
I will follow the course of the river

I know both yesterday and tomorrow
And it is today that I must build).

The paramount theme is one of belonging to Quebec, the fatherland, the metonymy of the American continent. Its effectiveness stems from the recurrent declaration of the image of the river in Quebec culture. For Quebeckers, there is only one "great river," and majestic descriptions of the St. Lawrence go back in Quebec tradition as far as Jacques Cartier's *Brefs Récits* (1545), and include Louis Fréchette's *Légende d'un peuple* (1887), Charles Gill's *Cap Eternité* (1919), Gustave Lamarche's "Ode au Saint-Laurent" (1944), folklore, patriotic songs, religious hymns, and even the French version of "O Canada" with its mention of the "fleuve géant." Throughout Quebec history, the river has been an *image* of self; in Lapointe's poem it becomes the language, the speech of self as well.

The formal features of Lapointe's unrhymed, three-part, 493-line poem stress the poet's awareness of his belonging to the resounding national chorus. A stanza of 8 lines is followed by a single line and a distich. The single line and the distich either echo the theme of the preceding stanza or announce the following. The three movements develop five themes: the origin of the poetic universe, the supremacy of Earth, the word as creator of the world, the country as ultimate objective, and the failure of man when confronted by his own mystery.

Lapointe's 1967 volume, *Le Premier Mot*, includes a prose piece, *Le Pari de ne pas mourir* (Wager to Never Die), in which the author outlines his poetics: poetry is the negation of death; human dignity is the only possible response to fate. Lapointe's subsequent collections are more experimental insofar as they rely upon typographical effects, artwork, and musical scores. *Arbre-radar* (Radar Tree, 1980), written in the tradition of Rimbaud's poem "Voyelles" (Vowels), reveals a poet haunted by Friedrich Hölderlin, Gérard de Nerval, Stéphane Mallarmé, Guillaume Apollinaire, Paul Eluard, René Char, Octavio Paz, Emile Nelligan, and Yves Bonnefoy. *Barbare inouï* (Incredible Barbarian, 1981) consists of a poem in thirteen sections, each printed on a loose black sheet with typography in white. The poems of the 1981 volume *Corps et graphie* develop the play on words in the title, Body and Writing–Choreography. *Corps transistor* (Transistor-Body, 1981) and *Le Premier Passage* (First Passage, 1983) were conceived as parts of a larger project that Lapointe began in 1976. Although critics have pointed out a continuity in the poetry of Lapointe and praised the later experimental verse, *Ode au Saint-Laurent* is likely to remain his most enduring achievement.

References:

Joseph Bonenfant, "La Passion des mots chez Gatien Lapointe," *Livres et Auteurs Québécois* (1970): 248-254;

Cécile Cloutier-Wojciechowska, "The St. Lawrence in the Poetry of Gatien Lapointe," in *Poetics of the Elements in the Human Condition*, edited by Anna-Teresa Tymieniecka (Dordrecht: Reidel, 1985), pp. 261-265;

Gérald Gaudet, *Les Ecrits des Forges: Une Poésie en devenirs* (Trois-Rivières, Que.: Ecrits des Forges, 1983);

Eva Kushner, "La Seconde Jeunesse de Gatien Lapointe," *La Poésie québécoise depuis 1975*, special issue of *Dalhousie French Studies* (1985): 108-114;

Maximilien Laroche, "Notes sur le style de trois poètes, Roland Giguère, Gatien Lapointe, Paul Chamberland," *Voix et Images du Pays*, 2 (1969): 90-106;

Laroche, "Le Pays: un thème et une forme," *Cahiers de Sainte-Marie*, 4 (1967): 103-124;

Laroche, "Sentiment de l'espace et image du temps chez quelques écrivains québécois," *Voix et Images du Pays*, 7 (1973): 167-182;

Henri-Dominique Paratte, "Gatien Lapointe: ouïr l'inouï," *La Poésie québécoise depuis 1975*, special issue of *Dalhousie French Studies* (1985): 31-42;

Bernard Pozier, *Gatien Lapointe: L'Homme en marche* (Trois-Rivières, Que.: Ecrits des Forges / Cesson-la-Forêt, France: Table Rase, 1987).

Paul-Marie Lapointe

(22 September 1929‑   )

Roger Chamberland
Université Laval

BOOKS: *Le Vierge incendié* (Montreal: Editions Mithra-Mythe, 1948);

Choix de poèmes: Arbres (Montreal: Editions de l'Hexagone, 1960);

Pour les âmes (Montreal: Editions de l'Hexagone, 1964);

Le Réel absolu: Poèmes 1948-1965 (Montreal: Editions de l'Hexagone, 1971);

Tableaux de l'amoureuse, suivi de Une, unique; Art égyptien; Voyage et autres poèmes (Montreal: Editions de l'Hexagone, 1974);

Bouche rouge (Outremont, Que.: L'Obsidienne, 1976);

The Terror of the Snows: Selected Poems, translated by D. G. Jones (Pittsburgh: University of Pittsburgh Press, 1976); revised and enlarged as *The 5th Season* (Toronto: Exile, 1985);

Tombeau de René Crevel (Outremont, Que.: L'Obsidienne, 1979);

Ecritures (Outremont, Que.: L'Obsidienne, 1980).

The son of a banker, Antoine Lapointe, and his wife, Antoinette Rousseau Lapointe, Joseph-Auguste-Julien-Paul-Marie Lapointe was born 22 September 1929 at Saint-Félicien in the Lac Saint-Jean region of Quebec. He studied at the Séminaire de Chicoutimi and at the Collège Saint-Laurent and the Ecole des Beaux-Arts in Montreal. After leaving school, he became a journalist with *Evénement-Journal* in Quebec City in 1950, staying there for four years. In Quebec he married Gisèle Verreault, an artist, on 29 November 1952; they have two children, Michèle and Frédéric. In 1955 Lapointe moved to *La Presse* in Montreal, working with the paper until 1960. With Jean-Louis Gagnon he helped found the *Nouveau-Journal* in Montreal in 1961, occupying the post of director of information. Moving to *Le Magazine Maclean*, serving as general editor from 1963 to 1968, he then joined Radio-Canada, where he has in turn been head of the news service, head of radio information, and director of radio programming, the post he now occupies. Parallel to these professional activities, he has

Paul-Marie Lapointe (photograph by Kèro)

also followed a literary career, publishing several collections of noteworthy poetry, which have won for him various prizes and honors: the Prix David and a Governor General's Award (both in 1972), the International Poetry Forum Prize (1976), and the Prix de La Presse (1980).

Scarcely turned eighteen, in 1947 Lapointe wrote his first book, *Le Vierge incendié* (The Virgin Burned), influenced by Paul Eluard's *Capitale de la douleur (Capital of Pain)* and Arthur Rimbaud's *Illuminations*. The book was published in 1948 by Editions Mithra-Mythe, the same publisher that, the same year, had produced the manifesto *Refus Global (Total Refusal)* and other texts of the *automatiste* group associated with the painter Paul-Emile Borduas. Lapointe's book employs the techniques of surrealism and to some degree displays the same formal and ideological preoccupations as the works of the *automatistes*. He had some ties with the group, principally with Claude and Pierre Gauvreau, who had helped arrange the publication of *Le Vierge incendié*. Comprising about a hundred poems (most of them prose poems, some in free verse, and three of them rhymed), Lapointe's book is divided into five sections, the titles suggesting the most important motifs: "Crânes scalpés," "Vos ventres lisses," "On dévaste mon coeur," "Il y a des rêves," and "La Création du monde" (Scalped Heads, Your Flat Stomachs, My Broken Heart, Dreams Ago, and The Creation of the World).

Lapointe works here with themes of love, freedom, art, the city, and violence, and he is aware of the human condition in a world ravaged by World War II, especially of existence in a place (such as Quebec) that has closed itself off and allowed the force of religious order to be all-powerful. In one of the poems in *Le Vierge incendié*, "Nous sommes installés sous le tonnerre . . ." ("We Have Taken Our Places Under the Thunder," in D. G. Jones's 1976 translation of Lapointe's selected poems, *The Terror of the Snows*), the speakers assert, "nous sommes installés sous le tonnerre // les compagnons sont effarés leurs poitrines blanchiront / paroles de chaux // leurs squelettes debout supportent l'hiver" ("we have taken our places under the thunder // companions are frightened their breasts will go white / words become lime // their upright skeletons shoulder the winter"). These speakers take their places in a desolate world, one made desolate because various authorities insist on retaining power: "les capitales piétinent leur peuple" ("the capitals trample their people"). Poetry of revolt against the established order, poetry contesting traditional forms, *Le Vierge incendié* is a new kind of verse, one unfamiliar in Quebec at the time, characterized by, in André G. Bourassa's words in the *Dictionnaire des œuvres littéraires du Québec*, a "juxtaposition littérale d'images" in a network of metaphors. Such poems are written as a painter paints pictures, letting motifs, images, symbols spring up as the imagination allows.

This same process of writing is the source of "Nuit du 15 au 26 novembre 1948," a suite of poems written in 1948 but not published until they were included in a special *automatiste* issue of *La Barre du Jour* in 1969 and not collected until

Lapointe's retrospective volume, *Le Réel absolu* (The Absolute Real), appeared in 1971. As Jean-Louis Major emphasizes in his *Paul-Marie Lapointe: La Nuit incendiée* (1978), this suite of poems provides a counterpoint to *Le Vierge incendié*: the 1948 volume demonstrates "l'experience du 'je' à travers le langage, [et] les vingt-neuf poèmes de 'Nuit du 15 au 26 novembre 1948' expriment les limites du langage à travers le 'moi'" (the experience of "I" through language, [and] the twenty-nine poems of "The Nights of the 15th to the 26th of November 1948" express the limits of language through the experience of "myself"). Full of a spirit of denunciation and revolt, and at the same time conscious of the limits of language and of the tension between that which is and that which can be, these texts reflect one another, creating the effect of a "noyade spéculaire" (drowning in mirrors), to use Major's phrase. Lapointe's mode of composition, as he has pointed out, can be likened to the workings of jazz, with each musician improvising in turn from a given motif. The long poem "Arbres" (Trees), appearing in the collection *Choix de poèmes: Arbres* (Selected poems: Trees, 1960), uses this technique effectively. The poet takes as his point of departure the celebrated work *La Flore laurentienne* (Laurentian Flora, 1935) by Frère Marie-Victorin; from this, out of a description of some species of trees, Lapointe draws the basic material that is multiplied through association of ideas and images.

With *Pour les âmes* (For the Souls, 1964), his third collection, Lapointe more radically and profoundly expresses a sense of alienation–the kind felt by those who are derided or forgotten and by individuals threatened by the precariousness of fate, personal or communal. Evocative titles such as "Psaume pour une révolte de terre" (Psalm for Earth's Revolt), "le temps tombe" (time falls), "Fragile Journée de mica" (The Fragile Day of Mica), "Epitaph pour un jeune révolté" (Epitaph for a Young Revolutionary), and "ICBM (Intercontinental Ballistic Missile)" express clearly the general theme of this work. It is important in this context not to forget the title of the work, *Pour les âmes*, which suggests a mystical function to the poetry. The extremely diverse writing in this work reinforces this idea; among the forms Lapointe uses is that of the psalm, which in the opening poem, in an incantatory ritual, fixes one parameter for the whole.

Lapointe's retrospective, *Le Réel absolu*, brings together all the titles that had been writ-

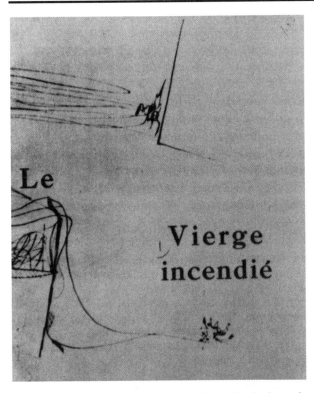

Front cover by Pierre Gauvreau for Lapointe's first book, a collection of one hundred poems that show the influence of Paul Eluard and Arthur Rimbaud (courtesy of Kenneth Landry)

ten from 1948 to 1965, including *Le Vierge incendié* and "Nuit du 15 au 26 novembre 1948." Premier Maurice Duplessis had died at the end of the 1950s, and there had been important social developments following the Quiet Revolution of the 1960s. Quebec had changed over the twenty years Lapointe had been writing, and readers of 1971 were more in tune with his poetic ideas. *Le Vierge incendié* won little notice in 1948; when it appeared in *Le Réel absolu* its mixture of the sacred and the erotic and its youthful and idealistic commitment to revolt commanded much greater attention. *Le Réel absolu* won for Lapointe his Governor General's Award and Prix David; it also earned him a new following.

The year 1974 saw the appearance of his next book, *Tableaux de l'amoureuse, suivi de Une, unique; Art égyptien; Voyage et autres poèmes* (Tableaux of the Lover, followed by One, Unique; Egyptian Art; Voyage and Other Poems). In this collection Lapointe steadily develops the themes of love and death—Eros and Thanatos indulging in their eternal combat. Suzanne Paradis, writing in the *Dictionnaire des œuvres littéraires du Québec*, finds in this work, as in that of Rina Lasnier and Alain Grandbois, "Une spiritualité exacerbée du réel érotique, par l'abolition des frontières autour de l'objet du culte amoureux et par l'émergence de l'âme pour l'agrandissement de la chair jusqu'à la démesure" (a spiritually exacerbated by erotic reality, by the abolition of the boundaries surrounding the object of love, and by the appearance of the soul, all for the purpose of enriching the self as much as possible). Three other publications soon followed. The first was *Bouche rouge* (Red Mouth [1976], translated in part by D. G. Jones in *The 5th Season*, his 1985 revision and enlargement of *The Terror of the Snows*). Like *Tableaux de l'amoureuse, Bouche rouge* was illustrated by the poet's wife, Gisèle Verreault. In 1979 *Tombeau de René Crevel* (Tomb of René Crevel) appeared, with watercolors by Betty Goodwin, and a year later Lapointe produced the monumental two-volume *Ecritures* (Writings). *Bouche rouge* celebrates femaleness, developing the theme of sensuality raised in his early writing and addressed in complex fashion in *Tableaux de l'amoureuse*. *Tombeau de René Crevel* pursues more radically the notion that language is independent from society; a tribute to a French surrealist poet who influenced Lapointe, the text consists entirely of selections from Crevel's work, the selection made according to an arbitrary system which allows the excerpts to be recombined into new arrangements. This commitment to the nonrepresentational function of language and the sense of the arbitrariness of formal arrangement (and therefore of "meaning") influence markedly Lapointe's next and longest work.

Over a thousand pages long, *Ecritures* is a difficult and ambitious book that examines the forms and the sense of poetic language; it is, one might say, a dance step using two typographies—"écRiturE"—allowing "writing" to be so free that chance itself seems definitive. In the collection eight of the nine parts covered by the title—that is, by the nine letters of the word *Ecritures*—are assigned one hundred poems; the last has thirty-six. These are followed by fifty-two nonrepresentational calligraphic designs entitled "Dactylologie." In this work Lapointe is attempting, he has said, to go "au bout de la forme et d'essayer d'éliminer toute subjectivité. Pour que l'écriture devienne une révolte de la langue même contre le discours habituel. C'est une révolte à l'intérieur même du langage. Je n'ai donc pas pris mes mots, j'ai éliminé toute possibilité de créer un discours cohérent qui puisse être comparé à une façon qu'on a de parler ou d'écrire normalement" (to the limits of form and to try to eliminate all subjectivity. In order that writing become a revolt on the part of language itself against ordinary discourse. It's a revolt at the very heart of language. I have not taken words in hand, I have eliminated all possibility of creating a coherent discourse that can be compared in any way to how one speaks or writes normally). This enterprise did not receive the response that Lapointe might have anticipated. Perhaps it was this modified welcome that since *Ecritures* has confined Lapointe to silence.

Lapointe occupies a special place in Quebec literature. His first works were written in a spirit of liberation that aligns him with the *automatise* group, with whom he had strong ties. His poetry, always independent of literary movements, modes, and school, has had as its primary concern the search for a language free from the constraints of codes–be they linguistic, social, or cultural. Lapointe is one of those writers of the 1940s and 1950s who helped begin the cultural revolution that came to fruition in the 1960s. His work, like that of Claude Gauvreau, has had an international influence.

References:

Pierre-André Arcand, "*Le Vierge incendié* de Paul-Marie Lapointe," *Voix et Images du Pays*, 8 (Spring 1974): 11-38;

André G. Bourassa, *Surréalisme et littérature québécoise: Histoire d'une révolution culturel* (Montreal: Les Herbes Rouges, 1988), pp. 285-298;

Etudes Françaises, special issue on Lapointe, 16, no. 2 (1980);

Jean Fisette, "*Le Vierge incendié* de Paul-Marie Lapointe: Pour une typologie des énoncés," *Brèches*, no. 4-5 (Spring-Summer 1975): 12-68;

Guy Laflèche, "Ecart, violence et révolte chez Paul-Marie Lapointe," *Etudes Françaises*, 6 (November 1970): 395-417;

Jean-Louis Major, *Paul-Marie Lapointe: La Nuit incendiée* (Montreal: Presses de l'Université de Montréal, 1978);

Pierre Nepveu, *Les Mots à l'écoute: Poésie et silence chez Fernand Ouellette, Gaston Miron et Paul-Marie Lapointe* (Quebec: Presses de l'Université Laval, 1979);

Georges-André Vachon, "Note sur Réjean Ducharme et Paul-Marie Lapointe (Fragment d'un Traité du vide)," *Etudes Françaises*, 11 (October 1975): 355-387.

Rina Lasnier
(6 August 1915-   )

Gwladys Downes
University of Victoria

BOOKS: *Féerie indienne: Kateri Tekakwitha* (Saint-Jean, Que.: Editions du Richelieu, 1939);

Images et proses (Saint-Jean, Que.: Editions du Richelieu, 1941);

Le Jeu de la voyagère (Montreal: Editions de la Société des Ecrivains Canadiens, 1941);

Les Fiançailles d'Anne de Noüe (Montreal: Secretariat de la Ligue Missionnaire des Etudiants, 1943);

Le Mère de nos mères (Montreal: Editions Messager Canadien, 1943);

Madones canadiennes (Montreal: Beauchemin, 1944);

Le Chant de la montée (Montreal: Beauchemin, 1947);

Notre-Dame du Pain, published with *Notre-Dame de la Couronne*, by Gustave Lamarche (Joliette, Que.: Editions des Paroliers du Roi, 1947);

Escales (Trois Rivières, Que.: Privately printed, 1950);

Présence de l'absence (Montreal: Editions de l'Hexagone, 1956);

La Grande Dame des Pauvres (Montreal: Editions les Soeurs Grises, 1959);

Mémoire sans jours (Montreal: Editions de l'Atelier, 1960);

Miroirs (Montreal: Editions de l'Atelier, 1960);

Les Gisants, suivi des *Quatrains quotidiens* (Montreal: Editions de l'Atelier, 1963);

L'Arbre blanc (Montreal: Editions de l'Hexagone, 1966);

Ces Visages qui sont un pays (Ottawa: Editions de l'O. N. F., 1968);

L'Invisible (Montreal: Editions du Grainier, 1969);

La Part du feu (Montreal: Editions du Songe, 1970);

La Salle des rêves (Montreal: Hurtubise HMH, 1971);

Poèmes, 2 volumes (Montreal: Fides, 1972);

Le Rêve du quart jour (Saint-Jean, Que.: Editions du Richelieu, 1973);

L'Echelle des anges (Montreal: Fides, 1975);

Les Signes (Montreal: Hurtubise HMH, 1976);

Rina Lasnier (courtesy of Kenneth Landry)

Matin d'oiseaux (Montreal: Hurtubise HMH, 1978);

Paliers de paroles (Montreal: Hurtubise HMH, 1978);

Entendre l'ombre (Montreal: Hurtubise HMH, 1981);

Voir la nuit (Montreal: Hurtubise HMH, 1981);

Le Soleil noir (Joliette, Que.: Editions de la Parabole, 1981);

Le Choix de Rina Lasnier: dans l'œuvre de Rina Lasnier (Notre-Dame-des Laurentides, Que.: Presses Laurientiennes, 1981);

Chant perdu (Trois-Rivières, Que.: Ecrits des Forges, 1983);

Etudes et rencontres (Joliette, Que.: Editions de la Parabole, 1984);

L'Ombre jetée, 2 volumes (Trois Rivières, Que.: Ecrits des Forges, 1987).

Rina Lasnier, daughter of Moise and Laura Galipeau Lasnier, was born on 6 August 1915, in Saint-Grégoire d'Iberville, Quebec. Educated at the Collège Marguerite Bourgeoys and the University of Montreal, she received degrees in French literature, English literature, and library science, although she has never used the last professionally. She has also worked as a journalist.

Before entering the university she was, most unusually for her time and provincial milieu, sent to a private school in England (Palace Gate, Exeter), an experience which profoundly influenced the direction of her poetic sensibilities by widening the scope of her reading in poetry as well as making her virtually bilingual. She has written poems in English in addition to her voluminous output in French, which includes two poetic dramas and two short stories as well as more than thirty volumes of verse.

A member of the Académie Canadienne Française since its inception (1945), she is the recipient of many literary awards, including the Prix David (1943 and 1974), the Prix Duvernay (1957), the Molson Prize (1971), the A. J. M. Smith prize (1972), the Prix France-Canada (1973), the Lorne Pierce Medal (1974), and the Prix Edgar Poe (France, 1979). She has also received an honorary degree from the University of Montreal (1977) and is a member of the Royal Society of Canada. Her home for many years has been Joliette, Quebec, where she continues to write and lecture.

In spite of these tangible proofs of recognition her work has not always met with approval or understanding in the Quebec literary world which became steadily more polarized after World War II when change in the universities replaced clerical with secular control and led to the extraordinary literary explosion of the 1960s. Poetry became suddenly part of the social and political ferment of the time against intellectual censorship and repression of all kinds, with the result that Lasnier, a deeply committed Catholic, was regarded with either indifference or hostility as an example of pious conventional thought. Neither the emotional and spiritual basis of her religious experience, which is universal, nor the literary

craft and point of view inherited from French poets of the previous hundred years, commended her to a new generation.

Lasnier is not an innovator in verse forms in spite of the great variety of metrical and stanza patterns she uses—including *vers libre* which, such was the cultural isolation of her environment, she was criticized for employing in the 1940s. Her particular skill has been to develop a long rhythmic line whose variations pile up like a series of waves against the reader's mind. It is very flexible, as effective in the love poems as in the complex analysis of the process of literary creation. "Tu es né mêlé à moi comme à l'archaïque lumière les eaux sans pesanteur" (You were born mingled with me of the first as light and misty creation). Coupled with a rich vocabulary and compressed imagery, this use of the long line, from the title poem in *Présence de l'absence* (1956), is reminiscent of both Paul Claudel's *versets* and St. John Perse.

In her first published work, *Féerie indienne: Kateri Tekakwitha* (An Indian Miracle Play: Kateri Tekakwitha, 1939), the theme which would dominate Lasnier's poetry during the next decades is stated very clearly. It is the struggle of the human soul to reach God, typified by the experiences of a saintly young Iroquois girl who refuses marriage to the son of the village sorcerer in order to give herself to the Christian faith. Although the work belongs, superficially speaking, to the romantic view of the American Indian, the intensity of Lasnier's vision and the biblical rhythms in the language signal from the outset that she is a writer capable of absorbing influences and fusing them with feeling in order to make a personal statement.

Her originality within Quebec lies in the way in which, without abandoning her profound Catholicism, she has elevated the "Christ folklorique" of the Quebec countryside into the incarnate principle of all creation, not only outside the poet's consciousness but inside it. She is not a mystic, but she has always been drawn to writers who, in any language, explore the various ways of communion with the ineffable. Reacting as a girl against "intellectual French poetry," she found, in England, her real spiritual nourishment in poets such as Francis Thompson and Gerard Manley Hopkins, along, later, with Edward Fitzgerald and the medieval Sufi poets who seemed closer than the French to her natural way of apprehending reality. Her continuing interest in other ways of approaching the divine has led her into reading, and occasionally writing, about the religion of ancient Egypt, as well as Hindu and Chinese philosophies.

She believes that "la poésie a toujours été intégrée au sacré; l'homme a toujours fait confiance à la poésie pour temoigner de son âme ou de Dieu" (poetry has always been an integral part of the sacred; man has always trusted poetry to bear witness to his soul or to his God). With the crucifixion as the central theme in her poetic consciousness, she explores both her inner and outer worlds. Poetry takes place in the area between *le sang et la lumière* (blood and light): "De ces cheveux liés de limon et de sang / l'infroissable pureté des astres et du feu" ("Out of his hair clotted with blood and clay / the scatheless purity of stars and fire" [from "Corps du Christ," translated by John Glassco as "The Body of Christ," *Ellipse*, 22, 1978]).

One does not have to be a symbolist to think in symbols. In Lasnier's poetry based on the natural life of the Quebec countryside–birds, flowers, trees, snow–there are few poems which do not carry overtones of symbolic meaning. Particularly noticeable are birds, which soar toward the light, and snow, which becomes either a sign of pure beauty or the equivalent of sterility and death. In "Le Pin solitaire" (The Solitary Pine) the poet identifies herself completely with the blasted pine rather than the softer forest growth around it; she is "cette mort au bout d'une epée de flamme" (this death on the point of a flaming sword). The actual object can be used with either positive or negative connotations depending on the poet's mood and intention.

Lasnier's love poetry is as effective–more so sometimes–as her religious verses and indeed is pervaded by an understanding of the relationships between human love and the divine. "Rien ne me porte aux confidences" (Personal confessions aren't my style), she says in the preface to *Poèmes* (1972), but the heart which is expressed in the poems obviously carries a great weight of anguish in the face of loss, absence, and death. Although many poems recall the joys of a lost paradise, the majority are full of deep sorrow and the

yearning for the unattainable, without a trace of the bitterness arising from sexual betrayal or jealousy. In "Le Champ du souvenir" (The Field of Memory), for example, the poet writes: "Ma peine précise ton absence,/l'ombre de falaise te repense" (My grief is the shape of your absence, / You return in the cliff's shadow). However, there is nothing passive in this poetry, where an undercurrent of rage and rebellion mingles with despair as the writer struggles to place her acceptance on the altar of the suffering Christ.

Rina Lasnier remains a unique figure in Quebec literature. Unlike many intellectuals before and after World War II she has never regarded herself as an exile from French culture, or established roots in France. She has not, however, been influenced by the popular Quebec movements toward feminism, totally free expression, or the use of *joual*, choosing rather to pursue a solitary vocation according to her own perception of poetry and the poet's role.

References:

Anne-Marie Alonzo, ed., *Rina Lasnier, ou, Le Langage des sources: Essais* (Trois Rivières, Que.: Estuaire, 1988);

Joseph Bonenfant and Richard Giguère, "Est-il une chose plus belle qu'une orange? Rencontre avec Rina Lasnier," *Voix et Images*, 4 (September 1978): 5-32; translated by M. L. Taylor as "Conversation with Rina Lasnier," *Ellipse*, no. 22 (1978): 32-61;

Ellipse, special issue on Lasnier and A. J. M. Smith, no. 22 (1978);

Sylvie Gelina-Sicotte, *L'Arbre dans la poésie de Rina Lasnier* (Sherbrooke, Que.: Cosmos, 1977);

Eva Kushner, ed., *Rina Lasnier* (Montreal: Fides, 1964);

Liberté, special issue on Lasnier, 18 (November-December 1976);

Claude Pelletier, ed., *Poétesses québécoises: Dossiers de presse* (Sherbrooke, Que.: Bibliothèque du Seminaire de Sherbrooke, 1986).

Papers:

Rina Lasnier's papers are at the Bibliothèque Nationale du Québec, in Montreal.

Irving Layton

(12 March 1912-   )

Ira Bruce Nadel
University of British Columbia

BOOKS: *Here and Now* (Montreal: First Statement, 1945);

Now Is the Place (Montreal: First Statement, 1948);

The Black Huntsmen (Montreal: Privately printed, 1951);

Cerberus, by Layton, Louis Dudek, and Raymond Souster (Toronto: Contact, 1952);

Love The Conqueror Worm (Toronto: Contact, 1953);

In The Midst of My Fever (Palma de Mallorca: Divers, 1954);

The Long Pea-Shooter (Montreal: Laocoön, 1954);

The Blue Propeller (Toronto: Contact, 1955);

The Cold Green Element (Toronto: Contact, 1955);

The Bull Calf and Other Poems (Toronto: Contact, 1956);

The Improved Binoculars (Highlands, N.C.: Jonathan Williams, 1956);

Music On a Kazoo (Toronto: Contact, 1956);

A Laughter in the Mind (Highlands, N.C.: Jonathan Williams, 1958; enlarged, Montreal: Editions d'Orphée, 1959);

A Red Carpet for the Sun (Toronto: McClelland & Stewart, 1959; Highlands, N.C.: Jonathan Williams, 1959);

The Swinging Flesh (Toronto: McClelland & Stewart, 1961);

Balls for a One-Armed Juggler (Toronto: McClelland & Stewart, 1963);

The Laughing Rooster (Toronto: McClelland & Stewart, 1964);

Collected Poems (Toronto: McClelland & Stewart, 1965);

Periods of the Moon (Toronto: McClelland & Stewart, 1967);

The Shattered Plinths (Toronto: McClelland & Stewart, 1968);

The Whole Bloody Bird: Obs, Aphs & Pomes (Toronto: McClelland & Stewart, 1969);

Selected Poems, edited by Wynne Francis (Toronto: McClelland & Stewart, 1969);

The Collected Poems of Irving Layton (Toronto: McClelland & Stewart, 1971);

Nail Polish (Toronto: McClelland & Stewart, 1971);

Engagements: The Prose of Irving Layton, edited by Seymour Mayne (Toronto: McClelland & Stewart, 1972);

Lovers and Lesser Men (Toronto: McClelland & Stewart, 1973);

The Pole Vaulter (Toronto: McClelland & Stewart, 1974);

The Darkening Fire: Selected Poems 1945-1968 (Toronto: McClelland & Stewart, 1975);

The Unwavering Eye: Selected Poems 1969-1975 (Toronto: McClelland & Stewart, 1975);

For My Brother Jesus (Toronto: McClelland & Stewart, 1976);

The Uncollected Poems, 1936-1959, edited by W. David John (Oakville, Ont.: Mosaic / Valley Editions, 1976);

The Poems of Irving Layton, edited by Eli Mandel (Toronto: McClelland & Stewart, 1977);

The Selected Poems of Irving Layton (New York: New Directions, 1977);

The Covenant (Toronto: McClelland & Stewart, 1977);

Taking Sides: The Collected Social and Political Writings, edited by Howard Aster (Oakville, Ont.: Mosaic / Valley Editions, 1977);

The Tightrope Dancer (Toronto: McClelland & Stewart, 1978);

Droppings from Heaven (Toronto: McClelland & Stewart, 1979);

For My Neighbours in Hell (Oakville, Ont.: Mosaic / Valley Editions, 1980);

The Love Poems of Irving Layton (Toronto: McClelland & Stewart, 1980);

Europe and Other Bad News (Toronto: McClelland & Stewart, 1981);

Shadows on the Ground (Oakville, Ont.: Mosaic / Valley Editions, 1982);

A Wild Peculiar Joy: Selected Poems 1945-1982 (Toronto: McClelland & Stewart, 1982);

The Gucci Bag (Oakville, Ont.: Mosaic / Valley Editions, 1983);

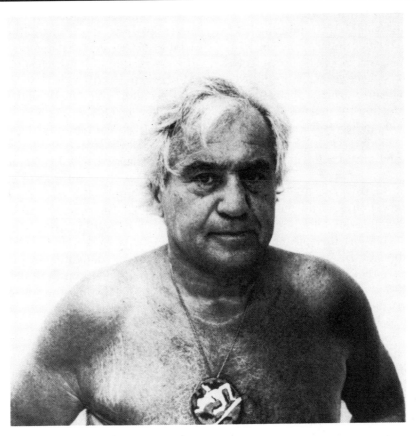

Irving Layton, 1983 (photograph by Arnaud Maggs)

The Love Poems of Irving Layton, with Reverence & Delight (Oakville, Ont.: Mosaic / Valley Editions, 1984);

A Spider Danced a Cosy Jig (Toronto: Stoddart, 1984);

Waiting for the Messiah: A Memoir, by Layton and David O'Rourke (Toronto: McClelland & Stewart, 1985);

Dance with Desire: Love Poems (Toronto: McClelland & Stewart, 1986);

Final Reckoning: Poems 1982-1986 (Oakville, Ont.: Mosaic / Valley Editions, 1987);

Fortunate Exile (Toronto: McClelland & Stewart, 1987).

OTHER: *Canadian Poems, 1850-1952,* edited by Layton and Louis Dudek (Toronto: Contact, 1952; revised and enlarged, 1953);

Pan-ic: A Selection of Contemporary Canadian Poems, edited by Layton (New York: Alan Brilliant, 1958);

Anvil: A Selection of Workshop Poems, edited by Layton (Montreal, 1961);

Poems for 27 Cents, edited, with an introduction, by Layton (Montreal, 1961);

Love Where the Nights Are Long: Canadian Love Poems, edited by Layton (Toronto: McClelland & Stewart, 1962);

Anvil Blood: A Selection of Workshop Poems, edited by Layton (Toronto: 1973);

Shark Tank, edited by Layton (Toronto, 1977).

Irving Layton is Canada's most prolific and pugnacious poet and has sustained a powerful if not to say domineering position in Canadian letters for over forty-five years. In the nearly fifty books he has published since 1945, Layton has been a writer of unflagging energy and undiminished anger who combines the rage of Jeremiah with the vitality of Nietzsche. Layton embodies his own idea of the poet as one who should "disturb and discomfort" society as well as the universe. This attitude, however, has frequently led to controversy. While some praise Layton's rambunctious style, others denigrate his pompous proclamations of self worth. Critics agree only that Irving Layton is a paradox: "each of his books both contradicts and affirms all that he has done before," Eli Mandel has written (*Globe and Mail,* 22 March 1969). Offset by an ironic point of view and often satiric tone, Layton's romantic sense of self provides a refreshing, invigorating dimension to contemporary Canadian writing. One of the few Canadian poets to perceive poetry as performance, Layton thrives in the role of showman, and William Carlos Williams's comment, in his introduction to Layton's *The Improved Binoculars* (1956), indicates the equally exuberant reaction of readers: "When I first clapped eyes on the poems of Irving Layton . . . I let out a yell of joy."

Outspoken and controversial for his poetic attacks on complacency, moral sterility, and Canadian indifference, Layton rarely fails to receive attention. He strives to reassert the spiritual values of life in the tradition of Blake, Shelley, Whitman, and Lawrence. A 1962 "epigram," included in *Taking Sides: The Collected Social and Political Writings* (1977), summarizes his position: "One cannot love life as much as I do . . . without abominating the pompous fools, the frustrated busybodies, the money lusting acquisitive dull clods, and lobotomized ideologues who make it difficult to live joyously." In the preface to *The Laughing Rooster* (1964) Layton declares that the concern of the poet is to "change the world; at any rate, to bear witness that another beside the heartless, stupid, and soul-destroying one men have created is possible." This attitude underlies almost all that he has written.

Although the satires and invectives have received most of the critical attention, Layton has also written lyrics of tender eloquence, verse that is classical in structure and technique. These poems replace hyperbole and exaggeration with carefully stated feelings for individual human beings. For Layton there is no unpoetic subject as passion and restraint battle over his poetic creativity. His single belief is that imagination can dominate reality, as he believes his personality can dominate his readers. His impact on Canadian writing has been profound as he seeks to cleanse the air of gentility and replace it with emotional electricity. "I want people to wake up, I want them to have an attack of personality," he declares in another of the epigrams in *Taking Sides*. His rapturous style, blunt criticisms, and flaunting sensuality have influenced several younger poets, notably Leonard Cohen and Seymour Mayne. Despite objections to his bombast and egotism, Layton's writing opened the eyes of Canadian poets to the spiritual energy and visionary force attainable from uniting romantic ideas with an ironic point of view.

Irving Layton was not trained to be a poet. After his birth in Neamtz, Rumania, in 1912 as Irving Lazarovitch, he immigrated to Canada at the age of one with his parents, Moses and Keine Moscovitch Lazarovitch. Educated in agriculture and economics at MacDonald College, St. Anne de Bellevue, Quebec, (B.Sc., 1939), he began to publish poetry while lecturing at the Jewish Public Library in Montreal in the early 1940s. In 1938 he married Faye Lynch, and in 1943 he finished his service with the Canadian army. In 1946 he completed a master's degree in economics and political science at McGill University; the same year he was divorced from Lynch and married to Betty Sutherland, with whom he subsequently had a daughter and a son, Naomi and Max, to both of whom Layton addressed sensitive lyric poems. He taught at Herziliah High School in Montreal (1945-1960) and as a part-time lecturer at Sir George Williams University (1949-1965), where he was also poet in residence (1965-1969). Divorced from Sutherland, in 1961 he married the writer Aviva Cantor; they had one son, David. Layton became poet in residence at the University of Guelph, 1969-1970, and professor of English at York University in Toronto in 1970. He remained at York until his retirement in 1978 to write full time. In that year Layton, whose marriage to Cantor had been dissolved, married Harriet Bernstein, a publicist, and moved to Niagara-on-the-Lake, Ontario. After the birth of a daughter, Samantha Clara, Layton was divorced in 1983. He is currently married to Anna Pottier. The recipient of several honorary degrees (Bishop's University, 1970; Concordia University, 1976; York University, 1979), the Order of Canada (1976), and many arts awards, Layton now lives in Montreal.

The 1940s mark the beginning of Layton's writing career. His first volume, *Here and Now*, was published at his own expense in 1945, and in 1943, with Louis Dudek and John Sutherland, he had become involved with editing *First Statement*. The periodical, later to merge with *Preview* to become *Northern Review*, became a means of improving his talent through exposure to the work of others. Layton's earliest poetry was satiric in tone and intent, mixing a "sense of adventure spiced with a refreshing cynicism," as A. M. Klein noted in the *Canadian Jewish Chronicle* (8 June 1945). The social awareness and political perspective of Layton's early writing gave him a point of view at once open to attack and definite in its focus. Hence, in "Letters in Canada" (*University of To-*

ronto Quarterly, April 1952), Northrop Frye reacted to Layton's 1951 volume, *The Black Huntsmen*, as a work of militant imagination of an intensely personal nature in which a poet is desperately trying to break out. The prevalence of stock sexual images and schematized political structures in these poems, even if they shocked readers by their subject matter, limited his readership and tempered Layton's critical success.

In the 1950s Layton was involved in the founding of Contact Press, joining Dudek and Raymond Souster. At this time Layton discovered a voice that could unite his skeptical vision and energetic, provocative language. Clarity, concision, and exactness of meaning began to define his work in such books as *The Long Pea-Shooter* (1954) and *The Cold Green Element* (1955). The mid to late 1950s signaled the maturing of Layton's writing, an achievement which he consolidated with his first critical and popular success, *A Red Carpet for the Sun* (1959).

In this volume, comprising work from 1942 to 1958, Layton makes clear his conception of poetry as he assumes his prophetic stance, "muscular" Judaism, and anti-philistinism–all in order to enunciate his simple but, for Canadian writing, radical attitude, articulated in the epigraph to the volume: "they dance best who dance with desire." Discovering and experiencing that desire is Layton's goal in the over two hundred poems that compose the book. In an important foreword to the collection, Layton reiterates his complaints against the destructiveness and corruption of men, wondering if the cause is in part the feeling that they are "objects of use and not of love." Explaining the contrasting elements of myth and reality, Layton describes a search for a "third realm" he hopes to locate on the "stilts of poetry." But he accepts the inevitable reality of life: "though art transcends pain and tragedy, it does not negate them, does not make them disappear."

For Layton, the poet is a commuter between heaven and hell with imagination his ticket. He alone can describe the dualities of the ideal and real, "the disorder and glory of passion. The modern tragedy of the depersonalization of men and women." Critical of women–"this is the inglorious age of the mass-woman. Her tastes are dominant everywhere"–Layton proclaims a certain poetic self dead with the poems from that previous period of "testing, confusion, ecstasy." What is left is "the ecstasy of an angry middle-aged man growing into courage and truth." These statements

are a testimony to the energy of Layton as well as to his commitment to a prophetic vision that cries out against the inhumanity of the past and reaffirms the ability of the poet to shape a future.

The poems in *A Red Carpet for the Sun* are those Layton sought to preserve from twelve previously published volumes and include several of his best-known works. "In the Midst of My Fever," for example, demonstrates his characteristic union of the personal and the universal: "In the depth of my gay fever, I saw my limbs / like Hebrew letters / Twisted with too much learning. I was / Seer, sensualist, or fake ambassador." The poem "The Birth of Tragedy" best articulates the pleasure and importance of poetry for Layton:

> And me happiest when I compose poems.
>   Love, power, the huzza of battle
>   are something, are much;
> Yet a poem includes them like a pool
>   water and reflection.

In "Orpheus" Layton glorifies the ability of poetry to "celebrate / Love equally with Death / Yet by its pulsing bring / A music into everything." The naturalistic "Bull Calf" and the mythical "On Seeing the Statuettes of Ezekiel and Jeremiah in the Church of Notre Dame" further highlight the mythic patterns of death and rebirth that exist throughout this collection, a work for which Layton received the Governor General's Award for Poetry in 1960.

During the 1960s Layton's writing took on a new dimension as a result of his meditations on the tragedy of European culture destroyed by war, mass murder, and the failure of Christian humanism. His foreword to *Balls for a One-Armed Juggler* (1963) calls for a new role for the poet, no longer the explorer of "new areas of sensibility" but the witness and judge of several hundred years of Western traditions that have been corroded. The opening sentences state his new concern: "Today, poets must teach themselves to imagine the worst. To apprehend the enormity of the filth, irrationality, and evil, they must have the severity to descend from one level of foulness to another and learn what the greatest of them had always known: there is, of course, no bottom, no end." The horrors of Belsen, Hiroshima, and Auschwitz must be faced. This approach is not a departure for Layton but a widening of his social awareness beyond his immediate society to the concerns of history. It also represents an expansion of a tradition of social protest in Canadian poetry, seen in the work of Dorothy Livesay and

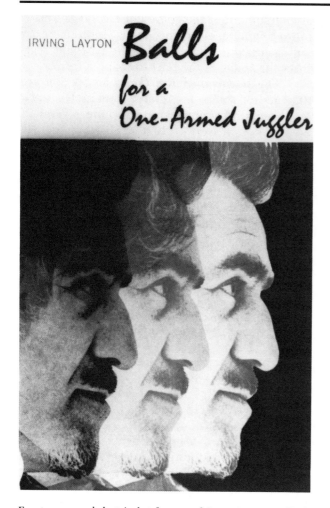

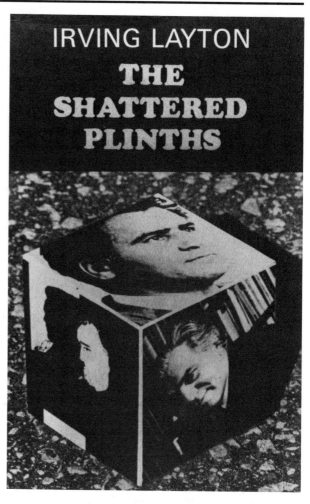

Front cover and dust jacket for two of Layton's verse collections from the 1960s. In both the poet addresses what he describes in the foreword to Balls for a One-Armed Juggler *as "the exceptionally heinous nature of twentieth-century evil."*

A. M. Klein, and illustrates the importance of the myth of return in Canadian-Jewish writing. As the poet begins to broaden his themes, he returns to his origins, for the Jewish poet, European sources, sadly altered in the twentieth century. The difference between Layton's earlier poems and those that follow *Balls for a One-Armed Juggler* is that he has become more conscious of a universal decay of values and morals. But, he argues, unlike contemporary fiction or drama, poetry has remained innocent of man's twentieth-century tragedies. The gravest error, Layton says, is that poets have forgotten that they are descended from prophets and have "swapped roles with entertainers and culture-peddlers." For Layton "the exceptionally heinous nature of twentieth-century evil" requires his total concentration as he stridently indicts the poets of the present age for failing to deal with this issue.

The poems in *Balls for a One-Armed Juggler*

demonstrate Layton's new perspective as he redefines his actions: "From hypocrisy, I weaved directness," he writes in "There Were No Signs." Exposing hypocrisy, as in the poem "The Real Values," or confronting death, as in "Thanatos," Layton displays a new courage in facing hard truths. He wants his readers to do the same: "When reading me," he tells them, "I want you to feel / as if I had ripped your skin off," he declares in "Whom I Write For." In an effort to engage the reader's anger he then lists the names of all those who have destroyed humanity: Polish machine gunners, Fidel Castro, Mao Tse-tung, Adolph Eichmann. In "A Tall Man Executes a Jig" Layton presents one of his most complex and controlled poems, one that embodies the contradictions of violence, its attraction and repulsion.

Other volumes in the 1960s continue Layton's broader political and social focus, although he still maintains his celebration of sexual love, as in *The Swinging Flesh* (1961). But it is the painful history of Europe that absorbs him, occasionally merged with the theme of sexuality, as in "An Old Nicoise Whore" from *Periods of the Moon* (1967). Travel becomes an important aspect of his writing at this time, and for his poems he uses Spanish, French, Greek, and Israeli settings from his various travels in the mid 1960s. Layton's Jewish heritage reemerges in the form of cultural identity, not just familial remembrances.

The Shattered Plinths (1968) most clearly summarizes these concerns. In "For My Two Sons" Layton provides a litany of destroyed, abused, and hated Jews, urging his sons to renounce passive forms of Judaism for a stronger, more active identity. "Be gunners in the Israeli Air Force," he concludes. Drawn to the reality of the struggling nation Israel, Layton confronts the problem of the poet's inability to alter reality. Temporarily defeated by his profession–"the wholly impractical art / of arranging words / on paper"–he nonetheless hopes for an effective spiritual activism. In this volume Layton repeatedly accuses passive poets who ignore the historical and political realities of the world. "The up-to-date poet / besides labouring at his craft / should be a dead shot," he writes in "The New Sensibility." Rejecting modernist poets such as Ezra Pound and T. S. Eliot for their lack of concern for the evils of the current century, Layton lambastes them in the foreword to *The Shattered Plinths* as secular replacements for "discredited clericals." He, alone, attempts to reclaim some honesty for poetry by rebuilding "the shattered plinths of christianity and humanism." "Art," he proclaims again, "has its roots in reality, personal and social." Political naivete and social ignorance can no longer exist for the poet.

During the 1970s Layton found only a moderate respite from his crusade for poetic honesty, social responsibility, and engagement with history. Love, imagination, and prophecy persist in his writing with characteristic Dionysian vigor in such volumes as *Lovers and Lesser Men* (1973) and *The Pole Vaulter* (1974), a work that successfully unites the themes of passion and politics. Writing poems and making love become identical acts for Layton in the 1970s collections, in which he again draws on his travels as a background for his thoughts. But intertwined with the celebration of love is danger–to Jews, exiles and the world.

The Pole Vaulter is dedicated to Nadezhda Mandelshtam and Heda Kovály, two women whose autobiographies clearly and horribly provide a despairing picture of communism and the complicity of Eastern European intellectuals. Opposing, in his foreword to the volume, a "heartless materialism, fixated on power and possessions," Layton states again his view of poetry as the salvation of mankind because it "insists on the validity of each individual's dream, on his inviolable right to it." The poet must clarify and illuminate those dreams and translate even hideousness through image and symbol. "For Anne Frank," "The Final Solution," and "The Transformation" are only three of many poems in the book that develop the relation of the poet to the age of atrocity. In "Adam and Eve" Layton blends "the poet / and Dionysian philosopher" he wishes to become with the sexuality that shapes so much of his writing.

For My Brother Jesus (1976) is the culmination of Layton's response to the malignant forces of the twentieth century. In an iconoclastic preface Layton accuses Christianity as the true source of anti-Semitism and reclaims Jesus for the Jews. Jesus, he remarked in an interview included in David O'Rourke's "The Lion in Winters" (*Canadian Literature*, Winter 1980), is "the archetypal poet–he stands for love, creativity and, most of all, joy and laughter." Reiterating his belief that poetry should "disturb the accumulated complacencies of people," Layton, in the foreword to *My Brother Jesus*, restates that Auschwitz and Gulag have been "the seminal and searing experiences of our time." Christianity, however, destroyed European culture and creativity. These controversial statements created a furor. The opening lines of the first poem, "Florence," demonstrate his attitude: "Here parasites thrive, niggardly worms, merchants / That grow sleek gnawing on sculptured stone." More polished in technique, the poems expand the idea of moral and cultural decay initiated in *The Shattered Plinths*. Expressing discontent and moral indignation like that set forth in the works of Elie Weisel and George Steiner, Layton, in "The Haemorrhage," articulates the tragedy of the Holocaust. Forever irreverent, however, Layton also mixes the comic with the tragic, identifying himself with the Jewish Jesus, plotting ways for his return, as in "Displaced Person" and "For Some of My Best Friends."

For My Brother Jesus also portrays a slightly mellowing Dionysus as Layton gradually begins to accept his status as an older but still attractive and vital man. There is also a new element of nostalgia and remembrance in these poems. "On Revisiting Poros After an Absence of Ten Years" carefully reexamines the past in a retrospective linked to death and Layton's recent loss of several friends, including the writer Desmond Pacey. Mortality and the past begin to enter his poems in ways not previously seen. Whether in the form of Jewish cemeteries, old mansions, or old friendships, the past begins to haunt Layton. But in memory he finds energy as well as comfort. "Act of Creation," a poem dedicated to Leonard Cohen, articulates the new energy discovered in the past, a vigor that is characteristic of his subsequent volumes.

The Covenant (1977), sustaining the religious impetus of *For My Brother Jesus; The Tightrope Dancer* (1978), recalling the vigor of *The Pole Vaulter;* and *Droppings from Heaven* (1979), with its varied poems on contemporary Canadian life all demonstrate the vitality that is typical of Layton's best writing. The bravado, however, is blended with ecstatic elegy, as Layton notes in the foreword to *The Tightrope Dancer:* the poet is "poised on a rope stretched tautly between sex and death." In *Droppings from Heaven* he continues the refrain set forth in *The Tightrope Dancer* of combating humbug, mediocrity, and gentility, demanding a "leavening" of wit and realism in "the cornstarch pudding of Anglo-Saxon Protestantism." But while the poet shouts, "I want to go into the sunset with both pitchforks blazing," he also uses an elegiac tone, asking to be remembered as "someone who believed that a great poem was the noblest work of man."

In poem after poem in *Droppings from Heaven* the message is clear: encounter unflinchingly the deadness of contemporary life and fight against it. To see the world as it is, with its cruel realities, while wearing what Layton calls in his poem "Freud With All His Knowledge" Nietzsche's "crown of thorns" made from "verities he could not make himself / forget" is Layton's goal. In this book Layton renounces the roles of satyr, prophet, and historian for that of "a cynical aging Jew / who knows much about men's / incurable viciousness and brutality," as he writes in "Father and Daughter." He also marvels at beauty and serenity, but with an ironic eye. He uses a fresh style in these poems, a style marked by lyrical diction and witty syntax. In "Takeoff," for example, he describes his pleasure in flight while "someone has strewn / an array of Chinese

Front cover for Layton's 1980 verse collection

letters in white / which the intrepid lanewise pilot takes for signs." In the affecting poem "Senile, My Sister Sings," less occupied with himself than usual, Layton achieves a clarity of vision and writing equal to his best work.

In 1980 a curious volume of letters, *An Unlikely Affair: The Irving Layton-Dorothy Rath Correspondence,* appeared. In these writings a poet with an "ageless heart" responds to the concerns and efforts of a new poet slowly locating her voice. Layton's letters include reading lists, poems, and aphorisms. His own poetry at this time, beginning with *For My Neighbours in Hell* (1980) and *Europe and Other Bad News* (1981), elaborates his now standard themes: social injustice, the death of the spirit in an age of materialism, energetic irreverence, and the lingering glow of passion. *For My Neighbours in Hell* is the weaker of these two books because Layton favors ephemeral moments in attempting to turn incident into event and moment into meaning. "The Burning Remnant," about Jewish survival, is an exception, and in his comic poem "Self-Interview" he admits that his outlook is bitter in order to prevent himself "from laughing at human misery."

Europe and Other Bad News is a book that Layton felt he had to write; his daimons, he explains in his foreword to the volume, forced the work on him. The foreword is an apologia in which he reviews the misreadings of his work by critics and restates his major themes, complaining that the Holocaust, the primary moral and psychological event of the twentieth century, is still neglected by contemporary poets. They have failed to see that "the 19th century slew God; the 20th century finished off man," he writes in the poem "An Ice Age."

In *Europe and Other Bad News* Layton singles out Jeremiah, Blake, Byron, Whitman, and Lawrence as his models. He resumes his indignant posture toward society's crimes, decrying the evil and celebrating the triumph of Jewish survival. But despite the horrors of the contemporary age, Layton upholds the divinity of man, although he recognizes the paradox of compassion and disgust in man's behavior. In "Credo" Layton celebrates the godliness of man; in "Reingemacht" he laments the prevalence of despair. Yet, in the future Layton anticipates "no war / between intellect and instinct" as thought and sexuality unite. *Europe and Other Bad News* includes one of Layton's most lyrical poems, the elegiac "Beginnings and Other Starts." This retrospective reconsideration of his work lends an important coda to the volume and to his writing as a whole.

In 1982 and 1983 Layton was nominated for a Nobel Prize. *A Wild Peculiar Joy: Selected Poems 1945-1982* appeared to general praise in 1982. This comprehensive selection of Layton's work, chosen by Layton and the Canadian poet and editor Dennis Lee, makes many of his early poems accessible to a new generation of readers. Approximately one dozen of the poems were revised for this publication. The following year saw the appearance of *The Gucci Bag*, a new collection of 105 poems that reaffirms Layton's belief, expressed in the foreword, that "poetry exists to give relief to those dark sensual impulses that our over-mechanized civilization has all but snuffed out." Responding to the "murderous times" of the present, the poet nails a Gucci bag to the outside wall of his house as a talisman against materialism and greed. But love and conflict, not pride or acquisitiveness, dominate the poems, supported by his powerful commitment

to poetry in the face of crumbling personal relations:

> I've had four mares
> shot from under me
> and I'm still riding hard for glory,
> but this time
> on no other horse than Pegasus.

In 1980 Layton had published a book of love poems; in 1984 an expanded volume, entitled *The Love Poems of Irving Layton, with Reverence & Delight*, appeared. Labeled "the definitive collection" of his expressions on love, the volume reflects multiple responses to the stages of love and includes most of Layton's best-known works, such as "The Day Aviva Came to Paris," "Seduction Of and By A Civilized Frenchwoman," and "Misunderstanding":

> I placed
> my hand
> upon her
> her thigh.
>
> By the way
> she moved
> away
> I could see
>
> her devotion
> to literature
> was not
> perfect.

Irving Layton: A Portrait appeared in 1985. A biography of the poet by Elspeth Cameron, the volume, written with Layton's cooperation, became an instant cause célèbre because Layton publicly and vociferously disputed many of Cameron's facts. Comprehensive and dispassionate, Cameron details numerous incidents in Layton's life while integrating, although not analyzing, his poetry. Layton called the book "the mating of the swift steed of fiction with the slow, stubborn donkey of fact, producing a lumpish mule of a book...." For her part, Cameron stood by her scholarship, citing hours of interviews with Layton and others, plus extensive documentation in the biography. But Layton had the last, extravagant word in his memoir, published shortly after the biography. Entitled *Waiting for the Messiah*, it covers the 1912-1946 period in his life with vibrant prose vividly bringing to life his youth in Montreal and his early efforts at being a poet. The memoir is an important primary text and a complement to Cameron's biography. In 1987, in the preface to his *Final Reckoning: Poems 1982-1986*, Layton continued his criticism of the biography, objecting to Cameron's non-Jewish background and general inaccuracies.

Dance with Desire: Love Poems (1986) is dedicated to "Miss Benjamin—the Grade Six teacher who awakened my erotic impulses and inspired my first sensual poem." Comprising mostly republications of works from earlier collections, the volume is chronologically arranged from 1953 to 1986 and includes several new works. Returning to an indictment of the sterile, WASP Canadian culture in *Final Reckoning*, Layton proclaims that the Jew is "at his best when he is the unsparing critic of his society's cultural values." The poems are longer and more narrative than in earlier books, with a touch of the humorous, as in "Socrates at the Centaur," depicting the philosopher at a Toronto theater. Poems dealing with the Holocaust, murder, and death ("love's pornographic twin") overshadow the comic. And, as usual, the mocking but endearing self of the poet proves irrepressible:

Like any civilized

Being in this century I want to be taken
for a Titan and to astonish everyone I meet
With my heroic compulsion and wisdom.

Marking Layton's seventy-fifth birthday, *Final Reckoning* shows the undiminished vigor and strength of Layton the poet and social critic.

Fortunate Exile (1987) gathers poems about Jewish history and experience. A summing up of Layton's long quest for the meaning of his religion, the volume draws from his entire oeuvre to give an overview of Jewish events and to celebrate Jewish people. Poems to A. M. Klein, Boris Pasternak, Nadezhda Mandelshtam, and Anne Frank appear with others such as "The Final Solution" and "Midsummer's Dream in the Vienna Stadpark." A powerful collection, *Fortunate Exile* confirms the persistent drives that shape Layton's poetry and provide its remarkable energy. The concluding stanza of "The Haemorrhage" is a case in point:

Dynasties, civilizations flutter past me
in a rain of blood: those that were, those yet to be.
Europe bleeding to death with its murdered Jews.
Finis.
The infected brown leaf crimson at the edges has
begun to fall

I listen for the noiseless splash in the immense blood-pool below.

A notable development in Layton's career has been the reception of his works in Italy. In 1974 Amleto Lorenzini translated *The Cold Green Element* into Italian (*Il freddo verde elemento*), and since then six volumes of Layton's poetry, often profusely illustrated, have appeared in Italian. The most recent is *Tutto considerato. Poesie 1945-1988* (1988), translated by Alfredo Rizzardi, with a preface by Leonard Cohen. Italian commentators have also produced an important volume, edited by Rizzardi, published in English as *Italian Critics on Irving Layton* (1988). The book comprises nine essays, one interview, and a bibliography of Layton's works available in Italian. Layton has long admired Italy, visiting often and often using Italian settings for his poems. In the interview included in Rizzardi's volume, Layton says that Italy generates for him "the immediate past, a history that is within my grasp. . . . Italian humanism provided an effective antidote to the puritanism and anti-eroticism that prevails in my own country." Calling himself "a 5000-year-old Canadian Jew," he expresses his feelings of exile and dislocation in a land of conservative and repressed emotions. At odds with prevailing attitudes, Layton has criticized Canada by declaring that "the morality of most people is nothing else but their / cloaked distaste for living." His view illustrates his obsession with challenging, contradicting, and overturning the conventional. As teacher, spiritual guide, and poet, Layton has had an important role as gadfly in the moral and literary landscape of Canada. He remains a stimulating, if uneven, writer who has created some fifty or sixty poems that "must rank with the best lyrical and reflective poems of the mid-century in English," according to A. J. M. Smith in *Contemporary Poets* (fourth edition, 1985). In what Wyndham Lewis referred to as the "sanctimonious icebox," Canada, Irving Layton has ignited the air with his robust and energetic concept of the poet—"someone," he writes in the foreword to his *Collected Poems*, (1965), "whom life knocks on the head and makes ring like a tuning fork."

Letters:

An Unlikely Affair: The Irving Layton-Dorothy Rath Correspondence (Oakville, Ont.: Mosaic / Valley Editions, 1980);
Wild Gooseberries: Selected Letters of Irving Layton, 1939-1989 (Toronto: Macmillan, 1989).

Bibliography:

Joy Bennet and James Polson, *Irving Layton: A Bibliography, 1934-1977* (Montreal: Concordia University Libraries, 1979).

Biography:

Elspeth Cameron, *Irving Layton: A Portrait* (Toronto: Stoddart, 1985).

References:

G. C. Ian Burgess, *Irving Layton's Poetry: A Catalogue and Chronology* (Montreal: McGill University, 1974);

Fred Cogswell, "Eros or Narcissus: The Male Canadian Poet," *Mosaic,* 1 (January 1968): 103-111;

Wynne Francis, *Irving Layton and His Works* (Toronto: ECW, 1984);

Francis, "Montreal Poets of the Forties," *Canadian Literature,* 14 (Autumn 1962): 21-34;

Eli Mandel, *Irving Layton* (Toronto: Forum House, 1969, revised, 1981);

Seymour Mayne, ed., *Irving Layton: The Poet and His Critics* (Toronto: McGraw-Hill Ryerson, 1978);

Bruce Meyer and Brian O'Riordan, "Irving Layton: Poet as Prophet," in their *In Their Words: Interviews With fourteen Canadian Writers* (Toronto: Anansi, 1984), pp. 10-25;

David O'Rourke, "The Lion in Winters: Irving Layton at York," *Canadian Literature,* 87 (Winter 1980): 52-65;

Alfredo Rizzardi, ed., *Italian Critics on Irving Layton* (Abano: Editore Piovan, 1988);

A. J. M. Smith, "The Recent Poetry of Irving Layton: A Major Voice," *Queen's Quarterly,* 62 (Winter 1955-1956): 587-591;

George Woodcock, "A Grab at Proteus," in his *Odysseus Ever Returning: Essays on Canadian Writers and Writing* (Toronto: McClelland & Stewart, 1970), pp. 76-92.

Papers:

Layton's papers, including manuscripts, notebooks, and correspondence, are at the library of Concordia University in Montreal.

Antoine-J. Léger

(16 October 1880-7 April 1950)

Hans R. Runte
Dalhousie University

BOOKS: *Les Grandes Lignes de l'histoire de la Société l'Assomption* (Quebec: Imprimerie Franciscaine Missionnaire, 1933);
Elle et lui: Tragique idylle du peuple acadien (Moncton, N.B.: L'Evangéline, 1940);
Une Fleur d'Acadie: Un Episode du grand dérangement (Moncton, N.B.: Imprimerie Acadienne, 1946);
Petitcodiac (Moncton, N.B., 1948).

Antoine-Joseph Léger served his native Acadia above all as a lawyer and politician and only marginally as the author of two historical novels and as an amateur historian. One of eleven children, he was born on 16 October 1880 in Memramcook, New Brunswick, to Julien-T. and Marie LeBlanc Léger. After attending elementary school and receiving his secondary and postsecondary education (B.A., Université Saint-Joseph, 1903) in Memramcook, he studied first at the teachers' college and then trained for a law career in the office of Alfred Laforêt in Edmunston, New Brunswick. In 1907 he was admitted to the bar; he established himself in Moncton, where he practiced, eventually in association with two of his sons, until his death. In 1910 he married Alvina M. Léger; they had four sons and one daughter.

He was named legal counsel and member of the executive board of the Société l'Assomption (since 1967 a mutual insurance company) in 1913 (positions he held until his death) and later adviser to what was to become the Société Nationale des Acadiens. In 1928 he earned an M.A. from Université Saint-Joseph, and in 1933 his alma mater awarded him an honorary doctorate in law. Léger was appointed King's Counsel in 1932.

Having run in the provincial elections, without success, as the Conservative candidate for Westmorland in 1917, he was elected in 1925 (and reelected in 1930) and named provincial secretary-treasurer until 1935, when he lost his seat and was appointed to replace Pascal Poirier

Antoine-J. Léger (Centre d'Etudes Acadiennes, Université de Moncton)

in the Canadian Senate. In 1946, two years after his wife's death, Léger married Marie Bourgeois, née Drisdelle. The following year, as parliamentary counsel, he accompanied the Canadian delegation to the second plenary session of the United Nations. On 7 April 1950, Léger died suddenly of cerebral hemorrhaging.

Keenly interested in the history and furtherance of his people, Léger played all his life a leading role in the political and civic affairs of his province. He strongly supported the establishment of an Acadian parish in anglophone Moncton; he was instrumental in the early planning for a site commemorating the expulsion of the Acadians (Grand-Pré National Historic Park, Nova Scotia); and he was an active member of many clubs and associations, including the Association Acadienne d'Education and the Société Nationale des Acadiens.

Léger's writings reflect his love of local history as well as the preoccupation of his era with the rediscovery of the Acadian past and with the "defense and illustration" of the French language in Acadia. As a reviewer of his second novel, *Une Fleur d'Acadie* (A Flower of Acadia, 1946), wrote in the Acadian newspaper *L'Evangéline* (14 November 1946): "Il faut aimer nos ancêtres . . . parce qu'ils ont été frappés par le malheur. . . . [Les] jeunes gens et [les] jeunes filles . . . semblent rougir de leur langue maternelle et lui préférer la langue du persécuteur de leurs ancêtres, le général Monckton . . . en . . . restant fidèles [à leur langue] ils vengent leurs ancêtres et leur donnent la victoire finale" (We must love our ancestors . . . because they were struck by misfortune. . . . Young people . . . seem to be ashamed of their native language and to prefer the language of their ancestors' persecutor, General Monckton . . . by . . . remaining faithful [to the French language] they avenge their ancestors and assure them of final victory).

Une Fleur d'Acadie is otherwise noteworthy for the fact that it has its roots in local oral traditions, the legendary feats of the young heroine having been retold from generation to generation in the Cormier family, and particularly by Léger's maternal grandmother, Nathalie Cormier. The Flower of Acadia is Marie-Hélène, from Chipoudie, who leads the resistance against the marauding English troops after they have separated her, on the eve of her wedding (25 August 1755), from her fiancé, René. Having fought throughout Acadia and with Lévis and Montcalm, René escapes prison in Halifax after the final loss of Acadia to the English, and, with the help of the Indians, makes his way back to Petitcodiac, New Brunswick, his parents, and Marie-Hélène whom he weds in 1762.

Léger's first novel, *Elle et lui: Tragique idylle du peuple acadien* (She and He: Tragic Idyll of the Acadian People, 1940), had as working titles "Jean" and "Jean dit l'Acadien" and was completed in 1938. It is the story of Jean, from France, and his wife Jeanne, daughter of Joseph and Madeleine, from Grand-Pré. Jean, whose father died on an Acadian battlefield in 1710, immigrates to Grand-Pré in 1716 and becomes one of the leaders of the Acadian community before, during, and after the expulsion. Upon their return from exile, Jean and Jeanne settle in Jemseg, New Brunswick, only to be menaced by a second expulsion when the Loyalists arrive seeking refuge from the American Revolution. Jean dies at the age of eighty-five, and his family (Jean and Jeanne had ten children) moves to Memramcook and into the Madawaska region in western New Brunswick.

More amateurish than *Une Fleur d'Acadie*, Léger's first novel is nevertheless noteworthy for containing transcriptions of several historical documents, although any attempts at fusing fact and fiction into a coherent story have clearly failed. While his novels are no longer widely read, his work is an example of a continuing Acadian literary tradition. Contemporary writers—most notably Antonine Maillet—have carried this tradition to the present, with greater narrative skill. Léger nonetheless occupies a position of some regard in Acadian cultural history.

References:
L.-M. Gouin, "Antoine Léger (1880-1950)," *Mémoires de la Société Royale du Canada*, 1 (1950): p. 87;

Maurice Lemire, *Les Grands Thèmes nationalistes du roman historique canadien-français* (Quebec: Presses de l'Université Laval, 1970), p. 113.

Papers:
Léger's papers, including the manuscript for *Elle et lui*, are at the Centre d'Etudes Acadiennes, Université de Moncton.

Roger Lemelin

(7 April 1919-)

Allison Mitcham
University of Moncton

BOOKS: *Au pied de la pente douce* (Montreal: Editions d'Arbre, 1944); translated by Samuel Putnam as *The Town Below* (New York: Reynal & Hitchcock, 1948; Toronto: McClelland & Stewart, 1961);

Les Plouffe (Quebec: Belisle, 1948); translated by Mary Finch as *The Plouffe Family* (Toronto: McClelland & Stewart, 1950);

Fantaisies sur les péchés capitaux (Montreal: Beauchemin, 1949);

Pierre le magnifique (Quebec: Institut Littéraire du Québec, 1952); translated by Harry Lorin Binsse as *In Quest of Splendour* (Toronto: McClelland & Stewart, 1955; London: Barker, 1956);

The Stations of the Cross, translation, by Mary Finch, of "Le Chemin de la croix" from *Fantaisies sur les péchés capitaux* (Toronto: Irwin, 1967);

Langue, esthétique et morale (Montreal: La Presse, 1977);

L'Ecrivain et le journaliste (Montreal: La Presse, 1977);

Les Voies de l'espérance (Montreal: La Presse, 1979);

La Culotte en or (Montreal: La Presse, 1980);

Le Crime d'Ovide Plouffe (Quebec: ETR, 1982); translated by Alan Brown as *The Crime of Ovide Plouffe* (Toronto: McClelland & Stewart, 1984).

MOTION PICTURES: *L'Homme aux oiseaux*, screenplay by Lemelin, National Film Board, 1952;

Les Plouffe, screenplay by Lemelin and Gilles Carle, International Cinema, 1981.

PERIODICAL PUBLICATIONS: "Leon Bloy, Chrétien et littérateur," *Regards*, 2 (March 1941): 32-37; 3 (May 1941): 130-136;

"L'Evolution du public en matière d'art," *L'Action Nationale*, 25 (February 1945): 90-100;

"My First Novel," *Queen's Quarterly*, 61 (Summer 1954): 189-194.

Roger Lemelin (courtesy of the author)

OTHER: "An Ill-Fitting Imported Ideology Won't Suit Canada," in *Divided We Stand*, edited by Gary Geddes (Toronto: PMA, 1977), pp. 180-184.

Lemelin's first awards, in 1946, were Le Prix David and Le Prix de la Langue Française de l'Académie Française for *Au pied de la pente douce*. These were followed by two Guggenheim fellowships (in 1946 and 1947) and a Rockefeller fellowship (1953), the Prix de l'Académie des Arts et des Lettres (1954), membership in the Royal Society of Canada (1949), the Prix de Paris (for *Pierre le magnifique*), a French-language medal from the Académie Française (1965), membership (as a foreigner) in France's Académie Goncourt (1975), an honorary degree in literature from Laurentian University, Sudbury (1976), and election to the Canadian News Hall of Fame (1978). He was made companion of the Order of Canada in 1980.

Lemelin's four novels have been translated into English: *Au pied de la pente douce* (1944) by Samuel Putnam as *The Town Below* (1948); *Les Plouffe* (1948) by Mary Finch as *The Plouffe Family* (1950); *Pierre le magnifique* (1952) by Harry Lorin Binsse as *In Quest of Splendour* (1955); and *Le Crime d'Ovide Plouffe* (1982), the sequel to *Les Plouffe*, by Alan Brown as *The Crime of Ovide Plouffe* (1984). The first two novels spawned a series of radio plays, and *Les Plouffe* served as the basis of a television series, though the series was not closely related to the book. In 1981 *Les Plouffe* was made into a movie, with screenplay by Lemelin and Gilles Carle.

Lemelin's career as a novelist has been only one of several successful endeavors. For four years (1948-1952) he worked as a journalist for *Time*, *Life*, and *Fortune*. Then, in the early 1950s he became a television writer; his best-known script is perhaps *L'Homme aux oiseaux* (1951), produced for the screen the following year by the National Film Board. Since 1972 Lemelin has been president and publisher of *La Presse*.

Roger Lemelin was born on 7 April 1919 in the district of Saint-Sauveur, Quebec City. The eldest of ten boys born to Joseph and Florida Dumontier Lemelin, he was obliged to leave school at the age of fifteen, in the midst of the Depression, to look for work. Both *Au pied de la pente douce* and *Les Plouffe* are set in Saint-Sauveur, and *Les Plouffe*, particularly, reflects the period just before World War II. Like Gabrielle Roy's Montreal novel of the same era, *Bonheur d'occasion* (*The Tin Flute*, 1945), *Les Plouffe* portrays with insight, tenderness, and humor the attitudes and plight of working-class individuals in the late 1930s.

Lemelin's first novel was written somewhat by chance, because in the early 1940s his focus was primarily on winning Canadian downhill ski championships. An accident in which he fractured an ankle removed him from the competitions and immobilized him for some time. During this period of forced inactivity he began *Au pied de la pente douce*. The vivid and moving depiction of the agony which one of the characters un-

dergoes because of a knee injury in this novel likely owes much to Lemelin's own suffering while writing this book.

This first novel is episodic, the characters numerous, the focus shifting. The inhabitants of the parish are divided into rival factions: "les mulots," who are members of the working class; and "les soyeux," who are "petits bourgeois." What unified story line there is is tied to the comings and goings, the hopes and fears of the protagonist, Denis Boucher.

Denis, like Lemelin, is a *mulot* from a large family and an athletic young man without much formal education, who dreams of becoming a writer. Throughout the book he is engaged in writing a first novel, for which he eventually wins first prize in a contest. As the book opens, Denis and his friends are in the process of escaping from a garden where they have stolen apples. This prank leads to the novel's central crisis. The youths avoid arrest because they are hidden by Lise Lévesque, a seventeen-year-old *soyeuse* beauty, fresh from the convent, who plays Chopin's nocturnes, who sings in a pure, clear soprano, and whose romantic notions are gleaned from Chateaubriand and Lamartine.

Lise is also rather insensitive and stereotypical–despite which, the narcissistic Denis is infatuated with her; his best friend, Jean, falls head over heels in love. Because Denis is articulate, good-looking, aloof, ambitious, and, above all, an aspiring writer, Lise returns his attentions, though it is Jean she should acknowledge. Lemelin's point, however, is that in this society appearance is of more consequence than substance.

Midway through the book, an incident occurs which is the turning point in the plot. Denis and Jean are invited to go to the beach with Lise and her parents. Once there, the boys go swimming, a sport at which Jean excels. Lise, however, watching from the distant shore, cannot tell which boy is which, and so mistakes Jean's prowess for Denis's. While Denis is in town on an errand, the inexperienced Lise takes the boat out, capsizes it, and begins to drown in clear sight of Jean and her father. The latter, a portly businessman who cannot swim, is transfixed, and although Jean swims to the rescue, he becomes too exhausted for them to reach safety. At this moment Denis appears and saves them both. When Lise regains consciousness, it is Denis whom she sees first and credits with the rescue. Jean, because he is modest and self-effacing, is once more put at a disadvantage by his friend. The re-

Dust jacket for Samuel Putnam's 1948 translation of Lemelin's first novel, Au pied de la pente douce

them. The helplessness and suffering of Jos, Jean's drunken jokester father, once he dimly realizes that he has been in some measure responsible for Jean's illness; Flora's pride in the "purity" of her crippled son, Jean's brother Gaston; the discovery that the prosaic Jos had in his youth written love poetry to his wife–these are circumstances which Lemelin treats with understanding and sympathetic humor.

Au pied de la pente douce is, however, an uneven work. The satire at times descends to slapstick, and it is as a predecessor of *Les Plouffe*, Lemelin's masterpiece, that the author's first novel is most significant. In his second novel Lemelin captures the relationships of the members of the Plouffe family: the loyalties, jealousies, tragedies, successes, pride, frustrations, and prejudices. *Les Plouffe* is one of Canada's great comic novels.

Maman Plouffe dominates the family from her kitchen. Although Mme Plouffe is a stout housewife of sixty and the mother of many children, she identifies with Joan of Arc. So strongly does her idol move her that she feels that if Joan of Arc could run the English out of France, she, Mme Plouffe, could, with the help of the curé Folbèche, do as much for Quebec.

The only "Anglais" she encounters in her kitchen is, however, almost more than she can handle. He is an American, and what is even more upsetting to Mme Plouffe, he is a Protestant minister, and one who is contemplating marriage. Mme Plouffe nearly fails in her mission to evict this heathen alien from her "country" because she fails to reckon with Quebeckers'–and indeed her own family's–fanatical love of sports. The preacher, Tom Brown, a baseball devotee and promoter, wins the support of the parishioners by sponsoring a baseball series with Guillaume Plouffe as the star. After a series of farcical events, the difficulties are solved, temporarily, to everyone's satisfaction.

The father of the family, and chief breadwinner, Théophile, who works as a typesetter for *L'Action Chrétienne*, occupies the background of the novel. His conversation focuses almost exclusively on politics. Théophile's political opinions and his diatribes are chiefly directed against the English, and his intense prejudice sparks many of the most comic and tragic scenes in the book. For instance, Théophile refuses to decorate his house or balcony for the 1939 visit of the king and queen. As a result of this small act of independence, Théophile loses his job, despite the fact

ally tragic repercussion is that Jean falls ill shortly after the return to town and in due course dies.

In *Au pied de la pente douce* Lemelin the satirist is at work. Lise's father is concerned only that the boys be recognized for saving his daughter's life; he gets their names in the newspapers and has medals made in honor of their bravery. Though well-meaning, he has no understanding of their immediate and pressing needs. He has offered Jean a dollar for risking his life, while Jean, unnoticed, is dying of neglect. Jean's family cannot afford a doctor, and the poverty and ignorance which prevail in Jean's household mean that he must suffer his extended agony while his family and their neighbors intensify his pain with remedies that are the ridiculous by-products of their ignorance and superstition. When at last the doctor, who is inexperienced, is sent for, it is too late. Tuberculosis of the bone has progressed too far for medical intervention.

Although Lemelin depicts the ignorance of his working-class characters, he does not blame that the owners of the press basically share his opinion. Behind the surface comedy Lemelin is once again the satirist, exposing the personal consequences of political inconsistency and expedience.

Family life, too, a much-prized feature of traditional Quebec life, is satirized. The Plouffe "children" range from nineteen to middle age, yet Mme Plouffe is unwilling to let them leave home, a circumstance that puts the offspring in some rather odd situations. The strangest is perhaps that of the middle-aged daughter, Cécile, who has never married because she has never been able to get away from home. Yet Onésime, the man who had once courted her and is now married to someone else, the father of a large family, still arrives every evening at the Plouffe residence promptly after supper to sit on the balcony with Cécile and to listen to Théophile talk politics. The "child" who dominates the Plouffe household is Ovide. Because Mme Plouffe has always felt that Ovide would become a priest, she has given him more attention than the others, a fact which has naturally upset the rest of the family. This favorite son eventually lands in a stormy and unfulfilling marriage with a flighty and insensitive woman named Rita Toulouse and becomes the central figure in the subsequent Plouffe novel.

Lemelin's strength in *Les Plouffe* is, above all, his loving treatment of the ridiculous, though often believable, antics of his characters. The naive Théophile pulls for the Germans to win the war and thus defeat "les Anglais" once and for all; the curé Folbèche announces that God has had enough of the sins of contemporary France and has sent the Germans as a punishment. Yet in Lemelin's hands nearly all of the characters in this book are sympathetic figures because of their vigor and valor. Absurd they may sometimes be, but they are rarely cold and never self-pitying. It is perhaps for these reasons especially that–animated on television and film–they attracted such an empathetic audience.

Pierre le magnifique has little in common with Lemelin's first two novels. It is much more carefully structured than the others. The episodic nature of the two early books has given way to a central focus on one dominant character, Pierre, at times a moody and egotistical youth whose idealistic dream is to do something "magnifique." The novel *Pierre le magnifique* also differs from Lemelin's earlier works in the degree to which it draws on other books as formal paradigms. In out-

line (though not in substance), Pierre resembles James Joyce's Stephen Dedalus in *A Portrait of the Artist as a Young Man*. As a child he is recognized for his scholastic ability and put through school at the expense of the church. He invariably stands first in his class and is filled with a belief that he is meant to fly above other mortals–that his destiny will be "magnificent." He suffers from the poverty of his home, sees the priesthood as his pure and heroic destiny until he graduates from school, and then, on the eve of making his commitment, he is turned from his vocation, partly by an awakened interest in women.

After the graduation exercises, Pierre embarks on a series of adventures, both lively and melodramatic, which occupy the rest of the book. Pierre is variously involved with priests, with the seductive lawyer Ferdinand, with the unrestrainable Denis Boucher, and with lumberjacks and Communist union organizers. The priests are often selfless and dedicated, and though they sometimes appear as comical and fallible human beings, they are not cold and calculating like Joyce's Jesuits. (Thus, in a contemporary context at least, one finds difficulty in understanding why in the early 1950's Lemelin was frequently labeled anticlerical.) And Pierre, who first flees northward into the wilderness to escape the past, eventually comes back to his original commitment, entering the seminary.

Lemelin's interest in the value of traditional social institutions further shows in his short-story collection, *Fantaisies sur les péchés capitaux* (Fantasies on Capital Sins, 1949). Of special interest is "Le Chemin de Croix," a tale about a poor parish priest whose obsession is to have the most beautiful and unusual church he can imagine. Lemelin makes full use of his comic gifts in developing the difficulties of the situation, and the story stands, with *Au pied de la pente douce*, as a proclamation of the originality and vitality of French Canada. Lemelin's expression of these characteristics, his understanding of ordinary people, and his ability to portray them vividly paved the way for others and gave him an important place in Canadian letters.

But the period in which these works were written was also that in which Lemelin-the-young-liberal of the Duplessis years was turning into Lemelin-the-older-conservative in an age of separatism, as his publications show. Increasingly he devoted himself to his journalism. *La Presse* published two pamphlets asserting conservative social positions, *Langue, esthétique et morale* (Language,

Aesthetics, and Morals) and *L'Ecrivain et le journaliste* (The Writer and the Journalist), both in 1977. The conclusion to the essay he contributed to Gary Geddes's *Divided We Stand* (1977), entitled "An Ill-Fitting Imported Ideology Won't Suit Canada," declares his federalist stance: "Considering that the Parti Quebecois has succeeded in generating such an impressive passion in Quebec behind a dead-end idea, wouldn't it be possible for the Canadian people to generate such a passion for something feasible which would be an inspiration for future generations?" Given the temper of the times, it is small wonder that a character named Lemelin should have turned up as a figure in Jacques Ferron's *Le Ciel de Quebec* (*The Penniless Redeemer*, 1969), as one of the architects of Quebec's political stasis. Yet Ferron's version of Lemelin can no more be accepted as an accurate picture of the writer than can the earlier images of him as a satirical and anticlerical reformer. The full picture is more complex. Lemelin, now part of the Quebec establishment, had not given up the cause of reform, but his tactics for achieving it were not those of 1960s and 1970s youths.

From 1952 to 1979 Lemelin published no new book-length works, but three volumes then appeared in succession: *Les Voies de l'espérance* (The Routes of Hope, 1979), *La Culotte en or* (The Golden Trousers, 1980), and *Le Crime d'Ovide Plouffe* (1982). The first of these collects pieces which Lemelin had published (mostly in newspapers) or presented orally between 1952 and 1979. It was characteristic of the day that this book was generally dismissed. The literary

critic François LaTravers of the Université du Quebec à Montréal, writing in *Livres et Auteurs Québécois* (1979), noted the work's humorous moments but described the general tone of *Les Voies de l'espérance* as pompous and self-indulgent. *La Culotte en or*, another collection of short pieces, primarily autobiographical, fared little better. With *Le Crime d'Ovide Plouffe*, however, Lemelin regained his touch. This novel, a continuation of the doings of the Plouffe family, shows the author to be as comical as ever. But what is chiefly surprising about this book is that Lemelin seems caught in a time warp. His story is set in 1948-1949 and seems to owe very little either thematically or stylistically to the kinds of change that affected the writing of fiction from 1960 to 1980, either in Canada or elsewhere. Hence, though he won and warrants a place in Canadian literary history, that place seems increasingly enclosed by the literary conventions and social attitudes of the Duplessis years.

References:

W. E. Collin, "Roger Lemelin: The Pursuit of Grandeur," *Queen's Quarterly*, 61 (Summer 1954): 195-212;

Luc Dufresne, "Québec chez Harvey et Lemelin," *Parti Pris*, 2 (May 1965): 31-36;

Jean-Charles Falardeau, *Notre Société et son roman* (Montreal: HMH, 1967), pp. 180-234;

Romanciers québécois: Dossier de presse, volume 3 (Sherbrooke, Que.: Bibliothèque du Séminaire, 1981);

Guy-N. Trottier, "Roger Lemelin, romancier et conteur," *La Revue Dominicaine*, 56 (September 1950): 92-97.

Jean Le Moyne

(17 February 1913-)

Antoine Sirois and Jean Vigneault
Université de Sherbrooke

BOOK: *Convergences* (Montreal: HMH, 1961); translated, with differing contents, by Philip Stratford as *Convergence: Essays from Quebec* (Toronto: Ryerson, 1966).

OTHER: Hector de Saint-Denys Garneau, *Poésies complètes: Regards et jeux dans l'espace; Les Solitudes,* edited by Le Moyne and Robert Elie (Montreal: Fides, 1949);

Garneau, *Journal,* edited, with a foreword, by Le Moyne and Elie (Montreal: Beauchemin, 1954);

Garneau, *Lettres à ses amis,* edited, with a foreword, by Le Moyne, Elie, and Claude Hurtubise (Montreal: HMH, 1967);

Au bout de mon âge, by Le Moyne and others (Montreal: Hurtubise HMH / Ici Radio-Canada, 1972).

Jean Le Moyne, best known in literary circles for his book, *Convergences* (1961), ranks with the most important essayists Quebec has produced. The book appeared when the so-called Quiet Revolution was beginning. It made an immediate appeal to Quebec intellectuals, and when it was translated into English in 1966, as *Convergence: Essays from Quebec,* it aroused widespread interest throughout anglophone Canada. In certain respects the book seemed out of tune with the times, but it impressed readers by the searching quality of its analysis and the elegant precision of its style. For this volume Le Moyne received three literary prizes: a Governor General's Award, the Prix France-Canada, and first prize of the Concours Littéraires de la Province de Québec.

Readers of *Convergences* find Le Moyne's most carefully considered views on an impressive variety of topics. He was not yet out of his teens when he joined, in 1929, a group of youths who wanted to set the intellectual and literary life of French Canada on the path of renewal. They founded the magazine *La Relève* in 1934; in 1941 the title was changed to *La Nouvelle Relève.* Le

Jean Le Moyne in 1988, on the day he retired from the Senate of Canada (courtesy of the author)

Moyne's articles in this publication are evidence of his budding literary aspirations. Prominent among his friends was the poet Hector de Saint-Denys Garneau, one of the first distinctly modern French-Canadian poets. Tragically for Quebec letters, Garneau died when he was quite young, and Le Moyne assumed responsibility for seeing his friend's *Poésies complètes* (1949), *Journal* (1954), and *Lettres à ses amis* (1967) through the press.

Le Moyne was born on 17 February 1913, in Montreal, to Méderic and Albine Geoffrion Le Moyne. The education the young Le Moyne received was such as to foster in him both the intellectual aspirations destined to become the dominant motive of his life and the religious feeling that permeates so much of his writing. He was enrolled for seven and a half years as a pupil in the Jesuit Collège de Sainte-Marie, which he left in 1933 because of a serious hearing impairment. His father, a doctor, took it upon himself to educate his son, awakening in him an interest in Greek culture and the Holy Scriptures. But Le Moyne had little need of teachers. Guided by an unerring intellectual instinct, he sought out a wide variety of thinkers on his own, from Spinoza to Jacques Maritain and Teilhard de Chardin. He was also a voracious reader of the classics of world literature and found time to delve into the history of music and mysticism. To Henry James he was particularly indebted. James taught him to value the peculiarly North American complexion of his own thought while acknowledging his ties to the European fountainhead.

The disparate occupations Le Moyne took up reflect his eclectic tastes in philosophy and literature. He became a journalist for the dailies *La Presse* (1941-1942) and *Le Canada* (1942-1944) and managing editor for the magazine *La Revue Moderne* (1953-1959), then served as researcher and scenarist for the National Film Board of Canada (1959-1969). Canadian prime minister Pierre Elliott Trudeau named him special assistant and senior adviser, a post he occupied for almost ten years (1969-1978). Appointed to the Senate of Canada in 1982, Le Moyne spent more than five years there, reaching the age of mandatory retirement in 1988. He is married to Suzanne Rivard, a painter who has served as head of the visual arts department at the University of Ottawa.

Convergences comprises twenty-eight articles published over a period of some twenty years. The title indicates that these articles, disparate as they are, convey a recognizably uniform view of the contemporary world. Le Moyne says as much in the foreword, pinpointing the unifying impulse of the collection: "C'est la considération théologale, plus ou moins explicite selon les sujets traités, mais constante, irrépressible . . . qui fait l'unité du présent recueil" (What gives the present collection of pieces its essential unity is the constant, irrepressible intention to work out, with greater or less explicitness, the theological implications of the different matters under study). In the essays Le Moyne treats the influences that have shaped his thinking, the dominant spiritual problems of the era, the status of women in soci-

ety, the literature of French Canada, critical appreciations of French and American writers, and of musicians, too (fully a quarter of the articles are devoted to them).

In *Convergences* there is a dominant preoccupation with the welfare of society in general and of Quebec society in particular. Preeminent among Le Moyne's concerns is the Incarnation. He plays up the tension between the spiritual and the temporal, between spirit and flesh, immanence and transcendence. From Teilhard de Chardin he has learned how that tension can be resolved. In "Teilhard et la réconciliation" he reflects on the proposition that Spirit is incarnated in matter; that flesh cannot occlude the Divine; that the universe is impregnated with Divinity. Even the machine, as Le Moyne was later to point out, fits into the framework of the Incarnation. The problem, which he addresses in his contribution to the 1972 volume *Au bout de mon âge* (At the End of My Age), can be traced to "un dualisme propre à notre vieille religion française" (a dualism inveterate to our old French religion) which has spawned in French Canada a morbidity, a neurosis that "apparaît chez nous à l'état culturel" (has with us achieved the solidity of a cultural manifestation).

Others of his articles berate further manifestations of this dualist attitude in Quebec. In "L'Atmosphère religieuse au Canada français" he writes: "nous ayant sauvés, l'autorité ecclésiastique en conservera l'habitude et tendra aussi à nous sauver de la vie" (Having ensured our survival, ecclesiastical authority seeks to perpetuate its role as savior, and ends up trying to save us from life). Moreover, as he notes in "La Femme dans la civilisation française," Canadienne-Quebeckers have exalted the role of the mother at the expense of that of the helpmeet with the result that they have taken too narrow a view of the marital relationship. Finally, Le Moyne caustically probes even the vibrant nationalism of his contemporary Quebec. It is his view, expressed in "Saint-Denys-Garneau, témoin de son temps" (Saint-Denys-Garneau, Witness of His Time), that this nationalism affronts specifically human values: "En effet l'humain prime le national et le national accidentel et secondaire n'est qu'un instrument aliénateur s'il prétend empêcher les risques de l'humain essentiel" (What is human, in fact, must take precedence over what is merely national. The national is only of accidental and secondary importance when set beside the human; it can accordingly become an alienating factor if it is in-

Front cover for Le Moyne's 1961 essay collection, winner of a Governor General's Award for Nonfiction, and dust jacket for Philip Stratford's English translation, published in 1966 (courtesy of the author)

voked in order to eliminate the risks inseparable from what is quintessentially "human" in the human condition). Le Moyne thus adopts positions that challenge the dominant ideology of the day. Yet he does believe in the emergence of a culture indigenous to Quebec, as he asserts in "Henry James et *Les Ambassadeurs*": "nous nous insérons dans la continuité européenne et notre originalité américaine fait son premier acte de pleine conscience créatrice" (from the European fountainhead we cannot be severed, but our North American originality asserts itself in a first, fully conscious creative act).

In *Convergences*, as well as in other writings, Le Moyne subjects Quebec society to the kind of lucid and rigorous criticism that has become his trademark. He deplores the overly religious atmosphere of decades past, but he does this with the genuine adherent's reluctance to impugn Christianity itself because of his belief in its essential worth. Furthermore, though he endorses the flowering of Quebec culture, he has no sympathy for

the strident nationalism of some of those who have shaped Quebec thought. What he would have them embrace, instead, is a form of Christian humanism that does not lose sight of the spiritual dimension in the pursuit of human happiness. The following passage from "La Femme dans la civilisation canadienne-francaise," in *Convergences,* is a characteristic utterance: "Mon héritage français je veux le conserver, mais je veux tout autant garder mon lien anglais et aller jusqu'au bout de mon invention américaine. Il me faut tout ça pour faire l'homme total" (My French heritage I of course want to preserve, but I am as eager to preserve my English affinities as well, and to avail myself to the utmost of the potential for cultural enrichment in the North American milieu. I need all of that to round out my idea of the total man).

Many of Quebec's best-known critics had enthusiastic praise for *Convergences*. Gilles Marcotte, in a review for *La Presse* (6 January 1962), capped a eulogistic commentary with the statement that the book is "la somme ... d'une pensée qui depuis plus de vingt ans s'exerce avec une admirable lucidité sur les problèmes essentiels de l'homme de ce temps, et de l'homme canadien-francais en particulier" (the concentrated expression of the thought of a man who, for the past twenty years or more, has been dissecting with admirable lucidity the most pressing problems confronting society today, and particularly Quebec society). Jean Hamelin, in *Le Devoir* (13 January 1962), summoned all the writers of Canada "de lire méthodiquement, lentement, attentivement, sans en passer une seule ligne, le livre capital que vient de publier ... M. Jean Le Moyne" (to read methodically, slowly, attentively, without skipping a single sentence, the landmark work just published ... by Mr. Jean Le Moyne). In 1968 Le Moyne received the Molson Prize, which is awarded to Canadians who have made a significant contribution to the cultural and intellectual life of their country.

Douglas LePan

(25 May 1914-   )

Wendy Robbins
University of New Brunswick

BOOKS: *The Wounded Prince and Other Poems* (London: Chatto & Windus, 1948);

The Net and the Sword (London: Chatto & Windus, 1953; Toronto: Clarke, Irwin, 1953);

The Deserter (Toronto: McClelland & Stewart, 1964);

Bright Glass of Memory: A Set of Four Memoirs (Toronto & New York: McGraw-Hill Ryerson, 1979);

Something Still to Find (Toronto: McClelland & Stewart, 1982);

Weathering It: Complete Poems 1948-1987 (Toronto: McClelland & Stewart, 1987).

OTHER: Chapters 1-7, in *Final Report of the Commission on Canada's Economic Prospects* (Ottawa, 1957);

"The Outlook for the Relationship: A Canadian View," in *The United States and Canada*, edited by John Sloan Dickey (Englewood Cliffs, N. J.: Prentice-Hall, 1964).

PERIODICAL PUBLICATION: "The Dilemma of the Canadian Author," *Atlantic Monthly*, 214 (November 1964): 160-164.

Diplomat, economist, poet, novelist, and professor of English, Douglas LePan has earned rec-

Douglas LePan (Thomas Fisher Rare Book Library, University of Toronto)

ognition both for his public service career and for his slender but distinguished body of creative writing, which has won two Governor General's awards–for poetry and for fiction.

Born to Arthur D'Orr and Dorothy Lucinda Edge LePan and raised in Toronto, LePan was an intelligent youth who, nevertheless, matured slowly and was made self-conscious by a severe stammer, as he notes in his memoirs, *Bright Glass of Memory* (1979), a work marked by his characteristic undertones of restraint, discretion, and humility. He graduated from the University of Toronto in 1935 with a B.A., first-class honors in English and history; he took a second B.A. at Merton College, Oxford, in 1937. An M.A. from Oxford was awarded in 1948. He spent one year teaching in the Department of English at the University of Toronto before moving to a lectureship at Harvard in 1938.

Despite the advent of World War II, these Harvard years constituted "one of the most lyric periods in my life," he recalls. Living at Winthrop House, he made the acquaintance of numerous young economists, including John Kenneth Galbraith, as well as of the poet Charles Olson, whose emphasis on the personal aspects of poetry contrasted sharply with the example of impersonality and perfection of form provided by LePan's most influential early mentor, T. S. Eliot, whom LePan first met in London in August 1943. During his final year at Harvard, LePan apparently had a brief, unhappy romance which left him in a state of "emotional crisis"; it was at this period that he began to write the verse of *The Wounded Prince and Other Poems* (1948), whose title work centers on imagery of "wounds / By love inflicted."

Like the coureurs de bois he praises in another early poem, LePan "sought for his wounds the balsam of adventure," sailing from Halifax to London to join the war effort in October 1941, initially taking a civilian job with the Canadian Legion Educational Services. In June 1942 he assumed the role of personal adviser on army education at Canadian Army Headquarters in Surrey, reporting directly to General Andrew McNaughton. He also worked briefly at Canada House under High Commissioner Vincent Massey, but he longed for action. Despite his shortsightedness, he managed to join the ranks of the artillery of the First Canadian Field Regiment and spent eighteen months as a gunner in Italy. A few months before the end of the war, he resumed diplomatic work in London, making economic analyses of the sterling area in the critical postwar years and meeting high-ranking international financiers and economists, including John

Maynard Keynes. At this time he completed the manuscript of *The Wounded Prince and Other Poems* which, through the intermediary of Elizabeth Bowen, was brought to the attention of Cecil Day Lewis at Chatto and Windus.

The year 1948 stands out in LePan's career: *The Wounded Prince* was published, receiving favorable notice in England and Canada; he was promoted to the rank of first secretary at Canada House; and he married Sarah Chambers, a technical illustrator from the United States. (They have two sons, born in the early 1950s; the marriage ended in separation in 1971.)

Cecil Day Lewis wrote the introduction to *The Wounded Prince*, praising LePan's traditionalist style and describing his technique as "the right word set unobtrusively in the right place." Frequent classical allusions and verbal echoes (particularly of Keats and Shakespeare) suggest how LePan can speak imitatively in "tones of borrowed eloquence." His most enduring and original poems, however, deal with Canadian landscape and its effect on the national psyche. Such celebrated psychological nature poems as "Coureurs de Bois," "Canoe-Trip," and "A Country Without a Mythology" have been frequently anthologized, and the last is singled out for special attention by Margaret Atwood in *Survival: A Thematic Guide to Canadian Literature* (1972).

In 1948-1949 LePan held a Guggenheim Fellowship which brought him back to Toronto where he wrote *The Net and the Sword*, (1953) a collection of poems which draw on his experiences as a soldier and which center on human agony, the breakdown of order, exile, and the loss of identity. As Northrop Frye noted in the *University of Toronto Quarterly* (April 1954), "the poems are not battlepieces but elegies." They tend to be eloquent, sonorous, heavily rhymed, and traditional in form, which prompted Irving Layton to label LePan the "Archibald Lampman of the battlefield." Notwithstanding this unresolved tension between a refined technique and the raw material of war, *The Net and the Sword* won a Governor General's Award for 1953.

In 1950 LePan joined the Department of External Affairs, Ottawa, serving initially as special assistant to the Honorable Lester Pearson, then as economic minister counsellor at the Canadian Embassy in Washington (1951-1955). In this capacity he participated in the drafting of the Colombo Plan. For three years he was secretary and director of research for the Royal Commission on Canada's Economic Prospects (the Gordon

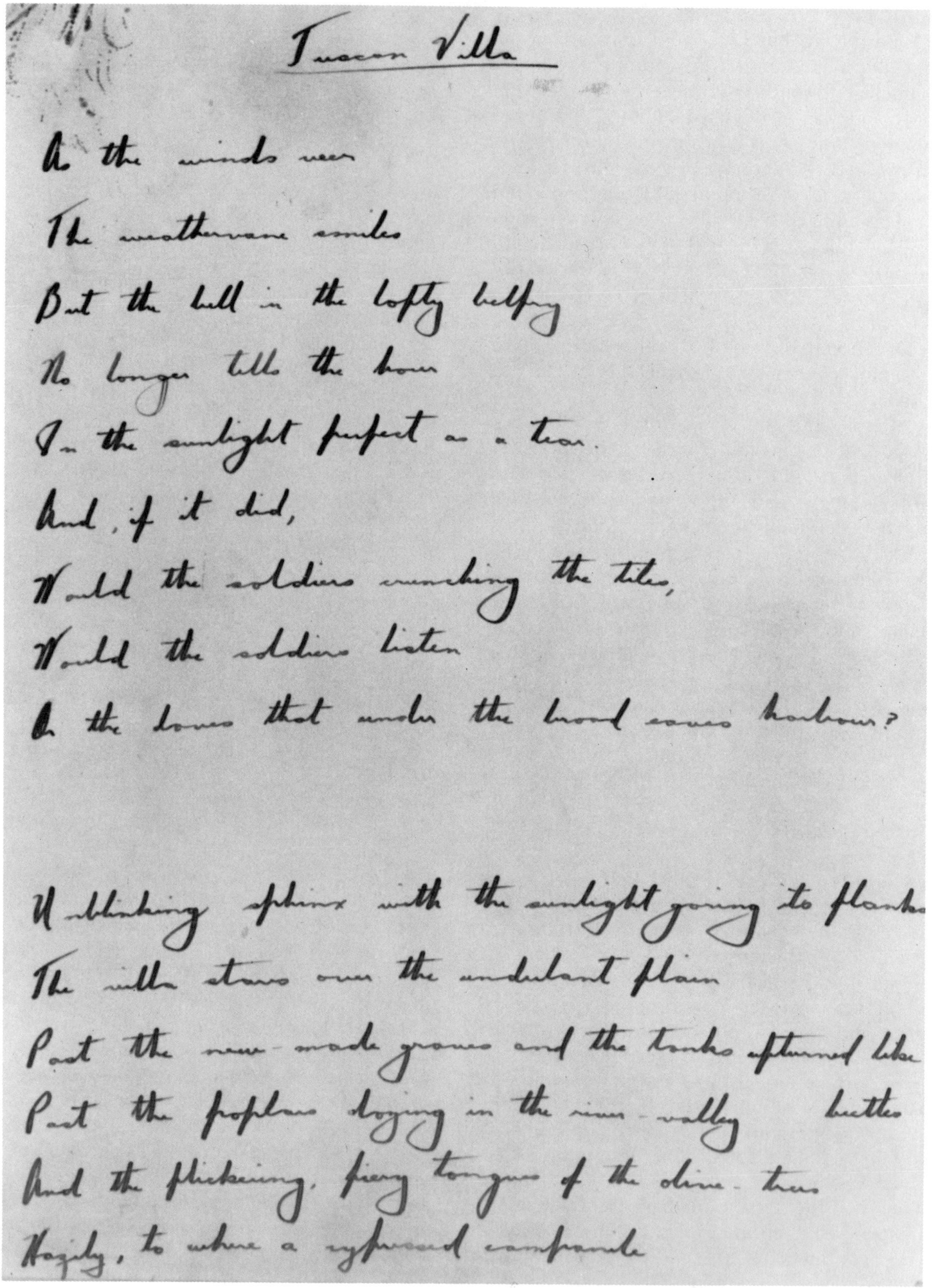

Tuscan Villa

As the winds veer

The weathervane smiles

But the bell in the lofty belfry

No longer tells the hour

In the sunlight perfect as a tear.

And, if it did,

Would the soldiers crunching the tiles,

Would the soldiers listen

Or the doves that under the broad eaves harbour?

Unblinking sphinx with the sunlight going to flash

The villa stares over the undulant plain

Past the new-made graves and the tanks upturned like

Past the poplars dying in the river-valley   beetles

And the flickering, fiery tongues of the olive trees

Hazily, to where a cypressed campanile

First page of the manuscript for one of the poems in LePan's second verse collection, The Net and the Sword
(Douglas LePan Papers, Thomas Fisher Rare Book Library, University of Toronto)

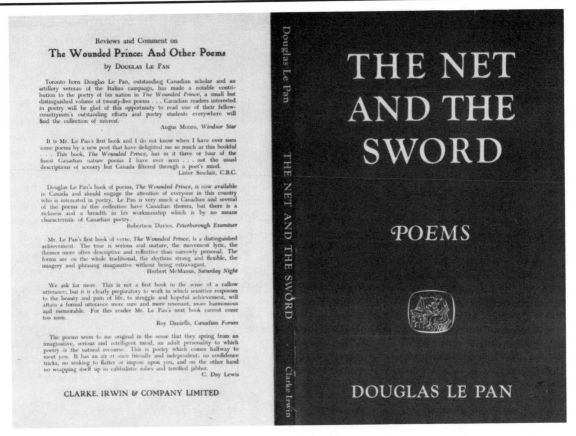

Dust jacket for LePan's collection of poems based on his experiences as a soldier during World War II. The Net and the Sword *won a Governor General's Award for 1953.*

Commission), and in 1958-1959 he held the position of assistant under secretary of state for external affairs.

Switching careers again, LePan returned to university life in 1959, taking an appointment as professor of English at Queen's University, Kingston. Here he set to work on his symbolic novel, *The Deserter* (1964). It is set in the period of demobilization following the war in an unnamed city (clearly London) and focuses on the conflict between individual freedom and social responsibility, between meaninglessness and commitment. The hero, Rusty, jettisons his regimented life as a soldier; separates himself from his friend, Mark, whose respectable diplomatic job sums up the anaesthetic world of "schedules and obligations"; and tries out the lonely, rootless life of a deserter and wanderer, finding himself unintentionally drawn into the underworld of crime. He seeks temporary respite from fear and pursuit in desperate friendships with a political refugee named Steve and a guilt-crazed woman named Anne, an imperfect reflection of the young woman Althea,

whom he idealizes as the epitome of perfection and completion. Following the mythic pattern, the wounded hero ascends from the underworld with new knowledge—that life includes imperfection, but also courage and friendship—and he turns himself in. Rusty's final action is both a surrender and an affirmation; D. G. Jones discusses this aspect of the novel in detail in "The Sacrificial Embrace" in *Butterfly on Rock: A Study of Themes and Imagery in Canadian Literature* (1970). The novel was immediately successful, though some critics complained about the literary quality of the dialogue even in its more realistic passages. *The Deserter* won a Governor General's Award for 1964 and was republished as a New Canadian Library paperback in 1973.

From 1964 to 1970 LePan was principal of University College, University of Toronto; from 1970 until his retirement in 1980, he held the position of University Professor. A suite of four poems won the Oscar Blumenthal Prize from *Poetry* in 1972, while his prose memoirs which highlight the decade from 1941 to 1951 were published as *Bright Glass of Memory* in 1979.

Yet a new burst of creativity was evident when LePan published another volume of poetry, *Something Still to Find*, in 1982, bringing together poems that had been appearing over several years in *Canadian Forum*, *Canadian Literature*, *Quarry*, *West Coast Review*, and other journals. The opening poem, "The Green Man," reads like a continuing tribute to the rejuvenating power of poetry, even among those who wear nonpoetic masks. The "green man," a natural Merlin, "watches the other animals, himself hidden / like an animal." But he is to be glimpsed "almost everywhere":

> In pale changing-rooms at the atomic energy
> plant
> the young technician is changed into a sylvan man,
> shadowed with mystery, and suffering from the sap,
> like a young green tree, quick thrall of earth and
> frenzy[.]

He, too, is vulnerable, however, and can bleed with "green wounds." Subsequent poems extend this intricate measure, this desire for repose in an unromantic world: they grieve for a lost kingdom, fear for the empty presence of a double, probe the blessings of romance, and praise the continuing triumph of love. Several poems look back at the Canadian wilderness LePan loves, finding still the "savagely trembling silence" that he praises and so names. These tendencies continue, however, to divide him from other poets writing in the 1980s. His formal diction, his net of European literary allusions, his occasional wit, his measured cadences and patterns of formal recurrence: these characteristics mark the later poems just as they do the early ones. His poetry is of a piece; *Weathering It*, a volume subtitled *Complete Poems 1948-1987*, appeared in 1987.

Douglas LePan ranks as a skilled poetic craftsman whose central concerns are the entanglement of life and death, the tension between freedom and necessity, and the conflict in the Canadian spirit between the claims of the land and those of European tradition. His nature poems tap a central root of the Canadian imagination, although his relatively limited output and his essentially conservative style have confined him to the middle slopes of postwar writing in Canada. His later poems, as he put it in *Bright Glass of Memory*, suggest a new commitment to "a looser and more personal manner." LePan describes himself (borrowing Rainer Maria Rilke's words) as an "eternal beginner."

References:

D. G. Jones, "The Sacrifical Embrace," in his *Butterfly on Rock: A Study of Themes and Imagery in Canadian Literature* (Toronto: University of Toronto Press, 1970);

Tom Marshall, *Harsh and Lovely Land* (Vancouver: University of British Columbia Press, 1979), pp. 80-82, 126-134;

Donald G. Priestman, "Man in the Maze," *Canadian Literature*, 64 (Spring 1975): 52-66.

Papers:

The Public Archives of Canada, Ottawa, holds LePan's diplomatic papers. His literary papers are at the Thomas Fisher Rare Book Library, University of Toronto.

Norman Levine
(22 October 1923-)

Ira Bruce Nadel
University of British Columbia

BOOKS: *Myssium* (Toronto: Ryerson, 1948);
The Tight-rope Walker (London: Totem, 1950);
The Angled Road (London: Laurie, 1952; Toronto: McClelland & Stewart, 1953);
Canada Made Me (London: Putnam's, 1958; Ottawa: Deneau & Greenberg, 1979);
One Way Ticket: Stories (London: Secker & Warburg, 1961; Toronto: McClelland & Stewart, 1961);
From a Seaside Town (Toronto: Macmillan, 1970);
I Don't Want to Know Anyone Too Well, and Other Stories (London & Toronto: Macmillan, 1971);
Selected Stories (Ottawa: Oberon, 1975);
I Walk by the Harbour (Fredericton: Fiddlehead, 1976);
In Lower Town (Ottawa: Commoners', 1977);
Thin Ice (Ottawa: Deneau & Greenberg, 1979; London: Wildwood House, 1980);
Why Do You Live So Far Away? (Ottawa: Deneau & Greenberg, 1984);
Champagne Barn (Markham, Ont.: Penguin, 1984).

OTHER: *Canadian Winter's Tales*, edited by Levine (Toronto & London: Macmillan, 1968).

PERIODICAL PUBLICATIONS: "Why I am an Expatriate," *Canadian Literature*, 5 (Summer 1960): 49-54;
"The Girl in the Drugstore," *Canadian Literature*, 41 (Summer 1969): 49-52.

Toronto Star

Novelist and short-story writer Norman Levine is best known for his autobiographical work, *Canada Made Me* (1958). A critical account of a 1956 visit to Canada during a thirty-one-year exile in England (1949-1980), *Canada Made Me* remains an important and provocative account of social life, cultural values, and personal reassessment. "To be a writer I had to be an exile," Levine has stated, and this condition of displacement and rootlessness has shaped his entire body of writing. Because of his foreign residence, Levine's popularity has been primarily in Europe, with his largest readership in Germany, where his translator has been, Heinrich Böll, the 1972 winner of the Nobel Prize for Literature. In Canada where Levine has lived since 1980, his works have achieved only modest recognition.

Norman Levine was born to Moses Mordecai and Annie Gurevich Levine in Ottawa and grew up in the Jewish section known as Lower Town, an experience he recalls in *Canada Made Me* and various short stories. Impoverished and limited in his educational opportunities, Levine began a job with the Department of National Defence immediately upon graduating from high school. In 1942, at the age of eighteen, he joined the RCAF and, after training in western Canada, went to Yorkshire, England, where he flew six bombing raids over Germany. Waiting to return to Canada after World War II, he attended Trin-

189

ity College, Cambridge, for a few months. In Canada he entered Montreal's McGill University, where he majored in English, earning a B.A. with honors in 1948. The same year his first book, *Myssium*, a chapbook of verse, was published. In 1949, with a thesis on Ezra Pound, he received an M.A. from McGill. For one year at McGill he was editor of the literary magazine.

Winning a fellowship, he attended King's College, London, in 1949 and 1950 but gave up academics for a career as a writer. He arrived in England with the manuscript of his first novel, *The Angled Road* (1952), begun as a writing project at McGill. Levine left Canada in 1949 because, in his words, "to be the kind of writer I wanted to be in Canada was impossible. The centre was either London or New York." The Canadian publisher Jack McClelland had agreed to handle Levine's novel if he would first find a foreign publisher. Participating in the postwar romanticism of England that celebrated art as well as ideology, Levine associated with painters and, most important, perhaps, spent time observing nature. Moving from London to Cornwall began a new phase in his work. As he told John D. Cox in a 1970 interview: "A hard new physical world seemed to have suddenly opened before me and in such splendid colour."

In 1950 Levine published a poetry collection, *The Tight-rope Walker*. In 1952 he married Margaret Payne, an Englishwoman, and settled in St. Ives, Cornwall, where they raised three daughters. *The Angled Road* appeared that same year, following the publication of various short stories in such magazines as *Vogue* and *Harper's Bazaar*. Written in what would become his characteristic staccato style, *The Angled Road* describes the youth of an English-Canadian, son of a peddler, who joins the RCAF and is sent to England, where he has a series of love affairs during the war. Returning home, he feels lost and departs from his parents to begin an uncertain future at university. This autobiographical novel made little impact in Canada.

In 1953 and 1954 Levine headed the English department at a boys' grammar school in Devon but devoted himself principally to writing, with trips to Canada in 1956 and 1965. After the death of his wife in 1978, he decided in 1980 to return to Toronto, where he now spends most of the year. In August 1983 he married Anne Sarginson.

Levine's novels and short stories deal with close observations of the self and its immediate surroundings. Personal relations dominate his writing, which often combines Canadian and English settings in a single work. Influenced by Anton Chekhov, James Joyce, and Graham Greene, Levine's work concentrates on psychological and domestic realism, avoiding experimentalism, exoticism, or myth. Much of his writing reflects his personal admission, made in his 1969 essay "The Girl in the Drugstore," that at McGill he ran away from being a Jew and in England he ran away from Canada. A result of his escape was, he told Cox, that his early stories were "pale" and "unreal" because he consciously altered their natural Canadian setting and experiences to those of England. Levine has always felt an exile–as a Jew, the son of Orthodox parents in Ottawa, as a poor student among the rich at McGill, and as a Canadian living in England. Only when he wrote *Canada Made Me* did he begin to accept his past and adjust his attitude to his state of exile.

Canada Made Me was initially to be a travelogue but it quickly became a unique Canadian autobiography. In 1956 Levine made a cross-country trip from Halifax to Ucluelet on Vancouver Island. Instead of merely recording his responses to the surface, however, he confronted his past and in realistic descriptive prose analyzed the meaning of his departure. Whether in Ottawa where his parents lived, the mining town of Ile-aux-Noix where he had worked in the summer of 1948, or Montreal where he had been a student, Levine blended the essence of the immediate with the truth of the past. Flashbacks and biographies of various individuals create an absorbing text, although his portrait of the country is unsympathetic. In Canada he sees optimism and energy replaced by unhappiness and boredom. The countryside is desolate, the cities barren.

Analyzing his own isolation and departure from Canada, Levine remarks that he left for the sake of change, because of his lack of any patriotic feeling, the unpleasant reminders of his childhood, and the absence of any distinctive culture: "ours is still a mixture of other cultures which hasn't fused into anything separate," he asserts in *Canada Made Me*. Attracted to the poorer areas of the cities because "they represent failure, and for me failure here has a strong appeal," Levine focuses on the seediness of the country, the flophouses, mining towns, and bars he revisits. Giving detailed descriptions of place while superimposing the past on the present, Levine constructs a complexly patterned book that is ulti-

I went back to the Y.M.C.A. and asked the young boy with the well groomed hair, and s rious suit, where could I buy a pair of socks. He thought. Sdd everywhere would be closed now. But you could try old Pop down in the gym stores, he might have a pair of gym socks. I went down the stairs to the basement. And opened a door. Hot. Smelling of sweat. Men puttingon their jockstraps, walking around with a towel to the shower room. Sound of water hissing down. I asked for Pop, one told me first door to the left. He was there behind a worn wooden counter trying to fix a combination lock for a boy in sweatshirt, and shorts. He was the Pop I've remembered. The one that's always there. At Boys Clubs, schools gyms. Behind him, from p lleys on the ceiling were the gym clothes hanging down like a miner's washroom. Pop, the friend of the boys, leave a message with Pop, let Pop take care of it. Everywh re the same. Pop kept there because of some physical disability. He had two fingers missing on his left hand. He sold me a pair of white basketball gym socks, and I went back to the doctors room, and took of the wet dark woolen ones threw them away in the we tepap r basket and put these on. Shaved. And went outside It was freezing cold. The slush froze up and it was difficult walking. I shuffled sliding along. Some kids had made a slide in one part I went down it going twice as fast on the leather soles and heels. The snow banks had an envelope of frost, had a crust of frost. I couldhear the whistle of a boat. Down the main street. Two service police, army walked by. Then two more, navy walked by. Young boys, tall, well built. The shops were lit up, the restaurents. I went in and had a hamburg r in one. There were several young boys from the navy trying to flirt with the young girl behind the counter. The hamburger was raw, but there was lots of onions. It was time to catch the plane. I took a bus back to the hotel by the railway station and waited. Blacl limousine. I had caun

Page from an early draft for Canada Made Me, *Levine's critical account of his 1956 visit to Canada during a thirty-one-year exile in England (The Norman Levine Papers, York University Archives; by permission of the author)*

mately a work of self-discovery. Dominating the work is the feeling that he does not belong anywhere, and his final view of Canada is bitter because the country has failed to realize the dream of a golden future and new beginning for its immigrants. A controversial book, *Canada Made Me* remained unpublished in Canada until 1979, although five hundred copies of the English edition were distributed by a Canadian publisher in 1958.

Six volumes of short stories, a book of poems, and a second novel appeared between 1958 and 1984. The short stories display a crafted but plain style and reflect a realistic rather than romantic world. They deal with encounters, personal concerns, and the past. The journey motif and atmospheric descriptions of place dominate the 1961 collection, *One Way Ticket*. *I Don't Want to Know Anyone Too Well* (1971) mixes adventures in England and Canada with problems of love, the desire but inability to communicate, and the obstructions that prevent complete understanding between people. Childhood experiences play an important role in both collections and in *In Lower Town*, a story which first appeared in *Encounter* (1973), was collected in *Selected Stories* (1975) and published separately, with photographs by Johanne McDuff, in 1977. The story draws on Levine's Ottawa childhood, but it is important to note that the documentary forms used—memoir and interview—function as elsewhere in his work to emphasize the subjectivity of experience and the imminence of change. Levine often fictionalizes events recounted in *Canada Made Me*.

A new sense of humor emerges in the stories of the 1970s, as in "A Canadian Upbringing," a comic portrayal of the "why I left Canada question." By implication autobiographical, the story identifies the current themes of Levine's work: the ghetto childhood, rootlessness, and travel. *Thin Ice* (1979) continues these well-constructed, realistic stories of personal encounters. His 1976 volume of poetry, *I Walk by the Harbour*, includes selections from Levine's 1948 poetry book plus several poems written in 1959. The modulated language and controlled verse express his response to the physical sense of place, specifically Cornwall.

Two more story collections, *Why Do You Live So Far Away?* and *Champagne Barn*, both published in 1984, shift focus only slightly, emphasizing his central character's contemporary role as husband and father more than his quest for his

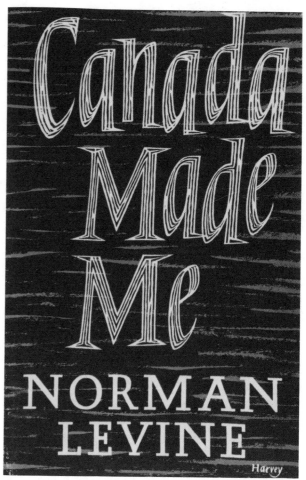

Dust jacket for Levine's best-known work (The Norman Levine Papers, York University Archives)

roots in the past. "By a Frozen River" (*Thin Ice*) talks of "autobiography written as fiction"; the stories of *Champagne Barn* are self-declaredly "a kind of autobiography." Yet in all his fiction Levine is drawing attention to the craft of expression more than to the life from which the expression stems. These are not stories making reference to a particular life so much as they are stories of a particular life lived in words.

From a Seaside Town (1970), Levine's second novel, is written with more energy than his first, although it deals with similar themes. Married to a non-Jewish Englishwoman, Joseph Grand, the hero, alternates between a bored life in the seaside town of Carnbray and a social and artistic life in London with his friends Albert, a Jew obsessed by the Holocaust, and Charles, a homosexual painter. In a first-person narrative the hero confesses his failings as a travel writer, lover, and husband while searching for something greater. His background is familiar: an immigrant to Ottawa, service in the RCAF, marriage to an English-woman. Searching, in part, for some deeper literary achievement, the hero muddles through a declining career as a travel writer. His life is enlivened only by an unexpected visit from his sister and her obnoxious husband from Montreal and a brief affair with a young actress. After a trip to Canada to revisit family and write about the country, the narrator returns a chastened man, accepting his relationship with his wife and mediocre career, although he turns from travel writing to short stories by the end of the work.

A novel of unpretentious aims and, in the narrator's words, "unconnected brief encounters," *From a Seaside Town* reflects the ambiguity of Levine's exile in the hero's comment on his early Canadian travel essays written in England: "I wrote about the violence, the mediocrity of the people, the provincialism, the dullness.... And all the time I wanted to be there." But the condition of exile and sense of separation that infuses so much of Norman Levine's writing does not isolate him as much as reestablish his attachment and identity as a Canadian.

Interviews:

John D. Cox, "Norman Levine: An Interview," *Canadian Literature*, 45 (Summer 1970): 61-67;

David McDonald, "Simplicity and Sophistication: A Conversation with Norman Levine," *Queen's Quarterly*, 83 (Summer 1976): 217-230;

Wayne Grady, "Interview: Norman Levine," *Books in Canada*, 9 (February 1980): 24-25.

References:

Michael Greenstein, "Between Ottawa and St. Ives: Norman Levine's Tight-rope Walkers," *Journal of Commonwealth Literature*, 23, no. 1 (1988): 61-75;

Ira B. Nadel, "*Canada Made Me* and Canadian Autobiography," *Canadian Literature*, 101 (Summer 1984): 69-81;

Michael Smith, "An Exile Comes Home," *Today* (11 October 1980): 11-13;

Donald Stephen, "Looking Homeward," *Canadian Literature*, 70 (Autumn 1976): 93-96;

Frederick Sweet, "Norman Levine," in *Profiles in Canadian Literature, 4*, edited by Jeffrey M. Heath (Toronto & Charlottetown: Dundurn, 1982), pp. 29-36.

Papers:

The York University Archives holds most of Levine's papers. The original manuscript for *Canada Made Me* is at the Harry Ransom Humanities Research Center, University of Texas at Austin.

John Marlyn

(2 April 1912-　)

Walter E. Swayze
University of Winnipeg

BOOKS: *Under the Ribs of Death* (Toronto: McClelland & Stewart, 1957; London: Barker, 1957);

Putzi, I Love You, You Little Square (Toronto: Coach House Press, 1981).

Since its publication in 1957, *Under the Ribs of Death* has been recognized as a vivid recreation of Winnipeg's multiethnic North End in the 1920s, a subtle analysis of racial prejudice and its consequences, and the first significant revelation of Hungarian immigrant experience in English Canada. As required reading for courses in Canadian literature, psychology, sociology, social history, and ethnic studies, it was long in print in the New Canadian Library edition, and for years it was the only volume in the series that contained no information about its author. Only when *Putzi, I Love You, You Little Square* was published in 1981 did Marlyn finally agree to interviews.

John Marlyn was born on 2 April 1912 in Debrecen, Hungary. His father, Adam, was a barber, a highly intelligent agnostic loner; his mother, Paula Kendal Marlyn, a Catholic, was the daughter of a wagon maker. Shortly after Marlyn's birth his father left Hungary and settled in Winnipeg, sending for his wife and child when Marlyn was six months old. Marlyn grew up in Winnipeg at 450 Henry Street, across from the CPR freight sheds, the slum setting for Sandor Hunyadi's childhood in *Under the Ribs of Death*. In an interview with Beverly Rasporich published in 1982, Marlyn said, "We felt that our family was a rampart against the fire which was raging outside–the poverty, crime, and prostitution. Learning was encouraged . . . not only in order to get a job, but for its own sake."

His father's illness forced Marlyn to quit school at the age of fourteen; for nearly five years he worked in the stockroom of Holt, Renfrew, a clothing retailer. He remembers envying a dog on the street because, he told David Arnason and Ken Hughes in an interview pub-

John Marlyn in 1957 (courtesy of the author)

lished in 1982, the animal "was free to go where he wanted to." Marlyn read widely and wrote constantly, and with private study he was able to enter the University of Manitoba in 1930, where, for a brief time, he reveled in literature and continued writing. He could not afford to stay on, and the only work he could get during the Depression was tutoring for twenty-five cents an hour. Eventually he took a cattle boat to England and found a job as an outside reader in the Gainsborough Studios of Gaumont British Films.

Ruth Miles, whom Marlyn had known in Winnipeg's North End, came to London, and

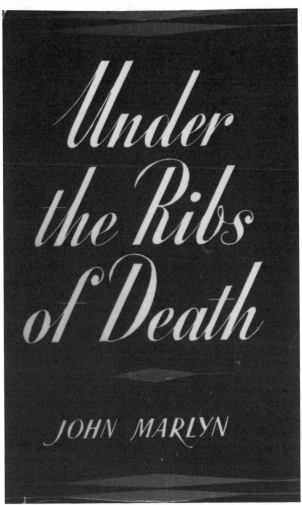

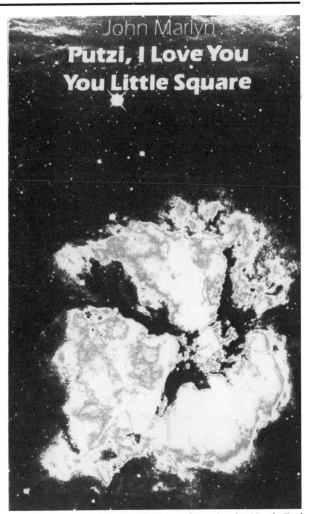

Dust jacket for Marlyn's first novel, about a Hungarian immigrant who comes of age in Winnipeg's North End

Front cover for Marlyn's 1981 novel, set in the North End and featuring the observations of a talking fetus

they were married on 16 August 1937. In 1938 they returned to Canada, first to Montreal and then to Ottawa, where they stayed. Marlyn has worked in a variety of civil-service writing positions with the Department of Labour, the National Film Board, and the Department of Secretary of State.

Under the Ribs of Death took five years to write and much longer to be published. The year after the book appeared under McClelland and Stewart's imprint, it won the Beta Sigma Phi First Novel Award. Marlyn's second book, *Putzi, I Love You, You Little Square*, took two years to write; it was composed first as a play, then as a short novel, but was not published until 1981. It was not as warmly received and disappointed admirers of the first novel who had waited so long for a second. A third novel, tentatively titled "Echoes from Afar," had been in progress long before *Putzi, I Love You, You Little Square*, but it has not ap-

peared. Marlyn has taught creative-writing classes in Ottawa and has also published stories in journals.

Under the Ribs of Death is often considered a bildungsroman in which the usual conflict between generations is exacerbated by the protagonist's association of his parents' Hungarian culture and humane values with grinding poverty and persecution, and the dominant WASP culture and commercialism with success and fulfillment. The young Sandor Hunyadi, rejecting his exploited, long-suffering father, fantasizes that his real father is an English lord and dreams of becoming English, rich, and powerful. When he gets his first job cutting grass in, to him, paradisiacal River Heights, he gives his name as Alex Humphrey, for its "quiet English elegance"; when he enters the cutthroat world of business, he rejects that name as "too soft . . . too harmless" and becomes Alex Hunter, painstakingly practicing a signature in which the lower-case letters look "something like the teeth of a buzz-saw." His strong desire to be assimilated engenders a mass of contradictions. He resents the English who coolly maneuver him into admitting his Hungarian origins, yet he worships the successful Hungarian Nagy, who exploits him more cruelly than the English. He considers the English Lawson's lack of prejudice against him a sign of weakness. Falling in love with his childhood playmate Mary Kostenuik, he reflects, "You'd never think from looking at her that her parents were foreigners."

Just as Alex seems about to achieve his dream of moving with his wife to River Heights, the 1929 stock-market crash occurs. Alex, unemployed in the ensuing Depression, trying to sell a couple of wicker baskets to buy stamps, stationery, and newspapers to apply for jobs, sees his dream house in River Heights "empty and deserted . . . gaping with the vacancy of death."

From childhood gang fights to manhood Sandor/Alex has ruthlessly crushed his humane instincts, which, in expressionistic nightmares, he fears threaten to destroy him, like the rat he crushes in terror with a shovel in his slum tenement. In the end, when the whole world seems a wasteland, he looks into his little son's eyes and "is filled . . . with a gladness such as he had rarely known, because in those mild depths . . . were all those things, miraculously alive, which he had suppressed in himself, stifled for the sake of what he had almost felt within his grasp, out there, over his son's head, out and beyond in the grey desolation." In the images of Ezekiel 37 and from Milton's *Comus* (lines 560-562), he has discovered a soul "Under the ribs of death." For all its local color and documentary realism, its kaleidoscopic vision of Hungarian festivities amid the drabness and cruelty of slum subsistence, and its terror of confrontation with oneself, the novel is primarily a powerful affirmation of the mystery of life.

In the explosive power of its image patterns *Under the Ribs of Death* is closer to expressionism than to realism. Similarly, while *Putzi, I Love You, You Little Square* has been called "humorous surrealism," it seems closer to expressionistic satire. In this short, witty novel set in the 1970s, a virgin named Ellen is pregnant with a precocious fetus who talks irrepressibly and embarrassingly, usually about Ellen's suitors. Putzi (a term of endearment that Marlyn had heard as a child and used as the name for a pet dog in *Under the Ribs of*

Death) is an absurd caricature of the little child that Wordsworth apostrophizes in the Immortality Ode as "best Philosopher," "Mighty Prophet!," "Seer blest!" Not only does Putzi relentlessly quote from or allude to Virgil, Shakespeare, Donne, Herbert, Samuel Johnson, Wordsworth, Tennyson, Wilde, Dylan Thomas, and Freud, but in a manner recalling Eliot's Tiresias, he sees and evaluates his mother, her suitors, and others in Winnipeg's North End. Through the wit and the slapstick emerges an awareness that children are born into a world already determined by decisions and circumstances for which they are later held responsible. If *Under the Ribs of Death* frightens with the image of the new gods, "buyers and sellers," turning "man into an animal with only a mouth to fill," *Putzi, I Love You, You Little Square* is even more frightening for its vision of technology's power and effects. In the form of ultrasound scans and amniocentesis, technology invades the privacy of the fetus. One of Ellen's suitors threatens Putzi that he will wire him to his computer with "a fine probe, shielded platinum actually, in the vicinity of your brain," in order to transform Putzi, an unborn child with all imaginable human potential, into "the only talking computer in the world." This image of dehumanization makes Marlyn's other satirical sallies on topics such as sexism, ethnic jealousy, pop psychology, and the youth cult, however subtle and humorous, seem incidental.

Putzi, I Love You, You Little Square does not develop the involvement in the problems of real people that Marlyn achieves in *Under the Ribs of Death*, nor does it have the emotional momentum of that novel. Until the novel in progress appears, John Marlyn's reputation will rest on the richly textured, compellingly humane *Under the Ribs of Death*.

Interviews:

David Arnason and Ken Hughes, "Between the Lines: Interview with John Marlyn," *NeWest Review*, 8 (November 1982): 12-15;

Beverly Rasporich, "An Interview with John Marlyn," *Canadian Ethnic Studies / Etudes Ethniques au Canada*, 14, no. 1 (1982): 36-40.

Reference:

Eli Mandel, Introduction to Marlyn's *Under the Ribs of Death* (Toronto: McClelland & Stewart, 1964).

Joyce Marshall

(28 November 1913-   )

W. H. New
University of British Columbia

BOOKS: *Presently Tomorrow* (Toronto: McClelland & Stewart, 1946; Boston: Little, Brown, 1946);

Lovers and Strangers (Philadelphia: Lippincott, 1957);

A Private Place (Ottawa: Oberon, 1975).

RADIO: *The Box of Fudge, Canadian Short Stories*, CBC, 27 January 1950;

Among the Lost, Bernie Braden Reads a Story, CBC, 21 March 1950;

The Old Woman, Canadian Short Stories, CBC, 12 May 1950;

All in the Winter's Cold, Canadian Short Stories, CBC, 16 June 1950;

The Pair of Gloves, Bernie Braden Reads a Story, CBC, 11 August 1950;

Belgium Avenue, Canadian Short Stories, CBC, 25 August 1950;

The World Again, Canadian Short Stories, CBC, 16 February 1951;

A Question of Numbers, Canadian Short Stories, CBC, 1 February 1952;

Wait for Me, Canadian Short Stories, CBC, 21 February 1953;

The Bicycle, Canadian Short Stories, CBC, 30 May 1953;

The One Who Asked, Canadian Short Stories, CBC, 8 February 1954;

The Ride Home, Anthology, CBC, 18 November 1958;

Snow on Flat Top, Anthology, CBC, 23 December 1960;

Ruin and Wrack, Anthology, CBC, 15 July 1972;

A Private Place, Anthology, CBC, 15 July 1973;

The Little White Girl, Anthology, CBC, 25 May 1974;

Summer, Anthology, CBC, 13 July 1974;

The Accident, Anthology, CBC, 13 December 1975;

The Escape, Anthology, CBC, 14 May 1977;

Copenhagen, Anthology, CBC, 12 November 1977;

The Case of Cassandra Dop, Anthology, CBC, 22 May 1982;

My Refugee, Anthology, CBC, 11 September 1982;

Avis de Vente, Anthology, CBC, 1983.

OTHER: "Come Ye Apart," in *Fiction* (Toronto: Toronto Writers' Club, 1936), pp. 5-10;

"Summer," in *75: New Canadian Stories*, edited by David Helwig and Joan Harcourt (Ottawa: Oberon, 1975), pp. 42-56;

" . . . a Difficult Country, and Our Home," in *Divided We Stand*, edited by Gary Geddes (Toronto: PMA, 1977), pp. 186-191;

"The Escape," in *Aurora: New Canadian Writing 1978*, edited by Morris Wolfe (Toronto: Doubleday, 1978), pp. 123-133;

"The Author Comments . . . [on 'The Old Woman']," in *Writers and Writing* (Toronto: TV Ontario, 1981), pp. 175-179;

"The Case of Cassandra Dop," in *Small Wonders*, edited by Robert Weaver (Toronto: CBC Enterprises, 1982), pp. 73-83;

"My Refugee," in *83: Best Canadian Stories*, edited by Helwig and Sandra Martin (Ottawa: Oberon, 1983), pp. 146-159.

TRANSLATIONS: Gabrielle Roy, *La Route d'Altamont*, translated as *The Road Past Altamont* (Toronto: McClelland & Stewart, 1966);

Word from New France: The Selected Letters of Marie de l'Incarnation, edited by Marshall (Toronto: Oxford University Press, 1967);

Eugène Cloutier, *Le Canada sans passeport*, abridged and translated as *No Passport: A Discovery of Canada* (Toronto: Oxford University Press, 1968);

Roy, *La Rivière sans repos*, translated as *Windflower* (Toronto: McClelland & Stewart, 1970);

Gérard Pelletier, *La Crise d'octobre*, translated as *The October Crisis* (Toronto: McClelland & Stewart, 1971);

Thérèse F. Casgrain, *Une Femme chez les hommes*, translated as *A Woman in a Man's World* (Toronto: McClelland & Stewart, 1972);

photograph by Patricia Starkey

Joyce Marshall

Roy, *Cet Eté qui chantait*, translated as *Enchanted Summer* (Toronto: McClelland & Stewart, 1976).

PERIODICAL PUBLICATIONS: "And the Hilltop was Elizabeth," *Queen's Quarterly*, 45 (Summer 1938): 186-194;

"How Not to Write," *Saturday Night*, 54 (30 September 1939): 20;

"The Hero," *Canadian Life*, 1 (March / April 1949): 9, 35;

"Nora–with Mercy," *Canadian Home Journal* (November 1949): 22-23, 44-52;

"Learn It Early," *Seventeen*, 9 (August 1950): 162, 245ff;

"Oh Jocelyn, My Friend," *Canadian Home Journal* (March 1953): 9, 72, 74-80;

"The Screaming Silence," *New Liberty*, 30 (October 1953): 29, 48-50;

"The Ride Home," *Montrealer*, 32 (October 1958): 28, 30, 32;

"In the Midst of Life," *Montrealer*, 33 (April 1959): 20-23;

" . . . In the Same Country . . . ," *Tamarack Review*, 13 (Autumn 1959): 121-124;

"Snow on Flat Top," *Montrealer*, 34 (December 1960): 24-26;

"Rightly Call[ed] the Nymph," *Montrealer*, 37 (May 1963): 30-35;

"Leaving Copenhagen," *Montrealer*, 38 (February 1964): 22-30;

"The Oasis," *Montrealer*, 38 (July 1964): 28-30;

"Canadian Poets and Their Mythologies," *Montrealer*, 39 (October 1965): 40-43;

"The Accident," *Fiddlehead*, 108 (Winter 1976): 62-69;

"The Gradual Day," *Canadian Fiction Magazine*, 20 (1976): 84-89;

"Paul and Phyllis," *Tamarack Review*, 72 (Fall 1977): 28-53;

"Windows," *Canadian Fiction Magazine*, 27 (1977): 102-112;

"Dorothy Livesay: A Bluestocking Remembers," *Branching Out*, 7, no. 1 (1980): 18-21;

"Gabrielle Roy 1909-1983," *Antigonish Review*, 55 (Autumn 1983): 35-46;

"Gabrielle Roy 1909-1983: Some Reminiscences," *Canadian Literature*, 101 (Summer 1984): 183-184;

"Avis de Vente," *Matrix*, 19 (Fall 1984): 2-8;

"The Tourist," *Canadian Forum*, 64 (March 1985): 30-33;

"Corridors," *Room of One's Own*, 10 (December 1985): 3-14;

"Rearing Horse," *Fiddlehead*, 145 (1985): 52-56;

"Senior Year," *Matrix*, 22 (Spring 1986): 15-22;

"Blood and Bone," *Canadian Forum*, 67 (August / September 1987): 18-23;

"Kat," *Canadian Woman Studies*, 8 (Fall 1987): 124-125;

"Jake's Leaps," *Dandelion*, 14 (Winter 1987): 62-71;

"The Writer as Translator: A Personal View," *Canadian Literature*, 117 (Summer 1988): 25-29;

"Ethel Wilson," *Brick*, 35 (Spring 1989): 32-36.

Born in Montreal on 28 November 1913, Joyce Marshall only slowly established the literary reputation she enjoys in the 1980s. Publishing as early as 1936, she was appreciated first as a meticulous prose stylist, and in due course she came to be known as a sensitive translator. But the literary form at which she excelled, the short story, was long dismissed as a minor genre, and for several decades many critics considered the subjects she frankly addressed (urban violence, female sexuality) to be irreconcilable with received definitions of art. Hence until the 1980s she occupied only a small space in literary history, an estimation that is being rectified as the body of her work is being anthologized, collected, and reread.

Her father, William Wallace Marshall, was a stocks-and-bonds dealer and an amateur singer. He and his wife, Ruth Winifred Chambers Marshall, had five children (four girls and a boy); they are the prototypes on which Marshall's stories of a little girl named Martha (or Marty–as in "The Little White Girl," collected in *A Private Place*, 1975) are based. In a letter dated 14 January 1988 Marshall remembers her mother as a woman who would have described herself as " 'just a housewife' . . . with considerable anger. The eldest of the 9 children of an Anglican clergyman, she was taken from school after the birth of the last, my grandmother having decided to spend the next year in bed. She always resented her lack of training and was determined that her daughters . . . should not suffer this lack."

Marshall's roots in Quebec go back four generations, and even after she had ceased to be a resident of the province, she continued to declare Quebec to be "home"; she alludes to these emotional connections, and to her childhood, in a passionate essay opposing Quebec's separation from Canada, published in Gary Geddes's anthology *Divided We Stand* in 1977. "What I really love," she writes, "is . . . the rub and bite of difference that keeps us alert and alive," and later: "Perhaps the best thing history has given us is the chance to shift, make new and partial adjustments, then shift and mesh again." Given the context of the 1970s, Marshall's essay is a plea for thoughtful social action, but it is a personal testament as well.

Marshall grew up in Montreal, attending Roslyn School (1920-1927), Westmount High School (1927-1929), and St. Helen's School (1929-1932)–the last of these an Anglican boarding school for girls, in Dunham, Quebec, where Marshall finished high school and took her senior matriculation year (instead of first year at university). She went on to McGill University, completing an Honours B.A. in English in 1935, winning the university's English language and literature medal. During these years she was also learning to write fiction.

She credits Harold G. Files of McGill's English department, who influenced more than one generation of Montreal writers, as an important mentor and as one of her most enthusiastic and supportive readers as she began to have her work published. As a student she also worked for the *McGill Daily* (she was the first female ever appointed to the senior editorial staff), reporting on campus events and reviewing plays and French films. To other campus magazines, such as the *Forge*, she contributed verse and fiction, and for one story won a five-dollar prize. There was a coterie of young writers at McGill at the time, but only Marshall went on to a literary career.

After graduation there were few opportunities for employment or travel; the Depression still limited people's lives. But as a non-Catholic, non-francophone female in the restrictive conservative Quebec of Premier Maurice Duplessis, she felt she was denied not only economic opportunities but also a political voice. So in 1937, with Europe beyond economic reach, she moved to Toronto. In contrast with Montreal, Toronto was to her eyes a politically more open city, though also more provincial, less sophisticated, less in touch with the rest of the world. But it was also a rapidly growing city, and as Toronto became the center for English-language radio broadcasting in Canada–another development of the 1930s–she began to find both a congenial literary medium and a literary voice.

Writing was always her full-time occupation, but it required support. Marshall worked at various clerical and sales jobs. She began to do freelance editing. She wrote occasional essays and reviews for *Saturday Night* and *Tamarack Review*. And she was publishing stories. "Come Ye Apart" had appeared in 1936 in *Fiction*, an anthology that emerged through the Toronto Writers' Club, after the American editor Edward J. O'Brien had visited Toronto and chastised writers there for not being adventurous. The Toronto Writers' Club primarily included journalists: William Arthur Deacon was a member; so was Dan McArthur, who founded the CBC's news department and later became one of Marshall's friends. Another story, "And the Hilltop was Elizabeth," which won the Canadian Women's Press Club fiction prize, appeared in *Queen's Quarterly* in 1938; it is a love story that declares a woman's need for independence, indicating already the direction that Marshall's writing was to take. (Virginia Woolf and Marcel Proust are among her favorite authors, and the influence of Woolf is particularly apparent in her earliest work.) She was also working on her first novel.

Presently Tomorrow appeared in 1946, to the consternation of some critics. J. R. MacGillivray, writing a survey of the year's fiction for "Letters in Canada" in the *University of Toronto Quarterly*, admired the style but ultimately dismissed the book; the climax, he averred, was unbelievable, and the sexual events of the closing pages were more designed for the marketplace than for "art." It was a judgment shaped by the very attitudes of the time that Marshall was trying to make clear in her novel–and so to oppose. Her novel, like many of her subsequent works, deals overtly with the realities of teenage female sexuality, and more fundamentally with the double standards that generally affect women in modern society, the social presumptions that cause them too often to lead repressed (because uninformed, or because deliberately misinformed) lives.

Presently Tomorrow grew out of the early story "Come Ye Apart." Set in an Anglican girls' school in Quebec's Eastern Townships, over a few weeks' time, it follows the lives of four girls who are completing their schooling that year, and the life of a young priest, politically too radi-

cal for his ecclesiastical superiors, who has been sent to the remote school to do penance and to lead a spiritual retreat for middle-aged matrons. The chapters of the book interpolate the meditations of the priest, Craig Everett, with the diary-like reflections of one of the girls, Ann Leslie. There are inexact parallels between the two. (In the early stream-of-consciousness story version, the two central narratives do not interconnect.) Craig struggles with his faith, as he recognizes that he is too preoccupied with himself to be of service to others; Ann, whose attention is taken up with the behavior of three of her friends, struggles to find maturity in her own way. She has, therefore, to learn to resist the models that others present to her, and he has to learn that some models make more sense for him than others do.

At the center of both their dilemmas is sexuality. One of Ann's friends, constantly wisecracking, seems sexually precocious; a second is all Oxford Group religiosity; a third seems mouselike and bland. Much hinges on puns on the word *lying*. Some characters tell untruths, to themselves or each other; others bed down; Ann Leslie represents a third option, for she is a storyteller, a would-be writer, who seeks to be able to express herself without being constrained by others' behavior or expectations. Unsatisfied with her teachers and friends, she seeks intellectual comfort from the priest. "It's very easy to remain a shadow once you start," he tells her; the lucky person is the one who can "start afresh, without a lot of ghosts trailing after. . . ." It is advice he might well give himself, for he finds that memories of his dead mother interfere with his growing up, despite what might be called his sociopolitical maturity–his concerns about unemployment, poverty, and a social role for the church. Sexually naive, he not only surrenders to the deliberate seductions of one of the girls–the bland one, it turns out, who is more adept at lying than the others realize–but he also, to the girl's amazement, tries to give up the church after he loses his virginity, in order to marry her. She refuses.

While she is a victim of a sort here (of an appetite for power, perhaps), he has been a victim, too: of her, of his stereotypical, male presumptions about innocent girlhood, and of his own ego and ignorance. In the end, it is Ann he can really help, and by helping her, help himself. For either of them to give up their first goals would be to fail. He decides to stay with the ministry, and Ann keeps open her artistic options. The ministry will not deny him his social commitment, he re-

Dust jacket for the first American edition of Marshall's novel set at an Anglican girls' school in the Eastern Townships of Quebec

We see ourselves always flat, arranged, she thought, so we do not know how the light strikes, how emotion takes and stretches these features we think of as our own. And suddenly there was a small broken thing she wanted to say to him. Have you ever felt that you were not quite real, that you were a little thinner and less solid than everyone else? That's what I want most in the world, she thought. To be solid. In myself first, then known as what I am.

She was afraid, she found, to take her eyes from her own face, to risk meeting his eyes, mirrored too, looking at her, finding something there, perhaps making something of what they found.

The novel begins when a woman, Katherine, meets a man, Roger, on a train. She likes him, responds to him partly because of his apparent strength, but responds even more when she recognizes that his overt manner masks some unhappiness; and she marries him. Over a period of several months, their Toronto marriage goes awry. She wants a "real" life; he appears to want only "a sort of life," and obliquely, through details of conversation and cocktail-party observation, the novel begins to question how normal the prevailing version of "normality" (i.e., married life) is. Roger admits at one point that "Nobody frightens us but ourselves," but he sees this comment more as advice for others than as self-recognition or revelation. His own insecurity is so well disguised and hence ill expressed that it constitutes the major cause of the marriage breaking down. He is unwilling to give himself away. For her part Katherine—who knows at least that he has grown up in a house that is a "tangle . . . of hurting and being hurt"—seeks fulfillment in various ways. First she tries passivity. She searches repeatedly for "what was required of her." But such a role does not satisfy her, just as it does not satisfy any of Marshall's female characters. Nor, of course, does it resolve Roger's problem. So she moves on. A victim of polio in childhood, Katherine limps, both actually and figuratively; late in the novel, discovering belatedly that she does not need Roger or Roger's covert hate any longer, she recognizes also that her weak leg can carry her better than she had thought. So she leaves him, for independence and for life, which at this point amount to the same thing.

alizes, even though political engagement will prove difficult in a conservative institution; artistry, for her, also leads in uncertain and sometimes paradoxical directions. As though in demonstration she is surprised when she, who is unimpressed by religious systems, discovers that Anglo-Catholic cadences affect her own voice, and she announces that she will "try . . . to remember . . . about the future being just today and then presently tomorrow."

Neither this novel nor Marshall's second, *Lovers and Strangers* (1957), has yet been republished. The overt subjects seem to have prevented some critics from appreciating the psychological perceptiveness of the narratives or the stylistic skill with which Marshall analyzes behavior. The stylishness of the second novel is apparent in the analytical phrasing of the "Prologue," which sets out the dimensions of the conflict to come:

From the 1940s to the 1980s Marshall's connection with CBC-Radio largely shaped the directions of her career. Like many other writers, she benefited when (to use her own phrase) "the incomparable Robert Weaver" joined the CBC in 1948. Weaver saw that radio was a potentially effective medium for the broadcast of short fiction. He worked with such programs as *Canadian Short Stories*, which had begun in 1946; this program led to an anthology Weaver edited with the radio producer Helen James in 1952: also called *Canadian Short Stories*, it included Marshall's "The Old Woman," later collected in *A Private Place*. Published again in Weaver's 1960 Oxford University Press anthology and later still in Margaret Atwood and Weaver's *Oxford Book of Canadian Short Stories in English* (1986), "The Old Woman" was for many years the single story by which Marshall was widely known. Weaver also established the CBC series *Anthology* in 1954, commissioning stories from writers he admired: Mordecai Richler and Mavis Gallant, as well as Marshall and others. (Such commissions and the payments attached to them, Marshall writes, often staved off "utter financial collapse.") "A Private Place" was written for *Anthology* and included in *The "Anthology" Anthology*, edited by Weaver in 1984.

Marshall edited various scripts for the CBC; she was also first reader for *Anthology* for almost the entire duration of that program. Many of her stories were broadcast over the CBC before appearing in print–which explains why anthologies such as the annual *New Canadian Stories* volumes edited by David Helwig often represented the first publications of her works. Some of Marshall's stories still remain unpublished, but others are lodged in a variety of journals and collections. Several stories appeared in the *Montrealer*, *New Liberty*, and the *Canadian Home Journal* during the 1950s, but few magazines at the time accepted short fiction, a fact which emphasizes the importance of radio as a medium of "publication." Yet another Weaver anthology, *Small Wonders* (1982), collected stories that were first broadcast on the CBC in 1981, including Marshall's "The Case of Cassandra Dop," a work which demonstrates the author's continuing interest in the forms of language and violence. It concerns, overtly, a college instructor's reaction to news of the sex-murder of her female assistant. As with Marshall's other stories it is not the declared subject which best describes the story, but the method, the forms and strategies of the language and expression. "The Case of Cassandra Dop" is a story in search of signs: a story that enacts two forms of indirect declaration–garrulity and taciturnity–as it shows characters attempting to interpret behavior that is familiar to their minds but beyond their understanding.

Marshall lived in Europe from July 1961 to October 1963. She had traveled to Europe before this time and has also visited Mexico and the United States, but the opportunity to live for about sixteen months in Copenhagen and for a year in Lillehammer, Norway (a special favorite: Norway was the birthplace of her paternal grandmother), led to other settings in her writing. "Any Time at All" and "A Private Place," for example, are both set in Denmark. ("Any Time at All" and "So Many Have Died" have their titles reversed in the first printing of *A Private Place*.) "The Tourist" (*Canadian Forum*, March 1985) deals with recollections of Greece; several others concern European refugees in Canada or, like "The Hero" (*Canadian Life*, March / April 1949), the ironic impact of European war on the patterns of normative Canadian behavior. Two travel essays also appeared in 1964 in the *Montrealer*. "Leaving Copenhagen" reflects on the character of a life lived in Denmark: "I loved this city. It does not overwhelm, as do the source-cities of our own history and the world's. I found no ghosts. . . . It is, above all, human, human and humane, not excessive in its demands, built entirely to our own scale. . . . Certain things [about Canada] I had missed–a sense of growth, disorder, something rangy and awkward. Or had I just, in trying to find Copenhagen, found an imaginary country?" Leaving the country, she found that:

> My life of sixteen months was condensed alarmingly as we darted and dashed along the streets. Now we were passing the one place I had made particularly my own. I always have such a place, choosing it or perhaps being chosen by it at the beginning. . . .
> I was not a tourist. I have lived here, must live a little longer, then must go.

From the 1950s to the 1970s Marshall was also earning some income as a translator from French of several articles and seven books, including the selected seventeenth-century letters of Mère Marie de l'Incarnation (*Word from New France*, 1967), Eugène Cloutier's Canadian travel book, *Le Canada sans passeport* (*No Passport*, 1968), and three novels by Gabrielle Roy, with whom she became friends: *La Route d'Altamont* (*The Road Past Altamont*, 1966), *La Rivière sans repos* (*Windflower*, 1970), and *Cet Eté qui chantait* (*Enchanted Summer*, 1976). She was also general editor of Patricia Claxton's translation of Roy's autobiography,

Enchantment and Sorrow (1987). Marshall pays tribute to Roy in reminiscences published in *Antigonish Review* in 1983 and in *Canadian Literature* in 1984; in a 1988 article for the latter journal she also comments on the delights and difficulties of translating. It was Weaver who got her involved in this activity. In the late 1950s Weaver asked her if she would translate a story by Roy, from *La Route d'Altamont*, for radio broadcast. Her technique, as she described it in the *Canadian Literature* piece, was to translate "fairly literally then fight . . . the results into English." At that stage translating turned into "an extended exercise in dialogue-writing." It taught her, she writes, things about English that she had not known before, and in particular to appreciate how the multiplicity of meanings of which English words are capable, and the interconnections among words in an English sentence, actually shape meaning and give resonance to a phrase. In the late 1970s, however, "having grown weary of scraping my mind raw over thoughts that weren't mine," she gave up translating and devoted herself to her own short stories and to a third novel, not yet completed.

A Private Place appeared in 1975, collecting seven stories, five of them first broadcast on *Anthology*. Of the seven, three have won particular attention: "The Enemy," "The Old Woman," and "So Many Have Died." The first of these (anthologized in W. H. New's *Canadian Short Fiction*, 1986) is a brilliant revelation of terror, especially of the indirect sort: a woman's apartment is ransacked; she becomes the victim of random violence; even more devastating is her realization that she is so ready to be upset, and that the chief victim of terror is trust. The second story, "The Old Woman," in some ways reverses "And the Hilltop was Elizabeth." In the earlier story a husband accusingly wonders why a woman, if she is a wife, needs another interest besides himself; "The Old Woman" tells of an English bride brought back to the Quebec bush by a man who proves less close to her than to "the old woman," the electric generator it is his job to maintain. Most commentary on the story stresses the man's madness. Marshall's focus is, however, as much on the woman as on the man. Whatever happens to him, the wife ultimately discovers resources she did not know she possessed, resources which free her into her own separateness. Symbolically she becomes a midwife in a francophone community, able to communicate to other women past a barrier of conventional language.

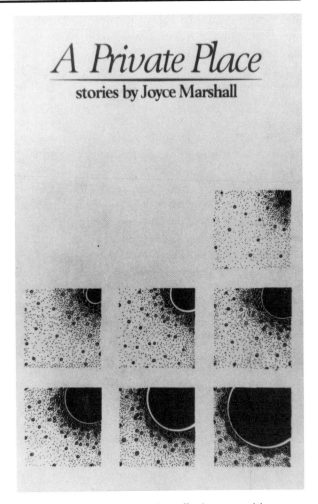

Dust jacket for Marshall's 1975 collection, comprising seven stories, five of which were first broadcast on the CBC-Radio series Anthology

"So Many Have Died" (which was anthologized in 1984 in Rosemary Sullivan's *Stories by Canadian Women*) is part of a triptych of stories. The other two sections—"Windows" and "Paul and Phyllis"—appeared in *Canadian Fiction Magazine* and *Tamarack Review*, respectively, in 1977. The first story in this group tells of the independent medical career of Aunt George, of her freedom of language, and of her freedom from both men and other women; it also tells of her murder, her vulnerability, despite her independence, to random action. The second story tells of Aunt George's granddaughter Phyllis, who seeks her grandmother in part because her own mother is so conventional, and because she has to pass her mother by if she is to establish a matrilineal connection, a route of meaning in her own life. That she arrives too late, that she instead meets with her grandmother's murderer, is a reminder that intentions do not guarantee results, and that there exists a kind of aberrant continuity in disorder. The third story promises some measure of love and freedom in Phyllis's life, but the point is that she has to claim it actively, just as her grandmother once did, and in her own way. It does not exist entirely outside herself.

The shifting speech patterns of the three Phyllis stories–the separate voices of the women: unconventional, faddish, uncertain–declare differences in attitude toward the world, differences in expectations of it. The stories' technique is in part an instruction in how to read them. Moreover, the control over speech rhythm redirects the reader from narrative events to the nature of the communication taking (or not taking) place. Communication–the power over it and the possibility of achieving it–is a recurrent issue in Marshall's work. Several recent stories probe its ramifications, both by considering it as a subject of commentary and by drawing attention implicitly to the power of the shapes of language.

The end of the 1985 story "The Tourist" demonstrates how communication sometimes gets thwarted in the act of communication itself. When a man recounts his travels through Greece, rewriting in his own memory the history of the woman to whom he is talking, she interrupts to try to tell her own story: "Damn it, I'm not in the least like you. I haven't wandered through life as a tourist, picking up this, picking up that. I left home when I was 18. Or rather home left me. My mother died and I didn't get on with my father. I had a devil of a time for years and years." But she breaks off, claiming the continuity of love and yet recognizing the limits on her own power to make herself understood or to maintain freedom, history, or experience in her own terms. The argument apparently goes silent. But that is an illusion; it rages on in her own head, and the story concludes: "She'd bring out one by one the details that had gathered in her head. . . . Pile them on. Then she'd say: It's a damned lie, I've staged this whole thing. Did you? he'd say. All of it? he'd say. And I'll say– But it wouldn't work. . . . It didn't matter what she said or didn't say. She'd boxed herself in. She couldn't say anything now that he couldn't use. Even if she was perfectly silent, he'd use that. And would. With all the details he'd assembled (or she'd given him) right from the beginning." Despite appearances, in other words, there has been no conversation going on; power intrudes into the character of the "exchange." The real communication is other-directed, between author and reader, both of them listening in on anger and impotence, and on the covert desires that mask and motivate human behavior.

Writer in residence at Trent University in Peterborough, Ontario, in 1980, Marshall is a founding member of the Literary Translators Association and also belongs to P.E.N. She won the *New Liberty* short-story prize in 1953, for "The Screaming Silence," and the Canada Council translation prize in 1976, for *Enchanted Summer*. She has also been a recipient of various Canada Council arts grants. She continues to live in Toronto and to write. During the 1980s new stories have been appearing frequently in established journals such as *Fiddlehead* and *Canadian Forum*, newer journals such as *Matrix* and *Dandelion*, and feminist journals such as *Canadian Woman Studies* and *Room of One's Own*. Two main themes–independence and violence–recurrently intertwine: they constitute two faces of a passionate engagement with the social character of contemporary life.

Reference:
W. H. New, *Dreams of Speech and Violence: The Art of the Short Story in Canada and New Zealand* (Toronto: University of Toronto Press, 1987), pp. 84-87.

Papers:
Joyce Marshall's papers are at the Bishop's University Library, Lennoxville, Quebec.

William C. McConnell
(12 February 1917-)

Ann Munton
University of British Columbia

BOOK: *Raise No Memorial: Selected Stories of William C. McConnell*, edited by Thomas S. Woods (Victoria, B.C.: Orca, 1989).

William C. McConnell, the son of George Arthur and Myrtle Louise Shaw McConnell, was born in Vancouver, British Columbia, 12 February 1917. One of six children, McConnell had an older and a younger brother, as well as three sisters, two older and one younger. They grew up in the ethnically mixed east side of Vancouver. Both parents were avid readers and created an atmosphere in which books and music were valued. McConnell's father was a hospital administrator who was born in Dublin and educated in Europe before immigrating to Canada. McConnell's mother was a registered nurse, whom he remembers as "the only person I knew who actually practised her Christianity." She was a fourth-generation Canadian, her father being one of the first settlers in Burnaby and its first reeve.

McConnell attended Lord Selkirk Elementary and John Oliver Secondary schools. The Latin and French he acquired lay the basis for the delight in language that is evident in his writing and the enjoyment he still receives reading French works in the original. Following World War II, as part of the Veterans' Programme, he enrolled in law school at the University of British Columbia. Rules were relaxed for the returning veterans, and McConnell was able to follow an eclectic and stimulating course of study, including classes on international debts and repayments, applied psychology, and Shakespeare, as well as the prescribed law courses.

McConnell's short stories, many of which have been collected under the title *Raise No Memorial* (1989), are marked by his experiences during the Depression and World War II, and by his legal career. In the Depression he had tasted insecurity, traveling across Canada by boxcar and turning his hand to a variety of different jobs, in logging camps and commercial fishery. This period is reflected in his writing in, for example, the de-

piction of the aloof wharfinger and crab fisherman in "Kaleidoscope" and in the careful delineation of coast landscape in "Runaway" and "Totem." Immediately before World War II McConnell was an accountant with Burrard Dry Dock, but the war cut short this career. Joining the Canadian army with both his brothers, McConnell became a sergeant. He spent part of his service at National Defence Headquarters in Ottawa and was discharged from the army in 1945. Three of the stories in *Raise No Memorial* reflect McConnell's wartime experiences. The title story was written the day after McConnell received the news of his younger brother's death in the Italian campaign. Together with "He Who was Alien Traces a Road" and "Montage," "Raise No Memorial" provides a detailed and realistic portrayal of the alienation and futility that war brings to the lives of refugees, common soldiers, and those waiting at home.

It was during the war that McConnell met Alice Parsons, an executive secretary, whom he married in April 1942. On 26 September 1944 their only child, Arthur, was born. In the 1940s and 1950s Alice McConnell published short stories in such journals as *Adelphi* and *Queen's Quarterly*. She died in 1982. Arthur McConnell, who studied at the Royal Academy of Music in London and at The Juilliard School in New York, is a violinist and director of strings at the Welsh College of Music and Drama in Cardiff.

After the war McConnell pursued both his literary and his legal careers. At first he wrote scripts for CBC-Radio to eke out the family income of the struggling student and apprentice lawyer, who was called to the bar in May 1949. Later, particularly during the 1970s and early 1980s, a busy law practice made it increasingly difficult to find time for writing. McConnell retired from law practice in 1984. Currently he is working on a second volume of short stories and a novella. The stories are experimental, primarily written as dialogue with little description.

Dust jacket for McConnell's 1989 collection, comprising twenty-two stories written from the 1940s through the 1980s

From 1961 until his retirement McConnell was a senior partner in Thompson and McConnell. He has argued cases before the Supreme Court of Canada and in the late 1960s defended Hubert Selby, Jr.'s *Last Exit to Brooklyn* against charges of obscenity. A series of stories, forming the last section of *Raise No Memorial*, is entitled "Life in the Law." There is a new irony and humor in these stories, as well as the familiar sensitivity to the suffering of others, found here in "Professional Courtesy," the depiction of the decline of a once-successful lawyer now in the grips of alcoholism.

McConnell early developed a sense of community with other writers. In the mid 1930s, at the height of the Depression, he met with other writers, including Dorothy Livesay and Jack Shadbolt, at English Bay. Calling themselves the Bath House Group, they read and commented upon each other's work, as well as such topical items as James Joyce's "Work in Progress," later published in its entirety as *Finnegans Wake*. During this time

McConnell had three stories broadcast on a Victoria radio station and his first story, "Kaleidoscope," published in the *Canadian Forum* for December 1940. The literary editor of the *Canadian Forum* at the time, Earle Birney, later became a friend. The war dispersed the Bath House Group, but by the late 1940s and into the 1950s a more informal group of writers, including McConnell and Birney, Ethel Wilson, Alice Munro, Margaret Laurence, and Jane Rule, had begun to meet in each other's homes for discussions and mutual support. At this time McConnell also became friends with Malcolm Lowry and his wife, Margerie. Lowry read the first draft of his novel *October Ferry to Gabriola* to the McConnells in his shack at Dollarton, and McConnell advised Lowry concerning the issues involving the law that run through that novel. Their relationship continued until Lowry's death in 1957. Alice McConnell helped Margerie Lowry with the editing of some of Lowry's posthumously published works, including short stories and *October Ferry to Gabriola*.

Over the years McConnell has published short stories in *Preview, First Statement, Northern Review, Canadian Forum, Queen's Quarterly,* and *Saturday Night*. His writing has also been included in several important anthologies. Some of his stories have been broadcast on the CBC-Radio programs *Wednesday Night* and *Anthology*, and he has taken part in literary discussions and conducted interviews with Lowry, Dylan Thomas, and others for the network.

McConnell also participated in the groundbreaking 1955 Canadian Writers Conference in Kingston, where those interested in the study of a Canadian national literature first convened, and helped with the establishment of *Canadian Literature* and *Prism International*. In fact, McConnell and Roy Daniells first discussed the prospect of creating these two journals on the plane on their way back to Vancouver from the Kingston conference. Perhaps McConnell's most important contribution in this area was the establishment of Klanak Press in 1958, which published early work by Marya Fiamengo, Robert Harlow, Florence McNeil, Henry Kreisel, and the first story by Jane Rule, as well as work by Ralph Gustafson and F. R. Scott. It also published the first English translations, by F. R. Scott, of poetry by Hector de Saint-Denys Garneau and Anne Hébert. In addition to pioneering in the publication of unknown writers, McConnell's Klanak Press has produced beautifully designed volumes. With the exception of *Klanak Islands*, a 1959 story anthology, all the books are limited editions of about eight hundred, printed by letterpress.

McConnell's 1989 volume of selected stories is a welcome compilation, recognizing his mastery of the genre and his ability to re-create the epiphanic moments that make individual lives unique. Editor Thomas S. Woods has grouped the stories into four sections: "Coastal Images," "Five Seasons," "Images of War," and "Life in the Law." The stories in the last two sections are the most realistic and traditional, but they share with the other stories McConnell's concern for justice and personal peace as well as his sensitivity to language and detail. For instance, early stories in the first section deal with the displacement of coastal native peoples without providing pat solutions; the dense language reflects the richness of the coastal environment. According to Carole Gerson in the preface to the collection, "the language of 'Love in the Park,' 'Kaleidoscope,' and 'Runaway' so deeply enfolds the swirling rhythms of an Emily Carr painting that it hardly comes as a surprise to encounter a figure of Carr herself (renamed Phoebe) in 'Totem,' a piece that could almost belong to Carr's own *oeuvre*."

Along with impressionistic language, McConnell uses montage style, emphasizing the short story's ability to focus on specific, intense moments by juxtaposing related quick takes. Although he employs this technique in all of the sections of the book, it is most pronounced in "Five Seasons," in which the seasonal stages and changes reflect similar ones in the lives of characters engaged in various relationships.

McConnell at times, as in "Kaleidoscope," creates a sense of immediacy by the exclusion of unnecessary connective words and articles, and often his images and metaphors are arresting. He describes "day . . . rubbing its eyes" in "White Legacy," "gnats and bluebottles stitching the air" in "Love in the Park," a natural tea as "smoky and succulent" in "Totem," and, in "Montage," he portrays a soldier making his awkward farewells to family members, kissing them "tentatively like a chicken at suspicious grain." McConnell's characters delight in language and play word games, as in "Second Season": "Androcles is . . . a common disease like Adenoids"; "Greed's a sad Greek." Writing about legal matters in "You Can't Win," McConnell further demonstrates his playfulness: "Generally accomplished liars are glib, hesitant witnesses not necessarily truthful. It's the whorls and their interruptions which give the feel and you persist, return, re-read, conjure, try a new route till you find or lose a trail." So with McConnell's own writing: "It's the whorls and their interruptions which give the feel and you persist, return, re-read, conjure."

Reference:

Thomas S. Woods, Introduction to McConnell's *Raise No Memorial* (Victoria, B.C.: Orca, 1989), pp. iii-xiii.

Edward McCourt
(10 October 1907-6 January 1972)

Paul Denham
University of Saskatchewan

BOOKS: *Music at the Close* (Toronto: Ryerson, 1947);

The Flaming Hour (Toronto: Ryerson, 1947);

The Canadian West in Fiction (Toronto: Ryerson, 1949; revised, 1970);

Home is the Stranger (Toronto: Macmillan, 1950; London: Macmillan, 1951);

Buckskin Brigadier: The Story of the Alberta Field Force (Toronto: Macmillan, 1955);

The Wooden Sword (Toronto: McClelland & Stewart, 1956);

Walk Through the Valley (Toronto: McClelland & Stewart, 1958; London: Barker, 1959);

Revolt in the West: The Story of the Riel Rebellion (Toronto: Macmillan, 1958; New York: St. Martin's, 1958; London: Barker, 1959);

Fasting Friar (Toronto: McClelland & Stewart, 1963); also published as *The Ettinger Affair* (London: Macdonald, 1963);

The Road Across Canada (Toronto: Macmillan, 1965; New York: St. Martin's, 1965; London: Murray, 1965);

Remember Butler: The Story of Sir William Butler (Toronto: McClelland & Stewart, 1967; London: Routledge & Kegan Paul, 1967);

Saskatchewan (Toronto: Macmillan, 1968; New York: St. Martin's, 1968; London: Macmillan, 1969);

The Yukon and Northwest Territories (Toronto: Macmillan, 1969; New York: St. Martin's, 1969; London: Macmillan, 1970).

RADIO: *Songs My Mother Taught Me*, CBC, 19 March 1959;

Cranes Fly South, CBC, 16 April 1959.

OTHER: "The White Mustang," in *Canadian Short Stories*, edited by Robert Weaver and Helen James (Toronto: Oxford University Press, 1952), pp. 14-26;

William Francis Butler, *The Wild North Land*, introduction by McCourt (Edmonton: Hurtig, 1968).

Edward McCourt (University Archives, University of Saskatchewan)

PERIODICAL PUBLICATIONS: "Roughing it with the Moodies," *Queen's Quarterly*, 52 (Spring 1945): 77-89;

"High Sierras," *Maclean's*, 61 (1 September 1948): 22-23, 59-60;

"Dance for the Devil," *Saturday Evening Post*, 225 (18 October 1952): 26-28;

"Cranes Fly South," *Weekend Magazine*, 5 (16 April 1955): 42-43;

"The Medicine Woman," *Queen's Quarterly*, 73 (Spring 1966): 75-84.

Edward McCourt's popular reputation rests largely on his travel books and his literary reputation on his five novels, but he also wrote biography, short stories, juvenile fiction and history, literary criticism, and radio plays. His major critical writing deals with Canadian literature, but he was also interested in the British novel (especially Thomas Hardy) and Anglo-Irish literature. At the time of his death he was working on a biography of Sir William Gregory, husband of Lady Augusta Gregory, patron of William Butler Yeats.

Edward Alexander McCourt was born on 10 October 1907 in Mullingar, Westmeath, Ireland, the youngest of three sons. His parents were William Alexander and Elizabeth Gillespie McCourt. The family moved to Canada in 1910 to take up a homestead near Kitscoty, Alberta. McCourt's early education at the local one-room school was followed by high-school courses taken by correspondence. He graduated with a B.A. (honors) in English from the University of Alberta in 1932 and won a Rhodes Scholarship. He took a B.A. at Merton College, Oxford.

Returning to Canada in 1935 he taught at Ridley College, St. Catharines, Ontario (1935-1936), Upper Canada College, Toronto (1936-1938), Queen's University (1938-1939), and the University of New Brunswick (1939-1944). In 1944 he moved back to the prairies to take a post teaching English at the University of Saskatchewan, where he remained until his death. He married Anna Margaret Mackay on 12 September 1938. They had one son, Michael William.

As a writer of fiction McCourt has usually been considered a prairie realist, strong on documentary detail but weak on characterization and occasionally melodramatic. His novels were politely received during his lifetime but have largely been forgotten since his death, and his short stories are seldom anthologized. *Music at the Close* and *The Wooden Sword* have, however, been republished in paperback, and it is *Music at the Close* which is most often mentioned in critical discussions. He has had effective and articulate admirers, such as R. G. Baldwin, Winnifred Bogaards, and Elizabeth Brewster, and is accorded respectful treatment in Dick Harrison's *Unnamed Country* (1977). Nevertheless, contemporary critical reaction is more accurately illustrated by the half-hearted enthusiasm of John Moss, who in *A Reader's Guide to the Canadian Novel* (1981) characterized *Music at the Close* as "somberly effective" and commented on its "stolid thoroughness" and its "serviceable" prose.

McCourt's writing reflects a continuing interest in the relationship between people and the places in which they live. His fiction is usually considered regional, and his important critical book, *The Canadian West in Fiction* (1949; revised, 1970), defines the literature of the Canadian prairies in terms of its preoccupation with "the subtle modifications of character which inevitably result from the influence upon ordinary men and women of a highly distinctive environment." The first major study of this literature, it influenced subsequent criticism, such as Henry Kreisel's article "The Prairie: A State of Mind" (*Transactions of the Royal Society of Canada*, June 1968) and Laurence R. Ricou's *Vertical Man / Horizontal World* (1973). Eli Mandel, however, found McCourt useful primarily as someone with whom to disagree; in *Another Time* (1977) he argues that McCourt, in assuming the primacy of the environment and the writer's obligation to be true to external fact, mistook the conventions of literary realism for universal principles. Mandel offers instead a notion of the Canadian prairies in literature as primarily a set of attitudes, a mythical framework, an imaginative construct. It is Mandel's view rather than McCourt's which dominates current critical discussion of prairie literature in Canada.

Music at the Close (1947), McCourt's first novel, has as its protagonist Neil Fraser, an imaginative boy growing up in an isolated prairie community in the 1920s. He finds the prairie an unsatisfactory place because it does not offer the romantic stimulus that literature does; in comparison it seems dull, even sordid. The novel offers McCourt's critique of a colonial culture that measures local conditions by imported standards. Neil's imagination remains out of phase with the realities of university life, of farming, of marriage and family life, until at last he joins the army at the outbreak of World War II and dies on the beach at Normandy. One is never sure whether in his death he finally faces the nature of his failure or whether he is still evading the meaning of his life.

The ambiguous ending gives the book considerable power, but McCourt seems to have been unsatisfied with it, for in his later fiction he was more careful to make his endings clear. His subsequent novels are competent, carefully crafted works, with the difficulties of the characters resolved in a comic rather than an ironic mode. The tension between imagination and reality continues to be played out in the prairie landscape. In *Home is the Stranger* (1950) Norah, an the old country."

No, there was nothing quite like it in the old country. Not the race meets she had occasionally gone to with her father, before Aunt Lucy had had power enough over him to forbid his going; or the monthly fairs at Innishcoolin where farmers for miles about chaffered long and loud with the prospective buyers of their pigs and cattle- some of them from as far away as England- and afterwards drank up their luckpennies in smelly taverns and turned the usually quiet night-time into a bedlam of noise and confusion and unaccustomed bucolic merriment. The race-meets and the fairs at home were somehow an accepted part of living; the sports day at Twin Buttes was an exotic addition- an Event. Even from the last cross-road a mile from the first elevator they could see that the town was en fête. A tattered flag-fluttered from the tall pole atop the ugly dutch-roofed building called the Town Hall- perhaps because it served as the centre of nearly every village function from a concert to a funeral; and the wind, blowing with inexorable persistence, brought to their ears the wavering sounds of music being played over some invisible but powerful loud-speaker.

" Public address system," Jim explained.

The pretentiousness of the name stirred her to silent laughter, but she did not say anything for Jim would not have understood her mirth. They drove down the main street of the village and over the rutted trail leading to the sports ground behind a steady stream of cars that advanced like

Page from "The Earth's Hunger," a draft for McCourt's 1950 novel, Home is the Stranger *(University Archives, University of Saskatchewan)*

Irish war bride transplanted to Alberta, finds both the prairie and its people one-dimensional in comparison to the romantic hills of her homeland, but she eventually understands and accepts both the love of her husband and the validity and sufficiency of the prairie. *Walk Through the Valley* (1958), set in the Cypress Hills near the United States border, is about young Michael Troy, who idolizes the glamorous Blaze Corrigal. Blaze turns out to be a sleazy rumrunner, leads Michael's father into a partnership that eventually destroys him, and seduces Michael's sister. The youth's sternly old-fashioned mother is the only one who sees Blaze clearly. Michael's maturing requires that he temper his youthful romanticism with the practical realities of farm life.

The Wooden Sword (1956) and *Fasting Friar* (1963) are novels about professors of English, but though their settings are urban and academic, the prairie is never far away. Steve Venner in the former is the most troubled of McCourt's protagonists, for the gap between his ideals of courage and the knowledge of his own limitations—the reality symbolized by the "featureless face" of the prairie—drives him to mental illness. Finally, a recognition of the courage required to live ordinary life enables him, like Michael and Norah, to move toward maturity and acceptance. In *Fasting Friar*, which offers some delightful comedy at the expense of academic preoccupations, Walter Ackroyd immures himself in scholarship because he can control it; the prairie beyond the walls of the academy is frightening because it represents the emotional freedom that he avoids. He achieves maturity through his affair with Marion Ettinger, which leads to an acceptance of that freedom.

Music at the Close, in addition to its own merits, is a work which stands squarely at a significant turning point in the development of prairie literature. The fiction which preceded it—the work of Frederick Philip Grove, Robert J. C. Stead, Martha Ostenso, and Sinclair Ross—presented the prairie as a place with a lot of geography but no history. For subsequent writers of poetry, fiction, and drama, such as Margaret Laurence, Rudy Wiebe, Robert Kroetsch, John Newlove, Andrew Suknaski, and Sharon Pollock, geography has receded in importance, and the prairie is more often defined as a place with a distinctive history. The shift is signaled in *Music at the Close*, in which Neil is dimly aware that there are still people in the district who remember the Riel Rebellion and the Frog Lake Massacre—in

Dust jacket for the first British edition of McCourt's fifth novel, set in western Canada's Cypress Hills

other words, that there is a rich history here, and the prairie is not as dull as he thinks it is. As well, McCourt's portrayals of the 1931 Estevan Strike and the rise of Social Credit give the novel a political dimension heretofore lacking in prairie literature.

McCourt did not explore these possibilities in his later fiction, though other writers did in theirs. But they inform much of his other work, which exhibits an intensely historical as well as geographical imagination. *Buckskin Brigadier* (1955) and *Revolt in the West* (1958) are narratives for young people about the Riel Rebellion of 1885, and *The Flaming Hour* (1947) is a juvenile novel set in the same period. *Remember Butler* (1967) is a biography of William Francis Butler, an Irish soldier and adventurer whose journeys across the winter-bound prairies in 1870-1871 and 1873 produced two of the finest early books about the region, *The Great Lone Land* (1872) and *The Wild*

North Land (1873). As well as being interested in a fellow Irishman on the Canadian prairie, McCourt saw in Butler a "champion of lost causes and seeker of impossible goals," a writer of clear and memorable prose about the region and the people who lived there, and a man who faced difficult circumstances with grace and practicality.

McCourt's travel books, *The Road Across Canada* (1965), *Saskatchewan* (1968), and *The Yukon and Northwest Territories* (1969), are effective because they combine an ability to render both the geography and history of the areas described, a fiction writer's interest in tales, legends, and anecdotes, and a skillful teacher's aptness with quotation.

References:

R. G. Baldwin, "Pattern in the Novels of Edward McCourt," *Queen's Quarterly*, 68 (Winter 1962): 574-587;

Winnifred Bogaards, "Edward McCourt: One Man's View of Alberta and Saskatchewan," *Prairie Forum*, 5 (Spring 1980): 35-50;

Bogaards, "Edward McCourt: A Reassessment," *Studies in Canadian Literature*, 5 (Fall 1980): 181-208;

E. W. Brewster, "Memoirs of a Romantic Ironist," *Canadian Literature*, 70 (Autumn 1976): 23-31.

Papers:

The McCourt Papers are at the Archives, University of Saskatchewan, Saskatoon.

Leslie McFarlane

(25 October 1902-6 September 1977)

J. Kieran Kealy
University of British Columbia

BOOKS: *Dave Fearless under the Ocean*, as Roy Rockwood (Garden City, N.Y.: Garden City Publishing, 1926);

Dave Fearless in the Black Jungle, as Rockwood (Garden City, N.Y.: Garden City Publishing, 1926);

Dave Fearless Near the South Pole, as Rockwood (Garden City, N.Y.: Garden City Publishing, 1926);

Dave Fearless Among the Malay Pirates, as Rockwood (Garden City, N.Y.: Garden City Publishing, 1926);

Dave Fearless on the Ship of Mystery, as Rockwood (Garden City, N.Y.: Garden City Publishing, 1926);

Dave Fearless on the Lost Brig, as Rockwood (Garden City, N.Y.: Garden City Publishing, 1926);

Dave Fearless at Whirlpool Point, as Rockwood (Garden City, N.Y.: Garden City Publishing, 1926);

The Tower Treasure, as Franklin W. Dixon (New York: Grosset & Dunlap, 1927; Newcastle-upon-Tyne: Harold Hill, 1951);

The House on the Cliff, as Dixon (New York: Grosset & Dunlap, 1927; Newcastle-upon-Tyne: Harold Hill, 1951);

The Secret of the Old Mill, as Dixon (New York: Grosset & Dunlap, 1927; Newcastle-upon-Tyne: Harold Hill, 1951);

The Missing Chums, as Dixon (New York: Grosset & Dunlap, 1928; Newcastle-upon-Tyne: Harold Hill, 1951);

Hunting for Hidden Gold, as Dixon (New York: Grosset & Dunlap, 1928; Newcastle-upon-Tyne: Harold Hill, 1951);

The Shore Road Mystery, as Dixon (New York: Grosset & Dunlap, 1928; Newcastle-upon-Tyne: Harold Hill, 1953);

The Secret of the Caves, as Dixon (New York: Grosset & Dunlap, 1929; Newcastle-upon-Tyne: Harold Hill, 1953);

Leslie McFarlane (photograph by Harold Whyte, courtesy of Canada Wide)

The Mystery of Cabin Island, as Dixon (New York: Grosset & Dunlap, 1929; Newcastle-upon-Tyne: Harold Hill, 1953);

The Great Airport Mystery, as Dixon (New York: Grosset & Dunlap, 1930; Newcastle-upon-Tyne: Harold Hill, 1953);

Streets of Shadow (New York: Dutton, 1930; London: Stanley Paul, 1930);

The Murder Tree (New York: Dutton, 1931; London: Stanley Paul, 1931);

What Happened at Midnight, as Dixon (New York: Grosset & Dunlap, 1932; Newcastle-upon-Tyne: Harold Hill, 1955);

While the Clock Ticked, as Dixon (New York: Grosset & Dunlap, 1932; Newcastle-upon-Tyne: Harold Hill, 1955);

Footprints Under the Window, as Dixon (New York: Grosset & Dunlap, 1933; Newcastle-upon-Tyne: Harold Hill, 1957);

The Mark on the Door, as Dixon (New York: Grosset & Dunlap, 1934; Newcastle-upon-Tyne: Harold Hill, 1957);

By the Light of the Study Lamp, as Carolyn Keene (New York: Grosset & Dunlap, 1934; London: Low, 1959);

The Secret of Lone Tree Cottage, as Keene (New York: Grosset & Dunlap, 1934; London: Low, 1959);

In the Shadow of the Tower, as Keene (New York: Grosset & Dunlap, 1934; London: Low, 1959);

The Hidden Harbor Mystery, as Dixon (New York: Grosset & Dunlap, 1935; Newcastle-upon-Tyne: Harold Hill, 1957);

A Three-cornered Mystery, as Keene (New York: Grosset & Dunlap, 1935; London: Low, 1959);

The Sinister Sign Post, as Dixon (New York: Grosset & Dunlap, 1936; London: Low, 1959);

A Figure in Hiding, as Dixon (New York: Grosset & Dunlap, 1937; London: Low, 1959);

The Secret Warning, as Dixon (New York: Grosset & Dunlap, 1938; London: Low, 1959);

The Flickering Torch Mystery, as Dixon (New York: Grosset & Dunlap, 1943; London: Low, 1963);

The Short Wave Mystery, as Dixon (New York: Grosset & Dunlap, 1945);

The Secret Panel, as Dixon (New York: Grosset & Dunlap, 1946);

The Phantom Freighter, as Dixon (New York: Grosset & Dunlap, 1947; Newcastle-upon-Tyne: Harold Hill, 1951);

The Last of the Great Picnics (Toronto: McClelland & Stewart, 1965);

McGonigle Scores! (Toronto: McClelland & Stewart, 1966);

Fire in the North (Cobalt, Ont.: Highway Book Shop, 1972);

A Kid in Haileybury (Cobalt, Ont.: Highway Book Shop, 1975);

Agent of the Falcon (Toronto: Methuen, 1975);

The Dynamite Flynns (Toronto: Methuen, 1975);

The Mystery of Spider Lake (Toronto: Methuen, 1975);

Squeeze Play (Toronto: Methuen, 1975);

Ghost of the Hardy Boys (Toronto: Methuen / New York: Two Continents, 1976);

Breakaway (Toronto: Methuen, 1976);

The Snow Hawk (Toronto: Methuen, 1976).

Leslie McFarlane's 1976 autobiography, *Ghost of the Hardy Boys*, includes a scene in which his son asks him if he had actually read all the children's books in his library. "Read them?" he answers. "I wrote them." Thus does his son learn that his father is probably the best-selling Canadian author of all time.

Leslie Charles McFarlane was born in Carleton Place, Ontario, on 25 October 1902. The son of John Henry McFarlane, an elementary-school principal, and the former Rebecca Barnett, McFarlane began his literary career as a reporter for the *Haileyburian*, the local newspaper of Haileybury, the small town in northern Ontario where he spent his childhood. From there, he went on to other Canadian newspaper jobs and finally moved to Massachusetts, where he became a writer for the *Springfield Republican*. In 1926 he answered an advertisement seeking an experienced fiction writer who was willing to work from the publisher's outlines. Within months, McFarlane had written his first book, *Dave Fearless under the Ocean*, receiving for his work a flat fee of one hundred dollars. The book appeared under the Stratemeyer house pseudonym Roy Rockwood, thus beginning McFarlane's twenty-one-year career with Edward Stratemeyer's publishing syndicate.

Encouraged by the security which this new work promised, McFarlane returned to Canada, hoping to use his income to finance more serious writing. In 1927 Stratemeyer asked him to ghost a new type of adventure series, in which the heroes would be the two sons of a private investigator. He quickly agreed and thus began, under the pseudonym of Franklin W. Dixon, an association with Frank and Joe Hardy which would last for the first twenty-one books of the series. During this period McFarlane also ghosted other Stratemeyer plots including several texts in the Dana Girls series. These were published under the pseudonym Carolyn Keene, first used by McFarlane and later identified with the Stratemeyer Syndicate's Nancy Drew books. In addition, under his own name, McFarlane published two adult murder mysteries, *Streets of Shadow* (1930) and *The Murder Tree* (1931), and numerous short stories, some of which have been "modernized" for the Methuen Checkmate Series, which includes six books by McFarlane—hockey and adventure stories—published in 1975 and 1976.

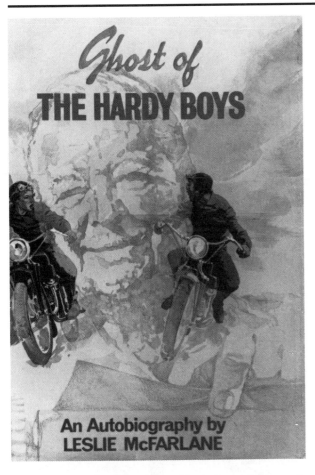

Dust jacket for McFarlane's autobiography, written nearly fifty years after he completed the first of the Stratemeyer Syndicate's Hardy Boys books

in 1959 and 1960 he served as chief editor of television drama for the CBC. His first wife, Amy Ashmore McFarlane, with whom he had had three children, died in 1955. In 1957 he married Beatrice Greenaway Kennedy. Because of his extensive work in television and films, McFarlane wrote no books during the 1950s and only two in the 1960s: *McGonigle Scores!* (1966), a boys' adventure story, and *The Last of the Great Picnics* (1965), a nostalgic account of a nineteenth-century Dominion Day picnic which concludes with a moving account of the young protagonist's meeting with Sir John A. Macdonald.

In 1976 McFarlane published probably his finest book, an autobiography entitled *Ghost of the Hardy Boys*, which includes a memorable recreation of the world of his childhood, a subject he had fictionalized a year earlier in *A Kid in Haileybury*. This title suggests that McFarlane fully realized that, despite a lifetime of writing under his own name, he would be best remembered for the books he ghosted. But he also suggests that one should not underestimate his contributions to these formulaic texts. Moreover, when one compares the rather bland, humorless boys' adventures being published today by a more "modern" stable of ghostwriters with the original Hardy Boys adventures, one is inclined to agree with McFarlane's own appraisal of the boys' first exploits: "I thought that I had written a hell of a good book—of its kind. . . . "

Following his departure from Stratemeyer in 1947, McFarlane concentrated his attention on radio, films, and television, writing dozens of radio plays and more than seventy television plays for CBC and producing or directing more than fifty films for the National Film Board of Canada. He had returned to Canada to live, and

References:

David Palmer, "A Last Talk with Leslie McFarlane," *Canadian Children's Literature*, 11 (1978): 5-19;

Robert Stall, "The Hardy Boys: the Ghost and the Old Books," *Weekend Magazine*, 23 (15 December 1973): 12-15.

Marshall McLuhan

(21 July 1911-31 December 1980)

Susan Jackel
University of Alberta

BOOKS: *The Mechanical Bride: Folklore of Industrial Man* (New York: Vanguard, 1951; London: Routledge & Kegan Paul, 1967);

Verbi-Voco-Visual Explorations, by McLuhan and others, *Explorations*, 8 (October 1957); republished (New York: Something Else Press, 1967);

Understanding News Media: A Report to U.S. Office of Education (Washington, D.C.: National Association of Educational Broadcasters for the U.S. Department of Health, Education, and Welfare, 1960);

The Gutenberg Galaxy: The Making of Typographic Man (Toronto: University of Toronto Press, 1962; London: Routledge & Kegan Paul, 1962; New York: New American Library, 1969);

Understanding Media: The Extensions of Man (New York: McGraw-Hill, 1964; London: Routledge & Kegan Paul, 1964);

The Medium is the Massage: An Inventory of Effects, by McLuhan and Quentin Fiore (New York: Bantam, 1967; London: Lane, 1967);

Through the Vanishing Point: Space in Poetry and Painting, by McLuhan and Harley Parker (New York: Harper & Row, 1968);

War and Peace in the Global Village: An Inventory of Some Current Spastic Situations That Could Be Eliminated by More Feedforward, by McLuhan and Fiore (New York: McGraw-Hill, 1968);

Counterblast (Toronto: McClelland & Stewart, 1969; New York: Harcourt, Brace & World, 1969; London: Rapp & Whiting, 1970);

The Interior Landscape: The Literary Criticism of Marshall McLuhan, 1943-1962, edited by Eugene McNamara (New York: McGraw-Hill, 1969);

Culture Is Our Business (New York: McGraw-Hill, 1970);

From Cliché to Archetype, by McLuhan and Wilfred Watson (New York: Viking, 1970);

Take Today: The Executive as Dropout, by McLuhan and Barrington Nevitt (New York: Harcourt Brace Jovanovich, 1972; Don Mills, Ont.: Longman, 1972);

Marshall McLuhan in 1967 (photograph by John Reeves)

City as Classroom: Understanding Language and Media, by McLuhan, Eric McLuhan, and Kathryn Hutchon (Agincourt, Ont.: Book Society of Canada, 1977);

Autre Homme, autre chrétien à l'âge électronique, by McLuhan and Pierre Babin (Lyons: Chalet, 1978);

Laws of Media, by McLuhan and Eric McLuhan (Toronto: University of Toronto Press, 1989).

OTHER: Hugh Kenner, *Paradox in G. K. Chesterton*, introduction by McLuhan (New York: Sheed & Ward, 1947);

Alfred Tennyson, *Selected Poetry*, edited, with an introduction, by McLuhan (New York: Rinehart, 1956);

Explorations in Communication, edited by McLuhan and Edmund Carpenter (Boston: Beacon, 1960);

Voices of Literature, 2 volumes, edited by McLuhan and Richard J. Schoeck (New York: Holt, Rinehart & Winston, 1964, 1965);

Harold Adams Innis, *Empire and Communications*, revised by Mary Quayle Innis, introduction by McLuhan (Toronto: University of Toronto Press, 1972).

Literary studies in Canada and throughout the world received a severe shaking-up in the 1960s with the work of Marshall McLuhan. Delighted with the controversy he aroused, for he took it as a sign of awakening consciousness to the ills of his time, McLuhan combined the roles of literary critic, social psychologist, historian of sensibility, and prophet. His own phrase for what he was was media analyst; because of the central importance in human affairs that he assigned to modes of communication, the term is hardly a limiting one. No one, however, was more adamant than McLuhan on the pointlessness of the urge to classify; he abhorred the specialization of the academy, which he saw as the institutionalized expression of a doomed mentality. To the extent that he even yet escapes easy classification, McLuhan's belief in his own uniqueness as a thinker is vindicated.

Herbert Marshall McLuhan was born in Edmonton, Alberta, on 21 July 1911; his parents, Herbert Ernest McLuhan, a real estate and insurance salesman, and Elsie Hall McLuhan, an actress, moved the family to Winnipeg during his boyhood. McLuhan entered the University of Manitoba to study engineering but switched to English, obtaining a B.A. in 1932 and an M.A. in 1934, with a thesis on George Meredith. He spent the next two years at Cambridge, absorbing lectures by I. A. Richards and F. R. Leavis, among others. His doctoral dissertation for Cambridge, titled "The Place of Thomas Nashe in the Learning of His Time," was submitted in 1942. In 1939 he had married Corinne Keller Lewis; they eventually had six children.

McLuhan's first published article, appearing in *Dalhousie Review* in 1936, addressed the "practi-

cal mysticism" of G. K. Chesterton. Although of Protestant parentage, McLuhan, influenced by Chesterton's essays, became a convert to Catholicism. He began his teaching career in 1936 at the University of Wisconsin in Madison, and then moved to the University of St. Louis from 1937 to 1944. After two years at Assumption University in Windsor, Ontario, McLuhan made his final move to St. Michael's College at the University of Toronto, where he taught for the next thirty-four years.

Throughout the 1940s McLuhan published articles in the New Critical mode on John Keats, George Herbert, Edgar Allan Poe, T. S. Eliot, Wyndham Lewis, Gerard Manley Hopkins, and others in such respected literary periodicals as the *Kenyon Review* and the *Sewanee Review*. In 1947 he provided an introduction to Hugh Kenner's *Paradox in G. K. Chesterton* and followed with more articles on literary subjects, primarily Eliot, Ezra Pound, and James Joyce. A selection of McLuhan's literary criticism is available in a collection edited by Eugene McNamara, *The Interior Landscape* (1969).

Although he had published comments on comics from 1944 on, and an article on American advertising as early as 1947, McLuhan's first major work on mass communications was *The Mechanical Bride: Folklore of Industrial Man*, published in 1951, a satirical look at newspaper and magazine advertising as keys to contemporary society and culture. In his preface McLuhan states his intention to "apply the method of art analysis to the critical evaluation of society." Yet, few readers can have been adequately prepared for what followed, for although the object is indeed society, and the evaluation slashingly critical in tone, the method is entirely McLuhan's own. As he warns the reader, he does not expect to prove a case, nor honor the convention that requires a book to have a single unifying idea. Rather, he will line up a series of exhibits–illustrated advertisements reproduced from the popular press–and provide his own sardonic commentary on the buried assumptions they contain, the hopes and desires they simultaneously reveal and confirm.

The element of evaluation and criticism in *The Mechanical Bride* stems from McLuhan's view that industrial civilization, in contrast to its nomadic and agricultural predecessors, is restrictive, unbalanced, ultimately inhumane. The mechanization which has made possible the cornucopia of industrially produced consumer goods has not stopped at the outer forms of human existence but has crept into the inner lives, the very psychic structure, of North Americans and all who pattern themselves on North American ideals. McLuhan's self-defined task was to awaken a sleeping generation from a nightmare of standardized tastes, aspirations, and opinions–standardized not only in their content but in their vulgarity as well.

McLuhan's professional background emerges in this book in his call for independent critical minds in the face of the dismaying disproportion between the amount of money spent on forming young minds through advertising, and that available for education in schools and colleges. Furthermore, his training in literary studies enables him to interpret the visual imagery and verbal clichés of his exhibits through a wide range of literary forms and figures: in one instance, he uses the historical romance from Sir Walter Scott to Thornton Wilder, in another, the detective fiction of Poe, Arthur Conan Doyle, and Raymond Chandler. In *The Mechanical Bride*, too, there is the first of McLuhan's many tributes to the preeminence of Joyce as both a literary artist and a social critic, *Finnegans Wake* being described as "a great intellectual effort aimed at rinsing the Augean stables of speech and society with geysers of laughter."

This pronouncement on Joyce affords a sample of McLuhan's neo-Swiftian phrasing in this book, as does his remark that "Doyle, in common with his age and ours, was obsessed with the psychic stench that rose from his own splintered ego." In pungent aphorisms McLuhan repeatedly indicts mid-century America for its rejection of spontaneity in obeisance to the inner logic of mechanism, seeing corsets and high-heeled shoes as the visible tokens of the mechanical bride, the voluptuously designed automobile as simultaneously a womb figure and a phallic symbol. It is in terms such as these that he traces throughout his book "the curious fusion of sex, technology and death" that seems to fascinate North Americans. The danger that McLuhan sees in this fascination is not simply its dominance of American social values, but its invisibility to those caught up in the trance. Hence the need for a prince, using "the habit of dissociation [from which] the means of recreating shop-worn values can come," to awaken the mechanical bride from her tranced sleep and so restore the possibility of integration and health to human consciousness.

That such has been the traditional role of the humanist critic has not escaped commentators on this book, but even critics quite unsympathetic to McLuhan's later work have recognized that in focusing on the popular mythology of contemporary society, in however flippant a tone, McLuhan raised for discussion a complex and deeply serious issue. *The Mechanical Bride* had relatively little impact in 1951–the author himself bought a thousand remaindered copies of the first edition to sell and give away–but it provided the basis for his subsequent investigations, at once wildly eclectic and increasingly single-minded, into the effects of communications media on human consciousness.

Eleven years separated McLuhan's first book and his second. In this interval were two years (1953-1955) as chairman of a Ford Foundation Seminar on Culture and Communications, and an appointment (1959-1960) as director of a media project undertaken jointly by the U. S. Office of Education and the National Association of Educational Broadcasters. McLuhan's report on this project, entitled *Understanding News Media*, appeared in 1960. During this period articles on Joyce, Pound, Eliot, John Dos Passos, and Wyndham Lewis continued to appear, as well as others on more popular themes: "Comics and Culture," "Classroom T.V.," and (reversing a hoary chestnut) "Why the C.B.C. Must Be Dull." But the main channel for McLuhan's speculations between 1953 and 1957 was *Explorations*, a journal which he edited in collaboration with the anthropologist Edmund Carpenter. Number eight of this journal (October 1957), with contributions by McLuhan and others, contains in capsule form much that would reappear in McLuhan's *The Gutenberg Galaxy: The Making of Typographic Man*, winner of a Governor General's Award in 1963. *Explorations in Communication*, edited by Carpenter and McLuhan and also containing seeds of later books, appeared in book form in 1960.

"Does the interiorization of media such as letters alter the ratio among our senses and change mental processes?," McLuhan asks in one of the early chapter glosses of *The Gutenberg Galaxy*, published in 1962. His answer is yes, it does, and from this alleged fact of historical and biological experience has flowed an astounding range of social and cultural effects: the visual organization of knowledge and the discovery of perspective; the rise of Baconian science and the uniform, centralizing forces of nationalism; the replacement of the polyphony of Renaissance prose with the equitone of Joseph Addison and after; the denuding of conscious life in typographic man; and finally the imminent retribalization of all modern peoples in the collective unconscious. These are only a few of the arresting concepts that made McLuhan and McLuhanism common currency in the 1960s upon the publication of *The Gutenberg Galaxy* and its successor, *Understanding Media: The Extensions of Man* (1964).

McLuhan's contention in *The Gutenberg Galaxy* is that habits of perception and analysis that Western thinkers take for granted as natural and universal are really the transitory and limited effects of a single technological development. "Gutenberg" in the book's title refers to the inventor of movable type. With the widespread deployment of alphabetic literacy through print, McLuhan argues, Renaissance thinkers and writers entered a new mechanical age fundamentally changed from the manuscript culture of the Middle Ages, which had in its turn supplanted the oral culture of the Greeks. The printed page enabled knowledge to achieve uniform, repeatable, and portable transmission, leading to increasing emphasis on standardized units not only in the mechanical production of goods but in social organization as well. Furthermore, by appealing to the eye rather than the ear, as both oral and manuscript cultures had done, print created a sensory orientation that exalts seeing at the expense of hearing and touching. Finally, the very form of the printed page, with its sequence of symbols lineally arranged, created a climate of thought which favors linear, cause-and-effect reasoning as the only legitimate source of intellectual conviction.

Reviewing *The Gutenberg Galaxy* for *Encounter* in 1963, Frank Kermode remarked that "in a truly literate society his book would start a long debate." It did just that. Reviewers were baffled, delighted, outraged, impressed, and the lines of battle quickly formed. On one front admirers praised the brilliance of McLuhan's insights into the relations between the arts and technological change. On the whole these commentators were willing to grant McLuhan's central assumption, that modes of communication do have measurable biological effects: the much-discussed alteration of sense ratios in the human organism. Others demurred, however, challenging the scientific basis of this claim and looking askance at McLuhan's wide-ranging but wholly unscientific marshalling of evidence.

This viewpoint raised a second area of contention, McLuhan's use of the scholarship of oth-

Dust jacket for a later printing of the 1964 book in which McLuhan explicates in detail his adage "The medium is the message" and introduces his concept of "hot" and "cool" media

ers. While some readers were prepared to treasure *The Gutenberg Galaxy* as a kind of exploding commonplace book, a repository of arcane and provocative quotations from a truly encyclopedic range of specialized studies, critics such as Nathan Halper and Patrick D. Hazard called McLuhan to task for misrepresenting or misunderstanding the experts he quoted at such length.

McLuhan shrugged off such cavils; his detractors, he said, were blinkered, irrelevant, hopelessly mired in outdated, nineteenth-century modes of thought. By calling for logic when what he offered was a mosaic or field approach to problems, they showed nothing more than the typical inflexibility of the Gutenberg mentality. Never conciliatory, his intransigence in the face of criticism led to charges of charlatanism or worse. John Symons, for example, complained that McLuhan's worst failing was his "wholesale reinterpretation of texts to prove his preconceived argument," a cardinal sin in the academic community; to George P. Elliott, McLuhan was a double agent inviting scholars to throw open the gates to the barbarian hordes. Also a target was McLuhan's idiosyncratic vocabulary; probes, configurations, implosions, interfaces became the badge of the McLuhanites, the bane of the purists. In 1968 editor Raymond Rosenthal of the college casebook *McLuhan: Pro & Con* felt impelled to include a glossary of McLuhanisms.

Perhaps the most balanced contributions to the debate over *The Gutenberg Galaxy* were Kermode's, and one by Raymond Williams in the *University of Toronto Quarterly* in 1964. Williams, who allowed more than a year before pronouncing his judgment, saw, as Kermode had, that the mosaic construction of the book was McLuhan's deliberate but necessarily ineffectual attempt to escape the paradox of his own predictions regarding the end of print culture. Williams ended his review, however, by calling *The Gutenberg Galaxy* "a wholly indispensable book," and McLuhan's work a "radically important revaluation of our world." Williams's essay and other important contributions to the controversy surrounding McLuhan's book have been collected in Rosenthal's *McLuhan: Pro & Con* and in *McLuhan: Hot & Cool*, edited by Gerald Stearn (1967).

Understanding Media brought the story of typographic man into the electronic present. "Rapidly we approach the final phase of the extensions of man," McLuhan wrote in the introduction, sustaining the apocalyptic note that had characterized *The Gutenberg Galaxy*. Here the best-known McLuhanism, "the medium is the message," receives exhaustive explication. The word *medium* expands in McLuhan's hands to take in phenomena as diverse as money, clocks, houses, roads, clothes, and games, as well as those more narrowly associated with the movement of information. Here, too, McLuhan introduces his controversial distinction between "hot" media (high in definition, leading to minimal involvement of the human emotions) and "cool" media (low in definition, inviting completion and intense participation). Examples of hot media are movies, radio, and books, while television is the cool medium par excellence. In the chapter on television, the book's longest, McLuhan plays innumerable variations on the theme of "the indomitable tactile promptings of the TV image," insistently distinguishing between the sensory effects of the image itself and the programs which are television's content.

Shorn of the long quotations from authorities that made *The Gutenberg Galaxy* so formidable, *Understanding Media* was widely reviewed and discussed. It confirmed McLuhan's status as the first pop philosopher, the media guru, the oracle of the electronic age (all stock phrases of the caption writers). If increasingly under fire from his academic peers, the nondescript English professor from Toronto (another standard label for McLuhan) became the toast of sophisticates from New York to San Francisco, delivering his gnomic utterances to rapt audiences of teachers, bankers, television and advertising executives, and assorted intellectuals. Journalists and television talk-show hosts vied for interviews, and McLuhan became a celebrity. Tom Wolfe's ebullient essay "What If He Is Right"–in *The Pump House Gang* (1968)–half satirically and half admiringly traces this stage in McLuhan's career.

In response to questions, McLuhan invariably explained the origins of his media studies in terms of his work in the classroom. Having chosen to teach, he felt compelled to try to understand the milieu of his students, if only as a strategy for survival. Although he confessed in an interview with Stearn (collected in *McLuhan: Hot & Cool*) that the electronic age constituted a "cultural gradient" for which he felt "complete personal distaste and dissatisfaction," his insistence that popular culture deserved extended and serious study inevitably identified him as that culture's champion and apologist. It seems likely, however, that Donald Theall, a former student of McLuhan's, is at least partly right to explain (in *The Medium is the Rear View Mirror*, 1971) McLuhan's academic nonconformism as a reaction against the literary-historical scholarship that dominated Toronto's graduate English department.

If the University of Toronto was his scholarly environment, McLuhan was a one-man anti-environment, a fact officially recognized and sanctioned when he was appointed by the university in 1963 to set up and head a Centre for Culture and Technology to further the study of the psychic and social consequences of technologies and media. Here in an old coach house McLuhan presided over graduate seminars of legendary unpredictability. Theall, who was secretary of the first Culture and Communications seminar in 1965, testifies to McLuhan's inspiration as a "masterly teacher," even as he prepares to catalogue the master's strengths and weaknesses in his book-length study.

The apogee of McLuhan's fame came in 1967 when he was appointed for a year to the Albert Schweitzer Chair of the Humanities at

Fordham University, New York. That same year he was awarded the Canada Council's Molson Prize for outstanding achievement in the social sciences. McLuhan marked his return to Toronto in 1968 by initiating, for people in government, business, and academia, *McLuhan's Dew-Line Newsletters*, the title adverting to his belief that he could study America the better for being physically removed from it. In Toronto he could act as the modern world's Distant Early Warning system, a first line of defense against the effects of media fallout on behalf of the numbed inhabitants of the electronic age.

McLuhan was the recipient of several honorary degrees in the 1960s, from the University of Windsor, Simon Fraser University, the University of Western Ontario, and other institutions. Television programs, magazine articles, and books about McLuhan flooded the later 1960s, while McLuhan, in collaboration with Quentin Fiore, put together a trimmed-down primer of McLuhanism in 1967 (*The Medium is the Massage*: the pun is on *mass age*, as well as on the supposed working over of the senses by media). Also with Fiore McLuhan produced *War and Peace in the Global Village* (1968). Another collaboration, this time with poet Wilfred Watson, produced *From Cliché to Archetype* in 1970, while *Take Today: The Executive as Dropout*, by McLuhan and Barrington Nevitt, followed in 1972. In 1970 McLuhan was made a companion in the Order of Canada.

But enthusiasm for both the medium and the message was waning; Dwight Macdonald's complaint about *Understanding Media*—"a book that lacks the virtues of its medium, being vague, repetitious, formless, and, after a while, boring"—gained increasing assent. "Marshall McLuhan fad appears to be fading" was the heading of a *Toronto Star* article of 21 November 1970; the writer was Dennis Duffy, whose small book on McLuhan had appeared the previous year. The magazine articles continued, the doctoral dissertations made their ominous appearance; by the mid 1970s, however, it was clear that McLuhan's probes and insights were essentially complete. When he retired from teaching in June 1980 after a severe stroke, his Centre for Culture and Technology was closed. He died at his home in Toronto on 31 December 1980. After an initial flurry of tributes, McLuhan's name—or at least McLuhanism—appeared to fade from public notice. But the publication of the *Letters of Marshall McLuhan* in 1987 renewed interest in the man

and drew attention to the impact that he had upon institutions, politics, and language. *Laws of Media* (1989), an attempt by Eric McLuhan to pursue the implications of some of his father's notebook entries, did not receive the same positive critical attention.

Letters:
Letters of Marshall McLuhan, edited by Matie Molinaro, Connie McLuhan, and William Toye (Toronto: Oxford University Press, 1987).

Bibliography:
The Writings of Marshall McLuhan and What Has Been Written About Him, 1934-1977: A Bibliography (Fort Lauderdale, Fla.: Wake-Brook House, 1977).

Biography:
Philip Marchand, *Marshall McLuhan: The Medium and the Messenger* (Toronto: Random House, 1989).

References:
James M. Curtis, *Culture as Polyphony* (Columbia: University of Missouri Press, 1978);
Dennis Duffy, *Marshall McLuhan* (Toronto: McClelland & Stewart, 1969);
Sidney Finkelstein, *Sense and Nonsense of McLuhan* (New York: International Publishers, 1968);
Arthur Kroker, *Technology and the Canadian Mind* (Montreal: New World Perspectives, 1984);
Juan Riviano, *The Ideas of Marshall McLuhan*, translated, with an introduction, by Iván Jaksic (Amherst, N.Y.: Council on International Studies, State University of New York at Buffalo, 1979);
Raymond Rosenthal, ed., *McLuhan: Pro & Con* (New York: Funk & Wagnalls, 1968);
Gerald Stearn, ed., *McLuhan: Hot & Cool* (New York: Dial, 1967);
Donald Theall, *The Medium is the Rear View Mirror: Understanding McLuhan* (Montreal & London: McGill-Queen's University Press, 1971).

Papers:
Marshall McLuhan's papers are at the Public Archives of Canada in Ottawa.

W. O. Mitchell

(13 March 1914-   )

Margery Fee
Queen's University at Kingston

BOOKS: *Who Has Seen the Wind* (Toronto: Macmillan, 1947; Boston: Little, Brown, 1947);
Jake and the Kid (Toronto: Macmillan, 1961);
The Kite (Toronto: Macmillan, 1962);
The Black Bonspiel of Wullie MacCrimmon (Calgary: Frontiers Unlimited, 1965);
Centennial Play, by Mitchell, Robertson Davies, Arthur L. Murphy, Eric Nicol, and Yves Thériault, music by Keith Bissell (Ottawa: Centennial Commission, 1967);
The Vanishing Point (Toronto: Macmillan, 1973);
The Devil's Instrument (Toronto: Simon & Pierre, 1973);
How I Spent My Summer Holidays (Toronto: Macmillan, 1981);
Dramatic W. O. Mitchell: The Devil's Instrument, The Black Bonspiel of Wullie MacCrimmon, Back to Beulah, The Kite, For Those in Peril on the Sea (Toronto: Macmillan, 1982);
Since Daisy Creek (Toronto: Macmillan, 1984);
Ladybug, Ladybug . . . (Toronto: McClelland & Stewart, 1988).

PLAY PRODUCTIONS: *Royalty Is Royalty,* Saskatoon, Greystone Theatre, University of Saskatchewan, 1 June 1959;
Centennial Play, by Mitchell, Robertson Davies, Arthur L. Murphy, Eric Nicol, and Yves Thériault, music by Keith Bissell, Lindsay, Ontario, 11 January 1967;
Wild Rose, book and lyrics by Mitchell, Calgary, Mac 14 Theatre Society at the Jubilee Auditorium, 24 May 1967;
The Devil's Instrument, Peterborough, Ontario Youtheatre at The Guildhall, 27 August 1972;
Back to Beulah, Calgary, Theatre Calgary, 9 January 1976;
The Black Bonspiel of Wullie MacCrimmon, Regina, Stoneboat Theatre, 27 February 1976;
The Kite, Calgary, Theatre Calgary, 30 April 1981;
For Those in Peril on the Sea, Calgary, Theatre Calgary, 11 February 1982.

MOTION PICTURES: *Face of Saskatchewan,* screenplay by Mitchell, Crawley Films, 1955;
Fires of Envy, screenplay by Mitchell, National Film Board, 1957;
Political Dynamite, screenplay by Mitchell, National Film Board, 1958.

TELEVISION: *The Black Bonspiel of Wullie MacCrimmon, Folio,* CBC, 9 October 1955;
The Devil's Instrument, Folio, CBC, 21 November 1956;
Honey and Hoppers, Folio, CBC, 7 November 1957;
Earn Money at Home, First Person Series, CBC, 10 August 1960;
Jake and the Kid, 12 scripts, CBC, 1961;
The Goose Hunt, Man in the Landscape, CBC, 8 May 1963;
A Saddle for a Story, 20/20, CBC, 14 July 1963;
The Kite, Show of the Week, CBC, 26 April 1965;
East End Was Just Beginning, Telescope, CBC, 17 November 1966;
Beef and Greens, 20/20, CBC, 16 March 1967;
The White Christmas of Archie Nicotine, To See Ourselves, CBC, 16 December 1971;
Back to Beulah, The Play's the Thing, CBC, 21 March 1974;
Joys of Saskatchewan Summer, Variety Special, CBC, 16 September 1977;
Sacrament, CBC, 1 January 1978.

RADIO: *The Devil's Instrument, Stage,* CBC, 27 March 1949;
Chaperone for Maggi, Stage, CBC, 1 May 1949;
Jake and the Kid, some 150 scripts, 1950-1956;
The Liar Hunter, Stage, CBC, 21 May 1950;
Out of the Mouths, Summer Theatre, CBC, 2 July 1950;
The Black Bonspiel of Wullie MacCrimmon, Summer Theatre, CBC, 30 July 1950;
Who Has Seen the Wind, CBC, 2 July 1955;
Time Is My Enemy, CBC, 5 February 1956;
Ingredient "H," CBC, 20 September 1959;
The Alien, Summer Stage, CBC, 10 July 1960;
Prairie Chicken Dance, CBC, 29 August 1960;

W. O. Mitchell (courtesy of the National Film Board of Canada)

Foothill Fables, 14 scripts, 1961-1964;

Open the Door and Let Her Come Right In, Summer Stage, CBC, 16 September 1962;

The White Christmas of Raymond Shotclose, CBC Christmas Special, 24 December 1962;

Royalty Is Royalty, Summer Stage, CBC, 23 June 1963;

Weather, Weather, Weather, Summer Fallow Series, CBC, 30 March 1964;

The Kite, Summer Stage, CBC, 12 June 1964;

Back to Beulah, Stage, CBC, 26 October 1974.

PERIODICAL PUBLICATIONS: "The Alien," *Maclean's,* 66 (15 September 1953)–67 (15 January 1954);

"Three Random Scenes–Complete with Cast and Plot from the Unfolding Drama of W. O. Mitchell," *Maclean's,* 77 (2 May 1964): 21-24;

"Debts of Innocence," *Saturday Night,* 91 (March 1976): 36-37.

Crocus, the small prairie town that W. O. Mitchell has created in his novels and stories, like Stephen Leacock's Mariposa, has been mapped in the Canadian imagination. The original of this mythic place is Weyburn, Saskatchewan, a town of about five thousand people when Mitchell spent his first twelve years there. Its notoriety was assured when Mitchell's first novel, *Who Has Seen the Wind,* appeared in 1947 to instant popular and critical acclaim. The novel has since sold more than half a million copies.

William Ormond Mitchell, born 13 March 1914, was the second of four sons of Ormond Skinner and Margaret Letitia McMurray Mitchell. In 1921 Mitchell's father, the Weyburn druggist and a popular elocutionist, died suddenly. In 1928 Mitchell had to withdraw from school for over a year because of a tubercular wrist. As Mitchell, quoted in *Canadian Heritage* (December 1980), recalled this period: "Billy Mitchell ... who ... was, between nine and four on a school day, the only living boy in Weyburn, Saskatchewan–the only living boy in the *world*–used to go out of the town and into the prairie." Because of Mitchell's illness the family moved to a healthier climate, first to Long Beach, California (1928-1929), and soon after to St. Petersburg, Florida, returning to Canada in the summers.

In 1931 Mitchell began premedical training at the University of Manitoba. His problem with his wrist forced him to transfer into arts for his second year. He majored in psychology but did not complete the degree. In 1934, after traveling in Europe and North America, Mitchell went to Seattle, planning to ship out to South America. A dock strike kept him in Seattle, however, and for two years he worked for the *Seattle Times*, wrote and acted for the Penthouse Players, and took courses in journalism, psychology, and creative writing at the University of Washington. After his sojourn in Seattle, Mitchell entered the University of Alberta in 1940. He received a B.A. and a certificate in education in 1942. In August of that year he married Merna Lynne Hirtle. He then worked for two years as principal and teacher at two Alberta schools, at Castor and New Dayton. At the same time he was publishing short stories in *Maclean's*, *Canadian Forum*, and *Atlantic Monthly*. In 1944 Mitchell decided to become a free-lance writer. In 1945 he moved his family to High River, Alberta, where his three children, Ormond Skinner (born 11 July 1943), Hugh Hirtle (born 1 June 1946), and Willa Lynne (born 31 July 1954), grew up. High River remained the family home until 1968, except for Mitchell's years as fiction editor of *Maclean's* in Toronto from 1948 to 1951. In High River, Mitchell completed his best-known novel, *Who Has Seen the Wind*.

During the 1950s Mitchell conducted summer writing workshops for the Saskatchewan Board at Fort Qu'Appelle (1952 to 1955, 1957); he also taught at Okanagan, British Columbia (1960), and for many summers at the Banff School of Fine Arts. In 1975 he became the director of creative writing at Banff, a position from which he retired in 1986. Mitchell's main source of income in the 1950s and early 1960s was the CBC. From 1950 to 1956 he wrote weekly half-hour scripts for CBC-Radio's *Jake and the Kid*, and from 1961 to 1964 he provided scripts for *Foothill Fables* and read his work on his own *W. O. Mitchell Reading* series. In 1961 the National Film Board produced *Jake and the Kid* in twelve half-hour shows for CBC-TV. He was writer in residence at the University of Calgary (1968-1971); the University of Alberta (1971-1973); Massey College, University of Toronto (1973-1974); York University (1976-1978); and the University of Windsor (1979-1987). Mitchell's home is currently in Calgary.

Dust jacket for Mitchell's second novel, published in 1962 and later adapted by the author for radio, television, and the stage

Who Has Seen the Wind seems, like most of Mitchell's novels, to be partly autobiographical: he remarked to David O'Rourke in an interview published in the early 1980s, "every bit's the truth, but the whole thing's a creative leap/lie." Brian's father, the town druggist, dies suddenly while his children are young, and the impetus for many of Mitchell's plots is a quest for a father. The quest is often impelled by the loss of a power struggle with a female figure. Brian, in the first pages of *Who Has Seen the Wind*, sets out "to get God after my gramma" and collects many substitute fathers. Ultimately, however, this quest belongs to literary tradition: at the heart of the Western are *male* relationships. As Robert Kroetsch has pointed out, in his "Fear of Women in Prairie Fiction: An Erotics of Space" (in *Crossing Frontiers: Papers in American and Canadian Western Literature*, edited by Dick Harrison, 1979), in prairie fiction men "are obedient to versions of self that keep them at a distance" from women: "the male as orphan, as cowboy, as outlaw."

In the Western the conflict is not simply between the civilizing and thus repressive mother figure and the chaotic but vital father figure, although this conflict resonates at the heart of some powerful prairie fictions. Ultimately the struggle is between order and energy, and neither must win. The giant and heroic figures that struggle over the soul of the child in Mitchell's works are not "real" fathers and mothers: these are generally kind, even idealized. For Mitchell the psychic action is with the substitute fathers, who are often outlaws or outsiders. Others are religious visionaries. Still others have native blood or marry natives. They go to comic extremes: for example, Daddy Sherry in the 1962 novel *The Kite* is the oldest man in the world, and the Old Ben in *Who Has Seen the Wind* claims to have 133 children. All tell tall tales.

Who Has Seen the Wind and several later works attempt to re-create the perceptual and psychic world of the child. Mitchell had studied the work of Swiss psychologist Jean Piaget at the University of Alberta, and these studies inform much of Brian's development. Encouraged by his mentor F. M. Salter, Mitchell, in fact, wrote part of *Who Has Seen the Wind* in a creative-writing course he took at Alberta. Salter's influence on the novel has been traced by Mitchell's daughter-in-law Barbara Mitchell in a 1988 article for *Canadian Literature*.

The novel is structured by Brian's attempts to come to terms with the meaning of death and by his attempts to understand God. Brian experiences the onset of a kind of transcendence—what he calls "the feeling"—while looking at a drop of rain on a spirea leaf. Gradually this mystical comprehension of nature fades, and Brian begins to replace "the feeling" with an attempt at intellectual, even philosophical inquiry. Despite Mitchell's talent for making people laugh, he has always written from a firm moral position. He attempts, at least in his early novels, to present a single universal truth, an absolute. The search in *Who Has Seen the Wind* seems to be for a way of life that can accommodate the awareness of both the beauty of nature and its utter indifference to man. Energy and order are engaged in a Blakean struggle throughout the book. A good (and humorous) demonstration of this struggle, and of the hypocrisy and narrow-mindedness that Brian encounters in Crocus, is the episode in

which the Old Ben's still explodes in the basement of the Presbyterian church, whose members control the moral outlook of the town. Although his spirits inspire many of the town's most respected men, including the judge, the Old Ben, himself an energetic force in the town, is finally locked up in the local jail.

Mitchell has been criticized for betraying the struggle in a deus ex machina ending. Nature in the form of a windstorm that seems to serve as an instrument of God's wrath easily defeats the forces of pettiness and hypocrisy. It almost seems as if Mitchell had to trivialize so as to make Brian's necessary compromise with order more palatable. Brian cannot remain innocent because he must grow up. Mitchell's resolution is in the mediation of energy and order by education: Brian's decision to become a "dirt doctor" means he will be able to apply the enlightenment of science to nature. *Who Has Seen the Wind* is also noteworthy for the lyric beauty of its descriptive passages, the creation of a set of unforgettable comic characters, and the apt and funny use of dialect. Richard Sullivan, in the *New York Times Book Review*, called the novel "a piece of brilliantly sustained prose"; Lloyd Wendt of the *Chicago Tribune* compared it to *Tom Sawyer*; Robertson Davies wrote in the *Peterborough Examiner* that Mitchell "so thoroughly captured the feeling of Canada and the Canadian people that we feel repeated shocks of recognition as we read. . . ."

Although *Jake and the Kid* was published in 1961, its characters had long been familiar to Mitchell's audience because they had frequently appeared in his short stories and radio scripts. The book's first story, "You Gotta Teeter," was the second Mitchell published; it appeared in *Maclean's* for 15 August 1942.

Although the publisher described *Jake and the Kid* as a novel, it is a series of thirteen sketches that Mitchell selected and revised from the mass of material he had written. The book won the Leacock Medal for Humour in 1962 and perhaps is closer to "pure" humor than any of Mitchell's long works. Yet a concern that is central in the works of other prairie writers such as Margaret Laurence, Robert Kroetsch, and Rudy Wiebe emerges in the sketches of *Jake and the Kid*: the relation of factual or "book" history to popular or "folk" history. The Kid's complaints about his teacher Miss Henchbaw exemplify this theme. Believing everything she reads, she finds the history the Kid learns from Jake, a hired hand on the Kid's mother's farm, unsatisfactory:

"Whenever I write down Looie Riel was a tall, hungry-looking fellow that wore gold cuff links, chewed Black Judas tobacco, and had a rabbit's foot fob to his watch, she gives me a D." Also common to much prairie literature is the book's fascination with the local landscape of correction lines, sloughs, coulees, quarter sections, coyotes, crocuses, and windbreaks, and the recounting, often in dialect and in the mode of the tall tale, of local pastimes: going to auctions, racing horses, making rain, singing in the church choir, and hunting gophers.

Jake and the Kid was well received, but *The Kite,* published in 1962, did not meet with much critical or popular approval. Loosely structured, the novel is unified by the attempts of David Lang, a middle-aged reporter, to write a magazine story about Daddy Sherry, the oldest man in the world. The narrative is mainly composed of Lang's interviews with various townspeople, each recounting some fantastic incident from Daddy Sherry's past, each purporting to reveal the secret of his long life. Daddy is so vividly drawn that he steals the show, and Lang's obsession with immortality, his quest for truth and for a father fade; instead Mitchell provides a series of vignettes which cannot bear the philosophic weight the author attempts to give them.

In *The Vanishing Point* (1973) Mitchell tries to deal with flux rather than to produce answers. Mitchell remarks on the change in his viewpoint in a 1971 interview with Donald Cameron (collected in Cameron's *Conversations with Canadian Novelists,* 1973): "for a long time I thought of myself as a Platonist, with Presbyterian overtones, but at some point in my writing apprenticeship I suddenly realized that it wouldn't do, there could be no closed systems in art. Since it rests upon life, it is made up of contradiction, of dilemma, of not either/or but of both." In 1953 Mitchell won the Maclean's Fiction Award for "The Alien," an unpublished novel. An abridged version of its third part was serialized in *Maclean's* from 15 September 1953 to 15 January 1954, and Mitchell's 1973 novel, *The Vanishing Point,* was based on the serialization. The novel's hero, Carlyle Sinclair, teaches on the Paradise Valley Reserve, as Mitchell taught on the Eden Valley Reserve in Alberta in 1951 and 1952. Carlyle Sinclair has, as foil and antihero, the maddening, argumentative, drunken, enterprising, religious, and ultimately triumphant Indian Archie Nicotine. Together Carlyle and Archie illustrate the contrast between white and Indian culture that

Mitchell is trying to illuminate. From the white point of view, the Stonies are filthy, inefficient, diseased, alcoholic, immoral, and lazy; from the Indian point of view, the whites are clean, productive, pure, authoritarian, and in the end coldhearted and estranged from their own and others' feelings. Carlyle unhesitatingly attempts to impose his viewpoint, Presbyterian and puritan, on his students, although he hates the ultimate result of this posture: the modern metropolis, which, surrounded by oil refineries and filled with prostitutes and false prophets, resembles a doomed city of the Old Testament.

Carlyle is told by his superior that "Paradise needs tidying up," but he fails to reduce the chaos: as Archie says, "Indians don't herd well." Carlyle's prize student, Victoria Rider, is pushed through school by her parents' ambitions and Carlyle's unconscious need to mold her into a replica of his mother. Defeated on so many issues, Carlyle eases his frustrations by pointing to her success as a student nurse as an example of what can be achieved. That she finally, disgraced and pregnant, leaves the hospital, that symbol of purity, order, and health, is, in the context of the novel, a victory. In a final scene, set in the dance tent, Carlyle joins Victoria in a ritual Indian dance; he discovers that he, not Victoria, is the lost one. Mitchell's description of the dance makes clear that Carlyle has given up his desire to change the Indians' self-image and has come to accept them for themselves. As W. J. Keith has noted in a 1987 article in *WLWE,* the romance of Victoria and Carlyle does not really solve the larger sociopolitical issues raised in the novel, especially the "issue of one race controlling and ruling another."

The narrator of Mitchell's 1981 novel, *How I Spent My Summer Holidays,* Hugh, is a man over sixty remembering the summer when he was twelve. Here the child-adult relationship is much darker and more problematic than it is in Mitchell's earlier novels. Hugh's recollections begin with a recurrent nightmare, redolent of sin, sexuality, and child abuse. The secret cave that Hughie and his friend Peter dig becomes a symbol for the child's world that is violated by adults: "We simply hadn't noticed the adult footprints in our child caves, but they were there all the time, left by guardian trespassers. They entered uninvited because they loved us and they feared for us. . . . They did not know, nor did we, that they could be carriers, unintentionally leaving serpents behind, coiled in a dark corner, later to bite and poison and destroy." It is significant that Hugh's father is not one of the trespassers–"I did not have to defend my interior from my father"–while his mother clearly is, "coming on strong, right through neutral territory and into my own." But Hugh's father substitute, King Motherwell, intrudes most violently of all.

This "oft-decorated hero of the Great War," whose name reveals his odd combination of heroism and tenderness, owns the pool hall, coaches the hockey team, and runs liquor across the border into Montana. He also marries a beautiful whore, Bella, whose infidelities finally drive him to murder, insanity, and suicide. Unlike Brian's father substitutes in *Who Has Seen the Wind,* King is neither comic nor harmless. And yet he is profoundly attractive, sheltering an insane sheepherder in the boys' cave, carving beautiful duck decoys, and loving Bella. She is compared to Persephone, and he, hiding her battered body in the cave, becomes King of the Underworld. As Guy Hamel wrote, reviewing the novel for *Fiddlehead* (July 1982), it is King Motherwell's destruction that makes *How I Spent My Summer Vacation* Mitchell's most somber novel: "Hugh finds, as all of us really know, that any stopping place short of death is artificial, that once we are one person and now we are another while yet remaining in essence the same being and inescapably the heirs of our own beginnings. . . ."

In her entry on Mitchell for *The Annotated Bibliography of Canada's Major Authors* (volume 3, 1981), Sheila Latham lists 174 radio and television plays by Mitchell and notes that Mitchell himself mentions having written 320 scripts for *Jake and the Kid,* although she was unable to unearth all of them in the CBC archives. But whatever the figures, Mitchell is as important as a dramatist and actor as he is for his novels. Following in his father's footsteps, and a venerable prairie tradition of tall-tale telling, Mitchell is a popular performer of his own works; he has traveled across Canada giving readings. He confesses to scanning many of the lines in his fiction: his works have been written to be read aloud.

Two of his early theatrical works, the collaborative *Centennial Play* and the operetta *Wild Rose,* were produced in 1967 to mixed reviews. Mitchell adapted the latter from his 1959 stage play, *Royalty Is Royalty,* which in turn was adapted from "The Princess and the Wild Ones," a story for which Mitchell received the President's Medal from the University of Western Ontario in 1953.

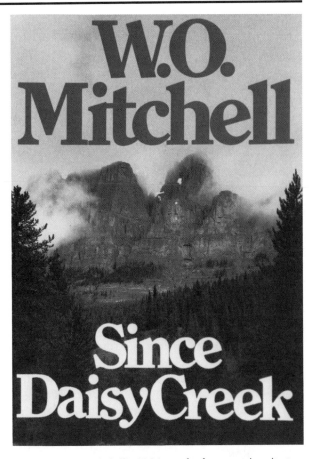

Dust jacket for Mitchell's 1984 novel, about a university professor who learns to make "loving allowances" for the frailties and failures of others

In 1982 five of Mitchell's plays were collected under the title *Dramatic W. O. Mitchell.*

The Devil's Instrument is set in a prairie Hutterite community. The devil's instrument is the harmonica that the main character, Jacob, an orphaned sixteen-year-old, learns to play. He is discovered and punished: the elders destroy the harmonica and propose to send him to Coventry, but he flees the community. The play was first produced for CBC-Radio, 27 March 1949, televised by CBC, 21 November 1956, and produced on stage in Peterborough, Ontario, 27 August 1972.

In *The Black Bonspiel of Wullie MacCrimmon* MacCrimmon's rink curls against the Devil's: Guy Fawkes, Judas Iscariot, and Macbeth. Wullie wagers his soul against a sure win. Mitchell's dislike of narrow-minded religion again surfaces when the local campaign against curling on the Sabbath almost causes Wullie's downfall. But Wullie is as wily as the comic spirit is high in this play, and the Devil, that noted poor loser, has to return to hell once more defeated. This play was first produced by CBC-Radio, 30 July 1950, and televised by CBC, 9 October 1955. It was adapted and separately published as a story in 1965.

In *Back to Beulah,* which won the Chalmers Award in 1976, Mitchell creates a surrogate family in a halfway house for the mentally ill. Harriet, Betty, and Agnes live together, supervised by Dr. Margaret Anders. Agnes, under pressure at Christmas, shoplifts a doll for the crèche, and she and Betty fantasize that it is real. The discovery of this aberration of the "mother instinct" brings Harriet and Dr. Anders into a conflict that Mitchell, in his notes on the cast of characters, also connects with motherhood: "Power and ascendancy are paramount for Harriet; the mother instinct is very strong for her. Agnes and Betty are her young, and she will defend them to the death." Dr. Anders, who has, according to the notes, chosen her profession to emulate her domineering mother, "needs power as badly as does Harriet." Rather brutally stripped of her pretensions by the ironic reversal of Harriet's experienced psychoanalytic interrogation, the distraught and hallucinating Dr. Anders is taken "back to Beulah," the mental institute, at the play's end. This play was produced for CBC-TV, 21 March 1974, and later adapted for broadcast on CBC-Radio, 26 October 1974.

The Kite, adapted from Mitchell's second novel, is more successful in its later version, perhaps because the somewhat dreary David Lang has been cut. *The Kite* was produced by CBC-Radio, 12 June 1964, televised, 26 April 1965, and produced on stage in Calgary, 30 April 1981. Some of Lang's story from the novel has been revised and transferred with good effect to the final play included in *Dramatic W. O. Mitchell, For Those in Peril on the Sea,* which had its premiere 11 February 1982 in Calgary. The television version of this play, entitled *Sacrament,* was shown on CBC, 1 January 1978. The play makes use of several of Mitchell's familiar themes and situations: it begins with a retarded boy's nightmare about his father, who has deserted him and his mother, and elaborates the boy's relationships with a series of father figures, emphasizing Mitchell's constant belief in the importance of what Annie, a character in the author's 1984 novel, *Since Daisy Creek,* calls making "loving allowances" for the frailties and failures of others.

Although Colin Dobbs has no idea who his father is, *Since Daisy Creek* is less a quest for the father than a struggle with the mother. Since his marriage failed and his teenaged daughter ran

away, Dobbs, a creative-writing professor, has been unable to write. Instead, he has been going up Daisy Creek, guided by Archie Nicotine, to hunt a bear. He uses the myth of the lone hero against the wilderness to compensate for his failure to deal with the "female" side of himself, the side that loves and creates. Dobbs manages to shoot the bear, significantly a female bear of enormous size, but is mauled terribly before Nicotine saves him. His daughter Annie returns, rescues Dobbs from a hospital, and alternately bullies and mothers him back to health. Dobbs gradually relinquishes his grip on the myth when he decides he does not need the bearskin as a trophy, and finally learns to make "loving allowances." A large part of the novel is taken up with a splendidly satirical account of university and departmental politics, featuring a novel-writing university president with forged academic credentials, and a female professor who blackmails and beds her way to tenure and an associate professorship.

Mitchell's most recent novel, *Ladybug, Ladybug* (1988), begins as Professor Emeritus Kenneth Lyon loses the use of his office in the chaotic English department introduced in *Since Daisy Creek.* Lonely, he hires as his housekeeper a pool-playing actress with a six-year-old daughter. The actress is being stalked by a psychotic graduate student, and the plot develops predictably. The novel was poorly received because it fails in precisely the ways that *How I Spent My Summer Holidays* succeeds: the violence seems arbitrary and the theme of child abuse merely trendy, unintegrated into the narrative form.

Mitchell's work is important in any discussion of Canadian literature, but his comic vision seems to have made him odd man out in a tradition that includes the somewhat gloomy realism of Frederick Philip Grove and Sinclair Ross. Thus, he has not been studied as extensively as they have by academic critics. *Who Has Seen the Wind* is unquestionably as much of a classic as Sinclair Ross's *As For Me and My House* (1941). Perhaps the use of a comic vision in the works of more recent prairie writers such as Ken Mitchell and Robert Kroetsch will allow for fuller recognition of Mitchell's part in the tradition of prairie literature.

Interviews:
Patricia Barclay, "Regionalism and the Writer: A Talk with W. O. Mitchell," *Canadian Literature,* 14 (Autumn 1962): 53-56;

Donald Cameron, "W. O. Mitchell: Sea Caves and Creative Partners," in *Conversations with Canadian Novelists*, part 2 (Toronto: Macmillan, 1973), pp. 48-63;

David O'Rourke, "An Interview with W. O. Mitchell," *Essays in Canadian Writing*, 20 (Winter 1980-1981): 149-159.

Bibliographies:

Sheila Latham, "W. O. Mitchell: An Annotated Bibliography," in *The Annotated Bibliography of Canada's Major Authors*, volume 3, edited by Robert Lecker and Jack David (Downsview, Ont.: ECW, 1981), pp. 323-364;

Marlys Chevrefils, Sandra Mortensen, and others, *The W. O. Mitchell Papers: An Inventory of the Archive at the University of Calgary Libraries*, edited by Jean F. Tener and Apollonia Steele (Calgary: University of Calgary Press, 1986).

References:

Donald R. Bartlett, "Dumplings and Dignity," *Canadian Literature*, 77 (Summer 1978): 73-80;

Arnold E. Davidson, "Lessons on Perspective: W. O. Mitchell's *The Vanishing Point*," *Ariel*, 12 (January 1981): 61-78;

S. A. Gingell-Beckmann, "The Lyricism of W. O. Mitchell's *Who Has Seen the Wind*," *Studies in Canadian Literature*, 6, no. 2 (1981): 221-231;

W. J. Keith, "W. O. Mitchell from 'The Alien' to *The Vanishing Point*," *WLWE: World Literature Written in English*, 27 (1987): 252-262;

Catherine McLay, "Crocus, Saskatchewan: A Country of the Mind," *Journal of Popular Culture*, 14 (Fall 1980): 333-349;

Barbara Mitchell, "The Long and the Short of It: Two Versions of *Who Has Seen the Wind*," *Canadian Literature*, 119 (Winter 1988): 8-22;

O. S. Mitchell, "Tall Tales in the Fiction of W. O. Mitchell," *Canadian Literature*, 108 (Spring 1986): 16-35;

W. H. New, "A Feeling of Completion: Aspects of W. O. Mitchell," *Canadian Literature*, 17 (Summer 1963): 22-33;

Laurence Ricou, "The Eternal Prairie: The Fiction of W. O. Mitchell," in his *Vertical Man/Horizontal World: Man and Landscape in Canadian Prairie Fiction* (Vancouver: University of British Columbia Press, 1973), pp. 95-110;

Ricou, "Stages of Language and Learning in W. O. Mitchell's *Who Has Seen the Wind*," in his *Everyday Magic: Child Language in Canadian Literature* (Vancouver: University of British Columbia Press, 1987).

Papers:

The University of Calgary, Alberta, has Mitchell's papers, including the manuscript of his unpublished novel "Roses Are Difficult Here" and scripts for the *Jake and the Kid* series.

Mavor Moore
(8 March 1919-   )

Chris Johnson
University of Manitoba

BOOKS: *And What Do YOU Do?: A Short Guide to the Trades & Professions* (London: Dent, 1960);

Louis Riel: An Opera in Two Acts, libretto by Moore and Jacques Languirand, music by Harry Somers (Toronto: Canadian Music Centre, 1967);

Getting In (New York: French, 1973);

Four Canadian Playwrights: Robertson Davies, Gratien Gélinas, James Reaney, George Ryga (Toronto: Holt, Rinehart & Winston, 1973);

The Pile. Inside Out. The Store (Toronto: Simon & Pierre, 1973);

Six Plays by Mavor Moore (Vancouver: Talonbooks, 1989)–comprises *The Apology, The Store, The Pile, Getting In, The Argument*, and *Come Away, Come Away*.

PLAY PRODUCTIONS: *I Know You*, Toronto, Toronto Arts and Letters Club, 1944;

Who's Who, script and direction by Moore, Toronto, New Play Society, 16 September 1949;

Sunshine Town, adapted from Stephen Leacock's *Sunshine Sketches of a Little Town*, book, lyrics, music, and direction by Moore, Toronto, New Play Society, 1955;

The Optimist, adapted from Voltaire's *Candide*, book, lyrics, and music by Moore, Toronto, New Play Society, 1956;

The Ottawa Man, adapted by Moore from Nikolai Gogol's play *The Inspector General*, direction by Moore, Toronto, Crest Theatre, 21 May 1961;

Louis Riel, libretto by Moore with Jacques Languirand, music by Harry Somers, Toronto, Canadian Opera Company at the O'Keefe Centre, 23 September 1967;

Johnny Belinda, adapted from Elmer Harris's play, music by John Fenwick, Charlottetown, Prince Edward Island, Charlottetown Festival, 1 July 1968;

photograph by Robert C. Ragsdale

Abracadabra, libretto by Moore, music by Harry Freedman, Courtenay, British Columbia, Courtenay Youth Festival, 1979;

Love and Politics, adapted from Nicholas Flood Davin's play *The Fair Grit*, book, lyrics, and music by Moore, St. Catharines, Ontario, Press Theatre, 1979;

Fauntleroy, adapted from Frances Hodgson Burnett's novel *Little Lord Fauntleroy*, music by Johnny Burke, Charlottetown, Prince Edward Island, Charlottetown Festival, 4 July 1980;

A Christmas Carol, adapted from Charles Dickens's novel, book, lyrics, music, and direction by Moore, Vancouver, Carousel Theatre, 1988.

SELECTED TELEVISION: *The Inspector General*, adapted from Nikolai Gogol's play, *Television Theatre*, CBC, 2 October 1952;

To Tell the Truth, adapted from Morley Callaghan's play, *Television Theatre*, CBC, 23 October 1952;

The Coventry Miracle Play, adaptation, CBC, Autumn 1952;

The Black Eye, adapted from James Bridie's play, *General Motors Presents*, CBC, 16 November 1954;

Sunshine Town, adapted from Moore's radio play *The Hero of Mariposa, Scope*, CBC, 19 December 1954;

Catch a Falling Star, General Motors Presents, CBC, 1 November 1955;

The Ottawa Man, adapted from Gogol's play *The Inspector General, Folio*, CBC, 20 February 1958;

The Man Who Caught Bullets, First Performance, CBC, 4 November 1958;

The Master of Santiago, adapted from Henry de Montherlant's play *Le Maître de Santiago, Folio*, CBC, 3 March 1959;

The Crucible, adapted from Arthur Miller's play, *Ford Startime*, CBC, 7 October 1959;

The Well, General Motors Presents, CBC, 12 June 1960;

Wise Guy, adapted from a story by Christopher Isherwood, *First Person*, CBC, 25 January 1961;

The Man Born to be King, adapted from Dorothy L. Sayers's radio plays, CBC, 31 March 1961;

Mary of Scotland, adapted from Maxwell Anderson's play, *Festival*, CBC, 28 September 1966;

The Puppet Caravan, adapted from Marie Claire Blais's play *La Roulotte aux poupées, Festival II*, CBC, 1 March 1967;

Enoch Soames, adapted from Max Beerbohm's story, *Festival*, CBC, 15 March 1967;

Yesterday the Children Were Dancing, translated and adapted from Gratien Gélinas's play *Hier, les enfants dansaient, Festival*, CBC, 6 November 1967;

The Best of All Possible Worlds, adapted from Voltaire's *Candide*, book, lyrics, and music by Moore, Festival, CBC, 17 January 1968;

Louis Riel, adapted from the libretto by Moore and Jacques Languirand, music by Harry Somers, CBC, 29 October 1969;

Getting In, Program X, CBC, 27 May 1971;

Inside Out, Program X, CBC, 23 December 1971;

The Store, Program X, CBC, 23 March 1972;

The Argument, BBC, 1973;

Come Away, Come Away, Program X, CBC, 16 February 1973;

The Lyons Mail, adapted from Charles Reade's play, *Purple Playhouse*, CBC, 18 March 1973;

The Roncarelli Affair, by Moore and F. R. Scott, CBC, 14 March 1974;

Johnny Belinda, adapted from Moore's musical, CBC, 1976.

SELECTED RADIO: *Christmas Carol–1941*, adapted from Charles Dickens's story, CBC, 25 December 1941;

The Great Flood, music by John Weinzweig, *Wednesday Night*, CBC, 28 July 1948;

The Government Inspector, adapted from Nikolai Gogol's play, *Wednesday Night*, CBC, 25 August 1948;

William Tell, adapted from Friedrich von Schiller's play, *Wednesday Night*, CBC, 27 April 1949;

To Tell the Truth, adapted from Morley Callaghan's play, *Wednesday Night*, CBC, 25 May 1949;

Call It a Day, adapted from Dodie Smith's play, *Ford Theatre*, CBC, 8 December 1950;

The First Mrs. Fraser, adapted from St. John Ervine's play, *Ford Theatre*, CBC, 9 February 1951;

The Drums Are Out, adapted from John Coulter's play, *Wednesday Night*, CBC, 11 July 1951;

The Best of All Possible Worlds, adapted from Voltaire's *Candide*, *Wednesday Night*, CBC, 9 January 1952;

The Hero of Mariposa, adapted from Stephen Leacock's stories, *Wednesday Night*, CBC, 31 March 1954;

The Son, Stage, CBC, 26 October 1958;

Old Moore's Almanac, by several hands, edited by Moore, *Wednesday Night*, CBC, 31 December 1958;

Don Juan in Hell, adapted from Bernard Shaw's *Man and Superman, Four's Company*, CBC, 23 May 1959;

Our Emblum Dear, Wednesday Night, CBC, 1 July 1959;

Catch My Death, Summer Stage, CBC, 30 August 1959;

Gulliver's Travels, adapted from Jonathan Swift's satire, *Four's Company*, CBC, 5 September 1959;

The Ottawa Man, adapted from Gogol's play *The Inspector General*, *Stage*, CBC, 1 May 1960;

Brave New World, adapted from Aldous Huxley's novel, *Four's Company*, CBC, 21 May 1960;

Fact or Fancy, adapted from Oscar Wilde, *Four's Company*, CBC, 17 June 1961;

The Rise and Fall of Witchcraft, *Four's Company*, CBC, 1 July 1961;

The Cachalot, adapted from Edwin John Pratt's poem, *Cameos*, CBC, 14 August 1961;

Fast Forward, CBC, 1968;

The Argument, CBC, 1970;

The Pile, CBC, 1970;

A Matter of Timing, CBC, 1971;

Come Away, Come Away, *Tuesday Night*, CBC, Fall 1972;

Freak, CBC, 1975.

OTHER: "Biography," in *Twentieth Century Canadian Poetry: An Anthology*, edited by Earle Birney (Toronto: Ryerson, 1953), p. 51;

"Theatre in English Speaking Canada" and "Radio and Television," in *The Arts in Canada: A Stock-Taking at Mid-Century*, edited by Malcolm Ross (Toronto: Macmillan, 1958), pp. 68-76, 116-124;

"Togetherness," in *A Treasury of Canadian Humour*, edited by Robert Thomas Allen (Toronto: McClelland & Stewart, 1967), pp. 71-73;

Gratien Gélinas, *Hier, les enfants dansaient*, translated by Moore as *Yesterday the Children Were Dancing* (Toronto: Clarke, Irwin, 1967);

The Awkward Stage: The Ontario Theatre Report, edited by Moore (Toronto: Methuen, 1969);

Murray Edwards, *A Stage in Our Past*, introduction by Moore (Toronto: Methuen, 1970);

"The Decline of Words in Drama," in *Dramatists in Canada: Selected Essays*, edited by W. H. New (Vancouver: University of British Columbia Press, 1972), pp. 97-104;

Come Away, Come Away, in *Encounter: Canadian Drama in Four Media*, edited by Eugene Benson (Toronto: Methuen, 1973), pp. 100-119;

The Roncarelli Affair, by Moore and F. R. Scott, in *The Play's the Thing: Four Original Television Dramas*, edited by Tony Gifford (Toronto: Macmillan, 1976), pp. 121-164;

Customs, in *Cues and Entrances: Ten Canadian One-Act Plays*, edited by Henry Beissel (Toronto: Gage, 1977), pp. 63-67;

George Ryga, *Two Plays: Paracelsus and Prometheus Bound*, introduction by Moore (Winnipeg: Turnstone, 1982), pp. 1-7;

Arthur L. Murphy, *Three Bluenose Plays*, introduction by Moore (Hantsport, N.S.: Lancelot, 1984);

"Culture as Culture," in *Organizational Culture: The Meaning of Life in the Workplace*, edited by Peter J. Frost and others (Beverly Hills, London & New Delhi: Sage Publications, 1985), pp. 373-378.

PERIODICAL PUBLICATIONS: "The Canadian Theatre," *Canadian Forum*, 30 (August 1950): 108-110;

"A Theatre for Canada," *University of Toronto Quarterly*, 26 (October 1956): 1-16;

"Canada's Great Theatre Prophet! Roy Who?," *Canadian Theatre Review*, 1 (Winter 1974): 68-71;

"History of English Canadian Amateur and Professional Theatre," *Canadian Drama/L'Art Dramatique Canadien*, 1 (Fall 1975): 60-67;

"An Approach to Our Beginnings: Transplant, Native Plant or Mutation," *Canadian Theatre Review*, 25 (Winter 1980): 10-16;

"Cultural Myths and Realities," *Canadian Theatre Review*, 34 (Spring 1982): 23-27;

"The Arts Centre: Dodo or Harbinger?," *Performing Arts in Canada*, 22 (Fall 1985): 5.

Mavor Moore has had a long and distinguished career as a playwright, composer, actor, director, radio and television producer, and arts administrator. Much of his dramatic writing has been for radio and television; indeed, he was a pioneer of Canadian television. He has been extraordinarily prolific, the author of more than a hundred radio plays and more than fifty produced television scripts. He was also instrumental in the formation of some influential theater companies. Distinctions include three Peabody awards and the Centennial Medal awarded in 1967; Moore was made an Officer of the Order of Canada in 1973; he became a Companion in 1988. In 1977 he received the Queen's Medal.

James Mavor Moore was born in Toronto in 1919 to Francis John Moore, an Anglican minister, and Dora Mavor Moore, a professional actress who had toured for a time with Sir Philip Ben Greet in America. She later played at

The Pile,
The Store,
Inside Out.
Mavor Moore

Dust jacket for Moore's 1973 play collection

London's Old Vic, afterward becoming a drama teacher and influential director and producer in Canada. (The awards distributed annually in the Toronto theater community are known as the Dora Mavor Moore Awards.) Inspired by his mother, the theatrical "godmother," Moore became involved in theater as a child, making his professional acting debut on radio at fourteen. While a student at the University of Toronto, he wrote and acted for the Canadian Broadcasting Corporation, was involved in student theater at Hart House, and joined the Village Players, a student company formed by his mother to take plays to Ontario schools. Moore made his professional stage debut with a summer-stock company in 1940. After graduating from the University of Toronto in 1941 with a degree in philosophy and English, he produced features and documentaries for the CBC, and in 1943 he joined the military, serving in the psychological warfare division of the Canadian Army Intelligence Corps.

Also in 1943 he married Darwina Faessler, by whom he had four daughters before the marriage was dissolved in 1967. In 1969 he married biographer Phyllis Grosskurth; they later divorced. (Her publications include: *John Addington Symonds: A Biography*, 1964; *Havelock Ellis: A Biogra-*

phy, 1980; and *Melanie Klein: Her World and Her Work*, 1986.) His third marriage was to soprano Alexandra Browning in 1980.

In 1946 Moore helped his mother establish the New Play Society (which Dora Mavor Moore ran until it was disbanded in 1971). Moore was for many years associated with NPS, serving as general manager from 1946 to 1950 and from 1955 to 1958, and making an extensive contribution as an actor (he played the title role in the premiere production of John Coulter's *Riel* in 1950), director, and playwright. The company represented a milestone in the evolution of Canadian theater: it trained a generation of actors, developed many Canadian plays (including works by Coulter, Andrew Allan, Lister Sinclair, Morley Callaghan, Harry Boyle, and Moore himself), and introduced Canadian audiences to the new European drama. In 1947, with Moore writing much of the material and producing, the first *Spring Thaw* was mounted; the extremely popular revue was an annual event for many years and launched the careers of many Canadian singers and comedians.

In 1949 the Society produced Moore's first full-length stage play, *Who's Who* (an earlier, short play, *I Know You*, had been produced by the Toronto Arts and Letters Club in 1944). In *Who's Who* Robert Murray, just deceased, is remembered in entirely different ways by his wife, son, and daughter. Yet more perspectives are added with the appearance of one of Murray's friends from the audience, the contributions of playwright and director, and, ultimately, the arrival of Murray himself. Drama of ideas, examination of reality and illusion, and Pirandellian structure which moves the audience's perception through a series of "realities" are characteristic of much of Moore's subsequent work.

In addition to his work for NPS, Moore worked for the United Nations Information Division as executive producer. Moore was chief producer when CBC television began operations in 1950, and in 1953 he was, with his mother, an initiator of the Stratford Shakespeare Festival, joining the Stratford company as an actor in 1954 for one season. In 1958, 1961, and 1963 he acted and directed with the Crest Theatre in Toronto, a theater like NPS and Stratford in that it was important in the reestablishment of professional theater in Canada. Moore was the drama critic for the Toronto *Telegram* from 1958 to 1960. He was founding chairman of the Canadian Theatre Centre in 1955 and in 1977 was elected first chairman of the Guild of Canadian Playwrights.

During this period Moore still found time to write, turning out dozens of radio, television, and stage plays. Among the most memorable was *The Best of All Possible Worlds*, a musical adaptation of Voltaire's *Candide*, with both book and music by Moore, broadcast by CBC-Radio in 1952 and, under the title *The Optimist*, staged in 1956 by the New Play Society. A musical based on the short stories of Stephen Leacock, *The Hero of Mariposa*, with book and music by Moore, was first broadcast on radio (1954) and later the same year became a television play, *Sunshine Town;* shortly after, it was produced in Toronto, London (Ontario), and Montreal in 1955 as a stage musical titled *Sunshine Town. The Ottawa Man*, a loose adaptation of Nikolai Gogol's *The Inspector General*, was first produced as a television play in 1958 and subsequently staged by the Crest Theatre in 1961. *The Ottawa Man* is set in a Manitoba town in the 1870s. The fraudulent official, a remittance man, exposes misgovernment of a sort seldom mentioned in history books, and Moore directs some pointed satire against Canadian racism.

From 1964 to 1968 Moore was founding artistic director of the Charlottetown Festival. Three of his musicals have been produced there: *Johnny Belinda*, with music by John Fenwick (subsequently produced as *Belinda*), premiered on 1 July 1968; *Sunshine Town* was mounted also in 1968; and *Fauntleroy*, with music by Johnny Burke, adapted from the novel *Little Lord Fauntleroy* by Frances Hodgson Burnett, was first produced 4 July 1980. One of Moore's most ambitious pieces of dramatic writing is the libretto for the opera *Louis Riel*, which he wrote with the assistance of Jacques Languirand. The opera, with music by Harry Somers, was first performed by the Canadian Opera Company in 1967. Moore and Languirand take more liberty with historical fact than did John Coulter in his play *Riel*, creating larger-than-life figures, and giving more tangible stage presence to the mythic and historical forces inherent in the story. Extensive use of the French language in the libretto emphasizes the sectarian and linguistic conflict and makes the opera one of Canada's earliest bilingual dramas.

Moore was one of the planners of the St. Lawrence Centre in Toronto and was that theater's first general director from 1965 to 1970. In the early 1970s Moore wrote most of his short plays which have been published; most were first presented on the electronic media and later published in their stage versions. All are distinguished by a focus on idea and by shifts in the audience's perception of the dramatic reality. In *The Pile* (collected in 1973) an engineer and a businessman debate methods of disposing of a pile of something; what the something is is never identified, but the structure of the piece puts the audience in the position of the pile itself. In *Come Away, Come Away* (in Eugene Benson's 1973 anthology, *Encounter: Canadian Drama in Four Media*), an old man meets a little girl, who encourages him to relive portions of his life. Gradually the audience becomes aware that the little girl is death. In *Inside Out* (collected in 1973) an actor father and an actress daughter cope with a crisis, each playing a series of roles; in the original television production (1971) the Pirandellian quality was intensified by Moore's playing the father with his actress daughter, Tedde, as the fictional daughter. Moore is fascinated by the relationship between the large organization and the individual. In *The Store* (collected in 1973) a department-store manager confronts a neurotic shopper, but the shopper is soon revealed as a personification of the manager's own neuroses. *Getting In* (1973) and *Customs* (in Henry Beissel's *Cues and Entrances: Ten Canadian One-Act Plays*, 1977) have an initially Kafkaesque tone as a prospective employee and a traveler in turn encounter a faceless bureaucracy, but in both cases the real menace is within the individuals concerned and is merely exposed by the encounter with bureaucracy.

Moore taught in the Departments of English and Theatre at York University from 1970 to 1984 and is now professor emeritus of that institution, as well as adjunct professor at the Universities of Lethbridge and Victoria. In 1979, after serving on the executive committee for five years, he was appointed chairman of the Canada Council, serving until 1983; he was the first artist to hold that position. Moore's writing for the stage during the last ten years includes: *Love and Politics*, a musical produced in 1979 based on Nicholas Flood Davin's 1876 play *The Fair Grit*; a one-act opera, *Abracadabra*, with music by Henry Freedman, commissioned by the Courtney, British Columbia, Youth Festival in 1979; *Fauntleroy;* and a musical version of Dickens's *A Christmas Carol* for Vancouver's Carousel Theatre in 1988. He hosted the CBC television program *Performance* from 1981 to 1984 and for several years has written columns examining the reciprocal influence of art and society for the Toronto *Globe and Mail*. In 1989 Talonbooks published *Six Plays by Mavor*

Moore, a collection of plays for two actors which includes *The Apology*, a new version of Socrates' trial. His work to this point suggests that his future writing will be divided between popular musical entertainment and pithy drama of ideas, a form of drama whose importance he defends eloquently in his essay "The Decline of Words in Drama," included in *Dramatists in Canada* (1972), edited by W. H. New.

References:

J. Frederick Brown, "The Charlottetown Festival in Review," *Canadian Drama/L'Art Dramatique Canadien*, 9 (1983): 254-267, 343-351;

Wayne Edmonstone, "Toward a National Theatre," in his *Nathan Cohen: The Making of a Critic* (Toronto: Lester & Orpen, 1977), pp. 153-182;

"Guilding the Writers: Interview with Mavor Moore," *Canadian Theatre Review*, 17 (Winter 1978): 94-98;

Margaret Gail Osachoff, "Riel on Stage," *Canadian Drama/L'Art Dramatique Canadien*, 8 (1982): 129-144;

Bill Tepper, "The Forties and Beyond: The New Play Society," *Canadian Theatre Review*, 28 (Fall 1980): 18-33;

Herbert Whittaker, "Spring Thaw" and "Sunshine Town," in *Whittaker's Theatre: A Critic Looks at Stages in Canada and Thereabouts, 1944-1975*, edited by Ronald Bryden (Greenbank, Ont.: The Whittaker Project, 1985), pp. 45-51.

Papers:

Moore's papers are at the library of York University in Toronto.

Desmond Pacey
(1 May 1917- 4 July 1975)

Fred Cogswell
University of New Brunswick

BOOKS: *Frederick Philip Grove* (Toronto: Ryerson, 1945);

Creative Writing in Canada: A Short History of English-Canadian Literature (Toronto: Ryerson, 1945; revised, 1961);

The Cow with the Musical Moo and Other Verses for Children (Fredericton: Brunswick Press, 1952);

Hippity Hobo and the Bee and Other Verses for Children (Fredericton: Brunswick Press, 1952);

Ten Canadian Poets: A Group of Biographical and Critical Essays (Toronto: Ryerson, 1958);

The Picnic, and Other Stories (Toronto: Ryerson, 1958);

The Cat, the Cow and the Kangaroo: The Collected Children's Verse of Desmond Pacey (Fredericton: Brunswick Press, 1968);

Ethel Wilson (New York: Twayne, 1968);

Essays in Canadian Criticism, 1938-1968 (Toronto: Ryerson, 1969);

Waken, Lords and Ladies Gay: Selected Stories of Desmond Pacey, edited by Frank M. Tierney (Ottawa: University of Ottawa Press, 1974).

OTHER: *A Book of Canadian Stories*, edited, with an introduction and notes, by Pacey (Toronto: Ryerson, 1947; revised, 1950);

New Voices: Canadian University Writing of 1956, edited by Pacey, Earle Birney, Ira Dilworth, Jean-Charles Bonenfant, and Roger Duhamel (Toronto: Dent, 1956);

The Selected Poems of Charles G. D. Roberts, edited by Pacey (Toronto: Ryerson, 1956);

Selected Poems of Dorothy Livesay, introduction by Pacey (Toronto: Ryerson, 1957);

Literary History of Canada: Canadian Literature in English, edited by Carl F. Klinck, with the collaboration of Pacey and others (Toronto: University of Toronto Press, 1965; revised, 1976);

Our Literary Heritage, edited by Pacey (Toronto: Ryerson, 1966);

Frederick Philip Grove, edited, with an introduction, by Pacey (Toronto: Ryerson, 1970);

Desmond Pacey (photograph by Harvey Studios Ltd., courtesy of Harriet Irving Library, University of New Brunswick)

Tales from the Margin: The Selected Short Stories of Frederick Philip Grove, edited by Pacey (Toronto: McGraw-Hill Ryerson, 1971);

Selections from Major Canadian Writers: Poetry and Creative Prose in English, edited by Pacey (Toronto: McGraw-Hill Ryerson, 1974);

The Letters of Frederick Philip Grove, edited by Pacey (Toronto: University of Toronto Press, 1976);

The Collected Poems of Sir Charles G. D. Roberts, edited by Pacey (Wolfville, N.S.: Wombat, 1985).

Intelligence, practical shrewdness, vital energy, and persistence were the predominant qualities associated with Desmond Pacey. These were displayed in his own writing and editing, in his family and community life, and in academic administration. He was essentially a pioneer, an initiator and inspirational force during a period of changing attitudes within English literature in Canada and changes in the nature and development of Canadian universities. Although he was the author of a few children's poems and a moderately well-received volume of short fiction, he is best remembered as the critic and literary historian who outlined the territory covered by the designation *English-Canadian literature.*

William Cyril Desmond Pacey was born in Dunedin, New Zealand, son of William Pacey of that city and Mary Elizabeth Hunt Pacey of Nottingham, England. His father's early death led to his mother's return to England where Pacey was educated at Magnus School in Newark. His mother subsequently married a Canadian farmer living near Hamilton, Ontario. There Pacey attended Caledonia High School, where he did so well that on graduation he received a scholarship to attend Victoria College, the University of Toronto. Earning an honors B.A. in 1938, he then attended Trinity College, Cambridge, on a Massey fellowship and a Dominion and Colonial Exhibition from Trinity. From this institution he received his Ph.D. in 1941.

Before his graduation, however, Pacey returned to Canada as professor of English at Manitoba's Brandon College (now Brandon University), a position which he held from 1940 to 1944, interspersed with one year as editor for the Wartime Information Board at Ottawa in 1943 and 1944. Before accepting the Brandon position, Pacey married, on 17 June 1939, Mary Elizabeth Carson. The couple had three sons and four daughters.

In 1944 Pacey terminated his service at Brandon College to become chairman of the Department of English at the University of New Brunswick, in Fredericton. This institution and the community that housed it became, for the rest of his life, his principal raison d'être. He presided over the growth of his own department during a period of unprecedented expansion and directed that growth toward the then unheard-of channel of research and teaching in Canadian literature. In addition to publishing articles and books in this field, Pacey inspired his students to pursue Canadian subjects; the eclectic notice he gave to the work of Canadian writers proved inspiring to the authors as well. His influence did not stop there. Along with Professor Roy Daniells of the Univer-

sity of British Columbia, he broke the academic stranglehold which the University of Toronto held on higher education in Canadian universities by having the University of New Brunswick and the University of British Columbia simultaneously initiate Ph.D. courses and degrees in English literature. Much later, cognizant of the need for sound scholarly texts and biographical materials, Pacey pioneered and found funding for research on the letters of Frederick Philip Grove and Sir Charles G. D. Roberts and a variorum edition of the complete poems of Roberts. Only one of these works was completed in his lifetime; *The Letters of Frederick Philip Grove* appeared in 1976, the year after Pacey's death, and *The Collected Poems of Sir Charles G. D. Roberts* was published in 1985. The Roberts letters remain unpublished.

Pacey's force and organizing ability were by no means confined to his department. As dean of graduate studies, 1960-1969, academic vice-president (1970 till his death), and acting president, 1972-1973, he was a continuing force in the shaping and development of the university. Unfortunately, he became ill with cancer, and his activities during the last two years of his life were increasingly curtailed. He fought a persistent, heroic battle against this disease, actually overcoming one type of cancer, only to fall prey at last to another. Throughout his life he gave unstintingly to the causes he championed and the ideals in which he believed. His efforts were not without incidental acknowledgments. He became a fellow of the Royal Society of Canada in 1955, and in 1972 he received the Society's Lorne Pierce Medal. Both the University of New Brunswick and Mount Allison University granted Pacey honorary degrees in 1973. In his further honor, the University of New Brunswick initiated a series of lectures given annually in the humanities and social sciences by distinguished scholars.

As a shaping force in the development of scholarship in Canadian literature, Pacey singlehandedly mastered an enormous amount of literary material, but its very bulk precluded, in most instances, more than the most obvious judgments. Although his work is biased on the side of realism in fiction and modernism in poetry, it is always characterized by common sense and the then unusual conviction that the Canadian material examined was worthy of respect. *Creative Writing in Canada* (1945; revised, 1961) long remained the standard history of anglophone Canadian literature; *Ethel Wilson* (1968) paid sensi-

Dust jacket for Pacey's 1947 anthology of "Canadian stories, written by Canadians, mostly about the Canadian scene"

tive tribute to an elegant stylist; *Ten Canadian Poets* (1958) and *Essays in Canadian Criticism, 1938-1968* (1969), selections from the many articles he had published, ran counter to some current trends in criticism by favoring biographical and cultural contexts in which to read writers' works. In the essay collections perhaps Pacey's most original and insightful articles are those on Archibald Lampman *(Ten Canadian Poets)* and Leonard Cohen *(Essays in Canadian Criticism)*. Perhaps the most attractively surprising of the many enthusiasms displayed in Pacey's writings is the appreciation of Irving Layton displayed in letters to that poet.

Of Pacey's own creative work, the short stories are solid, well-constructed examples of realism. When Roy Daniells wrote the foreword to *The Picnic, and Other Stories* (1958), he praised many of the qualities that defined Pacey's fiction as regional and realistic; paradoxically, these fea-

tures are among the reasons that have led to the subsequent eclipse of Pacey as a fiction writer. The sixteen stories in this volume tell conventionally of love, death, and discovery; they are set variously in Ontario, England, and the Maritimes. A recurring figure–a boy or young man on the farm, discovering at school the exigencies of life–is, Daniells observes, readily perceived as the author's alter ego.

The expectation that there can be orderly solutions to crises, that society is not intrinsically opposed to individual progress, that rage is not an inevitable consequence of conflict, marks Pacey's writing for its humane conservatism. It also accurately reflects the hopes of the later 1940s and 1950s. Daniells: "The melancholy or disillusion presented in these pages is that of youth but of youth not without resource (if only that of all the days to come). . . . Good, indeed, never really succumbs." Daniells also praises Pacey's technique in the stories, their "Simplicity, sensitiveness to the assaults of the world, and suffusing optimism" and their chronological structure and documentary form: "Each of them recounts a brief excursion along the road of experience, the events being related in the order of their occurrence without benefit of flash-back, montage or even stream-of-consciousness. This immemorial method of story-telling now strikes us as an innovation, calculated to restore the objective world to us."

Pacey published just over thirty stories altogether, most of the later ones in the *Fiddlehead* and *Atlantic Advocate*. (A full bibliography is contained in Frank M. Tierney's edition of Pacey's stories, *Waken, Lords and Ladies Gay*, 1974.) When Tierney assembled this collection, he chose only two of the later stories ("When She Comes Over," from *Fiddlehead* [1962], and "On the Roman Road," from *Atlantic Advocate* [1966]) to go with twelve of the stories from *The Picnic*. Tierney's response to Pacey's work, in his introduction to the 1974 volume and in a 1982 article that is the only extended comment on Pacey's writing, echoes that of Daniells in that it hinges on an appreciation for a set of values: wisdom, charity, tolerance, love. These values are highlighted by the somber tone of some of the stories, the sense of human fragility and vulnerability, and the refusal to give in to violence or despair. Although Tierney classifies character and plot types, neither he nor Daniells examines how these values derive from a set of assumptions about the natural order of society or about the way in which these assumptions affect literary form. Hence Tierney admires the authenticity of Pacey's descriptive detail. The conventional handling of narrative form raises questions about the nature of authenticity, but the values espoused in Pacey's fiction say a great deal about the character of the author. Where the stories are weakest is in their dialogue, which reflects the linguistic uncertainty of a writer whose boyhood was spent in three different countries. Pacey's children's poems are attractive and, although more limited in range, are comparable to those of Dennis Lee. They exemplify the warm, happy, domestic areas of his being.

Although in the last analysis, no change in cultural perspective can be attributed to one man alone, the fact that the study of Canadian literature was nonexistent in 1940 when Desmond Pacey began to teach and was by 1975 a principal occupation in English departments of many universities in Canada is much more than coincidence. For the generation that followed him, Pacey shaped a canon and set in motion the process of critical reinterpretation that has marked the years since his death.

References:
Roy Daniells, Foreword to Pacey's *The Picnic, and Other Stories* (Toronto: Ryerson, 1958);
Frank M. Tierney, Introduction to Pacey's *Waken, Lords and Ladies Gay* (Ottawa: University of Ottawa Press, 1974), pp. 9-15;
Tierney, "The Short Fiction of Desmond Pacey," *International Fiction Review*, 9 (Winter 1982): 3-16.

Len Peterson
(15 March 1917-   )

Jill Tomasson Goodwin
University of Waterloo

BOOKS: *Chipmunk* (Toronto: McClelland & Stewart, 1949);

Adolescent Rebellion, In Search of Ourselves, pamphlet no. 4 (Toronto: McClelland & Stewart, 1949);

Brotherly Hatred, In Search of Ourselves, pamphlet no. 2 (Toronto: McClelland & Stewart, 1949);

The Careful Boy, In Search of Ourselves, pamphlet no. 3 (Toronto: McClelland & Stewart, 1949);

Sex Education, In Search of Ourselves, pamphlet no. 1 (Toronto: McClelland & Stewart, 1949);

The Grin on the Moon (New York: Friendship Press, 1966);

The Great Hunger (Agincourt, Ont.: Book Society of Canada, 1967);

Burlap Bags (Toronto: Playwrights Co-op, 1972);

Women in the Attic (Toronto: Playwrights Co-op, 1972);

Let's Make a World (Toronto: Playwrights Co-op, 1973);

Almighty Voice (Agincourt, Ont.: Book Society of Canada, 1974);

They're All Afraid (Agincourt, Ont.: Book Society of Canada, 1981).

PLAY PRODUCTIONS: *Burlap Bags*, Toronto, Toronto Workshop Productions, 1960;

The Great Hunger, Toronto, Arts Theatre, November 1960;

All About Us, Winnipeg, Manitoba Theatre Centre, 28 October 1964;

Almighty Voice, Toronto, Young People's Theatre, August 1970;

The Queen Street Scrolls, Regina, Globe Theatre, 11 November 1971;

Let's Make a World, Toronto, Young People's Theatre, 1971;

The Workingman, Toronto, Toronto Workshop Productions, 1972;

Billy Bishop and the Red Baron, Toronto, Young People's Theatre, 1975;

Len Peterson (photograph by Robert C. Ragsdale, courtesy of the Canadian Broadcasting Corporation)

Etienne Brulé, Toronto, Young People's Theatre, 1977;

Eye of the Storm, Regina, Globe Theatre, 2 November 1985.

SELECTED TELEVISION: *They're All Afraid*, *Playbill*, CBC, Summer 1953;

Divorce Granted?, CBC, 10 August 1954;

Electra, CBC, 30 October 1955;

'55 in Review, CBC, 1 January 1956;

The Widow of the Mississagi, CBC, 6 May 1956;

Goodbye to Utopia, CBC, 1 January 1957;

Ice on Fire, *First Performance*, CBC, 10 October 1957;

The Trial of James Whelan, CBC, 21 November 1957;

Burlap Bags, *Q for Quest*, CBC, 3 January 1960;

Bombshelter in Braemar, Heritage, CBC, 20 March 1960;

The Long Road Back, GM Presents, CBC, 11 December 1960;

The Two-Faced Angel, CBC, 30 November 1962;

With My Heart Tucked Underneath My Arm, CBC, 28 October 1963;

Between the Silences of Love, CBC, 26 October 1964;

The Desperate Search, Show of the Week, CBC, 31 January 1966;

Not All By Myself, CBC, 15 May 1971.

SELECTED RADIO: *Mr. Warren's Profession*, Winnipeg Drama, CBC, 22 May 1941;

Brave Calvin, Theatre Time, CBC, 10 February 1942;

How Fame Came to Archie McFee, Theatre Time, CBC, 21 July 1942;

Look at One of Those Faces, Pacific Playhouse, CBC, 18 November 1942;

The End of the Line, Pacific Playhouse, CBC, 25 November 1942;

The City, Pacific Playhouse, CBC, 6 January 1943;

Now, Does He Know What He's Getting?, Stage, CBC, 13 February 1944;

Within the Fortress, Stage, CBC, 20 February 1944;

They're All Afraid, Stage, CBC, 27 February 1944;

Maybe in a Thousand Years, Stage, CBC, 19 November 1944;

Mr. Mulrooney's New Year's Party, Stage, CBC, 1 January 1945;

Love Story, Red Cross Show, CBC, 7 March 1945;

My Room Mate, Stage, CBC, 20 May 1945;

Burlap Bags, Stage, CBC, 3 February 1946;

White Collar, Stage, CBC, 3 March 1946;

Paper in the Wind, Stage, CBC, 5 May 1946;

Olli and the Troll, It's a Legend, CBC, 13 July 1947;

Cervantes of the Woeful Figure, Stage, CBC, 12 October 1947;

Assembly Line, Men at Work, CBC, 14 November 1947;

Adolescent Rebellion, In Search of Ourselves, CBC, 16 January 1948;

The Man Who Is Different, In Search of Ourselves, CBC, 20 February 1948;

Brotherly Hatred, In Search of Ourselves, CBC, 11 January 1949;

Sex Education, In Search of Ourselves, CBC, 25 January 1949;

The Girl Who Doesn't Care, In Search of Ourselves, CBC, 1 February 1949;

The Careful Boy, In Search of Ourselves, CBC, 8 February 1949;

A Little Girl in a Fabulous Fable, Vancouver Theatre, CBC, 5 August 1949;

Everybody Likes Me, Summer Theatre 2, CBC, 18 September 1949;

The Unwanted Father, In Search of Ourselves, CBC, 28 February 1950;

Chipmunk, Wednesday Night, CBC, 1 March 1950;

A Terrible Secret, In Search of Ourselves, CBC, 9 May 1950;

Don Juan of Toronto, Stage, CBC, 11 March 1951;

D'Arcy McGee, Trans-Canada Theatre, CBC, 1 July 1951;

Man with a Bucket of Ashes, Stage, CBC, 4 May 1952;

The Ghost in the Corpse, Playhouse, CBC, 10 June 1952;

Your World is a Plastic Platter, Stage, CBC, 1 March 1953;

Stand-in for a Murder, Ways of Mankind, CBC, 16 April 1953;

Desert Soliloquy, Ways of Mankind, CBC, 23 April 1953;

Sticks and Stones, Ways of Mankind, CBC, 14 May 1953;

Cold Comfort and Candy Floss, Stage, CBC, 1 November 1953;

Erkki's Boots, Dominion Radio Theatre, CBC, 18 May 1954;

Down Payment for a House, Summer Stage, CBC, 4 July 1954;

Cottage for Sale, Wednesday Night, CBC, 10 August 1955;

A Girl Named Pearl, Summer Stage, CBC, 4 September 1955;

The Widow of the Mississagi, Stage, CBC, 8 January 1956;

The Death of a Bitter Dream, Famous Canadian Trials, CBC, 24 September 1958;

The Cry of a Loon over the Water, Premiere on the Air, CBC, 11 November 1958;

Tomorrow We Hunt, 2 parts, Stage, CBC, 25 January and 1 February 1959;

Lilith, Stage, CBC, 6 December 1959;

Smallears, Stage, CBC, 17 January 1960;

Lukasee, Stage, CBC, 10 June 1960;

Passenger Pigeon Pie, Stage, CBC, 2 October 1960;

Joe Katona, Stage, CBC, 5 November 1961;

The Great Hunger, Stage, CBC, 20 March 1962;

Mathematics Tea, Late Night Theatre, CBC, 16 November 1962;

Shadow of Doubt, Famous Canadian Trials, CBC, 17 February 1963;

The Winter Nobody Got Younger, Sunday Night, CBC, 31 May 1964;

François' Mother, Mid-Week Theatre, CBC, 23 December 1964;

The Two-Faced Angel, Mid-Week Theatre, CBC, 12 May 1965;

The Old Man's House, Sunday Night, CBC, 29 August 1965;

Congreve with Bullet Holes, Stage, CBC, 13 February 1966;

Sunflowers in the Sea, Stage, CBC, 8 May 1966;

Architects, Stage, CBC, 8 January 1967;

The Trouble with Giants, Stereo Theatre, CBC, 17 February 1967;

Some Days You Have to Hit Somebody, Playhouse, CBC, 18 February 1967;

John A's Alchemist, FM Theatre, CBC, 6 March 1967;

Gently, Gently, My Countrymen, Stage, CBC, 28 May 1967;

The Private War on Nan White Beach, Stage, CBC, 1 June 1969;

Somebody at the Door, Studio, CBC, 5 October 1969;

Sir John Alexander Macdonald, Canadian School Broadcasts, CBC, 30 January 1970;

Sir Wilfred Laurier, Canadian School Broadcasts, CBC, 6 February 1970;

Sir Robert Borden, Canadian School Broadcasts, CBC, 13 February 1970;

To Keep the Lightning Out, Tuesday Night, CBC, 10 March 1970;

Miss Flowers Loves Mr. Death, Stage, CBC, 7 August 1971;

The Workingman, Stage, CBC, 1 September 1973;

Women in the Attic, Tuesday Night, CBC, 5 November 1974;

Return to Saint Malo, Stage, CBC, 3 November 1975;

Virgil Kelley, Stage, CBC, 22 November 1975;

Etienne Brule, Playhouse, CBC, 11 January 1976;

Dreamy, Nightfall, CBC, 25 December 1981;

Evariste Galois, Saturday Theatre, CBC, 19 November 1983;

Heroes of Science, Morningside, CBC, 28 May 1984;

The Life and Times of Cervantes, Morningside, CBC, 9 September 1985;

Perfect Game, Sunday Matinee, CBC, 6 April 1986.

OTHER: *Stand-in for Murder, Desert Soliloquy, Home Sweet Home,* and *Sticks and Stones,* in *Ways of Mankind: Thirteen Dramas of Peoples of the World and How They Live,* edited by Wal-

ter Goldschmidt (Boston: Beacon, 1954), pp. 11-19, 53-62, 95-105, 166-174;

Billy Bishop and the Red Baron, in *A Collection of Canadian Plays,* volume 4, edited by Rolf Kalman (Toronto: Simon & Pierre, 1975), pp. D26-D62;

Man with a Bucket of Ashes, in *All the Bright Company: Radio Drama Produced by Andrew Allan,* edited by Howard Fink and John Jackson (Kingston, Ont.: Quarry / Toronto: CBC Enterprises, 1987), pp. 139-169.

PERIODICAL PUBLICATIONS: *Return to Saint Malo, Quarry,* 28 (Summer 1979): 31-43;

"With Freedom in Their Eye . . . ," *Canadian Theatre Review,* 36 (Fall 1982): 23-29.

One of Canada's most prolific and varied playwrights, Len Peterson has written more than one thousand radio plays (original and adaptations), forty television scripts, several film scripts, musicals, and stage plays (many of them unpublished), for both adults and children. He is also one of Canada's first playwrights to make a living writing full-time, beginning his career in radio in 1939. Peterson is best known for his socially critical plays: for radio, *They're All Afraid* (1944), *Burlap Bags* (1946), and *Joe Katona* (1961); for television, *Ice on Fire* (1957); for the stage, *The Great Hunger* (1960).

Leonard Byron Peterson was born in Regina on 15 March 1917, the only son of Nels and Marion Peterson. He was educated at Regina's Kitchener Public School and Scott Collegiate, from which he graduated in 1935. In high school Peterson excelled at many sports, including football and wrestling. He went on to a general arts degree at Luther College (1935-1936) in Regina but left the program disillusioned and, in 1936, enrolled in mathematics and science at Northwestern University, Chicago, where he received a bachelor of science degree in three years.

During his time in Chicago, Peterson began to write, no doubt touched by the golden age of radio in the United States. Encouraged by his professors, he decided to make writing his career and, in 1939, moved to Toronto to realize his goal. In 1942 Andrew Allan, then head of drama for the CBC in Vancouver, produced Peterson's play *Look at One of Those Faces,* which he had sent from army camp in Ontario. During his service Peterson continued to send scripts to Allan and to Esse Ljungh, who was producing plays out of the Winnipeg studio. On the recommendation of

RETURN TO SAINT-MALO

RONSARD AND MARGUERITE SITTING LEFT AND RIGHT

1

SOUND: Bells: move from the to:

RONSARD: Speak up, confess louder, my child. I cannot hear you, God cannot hear you.

Marguerite: Father, I have sinned too ...

RONSARD: It is a long list you have —

SOUND:

Marguerite:

RONSARD: Island of Demons?

marguerite: (Excitedly) In that big gulf, St. Lawrence? Your uncle put you on that island and left you? You are Marguerite de La Rocque.

marguerite: No! How do you know me?

Ronsard: And your uncle Jean-François de La Rocque de Roberval?

SOUND: Marguerite climbing out of the confession box

Marguerite: no, no, no, no

Ronsard: Wait! Marguerite! Don't run away!

SOUND: Bells suddenly loud and clamorous and out!

marguerite: (Startled, half-screams) Ohh! Let go of me!

Ronsard: Where is my son? ... will you? Here in Saint-Malo

marguerite: your son?

Ronsard: André?

marguerite: you? André's father?

Ronsard: Pierre Ronsard, yes!

Marguerite: But a monk?

Ronsard: No, no.

marguerite:

Ronsard:

marguerite:

Page from the manuscript for Peterson's radio play Return to Saint Malo, *broadcast on the CBC series* Stage *in November 1975 (Len Peterson Papers, Special Collections Division, University of Calgary Library; by permission of the author)*

243

his commanding officer, Peterson was sent to Ottawa to write documentaries about the war and army life.

In 1943, while stationed in Ottawa, Peterson met Allan. Allan had just been appointed the national supervisor of drama for the CBC and was asking writers about the kind of drama series to which they might want to contribute. Peterson influenced Allan's opinion about the series greatly: in his autobiography, *Andrew Allan: A Self-Portrait* (1974), Allan notes that these conversations had "more than any other factor, moved me to undertake a series which would give writers the chance they wanted." In fact, the *Stage* series, as it was to be called, gained its fame–and notoriety–because its writers wrote as they thought, and none more than Peterson.

Stage aired in January 1944, and Peterson wrote the fourth, fifth, and sixth plays in the first half-season. Of the three–*Now, Does He Know What He's Getting?* (which aired 13 February), *Within the Fortress* (20 February), and *They're All Afraid* (27 February)–the last play provoked public controversy. The play chronicles a young man's discovery of fear in Canada–in the workplace, at home, and in personal relationships. The subject matter angered listeners who wrote and called the CBC. CBC officials complained to Allan, saying that the play undermined wartime morale, but Allan staunchly defended Peterson and his script. In fact, Allan submitted the script to the Ohio State radio competitions where it won first prize, displacing all the American entries.

This episode characterizes both Peterson as a writer and Canadian radio in the 1940s and 1950s: bold and socially critical. Peterson continued to write these kinds of plays, the most important of which were: *Maybe in a Thousand Years* (1944), about an interracial marriage; *Burlap Bags* (Ohio State winner, 1946); *Man with a Bucket of Ashes* (1952), about a father's sacrifice of his son; and *Joe Katona*, about a falsely imprisoned farm hand (commissioned for CBC's twenty-fifth anniversary and an Ohio State winner, 1961). During CBC's Golden Age, Peterson wrote almost two hundred original plays and twenty adaptations, often completing a script every two weeks. Through the 1960s he wrote for, among others, Ljungh, Allan's successor on *Stage*. He won an ACTRA award for his radio play *The Trouble with Giants* (1967), about the erosion of Lithuanian culture under Germany and Russia. Peterson's compassion for, and interest in, the figure of the un-

derdog struggling against impersonal forces, exhibits itself in all these plays.

Peterson wrote documentary dramas for both radio and film. In radio he wrote for the entire run of *In Search of Ourselves* (1948-1954), a series produced by CBC's Talks and Public Affairs Department with the help of the Canadian Mental Health Association. These plays were educational: they dramatized case histories of fictional characters who were then analyzed by Dr. J. D. M. Griffin, the consulting psychiatrist for the program. Like other series of the era, *In Search of Citizens* (about new immigrants), *Return Journey* (about prisoners and ex-prisoners), *What Makes You Sick* (about psychosomatic illness), *In Search of Ourselves* represents the CBC's strong commitment to social issues and public education.

Similarly, the National Film Board borrowed documentary techniques and educational goals from its war propaganda programs. Peterson worked briefly for the NFB immediately after World War II on such projects as *Summer's for Kids* but wrote less than a dozen scripts by the time he stopped working for the Board in the 1950s. In 1948 his film *The Bell Singers*, a documentary on the singing group, won first prize at the international Milan Film Festival.

In 1951 Peterson married Iris Rowles, and they had a daughter, Teresa, in 1952. (She died in 1958.) Other children followed: Ingrid (1954), Jill (1956), Wendy (1959), and Anthony (1964). While his family was young, Peterson became active in the Toronto theater. In 1951 a group of CBC radio writers, actors, and directors–principally Peterson, John Drainie, Lorne Greene, and Glen Frankfurter–founded the Jupiter Theatre "to produce plays of repute, both classic and contemporary, and to promote the production of plays by Canadian dramatists." In its three years of productions, Jupiter Theatre, which opened with Bertolt Brecht's *Galileo*, staged plays by Jean-Paul Sartre, Christopher Fry, Eugene O'Neill, Tennessee Williams, and Luigi Pirandello, as well as Canadian works by such writers as Lister Sinclair, Ted Allan, and Nathan Cohen. Two years after the dissolution of Jupiter Theatre in 1954, Peterson helped to found the Canadian Theatre Centre (a branch of the International Theatre Institute) which promoted an "international exchange of knowledge and practice in theatre arts"; he was its president when it disbanded in 1972. In promoting Canadian plays, in January 1972 Peterson helped found Playwright's Co-op,

*Dust jacket for Peterson's play about a Cree Indian who steals
a cow to feed his starving people*

which "exists to serve the Canadian playwright and the Canadian theatrical community," primarily through publishing contemporary Canadian plays in script form. Playwright's Co-op has published his plays *Burlap Bags* (1972), *Women in the Attic* (1972), and *Let's Make a World* (1973).

In the 1950s, too, Peterson wrote for the newly created CBC-TV. In 1953 he adapted his radio play *They're All Afraid* for television. The play was broadcast during the first season of the live series *Playbill;* it was published in book form in 1981. In 1957 Peterson wrote for the drama series *First Performance* which commissioned television scripts from Canadian writers. *Ice on Fire*, a look at violence in hockey, is considered his best television script. Peterson also contributed to CBC's *Q for Quest*, an anthology series of experimental, half-hour dramas, and to such series as *GM Presents;* he continued to write for television into the 1970s.

Like his work in radio and television, Peterson's stage work spans several decades. In November 1960 the Arts Theatre in Toronto produced one of his best-known works, *The Great Hunger*. Set in an Eskimo camp in the Arctic, the play dramatizes the fulfilling of an Eskimo law of retribution when a father kills his adopted son, despite a white man's teachings of Christian forgiveness. In August 1970 the Young People's Theatre in Toronto produced Peterson's best children's play, the one-act *Almighty Voice*, about the government's hunt for Almighty Voice, a Cree Indian who stole a cow to feed his starving people. Peterson has said that *The Ways of Mankind*, a CBC radio series for which he wrote in 1953, contributed significantly to his appreciation of, and interest in, anthropology, an influence on both *The Great Hunger* and *Almighty Voice*.

Of Peterson's many plays, *Burlap Bags* has been presented in three of the media Peterson has tried: radio, television, and the stage. First broadcast on Andrew Allan's *Stage* series on 3 February 1946, *Burlap Bags* received mixed reviews: some listeners applauded its bold and exciting new techniques which depicted the dehumanization of people in contemporary society; others condemned the theme and the suppressed anger they perceived in the presentation. (It was broadcast four more times on radio; twice on *Stage*, in 1949 and 1965; twice on other CBC drama programs, in 1952 and 1954.) The play dramatizes the diary of a tramp named Tannahill who has committed suicide in a rooming house. The diary is read aloud by two other roomers who have gone through his possessions. It chronicles an absurd world filled with disembodied, nonsensical voices, people wearing shackles, characters whose names are Frustrated, Bored, Cautious, Bewildered, and Disillusioned. All don burlap bags to hide from the frustration, boredom, disillusionment, and absurdity of life. Thwarted in his attempts to help these people, Tannahill looks for a burlap bag himself, finds they are all taken, and kills himself. Having finished the diary, the roomers dismiss Tannahill's nightmare vision and make plans to go to the beer parlor and sneak into a movie. Many critics have identified the play as an early example of the theater of the absurd; others see its techniques as primarily expressionistic. In either case Peterson touched on postwar anxiety in a striking, and radiophonically successful, way.

Primarily because the play presents the mental workings of Tannahill's mind–in a series of distorted images and fragments of dialogue–its adaptation to the television screen was not entirely successful. Broadcast on 3 January 1960 on CBC's *Q for Quest* (directed by Harvey Hart), the television version tries to re-create the fluidity of the radio original with techniques such as a wavy scrim and gobbos, or patterns of light. Despite strong performances, the play is more hampered than aided by the visual medium. Peterson also adapted the play for the stage the same year, which was produced by Toronto Workshop Productions.

Peterson continues to write for radio. Recently, he has been working on "The Magic Mirror," a children's play, which is scheduled for production by the Carousel Players of Saint Catharines, Ontario, during their 1989-1990 season. Given his interest in social criticism and his prolific career, Peterson will no doubt provide his audiences with many more plays which challenge and disturb.

Reference:

Sheila Sim, "Tragedy and Ritual in *The Great Hunger* and *Rita Joe*," *Canadian Drama*, 1 (Spring 1975): 27-32.

Papers:

Len Peterson's papers are at the University of Calgary Library.

Al Purdy

(30 December 1918-   )

George Woodcock

BOOKS: *The Enchanted Echo* (Vancouver: Clarke & Stuart, 1944);

Pressed on Sand (Toronto: Ryerson, 1955);

Emu, Remember! (Fredericton: Fiddlehead Poetry Books, 1956);

The Crafte So Long to Lerne (Toronto: Ryerson, 1959);

Poems for All the Annettes (Toronto: Contact, 1962; enlarged edition, Toronto: Anansi, 1968; enlarged again, 1973);

The Blur in Between: Poems 1960-61 (Toronto: Emblem Books, 1962);

The Cariboo Horses (Toronto: McClelland & Stewart, 1965);

North of Summer (Toronto: McClelland & Stewart, 1967);

Wild Grape Wine (Toronto: McClelland & Stewart, 1968);

Love in a Burning Building (Toronto: McClelland & Stewart, 1970);

The Quest for Ouzo (Trenton, Ont.: Kerrigan Almy, 1971);

Hiroshima Poems (Trumansburg, N.Y.: Crossing, 1972);

Selected Poems (Toronto: McClelland & Stewart, 1972);

On the Bearpaw Sea (Burnaby, B.C.: Blackfish, 1973);

Sex and Death (Toronto: McClelland & Stewart, 1973);

In Search of Owen Roblin (Toronto: McClelland & Stewart, 1974);

The Poems of Al Purdy: A New Canadian Library Selection (Toronto: McClelland & Stewart, 1976);

Sundance at Dusk (Toronto: McClelland & Stewart, 1976);

A Handful of Earth (Coatsworth, Ont.: Black Moss, 1977);

At Marsport Drugstore (Sutton West, Ont.: Paget, 1977);

Moths in the Iron Curtain (Cleveland: Black Rabbit, 1977; Sutton West, Ont.: Paget, 1979);

No Other Country (Toronto: McClelland & Stewart, 1977);

No Second Spring (Coatsworth, Ont.: Black Moss, 1977);

Being Alive: Poems 1958-78 (Toronto: McClelland & Stewart, 1978);

Al Purdy in 1965 (photograph by John Reeves)

The Stone Bird (Toronto: McClelland & Stewart, 1981);

Birdwatching at the Equator: The Galapagos Islands Poems (Sutton West, Ont.: Paget, 1982);

Bursting Into Song: An Al Purdy Omnibus (Windsor, Ont.: Black Moss, 1982);

Morning and It's Summer: A Memoir (Dunvegan, Ont.: Quadrant Editions, 1983);

Piling Blood (Toronto: McClelland & Stewart, 1984);

The Collected Poems of Al Purdy, edited by Russell Brown (Toronto: McClelland & Stewart, 1986).

OTHER: *The New Romans: Candid Canadian Opinions of the U.S.*, edited by Purdy (Edmonton: Hurtig, 1968);

Fifteen Winds: A Selection of Modern Canadian Poems, edited by Purdy (Toronto: Ryerson, 1969);

I've Tasted My Blood: Poems of Milton Acorn, edited by Purdy (Toronto: Ryerson, 1969);

Storm Warning: The New Canadian Poets, edited by Purdy (Toronto: McClelland & Stewart, 1971);

Storm Warning 2: The New Canadian Poets, edited by Purdy (Toronto: McClelland & Stewart, 1976);

Wood Mountain Poems, edited by Purdy (Toronto: Macmillan, 1976);

R. G. Everson, *Everson at Eighty*, introduction by Purdy (Ottawa: Oberon, 1983).

When Al Purdy published his fourth book of poems in 1959 (the first book of his that critics took seriously) under the title of *The Crafte So Long to Lerne*, he was wryly celebrating the long period of apprenticeship in which he had begun to find his own poetic voice. He was then forty-one, having been born in 1918 in the small agricultural community of Wooler in southeastern Ontario. His father was a farmer, and his Loyalist ancestors, who came to Upper Canada in the 1780s during the years after the American War of Independence, had lived in that area for a century and a third. Much of his poetry has celebrated these forebears and the land which they won from the wilderness and which by the time of his early manhood the bush was already reclaiming. As he wrote in "My Grandfather's Country" (collected in *Being Alive,* 1978):

> and if I must commit myself to love
> to any one thing
> it will be here in the red glow
> where failed farms sink back into earth
> the clearings join and fences no longer divide
> where the running animals gather their bodies
>   together
> and pour themselves upwards
> into the tips of falling leaves
> with mindless faith that presumes a future.

Purdy was already writing poems at the age of thirteen, but it took half a life of experience for him to find, in middle age, that characteristic and colloquial voice which has made him, in two senses of the word, one of the most popular of modern Canadian poets. He has claimed, doubtless ironically, that he came of "degenerate Loyalist stock," though his father, Alfred Wellington Purdy, seems to have been a capable and successful farmer, running a large apple orchard as well as an efficient mixed farm. But he was fifty-eight when Al was born, and two years later he died of cancer.

Al and his mother, Eleanor Louisa Ross Purdy, moved to Trenton, into a red brick house that in 1921 was more than a hundred years old. As Purdy remembered in *Morning and It's Summer* (1983): "The floors were sagging upstairs and down, as if the house was tired from all these years and couldn't stand properly upright any longer. Some of the doors wouldn't open or close without a struggle. At night when I was awake and listening, small noises came from everywhere: the sound of old floor joists, boards and square-headed nails talking together." (The house was still standing, more or less as Purdy described it, in 1968.)

Purdy grew up in Trenton. He was educated at the Dufferin Public School there, and later at Albert College in Belleville and at the Trenton Collegiate Institute, but like several of the best contemporary Canadian poets, he had no university training. Indeed, he left school after grade ten, and at the age of seventeen he rode the rods to Vancouver. Returning to Trenton, he took whatever small odd jobs were available during the Depression years. In 1940 he

joined the Royal Canadian Air Force, and in 1941 he married Eurithe Parkhurst, to whom, forty-five years later, he would dedicate his *Collected Poems* (1986). Purdy's service was noncombatant. Indeed, he spent some of it at the remote airbase of Woodcock, beside the Skeena River in British Columbia, and did other stints at Vancouver and Ottawa.

After the war Purdy lived partly in British Columbia but mostly in Ontario where, at Ameliasburgh, in the country of his ancestors he built with his own hands in 1957 the house that figures in his many poems and to which he returns, as to a spiritual retreat, after his travels. He worked at many jobs, including a period of five years in a Vancouver mattress factory; he never settled into any regular job, and perhaps the principal reason for this was that, even though he did not have much early success, he increasingly regarded the writing of poetry as his true vocation.

It was not until the 1960s, when the Canada Council began operation with programs that enabled writers to work without always being concerned about earnings, that Purdy began to be liberated from the need to find casual jobs to keep himself alive while he wrote. He won his first Canada Council fellowship in 1960 and others later in the decade, and as his work became better known he was able to supplement his small income from publishing poems by lecturing and reading poetry. During the later 1960s, indeed, he became a popular reader at Canadian universities and also a restless traveler. Over the years he has journeyed through Canada from Newfoundland to the west coast of Vancouver Island, and north to Baffin Island; to Cuba, Mexico, Turkey, Greece, Italy, France, Spain, Japan, and Africa. He is a writer "for whom the visible world exists" (to borrow Théophile Gautier's phrase) palpably and directly, and travel has always played a role in shaping much of his poetry, just as the combination of his literary ambitions and a working-class style of living have helped him develop its earthy anecdotal quality. But Purdy's world, however broad his wanderings may have made it, still swings inward to the place that gives a name to so many of his poems and appears as the symbolic center of his imaginative world, Roblin Lake in deep Loyalist country near Ameliasburgh.

Purdy's first book, *The Enchanted Echo*, is a sixty-two-page volume which he paid a Vancouver printer to produce in 1944; there were five-hundred copies and for years they hung on

Purdy's hands, though now a copy fetches a high price in the rare-book market. It was a conservatively traditional book, clearly written by a young poet who was unaware of the kind of poetry being published in such Canadian magazines of the 1940s as *First Statement* and *Preview,* and who had not even advanced to the standpoint of modernism which had been established in Canada in the 1930s by F. R. Scott, A. J. M. Smith, and the other poets associated with the *McGill Fortnightly Review.* In this first book Purdy presented himself as the student of Rudyard Kipling and G. K. Chesterton (in this–let us not forget–agreeing with Jorge Luis Borges) and a disciple of the so-called Confederation poets–or, to be more specific, of the two Confederation poets who are now less highly regarded, Charles G. D. Roberts and Bliss Carman. The title poem of *The Enchanted Echo* in fact reads like a good Carman poem; and if it did not proclaim the originality of the writer, it did at least show Purdy's sensitivity and his potential skill.

> I saw the milkweed float away,
> To curtsy, climb and hover,
> And seek among the crowded hills
> Another warmer lover.
>
> Across the autumn flushing streams,
> Adown the misty valleys,
> Atop the skyline's sharp redoubts,
> Aswarm with coloured alleys–
>
> I caught an echo in my hands,
> With pollen mixed for leaven–
> I gave it half my song to hold,
> And sent it back to heaven.
>
> Now oft, anon, as in a dream,
> O'er sculptured heights ascending,
> I hear a song–my song, but now,
> It has another ending.

That is fairly competent pastiche rather than good poetry, but it shows already that ability to absorb and use–and then finally reject–influences that in the end would make Purdy one of the most difficult poets to relate to any school or movement.

More than a decade passed before Purdy was heard from again, except in occasional poems in fugitive periodicals. Then in the mid 1950s two publishers took risks on his work–but very small ones. Ryerson Press published as a sixteen-page chapbook in 1955 his *Pressed on Sand,* and the year after, Fred Cogswell at Fiddle-

head Books brought out his *Emu, Remember!,* also sixteen pages. A touch of Purdy casualness began to appear in these brief booklets, but they were still largely dominated by the sentimental and formal criteria of an earlier age. Yet somewhere within this carapace of convention a true poet was waiting to find the voice that would give expression to his experience and his special view of existence. That discovery took place somewhere between the publication of *Emu, Remember!* in 1956 and that of *The Crafte So Long to Lerne,* with its ironically archaic title, in 1959, as Purdy's second Ryerson chapbook. In his afterword to *The Collected Poems of Al Purdy* Dennis Lee convincingly places the beginning of Purdy's emergence in the period from 1955 to 1957 when Purdy lived in Montreal and for the first time seems to have entered a real circle of poets. They were, largely, the poets who had made Montreal a center of poetic modernism during the 1940s, notably Irving Layton and Louis Dudek, and to a lesser extent Milton Acorn, who was a working-class apprentice poet rather like Purdy himself. These poets were catalysts rather than influences so far as Purdy was concerned. They encouraged him to shed the archaic manner and the formal conventions of his earlier work and to discover his own voice, which he did–surprisingly–without adopting theirs on the way.

By the time Purdy left Montreal in 1957 and built his house at Ameliasburgh, he had decided to dedicate himself wholly to writing, while, with a faith in her husband perhaps greater than his own, Eurithe Purdy worked to keep a minimum of cash flowing into the house on Roblin Lake. Having been content to serve his apprenticeship under the Victorian and Georgian minor masters, he now set out to create a style and a poetic persona that were entirely individual. He was open to learn from other poets, and he had admitted to many influences, "including the usual big names (Pound, Eliot, Yeats); also César Vallejo, Neruda, Superveille, Charles Bukowski, Robinson Jeffers, etc., etc." (It is significant of his universalist attitude toward the craft of poetry, as distinct from his regionalist attitude toward its content, that he includes no Canadian on this list.) But he has avoided the group loyalties of schools and cenacles and indeed has deliberately avoided creating a single style of his own. Talking of the Black Mountain poets, he once said: "I do not dismiss these people and believe it is possible to learn much from them but only IF one remains oneself, something most of them ap-

GOVERNOR-GENERAL'S AWARD 1966
PRESIDENT'S MEDAL 1964

AL PURDY

poems
for all the Annettes

$2.50

Poems for all the Annettes has been unobtainable for years. First published in 1962 by Contact Press, it was the culmination of two decades of development and exploration. In the 1968 Ansnsi edition, Purdy has revised many poems, dropped others, and carried in still others from his early chap-books and pamphlets. The result is a robust and dazzling collection from the leading poet in Canada.

photograph by Michael Ondaatje

"One of the few very good poets since 1900."
- Charles Bukowski

"Purdy is the hottest poet in the country."
- Robert Weaver

"Purdy is now on common grounds with the very best of North America's poets."
- Alan Bevin

"Al Purdy, of all Canadian poets publishing today, is surely the most admired for the originality and honesty and power of his voice."
- Earle Birney

Covers for the 1968 edition of a collection described by Purdy as marking "the transitional period between what I was and am and change into"

parently find difficult. I believe that when a poet fixes on one style or method he severely limits his present and future development. By the same token I dislike the traditional methods of rhyme and metre when used without variation, ditto traditional forms. But I use rhyme, metre and (occasionally) standard forms when a poem seems to call for it."

The remaking of himself as a poet was a slow process, as is apparent when one compares his limited output in the late 1950s and early 1960s with the flood of writing he achieved from the mid 1960s onward when he became certain of his directions. From 1965, when he published *The Cariboo Horses,* he has published steadily; in some years he has produced more than one volume. But during the period of self-discovery he moved less certainly. *The Crafte So Long to Lerne*–a tiny book–appeared in 1959; *Poems for All the Annettes,* accompanied by another tiny book, *The*

Blur in Between, in 1962. *The Cariboo Horses* established him as a major presence in Canadian poetry and won him his first Governor General's Award, and from that point he moved rapidly forward.

Some critics have seen *The Cariboo Horses* as the book in which Purdy emerges as an individual voice. He himself saw *Poems for All the Annettes* and *The Blur in Between* as marking, three years earlier, "the transitional period between what I was and am and change into." Until that time, he felt "other people's styles were apparent in my stuff." But to many close readers the opening of forms and the establishment of a philosophic continuum that are characteristic of the later Purdy first became evident in *The Crafte So Long to Lerne.*

Dipping into those crucial years of the mid 1950s from which that book emerged, one finds characteristic Purdy themes and tropes develop-

250

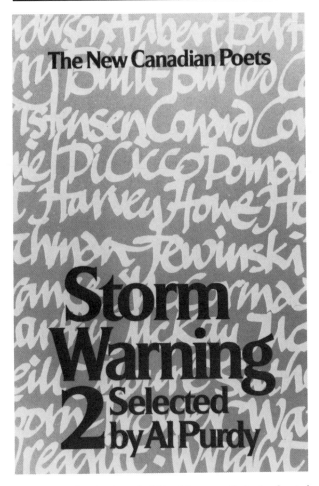

Front cover for the second of Purdy's two anthologies devoted to the works of young poets. "It attempts," he writes in the introduction, "to sneak a glance at the future like a storm warning, alerting us to some of the people who may rock literary boats in Canada at some distant date."

ing. Take, for example, "Elegy for a Grandfather," from *Emu, Remember!*:

> Well, he died, didn't he? They said he did.
> His wide whalebone hips will make a prehistoric
>   barrow,
> A kitchen midden for mice under the rough sod,
> Where relatives stood in real and pretended sor-
>   row
> For the dearly beloved gone at last to God,
> After a bad century–a tough, turbulent Pharaoh
> With a deck of cards in his pocket and a Presby-
>   terian grin.
>
> Well, maybe he did die, but the boy didn't see it;
> The man knows now and the whimsical tale is told
> Of a lying lumberjack with a fist like a piece of
>   suet,
> A temper like toppling timber and splinter-
>   ing words to scald

> The holy ears of an angel–and a beautiful man
>   in a riot;
> But a bright, bragging boy's hero with a pocket
>   full of gold.
> Like a neolithic swear word from the opposite
>   end of time.
>
> No doubt at all that he's dead: a sadly virtu-
>   ous voice
> Folded tragedy sideways and glossed his glitter-
>   ing sins.
> Old in his ancient barrow and no-one could
>   ever guess
> If the shy fox people play with his gnarled
>   grey bones,
> Or a green Glengarry river sluices his grave
>   and sighs.
> And earth has another tenant involved in her
>   muttering plans,
> With a deck of cards in his pocket and a Presby-
>   terian grin.

The form is still only half liberated: iambics lapsing into irregularity and half-rhymes rather than full ones. But the way of speaking has changed. The tone is conversational moving toward the familiar or colloquial, and the lines are freer than before. But more important are the characteristic Purdy themes and philosophic stances beginning to fall into shape. There is the sense of a personal, and familial, history (the grandfather will appear in Purdy's poems again and again) that expands into Loyalist and Canadian history. There is the sense of a local geography that illuminates a familiar landscape, a sense of locality transplanted from southeastern Ontario to the high Arctic and the Aegean Sea. And there is the inclination to relate proximate and therefore reasonably precise history to ancient history where actuality blurs into myth; Grandfather becomes a Pharaoh as well as a Presbyterian (a typical Purdy comic incongruity here!) and ends up "a neolithic swear word from the opposite end of time."

Historic Purdy, erudite Purdy, two aspects of the poetic persona that will become familiar in later volumes, are already evident in poems of the later 1950s, in the pastiche in the manner of the Chinese T'ang poets, "From the Chi P'ing Mei," and in the ironic gloss on the disappointing nature of the Minoan documents–account books mostly–revealed when Michael Ventris finally deciphered "Linear B." In the latter poem, entitled "On the Decipherment of Linear B," the pedant's vision and the poet's vision are clearly–and characteristically–contrasted when Purdy ends, having had his fun with the earnest scholars, with a romantic declaration that reveals another side of his emerging poetic persona:

> But Knossos did burn, its flaming windows
> signalled the stars 3,000 years ago:
> when men died foetal, rolled into blackened balls,
> and women, abandoned by children and lovers,
> fled to the palace upper rooms with skirts on fire:
> and over the island a south wind blowing[.]

By the early 1960s the style is liberated, and the persona has moved toward full development. In *Poems for All the Annettes* the traditional rigors of form are no longer there even as vestiges, and the historic and erudite Purdy is subsumed in the comic, lecherous, scatological, bibulous Purdy living out his disreputable pastorals beside Roblin Lake. Mockery and self-mockery emerge as dominant elements and continue to characterize one of Purdy's poetic voices. They are exemplified in the parodic structure of "Spring Song," with the poet as lecherous rustic god and the farm girl as provocative nymph:

> Old father me
> in the classic rural tradition
> listening to frogs
> larrup loopholes in silence
> making sexual abstinence the ultimate
> BLASPHEMY
> Rabbits turn annoyed
> having shat in the garbage all winter
> they dislike this noisy interruption
> and skitter into the willows
> Crying birds of passage
> are overheard in the clouds plotting
> a better world for starlings
> Old father me
> doing pushups under an ancient Pontiac
> attempting to change the oil

> Include me out of it all?
> Never
>   so long as the farm girl has
> my two soft-boiled eyes twinkling
> hard against her jiggling jelly buttocks
> swaying down the lane to the mailbox
> wearing shorts in figleaf weather
> I'm obscurely gratified but rueful too
>   at the young man's vehement twitching
> lechery
>   inside an old man's
>   voyeur-masochistic morals
> under a senile Pontiac in the butter-yellow
> sunlight attempting to change the oil[.]

Certainly with the appearance of *The Cariboo Horses* Purdy was writing at the top of his individual form, having developed a long-lined and colloquially free manner and an ability to be intellectually direct—even at times didactic—without sacrificing the suggestive depths of poetic imagery. He was drawing freely on the funds of miscellaneous knowledge that a generalizing and self-educated mind tends to accumulate. Yet though he was densely allusive, he was never obscure. As a reader he moved through history, just as a traveler he wandered physically over a great part of the twentieth-century world. Many of his poems show a remarkable ability to bring images drawn from great sweeps of time and space into a meaningful relationship with what he sees before him in the everyday contemporary world. For example, watching cowboys' horses in a British Columbia inland village, he can end that crucial poem "The Cariboo Horses" with an extraordinary evocation of the equine past and present, seen as an oblique gloss on human history:

> Only horses
>   no stopwatch memories or palace
>   ancestors
> not Kiangs hauling undressed stone in the Nile
>   Valley
> and having stubborn Egyptian tantrums or
> Onagers racing through Hither Asia and
> the last Quagga screaming in African highlands
>   lost relatives of those
>   whose hooves are thunder
> the ghosts of horses battering thru the wind
> whose names were the wind's common usage
> whose life was the sun's
>   arriving here at chilly noon
>   in the gasoline smell of the
>   dusk and waiting 15 minutes
>   at the grocer's.

Purdy's arrival at maturity as a poet corresponded with a shift in his life-style. He ceased completely to be the itinerant casual worker, and from then on his travels became the wanderings of a writer committed to earn his living by his craft. He has, most important, continued to write poems until, with his *Collected Poems*, the number of volumes has reached beyond two dozen (twenty-six), not counting broadsheets and pamphlets. He has written more than a dozen radio and television plays, but radio and television are ephemeral media, and up to now none of his drama has been published. He has commented with a poet's judgment, in reviews written for such journals as *Canadian Literature*, on the work of other poets, though he has never ventured on major critical articles. During the 1970s he wrote travel essays and anecdotal portraits of people and places which were published in such journals as *Maclean's* and *Weekend* magazine, and a collection of them eventually appeared under the title of *No Other Country* (1977); they were idiosyncratic and impressionistic, and occasionally, as in his account of a meeting with Roderick Haig-Brown ("Cougar Hunter") or in his sympathetic account of the alcoholic troubles of Malcolm Lowry ("Malcolm Lowry"), they showed great psychological insight into the minds and moods of fellow writers. A later work, half prose, half verse, that is important in the Purdy canon is *Morning and It's Summer*, which consists of a long essay about his childhood–his only published autobiographical work in prose–and a group of poems about figures from his childhood which show how strongly autobiographical his verse also is.

In addition he has edited three verse anthologies–*Fifteen Winds: A Selection of Modern Canadian Poems* (1969), *Storm Warning: The New Canadian Poets* (1971), and *Storm Warning 2* (1976)–and a polemical prose anthology, *The New Romans: Candid Canadian Opinions of the U.S.* (1968), which evokes echoes of his Loyalist past, since it is essentially a critique of the United States and by implication supports Canadian nationalism, which Purdy endorsed during the later 1960s (one of his few overt political stands) with his active membership on the Committee for an Independent Canada. A volume of correspondence with the American poet Charles Bukowski (whom he admits was an early influence) appeared as *The Bukowski/Purdy Letters, 1964-1974: A Decade of Dialogue* in 1983, and another volume of his correspondence, with the Canadian critic and man-of-letters George Woodcock, was published as *The George Woodcock-Al Purdy Letters* in 1987.

In addition to these excursions into the extrapoetical areas of literature, Purdy in recent years has been turning toward academic employment rather than Canada Council grants to supplement his income from poetry and other writings. He was a visiting associate professor at Simon Fraser University in 1970 and since then has taught creative writing or acted as writer in residence at a number of institutions, including the University of Manitoba, the University of Western Ontario, Loyola College, and the Banff School of Fine Arts.

In a general sense one might say that Purdy's poems since the publication of *The Cari-*

boo Horses have alternated between those that describe his wide rovings (some volumes, like the 1967 *North of Summer*, being devoted entirely to strange places) and those that reflect Purdy's probings into the past of his country and his own relationship to it. Many of the latter class of poems–"Roblin's Mill [II]," for example–are strongly elegiac in tone, celebrating the men and women who first colonized Upper Canada and created its special way of life, which itself has vanished with the men who built the old mills that have so fascinated Purdy as the last monuments to an evanescent way of life.

> The black millpond
>   holds them
> movings and reachings and fragments
> the gear and tackle of living
> under the water eye
> all things laid aside
>   discarded
>   forgotten
> but they had their being once
> and left a place to stand on.

The idea of "a place to stand on" is important to Purdy, perhaps because he realized so deeply, as he expressed it in "Wilderness Gothic," the impermanence of human ways of life:

> An age and a faith moving into transition,
> the dinner cold and new-baked bread a failure,
> deep woods shiver and water drops hang pendant,
> double-yoked eggs and the house creaks a little–
> Something is about to happen. Leaves are still.
> Two shores away, a man hammering in the sky.
> Perhaps he will fall.

Within this vision of the changing world revolving around paradoxically lasting values, Purdy pursues what he has declared to be his principal themes: "Sex and death (which last naturally includes life)," and when he unites the joy of love with the sadness of death he writes with a peculiarly romantic intensity, as in the closing stanza of one of his best poems, "Necropsy of Love":

> If death shall strip our bones of all but bones,
> then here's the flesh, and flesh that's drunken-
> sweet
> as wine cups in deceptive lunar light;
> reach up your hand and turn the moonlight off,
> and maybe it was never there at all,
> so never promise anything to me:
> but reach across the darkness with your hand,
> reach across the distance of tonight,

and touch the moving moment once again
before you fall asleep[.]

But Purdy is a poet of Protean aspects, and, as George Woodcock remarks in *The World of Canadian Writing* (1980): "after having said so much about Purdy as the history-conscious poet, the philosopher of the human condition, the geographer of the imagination, one is suddenly aware of a noisy fellow dragging at one's legs under the impression that they are wild-grape vines, and Purdy pulls one down to the earth on which, however high his head and wide his scope, his feet are surely set. For he is also the poet of comedy: picture postcard domestic comedy with nagging wives and plundering husbands; Sancho Panza greedy comedy; high low comedy as when the poet makes a mock epic out of trying to defecate in the presence of Eskimo huskies hungry for human excrement; original Dionysiac comedy in that wild drunken poem, 'The Winemaker's Beat-Etude.' "

This is the world of Purdy the plain man, the man of direct, colloquial speech, and it is a world in which sardonic comedy can flourish beside a grim sense of human actuality which makes an old woman in one poem die stuffing her false teeth up her rectum and an old man—in "Old Alex"—leave behind him a memory of venomous malice that does not entirely dissolve Purdy's sympathy for him as a human being whose individuality life did not destroy.

> I don't mourn, Nobody does. Like mourning
>   an ulcer.
> Why commemorate disease in a poem then?
> I don't know. But his hate was lovely,
> given freely and without stint. His smallness
> had the quality of making everyone else feel
>   noble,
> and thus fools. I search desperately
> for good qualities, and end up crawling
> inside that decaying head and wattled throat
> to scream obscenities like papal blessings,
> knowing now and again I'm at least God.
> Well, who remembers a small purple and yel-
>   low bruise long?
> But when he was here he was a sunset!

Good poets tend to progress until they have found their own voices, and by that time their imaginative insights and their technical abilities have reached such a harmony that they now exist on a kind of plateau of self-consistency and do not ascend any longer as much as they explore the level they have attained, and often this explora-

tion continues for many years. With Purdy it has continued since he reached his evident poetic maturity with *The Cariboo Horses* in 1965. From that time onward, numerous as his collections of poems have been, their quality has remained surprisingly consistent from volume to volume. And as long as the human character and human destiny and the natural environment continue to fascinate Purdy with their infinite variety, it is unlikely, given his accumulated skill, that he will cease to write good poetry.

A book of the 1980s, *The Stone Bird* (1981), confirms this judgment with its haunting messages of the rejuvenative power of the natural world which man has sought so hard–but up to now so fortunately in vain–to destroy. In the last verse of the first poem of this collection, "The Dead Poet" (which he would later use as the epilogue for his *Collected Poems*), Purdy's credo, with its music and wisdom and its suggestion that we are welcome back to the earth from which we came, is encompassed:

> Sleep softly spirit of earth
> as the days and nights join hands
> when everything becomes one thing
> wait softly brother
> but do not expect it to happen
> that great whoop announcing resurrection
> expect only a small whisper
> of birds nesting and green things growing
> and the brief saying of them
> and know where the words come from[.]

In the mid 1980s, as Purdy approached seventy, a volume of his poems tended to include a number of fairly constant components, and in the last collection before his *Collected Poems, Piling Blood* (1984), they are there once again: the comic poems of henpecked husband or aging, cautious lecher; the historic reconstructions of the Loyalist past; the autobiographical pieces, which in *Piling Blood* touch on every period of Purdy's life from boyhood to the present, pondering the nature of memory, the way self as well as body changes, and treating the lives of the losers who seem to have populated Purdy's life in exceptional numbers, with an even deeper compassion, more honest because more bewildered, than in the past. One especially moving poem, "My Cousin Don," is about a companion from the distant orchards and gardens of childhood whom war destroyed:

> I insist there was something, a thing of value.
> It survived when death came calling

for my friend on a Italian battlefield:
not noble, not heroic, not beautiful–
It escapes my hammering mind,
eludes any deliberate seeking,
and all I can think of
is apples apples apples[.]

The most memorable among these *spätlese*
poems are those in which the philosophical ruminations are mingled with a lyrical vision, and at
the same time the elegiac mood is suddenly light-
ened by an expression of joy in living. Typical is
the last poem in *Piling Blood*, "In the Early Creta-
ceous," in which Purdy imagines the first appearance of flowers in the age of the dinosaurs and
sees in it the splendor of unrecorded history, the
great sweep of time so vast that it becomes incomprehensible in its linking of all the world's processes in vast, inevitable, and unrememberable sequence:

> But no one will ever know
> what it was like
> that first time on primordial earth
> when bees went mad with pollen fever
> and seeds flew away from home
> on little drifting white parachutes
> without a word to their parents–
> no one can ever know
> even when someone is given
> the gift of a single rose
> and behind that one rose
> are the ancestors of all roses
> and all flowers and all the springtimes
> for a hundred thousand years
> of summer and for a moment
> in her eyes an echo
> of the first tenderness

In *Piling Blood*, as in other recent Purdy volumes, one is aware, with a feeling that grows
from page to page, not only of a general triumph of poetic workmanship but also of a depth
of vision and wisdom that few of Purdy's contemporaries have equaled. In a trope that recalls his
own images of a vanished Loyalist past, one sees
him as resembling one of those apples of vanished varieties from the orchards of our child-
hoods that ripened late and in their lofts sweet-
ened inward long into the winter. As a poet he
has aged well.

And so *The Collected Poems of Al Purdy*, which
appeared in 1986 and in the next year won him
his second Governor General's Award, was not
merely the bringing together–penultimately one

hopes–of a life's work, but also an assertion of
Purdy's position in the tradition of Canadian writing. There were other, more tentative, collections
before it: *Selected Poems* in 1972; *Being Alive:
Poems 1958-78* in 1978; *Bursting into Song: An Al
Purdy Omnibus* in 1982. But none of these has the
definitive intention of *The Collected Poems*, which
is virtually a "complete poems."

One distrusts the conventional definitions,
and when the questions arise–Is Purdy a truly
great poet? Is he a major poet?–one may be inclined to leave them unanswered and ask other
more relevant ones. Has he mastered his craft?
Does he present a self-consistent vision? Has he
produced a body of work that commands sustained respect from his peers? Has he won
Stendhal's lottery–to be read in a hundred years'
time?

Reading the thick volume of *The Collected
Poems*, four hundred pages long, in which almost
every poem still throbs with immediacy, one can
answer "Yes" to all these questions. Purdy is a
true poet, of remarkable breadth of vision and authenticity of voice. There are not many of his bet-
ters writing in English today. And one of the
signs of his ultimate success is that, while his poetic persona was dominant in the work of his middle period, in his later work it is the poem rather
than the creator that comes into the reader's vision, the artifact rather than the artificer. Purdy
in his own way recognizes this–that the poet and
even the poetic persona can die and the poem
can live–and so, in the last of the new pieces he includes in *The Collected Poems*, "Pre-Mortem," he
grants that: "A poem can have a soul / just as a
man can / the man's soul of course is unknowable /
the poem's soul may be known obliquely[,]" and
in a remarkable last verse he envisages the point
of death, when the poet is beyond awareness, but
the poem survives and continues its own life:

> For the dying man
> the world's marvelous clichés
> fade and revivify
> flush into pallor
> as the cancer feeds
> and like little lambs in springtime
> his heart skips apace
> A name is spoken in the silence
> then only the soul
> hears the name which is the poem's
> soul and no writer
> listens but the poem listens
> in a coldness which obtains
> at the fire's centre[.]

Purdy's poems will survive and are likely to remain among the classics of Canadian writing. And so *The Collected Poems of Al Purdy* is not merely a personal document, the commemoration of a life's work; it is also one of the milestones in the development of a nation's literary traditions.

Letters:

The Bukowski/Purdy Letters, 1964-1974: A Decade of Dialogue, by Purdy and Charles Bukowski, edited by Seamus Cooney (Sutton West, Ont.: Paget, 1983);

The George Woodcock-Al Purdy Letters, edited by George Galt (Toronto: ECW, 1987).

Interviews:

Alan Twigg, "Al Purdy: One of a Kind," in his *For Openers: Conversations with 24 Canadian Writers* (Madeira Park, B.C.: Harbour, 1981), pp. 1-12;

Bruce Meyer and Brian O'Riordan, "Al Purdy: The Phony, the Realistic, and the Genuine," in their *In Their Words: Interviews with Fourteen Canadian Writers* (Toronto: Anansi, 1984).

Bibliography:

Marianne Micros, "Al Purdy: An Annotated Bibliography," in *The Annotated Bibliography of Canada's Major Authors,* edited by Robert Lecker and Jack David, volume 2 (Downsview, Ont.: ECW, 1980), pp. 221-277.

References:

Margaret Atwood, "Love is Ambiguous . . . Sex is a Bully," review of *Love in a Burning Building, Canadian Literature,* 49 (Summer 1971);

George Bowering, *Al Purdy* (Toronto: Copp Clark, 1970);

Bowering, "Purdy: Man and Poet," *Canadian Literature,* 43 (Winter 1970);

Gary Geddes, "A. W. Purdy: An Interview," *Canadian Literature,* 41 (Summer 1969);

Dennis Lee, "The Poetry of Al Purdy: An Afterword," in *The Collected Poems of Al Purdy,* edited by Russell Brown (Toronto: McClelland & Stewart, 1986);

Peter Stevens, "In the Raw: The Poetry of Al Purdy," *Canadian Literature,* 28 (Summer 1966);

David Stouck, "Al Purdy," in his *Major Canadian Authors* (Lincoln: University of Nebraska Press, 1984);

George Woodcock, "On the Poetry of Al Purdy," in his *The World of Canadian Writing* (Vancouver: Douglas & McIntyre, 1980).

Papers:

Collections of Purdy's papers are at the Douglas Library, Queen's University, Kingston, Ontario, and the University of Saskatchewan Library, Saskatoon. The University of British Columbia Library, Vancouver, the Lakehead University Library, Thunder Bay, Ontario, and the Thomas Fisher Rare Book Library, University of Toronto, hold some manuscripts and drafts for Purdy's works.

John Reeves
(1 December 1926-   )

Jill Tomasson Goodwin
University of Waterloo

BOOKS: *A Beach of Strangers: An Excursion* (Toronto: Oxford University Press, 1961);
Triptych (Toronto: CBC Enterprises, 1972);
The Arithmetic of Love (Toronto: 68 Publishers, 1975);
Murder by Microphone (Toronto & Garden City, N.Y.: Doubleday, 1978);
Murder Before Matins (Toronto & Garden City, N.Y.: Doubleday, 1984);
Murder with Muskets (Toronto & Garden City, N.Y.: Doubleday, 1985);
Death in Prague (Toronto: Doubleday, 1988).

PLAY PRODUCTIONS: *A Beach of Strangers*, Toronto, York University, 1973-1974 season;
The Arithmetic of Love, Toronto, St. Lawrence Centre, 28 October 1975.

SELECTED RADIO: *Indian Summer, Thursday Playhouse*, CBC, 9 July 1953;
The Book of Job, Four's Company, CBC, 23 April 1959;
Autumn Nocturn, Wednesday Night, CBC, 26 October 1960;
Five Joys of Mary, Wednesday Night, CBC, 7 December 1960;
A Fourteenth Century Life of Christ, Four's Company, CBC, 22 July 1961;
Bits and Pieces, Wednesday Night, CBC, 6 March 1963;
Passion of Christ, Stage, CBC, 7 April 1963;
Beowulf, Sunday Night, CBC, 21 June 1964;
The Pooh Perplex, Sunday Night, CBC, 23 August 1964;
Play of Jesus, 2 parts, *Tuesday Night*, CBC, 30 November and 7 December 1965;
Tyson's Log, Stage, CBC, 17 April 1966;
Ideal Newspaper, Fourth Estate, CBC, 26 September 1966;
Redemption of Man, FM Theatre, CBC, 20 March 1967;
The Last Summer of Childhood, Tuesday Night, CBC, 29 August 1967;
Resurrection, CBC, 14 April 1968;

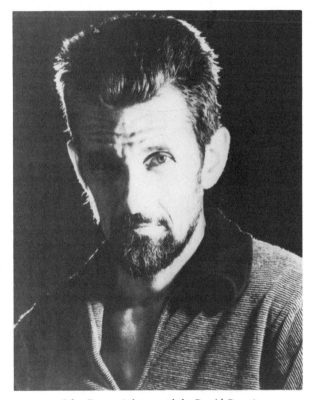

John Reeves (photograph by David Street)

When Demirgian Comes Marching Home Again, Tuesday Night, CBC, 9 July 1968;
Him, Summer Stage, CBC, 21 July 1968;
Play of Jesus, Tuesday Night, CBC, 17 December 1968;
Vision of William, Theatre 10:30, CBC, 31 March 1969;
Southern Passion, Theatre 10:30, CBC, 1 April 1969;
Meditation on the Passion, Theatre 10:30, CBC, 2 April 1969;
Complaint of Christ, Theatre 10:30, CBC, 3 April 1969;
Crucifixion of Jesus, Theatre 10:30, CBC, 4 April 1969;
Land of Lost Content, Tuesday Night, CBC, 21 October 1969;

Black Hallelujah, Stage, CBC, 10 April 1971;

Triptych, Tuesday Night, CBC, 7 September 1971;

House of Atreus, Tuesday Night, CBC, 27 March 1973;

Yah! Ho! The Echo of No Return, Radio International, 6 April 1973;

Duo, Tuesday Night, CBC, 28 August 1973;

Parallelogram, Tuesday Night, CBC, 25 June 1974;

Year of the Lord, Stage, CBC, 30 November 1974;

Deluge, adapted from Shakespeare, *Best Seat in the House,* CBC, 6 June 1976;

Polyglot Shakespeare, Best Seat in the House, CBC, 23 August 1977;

A Prayer for the Dying, adapted from Jack Higgins's novel, *Celebration,* CBC, 17 March 1985.

OTHER: "The Various Voices: Poems of the Unofficial Cultures," compiled, with an introduction, by Reeves, *Canadian Literature,* 42 (August 1969): 37-47.

John Reeves is part of the second generation of powerful and talented CBC-Radio producer-directors, following in the tradition of Andrew Allan, Esse Ljungh, Rupert Caplan, and J. Frank Willis. Reeves's reputation also rests on his inventive radio plays, noteworthy for their linguistic acrobatics, as well as their use of verse and prose, music, and shifting points of view. Some of these plays were published in the 1960s and 1970s. In the course of his career Reeves has also composed more than thirty pieces of religious music and several opera librettos. Most recently he has become a mystery-fiction writer.

John Michael Reeves, son of Albert George and Doris Helen Swinburn Reeves, was born in Merritt, British Columbia, on 1 December 1926. At the age of three he moved with his family to England, where his father, an Anglo-Catholic minister, took a parish in Lincolnshire. There, Reeves discovered a lifelong love for music. He attended Marlborough College, where he sang in the choir and conducted a small choral group. In 1945, on a choral scholarship, he went to St. John's College, Cambridge, where he took classics, graduating with a bachelor of arts degree in 1948.

In 1944 Reeves had volunteered for the British air force, but his service was deferred so that he could attend university. Beginning in 1948 he served with the British Intelligence Corps, but after one year he requested an early leave to teach classics at the University of British Colum-

bia. Reeves remained at UBC for two years. Finding that teaching was not his vocation, he accepted a position as a trainee producer-director at CBC-Radio in Toronto. In 1952 he became a music producer for the CBC.

Over his thirty-five-year tenure at the CBC, Reeves produced and directed an impressive variety of musical, religious, literary, and dramatic series. In the 1950s he was an assistant producer of *CBC Opera Company* and *CBC Symphony* and producer of *CBC String Quartet;* producer and host of *A Word in Your Ear,* a weekly series presenting recorded poetry and prose; producer of *Focus,* an hour-long weekly series of drama, music, and documentary; and producer and writer for *Four's Company,* an hour-long series featuring the Toronto Drama Quartet (John Drainie, Mavor Moore, Diana Maddox, and Ruth Springford). In the 1960s he produced *A Report on the Arts,* a half-hour weekly radio magazine on the arts in Canada; *The Fourth Estate,* a half-hour weekly series on journalism; and *Canadian Short Stories* (entitled *Stories with John Drainie* until the actor's death in 1966), a fifteen-minute daily series which broadcast short stories by new and established Canadian writers. In the 1970s Reeves produced *The Best Seat in the House,* a series which featured *Kunstkopf* (artificial head) programming. This technologically experimental program, featuring music and drama, was the first of its kind in North America. In the 1980s Reeves produced *Celebration,* a weekly series of interfaith religious programs, which featured music, drama, literature, and documentary; was a contributing producer to *Ideas,* the nightly program hosted by Lister Sinclair; and was a contributing producer to *Stereo Theatre.* He retired from CBC-Radio on 1 January 1987, the year after his marriage to his third wife, Cathryn Kester. His final project as both producer and author was *The Human Face,* a documentary about idealism in Czechoslovak history. From 1953 to 1975 Reeves was a contributing producer to such well-known CBC series as *Wednesday Night, Stage,* and *Anthology.* Reeves has received the Gabriel Prize for religious programs (1977), the John Drainie Award for distinguished contribution to broadcasting (1978), the Canadian Music Council Award for best choral broadcast of the year (1982), and the Masaryk Award from the Czechoslovak Association of Canada (1989).

Reeves's writing interests parallel those which he demonstrated as a producer: music, poetry, drama, and the novel. After some of his

As the curtain is about to fall
on the last act of *Tosca*. . . .

Murder With Muskets

JOHN REEVES

*Dust jacket for Reeves's third mystery novel featuring Toronto
police detectives Andrew Coggin and Fred Sump*

verse was recorded and released as *Poems of John
Reeves* (Hallmark Recordings, 1954), he began to
incorporate poetry into his work in radio drama.
Reeves is best known for his experiments in
sound, music, and language in radio drama. His
unpublished plays, all produced by CBC-Radio,
present a skillful blending of these components.
Argive Soliloquies, for instance, retells the Trojan
War and its aftermath in verse drama. *Concerning
Grimoldby*, a portrait of Reeves's father's Lincolnshire Church, combines verse and prose. *Black Hallelujah* (1971) incorporates a live musical presentation broadcast from a church. Reeves has also
written dozens of adaptations from classic and contemporary literature.

Written from 1960 to 1975, Reeves's three
published plays show some of his technological
and topical preoccupations. *A Beach of Strangers*
(broadcast on *CBC Wednesday Night* in 1959 and
published in 1961), which won the Italia Prize
for drama in 1959, is a play in verse and prose
about three sets of characters who relate their dif-

ferent views of a day at the beach. Indebted to
Dylan Thomas's radio play *Under Milk Wood*
(1954), *A Beach of Strangers* experiments with
sound and language and presents a kaleidoscope
of views. Directed by Mavor Moore, it was staged
at York University, Toronto, in the early 1970s; it
was also produced at Toronto's Ryerson College
in 1986. It has been translated into German,
French, Italian, Serbo-Croatian, Japanese, Polish,
Finnish, Norwegian, and Czech. *Triptych* (broadcast in 1971 and published in 1972) is the world's
first quadraphonic radio drama. It is a trilogy
which examines Christmas, Good Friday, and Easter from religious and secular perspectives, combining medieval and modern prose, music for electric and pipe organ (which Reeves composed),
and folk tunes from different parts of the world.
The Arithmetic of Love, published in 1975 in a bilingual edition in English and Czech, gives voice to
Reeves's political interest, which was sparked by
events of the Prague Spring in 1968. In verse
and prose it chronicles the history of Czechoslovakia's continual struggle for freedom. This play
was staged in Czech on 28 October 1975 at the
St. Lawrence Centre, Toronto, and given a radio
broadcast in English on the CBC in 1975.

Reeves's most recent writing comprises a series of five mystery novels, in which he describes
the sleuthing of Toronto police detectives Andrew Coggin and Fred Sump. *Murder by Microphone* (1978) is set in a CBC building; *Murder Before Matins* (1984) at an abbey; *Murder with
Muskets* (1985) at an opera house; and *Death in
Prague* (1988) in Czechoslovakia. Reeves's final
novel in the series, as yet unpublished, is tentatively entitled "Final Lap" and concerns the
world of track and field. The work reflects
Reeves's interest in running, a sport in which he
has held Canadian records for his age group in
all distances from the half-mile to ten miles, and
the world record for two miles.

In addition to "Final Lap," Reeves is at
work on "The St. Matthew Trio," a cycle of
poems about Johann Sebastian Bach's *St. Matthew
Passion*; "Calendar," a cycle of poems with accompanying motet, recording significant incidents in
Czech history; and "The Pankrác Requiem," a libretto for an opera he is composing, set in the
Pankrác prison in Prague. He has also written
the first draft of his autobiography.

Papers:
The John Reeves papers are at the Centre for
Broadcasting Studies, Concordia University.

Gwen Pharis Ringwood

(13 August 1910-24 May 1984)

Chris Johnson
University of Manitoba

BOOKS: *Dark Harvest* (Toronto: Nelson, 1945); revised version, *Canadian Theatre Review*, 5 (Winter 1975): 70-128;

The Courting of Marie Jenvrin (Toronto: French, 1951);

Still Stands the House (Toronto: French, 1955);

Younger Brother (New York: Longmans, Green, 1959);

The Rainmaker (Toronto: Playwrights Co-op, 1975);

Widger's Way (Toronto: Playwrights Co-op, 1976);

The Sleeping Beauty: A New Version of the Old Story, and The Golden Goose: Two Plays for Young People (Toronto: Playwrights Co-op, 1979);

The Collected Plays of Gwen Pharis Ringwood, edited by Enid Delgatty Rutland (Ottawa: Borealis, 1982)—comprises: *One Man's House; Chris Axelson, Blacksmith; Still Stands the House; Pasque Flower; Dark Harvest; Red Flag at Evening; The Days May Be Long; Saturday Night; The Courting of Marie Jenvrin; The Rainmaker; Stampede; A Fine Coloured Easter Egg; Widger's Way; Lament for Harmonica; The Deep Has Many Voices; Wail, Wind, Wail; Compensation Will Be Paid; The Stranger; A Remembrance of Miracles; The Lodge; Mirage; Garage Sale;* and *The Furies.*

PLAY PRODUCTIONS: *The Dragons of Kent*, Banff, Alberta, Banff School of Fine Arts, 1935;

One Man's House, Chapel Hill, Carolina Playmakers at the University of North Carolina, December 1937;

Still Stands the House, Chapel Hill, Carolina Playmakers at the University of North Carolina, 3 March 1938;

Chris Axelson, Blacksmith, Chapel Hill, Carolina Playmakers at the University of North Carolina, 26 May 1938;

Pasque Flower, Chapel Hill, Carolina Playmakers at the University of North Carolina, 2 March 1939;

Red Flag at Evening, Edmonton, Youth Training Schools, 1939;

Gwen Pharis Ringwood (courtesy of Patrick Ringwood)

The Courting of Marie Jenvrin, Banff, Alberta, Banff School of Fine Arts, 25 August 1941;

The Jack and the Joker, Banff, Alberta, Banff School of Fine Arts, Summer 1944;

Dark Harvest, Winnipeg, University of Manitoba Dramatic Society, 17 January 1945;

The Rainmaker, Banff, Alberta, Banff School of Fine Arts, 22 August 1945;

Stampede, Edmonton, University of Alberta Dramatic Society, March 1946;

A Fine Coloured Easter Egg, Banff, Alberta, Banff School of Fine Arts, 1946;

Widger's Way, Edmonton, University of Alberta Studio Theatre, March 1952;

Maya, Ottawa, Ottawa Little Theatre, 1959;

Look Behind You, Neighbour, music by Chet Lambertson, Edson, Alberta, Edson High School, 2 November 1961;

The Sleeping Beauty, Williams Lake, British Columbia, Cariboo Indian School at the Williams Lake Festival, April 1965;

The Three Wishes, Williams Lake, British Columbia, 25 December 1965;

The Road Runs North, music by Art Rosoman, Williams Lake, British Columbia, Williams Lake Junior High School, 7 June 1967;

Jana, Williams Lake, British Columbia, Gwen Ringwood Theatre, 19 June 1971;

The Deep Has Many Voices, Williams Lake, British Columbia, Gwen Ringwood Theatre, 19 June 1971;

The Magic Carpets of Antonio Angelini, Winnipeg, Winnipeg Multicultural Festival, July 1976;

The Lodge, West Vancouver, West Vancouver Little Theatre, 1977;

Mirage, music by Gary Welsh and Alvin Cairns, Saskatoon, Greystone Theatre, University of Saskatchewan, 24 May 1979;

Garage Sale, Vancouver, New Play Centre, DuMaurier Festival, 14 April 1981;

Drum Song, Victoria, British Columbia, Phoenix Theatre, University of Victoria, 22 June 1982—comprises *Maya*, *The Stranger*, and *The Furies*.

TELEVISION: *Lament for Harmonica, Shoestring Theatre*, CBC, 14 February 1960;

The Deep Has Many Voices, Teleplay, CBC, 4 December 1967.

RADIO: *New Lamps for Old*, ten scripts for the series by Ringwood (*Beethoven, The Man who Freed Music; Christopher Columbus; Florence Nightingale; Galileo, Father of Science; Henry, The Navigator; Nansen of the North; Oliver Cromwell; Socrates, Citizen of Athens; Threat to Planet Earth;* and *Valley of Ignorance*), ten by Elsie Park Gowan, CKUA, Edmonton, 1936-1937;

A Fine Coloured Easter Egg, adapted from Ringwood's play, *Prairie Playhouse*, CBC, 12 February 1953;

Still Stands the House, adapted from Ringwood's play, *Prairie Playhouse*, CBC, 5 March 1953;

The Wall, music by Bruce Haak, *Prairie Playhouse*, CBC, 21 January 1954;

So Gracious the Time, CBC, 25 December 1955;

Restez, Michelle, Don't Go, CBC, 1977;

Lament for Harmonica, adapted from Ringwood's play, CBC, 1979;

A Remembrance of Miracles, CBC, 1979;

Garage Sale, adapted from Ringwood's play, *Saturday Matinee*, CBC, 24 May 1981.

OTHER: "Get Along Little Dogie," in *Wide Open Windows*, edited by Franklin L. Barrett (Vancouver, Toronto & Montreal: Copp Clark, 1947), pp. 212-225;

"The Little Ghost," in *Canadian Short Stories*, edited by Robert Weaver and Helen James (Toronto: Oxford University Press, 1952), pp. 68-75;

"The Last Fifteen Minutes," in *Stories With John Drainie*, edited by John Drainie (Toronto: Ryerson, 1963), pp. 36-41;

"Some People's Grandfathers," in *Stories From Across Canada*, edited by Bernard L. McEnvoy (Toronto: McClelland & Stewart, 1966), pp. 9-14;

"On 'Still Stands the House,'" in *Transitions I: Short Plays*, edited by Edward Peck (Vancouver: Commcept Press, 1978), pp. 271-274;

Introduction to *The Rainmaker*, in *Canada's Lost Plays*, volume 3, *The Developing Mosaic: English-Canadian Drama to Mid-Century*, edited by Anton Wagner (Toronto: Canadian Theatre Review Publications, 1980), pp. 146-148;

The Magic Carpets of Antonio Angelini, in *Kids' Plays: Six Canadian Plays for Children* (Toronto: Playwrights Press, 1980), pp. 151-185.

PERIODICAL PUBLICATIONS: "Women and the Theatrical Tradition" and "Afterwords," *Atlantis: A Women's Studies Journal / Journal d'Etudes sur la Femme*, 4 (Fall 1978): 154-158;

"Questions (Lines written for my grand-daughter soon to be 13)," *Atlantis: A Women's Studies Journal / Journal d'Etudes sur la Femme*, 6 (Spring 1981): 134-135.

Gwen Pharis Ringwood was the first Canadian playwright to make a prolonged effort to translate the lives of western Canadians into dramatic form. Her best-known plays, *Still Stands the House* and *Dark Harvest*, develop techniques to dramatize conflict between man and environment, a theme long used by Canadian novelists and poets but one which had for the most part eluded the dramatists.

Ringwood was born Gwendolyn Margaret Pharis in Anatone, Washington, to Leslie Pharis, a schoolteacher and farmer, and his wife, Mary Bowersock Pharis, also a teacher. The Pharis family moved to Alberta to farm in 1913 and crossed the international boundary again to try cattle ranching near Valier, Montana, in 1926. Gwen Pharis entered the University of Montana in 1927, but when the family moved back to Canada in 1929, she transferred to the University of Alberta, graduating in 1934.

While at university Ringwood became involved in theater through working as a secretary for Elizabeth Sterling Haynes, director of drama in the provincial government's department of extension, a pioneer in Albertan community theater, and a moving force behind the Banff School of Fine Arts. That institution produced Ringwood's first play, *The Dragons of Kent*, in 1935. In 1936 and 1937 she wrote ten radio plays for the University of Alberta station. In 1937 she went to the University of North Carolina, where she worked with Frederick Koch and his Carolina Playmakers. She earned an M.A. in 1939 and was winner of the Roland Holt Cup for outstanding work in drama.

Much of Ringwood's subsequent work shows the influence of Koch's emphasis on "folk drama," which, in his words, centers on dramatic action arising from "man's desperate struggle for existence and his enjoyment of the world of nature." Three of Ringwood's Carolina plays, *Still Stands the House* (first produced in 1938 and published that year in *The Carolina Playbook*), *Pasque Flower* (produced in 1939 and published that year in the *Carolina Playbook*), and *Dark Harvest* (written in 1939, produced and published in 1945), depict conflict between these two "folk" reactions to nature. (All three are in *The Collected Plays of Gwen Pharis Ringwood*, edited by Enid Delgatty Rutland, 1982.) Set on an Alberta farm, like the other two, *Still Stands the House* is a one-act confrontation between Hester Warren, a woman determined to stay on her father's farm, and her sister-in-law, Ruth, who longs for a more cultured life. Fearful of losing the farm and betraying her dead father, Hester engineers the death of her brother and his wife in a blizzard, enlisting as her ally the harsh environment with which she identifies completely. The pioneer figure is treated more sympathetically in *Pasque Flower*. Jake Hansen's hunger for land and the appar-

ently cold-hearted manner in which he heeds the harsher necessities of farm life set him in conflict with his sensitive wife and his younger brother. However, Jake is capable of responding to beauty, and when this capacity is demonstrated, a romance between wife and brother is abandoned.

The same triangular relationship with the same metaphorical implications is explored in greater detail in Ringwood's first full-length play, *Dark Harvest*. (Indeed, the brief *Pasque Flower* seems like a preliminary sketch for the three-act play.) Gerth Hansen, the "Wheat King," is potentially a fascinating character, and the exploration of hubris in Ringwood's Alberta farm setting should result in a play of some significance in the Canadian context. However, the land and Gerth's obsession are diminished by an overly complicated plot, superfluous characters, distracting subplots, and an unsatisfying ending. Some of these difficulties were mitigated in a revised version published in *Canadian Theatre Review* in 1975.

While at the University of North Carolina, Ringwood also wrote *One Man's House* (produced in 1937), a one-act social protest play presenting the suffering of a union activist's family during the Depression, and the first of her country comedies, *Chris Axelson, Blacksmith* (produced in 1938). Most of these comedies show characters engaging in deception for the sake of love–familial love, as in the case of *Chris Axelson, Blacksmith*, or romantic love, as in *In The Courting of Marie Jenvrin* (produced at Banff in 1941, published in 1951), in which a clever countryman outwits his businessman rival. In *A Fine Coloured Easter Egg* (first produced in 1946), a Ukrainian farmer fakes suicide in an attempt to win his wife away from her materialistic dreams. *Widger's Way* (first produced in 1952 and published in a mimeographed acting edition by Playwrights Co-op in 1976) is probably Ringwood's most successful work in this vein, a long one-act piece whose delightful intricacies of plot and preposterous stage action take it into the realm of farce, sometimes almost into the realm of theater of the absurd; Widger, a miserly old farmer, is almost undone by his greed and by coincidence let loose by a prospector's cache of gold, but virtue accidentally triumphs. All the comedies discussed above, as well as *One Man's House*, are in Ringwood's *Collected Plays*.

She returned to Alberta in 1939, becoming, like Haynes before her, director of drama in the department of extension as well as a teacher of acting and playwriting at the Banff school. That same year, she married John Brian Barney

Laughter.

Laughter, just like rays of sunlight
    That come sparkling, falling through rain.
Laughter, though with tears entermingled
    Though it comes from a heart filled with pain.

Laughter from the lips of a baby
    Like the sound of a wee fairy bell.
Perhaps that's where we got sunbeams.
    Perhaps - for you never can tell.

The laughter of gay, happy children;
    The laughter of mothers and men.
Who've fought and often have suffered,
    But have laughed and gone on once again.

Laughter, 'tis God's greatest blessing
    The power to smile and go on.
'Till we reach once again the beginning
    Till we wake at the breaking of dawn.

Manuscript for an unpublished poem by Ringwood (Gwen Ringwood Papers, University of Calgary Library, Special Collections; by permission of Patrick Ringwood)

Ringwood, a medical doctor; in 1940 they moved to Goldfields, a mining town in the north of Saskatchewan, and the first of their four children was born in 1941, the same year she was awarded the Governor General's medal for outstanding service to Canadian drama. Ringwood returned to Edmonton in 1942 when her husband joined the Army Medical Corps, and was commissioned by the Alberta Folklore and History Project to write three plays: *The Jack and the Joker* (produced in 1944), a one-act comedy based on an incident in the life of a pioneer newspaper editor; *The Rainmaker* (produced in 1945, published in 1975), another short country comedy, in which an itinerant rainmaker changes lives in a farming community; and *Stampede* (produced in 1946), a melodrama about the legendary black cowboy, John Ware, and the beginning of the commercialization of the Calgary Stampede. (All three are in *The Collected Plays*.)

The most modest of major Canadian playwrights, Ringwood showed little interest in acquiring a broad or metropolitan audience, concentrating instead on portraying, in local productions, the small communities she knew well. This quality is particularly clear in her "community pageants." *Look Behind You, Neighbour*, a musical, combines domestic drama and local history; it was written to celebrate the fiftieth anniversary of Edson, Alberta, in 1961. *The Road Runs North*, a "historical" musical based on the life of Billy Barker of gold-rush fame, was written to commemorate the centennial of Williams Lake, British Columbia, in 1967.

After her move to British Columbia with her family in 1953, there was a marked shift in Ringwood's work. The Williams Lake area to which the Ringwoods moved has a large native Indian population, renewing an interest that began when Ringwood lived near a Blackfoot reservation in Montana; Indians appear as characters in Ringwood's plays, and the social conditions she observed resulted in a sharper note of protest. In *Lament for Harmonica*, an Indian girl is corrupted and destroyed by a white lover and the white world. The play was included in *The Collected Plays* as *Lament for Harmonica*, but it was first produced as *Maya* in 1959, and has sometimes been presented under that title in subsequent productions. In a different mood, Ringwood wrote several children's plays for production at the Indian School in Williams Lake. Some, like *The Sleeping Beauty* (first produced in 1965, first published with another children's play, *The Golden Goose*, in

1979), combine the European fairy-tale tradition and Indian legend. A similar blending of traditions is used in her tragedy, *The Stranger* (first produced as *Jana* in 1971 and included in *The Collected Plays*), in which the Medea myth is given an Indian setting and a contemporary social message.

Concern for the plight of the native people of Canada is also evident in *Younger Brother*, Ringwood's 1959 novel for young people. Set in the foothills of the Rockies in Alberta during the 1940s, the novel presents its young protagonist, Brandt Merrill, with a series of tests, physical and moral; Brandt's loyalties are tested when an Indian is falsely accused of cattle theft perpetrated by the best friend of and substitute for Jules, the older Merrill brother killed in the war. The novel is distinguished by a convincing and pervasive sense of place. (A second novel, "Pascal," has not been published.)

Social concern characterizes much of Ringwood's later work. *The Deep Has Many Voices* (produced in 1971), an experimental piece, uses media and music to give theatrical shape to the confusion experienced by contemporary young people. (Ringwood had been closely involved with young people as a drama teacher and adjudicator most of her life, teaching courses in drama and theater at Cariboo College in Williams Lake from 1968 to 1975.) *A Remembrance of Miracles* (first produced as a radio play in 1979) attacks small-town bigotry unleashed by a schoolteacher's choice of books for class, and *The Lodge* (produced in 1977) uses family conflict to expose the destructiveness of materialism. These plays are all included in *The Collected Plays*.

The Association for Canadian Theatre History recognized Ringwood's pioneering contribution to theater in Canada by making her an honorary member of the association at their Saskatchewan conference in 1979; that occasion also saw the first production of *Mirage*, a full-length play in eleven scenes depicting the history of Saskatchewan through events in the lives of three generations of a representative farm family. It is the most ambitious, complex, and perhaps best of her "community pageants"; protest and doubt relieve the sunniness of the form. It, and the other two plays written late in Ringwood's life, are included in *The Collected Plays*. Ringwood's last plays were *Garage Sale*, a one-act bittersweet comedy about the reminiscences of an elderly couple, produced as part of the annual DuMaurier Festival in Vancouver in 1981, and *The Furies*, a one-act tragedy, again with an Indian theme: native women take revenge for sexual exploitation in the intertwined stories of two incidents occurring decades apart. *The Furies* was first produced with two other plays, under the collective title *Drum Song*, at the University of Victoria, on 22 June 1982, at the opening of that institution's Phoenix Theatre.

Ringwood's artistic roots remained in her own community (the little theater in Williams Lake was named after her long before her death on 24 May 1984), but the stylistic experiments and concern with social issues characteristic of her later work suggest an artistic vision which increasingly sought to integrate the tangibly local with the larger society and its universal questions.

References:

Geraldine Anthony, *Gwen Pharis Ringwood* (Boston: Twayne, 1981);

Anthony, "Gwen Pharis Ringwood," in her *Stage Voices: Twelve Canadian Playwrights Talk About Their Lives and Work* (Toronto: Doubleday, 1978), pp. 85-110;

Anthony, "The Magic Carpets of Gwen Pharis Ringwood," *Canadian Children's Literature*, 8 (1977): 84-89;

Michael Benazon, "Ringwood's Saskatchewan Mirage," *Canadian Theatre Review*, 24 (Fall 1979): 122-123;

George Broderson, "Gwen Pharis–Canadian Dramatist," *Manitoba Arts Review*, 3 (Spring 1944): 3-20;

L. W. Conolly, "The Collected Plays of Gwen Pharis Ringwood: A Review Essay," *Canadian Drama / L'Art Dramatique Canadien*, 9 (1985): 514-520;

Conolly, "Modern Canadian Drama: Some Critical Perspectives," *Canadian Drama / L'Art Dramatique Canadien*, 9 (1985): 216-217, 219-221;

Judith Hinchcliffe, "*Still Stands the House*: The Failure of the Pastoral Dream," *Canadian Drama /*

L'Art Dramatique Canadien, 3 (Autumn 1977): 183-191;

Margaret Laurence, Foreword to *The Collected Plays of Gwen Pharis Ringwood*, edited by Enid Delgatty Rutland (Ottawa: Borealis, 1982), pp. xi-xiv;

Denyse Lynde, "The Dowser Characters in the Plays of Gwen Pharis Ringwood," *Ariel*, 18, no.1 (1987): 27-37;

Richard Perkyns, Introduction to *Drum Song*, in his *Major Plays of the Canadian Theatre 1934-1984* (Toronto: Irwin, 1984), pp. 328-334;

Margaret Loewen Reimer, "Regionalism as a Definitive Characteristic in Four Canadian Dramas," *Canadian Drama / L'Art Dramatique Canadien*, 2 (Autumn 1976): 144-153;

George Ryga, Preface to *The Collected Plays of Gwen Pharis Ringwood* (Ottawa: Borealis, 1982), pp. xv-xviii;

Ann Saddlemyer, "At Home in the Theatre: Ireland's Lady Gregory and Canada's Gwen Pharis Ringwood," in *Literary Interrelations: Ireland, England and the World*, edited by Wolfgang Zach and Heinz Kosok (Tubingen: Narr, 1987), II: 111-120;

Anton Wagner, "Gwen Pharis Ringwood Rediscovered," *Canadian Theatre Review*, 5 (Winter 1975): 63-69;

Wagner, Introduction to *Canada's Lost Plays*, volume 3, *The Developing Mosaic: English-Canadian Drama to Mid-Century*, edited by Wagner (Toronto: Canadian Theatre Review Publications, 1980), pp. 4-39;

Wagner, ed., *Canada's Lost Plays*, volume 2, *Women Pioneers* (Toronto: Canadian Theatre Review Publications, 1979), pp. 4-19, 184-185.

Papers:

Gwen Pharis Ringwood's papers are at the University of Calgary Library, Special Collections Divison.

Dorothy Roberts
(6 July 1906-)

Louis K. MacKendrick
University of Windsor

BOOKS: *Songs for Swift Feet*, as Gostwick Roberts
     (Toronto: Ryerson, 1927);
Dazzle (Toronto: Ryerson, 1957);
In Star and Stalk (Toronto: Emblem Books, 1959);
Twice to Flame (Toronto: Ryerson, 1961);
Extended (Fredericton: Fiddlehead, 1967);
The Self of Loss: New and Selected Poems (Frederic-
     ton: Fiddlehead, 1976).

Dorothy Gostwick Roberts was born in Fredericton, New Brunswick, on 6 July 1906, the
daughter of the poet Theodore Goodridge Roberts and Frances Allen Roberts. Her uncle was
Charles G. D. Roberts. During her early years
she spent time in England, France, Ottawa, and
Toronto; she was educated principally in Fredericton and at the University of New Brunswick
(1926-1928). She was a reporter for the Fredericton *Daily Mail* and in 1929 married August R.
Leisner. Their daughter, Anne, was born in
1931, and their son, John, in 1937. From 1938 to
1954 Roberts sold stories, generally of family situations, to various publications and worked on a
novel that has never been published. Her married life was spent in Toronto from 1934 to late
1940, in Ithaca, New York, and, after 1945, in
State College (later University Park), Pennsylvania. She has held poetry discussions and readings
at Pennsylvania State University, where her husband was professor of English, and at its branch
campuses, and she has often participated in the
Central Pennsylvania arts festival. Her poetry,
which she began to pursue seriously in the 1950s,
after an early chapbook of juvenilia, has appeared in a variety of Canadian and American periodicals and anthologies. She is a member of the
League of Canadian Poets and has completed
what she calls "a long collection of later life
poems," "In the Flight of Stars."

Roberts's poetry, not great in volume, has
been generally overlooked except for rare but generous reviews, one critical analysis, and the inclusion of some of her poems in anthologies. Appreciations have variously pointed to some predom-

inant themes in her work: Martin Ware (*Dalhousie
Review*, Winter 1976-1977) notes a separation
from warmth, a preoccupation with common
shapes subject to sudden transformation, and an
affinity for the earthbound; Robert Gibbs (*Fiddlehead*, Spring 1977) focuses on her use of distance
in time and space, and her reaching from particular experience to a view of the large and impersonal; and Emily Grosholz (*Cumberland Poetry Review*, Spring 1985) comments on her austere
northern landscapes, alienation, the mind's confrontation with nature, and the small order of

the domestic circle. Roberts herself has acknowledged her attention to the forces of dissolution and forces that bind, to love and sensory life under the aspect of the tremendous, and to the condition of exile as a complement of her childhood's confinements.

Much of Roberts's poetry observes the immutable and distinctive forms and patterns of the natural world, as well as the transitions between successive states of existence. In "Ours" (collected in *Extended*, 1967) she testifies that "not only place is here but form to enact it," a double focus which recurs with local variations throughout her work. In "A Pattern" (*Twice to Flame*, 1961) she best articulates the eternity and energy of the predominantly natural phenomena she observes: "A pattern rests, a pattern reaches plenty, / A pattern holds its seasons in assembly / And finishes itself in constant freedom." There is an ineluctable side of the natural cycle which holds equally true for the pastoral homeland of actuality and memory. Objects are fixed in their patterns, yet they are constantly kinetic. Her poetry is full of motion, with the frequent gesture of thrusting upward and its complement of descent. Transience is never far from this poet's awareness. Like islands which "coerce the things in flux to stay awhile" ("Staying," *The Self of Loss*, 1976), dissolution is generally balanced by the complementary persistence of essential, even transcendent, form: "I house my uncertain self in the star and stalk" ("Early Morning," *In Star and Stalk*, 1959). Human life, too, is seen as part of a grander design. Unlike the woods in "Winter," (*The Self of Loss*), humans "must go on to real death."

Nature and existence are necessarily two-sided in Roberts's outlook, a sequence of "possibilities and confinements" ("Boat on the Beach," *The Self of Loss*). She treats unhesitatingly the great polarities of death and decay, birth and renewal, and the transitions between such states. She is no sentimentalist about passage, but a realist. The anthologized poem "Dazzle" (*Dazzle*, 1957) epitomizes her acknowledgment of the inevitability and the glory of natural process: "Light plays with the chorus of the living / While the dead hurry down / Earthward to lift to the dazzle / Any answering form." This celebration of natural succession is also expressed in "Outburst of May," (*Dazzle*), in which spring's dramatic surge provokes thoughts of the inevitable: "To dampen down explosion / Autumn will have to come, the

chilling fall / Of spent particulars before another tension."

Her poetry often confirms "a lease on dislocations"–the subtitle of one section in *The Self of Loss: New and Selected Poems*. Time and distance appear often, even in relatively undemonstrative circumstances: in "Turnpike" (*Dazzle*) road signs engage the timeless, so that "each strict injunction / We follow, follow, till the ultimate wheel / Turning in the infinite O turns to God." Roberts's poetry also possesses a metaphysical dimension: images of light and heavenly bodies are frequent, and immediate phenomena may suggest a continuum that reaches beyond the particular: "to feel this depth of time that we could acknowledge / Only in substance that our senses encountered . . . " ("House in the Past," *Extended*). Although individual poems can be strongly conceptual, they rarely lose their basis in specific and detailed substance.

Roberts has a singular ease of language; she is able to combine idea and carefully restrained but apt metaphor in a seemingly effortless way, as in a graveyard "where names are pooled and the deep well of time / Is known because supported by the stones" ("Time in the Cemetery," *Extended*). Her persistent theme of mortal condition balanced by resurgence is most often evident in her careful selection of subject, a realization of its inherent shifting qualities, and a rigorous, disciplined expression. Throughout her work the impression is of firm intelligence: the poetry is not complex or ambiguous but thoughtful and objective. It is formal without being reserved, austere, or inaccessible, and it is often strongly meditative in tone. Her images derive from common, usually organic, objects and events, which are often seen to act as epitomes, and her subtle sound values are significantly understated. Her verbs are definite, chosen both for meaning and movement; her verse has a muscular weight, and, paradoxically, a singular delicacy and sensuousness.

Reference:
Emily Grosholz, "Form, Flux, and Pattern: The Poetry of Dorothy Roberts," *Cumberland Poetry Review* (Spring 1985): 22-34.

Papers:
Dorothy Roberts's papers are at the Pattee Library, Pennsylvania State University.

Sinclair Ross

(22 January 1908-   )

Lorraine McMullen
University of Ottawa

BOOKS: *As For Me and My House* (New York: Reynal & Hitchcock, 1941; Toronto: McClelland & Stewart, 1957);

The Well (Toronto: Macmillan, 1958);

The Lamp at Noon and Other Stories (Toronto: McClelland & Stewart, 1968);

Whir of Gold (Toronto: McClelland & Stewart, 1970);

Sawbones Memorial (Toronto: McClelland & Stewart, 1974);

The Race and Other Stories by Sinclair Ross, edited by Lorraine McMullen (Ottawa: University of Ottawa Press, 1982).

OTHER: "Just Wind and Horses: A Memoir," in *The Macmillan Anthology*, volume 1, edited by John Metcalf and Leon Rooke (Toronto: Macmillan, 1988).

Sinclair Ross is best known for his prairie fiction. His first novel, *As For Me and My House* (1941), and his most recent, *Sawbones Memorial* (1974), along with his short stories are his most memorable works.

James Sinclair Ross was born on 22 January 1908, to Peter and Catherine Foster Fraser Ross on a homestead in northern Saskatchewan, twenty-five miles from Prince Albert. After completing high school in 1924, he began working for the Union Bank of Canada (later taken over by the Royal Bank of Canada) at Abbey, Saskatchewan. In 1928 he was transferred to Lancer and in 1929 to Arcola, both in Saskatchewan. In 1933 he moved to Winnipeg. Ross's first published story, "No Other Way," appeared in *Nash's Pall-Mall* (October 1934) after winning third prize in the magazine's short-story competition for previously unpublished writers. From 1934 to 1941, when he joined the Canadian army, Ross published several short stories, almost all of them in *Queen's Quarterly*.

Ross roots his fiction in a particular and vividly realized place and time–the Saskatchewan prairie of the 1930s. Setting is integral to theme

Sinclair Ross (photograph by Schiffer Photography, Ltd.)

and narrative. The beauty and violence of the landscape come alive through his writing, and the prairie becomes a region of the mind. His regionalism makes Ross an important figure in Canadian literature, while his thematic concerns–alienation and loneliness, the ever-presentness of the past, the artistic and imaginative struggle, the search for meaning in an incomprehensible universe–belong to the mainstream of twentieth-century writing.

Ross's stories, ten of which are collected in *The Lamp at Noon and Other Stories* (1968) and nine in *The Race and Other Stories* (1982), are among his most successful works. Most are set on the prairie of the 1930s during the drought and Depression. The stories focus on the effects of loneliness, hardship, and poverty on individuals and their relationships. Thus, while Ross portrays the harshness of the land vividly and realistically, his focus is on inner rather than outer landscape. As Margaret Laurence wrote in her introduction to the first edition of *The Lamp at Noon and Other Stories,* "the outer situation always mirrors the inner. The emptiness of the landscape, the bleakness of the land, reflect the inability of these people to touch one another with assurance and gentleness."

The struggle against nature in Ross's stories is often bitterly ironic. In "Not by Rain Alone," for example, a young farmer survives a blizzard by crawling into a haystack for protection. He returns home to find that his young wife, whom he had left alone, has died in childbirth. The indifference of nature to man is often revealed as an aspect of cosmic indifference. To the young wife in "A Lamp at Noon," the farmyard during a dust storm appears as "an isolated acre, poised aloft above a sombre void." The sensation of being on the edge of a void recurs frequently in Ross's fiction.

In stories told from a woman's point of view the failure of communication and sense of isolation are paramount. In "The Lamp at Noon" years of poverty and hardship culminate in a three-day dust storm which drives a young woman insane. In "The Painted Door" a lonely woman, isolated during a blizzard, capitulates to the advances of a handsome neighbor, with tragic results. Stories of childhood are less bleak and are interlaced with humor. Several of these, based on Ross's childhood experiences, are among his best works. Those involving adolescents are clearly initiation stories. Stories of younger children show them caught up in the world of the imagination, not yet completely aware of the drabness of the present. Written in a style characterized by economy, precision, rhythm, and repetition, Ross's stories render significant the experiences of prairie life.

In 1941 Ross published his first novel, *As For Me and My House.* The novel consists of the journal recordings of a prairie minister's wife from the time of her arrival with her husband in the small town of Horizon until their departure the following year. The conflict is complex, involving the relationship between Mrs. Bentley and her husband, Philip, the couple's conflict with the narrow, puritanical town, and Philip's growing

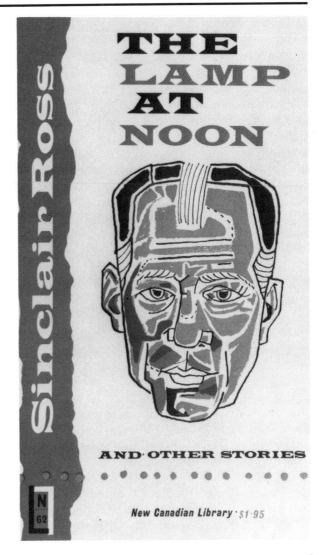

Front cover for Ross's 1968 collection, ten stories, most of which are set on the drought-ridden prairie during the Great Depression

frustration and sense of guilt as minister of a religion in which he no longer believes and as a would-be artist lacking the opportunity to develop his talent. After twelve years of marriage, the Bentleys are childless, another source of unhappiness. Because Philip longs for a son, his wife suggests that they adopt a twelve-year-old whose father has deserted him. The boy's presence only complicates the situation between husband and wife. When the child is taken away in a short time, Philip, more bitter and resentful than ever, has an affair with a young choir member who dies in childbirth. The Bentleys then adopt her son. As the novel ends Philip has resigned from the ministry, and the Bentleys are leaving for the city, where Philip will have an opportunity to try to develop his artistic talents.

Mrs. Bentley is an eyewitness narrator who records events almost as they occur. The reader must attempt to establish the accuracy of her assumptions and her interpretations of others, including her husband, who says little, preferring to avoid emotional scenes by walking tight-lipped into his study, shutting the door behind him. Evocation of mood through weather–wind, dust, drought, snow–and Ross's constant mirroring of the Bentleys' inner states through climate and surroundings contribute to the novel's intensity. From the beginning, wind and rain convey the indifference of nature, and the town's huddled houses are projections of Mrs. Bentley's feelings of helplessness in the face of cosmic indifference. On her first day in Horizon she notes in her journal: "Above, in the high cold night, the wind goes swinging past, indifferent, liplessly mournful. It frightens me, makes me feel lost, dropped on this little perch of town and abandoned." Her sensations are reinforced by the prairie; on her lonely evening walks, snow in the winter and dust in the summer obscure her vision: "The dust is so thick that sky and earth are just a blur. You can scarcely see the elevators at the end of town. One step beyond, you think, and you'd go plunging into space." On one level space is the immediate unknown future of the Bentleys, on another, the vast unknown beyond life itself.

As For Me and My House received little attention on first publication, partly, perhaps, because it appeared during World War II. Since publication of the New Canadian Library edition in 1957, the novel has received increasing recognition, and it is now generally accepted as a Canadian classic. The style of the novel, which is compressed, metaphorical, and indirect, is largely responsible for its density and complexity. Mrs. Bentley is an ambiguous figure, about whom critics are divided; to some she appears as an overly possessive wife, to others a patient, long-suffering one. Laurence Ricou, in his *Vertical Man/Horizontal World* (1973), writes: "Ross is the first writer in Canada to show a profound awareness of the metaphorical possibilities of the prairie landscape. More particularly, and hence the term 'internalization' is appropriate, Ross introduces the landscape as a metaphor for man's mind, his emotions, his soul perhaps, in a more thorough and subtle way than any previous writer."

In 1942 Ross joined the Canadian army and was sent overseas with the Ordnance Corps. He served at army headquarters, London, England, until 1946. Despite bombing raids and the buzz bombs of the last days of the war, Ross enjoyed London with its theaters and symphonies. In October 1946, shortly after his return to Canada, he was transferred to the head office of the Royal Bank, where he remained until his retirement on 31 January 1968. For the last nine or ten years he worked in the advertising department. While in Montreal, Ross published two stories relating experiences of Canadian soldiers during the war years, "Barrack Room Fiddle Tune" and "Jug and Bottle," and several more stories with Saskatchewan backgrounds. In 1958 Ross published his second novel, *The Well*.

In *The Well* Ross focuses on a twenty-year-old who moves from an urban to a rural environment. After shooting a man, perhaps mortally, in a robbery attempt, Chris Rowe flees from the Montreal police. He jumps off a freight train in a small prairie town and hides out with an elderly farmer who offers him a job. The plot revolves around Chris's relationship with the farmer, Larson, and Larson's young wife, Sylvia.

For Larson, whose only son was killed in childhood, Chris becomes a surrogate son. For Sylvia, thirty years younger than Larson yet older than Chris, Chris becomes a possible means of escape from a loveless marriage. For Chris, Sylvia, who seduces him, is in many ways a mother figure. The romantic triangle thus takes on aspects of an oedipal situation as Sylvia tries to involve Chris in a plan to murder her husband. For Chris, whose background in Montreal is that of a member of a young street gang regularly involved in petty crime, nature becomes a regenerative force. In his interaction with the landscape, the farm animals, and the simple activities of farm life, and with Larson's acceptance of him, Chris's sense of values alters so that finally he has the strength to reject Sylvia. The central symbol of the novel is the well which Larson and his first wife had dug years earlier. For Larson, the well represents past happiness. Showing Chris the old well, Larson indicates his wish to link Chris with this past and perhaps through him to find it again. *The Well* is not as successful as Ross's first novel. It is structurally weak, and the ending is melodramatic. It lacks the intensity and the metaphoric language of his earlier work.

In 1968 Ross retired from the bank and moved to Athens, Greece. It was there that he completed his third novel, *Whir of Gold* (1970), begun some years earlier in Montreal. This novel takes up the story of Sonny McAlpine, the prairie farm boy of an earlier story, "The Outlaw." Sonny,

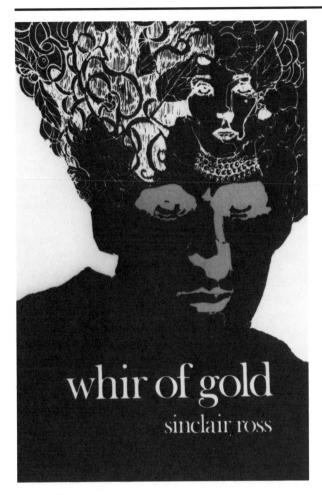

Dust jacket for Ross's third novel, written in Athens, Greece, shortly after his retirement there in 1968

who has become a clarinetist, has moved to Montreal, hoping to be a success in the big city. Now, lonely and discouraged, he is on the verge of returning west. He meets Mad, a Nova Scotian girl who is as lonely in the city as he is. Mad, who works as a waitress and at times as a prostitute, moves in with Sonny. A third individual of significance in the plot is a small-time crook named Charlie who lives across the hall in Sonny's rooming house. Charlie persuades Sonny to join him in a robbery. The robbery attempt fails; Sonny is injured and is nursed back to health by Mad. Sensing his rejection of her, Mad leaves, while Sonny seems about to get a job with a band, as he had hoped. Sonny, like Philip Bentley the would-be painter, is an image of the struggling artist. Like Philip, he is a lonely figure lacking the stimulus or opportunity to practice his art. Yet music remains his world.

The story is told retrospectively by Sonny as he attempts to understand the significance of what has happened. Scenes from Sonny's prairie childhood are interwoven with more immediate Montreal events. The two loves of Sonny's life, his music and his horse, Isabel, coalesce in the liveliest incident of the novel, a horse race. Defying his parents' prohibition, the young Sonny enters his horse in a race at the town fair. She wins, and the prize provides the money for Sonny's music lessons. The incident is told with the humor and economy characteristic of Ross's stories of childhood.

The title of the novel is central to its meaning. The term comes from a childhood incident in which Sonny is entranced by a flicker, which in movement seems to be "flashing like a whir of gold, a gust of feathered light." He attempts to capture the bird, "to run the miracle to earth, lay hands on it, for all time make it mine." The whir of gold becomes the symbol of a fleeting, elusive beauty. For Mad, a big, generous, warm-hearted woman, the elusive beauty is her dream of one day settling down to a simple life in Nova Scotia with "a right one." For Sonny, it is the successful musical career which so far has eluded him.

Whir of Gold is a mood story. The introspection, the questioning, the haunting sense of guilt and regret which Sonny has about his treatment of Mad are conveyed with skill. Yet the novel has received little attention, except for some praise for Ross's handling of Sonny's early life in Saskatchewan.

In March 1971 Ross moved from Athens to Barcelona, Spain, and in 1973 from Barcelona to Málaga. The following year he published *Sawbones Memorial*, a novel which returns to the prairie to tell the story of an entire community. On 20 April 1948 the townspeople of Upward gather to honor "Sawbones" Hunter, their doctor who is retiring after forty-five years of service, and to open the new hospital which is dedicated to him. Despite the brief period in which the action takes place, Ross manipulates time to reveal four generations of townspeople through the thoughts and memories of those present.

Ross crowds his novel with more than thirty characters. The most interesting are those judged by the town to be outsiders: Benny Fox, the homosexual town musician; Nick Miller, the Ukrainian boy returning to take over Hunter's practice; Caroline Gillespie, an English war bride married to Upward's leading citizen; Maisie Bell, reputed to be the town's scarlet woman. Doc Hunter, the center of attention, despite being something of an outsider himself, has been involved through his profession with most of the crucial events of the town and is privy to most of the town's secrets.

Sawbones Memorial is more positive in tone than Ross's previous works and possesses more humor than his earlier novels. Although ostensibly about Hunter, the novel is really concerned with universal human experience: love and sexuality, birth and death, youth and old age. A major theme is communication. The town becomes a microcosm of the world through which the author reveals that although modern life has materially changed, human nature remains the same. The town's name, Upward, is, then, ironic.

The novel is composed solely of dialogue and monologue. Claude Mauriac's *Le Dîner en ville* (*The Dinner Party*, 1959) gave Ross the idea of writing a novel about a group gathered together for a few hours. Through his townspeople, Ross explores the universal aspects of the human condition with skill and economy, interweaving the tragic with the comic. Much of the tension of the novel evolves from the contrasting and counterpointing of the two polarities of man's experience: frustration and fulfillment, pettiness and generosity. Although not yet as well known as *As For Me and My House, Sawbones Memorial* has been praised for its effective use of innovative techniques.

After seven years in Málaga, Ross returned to Canada in March 1980, settling first in Montreal, and then moving the following year to Vancouver. In the chronology of Canadian prairie writers, Ross follows early realists such as Frederick Philip Grove and precedes the generation of Robert Kroetsch, Margaret Laurence, and Rudy Wiebe. Ross's protagonists are unlike the heroic patriarchal figures which Grove depicts. Ross most often gives voices to man's awareness of his insignificance, whether in the claustrophobic atmosphere of the small town or in the unlimited space of the prairie. Alienation, failure of communication, the problem of the imagination are all tied to Ross's overriding concern, man's predicament as a finite being in a world in which he can achieve only limited understanding, and in a life over which he has only limited control. Ross's masterly control of form, his metaphoric use of landscape to mirror the psychic lives of his characters, the taut, economical rhythm of his prose, the complex interweaving of action, character, and landscape–all contribute to the intensity with which he voices these concerns.

Bibliography:

David Latham, "Sinclair Ross: An Annotated Bibli-

ography," in *The Annotated Bibliography of Canada's Major Authors*, volume 3, edited by Robert Lecker and Jack David (Downsview, Ont.: ECW, 1981), pp. 365-395.

References:
Karen Bishop, "The Pegasus Symbol in The Childhood Stories of Sinclair Ross," *Ariel: A Review of International Literature*, 16 (July 1985): 67-87;

Richard Cavell, "The Unspoken in Sinclair Ross's *As For Me and My House*," *Letteratura Lingue Idee*, 14 (1980): 23-30;

Robert D. Chambers, *Sinclair Ross and Ernest Buckler* (Toronto: Copp Clark, 1975);

Marilyn Chapman, "Another Case of Ross's Mysterious Barn," *Canadian Literature*, 103 (Winter 1984): 184-186;

Paul Comeau, "Sinclair Ross's Pioneer Fiction," *Canadian Literature*, 103 (Winter 1984): 174-184;

Wilfred Cude, "Beyond Mrs. Bentley: A Study of *As For Me and My House*," *Journal of Canadian Studies*, 8 (February 1973): 3-18;

Cude, "Turn It Upside Down: The Right Perspective on *As For Me and My House*," *English Studies in Canada*, 5 (Winter 1979): 469-488;

Roy Daniells, Introduction to Ross's *As For Me and My House* (Toronto: McClelland & Stewart, 1957);

Paul Denham, "Narrative Techniques in Sinclair Ross's *As For Me and My House*," *Studies in Canadian Literature*, 5 (Spring 1980): 116-124;

Sandra Djwa, "False Gods and the True Covenant: Thematic Continuity between Margaret Laurence and Sinclair Ross," *Journal of Canadian Fiction*, 1, no. 2 (1972): 43-50;

Djwa, "No Other Way: Sinclair Ross's Stories and Novels," *Canadian Literature*, 47 (Winter 1971): 49-66;

Keath Fraser, "Futility at the Pump: The Short Stories of Sinclair Ross," *Queen's Quarterly*, 77 (Spring 1970): 72-80;

Thomas M. F. Gerry, "Dante, C. D. Burns and Sinclair Ross: Philosophical Issues in *As For Me and My House*," *Mosaic*, 22 (Winter 1989): 113-122;

Barbara Godard, "El Greco in Canada: Sinclair Ross's *As For Me and My House*," *Mosaic*, 14 (Spring 1981): 54-75;

Takao Hagiwara, "The Role of Nature in *An'ya koro* (A Dark Night's Passing) and *As For Me and My House*," *Selecta*, 3 (1982): 1-8;

Evelyn J. Hinz and John J. Teunissen, "Who's the Father of Mrs. Bentley's Child? *As For Me and My House* and the Conventions of the Dramatic Monologue," *Canadian Literature*, 111 (Winter 1986): 101-113;

Frances W. Kaye, "Sinclair Ross's Use of George Sand and Frederic Chopin as Models for the Bentleys," *Essays on Canadian Writing*, 33 (Fall 1986): 100-111;

Margaret Laurence, Introduction to Ross's *The Lamp at Noon and Other Stories* (Toronto: McClelland & Stewart, 1968);

T. J. Matheson, " 'But Do Your Thing': Conformity, Self-Reliance, and Sinclair Ross's *As For Me and My House*," *Dalhousie Review*, 66 (Winter 1986-1987): 497-512;

E. A. McCourt, *The Canadian West in Fiction* (Toronto: Ryerson, 1949; revised, 1970);

Lorraine McMullen, Introduction to Ross's *Sawbones Memorial*, New Canadian Library, no. 145 (Toronto: McClelland & Stewart, 1978);

McMullen, *Sinclair Ross* (Boston: G. K. Hall, 1979);

Ken Mitchell, *Sinclair Ross: A Reader's Guide* (Regina: Thunder Creek Publishing, 1981);

W. H. New, "Sinclair Ross's Ambivalent World," *Canadian Literature*, 40 (Spring 1969): 26-32;

Laurence Ricou, *Vertical Man/Horizontal World: Man and Landscape in Canadian Prairie Fiction* (Vancouver: University of British Columbia Press, 1973);

L. Morton Ross, "The Canonization of *As For Me and My House:* A Case Study," in *Figures in a Ground: Canadian Essays on Modern Literature Collected in Honor of Sheila Watson*, edited by Diane Bessai and David Jackel (Saskatoon: Western Producer Prairie Books, 1978), pp. 189-205;

Meena Shirdwadkar, "Conscience and Conflict in Sinclair Ross," *Indian PEN*, 46 (May / June 1984): 12-16;

Donald Stephens, "Wind, Sun, and Dust," *Canadian Literature*, 23 (Winter 1965): 17-24;

David Stouck, Introduction to *As For Me and My House* (Lincoln: University of Nebraska Press, 1978);

Stouck, "The Mirror and the Lamp in Sinclair Ross's *As For Me and My House*," *Mosaic*, 7 (Winter 1974): 141-150;

Warren Tallman, "Wolf in the Snow," *Canadian Literature*, 5 (Summer 1960): 7-20; 6 (Autumn 1960): 41-48;

F. H. Whitman, "The Case of Ross's Mysterious Barn," *Canadian Literature*, 94 (Autumn 1982): 168-169;

David Williams, "The 'Scarlet' Rompers: Toward a New Perspective on *As For Me and My House*," *Canadian Literature*, 103 (Winter 1984): 155-166;

Lorraine M. York, " 'It's better nature lost': The Importance of the Word in Sinclair Ross's *As For Me and My House*," *Canadian Literature*, 103 (Winter 1984): 166-174.

W. W. E. Ross

(14 June 1894-26 August 1966)

Frank Davey
York University

BOOKS: *Laconics*, as E. R. (Ottawa: Overbrook, 1930);
Sonnets, as E. R. (Toronto: Heaton, 1932);
Experiment, 1923-29, edited by Raymond Souster (Toronto: Contact, 1956);
Shapes and Sounds, edited by Souster and John Robert Colombo (Don Mills, Ont.: Longmans, 1968).

PERIODICAL PUBLICATION: "On National Poetry," *Canadian Forum*, 24 (July 1944): 88.

"The first poet in Canada to use real factual things unadorned by metaphor," critic Peter Stevens has called W. W. E. Ross. Ross was born in Peterborough, Ontario, on 14 June 1894 to Ralph and Nellie Creighton Ross. He grew up in Pembroke, Ontario, and earned a degree in chemistry from the University of Toronto in 1914. His interest in the natural world took him on two surveying trips in the summers of 1912 and 1913, both to northern Ontario wilderness regions–Algonquin and Algoma–later made famous by the paintings of the Group of Seven. He served with the Canadian Expeditionary Force in World War I as a private in the signal corps. On his return, he took up lifelong employment as a geophysicist at the Dominion Magnetic Observatory at Agincourt, Ontario, a few miles north of Toronto. He married Mary Lowrey on 3 June 1924, and they had two children, Mary Loretto and Nancy Helen. The family settled in Toronto at the Delaware Avenue house at which he died, of cancer, in 1966.

His earliest works, dated 1923-1925 by his editors, are written in free verse and reflect a knowledge of both imagism and Japanese poetry. Although acquainted with the works of numerous American writers, including William Carlos Williams, Robert Frost, Ezra Pound, Vachel Lindsay, Carl Sandburg, and Amy Lowell, his chief American influences were E. E. Cummings and Marianne Moore. He objected to both difficult and ornate verse and found the conventional ro-

W. W. E. Ross

manticism of Canada's Confederation poets particularly unappealing. His first publications were in Marianne Moore's *Dial* (in 1928) and in *Poetry* (Chicago). These were followed by two slim collections, *Laconics* (1930) and *Sonnets* (1932), both of which he signed with the initials E. R.

Laconics collects the imagist poems Ross is best known for, poems constructed of discrete two-

274

stress lines and direct, factual images; many of these poems present the northern Ontario landscape in the stark manner of the Group of Seven. *Sonnets* reveals a lesser-known side of Ross— the classicist and traditional metricist concerned not only with factual reality but also with spiritual truth.

In the 1930s Ross's interest in things spiritual led him to translate work by the surrealist Max Jacob and to write prose poems influenced by Jacob and Franz Kafka; some of the prose poems were published in *New Directions in Prose & Poetry* for 1937. His work in this period incorporates elements of automatic writing, transcendentalism, mysticism, and archetypal imagery.

An extremely private man, Ross did little to bring his writing to attention and offered very little of it for publication. Most of his publications after 1930 were solicited by anthologists or magazine editors. Critic Barry Callaghan suggests that he wrote "only when strenuously urged by an anthologist or literature student." Such urging from poet Raymond Souster resulted in the collection *Experiment, 1923-29*, published in 1956 by Souster in a mimeograph edition under the Contact Press imprint. (Ross felt this collection misrepresented him in its emphasis on his imagist work.) Similar encouragement by Callaghan led to his writing of the poems included in the posthumously published collection, *Shapes and Sounds* (1968).

While Ross's private and somewhat trenchant nature, together with his diffidence toward publishing and the publicly lived literary life, caused him to be little known during his lifetime except to fellow poets, it could bring to his work an austerity of diction and simplicity of syntax close to the imagist ideal. His strongest work is undoubtedly this early imagist-oriented poetry, work that derives its strengths from his restrained, skeptical personality, from his scientist's preference for objective, factual material, and from his affection for the Canadian wilderness landscape. This is poetry which, as he wrote in "On National Poetry" (*Canadian Forum*, 1944), is "distinctly located" in a geographic "locale." Ross's writing became of special importance in the 1950s and 1960s when new generations of Canadian poets sought their precursors in the modernist goals of restraint, precision, organic rhythm, and the factual image.

Letters:

A Literary Friendship: The Correspondence of Ralph Gustafson and W. W. E. Ross, edited by Bruce Whiteman (Toronto: ECW, 1984).

References:

Barry Callaghan, "Memoir," in Ross's *Shapes and Sounds*, edited by Raymond Souster and John Robert Colombo (Don Mills, Ont.: Longmans, 1968), pp. 1-7;

Peter Stevens, "On W. W. E. Ross," *Canadian Literature*, 39 (Winter 1969): 43-61.

Simone Routier

(4 March 1901-6 November 1987)

Louise H. Forsyth
University of Western Ontario

BOOKS: *L'Immortel Adolescent* (Quebec: Le Soleil, 1928; revised and enlarged, 1929);

Ceux qui seront aimés (Paris: Pierre Roger, 1931);

Paris–Amour–Deauville (Paris: Pierre Roger, 1932);

Les Tentations (Paris: La Caravelle, 1934);

Adieu, Paris! Journal d'une évacuée canadienne, 10 mai-17 juin 1940 (Ottawa: Le Droit, 1940; revised and enlarged edition, Montreal: Beauchemin, 1944);

Réponse à "Désespoir de vieille fille," as Marie de Villiers (Montreal: Beauchemin, 1943);

Les Psaumes du jardin clos (Paris: La Lyre et La Croix / Montreal: Editions du Lévrier, 1947);

Je te fiancerai (Paris: La Lyre et La Croix, 1947); republished as *Le Long Voyage* (Paris: La Lyre et La Croix, 1947);

Notre Dame du bel amour, by Routier and Soeur Paul-Emile (Ottawa: Le Droit, 1947);

Le Choix de Simone Routier dans l'œuvre de Simone Routier (Notre-Dames-des-Laurentides, Que.: Presses Laurentiennes, 1981).

PERIODICAL PUBLICATION: "La Ferveur d'une débutante en poésie," *Ecrits du Canada Français*, 44 / 45 (1982): 213-225.

Simone Routier (photograph by Victor Barbeau, courtesy of Kenneth Landry)

Simone Routier's name is usually cited among those of the significant poets of the first half of the twentieth century. She was the respected associate of many Quebec authors and critics, both those who stayed in Canada and those who traveled to France between World War I and World War II. Her work offers an account of her personal search for knowledge, of her travels and involvement in literary discussions, ideological debates, and historical events. In her early writings she demonstrated a strong sense of her material presence as a woman in the world. She was one of the first Quebec poets to explore fully the theme of love. Her work is also significant as a lucid account of the act of creation. In her later volumes the theme of fervent religious faith is dominant.

Routier's work shows the influence of the French symbolists, of the French moralist tradition, of such French writers of the twentieth century as Paul Valéry and Paul Claudel, and of the Quebec poets who rejected the moralistic and literary conventions of the landscape writers of the early twentieth century. Routier was born in Quebec City, daughter of Zélia Laforce Routier and Alfred-Charles Routier, a jeweler. She was the great-niece of historian François-Xavier Garneau. She completed her primary and secondary educations with the Ursulines.

Her first book, *L'Immortel Adolescent* (1928), is an expression of wonder felt by a young woman when she first experiences the emotions associated with romantic love. Routier's own first amorous experience may have been with the poet Alain Grandbois, whom Routier met when she was invited by his sister, Gabrielle, to visit the family's summer home on Lac Clair in Saint-Casimir. A close relationship seems to have developed between the two young poets, which lasted for two years (1920-1922) and then dissolved with some measure of bitterness and misunderstanding. This was an important episode for Routier. When she and Grandbois met in Paris ten years after their separation, she was struck by the spiritual closeness which she still felt between them: "Nous avons tous les deux une main si semblable et des goûts et des réactions tellement identiques que notre dialogue me donne parfois l'impression d'un monologue" (We are so similar in taste and response that our dialogue sometimes seems like a monologue to me). At the time of Grandbois's death in 1975, Routier wrote a poem, "Triste étrangement," in which she evokes the bond they shared. Published in the autumn 1975 issue of *Poésie*, the poem concludes with her question to Grandbois, "Alain, te souviens-tu de nos vingt ans emmêlés?" (Alain, do you remember our intertwined twenty years?). However, the relationship which was to prove decisive for Routier was one she had a few years later with a young English-speaking, Protestant Canadian whom her family found unsuitable for marriage. This loss of promised happiness seems to have led her, after the publication of her first book, to travel to France and to pursue her career there.

In *L'Immortel Adolescent* the unhappy love affair is transmuted into a profound spiritual experience whereby a young woman becomes a poet. The thematic structure of the volume reflects this development. The two introductory poems lead into the volume's four sections in which the adolescent who first showed her love and suffering is transformed into her muse, becoming a symbol of youth, beauty, and life. The major themes of the volume are love, solitude, travel, and creativity. These remain the central themes throughout Routier's works, although they are transformed through the years.

In the first introductory poem, the poet addresses "l'immortel adolescent," whom, as a sculptor, she has formed with her own creative powers; she urges him to speak and show his lasting vitality to her. His silence until the end of the volume makes the work a quest for the source of vision. The second introductory poem, "Le Coffret de mosaïque" (The Mosaic Chest), sets forth in miniature all that is contained in the following four sections of the work, including the title of each section. The poet introduces the theme of life as exile. The delicate and troubling beauty of the mosaic chest is a symbol of the power of human creativity to overcome misfortune and reproduce lost riches.

In the first section, "Fauves Entrelacs" (Untamed Tracery), the poet recaptures the experience of love, from intoxication to loneliness and doubt. In the second section, "Sombre Apothéose," the movement is reversed, with the poet returning from despair to the hope and serenity of new wisdom. However, it is first necessary to traverse a period of dark and painful solitude. The creative process and an opening out to new experience–travel, in this case, as in many of Routier's works–offer joyous consolation in section three, "La Flore exhubérante" (Exuberant Flora). In the final poems, those of the section entitled "Veines aux reflets variés" (Sparkling Veins), she reflects on the nourishment needed by her soul if her writing is to capture beauty. The pattern of the intoxication of love, followed by solitude and despair and then new vision with enlarged spaces, is constant in Routier's writing.

L'Immortel Adolescent was an immediate success. The first edition was sold out within three months. The Province of Quebec selected it for the Prix David in 1929, and the Société des Poètes Canadiens-Français invited Routier to become a member the same year. The following year she moved to Paris, where she registered at the Sorbonne to study phonetics and literature. In Paris, from 1930 to 1940, she worked as draughtswoman-cartographer at the Archives Publiques du Canada. In 1931, with the publication of her second book of verse, she received the Quebec lieutenant-governor's medal, the *diplôme d'honneur* from the Société des Poètes Canadiens-Français, and the *diplôme des Jeux Floraux du Languedoc*.

Her second volume, *Ceux qui seront aimés* (Those Who Will Be Loved), with a preface by Louis Dantin, is a slender collection which is close in form and theme to *L'Immortel Adolescent*: love, separation, despair, new horizons. Routier's first book of prose appeared in 1932: *Paris–Amour–Deauville*. The title reflects the three major divisions of the book; a fourth section, "Et Autres Choses" (And Other Things), is divided into thematic groupings: writing and philosophy, morality, personal experience. Each section includes several brief paragraphs, each presenting a concise and witty statement. In "Paris" Routier evokes the sites of Paris and its unique character as a great city. By way of contrast, "Deauville," in which she reflects on the famous Normandy resort, offers the follies of bourgeois social life, which Routier enjoys holding up to gentle ridicule. "Amour" offers personal insight into the most universal of human desires. The first subsection of "Et Autres Choses" is particularly interesting for an understanding of Routier's theories regarding literary creation and shows her eager to avoid banal convention.

Routier's finest and most original volume of poetry, *Les Tentations* (Temptations), appeared in 1934, with pen drawings by Bernard Laborie and woodcuts by André Margat. The frank sensuousness and awakening are expressed by the poet in fresh images. The dominant themes of the volume are travel and love, with the introductory poem presenting the irresistible call of intoxication. In the first section the poet evokes places she has visited in France, other countries of Europe, and Africa.

By the time she published *Les Tentations*, Routier had achieved mastery of her craft. In this volume she explores a wide variety of poetic forms, ranging from fixed medieval forms to free verse, a daring innovation for a Quebec writer of the time. She had already indicated the fascination she felt for the freedom of this verse form in *Paris–Amour–Deauville;* in "L'Antique Alexandrin," first published in *Le Choix de Simone Routier* (Selections of Simone Routier, 1981), she states how suitable it is in the modern world as an expression of the desire to live as fully as possible:

> Les vers-libristes ne garantissent rien, bien sûr;
>   ils n'ont que faire des routes trop sûres,
> Puisqu'ils veulent avaler la vie, toute la vie et
>   sauter, par-delà les étoiles, tous les murs

(The free-verse poets don't guarantee anything, it's true; / they want nothing to do with the too-safe roads, / Since they want to swallow life, all of life and / jump, beyond the stars, over all the walls).

The frank response to the call of adventure becomes even stronger in the second section, unified by the theme of love. However, as in her earlier volumes, the intoxication passes, perhaps because of the poet's inability to give herself fully to it, and she is left with solitude and weariness, finally alleviated by a return to the call of new departures.

Although in 1939 Routier represented the Société des Ecrivains Canadiens-Français in Liège at the Congrès International des Ecrivains de Langue Française, the early years of World War II were for her a period of tragedy. Her fiancé, Louis Courty, was killed by an exploding shell two days before their wedding. A short time later she had to leave France, abandoning all her belongings, including her manuscripts, the work of ten years. Her difficult departure is recounted in diary form in *Adieu, Paris! Journal d'une évacuée canadienne, 10 mai-17 juin 1940* (1940), covering the period between the German invasion of France at Sedan to the days following the occupation of Paris. Routier's personal experiences are thrown into relief by her description of others, particularly the thousands of refugees, and by her use of newspaper accounts to establish an accurate historical context. *Adieu, Paris!* was an extremely popular book, going through five editions by 1944.

Upon her return to Canada, Routier began a ten-year tenure as archivist at the Canadian Archives in Ottawa (1940-1950), where she also enrolled at the Institut Dominicain de Philosophie. A period of ten months spent at the Dominican Monastery at Berthierville showed that, despite her great need for tranquillity, she did not have a vocation for the secluded life. The central theme of her four subsequent books published during the 1940s is a warm and fervent religious faith. While this represents a new departure in her writing, Routier's sensitivity remains unchanged: spiritual fulfillment can come only through full acceptance of experience in the material world.

Réponse à "Désespoir de vieille fille" (Response to "Old Maid's Despair," 1943), written under the pseudonym of Marie de Villiers, is a reply to Thérèse Tardif's 1943 volume of "pensées" and a denunciation of the petty vision of a work in which the author turns her back on the beauties of life.

Les Psaumes du jardin clos (Psalms from the Closed Garden, 1947) was inspired by the garden of the convent at Berthierville. It is a fervent celebration of God's love. The first line of each of the 150 stanzas is taken from the book of Psalms. *Je te fiancerai* (I Will Become Engaged to You) appeared in 1947 and was republished the same year under the title *Le Long Voyage*.

Although thematically this volume is close to *Les Psaumes du jardin clos*, Routier's poetic language assumes new form here, with the poet influenced by the French writer Claudel in her use of long lines which are similar to biblical verse. *Notre Dame du bel amour* (Our Lady of Good Love), a collaboration of Routier and Soeur Paul-Emile, is a short text written to be accompanied by choral and orchestral music. It was composed to be performed at the Congrès Marial held in Ottawa in June 1947 and published later that year.

On 31 March 1947 Routier was named to the Académie Canadienne-Française. A warm speech of reception was made by Rina Lasnier, who drew special attention to Routier's literary and spiritual courage and her personal strength. Routier was named *attachée de presse* at the Canadian Embassy in Brussels in 1950. In 1955 she was appointed cultural attachée at the Canadian Consulate in Boston; she became vice-consul in 1957.

Routier retired from government service when she married J.-Fortunat Drouin on 8 April 1958. During her retirement she contributed articles and poems to various periodicals. The publication of *Le Choix de Simone Routier* made available for the first time some of her considerable unpublished material. Simone Routier died on 6 November 1987. She is an important Quebec writer whose works deserve more serious critical study than they have received to date.

Letters:
Routier and Louis Dantin, "Correspondance

1929 à 1941," *Ecrits du Canada Français*, 44 / 45 (1982): 227-274.

References:
Jacques Blais, "Les Recueils selon l'esprit nouveau," in his *De l'ordre et de l'aventure* (Quebec: Presses de l'Université Laval, 1975), pp. 67-70;

Louis Dantin, "Mlle Simone Routier," in his *Poètes de l'Amérique française*, second series (Montreal: Albert Lévesque, 1934), pp. 129-145;

Alfred DesRochers, *"L'Immortel Adolescent"* and "En écoutant parler Simone Routier," in his *Paragraphes* (Montreal: Action Canadienne-Française, 1931), pp. 123-150, 167-172;

Maurice Hébert, . . . *Et d'un livre à l'autre* (Montreal: Albert Lévesque, 1932), pp. 183-190;

Rina Lasnier, "Leurs figures: Simone Routier," *Liaison* (May 1947): 268-272;

Gilles Marcotte, "La Chair décevante," in his *Une Littérature qui se fait* (Montreal: HMH, 1962), pp. 121-139;

Séraphin Marion, *En Feuilletant nos écrivains* (Montreal: Action Canadienne-Française, 1931), pp. 89-96;

René Pageau, *Rencontres avec Simone Routier, suivies des Lettres d'Alain Grandbois* (Joliette, Que.: La Parabole, 1978).

Papers:
Routier's manuscripts, correspondence with many Quebec writers, and other documents are at the Bibliothèque Nationale du Québec.

F. R. Scott
(1 August 1899-31 January 1985)

Sandra Djwa
Simon Fraser University

SELECTED BOOKS: *Labour Conditions in the Men's Clothing Industry*, by Scott and H. M. Cassidy (Toronto: Thomas Nelson, 1935);

Canada Today: A Study of Her National Interests and National Policy (Toronto: Oxford University Press, 1938; revised and enlarged, 1939);

Make This Your Canada: A Review of C.C.F. History and Policy, by Scott and David Lewis (Toronto: Central Canada Publishing, 1943);

Overture (Toronto: Ryerson, 1945);

Events and Signals (Toronto: Ryerson, 1954);

The Eye of the Needle: Satires, Sorties, Sundries (Montreal: Contact, 1957);

Signature (Vancouver: Klanak, 1964);

Selected Poems (Toronto: Oxford University Press, 1966);

Trouvailles: Poems from Prose (Montreal: Delta, 1967);

Dialogue sur la traduction à propos du "Tombeau des rois," by Scott and Anne Hébert (Montreal: HMH, 1970);

The Dance Is One (Toronto: McClelland & Stewart, 1973);

Essays on the Constitution: Aspects of Canadian Law and Politics (Toronto: University of Toronto Press, 1977);

The Collected Poems of F. R. Scott, edited by John Newlove (Toronto: McClelland & Stewart, 1981);

A New Endeavour: Selected Political Essays, Letters, and Addresses, edited by Michiel Horn (Toronto: University of Toronto Press, 1986).

TELEVISION: *The Roncarelli Affair*, by Scott and Mavor Moore, CBC, 14 March 1974.

OTHER: *Social Planning for Canada*, edited by Scott (Toronto: Thomas Nelson, 1935);

New Provinces: Poems of Several Authors, edited by Scott and A. J. M. Smith, includes poems by Scott (Toronto: Macmillan, 1936);

Canada After the War: Studies in Political, Social, and Economic Policies for Post-war Canada, edited by Scott and Alexander Brady (Toronto: Macmillan, 1944);

The Blasted Pine: An Anthology of Satire, Invective and Disrespectful Verse, Chiefly by Canadian Writers, edited by Scott and Smith (Toronto: Macmillan, 1957; revised and enlarged, 1967);

St.-Denys Garneau & Anne Hébert: Translations / Traductions (Vancouver: Klanak, 1962);

Quebec States Her Case: Speeches and Articles from Quebec in the Years of Unrest, edited by Scott and Michael Oliver (Toronto: Macmillan, 1964);

The Roncarelli Affair, by Scott and Mavor Moore, in *The Play's the Thing: Four Original Television Dramas*, edited by Tony Gifford (Toronto: Macmillan, 1976), pp. 121-164;

Poems of French Canada, translated by Scott (Burnaby, B.C.: Blackfish, 1977).

F. R. Scott was one of the most important catalysts of modern English-Canadian poetry, partly because of the influence of his own poetry and partly because of a charismatic personality: he was instrumental in the founding of several literary groups and little magazines such as the *McGill Fortnightly Review*, the *Canadian Mercury*, and *Preview*. He was also a pioneer translator of Quebecois poetry. As a satirist in the late 1920s and early 1930s, he helped battle an outworn romanticism in order to introduce the new poetry. In such landscape poems as "Old Song," "Lakeshore," and "Laurentian Shield," he established a northern evolutionary view of Canadian nature which influenced contemporary poets, including Earle Birney, Al Purdy, and Margaret Atwood. As a commentator on the wider field of Canadian culture, F. R. Scott is a figure of extraordinary importance. He achieved distinction not only as a poet but also as a political activist and a leading constitutional lawyer. None of these activities can be neatly separated from the others: they all find expression in his poetry and all stem from the nationalist concerns of the 1920s.

Francis Reginald Scott was born in Quebec City on 1 August 1899. His father was Canon

F. R. Scott (photograph by William Toye)

F. G. Scott, an Anglican clergyman popularly known as the poet of the Laurentians, who gained distinction as the "beloved padre" of the Great War; his mother was Amy Brooks Scott. From his father he absorbed his religious and poetic impulses, a tradition of public service, and a love for the Canadian northland. At the turn of the century the northern landscape was strongly linked with national identity in Canada. On family camping trips the elder Scott would often comment on the great age of the Laurentian rock; a keen astronomer, he taught his son to chart the stars in the northern sky. The young Scott began to read astronomy, and this interest continued during his years at Quebec High School, from which he graduated in 1916. In the fall of this year he left home to attend Bishop's College at Lennoxville, near Montreal. There he developed a taste for poetry, especially that of Alfred Tennyson, and an interest in European history. In 1919 he received his B.A.

In 1920 he attended Oxford under a Rhodes scholarship. He studied history, and in his spare time read widely, especially in science, rowed for Magdalen, translated sonnets from the Old French and Italian, and wrote satirical verse. While still at Bishop's he had read Henri Bergson's *L'Evolution créatrice* (*Creative Evolution*, 1907). In his first year at Oxford he read Arthur Eddington's writings on the universe; later he began to read Albert Einstein. Little by little his religious vision of the world was modified by the new science. It was at Oxford that Scott first became interested in socialism, largely as an outgrowth of study sessions held by the Student Christian Movement, one on R. H. Tawney's *The Acquisitive Society* (1920). Tawney's Christian socialism augmented Scott's early religious training. He began to articulate his belief that a man's "rights" or profits in society ought to be commensurate with his "function" or contribution to it. In 1922 Scott received an Oxford B.A., and in 1923 he concluded his thesis for a B.Litt., "The Annexation of Savoy and Nice by Napoleon III, 1860." By the fall of 1924, as entries in his private journals confirm, he had come to the conclusion that he could not be happy unless his own life was dedicated to making a worthwhile contribution to society.

In October of 1923 Scott returned to Canada and a post as teacher at Lower Canada College in Montreal. He did so with the recognition that a "new era starts–Life, in fact. Period of assimilation is over: period of Expression, in every way that is good, must commence." In fact, his most important decade of assimilation was about to begin. He studied law at McGill University (1924-1927) and served an apprenticeship with the Montreal law firm of Lafleur, MacDougall, Macfarlane & Barclay. In 1927 he was called to the bar, and in 1928, the year he married Marian Mildred Dale, a painter, he began teaching law at McGill, where he remained until his retirement in 1968, serving as dean of law from 1961 to 1964.

Among Scott's important activities of the 1920s was his participation in a series of groups which afforded freewheeling discussion and the opportunity for self-expression. The first, simply named The Group (1925-1929), was a small gathering of friends who met regularly to discuss current events, literature, and art. It was through the Canadian nationalism of the 1920s, as reflected by this circle, that the foundation was laid for Scott's subsequent political, legal, and poetic character. Politically he became a moderate Canadian nationalist, rejecting the imperial and Victorian past. Artistically, like the painters known as the Group of Seven, he was turning for inspiration to Canada's northern landscape with its sharp, northern light. As he wrote in "New Paths," a poem written in the mid 1920s but unpublished until 1981:

> Here is a new soil and a sharp sun,
>
> Turn from the past,
> Walk with me among these indigent firs,
> Climb these rough crags . . . [.]

Then, through the poet A. J. M. Smith and the editorial board of the *McGill Fortnightly Review* (on which he served as a founding member from 1925 to 1927), he was introduced to modern poetry, especially that of T. S. Eliot and the imagists, and of equal importance, to the iconoclastic spirit of the 1920s. Scott's attacks on the orthodox were to range widely, but his first broadside was launched against the old poetry. In 1927, in the *McGill Fortnightly Review*, he published a first draft of "The Canadian Authors Meet," an indictment of the Canadian literary establishment: his jaunty roll call of the major poets of the Confederation group, "Carman, Lampman, Roberts, Campbell, Scott," presumably D. C. Scott, did not exclude his father, F. G. Scott:

> Shall we go round the mulberry bush, or shall
> We gather at the river, or shall we
> Appoint a poet laureate this Fall,
> Or shall we have another cup of tea?

Scott later became the Montreal representative to the editorial board of the *Canadian Forum*. In 1931, in two successive issues of the *Canadian Forum*, Scott published his own manifesto for the new poetry: "The old order of politics needs no consideration; the fact of the war was proof enough of its obsolescence. The old order of Deity was shown by anthropologists to be built not upon rock, but upon the sand of primitive social custom. Socialism and communism cast overwhelming doubt upon the value of the economic order. . . . The universe itself, after Einstein's manipulations . . . became a closed continuum as warped as the mind of man. . . . Amid the crash of systems, was Romantic poetry to survive?" Scott's own career exemplifies the transition from Victorian romanticism to the modern. But, as with most moderns, there was a strong infusion of romanticism in his own poetry: primarily in his use of nature as symbol but also as expressed in his belief that poetry can help to change society. In overall development his work can be seen in four successive stages. In the late 1920s he wrote a northern landscape poetry influenced by the imagists, by Eliot's fertility myth, and by Bergson's theory of the *élan vital*. In the 1930s, in response to the Depression, he wrote a basically socialist, often satiric, program poetry. Subsequently, in the late 1940s and early 1950s, both strains were fused into a more philosophical structure, as in "A Grain of Rice" (first published in *Events and Signals*, 1954), in which Scott's humanist reflections move from cell, to man, to the larger movements of the physical universe.

The earliest landscape poetry is best represented by "Old Song," first published in the *Canadian Mercury*, for which Scott served as an editor, in 1929. Here, the ephemerality of human life and vegetation ("far voices / fretting leaves") contrasts with the larger eternal processes given voice by the St. Anne River: "in the deep / Laurentian river / an elemental song / for ever":

> a quiet calling
> of no mind
> out of long aeons
> when dust was blind
> and ice hid sound.

This is a basically evolutionary vision, in which the land is associated with timeless process. Man, the microcosm, is evanescent: a brief interval in this continuing process. The chief attraction of the poem is not this surface imagist description but rather the animating force that lies beneath physical reality:

> only a moving
> with no note
> granite lips
> a stone throat

The force which animates nature, personified in the powerful last image, is evolutionary process, invested with Bergson's *élan vital*.

The next stage in Scott's poetry, the social verse of the 1930s and early 1940s, is first seen in "An Anthology of Up-to-Date Canadian Poetry," nineteen poems published in the *Canadian Forum* in 1932, and in "Social Notes," a series of thirteen poems which followed in the same journal three years later. After this date much of Scott's poetry had a political application. Again, as in the early nature poetry, Scott is focusing upon the land, but now his verse expresses a distinctly socialist vision, in particular, Tawney's belief that profit ought to be commensurate with a man's contribution to society. Consider "Natural Resources":

> Come and see the vast natural wealth of this mine.
> In the short space of ten years
> It has produced six American millionaires
> And two thousand pauperized Canadian families.

In these poems Scott begins to develop the characteristic technique of his later satiric verse: the presentation of a series of simple statements of fact which can have a cumulative power.

During the years when he was still finding his poetic voice, he was also emerging as a forceful champion of civil rights. He became involved with the politician J. S. Woodsworth, the historian Frank Underhill, and others in founding, in the early 1930s, the League for Social Reconstruction, a socialist study group. He also helped frame the "Regina Manifesto," which shortly brought the social democratic C.C.F. (Co-operative Commonwealth Federation) into being. National chairman of the C.C.F. from 1942 to 1950, he was often in conflict with the legal establishment at McGill. In the 1950s he successfully argued several court cases which have become landmarks in Canadian jurisprudence, and in 1952 he went to Burma (as a U.N. technical assistant) to help design the socialist state there.

The campaign for a new poetry continued in the 1930s when Scott and Smith together edited the first anthology of modern Canadian po-

Dust jacket for the 1966 volume that includes selections from Scott's nature poems, satires, metaphysical verse, and translations of French-Canadian poets

etry. In emulation of the British *New Signatures*, and published in 1936, it was called *New Provinces* and included poems by Robert Finch, Leo Kennedy, A. M. Klein, E. J. Pratt, Scott, and Smith. Scott wrote a brief preface in which he remarked that the search for new content in modern poetry was less successful than the search for new techniques: "By the end of the last decade the modernist movement was frustrated for want of direction." He contributed ten poems to *New Provinces*, and many are reworkings of traditional concepts: religion is parodied in "Teleological," organized charity in "Summer Camp," the old poetry in "The Canadian Authors Meet," and the capitalist economy in "Efficiency." "Teleological," a parody of the argument from design, is one of the most interesting poems in this anthology:

> Note, please, the embryo.
> Unseeing
> It swims into being.

Elan vital,
Thyroid, gonads *et al.*

Here, the casual scientific tone, pointing out the specimen in its implied laboratory setting, forces the reader to contrast the order and design of science with that of religion. In this reworking of the old myths and images of religion in terms of the new myths and images of science, Scott is characteristic of the moderns, for, as F. J. Hoffman has remarked in a piece published in *Backgrounds to Modern Literature* (edited by John Oliver Perry, 1969), the urge toward secularization is one of the outstanding characteristics of the writers of the 1920s. Scott's social concerns are brought to a synthesis in "Overture," his last poem in *New Provinces*, which blends aesthetic and social concerns within a larger humanist framework: the speaker listening to a Beethoven sonata in a darkened room under a cone of light, hears "the bright / Clear notes fly like sparks through the air / And trace a flickering pattern of music there."

But how shall I hear old music? This is an hour
Of new beginnings, concepts warring for power,
Decay of systems–the tissue of art is torn
With overtures of an era being born.

As the Spanish civil war gave way to the greater tragedy of World War II, the 1930s indeed proved to be a decade of "concepts warring for power." By 1941 the Phony War had accelerated into the battle to save Britain, and Scott, now at Harvard under a Guggenheim fellowship, writing on the Canadian constitution, had begun a series of war poems. These were first published in *Poetry* (Chicago) and then collected in his first book of poetry, *Overture* (1945). Five of these poems, printed in the March 1944 issue of *Poetry*, earned him the Guarantor's Prize for that year. As the title poem implies, this is program poetry: the book begins with "Dedication," a call for world brotherhood, and ends with "Villanelle for Our Time." The first part of the book, especially the Audenesque "Flux" and "Armageddon," is suggestive of the British war poets. In the second part the voice is more recognizably Scott's own in, for example, the meditative humanism of "Examiner" and "Passer-by." Also impressive is a group of northern landscape poems, some of which were written in the late 1920s and early 1930s.

Events and Signals is Scott's best book of poetry; it includes the much-anthologized poems "A Grain of Rice," "Lakeshore," "Laurentian Shield,"

"Last Rites," and the satiric "Bonne Entente." Several of these are key poems in the development of a modern tradition in English-Canadian poetry. In "Lakeshore" Scott is exploring the evolutionary myth which is so resonant a part of modern Canadian romanticism; in "Laurentian Shield" he is articulating a nationalist and socialist view of the northern landscape, an evolutionary landscape which has influenced such younger poets as Al Purdy and Margaret Atwood.

Hidden in wonder and snow, or sudden with
    summer,
This land stares at the sun in a huge silence
Endlessly repeating something we cannot hear
Inarticulate, arctic,
Not written on by history, empty as paper[.]

That part of the Laurentian Shield stretching between the Great Lakes and Winnipeg and leaning north to the Pole, the land is "inarticulate" because "arctic" or barren. Uncultivated, it is without history or language, man's tabula rasa. Yet, in the depths of its lakes, the land has "songs" of its own. At present there are rudimentary "pre-words, / Cabin syllables, / Nouns of settlement," but, ominously, the language is moving through "steel syntax" toward the "long sentence of its exploitation." Yet the conclusion affirms that the hope of the future is to be found in the warmth of human neighborhood and social cooperation:

But a deeper note is sounding, heard in the mines
The scattered camps and the mills, a language of
    life,
And what will be written in the full culture of
    occupation
Will come, presently, tomorrow,
From millions whose hands can turn this rock into
    children.

Scott's most characteristic poem is "A Grain of Rice." Here the framing evolutionary structure of the macrocosm / microcosm is introduced with the opening line, "Such majestic rhythms, such tiny disturbances." The larger rhythms are the great movements of the universe; by implication, the tiny disturbances are life, the grain of rice. In one sense, these disturbances are events such as the delicate emergence of a great Asian moth from its chrysalis, "radiant, fragile, / Incapable of not being born, and trembling / To live its brief moment." In another sense, the tiny disturbance is man–located between cell and galaxy but unnatural in his cruelty to his fellows:

"Today, while Europe tilted, drying the Baltic, / I read of a battle between brothers in anguish, / A flag moved a mile." The concluding stanza is a summation of the deep structure of Scott's poetics with reflections on religion, love, and science, a belief in the order of the universe as opposed to human order, and a reaching out to the frontiers of life and knowledge:

> Religions build walls round our love, and science
> Is equal of error and truth. Yet always we find
> Such ordered purpose in cell and in galaxy,
> So great a glory in life-thrust and mind-range,
> Such widening frontiers to draw out our longings,
> > We grow to one world
> > Through enlargement of wonder.

Events and Signals is prefaced by an epigraph– "between the event and the observer there must pass a signal–a wave, an impulse, or perhaps a ray of light"–and many of Scott's major metaphors (the great Asian moth, the northern lake, the dying man in his oxygen tent) send out signals to be grasped by the perceiving poet and his readers. Scott sees the poet's role as that of an interpreter. In an unpublished radio talk given in 1946 he suggested that the poet can "make us aware of life and our place in it . . . by discovering and expressing the significant and important relationships between man and his age."

In 1957 Scott published *The Eye of the Needle: Satires, Sorties, Sundries*, which includes the now classic "W.L.M.K.," a satiric view of the political fence-sitting of William Lyon MacKenzie King, prime minister of Canada for most of the period from 1921 to 1948: he "never let his on the one hand / Know what his on the other hand was doing." As the line indicates, King becomes both cause and symbol of a Canada without direction. In the same year, Scott and Smith edited *The Blasted Pine: An Anthology of Satire, Invective and Disrespectful Verse, Chiefly by Canadian Writers*, a book which became instantly popular. *Signature*, his 1964 collection, includes the impressive "Mount Royal" ("No things sit, set, hold. All swim, / Whether through space or cycle, rock or sea") and "A Lass in Wonderland," a ballad whose punning title expresses Scott's rueful dismay when defending D. H. Lawrence's *Lady Chatterley's Lover* against charges of obscenity in the Quebec Superior Court. *Selected Poems* appeared in 1966, and *Trouvailles: Poems from Prose*, a book of found poems, was published the following year. *The Dance Is One*, Scott's 1973 volume of verse, includes the memorable "On Saying Good-bye to My Room in Chancellor Day Hall," which, by itemizing the objects in Scott's office, recapitulates his life's work.

Scott began to translate Quebec poets in the late 1940s. In 1962 he produced *St.-Denys Garneau & Anne Hébert: Translations / Traductions. Dialogue sur la traduction à propos du "Tombeau des rois"* is an account of his correspondence with Anne Hébert regarding his translation of her poem "Tombeau des rois" ("The Tomb of the Kings"). This volume, with a foreword by Northrop Frye, was published in 1970. In 1978 he received the Canada Council's translation prize for his collected translations, *Poems of French Canada* (1977).

In the course of his career Scott was the recipient of many other awards and honors. He was elected to the Royal Society of Canada in 1947 and given the Lorne Pierce Medal for distinguished service to Canadian literature in 1962. During the 1960s he was a member of the Royal Commission on Bilingualism and Biculturalism. In 1965 he was awarded the Molson Prize, given by the Canada Council for outstanding achievements in the arts, humanities, and social sciences. He became Companion of the Order of Canada in 1967 and earned Governor General's awards for his *Essays on the Constitution: Aspects of Canadian Law and Politics* (1977) and *The Collected Poems of F. R. Scott* (1981). In 1986 Michiel Horn edited a collection of Scott's essays, letters, and addresses entitled *A New Endeavour* and supplied a helpful contextual introduction, "Frank Scott's Life in Politics." Scott was the recipient of honorary degrees from many institutions, including Dalhousie University, McGill University, the University of British Columbia, and the University of Toronto.

W. E. Collin in a pioneer book of criticism, *The White Savannahs* (1936), describes Scott, Smith, A. M. Klein, and Leo Kennedy as the Montreal Group. In the chapter entitled "Pilgrim of the Absolute" he relates Scott's early landscape poems to T. S. Eliot's *The Waste Land* (1922), noting their connection with the loss of Eden and the desire for an ideal. Louis Dudek, writing in the *Northern Review* in 1951, makes illuminating comparisons between the generations of F. G. and F. R. Scott, proposing the younger Scott as Canada's first representative "modern poet." He finds a sharp cleavage in Scott's poetry between the satiric verse, in which Scott is too obviously a socialist writing socialist verse, and the more personal lyrics, in which he finds a "hope" for Canadian poetry.

Desmond Pacey in his *Ten Canadian Poets* (1958) recognizes Scott's excellence in the three fields of law, literature, and politics, and he argues correctly that "the visionary centre for all of Scott's activities is still an aesthetic one." He writes intelligently of the problems experienced by both Scott and Smith in the attempt to create a national literature and analyzes several of Scott's reflective, meditative lyrics. Scott, he concludes, "will be remembered as a poet primarily for his social satire."

Pacey's judgment that the satiric is the most important aspect of Scott's poetry was accepted by most successive critics. Robin Skelton, writing in a special issue of *Canadian Literature* devoted to Scott (Winter 1967), identifies "intelligence" as the major factor in forming Scott's poetry, thus the satiric mode is dominant. Nonetheless, he hastens to correct what might appear to be a one-sided view by comparing Scott to the metaphysical poets: "Scott, like Donne, like Carew, and like Marvell, speaks as a complete man; his passion involves his intelligence, and his intelligence gives rise to passion." A. J. M. Smith, in the same issue of *Canadian Literature*, also speaks of Scott as a metaphysical, noting that " 'Lakeshore' may also serve as an exemplar both of the 'candid' style derived from Imagism and of the witty metaphysical style that, without being in the least derivative, recalls Marvell and Waller–or, if you prefer, Auden." K. Goodwin, in the *Journal of Commonwealth Literature* (December 1967), considers Scott a satiric poet but disagrees with the label "metaphysical," for Scott, unlike the metaphysicals, does not argue himself into a position during the course of the poem.

Stephen Scobie in "The Road Back to Eden: The Poetry of F. R. Scott," published in *Queen's Quarterly* (Autumn 1972), begins with a view of Scott's metaphysic not dissimilar to that of Collin; however, Scobie's article was written in response to Skelton and Smith, who "do not adequately suggest the degree to which Scott's outlook, in some of his most serious poems, is a profoundly ambiguous one. His clarity is often used to define an ambivalence, and his word play (especially the punning) to embody contrasting meanings in their most concise forms." A background to the McGill Movement in which Scott was so important a figure is found in *The McGill Movement* (1969), edited by Peter Stevens. Other noteworthy critical writing includes Elizabeth Brewster's "The 'I' of the Observer" (*Canadian Literature*, Winter 1978), Germaine Warkentin's "Scott's 'Lakeshore' and

Its Tradition" (*Canadian Literature*, Winter 1980), and the special issues of *Canadian Poetry* (Spring / Summer 1977) and *Brick* (Summer 1987) devoted to Scott.

In "F. R. Scott: Modernist and Romantic Poet" (*Fiddlehead*, January 1983) Terry Whalen argues that despite Scott's reputation as a modernist and a cosmopolitan, he is both romantic in his "strenuous hope for humanity" and uniquely Canadian in his guardianship "of the conscience and the memory of Canadian experience." Donald Winkler, director of *Rhyme and Reason*, a sixty-minute documentary on Scott's life and work, records his impressions of Scott's social wit in "Keeping Stride with F. R. Scott: Notes From A Film-maker's Diary" (*Books in Canada*, March 1983). In "Lives of the Poets" (*Saturday Night*, September 1983) George Woodcock reviews the published proceedings of the 1981 Scott conference at Simon Fraser University, a collection of essays entitled *On F. R. Scott: Essays on His Contributions to Law, Literature and Politics* (1983), and *The Collected Poems of F. R. Scott*. Woodcock argues that neither the volume of essays nor Scott's own poetry addresses the issue of regional pluralism in Canada: Scott's support of "strong central government" smacks of authoritarianism. Echoing other critics, he concludes that Scott's work may best be understood "in terms of polar opposites. The authoritarian exists beside the libertarian. The harshly didactic voice in his poetry exists beside the purely lyrical. The public ideal exists beside the private sensibility. The social planner exists beside the individual rebel. Such contradictions, rare in our staid society, mark Scott as an exceptional being in his time and place, a Canadian of historic importance as well as an historically important Canadian poet."

In a tribute occasioned by the poet's death in 1985, Hugh MacLennan ("F. R. Scott," in *Quill and Quire*, March 1985) recalls Scott's life and work. In another retrospective Michiel Horn ("The Future of Man Is My Heaven," *Canadian Forum*, April 1985) finds that "the driving force in Scott's long life was the ideal of service to humanity." Douglas Barbour, in "F. R. Scott 1899-1985" (*Canadian Literature*, Summer 1985), presents Scott as a man who, in all his careers, "always put himself on the line." Finally, in "King Gordon Remembers F. R. Scott" (*Saturday Night*, July 1985) Gordon, the son of novelist C. W. Gordon, celebrates Scott in an anecdotal account of their friendship. As a poet and political activist, Gordon says, Scott looked for "Order in nature, order in society. Not the imposition of an immutable structure but a process, ensuring the equitable meeting of human needs and the liberation of the creative spirit of mankind."

Bibliography:

Robert Still, "F. R. Scott: An Annotated Bibliography," in *The Annotated Bibliography of Canada's Major Authors,* volume 4, edited by Robert Lecker and Jack David (Downsview, Ont.: ECW, 1983), pp. 205-265.

Biography:

Sandra Djwa, *The Politics of the Imagination: A Life of F. R. Scott* (Toronto: McClelland & Stewart, 1987).

References:

Douglas Barbour, "F. R. Scott 1899-1985," *Canadian Literature,* 105 (Summer 1985): 196;

Elizabeth Brewster, "The 'I' of the Observer," *Canadian Literature,* 79 (Winter 1978): 23-30;

Brick, special issue on Scott, 30 (Summer 1987);

Canadian Literature, special issue on Scott, 31 (Winter 1967);

Canadian Poetry, special section on Scott, (Spring / Summer 1977);

W. E. Collin, "Pilgrim of the Absolute," in his *The White Savannahs* (1936); republished (Toronto & Buffalo: University of Toronto Press, 1975), pp. 177-204;

Sandra Djwa and R. St.-John Macdonald, eds., *On F. R. Scott: Essays on His Contributions to Law, Literature and Politics* (Kingston, Ont.: McGill / Queen's University Press, 1983);

Louis Dudek, "F. R. Scott and the Modern Poets," *Northern Review,* 4 (December / January 1950-1951): 4-15;

K. Goodwin, "A Canadian Satirist," *Journal of Commonwealth Literature,* 4 (December 1967);

King Gordon, "King Gordon Remembers F. R. Scott," *Saturday Night,* 100 (July 1985): 22-25;

Michiel Horn, "The Future of Man Is My Heaven," *Canadian Forum,* 65 (April 1985): 20-21;

Hugh MacLennan, "F. R. Scott," *Quill and Quire,* 51 (March 1985): 59;

Desmond Pacey, "F. R. Scott," in his *Ten Canadian Poets: A Group of Biographical and Critical Essays* (Toronto: Ryerson, 1958), pp. 223-253;

Stephen Scobie, "The Road Back to Eden: The Poetry of F. R. Scott," *Queen's Quarterly,* 79 (Autumn 1972): 314-323;

Peter Stevens, ed., *The McGill Movement: A. J. M. Smith, F. R. Scott and Leo Kennedy* (Toronto: Ryerson, 1969);

Germaine Warkentin, "Scott's 'Lakeshore' and Its Tradition," *Canadian Literature,* 87 (Winter 1980): 42-51;

Terry Whalen, "F. R. Scott: Modernist and Romantic Poet," *Fiddlehead,* 135 (January 1983): 96-100;

Donald Winkler, "Keeping Stride with F. R. Scott: Notes From A Film-maker's Diary," *Books in Canada,* 12 (March 1983): 3-4;

George Woodcock, "Lives of the Poets," *Saturday Night,* 98 (September 1983): 59-60.

Papers:

Scott's papers are at the National Archives of Canada in Ottawa, and at Queen's University in Kingston.

Reuben Ship
(18 October 1915-23 August 1975)

Gerry Gross
Concordia University

BOOK: *The Investigator: A Narrative in Dialogue* (London: Sidgwick & Jackson, 1956).

PLAY PRODUCTION: *We Beg to Differ*, lyrics by Ship as Reuben Davis, music by Mel Tolkin, Montreal, New Theatre Group at Victoria Hall, 1939.

TELEVISION: *My Wife's Sister*, episodes by Ship, Grenada-T.V., 19 September 1956-11 June 1957;
The Greatest Man in the World, adapted from James Thurber's story, *Armchair Theatre*, ABC, 9 November 1958;
Try a Little Tenderness, Redifussion, 18 July 1968.

RADIO: *The Life of Riley*, some three hundred half-hour episodes by Ship, NBC, 1944-1951;
The Night Before Christmas, adapted from the short play by Laura and S. J. Perelman, *Ford Theatre*, CBC, 18 December 1953;
The Man Who Liked Christmas, *Stage*, CBC, 27 December 1953;
The Investigator, *Stage*, CBC, 30 May 1954;
The Greatest Man in the World, adapted from James Thurber's story, *Stage*, CBC, 4 December 1955;
The Taxman Cometh, *Stage*, CBC, 27 April 1969.

OTHER: *The Investigator*, original version, in *All the Bright Company: Radio Drama Produced by Andrew Allan*, edited by Howard Fink and John Jackson (Kingston, Ont.: Quarry / Toronto: CBC Enterprises, 1987), pp. 235-268.

Reuben Ship is best known for *The Investigator*, an hour-long burlesque drama produced by CBC-Radio in May 1954. The broadcast caused much comment in Canada and the United States because it directed its satirical fire at Sen. Joseph McCarthy and the several committees of the U.S. Congress then investigating Communist subversion in education, the arts, industry, and government. Ship felt that he and other artists were the

Reuben Ship at his graduation from McGill in 1939

victims of a witch-hunt in the United States (and in Canada to a much lesser extent) and that many politicians were exploiting the Red Scare to enhance their political power or to curtail the freedom of those with whom they disagreed. In fact, the RCMP had investigated some CBC personnel, and one week after the broadcast Frank Lennard (P. C. Wentworth) interrupted the debate on CBC appropriations in the House of Commons to complain about Ship. He asked whether or not the CBC and his colleagues in the House knew that Ship had been deported from the United States, adding, "if they don't, it is about time they did, and it is about time the CBC screened their employees . . . to see who should not be there." While Lennard received no support at the time, his interjection does convey one part of the con-

288

text within which Ship was working in the 1950s.

Ship grew up during the Depression. His parents, Sam and Bella Davis Ship, lived in Plateau Mt. Royal, a section of central Montreal populated by many immigrants who had brought from Europe a tradition which embraced trade unionism and other socialist values. His family and those of his classmates believed in education as a way to a better life. Despite a lengthy illness for which he was hospitalized and which left him susceptible to infection for the rest of his life, he was able to go on to university. At McGill he studied English literature, joined the Players Club, and was entertainment editor of the *McGill Daily* in 1938-1939. After graduating in 1939 with a B.A., he worked with a group of dedicated amateurs in the YM-YWHA Little Theatre, producing antifascist plays, the proceeds from which were dedicated to the war effort. Ada Span, who became Ship's first wife, had been prominent in this group as an actress and director. She and Ship began working with the New Theatre Group, which had been performing primarily antifascist and left-wing plays since the early 1930s. The group had frequently been under the surveillance of the so-called Red Squad of the Quebec Provincial Police and for that reason sometimes had trouble finding performing space. In 1939 Ship wrote the lyrics for a musical revue called *We Beg to Differ* with music by Mel Tolkin. The New Theatre Group produced it with considerable success, and many of its songs mocking current political targets were played at Progressive Arts clubs in other Canadian cities.

During the summer of 1939 Ship and a few others entertained at resorts in the northeastern United States and then remained in New York, playing union halls at three dollars per meeting. Even a booking at the Village Vanguard provided little income, but Ship stayed on. Finally in 1944 he was hired as a scriptwriter for a new situation comedy which NBC was producing in Hollywood for broadcast over its Blue Network, which then extended nationwide in the United States and Canada. *The Life of Riley* concerned a hard hat "who paid his bills when he had the dough, raised good lively kids, went to church as often as his wife could drag him, [and] probably bowled Wednesday nights. . . ." In 1950 the show was transferred to television, but Ship's contract had expired, and he was not rehired. On 31 July 1951 he was interviewed by an officer of the U.S. Immigration and Naturalization Service and was informed that his immigration status was under re-

view. Subsequent hearings revealed that he had been named a Communist by two colleagues in the Radio Writers Guild.

Ship was required to appear before the subcommittee of the House Un-American Activities Committee (HUAC) then inquiring into communism in the motion-picture industry. At the hearing on 24 September 1951, Ship refused to cooperate and charged that the Committee had no right to ask about his beliefs. He volunteered the information that he had chosen not to become a U.S. citizen because "a shocking and frightening change has taken place in this country since the death of . . . Franklin Roosevelt. Hundreds of aliens have been thrown into jail, . . . have been persecuted because of their beliefs." He was dismissed summarily. Then, for about eighteen months, Ship struggled to remain in the United States; but after several hearings in Los Angeles and a fruitless journey to the Appeals Board in Washington, Ship was finally ordered deported to Canada on 12 January 1953. Ship settled near Toronto in 1953 and supported himself and his family, which now included three daughters, by working in an advertising agency and by writing radio drama for the CBC. He still wrote comedies, but now they all pointed satirically at hypocrisy in government, business, and other institutions.

The Night Before Christmas (1953) is a farce adapted from the stage play by Laura and S. J. Perelman concerning two bank robbers who masquerade as owners of a furniture store. Their plan to burrow through their basement wall into the bank on Christmas Eve fails when their store is robbed. *The Man Who Liked Christmas* (1953) concerns a mild man whose family treats him like a dog, except on Christmas day. He comes to believe that if every day were Christmas, all travail would vanish. But he is rebuked by everyone in a fashion which reveals their hypocrisy.

In his most important play, *The Investigator* (1954), Ship hit back at the exploiters of the Red Scare. The Investigator is on his way to a hearing when the plane crashes. He awakes in heaven and almost immediately finds fault with the Gatekeeper and others of the Immigration Service because, in his view, they are carelessly admitting subversives "up here." He forms a committee with Torquemada, Cotton Mather, and others in order to examine suspect residents. Socrates is examined, as are Voltaire, Milton, and others, and all are bullied in a manner which unmistakably resembles that of Joseph McCarthy. The witnesses are all deported "down there." The parade is interrupted by the entrance of the leader from below who is furious with the committee for sending him a succession of troublemakers, who are unionizing his citizens and generally "raising hell." But nothing stops the Investigator, and soon he wants to question "the Big Man, himself." When his committee tries to check him, he becomes incoherent, repeating again and again, "I am the boss!"

The CBC production, with John Drainie in the title role, was first-rate. Barry Morse, who played the Gatekeeper (according to Ship's instructions) "like an overburdened night clerk in a small hotel," remembers how busy the CBC switchboard was after the show. "While it was in progress, some people got sucked in and really thought it was happening for a bit. You see, they thought John Drainie was really McCarthy."

Within a month, tapes of the show were circulating in New York, and then a long-playing record of the production, bearing no credits, appeared on the *Discuriosity* label. Jay Gould, the *New York Times* radio and television critic, reported that perhaps as many as five thousand copies of the record were selling weekly. Marya Mannes, writing in the *Reporter*, so praised the production that a CBC executive had the article copied and distributed. The play was aired on the Home Service of the BBC on 24 August 1955, and the Australian Broadcasting Commission asked the CBC for broadcast rights. In 1956 a version of *The Investigator* was published in which the stage directions are set out as narrative and the dialogue has been changed to indirect discourse. But regardless of the work's success, Ship found it necessary to continue working in advertising, and not long afterward, he moved to England.

It does not seem that Ship's ambitions were fully realized in England. Like other blacklisted authors, he was probably still selling scripts in the United States under pseudonyms, but the extent of his output is unknown. In 1956 and 1957 he did contribute several scripts to a British television series entitled *My Wife's Sister*. This situation comedy concerned a family based in Manchester that suffers the consequences of the unwelcome re-

turn of a sister-in-law, who has been away many years. Ship also revised his successful radio play *The Greatest Man in the World* (1955) for television, and it was produced in 1958 for the series called *Armchair Theatre*.

In the early 1960s Ship wrote the scenarios for two films, *There Was a Crooked Man* and *The Girl on the Boat*, both starring the British comic Norman Wisdom. The former was the more successful commercially. Wisdom convincingly portrayed a former thief who has developed a social conscience, and Ship's satire reflects his anti-establishment position.

Ship's family had followed him to England, but his marriage failed. Soon after, he married Elaine Grand, the Canadian television journalist best known for her work on the show *Tabloid*. Ship continued to write radio drama, and in 1969 one of his best plays, *The Taxman Cometh*, was produced on *CBC Stage*. It concerns a writer of cavalier habits whose domestic situation includes a live-in mistress and ruinous debts. He courts disaster and the district tax officer's secretary in order to persuade her to steal his tax file, which contains the record of the main component of his debt. Ship's mastery of the form is evident especially in a section in which the writer dictates a play about a writer whose situation is identical to his own, a device which permits him to mock himself as rogue and fool. This show was his last for the CBC.

Ship continued to live in England until his death in 1975. The original version of *The Investigator* was published twelve years after his death, in *All the Bright Company: Radio Drama Produced by Andrew Allan*. No doubt his early promise was only partly fulfilled, but few Canadians have written dramatic satire for any medium with as much wit and conviction as one finds in Ship's radio drama.

Reference:

N. Alice Frick, *Image in the Mind: CBC Radio Drama 1944 to 1954* (Toronto: Canadian Stage and Arts Publications, 1987), pp. 134-143.

Lister Sinclair
(9 January 1921-   )

Chris Johnson
University of Manitoba

BOOKS: *A Play on Words and Other Radio Plays* (Toronto: Dent, 1948)–comprises *A Play on Words; The Blood is Strong; Day of Victory; Oedipus the King; The Faithful Heart; The Case Against Cancer; No Scandal in Spain; All About Emily; You Can't Stop Now; The New Canada; We All Hate Toronto;* and *Epitaph on a War of Liberation;*

The Blood is Strong: A Drama of Early Scottish Settlement in Cape Breton (Agincourt, Ont.: Book Society of Canada, 1956);

Socrates (Agincourt, Ont.: Book Society of Canada, 1957);

Democracy in America: Scripts of Fourteen Dramatizations by Lister Sinclair and George E. Probst Based on the Classic Work by Alexis de Tocqueville, edited by Probst (New York: National Educational Television and Radio Center, 1962)–comprises *Any Lady is a Lady: A Study in American Manners; The Aristocrats of Democracy: A Study in American Law and Lawyers*, by Sinclair and Probst; *The Ark of Civilization: A Study in American Character*, by Sinclair and Probst; *The Cement of Democracy: A Study in American Religion; The Chief Instrument of Freedom: A Study of the American Press; The Cold Water Army: A Study in American Progress; Common Sense and Moonshine: A Study in American Education; The Fourth of July in Albany, 1831: A Study in American Independence; The Governor in the Boarding House: A Study in American Equality; The Happy Republic: A Study in American Values*, by Sinclair and Probst; *The Heavenly Prison: A Study in American Reform; These Precious Premises: A Study in Political Optimism; The Tyranny of the Majority: A Study in American Freedom;* and *Where Could I Be Better Off ? A Study in Jacksonian America;*

Darwin and the Galapagos, by Sinclair and John Livingston (Toronto: CBC Publications, 1966);

The Art of Norval Morrisseau, by Sinclair and Jack Pollock (Toronto: Methuen, 1979).

Lister Sinclair (courtesy of the Canadian Broadcasting Corporation)

PLAY PRODUCTIONS: *The Man in the Blue Moon*, script and direction by Sinclair, Toronto, New Play Society, 1 May 1947;

Socrates, Toronto, Jupiter Theatre, February 1952;

The Blood is Strong, Toronto, Jupiter Theatre, 1952;

The World of the Wonderful Dark, Vancouver, Vancouver International Festival, Summer 1958.

SELECTED TELEVISION: *Hilda Morgan*, adapted from Sinclair's radio play, *Television Theatre*, CBC, 27 November 1952;

One John Smith, adapted from Sinclair's radio play, *Television Theatre*, CBC, 26 February 1953;

The Blood is Strong, adapted from Sinclair's radio play, *Television Theatre*, CBC, 5 January 1954;

The Odds and the Gods, by Sinclair, Charles Israel, and Roald Dahl, *Scope*, CBC, 16 January 1955;

Othello, adapted from William Shakespeare's play, *Folio*, CBC, 23 October 1955;

The Hand and the Mirror, *Folio*, CBC, 20 November 1955;

When Soft Voices Die, *Folio*, CBC, 29 January 1956;

The Small Rain, adapted from Sinclair's radio play, *Folio*, CBC, 11 March 1956;

The Haunted Post Office, *Folio*, CBC, 25 March 1956;

The Empty Frame, *Folio*, CBC, 27 February 1957;

Janey Canuck, adapted from Byrne Hope Saunders's biography of Emily Murphy, *First Performance*, CBC, 24 October 1957;

Socrates, adapted from Sinclair's radio play, *Folio*, CBC, 29 May 1958;

Pride and Prejudice, adapted from Jane Austen's novel, *General Motors Presents*, CBC, 21 December 1958;

Hedda Gabler, adapted from Henrik Ibsen's play, *Fort Startime*, CBC, 10 May 1960;

Galileo, adapted from Bertolt Brecht's play, *Festival*, CBC, 25 March 1963;

Bernard Shaw: Who the Devil Was He?, *Festival*, CBC, 6 April 1966;

Heritage Theatre (series), 1987.

SELECTED RADIO: *Refugee*, *Stage*, CBC, 1 May 1944;

The Man Who Wouldn't Die, *Stage*, CBC, 28 May 1944;

A Play on Words, *Stage*, CBC, 12 November 1944;

The Other Side, *Stage*, CBC, 31 December 1944;

The Blood is Strong, *Our Canada*, CBC, 2 February 1945;

All About Emily, *Stage*, CBC, 25 February 1945;

The Day of Victory, CBC, 8 May 1945;

No Scandal in Spain, CBC, 6 June 1945;

You Can't Stop Now, *Stage*, CBC, 11 November 1945;

Some of Our People Say, *Panorama*, CBC, 29 November 1945;

The Faithful Heart, *Stage*, CBC, 16 December 1945;

Epitaph on a War of Liberation, *Stage*, CBC, 6 January 1946;

We All Hate Toronto, *Panorama*, CBC, 17 January 1946;

The New Canada, CBC, 7 March 1946;

The Lunatic, the Lover and the Poet, *Stage*, CBC, 31 March 1946;

The Case Against Cancer, CBC, 3 April 1946;

Oedipus the King, adapted from Sophocles' play, *CBC Stage*, CBC, 20 October 1946;

One John Smith, *Stage*, CBC, 27 October 1946;

Socrates, *Stage*, CBC, 16 February 1947;

Antigone, adapted from Sophocles' play, *Stage*, CBC, 5 October 1947;

Fortune, My Foe, adapted from Robertson Davies's play, *Stage*, CBC, 17 October 1948;

A Day in the Life of Samuel Johnson, *Wednesday Night*, CBC, 2 February 1949;

The Night of Promises, *Stage*, CBC, 13 March 1949;

Hilda Morgan, *Stage*, CBC, 22 May 1949;

Saint Augustine of Canterbury, *Stage*, CBC, 23 October 1949;

The Man in the Blue Moon, adapted from Sinclair's stage play, *Stage*, CBC, 5 February 1950;

The Hand That Made the Mask, *Wednesday Night*, CBC, 8 February 1950;

World Affairs, 1900-1950, CBC, 2 May 1950;

General Science, 1900-1950, CBC, 9 May 1950;

Leisure and Entertainment, 1900-1950, CBC, 16 May 1950;

Power and Transportation, 1900-1950, CBC, 23 May 1950;

The Home, 1900-1950, CBC, 30 May 1950;

The Seven Diamond Girls, *Playhouse*, CBC, 20 May 1952;

The Hand and the Mirror, *Wednesday Night*, CBC, 1 October 1952;

Language, *Ways of Mankind*, CBC, 9 April 1953;

Athens and Sparta, *Ways of Mankind*, CBC, 30 April 1953;

The Case of the Sea Lion Flippers, *Ways of Mankind*, CBC, 7 May 1953;

A Legend of the Longhouse, *Ways of Mankind*, CBC, 21 May 1953;

But I Know What I Like, *Ways of Mankind*, CBC, 2 July 1953;

Museum of Man, *Ways of Mankind*, CBC, 2 July 1953;

Return to Colonus, *Stage*, CBC, 24 January 1954;

The Tale of the Talking Bird, *Dominion Radio Theatre*, CBC, 13 July 1954;

The Summit and the Tide, *Stage*, CBC, 23 January 1955;

When Soft Voices Die, *Stage*, CBC, 24 April 1955;

The Case of the Borrowed Wife, *Ways of Mankind*, CBC, 5 May 1955;

The Case of the Bamboo-Sized Pigs, Ways of Mankind,
CBC, 12 May 1955;

The Repentant Horse-Thief, Ways of Mankind, CBC,
19 May 1955;

Lion Bites Man, Ways of Mankind, CBC, 26 May
1955;

The Forbidden Name of Wednesday, Ways of Mankind,
CBC, 2 June 1955;

Laying Down the Law, Ways of Mankind, CBC, 9
June 1955;

The Isle is Full of Voices, Ways of Mankind, CBC, 14
July 1955;

The Small Rain, Wednesday Night, CBC, 6 Novem-
ber 1955;

The Golden Age, Stage, CBC, 13 October 1957;

Visions of Joan, Wednesday Night, CBC, 19 March
1958;

The Crystal and the Rose, Stage, CBC, 31 March
1959;

There Were Giants in the Earth, Stage, CBC, 20 De-
cember 1959;

The Last Refuge, Stage, CBC, 19 November 1961;

The View From Here Is Yes, Wednesday Night, CBC,
13 December 1961;

Where Could I Be Better Off?, adapted from Alexis
de Tocqueville, *Democracy in America,* NBC,
17 January 1962;

The Governor in the Boarding House, adapted from
de Tocqueville, *Democracy in America,* NBC,
17 January 1962;

The Fourth of July in Albany, 1831, adapted from
de Tocqueville, *Democracy in America,* NBC,
17 January 1962;

The Ark of Civilization, adapted from de Tocque-
ville, *Democracy in America,* NBC, 17 January
1962;

Any Woman is a Lady, adapted from de Tocque-
ville, *Democracy in America,* NBC, 17 January
1962;

The Cement of Democracy, adapted from de Tocque-
ville, *Democracy in America,* NBC, 17 January
1962;

The Cold Water Army, adapted from de Tocque-
ville, *Democracy in America,* NBC, 17 January
1962;

The Tyranny of the Majority, adapted from de
Tocqueville, *Democracy in America,* NBC, 17
January 1962;

Common Sense and Moonshine, adapted from de
Tocqueville, *Democracy in America,* NBC, 17
January 1962;

Enlightenment Through Deceit, adapted from de
Tocqueville, *Democracy in America,* NBC, 17
January 1962;

The Happy Republic, adapted from de Tocqueville,
Democracy in America, NBC, 17 January
1962;

Those Precious Premises, adapted from de Tocque-
ville, *Democracy in America,* NBC, 17 January
1962.

OTHER: *A Word In Your Ear, When Greek Meets*
Greek, The Case of the Sea Lion Flippers, Leg-
end of the Long House, All the World's a Stage,
But I Know What I Like, and *Museum of Man,*
in *Ways of Mankind: Thirteen Dramas of Peo-*
ples of the World and How They Live, edited by
Walter Goldschmidt (Boston: Beacon, 1954),
pp. 23-32, 67-76, 111-121, 126-136, 141-
150, 154-162, 180-185;

Return to Colonus, in *Canadian Anthology,* edited by
C. F. Klinck and R. E. Watters (Toronto:
Gage, 1955);

Hilda Morgan, in *All the Bright Company: Radio*
Drama Produced by Andrew Allan, edited by
Howard Fink and John Jackson (Kingston,
Ont.: Quarry/Toronto: CBC Enterprises,
1987), pp. 67-101.

Lister Sinclair was a prolific and distinguished radio dramatist during the golden age of
Canadian radio in the 1940s and 1950s. *Canadian*
National Theatre on the Air, 1925-1961, Howard
Fink's descriptive bibliography of broadcast radio
scripts, attributes 183 plays to Sinclair during the
period covered by the inventory. Sinclair has also
had a long career as a radio and television producer, actor, and program host.

The son of W. Shedden Sinclair, a chemical
engineer, and his wife, Lillie Agnes Sinclair,
Lister Shedden Sinclair was born on 9 January
1921 in Bombay, India. Sent back to England
when he was three to be raised in relatives'
homes and boarding schools, Sinclair came to Canada at the age of eighteen to study at the University of British Columbia in Vancouver. There he
met his first wife, Alice Mather, and married her
in 1942, the same year he earned his B.A. Alice
Mather Sinclair has made a significant contribution to the development of Canadian electronic
drama through her work as a story editor for the
CBC. One son was born to this marriage, which
ended in divorce; Sinclair had another son by his
second wife, Margaret Watchman, whom he married in 1965.

After completing his M.A. at the University
of Toronto in 1945, Sinclair was a lecturer in mathematics there until 1948. In 1944 he began to

Sinclair, Andrew Allan, and Alice Hill in the 1950s (courtesy of the Canadian Broadcasting Corporation)

work part-time as an actor and writer for the Canadian Broadcasting Corporation, a connection which has continued, with only short breaks, until the present. When CBC-Television was established in 1952, he became one of the first writers to contribute to that medium in Canada and has since written many scripts; he has served as executive producer of various television series; he became an executive producer in 1967; from 1972 to 1975 he was the CBC's executive vice-president; and from 1975 to 1980, vice-president in charge of program policy and development. He has returned to his original profession, teaching, from time to time, having been appointed to the staff of the Royal Conservatory of Music in Toronto in 1952 and of the Faculty of Fine Arts at York University in 1983.

Even more than stage plays, radio plays seem fated to disappear; still, some of Sinclair's scripts are held by the library of Concordia University in Montreal and an unusually large number have appeared in print. In 1948 twelve were published as *A Play on Words and Other Radio Plays.* The range of style is great: *All About Emily* and *We All Hate Toronto* are witty satires on contemporary values; *Oedipus the King* is a stark and vibrant retelling of the myth; and several, among them *No Scandal in Spain* and *You Can't Stop Now,* are strong pleas for a new and peaceful world. Walter Goldschmidt's 1954 anthology, *Ways of*

Mankind, includes thirteen playlets, seven by Sinclair, dramatizations of anthropological concepts broadcast by an American educational network. Sinclair's pieces demonstrate an unusual ability to combine documentary and dramatic material, a skill he later employed to write episodes for NBC's *Democracy in America,* based on Alexis de Tocqueville's book about his historic visit to investigate American society. Scripts by Sinclair and George E. Probst for this series were published in book form in 1962.

Sinclair's work on behalf of broadcasting in Canada has been recognized by the John Drainie Award for contributions to broadcasting and the Sandford Fleming Medal, which the Royal Canadian Institute awarded him in 1984. He has also won ten of the Ohio State Awards for Educational Radio and Television Programs and holds honorary doctorates from four Canadian universities, including the University of British Columbia and Memorial University of Newfoundland. In 1985 he was made an officer of the Order of Canada.

While most of his writing has been for the electronic media, Sinclair has rewritten some of the scripts for the stage. Only *The Man in the Blue Moon* was written first for the stage. A tragicomic piece about a meek mathematician who invents a death ray, it became, in 1947, the first Canadian play produced by Dora Mavor Moore's New Play

Society, in a production directed by Sinclair; on other occasions Sinclair acted for NPS. Summing up the 1947-1948 Toronto theater season in the *Canadian Jewish Weekly*, the influential Canadian critic Nathan Cohen identified Sinclair as foremost among postwar Canadian playwrights, but qualified his praise: "He is distinguished by a singular loveliness of language and brooding wit, but his plays as a whole are deficient in characterization, cloudy in meaning, and promiscuous in technique." *Socrates* was produced by the Jupiter Theatre in Toronto in 1952 and published in 1957; the familiar story of the philosopher's arrest on false charges is given fresh immediacy by Sinclair's sharp but homely dialogue and by some intriguing speculation concerning Socrates' friendship with Aristophanes.

The Blood is Strong is Sinclair's best-known stage play; the original script was for a radio play broadcast in 1945; the stage play premiered in 1952; a television version was produced in 1954. The central image is the family as "garrison" (to use Northrop Frye's term): the MacDonalds try to make a new home in the woods of Cape Breton Island after emigrating from the Isle of Skye in the early nineteenth century. Murdoch, the family patriarch, attempts to preserve Scottish values in an alien wilderness, but the wilderness becomes home instead to his family. Young love triumphs when daughter Kate marries Barney, an uncouth colonial hunter, and through the deaths of a son and his wife, MacDonald acquires another link to the new land, through "blood purchase." In form the play is quite orthodox, but Sinclair stretches the possibilities of realism by using Scots and colonial dialects, as well as song and Scripture, to heighten the language and sharpen the contrasts.

It has been some time since Sinclair has published creative work, although he collaborated with Jack Pollock to write *The Art of Norval Morrisseau* (1979), a study of the celebrated native Indian painter. A man of many parts and many arts, he has, of late, been devoting most of his time to music, as a musician, music critic, and producer of music programs on the CBC. He is currently president of the Canadian Conference of the Arts, host of the CBC-Radio program *Ideas*, and, since 1983, has been the host of the Festival of the Sound, an annual musical event held in Parry Sound, Ontario.

References:

Jane Chadder, "The Canada of Sinclair's *The Blood is Strong:* 'A Country Without a Mythology?,' " *Canadian Drama / L'Art Dramatique Canadien*, 3 (Fall 1977): 100-104;

N. Alice Frick, *Image in the Mind: CBC Radio Drama 1944 to 1954* (Toronto: Canadian Stage and Arts Publications, 1987), pp. 36-40, 79-81, 92-104;

Kathy Schepens, "The Presentation of Native People in *The Blood is Strong, At My Heart's Core,* and *The Great Hunger*," *Canadian Drama / L'Art Dramatique Canadien*, 2 (Fall 1976): 166-171;

William Solly, "Nothing Sacred: Humour in Canadian Drama in English," in *Dramatists in Canada: Selected Essays,* edited by W. H. New (Vancouver: University of British Columbia Press, 1972), pp. 39-52;

M. Joan Stainton, "The Canadian Immigrant in Drama," *Canadian Drama / L'Art Dramatique Canadien*, 2 (Fall 1976): 172-175.

Papers:

The scripts for some of Sinclair's radio plays are in the CBC collection assembled by the Centre for Broadcasting Studies at Concordia University, Montreal.

Elizabeth Smart
(27 December 1913-4 March 1986)

Lorraine Weir
University of British Columbia

BOOKS: *By Grand Central Station I Sat Down and Wept* (London: Nicholson & Watson, 1945; Toronto: Popular Library, 1977);

A Bonus (London: Polytantric Press, 1977);

The Assumption of the Rogues and Rascals (London: Cape, 1978);

Ten Poems (Bath: Bath Place Community Arts Press, 1981);

Eleven Poems (Bracknell, U.K.: Owen Kirtow, 1982);

In the Meantime (Ottawa: Deneau, 1984);

Necessary Secrets: The Journals of Elizabeth Smart, edited by Alice Van Wart (Toronto: Deneau, 1986);

Juvenilia: Early Writings of Elizabeth Smart, edited by Van Wart (Toronto: Coach House Press, 1987);

Autobiographies, edited by Christina Burridge (Vancouver: William Hoffer / Tanks, 1987).

Long neglected by Canadian critics, Elizabeth Smart suffered the fate of the expatriate whose literary career was interrupted and taken up again many years after her first publication. That volume, *By Grand Central Station I Sat Down and Wept* (1945), was itself an anomaly in terms of Canadian writing at the time. The rise of Canadian interest in the techniques of experimental fiction associated with modernism has, together with the publication of Smart's second novel in the late 1970s, produced a context within which her work may be seen and understood as a significant contribution to the small body of Canadian narratives in the lyrical mode.

Elizabeth Smart was born into the bourgeois family of Russel S. Smart, a barrister, and Emma Louise Parr Smart on 27 December 1913. She attended Hatfield Hall, a private school, and was brought up in a family which valued its place in the social circle of Ottawa diplomatic and political life. At the conclusion of her studies at Hatfield Hall, she and her sister were sent to England for a year since Smart was not permitted by her mother to enter university. In England

Elizabeth Smart in 1979 (photograph by John Reeves)

she fulfilled her role as debutante by studying music and violated it by attending King's College, London, for a time. On her return to Ottawa, she decided to pursue writing rather than music and wrote society notes and editorials for the *Ottawa Journal* before leaving for the more literary environment of New York. As a result of her submission of poems to Lawrence Durrell, she received an introduction to the poet George Barker, with whom she was to live on and off for many years. Returning to Canada in 1940, Smart lived at Pender Harbour in British Columbia and there, in August 1941, the first of her four children by Barker was born.

During her stay at Pender Harbour, Smart wrote *By Grand Central Station I Sat Down and Wept,* a lyrical novel in first person with a loosely biographical plot. The story of a passionate affair which meets with social and legal repression, this novel focuses far less on the presentation of events and clearly defined characters in the realistic mode than on the narrator's at times ecstatic, at times agonized reactions to her situation. Disjunct emotional reportage, Smart's prose moves through lyrical descriptions of the beloved and of love's alteration of the lover's senses of time and space, presentations of the agonies of jealousy (for her lover, like Barker, his original, is already married) and of separation as they cross a state border and are apprehended by police. Set in wartime, Smart's first novel depicts the impossibility of love in a brutalized world and the tragic predicament of a woman who views herself as condemned always to wait for a man over whose actions she can have no control.

Smart's second book, a volume of poems entitled *A Bonus,* was published in 1977. In the three decades between these two books she lived a peripatetic life. During World War II she lived with Barker in Washington, D.C., and worked at the British Army Office and then at the Information Office of the British Embassy until, in 1943, expecting her second child, she arranged a transfer from Washington to London. Though she was dismissed from her job on arrival because of her pregnancy, Smart resolved to stay in England and supported herself and her children over the next twenty years with a variety of journalistic jobs, including writing for fashion magazines and doing advertising copy writing. In 1966 she retired to a cottage in Flixton, north Suffolk, and devoted herself to gardening, raising two grandchildren, and to a long struggle with writer's block as evidenced by her journals during this period. Her first novel was republished, by Panther, in the same year. Like its predecessor, *A Bonus* reveals the preoccupations of Smart's life. It is an uneven book, reflecting its author's disdain for literary fashion and her ability to capture in an image or an epigram the wisdom and violence of her struggle. The great traditional theme of the garden dominates the book, its fertility and rampant energy moving the poet to meditations on her characteristic concerns of pain, futility, love, and death.

In 1978 Smart's second and best novel, *The Assumption of the Rogues and Rascals,* was published. Employing a first-person narrator who sporadically observes her world and reflects upon it, this novel comments much more sharply upon the position of women in modern society than had Smart's earlier published works. In its narrator's words, *The Assumption of the Rogues and Rascals* is a "social apotheosis" in which "every single word [is] evaporated to a mere rich residue." Out of this distillation come paradigmatic statements: "The womb's an unwieldy baggage. Who can stagger uphill with such a noisy weight?" The novel as a whole presents its narrator's episodic discovery of her own strength and command of the "eccentric genes" necessary for writing. Its sole character is the narrator: its setting, her life, ranges from the postwar period to the present time.

Published in 1984, *In the Meantime* is a collection of fugitive works–poems, an autobiographical sketch of childhood entitled "Scenes One Never Forgets," a 1979 extract from the journals published in 1986 as *Necessary Secrets,* and a biographical narrative which is one of Smart's finest works. "Dig a Grave and Let Us Bury Our Mother" (its title from William Blake's poem "Tiriel") is Smart's most direct and powerful attempt to transform into art her lifelong sense of being haunted and determined by her obsessively protective mother. Written in 1939, six years before the publication of *By Grand Central Station I Sat Down and Wept,* this novella (as Smart's editor, Alice Van Wart, classifies it) is a courageous narrative of the lesbian affair which punctuates a polymorphous ménage à trois. Encountering her lover, the narrator discovers both her mother and herself as child and mother: "I am kissing the one I fly from. It is a wailing child. I am older than the world, older and stronger." Though this narrative is uneven, it is the most powerful of Smart's published writings and has much in common stylistically and, as in the passage quoted, thematically with Djuna Barnes's novel, *Nightwood* (1936).

Among the poems collected in *In the Meantime* is a sequence concerned with another aspect of Smart's last years, her return to Canada as recipient of a Senior Arts Grant from the Canada Council in 1982-1983. Living first in Toronto and then taking up an appointment as writer in residence at the University of Alberta in Edmonton, Smart sought understanding from a new generation of readers. Touring the country giving readings, she was more warmly welcomed in the feminist com-

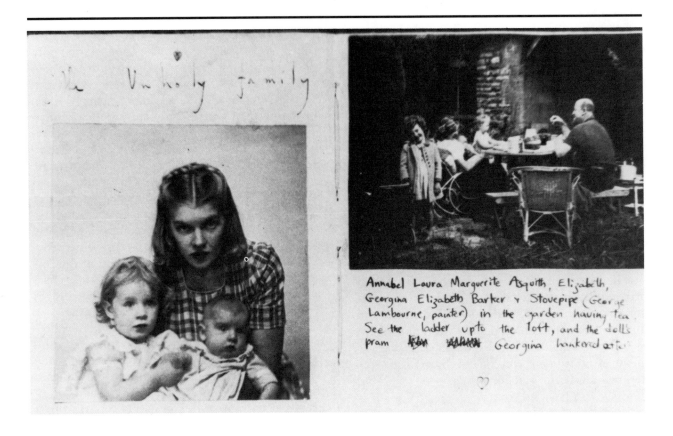

Annabel Laura Marguerite Asquith, Elizabeth,
Georgina Elizabeth Barker & Stovepipe (George
Lambourne, painter) in the garden having tea.
See the ladder up to the loft, and the doll's
pram ~~~~ ~~~~ Georgina hankered after

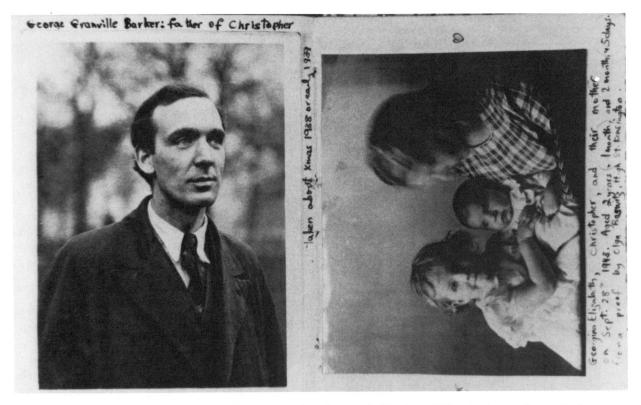

George Granville Barker: father of Christopher

Pages from the album Smart kept for her son Christopher, the second of her four children by the poet George Barker
(copyright © by Sebastian Barker)

munity than, as she put it, "In the whispering / hells of Academe." Finding Canadians still to be as "caged" as they had been in her youth, Smart returned to England. Her journals, *Necessary Secrets*, were the last of her works to appear in her lifetime and reveal the autobiographical basis of most of her works. Smart died in London on 4 March 1986. *Juvenilia: Early Writings of Elizabeth Smart* and her *Autobiographies* were published posthumously, in 1987.

Like her friend, the English poet Stevie Smith, Elizabeth Smart achieved little recognition in her lifetime. Like Barnes and Smith, she lived with intensity her failure to win readers, a failure as much the product of publishing fads as of the imposition of social norms unacceptable to her and inapplicable to her work. Smart's work awaits the attention of a sensitive editor who will allow the best to stand for critical scrutiny in the context of such writers as Smith, Barnes, and Jane Bowles.

Interviews:

Katherine Govier, "The Smart Woman," *Globe and Mail*, 12 April 1978, "Fanfare" section, pp. 10-11;

Eleanor Wachtel, "Passion's Survivor," *City Woman* (Summer 1980): 51-55;

Bruce Meyer and Bruce O'Riordan, "Elizabeth Smart: Fact and Emotional Truth," in their *In Their Words: Interviews with Fourteen Canadian Writers* (Toronto: Anansi, 1984), pp. 184-196.

Reference:

John Goddard, "An Appetite for Life," *Books in Canada*, 11 (June / July 1982): 7-12.

Papers:

Smart's papers are at the National Library of Canada.

A. J. M. Smith

(8 November 1902-21 November 1980)

Wynne Francis
Concordia University

SELECTED BOOKS: *News of the Phoenix and Other Poems* (Toronto: Ryerson, 1943; New York: Coward-McCann, 1943);

A Sort of Ecstasy: Poems New and Selected (East Lansing: Michigan State College Press, 1954; Toronto: Ryerson, 1954);

Collected Poems (Toronto: Oxford University Press, 1962);

Poems: New and Collected (Toronto: Oxford University Press, 1967);

Towards a View of Canadian Letters: Selected Critical Essays 1928-1971 (Vancouver: University of British Columbia Press, 1973);

On Poetry and Poets: Selected Essays of A. J. M. Smith with an Introduction by the Author (Toronto: McClelland & Stewart, 1977);

The Classic Shade: Selected Poems (Toronto: McClelland & Stewart, 1978).

OTHER: *New Provinces: Poems of Several Authors*, edited by Smith and F. R. Scott (Toronto: Macmillan, 1936); republished with "A Rejected Preface" by Smith (Toronto & Buffalo: University of Toronto Press, 1976);

The Book of Canadian Poetry: A Critical and Historical Anthology, edited, with an introduction and notes, by Smith (Chicago: University of Chicago Press / Toronto: Gage, 1943; revised, 1948; revised again and enlarged, Toronto: Gage, 1957);

Seven Centuries of Verse: English and American: From the Early English Lyrics to the Present Day, edited by Smith (New York: Scribners, 1947; revised and enlarged, 1957, 1967);

The Worldly Muse: An Anthology of Serious Light Verse, edited, with an introduction, by Smith (New York: Abelard Press, 1951);

Exploring Poetry, edited by Smith and M. L. Rosenthal (New York: Macmillan, 1955);

The Blasted Pine: An Anthology of Satire, Invective, and Disrespectful Verse Chiefly by Canadian Writers, selected, arranged, and with an introduction by Smith and Scott (Toronto: Macmillan, 1957; revised and enlarged, 1967);

A. J. M. Smith

The Oxford Book of Canadian Verse: In English and French, edited, with an introduction, by Smith (Toronto: Oxford University Press, 1960);

Masks of Fiction: Canadian Critics on Canadian Prose, edited, with an introduction, by Smith (Toronto: McClelland & Stewart, 1961);

Masks of Poetry: Canadian Critics on Canadian Verse, edited, with an introduction, by Smith (Toronto: McClelland & Stewart, 1962);

100 Poems, edited, with an introduction and glossary, by Smith (New York: Scribners, 1965);

The Book of Canadian Prose, volume 1: *Early Beginnings to Confederation*, edited by Smith (Toronto: Gage, 1965); republished as *The Colonial Century: English-Canadian Writing Before Confederation* (Toronto: Gage, 1973);

Modern Canadian Verse: In English and French, edited by Smith (Toronto: Oxford University Press, 1967);

The Collected Poems of Anne Wilkinson and a Prose Memoir, edited, with an introduction, by Smith (Toronto: Macmillan, 1968; New York: St. Martin's, 1968);

The Canadian Century: English-Canadian Writing Since Confederation, volume 2 of *The Book of Canadian Prose*, edited by Smith (Toronto: Gage, 1973);

The Canadian Experience: A Brief Survey of English-Canadian Prose, edited by Smith (Toronto: Gage, 1974).

In 1976 at Michigan State University, American and Canadian scholars and poets gathered to honor A. J. M. Smith, seventy-four-year-old doyen of Canadian letters. It is fitting that such a symposium should have been held at an American university, for Smith lived and taught in the United States for half a century, though he could hardly be called an expatriate. Much of his writing was done during long summers spent at his country home on Lac Memphremagog, Quebec, less than two hours' drive from Montreal. Moreover, through correspondence and frequent visits with Canadian editors, academics, and poet friends, he kept in touch with literary developments in Canada. He traveled widely in his native country and was frequently a guest lecturer or a visiting professor at various Canadian universities. The bulk of his critical essays and his most important anthologies focus on Canadian literature. He is credited with having, in the 1920s and 1930s, almost singlehandedly created a climate for modern poetry in Canada. He continued throughout his career to be an active participant in the various critical dialogues that have attended the progress of Canadian poetry.

Arthur James Marshall Smith was born on 8 November 1902 of British parents, Octavius Arthur and Louise Whiting Smith, in Westmount, Quebec. He attended Roslyn Avenue School in Westmount and was graduated from Westmount High School in 1921. By his own account he discovered modern poetry when, as a teenager, he came across Harriet Monroe and Alice Corbin Henderson's *New Poetry: An Anthology* (1917) in the Westmount Public Library. His sixteenth and seventeenth years were spent in England with his parents. During that time he frequented Harold Monro's bookshop in London and thus continued to immerse himself in the work of Pound, Eliot, Yeats, Sitwell, Stevens, and H. D. He was already imitating such models when, after his return to Canada, he entered McGill University in 1921. Out of a liking for chemistry, he registered as a science student; but a course in seventeenth-century English literature reinforced his predilection for poetry. He was strongly attracted to the metaphysical poets and found Marvell and Vaughan especially congenial to his own temperament.

With this awareness of the concerns of modernism the young Smith now turned his attention to Canadian poetry. What he found did not inspire him. Neither the reigning poets (Bliss Carman, Charles G. D. Roberts, Wilson Macdonald) nor the host of other poets in current Canadian anthologies gave convincing evidence of a modernist sensibility. During the early 1920s critics and historians, editors and reviewers, and especially the newly founded Canadian Authors Association, all favored a conservative, late-Victorian mode of verse. Canadian poets were valued not for intelligence and craft but in terms of moral uplift, agreeable sentiments, and nationalistic fervor. Smith despised the so-called Maple Leaf School. He resolved to study and practice writing and to test his work by submitting it to the best English and American literary magazines–and to the *Canadian Forum*, the only Canadian journal that promoted modernism both in poetry and in criticism. "Pagan," Smith's first poem to be published outside of a student paper, appeared in the *Forum* in February 1924.

During that academic year 1923-1924, as editor of the "Literary Supplement" of the *McGill Daily*, Smith began his campaign to establish modernism in Canada. He soon attracted other talented young Montreal writers. Leon Edel recalls Smith's influence on him at the time: "we would sit at the back of a classroom and pretend to listen ... while Smith wrote poems and gave me T. S. Eliot to read. ... Smith first taught me the meaning of literature. ... He made me feel the modern idiom, the use of this year's language shorn of the old accretions of meaning." F. R. Scott was another who was initiated into modernism by Smith. Scott had just entered law school at McGill. Son of a living Canadian poet, Scott had studied at Oxford and had written some poems himself, but until he met Smith he was unacquainted with the new poetry.

Scott and Smith formed an immediate friendship. Together they were mainly responsible for founding and editing the *McGill Fortnightly Review* (1925-1927). Ostensibly a campus paper, the *Fortnightly* was actually a showcase for a brilliant roster of Montreal writers: Eugene Forsey, John Glassco, Stephen Leacock, Otto Klineberg, Leon Edel, and Leo Kennedy, among others. The majority of the critical articles and poems, however, were written by A. J. M. Smith and F. R. Scott using their own names or various pseudonyms. Smith published at least forty-four of his own poems and numerous prose pieces on Yeats, on Eliot's *The Waste Land*, and on the importance for the contemporary poet of symbolism, mythology, and psychology. Smith and the McGill poets were not, of course, the only writers in Canada at the time to be sensitized to modernism; but Smith's enthusiasm, combined with his creative, critical, and editorial talents, made him the leader of the first concerted effort to establish the new poetry in Canada.

Smith received his B.Sc. degree from McGill in 1925. A year later he completed his master's at the same university, with a thesis on William Butler Yeats, who had just, in 1925, published *A Vision*. After teaching for a year at Montreal High School, Smith married Jeannie Dougall Robins. The years 1927-1929 were spent on a fellowship in education at Edinburgh University, where Smith studied under H. J. C. Grierson. He received his Ph.D. in 1931; his doctoral dissertation was entitled "Studies in the Metaphysical Poets of the Anglican Church in the Seventeenth Century." While abroad, Smith continued to write poems. Some were published in British magazines (*London Aphrodite*, *New Verse*, *Twentieth Century Verse*); others appeared in American journals (the *Dial*, *Poetry*). He also sent some poems and articles home; they appeared in the *Canadian Mercury* (1928-1929), which Scott edited, and in the *Canadian Forum*. It was in the latter that his most important early article appeared in April 1928. "Wanted—Canadian Criticism" (collected in *Towards a View of Canadian Letters*, 1973) was a scathing denunciation of the current state of Canadian poetry and an urgent call for higher, more stringent standards based on internationally recognized aesthetic criteria.

University posts were scarce when Smith returned to Canada in 1929. After a year of teaching at Baron Byng High School in Montreal, he

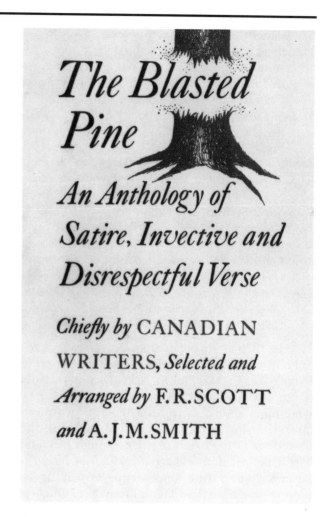

Dust jacket for Smith and F. R. Scott's second anthology. Their first was the ground-breaking New Provinces, *published in 1936.*

left to seek work in the United States. During the next several years of the Depression he held short-term jobs in various American schools and colleges. F. R. Scott carried on, meanwhile, with the practical aspects of a project originally conceived by himself, Smith, and Leo Kennedy. *New Provinces* was planned to be the first truly modern anthology of poetry in Canada. It was to contain samples of the work of four Montreal poets, Smith, Scott, Kennedy, and A. M. Klein. Two Toronto poets, E. J. Pratt and Robert Finch, were eventually added, although Smith's preference had been for Dorothy Livesay and W. W. E. Ross. Smith was moving from job to job in the United States while the anthology was in preparation; nevertheless, his austere standards determined the selection of poems. He also contributed a substantial and caustic introduction in which he deplored the dreamy romanticism of contemporary Canadian poets and argued for an intellectually rigorous "pure poetry," which he described as "objective, impersonal, and in a sense timeless and absolute." Pratt especially objected to this essay as being too extreme and iconoclastic. "I assured him," wrote Scott to Smith, "that you were the real leader of the young movement and that your word was law." But the publishers also objected. Scott finally substituted a brief note of his own. Three decades later Smith's essay was rescued from oblivion and published as "A Rejected Preface" in *Canadian Literature* (Spring 1965); it was also included in the 1976 republication of *New Provinces*. To read that preface today is to realize the passion of Smith's early militancy and to understand the spirit in which he undertook to redefine and redirect the Canadian poetic tradition.

New Provinces appeared in 1936. In the same year W. E. Collin published his impressive *The White Savannahs*, a collection of critical studies which dealt perceptively with the work of the Montreal poets and lauded Smith especially. But neither book sold well and neither was republished for several decades. The McGill movement collapsed in the mid 1930s mainly because of the drastic effect of the Depression on publishing in Canada. Only one of the original four poets was able to get a book into print before 1940. Smith had to wait until 1943 before his first collection, *News of the Phoenix and Other Poems*, appeared.

In 1936 Smith secured a job at Michigan State College (later Michigan State University) where he was to hold a full-time teaching position until his retirement in 1972. He lost none of his interest in Canadian literature. In 1941 (the year his son Peter was born) he obtained a Guggenheim Fellowship to prepare a historical and critical anthology of Canadian poetry. His research led him to modify some of his harsher judgments of older Canadian poets. By the time *The Book of Canadian Poetry* appeared in 1943 he had devised a way to honor the historicity of his subject matter while still insisting on his aesthetic absolutism. The Canadian tradition, he argued in his introduction, exhibited two persistent strains, the "native" and the "cosmopolitan." He ascribed merits to each but his obvious preference was for the latter, for a poetry that "from the beginning, has made a heroic effort to transcend colonialism by entering into the universal, civilizing culture of ideas." This preference led him to choose, especially from the work of the newest generation of poets in the 1940s, only those poems that reflected his tastes. The anthology was well received on the whole and proved to be widely influ-

Front cover for Smith's last poetry collection

ential as a textbook. But Smith's assumptions were vigorously attacked by John Sutherland, editor of the poetry magazine *First Statement*. In his introduction to *Other Canadians* (1947), an anthology designed to promote the work of those poets of the 1940s neglected by Smith, Sutherland reversed Smith's categories and argued that the best Canadian poets were "native" proletarian social realists who wrote out of their North American experience, whereas those British-oriented aesthetes who imitated "cosmopolitan" models were the real colonials. In later editions of *The Book of Canadian Poetry*, and in his more recent anthologies, Smith abandoned these categories; but his preferences remained obvious both in his selections and in his numerous critical articles.

Sutherland's challenge was an early indication that Canadian poets were outgrowing Smith's influence. When, as guest speaker at the Kingston Writers' Conference in 1955, Smith proposed that poets write primarily for other poets (a "restricted, knowledgeable and exacting audience"), his elitism was loudly repudiated by almost every poet present. In the 1960s when he advocated "eclectic detachment" as the appropriate stance for Canadian poets and substituted "universal" for "cosmopolitan" values, he was again challenged. Louis Dudek, for example, suggested that true universality emerged from "a local pride" (William Carlos Williams's phrase). In 1967 Dudek and Michael Gnarowski compiled a historical anthology of criticism, *The Making of Modern Poetry in Canada*, which was intended to redress the balance in favor of a tradition of social realism. By the end of the 1960s the younger poets who had emerged in that decade had passed beyond modernism into a more democratic, pluralistic, existential, and experimental mode of creativity. They were not attuned to Smith's values; nor could he respond to them sympathetically as a critic. Instead he now turned his attention to established poets whose work yielded to his critical methods. His studies of the poetry of Anne Wilkinson, Margaret Avison, and P. K. Page (all collected in *Towards a View of Canadian Letters*) are particularly valuable.

Smith's own published poetry is slim in volume and wholly exemplary of his critical principles. He chose to be remembered in his 1967 collection, *Poems: New and Collected*, by 121 short pieces. Among the best known are "Like An Old Proud King In a Parable," "The Creek," "The Lonely Land," and "The Archer." Smith practiced "a difficult lonely music"–precise, formal, elegant, ironic, and elegiac–though he could be witty, intense, and bawdy, too. Most of the poems are written to, about, or "in the manner of," other poets. In "A Self-Review" (*Canadian Literature*, Winter 1963, collected in *Towards a View of Canadian Letters*), he stated, "My poems are not autobiographical, subjective or personal. . . . None of them is reverie, confession or direct self-expression. They are fiction, drama, art; sometimes pastiche, sometimes burlesque, and sometimes respectful parody. . . ." And in "The Poetic Process" (1964; published in *Centennial Review of Arts and Science*, Fall, and collected in *Towards a View of Canadian Letters*) he remarked, "I suppose I am what is called an academic poet. . . . The *finished work* rather than the work of finishing is what I have valued most." One has only to place beside this statement some remarks made by George Bowering in a 1974 interview collected in Caroline Bayard and Jack David's *Out-Posts/Avant-Postes* (1977) to realize the gulf that exists between Smith's modernism and the postmodern sensibility: "I don't believe in art as a product or an artifact or in any of that business of polishing it. . . . I'm not interested in the results of thinking. I'm interested in the process of thinking itself, naturally." But to critics of Smith's own vintage (George Woodcock, Leon Edel, Roy Fuller, M. L. Rosenthal), and to others who still regard poetry as a high art, "pure, timeless and absolute," Smith's exquisitely crafted poems are among the best of their kind in any literature.

Paradoxically, even as Smith's conception of poetry was losing favor among poets, there emerged in Canada a large audience of nationally conscious readers eager to learn about their literature, past and present. As "Can Lit" courses became more popular, Smith's critical articles and anthologies found a widening audience. *The Book of Canadian Poetry* was twice revised (1948, 1957). *The Oxford Book of Canadian Verse: In English and French*, edited by Smith, appeared in 1960; *Modern Canadian Verse: In English and French* appeared in 1967. Two anthologies of criticism, *Masks of Fiction* and *Masks of Poetry*, were published in 1961 and 1962 respectively. *The Blasted Pine: An Anthology of Satire, Invective, and Disrespectful Verse Chiefly by Canadian Writers*, coedited with F. R. Scott, appeared first in 1957. It was revised and enlarged in 1967. A two-volume anthology of Canadian prose from colonial times to the present appeared as *The Book of Canadian Prose* (volume one) in 1965 and *The Canadian Century* (volume two) in 1973. A welcome selection of Smith's own critical essays, *Towards a View of Canadian Letters*, also appeared in 1973. Then in 1976, in the most personal piece of writing he ever published, Smith provided a relaxed and informative memoir of his career as an anthologist of not only Canadian but also American and British literature. "Confessions of a Compulsive Anthologist" (collected in *On Poetry and Poets*, 1977) is, among other things, a fascinating gloss on the history of modern poetry in Canada. His final selection of poems, *The Classic Shade*, containing an appreciative introduction by M. L. Rosenthal, appeared in 1978.

Canada has not failed to honor A. J. M. Smith. His first collection of poems, *News of the Phoenix*, received a Governor General's Award in 1944. Honorary degrees were bestowed on him by McGill (1958), Queen's (1966), Bishop's (1967), and Dalhousie (1969). He received the Lorne Pierce Medal of the Royal Society of Canada in 1966; the Dominion of Canada Centennial

Medal in 1967; and the Canada Council Medal in 1968. In 1976 he was named Claude Bissell Professor of Canadian-American Literature at the University of Toronto.

During the last two years of his life illness overtook him. He spent as much time as possible at his beloved home overlooking Lac Memphremagog, in the Eastern Townships of Quebec. During his last summer his eyesight failed so that he could not read; he was too weak to write. American and Canadian friends came to read to him, to give him the latest literary news, and to say goodbye. In the fall he returned to East Lansing, Michigan. He died on 21 November 1980.

Letters:

Anne Burke, "Some Annotated Letters of A. J. M. Smith and Raymond Knister," *Canadian Poetry: Studies/Document/Reviews*, 11 (Fall / Winter 1982): 98-135.

Interviews:

[Albert Tunis], "The *Fortnightly*'s Forthright Four," *McGill News*, 44 (Autumn 1963): 15-20, 30;

Richard Jansma, "Interview," *Red Cedar Review*, 3-4 (Summer 1971): 44-49;

Michael Darling, "An Interview with A. J. M. Smith," *Essays in Canadian Writing*, 9 (Winter 1977-1978): 55-61.

Bibliographies:

Michael E. Darling, *A. J. M. Smith: An Annotated Bibliography* (Montreal: Véhicule, 1981);

Anne Burke and Ellen Quigley, "A. J. M. Smith: An Annotated Bibliography," in *The Annotated Bibliography of Canada's Major Authors*, volume 4, edited by Robert Lecker and Jack David (Downsview, Ont.: ECW, 1983), pp. 267-370.

References:

Earle Birney, "A. J. M. S.," *Canadian Literature*, 15 (Winter 1963): 4-6;

John Malcolm Brinnin, "Views of Favourite Mythologies," *Poetry*, 65 (December 1944): 157-160;

E. K. Brown, "A. J. M. Smith and the Poetry of Pride," *Manitoba Arts Review*, 4 (Spring 1944): 30-32;

Canadian Poetry, special A. J. M. Smith memorial issue, edited by D. M. R. Bentley and Michael Gnarowski, 11 (Fall/Winter 1982);

W. E. Collin, "Difficult, Lonely Music," in his *The White Savannahs* (Toronto: Macmillan, 1936), pp. 235-263;

Sandra Djwa, "A. J. M. Smith: Of Metaphysics and Dry Bones," *Studies in Canadian Literature*, 3 (Winter 1978): 17-34;

Leon Edel, "The Worldly Muse of A. J. M. Smith," *University of Toronto Quarterly*, 47 (Spring 1978): 200-213;

Ellipse, special issue on Smith and Rina Lasnier, no. 22 (1978);

John Ferns, *A. J. M. Smith* (Boston: Twayne, 1979);

Michael Gnarowski, Introduction to *New Provinces: Poems by Several Authors*, edited by Smith and F. R. Scott (Toronto & Buffalo: University of Toronto Press, 1976);

Wayne Grady, "Who is This Man Smith?," *Books in Canada*, 7 (November 1978): 8-11;

Gordon Harvey, "A. J. M. Smith and The Classic Shadow," *Compass*, 8 (Winter 1980): 1-28;

W. J. Keith, "How New Was *New Provinces*?," *Canadian Poetry*, 4 (Spring/Summer 1979): 120-124;

I. S. MacLaren, "The Yeatsian Presence in A. J. M. Smith's 'Like an Old, Proud King in a Parable,'" *Canadian Poetry*, 4 (Spring/Summer 1979): 59-64;

Eli Mandel, "Masks of Criticism: A. J. M. Smith as Anthologist," *Canadian Poetry*, 4 (Spring/Summer 1979): 17-28;

Desmond Pacey, "A. J. M. Smith," in his *Ten Canadian Poets* (Toronto: Ryerson, 1958), pp. 194-222;

M. L. Rosenthal, "Poor Innocent: The Poetry of A. J. M. Smith," *Modern Poetry Studies*, 8 (Spring 1977); republished as the introduction to Smith's *The Classic Shade: Selected Poems* (Toronto: McClelland & Stewart, 1978), pp. 9-19;

Peter Stevens, ed., *The McGill Movement: A. J. M. Smith, F. R. Scott, and Leo Kennedy* (Toronto: Ryerson, 1969), pp. 95-143;

John Sutherland, "The Old and the New," introduction to *Other Canadians*, edited by Sutherland (Montreal: First Statement Press, 1947), pp. 5-20;

Germaine Warkentin, "Criticism and the Whole Man," *Canadian Literature*, 64 (Spring 1975): 83-91;

F. W. Watt, "The Plot Against Smith," *Canadian Literature*, 105 (Summer 1985): 111-131;

Milton Wilson, "Second and Third Thoughts About Smith," *Canadian Literature*, 15 (Winter 1963): 11-17;

George Woodcock, "Two Aspects of A. J. M. Smith: 1. The Poet; 2. Anthology as Epithalamion," in his *Odysseus Ever Returning: Essays on Canadian Writers and Writing* (Toronto: McClelland & Stewart, 1970), pp. 111-118.

Papers:

Smith's papers are at the Bata Library, Trent University, Peterborough, Ontario; the Thomas Fisher Rare Book Library, University of Toronto; and the McLennan Library, McGill University, Montreal.

Raymond Souster
(15 January 1921-   )

Frank Davey
York University

BOOKS: *When We Are Young* (Montreal: First Statement, 1946);

Go to Sleep, World (Toronto: Ryerson, 1947);

The Winter of Time, as Raymond Holmes (Toronto: Export Publishing, 1950);

City Hall Street (Toronto: Ryerson, 1951);

Cerberus, by Souster, Louis Dudek, and Irving Layton (Toronto: Contact, 1952);

Shake Hands with the Hangman (Toronto: Contact, 1953);

A Dream that is Dying (Toronto: Contact, 1954);

Walking Death (Toronto: Contact, 1954);

For What Time Slays (Toronto: Contact, 1955);

Selected Poems, edited by Dudek (Toronto: Contact, 1956);

A Local Pride (Toronto: Contact, 1962);

Place of Meeting: Poems, 1958-60 (Toronto: Gallery Editions, 1962);

The Colour of the Times: The Collected Poems of Raymond Souster (Toronto: Ryerson, 1964);

Ten Elephants on Yonge Street (Toronto: Ryerson, 1965);

As Is (Toronto: Oxford University Press, 1967);

Lost & Found: Uncollected Poems 1945-1965 (Toronto: Clarke, Irwin, 1968);

So Far, So Good: Poems 1938-1968 (Ottawa: Oberon, 1969);

The Years (Ottawa: Oberon, 1971);

Selected Poems of Raymond Souster, edited by Michael Macklem (Ottawa: Oberon, 1972);

On Target, as John Holmes (Toronto: Village Book Store Press, 1973);

Change-up: New Poems (Ottawa: Oberon, 1974);

Rain-check (Ottawa: Oberon, 1975);

Double-header (Ottawa: Oberon, 1975);

Extra Innings: New Poems (Ottawa: Oberon, 1977);

Hanging In: New Poems (Ottawa: Oberon, 1979);

Collected Poems of Raymond Souster, 6 volumes (Ottawa: Oberon, 1980-1988);

From Hell to Breakfast, by Souster and Douglas Alcorn (Toronto: Intruder Press, 1980);

Going the Distance: New Poems 1979-1982 (Ottawa: Oberon, 1983);

Jubilee of Death: The Raid on Dieppe (Ottawa: Oberon, 1984);

Queen City, photographs by Bill Brooks (Ottawa: Oberon, 1984);

Flight of the Roller Coaster: Poems for Children, edited by Richard Woollatt (Ottawa: Oberon, 1985);

Into This Dark Earth, by Souster and James Deahl (Toronto: Unfinished Monument, 1985);

It Takes All Kinds: New Poems (Ottawa: Oberon, 1986);

The Eyes of Love (Ottawa: Oberon, 1987);

Asking for More (Ottawa: Oberon, 1988).

OTHER: Ronald Hambleton, ed., *Unit of Five*, includes poems by Souster (Toronto: Ryerson, 1944);

Raymond Souster in 1964 (photograph by John Reeves)

Experiment, 1923-29: Poems by W. W. E. Ross, edited by Souster (Toronto: Contact, 1956);

Poets '56: Ten Young English-Canadians, edited by Souster (Toronto: Contact, 1956);

Michael Gnarowski, *Contact, 1952-1954*, comments on *Contact* by Souster (Montreal: Delta, 1966);

New Wave Canada: The New Explosion in Canadian Poetry, edited by Souster (Toronto: Contact, 1966);

Shapes and Sounds: The Poems of W. W. E. Ross, edited by Souster and John Robert Colombo (Don Mills, Ont.: Longmans, 1968);

Generation Now, edited by Souster and Richard Woollatt (Don Mills, Ont.: Longmans, 1970);

Made in Canada: New Poems of the Seventies, edited by Souster and Douglas Lochhead (Ottawa: Oberon, 1970);

Sights and Sounds, edited by Souster and Woollatt (Toronto: Macmillan, 1973);

100 Poems of Nineteenth-Century Canada, edited by Souster and Lochhead (Toronto: Macmillan, 1974);

These Loved, These Hated Lands, edited by Souster and Woollatt (Toronto: Doubleday, 1975);

Vapour and Blue: Souster Selects Campbell; The Poetry of William Wilfred Campbell, edited, with an introduction, by Souster (Sutton West, Ont.: Paget, 1978);

Comfort of the Fields: Archibald Lampman, edited, with an introduction, by Souster (Sutton West, Ont.: Paget, 1979);

Poems of a Snow-Eyed Country, edited by Souster and Woollatt (Don Mills, Ont.: Academic Press Canada, 1980);

Windflower: Poems of Bliss Carman, edited, with introductions, by Souster and Lochhead (Ottawa: Tecumseh, 1985);

Powassan's Drum: Selected Poems of Duncan Campbell Scott, edited, with an introduction, by Souster and Lochhead (Ottawa: Tecumseh, 1986).

Raymond Souster is best known for his short poems portraying Toronto street scenes and for his deceptively casual language and tone. During the 1950s and 1960s he was a close friend of the Montreal poets Louis Dudek and Irving Layton, and he collaborated with Dudek and Peter Miller in the founding and operating of Contact Press, the most significant Canadian small press of the 1950s.

Souster was born in Toronto in 1921 to lower-middle-class parents; his father, Austin Souster, was a clerk in the Canadian Bank of Commerce; his mother was the former Norma Baker. As a child Souster was an outstanding pitcher in bantam and juvenile baseball leagues, but on graduation from high school he took a clerking job with the Imperial Bank of Canada (later the Canadian Imperial Bank of Commerce) where he worked for forty-five years. In 1941 he enlisted in the Royal Canadian Air Force, hoping for both pilot training and overseas service. However, because of medical limitations, he was trained as ground crew and posted to Nova Scotia and later New Brunswick. A posting to Europe took him to Yorkshire for the last days of the war.

Souster had begun writing poetry while in his teens. His general feeling of being estranged from the wealth, educational opportunities, and literary establishment of his culture had led him to admire poetry, such as that of Kenneth Rexroth, written in direct speech and expressing social anger. While in the RCAF he published poems in John Sutherland's little magazine *First Statement;* he was impressed by the iconoclasm and anti-British sentiment of this magazine, and of its associate editors, the young poets Dudek and Layton. Almost immediately he and several friends began publishing the little magazine *Direction.* Mimeographed, using "borrowed" air-force equipment and supplies, the magazine included antiwar poems, attacks on members of the Canadian Literary establishment, and excerpts from the then-banned novel by Henry Miller, *Tropic of Cancer.*

On demobilization Souster returned to Toronto and his job at the Imperial Bank; he married Rosalia Lena Geralde, a bank clerk, on 24 June 1947 and settled in the Runnymeade area of Toronto in which he had grown up. In 1948 he attempted to publish another magazine, *Enterprise,* which he printed in typewriter carbon copies, but its six issues attracted almost no attention or contributors. His poetry, however, which had found its first significant publication in Ronald Hambleton's 1944 anthology *Unit of Five,* continued to find acceptance. His first book, *When We Are Young,* was published by John Sutherland's First Statement Press in 1946; a second and larger collection, *Go to Sleep, World,* appeared under the Ryerson Press imprint in 1947. A

vastly reduced version of a third manuscript, *City Hall Street,* was published by Ryerson in 1951.

Dudek's return to Canada from New York later that year found Souster disappointed with the failures of his magazines and the drastic editing of *City Hall Street,* and feeling totally isolated from other writers. Souster described Dudek's initial letter to him at this time as "a letter of acceptance while in a concentration camp." Inspired by an August meeting with Dudek and Layton, in October 1951 Souster announced the launching of his third magazine, *Contact;* Dudek provided articles and reviews and helped Souster obtain work from American writers such as Paul Blackburn and Robert Creeley. By March 1952, at Dudek's urging, Souster, Dudek, and Layton had become book publishers with the founding of Contact Press and the publication of its first volume, *Cerberus,* comprising poetry and polemic statements by the three editors. In May 1952 Dudek made a gift to Souster of a copy of *The Collected Later Poems of William Carlos Williams,* which moved him to undertake a radical revision of his own prosody.

These extraordinary changes in Souster's life continued during the next few years. Contact Press soon grew into the premier publisher of new poetry in Canada. From 1953 to 1956 Souster published five books through the press, the fifth *Selected Poems,* edited for him by Dudek. Through *Contact* magazine Souster became acquainted with the work of Charles Olson, Robert Creeley, Cid Corman, Denise Levertov, Wallace Stevens, and Octavio Paz, and began a long correspondence with Corman. When in 1957 he began yet another magazine, *Combustion* (he had discontinued *Contact* in 1954), he was able to draw on international writers, particularly from the U.S. Black Mountain group, and to publish Canadian writing in a truly cosmopolitan context.

In the 1960s Souster gradually withdrew from his editorial roles and published his strongest collections of poems. He discontinued *Combustion* in 1960, and in 1967, after editing a controversial anthology of younger poets, *New Wave Canada: The New Explosion in Canadian Poetry* (1966), agreed with Peter Miller that Contact Press had completed its task, particularly since several new houses had recently been founded to publish Canadian poetry. Souster's incorporation of Williams's prosody into his own became complete in his collections *A Local Pride* (1962) and *Place of Meeting: Poems, 1958-60* (1962). A new volume of collected poems which reflected this change in

BELIEVE ME, I'M NOT WAITING

believe me, I'm not waiting
until Death slips two shoes on your feet
that seem like the perfect fit at last
(no more rubbing at the toes, no weakness in the arch),
so that you find yourself getting up
and walking right out of this life
like a young girl without a care in the world
in her first high heels.

no, I'm not waiting
like Hardy to walk again Beeny Cliff
one year too late. I'm not waiting like Montale
to catalogue in a list of touching remembrance
the mystery that was his dear little mosca.

no, I'm squeezing down hard
on all the sweet-tasting orange pulp
that is today, leaving the tart
lemon rind of tomorrow for all those
so eager to suck dry
its mouth-puckering bitterness...

I'm seizing the present moment
to celebrate what we have, what we feel,
what we touch together now while our fingers
       still entwine,
while our bodies can still come alive,
glow, yes, even sing their strange, unreal
       beautiful song!

                   Raymond Souster

FROM THE EYES OF LOVE (OBERON PRESS, 1987)

Fair copy by Souster (by permission of the author)

style, *The Colour of the Times*, was awarded a Governor General's Award for poetry for 1964. Souster followed this book with two more memorable collections: *Ten Elephants on Yonge Street* (1965) and *As Is* (1967). The latter collection, along with *Lost & Found: Uncollected Poems 1945-1965* (1968), was later republished as *Double-header* (1975). During the late 1960s and the 1970s Souster devoted time to attempts to expand his range as a writer and to get previously unpublished early poems into print. From the start of his career he has had ambitions as a novelist; he wrote *The Winter of Time* under the pseudonym Raymond Holmes in 1950, and from 1967 to 1972 he wrote at least six drafts of that glamorized version of his war experiences, finally publishing the new work, entitled *On Target*, under the pseudonym John Holmes in 1973. He also experimented with the prose poem and serial poem (notably the series "Pictures of a Long-lost World") and, less successfully, with longer poems. His best work remains, however, the short lyric account, often whimsical, of street scenes, small animals, human love and pain, given in a laconic, colloquial voice–the common man speaking about everyday things. There is a pervasive sense of the minimal about Souster's best work: minimal poetic effects and commonplace subjects that assert the importance of the quotidian world. Apart from his Williams-influenced change in prosody in the early 1950s, there has been little evolution in Souster's poetry. Most of his poems have depended on a structural contrast between images of confinement, often associated with large commercial buildings, and ones of freedom, usually located outside such buildings. Linked to the latter have been baseball, Souster's favorite sport, jazz, small animals, and various human outcasts. A theme of nostalgia runs through many of these poems–for childhood, for youth, for simpler cultural patterns–a nostalgia that is also implicit in Souster's continuing to write poems in the language and style of his poems of the 1950s.

After his retirement, Souster became writer in residence at University College, Toronto (1984-1985). He continued to publish new volumes of poetry during the 1970s and 1980s. *It Takes All Kinds: New Poems*, published in 1986, is characteristic: lyrics of observed urban experience convey a sympathy for the plight of being human but find greater pleasure in the rural, the distant, and the past. The poet's continuing interest in World War II is central in another novel, *From Hell to Breakfast* (1980), coauthored with

Douglas Alcorn, which concerns RCAF operations, especially of the 418 Squadron. *Jubilee of Death: The Raid on Dieppe* (1984) is a more innovative work on the theme of war. It is a long poem for twenty-seven voices–ranging from a private to Lt. Gen. A. G. L. McNaughton to Winston Churchill–that reconstructs the human emotions behind the ill-fated Canadian attack on Dieppe on 19 August 1942.

Souster's inquiries into the Canadian past reiterate his nostalgic reading of history and literature. *Into This Dark Earth* (1985), a poem written with James Deahl, focuses on the 1837 Rebellion; in other works–individual poems–the poet revisits the homes of such literary figures as Stephen Leacock. Another example of Souster's literary activities during the 1970s and 1980s is the series of highly personal selections from the Confederation Poets, which he edited, or coedited, including *Comfort of the Fields: Archibald Lampman* (1979) and *Windflower: Poems of Bliss Carman* (1985). These collections, from the poet who was one of the editors for *New Wave Canada*, emphasize the romantic strain in Souster's writing. In the 1980s, too, his own poetry output has been honored through the publication of selections such as Richard Woollatt's edition of Souster's poems accessible to young readers, *Flight of the Roller Coaster* (1985) and the six volumes of *Collected Poems* Michael Macklem's Oberon Press had published by 1988.

Souster will be historically important for his participation, with Dudek and Layton, in the sudden movement of Canadian poetry toward North American language and prosody. He will be remembered also for his assistance to younger writers, and for his editorial work with Contact Press and *Contact* and *Combustion* magazines. *Combustion* single-handedly kept Canadian poetry in touch with the mainstream of contemporary American poetry, while Contact Press, operating as the only regularly publishing literary press of its period, produced first books by nearly all the Canadian poets who rose to prominence in the 1960s.

Bibliography:
Bruce Whiteman, *Collected Poems of Raymond Souster: A Bibliography* (Ottawa: Oberon, 1984).

References:
Frank Davey, *Louis Dudek and Raymond Souster* (Vancouver: Douglas & McIntyre, 1981);
Louis Dudek, "Groundhog among the Stars," *Canadian Literature*, 22 (Autumn 1964): 34-49;

Gary Geddes, "A Cursed and Singular Blessing," *Canadian Literature*, 34 (Autumn 1967): 63-70;

Bruce Meyer and Brian O'Riordan, "Raymond Souster: The Quiet Chronicler," in their *In*

Their Words: Interviews with Fourteen Canadian Writers (Toronto: Anansi, 1984), pp. 86-95;

Bruce Whiteman, *Raymond Souster and His Works* (Toronto: ECW, 1984).

Yves Thériault

(28 November 1915-20 October 1983)

Anne de Fabry
King's College

BOOKS: *Contes pour un homme seul* (Montreal: Editions de l'Arbre, 1944; enlarged edition, Montreal: HMH, 1965);

La Fille laide (Montreal: Beauchemin, 1950);

Le Dompteur d'ours (Montreal: Cercle du Livre de France, 1951);

Les Vendeurs du temple (Quebec: Institut Littéraire du Québec, 1951);

La Vengeance de la mer (Montreal: Publications du Lapin, 1951);

Aaron (Quebec: Institut Littéraire du Québec, 1954);

Agaguk (Quebec: Institut Littéraire du Québec, 1958); translated by Miriam Chapin (Toronto: Ryerson, 1963; London: Dent, 1964);

Alerte au camp 29 (Montreal: Beauchemin, 1959);

La Revanche du Nascopie (Montreal: Beauchemin, 1959);

Ashini (Montreal: Fides, 1960); translated by Gwendolyn Moore (Montreal: Harvest House, 1972);

L'Homme de la Papinachois (Montreal: Beauchemin, 1960);

La Loi de l'Apache (Montreal: Beauchemin, 1960);

Roi de la côte nord: La Vie extraordinaire de Napoléon-Alexandre Comeau (Montreal: Editions de l'Homme, 1960);

Amour au goût de mer (Montreal: Beauchemin, 1961);

Cul-de-sac (Quebec: Institut Littéraire du Québec, 1961);

Les Commettants du Caridad (Quebec: Institut Littéraire du Québec, 1961);

Séjour à Moscou (Montreal: Fides, 1961);

Le Vendeur d'étoiles et autres contes (Montreal: Fides, 1961);

La Montagne sacré (Montreal: Beauchemin, 1962);

Nakika (Montreal: Leméac, 1962);

Le Rapt du lac caché (Montreal: Beauchemin, 1962);

Si la bombe m'était contée (Montreal: Editions du Jour, 1962);

Les Aventures de Ti-Jean (Montreal: Beauchemin, 1963);

Avea, le petit tramway (Montreal: Beauchemin, 1963);

Les Extravagances de Ti-Jean (Montreal: Beauchemin, 1963);

Maurice le moruceau (Montreal: Beauchemin, 1963);

Naya, le petit esquimau (Montreal: Beauchemin, 1963);

Le Grand Roman d'un petit homme (Montreal: Editions du Jour, 1963);

Le Ru d'Ikoué (Montreal: Fides, 1963);

Ti-Jean et le grand géant (Montreal: Beauchemin, 1963);

La Rose de pierre: Histoires d'amour (Montreal: Editions du Jour, 1964);

Zibon et Coucou (Montreal: Leméac, 1964);

La Montagne creuse (Montreal: Lidec, 1965);

Le Secret de Mufjarti (Montreal: Lidec, 1965);

Les Temps du Carcajou (Quebec: Institut Littéraire du Québec, 1965);

Les Dauphins de Monsieur Yu (Montreal: Lidec, 1966);

Yves Thériault (photograph by Kèro)

Le Château des petits hommes verts (Montreal: Lidec, 1966);

Le Dernier rayon (Montreal: Lidec, 1966);

L'Appelante (Montreal: Editions du Jour, 1967);

La Bête à 300 têtes (Montreal: Lidec, 1967);

Centennial Play, by Thériault, Robertson Davies, Arthur L. Murphy, and Eric Nicol, music by Keith Bissell (Ottawa: Centennial Commission, 1967);

Les Pieuvres (Montreal: Lidec, 1967);

Kesten (Montreal: Editions du Jour, 1968);

Le Marcheur (Montreal: Leméac, 1968);

La Mort d'eau (Montreal: Editions de l'Homme, 1968);

L'Ile introuvable (Montreal: Editions du Jour, 1968);

Mahigan (Montreal: Leméac, 1968);

N'Tsuk (Montreal: Editions de l'Homme, 1968); translated by Moore (Montreal: Harvest House, 1972);

Les Vampires de la rue Monsieur-le-Prince (Montreal: Lidec, 1968);

Antoine et sa montagne (Montreal: Editions du Jour, 1969);

L'Or de la felouque (Quebec: Editions Jeunesse, 1969);

Tayaout, fils d'Agaguk (Montreal: Editions de l'Homme, 1969);

Textes et documents, edited by Renald Bérubé (Montreal: Leméac, 1969);

Valérie (Montreal: Editions de l'Homme, 1969);

Fredange, suivi de Les Terres neuves (Montreal: Leméac, 1970);

Le Dernier Havre (Montreal: L'Actuelle, 1970);

La Passe-au-Crahin (Montreal: René Ferron, 1972);

Le Haut Pays (Montreal: René Ferron, 1973);

Agoak, l'héritage d'Agaguk (Montreal: Quinze, 1975); translated by John David Allan as *Agoak: The Legacy of Agaguk* (Toronto: McGraw-Hill Ryerson, 1979);

Œuvre de chair (Montreal: Stanké, 1975); translated by Jean David as *Ways of the Flesh* (Montreal: Gage, 1977);

Moi, Pierre Huneau (Montreal: Hurtubise HMH,
1976);

Cajetan et la taupe (Montreal: Editions Paulines,
1979);

Les Aventures d'Ori d'Or (Montreal: Editions Paulines, 1979);

Popok, le petit Esquimau (Montreal: Québécor,
1980);

Les Aventures de Volpek (Montreal: Centre Educatif
et Culturel, 1980);

La Quête de l'ourse (Montreal: Stanké, 1980);

Le Partage de minuit (Montreal: Québécor, 1980);

La Femme Anna et autres contes (Montreal: VLB,
1981);

Kuanuten (Vent d'est) (Montreal: Editions Paulines,
1981);

L'Etreinte de Vénus: Contes policiers (Montreal: Québécor, 1981);

Valère et le grand canot (Montreal: VLB, 1981);

L'Herbe de tendresse (Montreal: VLB, 1983);

Yves Thériault se raconte (Montreal: VLB, 1985);

*Le Choix de Marie-José Thériault dans l'Œuvre
d'Yves Thériault* (Charlesbourg, Que.: Presse
Laurentiennes, 1986).

PLAY PRODUCTIONS: *Le Marcheur*, Montreal,
Théâtre du Gesù, 21 March 1950;

Berangère ou La Chair en feu, Notre-Dame de
Lorette, Quebec, Théâtre La Fenière, 17
June 1965;

Centennial Play, by Thériault, Robertson Davies,
Arthur L. Murphy, and Eric Nicol, music by
Keith Bissell, Lindsay, Ontario, 11 January
1967.

OTHER: *Pierre Gilles Dubois*, photographs by
Christian Dubois, text by Thériault (La
Prairie, Que.: M. Broquet, 1981).

Author of essays, newspaper articles, plays,
tales, short stories, and more than thirty novels,
Yves Thériault was one of the most prolific francophone writers in Canada. Although many of
his works are popular, *Agaguk* (1958; translated,
1963), the story of an Eskimo living a nomadic
and primitive life in the far North, has been
hailed as his masterpiece. It received the Prix de
la Province de Québec in 1958 and the Prix
France-Canada in 1961 and has been translated
into six languages. As of 1981 *Agaguk* was studied in all Quebec high schools and in many French-

Canadian literature courses across Canada and
abroad. Accordingly sales of Thériault's books
are high, and several of his works have had
more than one edition. The success of *Agaguk*
prompted Thériault to write sequels: *Tayaout, fils
d'Agaguk* was published in 1969, and *Agoak,
l'héritage d'Agaguk* appeared in 1975.

Yves Thériault was born to Alcide and
Aurore Nadeau Thériault on 28 November 1915.
He had an elder sister, Madeleine, who died at
the age of twenty-one. His ancestors were mostly
French-Acadian, but his paternal grandfather
was a Montagnais Indian. From his father he
learned to speak Montagnais Cree. Both his father and grandfather were carpenters who built
barns and churches. Thériault was born in Quebec City, but soon after his birth his family
moved to Montreal where the construction business was thriving. Thériault attended parish
schools and learned perfect English. Never an
enthusiastic student, he quit school during the
eighth grade, nourishing an everlasting resentment against teachers. Although it is a minor
theme, most of his works contain negative references to school curricula and authorities: even as
late as 1980, in his novel *La Quête de l'ourse* (The
Bear Hunt), he inserted a scene in which the
teacher of his young Indian hero is odious.
Thériault's pedagogical aversion extended to professors who wrote reviews of his publications.

In his years growing up in Quebec City's
Notre-Dame-de-Grâce district, he had the good
fortune to become acquainted with a neighbor
woman who lent him many interesting books. He
practiced sports and was particularly attracted to
boxing and tennis. Upon leaving school he
worked at a variety of odd jobs, including cheese
salesman, bartender, and truck driver. In 1934
he developed tuberculosis and remained for a
year and a half at the sanatorium of Lac-Edou-
ard, near Lac Saint-Jean. His condition improved
to the point that he was able to join a group of
trappers who gave him firsthand experience of a
skill that later proved useful to him as background for his Indian novels. Earlier he had traveled widely in Canada and acquired a knowledge
of the geography and folklore of the country.

From the mid 1930s until the early 1960s
Thériault was employed by several radio stations
and television networks, French and English: he
worked successively and intermittently for CHNC
in New Carlisle (Gaspésie), CHRC in Quebec
City, CHLN in Trois-Rivières, CJBR in Rimouski,
and CKCH in Hull, near Ottawa. He started writ-

ing his first radio skits in 1940. Concurrently he wrote short stories for the Montreal newspaper *Le Jour*, publishing his first in 1941. For a brief period he worked for a Toronto newspaper. In 1942 he was director of the publicity department in a factory. Thériault married Germaine-Michelle Blanchet on 21 April 1942. They had two children: Marie-José, now a poet and editor (who in 1986 compiled a selection of her father's work), and Yves-Michel, an archivist. Thériault and Blanchet met at the offices of *Le Jour*, where she was personal secretary to the editor in chief, novelist, and essayist Jean-Charles Harvey. In 1943 Thériault worked for a short time at the National Film Board of Canada as a scriptwriter and publicist, and from 1945 to 1950 he worked as a writer for Radio-Canada.

His career as a man of letters was set definitely on its course when in 1945 he noticed in the French-language paper *La Presse* an advertisement asking for writers to produce "ten-cent" novels. Thériault and his wife each undertook to contribute three detective stories and three love stories a week. These were published anonymously or pseudonymously. Working under pressure, both developed rapid methods of writing. They became so efficient that soon they were able to triple their production.

Curiously Thériault abhorred the physical act of writing. He once said that it was "through despair" that he was led to writing. When questioned about his talent, he referred to himself as primarily a *conteur* or storyteller. For him words were ultimately the means for underscoring gestures: "If one has conceived a series of codified gestures, gestures that *tell*," he declared, "one does not need words."

Most of his early writings are tales and short stories which mix humor and fantasy, treating problems with an economy of means. Many of his early tales have not been collected in book form. In all, he has written more than a thousand tales, and more than thirteen hundred play scripts, of which only a handful have seen print.

Thériault's first book bearing his name is a collection of twenty tales entitled *Contes pour un homme seul* (Stories for One Man Only), published in 1944. Another collection of tales, *Le Vendeur d'étoiles et autres contes* (The Star Seller), appeared in 1961, and a collection of short stories, *L'Ile introuvable* (The Unfindable Island), in 1968. In the last years of his life he returned to the *conte* form. *La Femme Anna et autres contes* and *Valère et*

Front cover for the English translation of Thériault's best-known work

le grand canot (Valère and the Longboat), both published in 1981, illustrate his penchant for swift narrative, economic plotting, moral point, and engaging voice.

In 1950 Thériault was offered a scholarship by the French government, which he declined because of work commitments. In that year he published his first novel, *La Fille laide* (The Ugly Girl), which was moderately praised by the critics. His second novel, *Le Dompteur d'ours* (The Bear Tamer), his third, *Les Vendeurs du temple* (The Sellers of the Temple), and his fourth, *La Vengeance de la mer* (The Vengeance of the Sea), appeared in 1951. Variously, they tell of melodramatic events and satirize the political circumstances of modern Quebec. Death and sexual frustration recur as themes. *Aaron*, one of his best novels, was published in 1954. In his years of residence in Montreal, Thériault had met many Jews; he sometimes accompanied them to the synagogue and had learned some Yiddish and some modern Hebrew. He read the Bible extensively. Having pondered the difficulties facing an orthodox Jew living in a North American culture, he first wrote a thirty-minute radio script which probed this theme; it was presented over CKAS in 1951. The novel version was written later, in 1954, while Thériault was in Florence, Italy.

Thériault traveled extensively outside Canada. In 1952 he went on a trip around the world aboard an Italian freighter. He visited Italy, France, Spain, Greece, and Yugoslavia. In 1961 he was invited by the Soviet government to attend the Second International Film Festival in Moscow. He remained seventeen days in the Russian capital and gave a detailed and generally positive account of his impressions in a two-hundred-page chronicle entitled *Séjour à Moscou* (Sojourn in Moscow, 1961). In the meantime he had published several significant works, among which were his two most highly acclaimed: *Agaguk* and *Ashini* (1960; translated, 1972). For the latter work Thériault was awarded the Governor General's Award for Fiction and the Prix France-Canada. He had been elected to the Royal Society of Canada in 1959. In 1964 he served a term as president of the Société des Ecrivains Canadiens. Subsequent honors included the Molson Prize in 1971 and the Prix David in 1979.

Agaguk is more restrained than most of Thériault's other work–more restrained even than the lyric sensibility of *Ashini*, which praises the richness of the Montagnais culture and bewails its decline under pressure from white Canada. *Agaguk* tells what is essentially a morality tale. The title figure, a young Inuit man, is caught between the traditional ways of his forebears and the pressures of the present, represented by whites and the law. Married young and soon to be a father, Agaguk is also constrained by the physical circumstances of the tundra. The moral test comes when his wife, Iriook, gives birth to a daughter. His trained traditional response would be to kill the girl. But his wife persuades him otherwise, turning Agaguk away.

In addition to *Agaguk* and *Ashini*, by 1965 Thériault had also written several melodramatic works and *Le Ru d'Ikoué* (1963), a novel in which he continued to upgrade the image of the Indians, denouncing their assimilation by the whites. He had become one of the most articulate (and most listened to) spokesmen for the native people. He was appointed director of Cultural Affairs in the Ministry of Indian Affairs in Ottawa, a position he held from 1965 to 1967. In 1968

Front cover for Thériault's lyric novel about the richness and decline of Montagnais Indian culture. Ashini *won a Governor General's Award and the Prix France-Canada for 1960.*

and 1969 many more novels and a volume of stories appeared. Although Thériault suffered a cerebral thrombosis in 1970, which left him paralyzed and unable to speak, he recovered enough to take up writing again within a matter of years. In 1977 he became codirector of a film company with Lorraine Boisvenue. And in the later 1970s he was experimenting more with fictional form, especially in *Moi, Pierre Huneau* (1976), a Gaspé fisherman's compelling soliloquy, and *La Quête de l'ourse*, another volume in his northern saga. In addition to *contes*, Thériault wrote tales for children in his last years, several works of detection, and erotic romance fantasies such as *Œuvre de chair* (1975; translated as *Ways of the Flesh*, 1977) and *Le Partage de minuit* (The Stroke of Midnight, 1980). Thériault died on 20 October 1983. He had been living at Rawdon, a small town some forty miles north of Montreal.

It is tempting to classify Thériault's novels in three main groups: the Montreal, the Indian, and the Acadian novels. Almost all his works of fiction are set in eastern Canada, yet Thériault cannot be labeled a regionalist or nationalist in the narrow sense of the terms. Manifestly the temporal and geographical settings give his works anthropological, sociological, and cultural qualities which distinguish his writing, but the problems he exposes are universal. His protagonists are not perfect, but most of them are admirable precisely because they fight to preserve their cultural heritage, their freedom, and their power. The forces of Eros–as opposed to the forces of Thanatos–inhabit his younger heroes, and their eroticism expresses their vital strength. Some Thériausian heroes are cruel, yet they win the sympathy of readers because they are courageous, intelligent, faithful, sincere, and because they pursue very high goals. Many of them lose in the end, but it is usually through no fault of their own; they are victims of powers stronger than man.

Thériault's work is abundant and diverse; few writers, in fact, possess his faculty for varying plots and characters. There is, however, a common denominator for most of his novels: the protagonist in conflict–physical, social, familial. Except for some of his later work Thériault's narrative technique is conventional, his style clear and direct. Because so much of his writing is still uncollected, it is difficult finally to assess his achievement. If one heeds the comments of Victor-Lévy Beaulieu, who wrote the prefaces for and published the 1981 story collections *La Femme Anna* and *Valère et le grand canot*, Thériault is one of the "giants" of Quebec literature.

References:

Victor-Lévy Beaulieu, Preface to Thériault's *La Femme Anna et autres contes* (Montreal: VLB, 1981);

Beaulieu, Preface to Thériault's *Valère et le grand canot* (Montreal: VLB, 1981);

Rénald Bérubé, "35 Ans de vie littéraire: Yves Thériault se raconte," *Voix et Images*, 5 (Winter 1980): 223-243;

Gérard Bessette, "Le Primitivisme dans les romans de Thériault," in his *Une Littérature en ébullition* (Montreal: Editions du Jour, 1968), pp. 109-216;

André Brochu, "Yves Thériault et la sexualité," *Parti Pris*, 1 (Summer 1964): 9-11, 141-155;

Nicole Dupré and Daniel Lemieux, *Yves Thériault, auteur* (Montreal: Société Radio-Canada, 1982);

Maurice Emond, *Yves Thériault et le combat de l'homme* (Montreal: Hurtubise HMH, 1973);

Hélène Lafrance, *Yves Thériault et l'institution littéraire québécoise* (Quebec: Institut Québécois de Recherche sur la Culture, 1984);

Jean Ménard, "Yves Thériault ou l'evolution d'un romancier," *La Revue Dominicaine*, 65 (November 1960): 206-215;

Jean-Paul Simard, *Rituel et langage chez Yves Thériault* (Montreal: Fides, 1979);

Jack Warwick, *The Long Journey* (Toronto: University of Toronto Press, 1968).

Papers:

Some of Thériault's correspondence is at the Public Archives of Canada.

Colleen Thibaudeau

(29 December 1925-   )

Jeanette Lynes
Mount Allison University

BOOKS: *Lozenges: Poems in the Shapes of Things* (London, Ont.: Alphabet, 1965);
Ten Letters (Ilderton, Ont.: Nairn, 1975);
My Granddaughters Are Combing Out Their Long Hair (Toronto: Coach House Press, 1977);
The Martha Landscapes (Ilderton, Ont.: Brick, 1984).

PERIODICAL PUBLICATIONS: *Brick 5* (Winter 1979), includes writing by Thibaudeau.

An author of poems, stories, and children's verse, Colleen Thibaudeau has been actively involved with Canadian small presses and the League of Canadian Poets since the mid 1960s. She has given numerous poetry readings, and her work has appeared in a wide variety of periodicals and anthologies. She is known as a children's poet, exploring such forms as concrete poetry and participation poetry, as well as a writer of thematically complex, linguistically demanding poetry for mature audiences.

It was not until the late 1970s that Thibaudeau's writing reached a wide readership. There were two events that helped bring about recognition of the literary merit of her work: the publication of Thibaudeau's poetry collection *My Granddaughters Are Combing Out Their Long Hair* in 1977 and the winter 1979 appearance of *Brick 5*, which featured writing by Thibaudeau and critical appraisals of it.

Thibaudeau was born on 29 December 1925 in Toronto. From the Markdale area of Grey County, Ontario, her father, Stewart Thibaudeau, was wounded during World War I at Vimy and met Thibaudeau's mother, Alice Pryce, from Belfast, during his convalescence. The Thibaudeaus are of Acadian descent. Thibaudeau's father studied at the University of Toronto and taught school in Flesherton and St. Thomas, Ontario.

Thibaudeau's family moved to St. Thomas during her first years of public school. Although in *Brick 5* she describes her years in St. Thomas

Colleen Thibaudeau (photograph by Janosz Meissner)

as "just a small town life," Thibaudeau, a young woman and maturing writer, felt the effects of World War II and the absence, in particular, of an extracurricular dramatic or literary society.

Thibaudeau's need to interact with others interested in writing was fulfilled when she entered the University of Toronto's University College, where she received a B.A. in English language and literature in 1948 and an M.A. in 1949, writing her master's thesis on contemporary Canadian poetry of the 1940s. At the university, Thibaudeau met several writers, including James Reaney, Jean McKay, Phyllis Gotlieb, Henry

317

Kreisel, Dorothy Cameron, Duncan Robertson, and Robert Weaver. Thibaudeau's own work appeared in the student literary magazine the *Undergrad*.

After completing her master's degree, Thibaudeau worked for one year in the advertising and publicity department of the publishing firm McClelland and Stewart. She then went abroad, teaching at a lycée in Angers, France, in 1950 and 1951. During this period Thibaudeau did a substantial amount of writing, much of which was not collected until 1977 in her book *My Granddaughters Are Combing Out Their Long Hair*. Her short story "How to Know the True Prince," which appeared in *Brick 5*, was also written during the early 1950s.

In 1951 Thibaudeau married James Reaney, a poet, playwright, and her fellow student at the University of Toronto. The couple lived in Winnipeg from 1951 to 1957, where their two sons, James and John, were born in 1952 and 1954. The family moved to Toronto in 1957, where Reaney studied for his doctoral degree. After the birth of their daughter, Susan, in 1959, the Reaneys settled in London, Ontario, where Reaney took a teaching post at the University of Western Ontario. In 1966 the Reaneys' son John died of meningitis. In moving to London, Thibaudeau had returned to southwestern Ontario, close to where she had spent her teenage years. She still resides in London.

From 1951 to 1962 Thibaudeau wrote under the pseudonym of M. Morris. When asked by Jean McKay in a *Brick 5* interview why she adopted a pseudonym, Thibaudeau replied that M. Morris was created mainly as an experiment, "a change" that would, she felt, give editors the opportunity to read her work more objectively. The creation of M. Morris has a certain appropriateness in the context of Thibaudeau's writing, which has always embraced the other or the different and which has continually uncovered the unexpected in its images of metamorphosis and its complex webs of shifting perceptions and identities.

Although her upbringing took place in "just a small town," Thibaudeau's writing is by no means ordinary or narrow in scope. In its revelation of how the ordinary is in fact extraordinary, Thibaudeau's work is reminiscent of other "small-town" Ontario writers, such as George Elliott, Reaney, and Alice Munro. Critics and reviewers of Thibaudeau's writing have consistently commented on her skillful interweaving of domestic and unusual, concrete and abstract, tangible and

intangible. Thibaudeau's talent lies in her ability to place the reader in a world of familiar, domestic security and then, with agility and speed, to undermine the reader's comfortable associations with that world. The surface of life, Thibaudeau's writing suggests, is in itself rich and sensuous, but it is also only the beginning point of perception and experience; unexplored dimensions of perception frequently "perforate" the surface at unexpected moments.

Because Thibaudeau's eye and ear are so attuned to the phenomenal and beyond, her work resembles, as Terry Griggs suggests in an article for *Brick 5*, a Breughel landscape, with its "energetic community, [its] entangled life," but, Griggs points out, Thibaudeau's vision is "ghostlier": "The focus is adjusted for the noumenal, the supernaturally delicate tracings one might come across of a day of life's cleaning, . . . the invisible webbing that holds things so lightly, so inviolably together." Caroline Bayard, in a review of *My Granddaughters Are Combing Out Their Long Hair*, traces Thibaudeau's literary lineage to the turn-of-the-century French poet Francis Jammes who wrote, in Bayard's words, "about the unusual, fragile occurrences in his otherwise conventional, middle-class life."

In her writing since her second book, *Ten Letters* (1975), Thibaudeau has explored a range of techniques, forms, and organizing principles. She has demonstrated her ability to work with a variety of rhyme schemes and line lengths and experimented with dialogue, narrative, cataloguing, and "found" poetry. *Ten Letters* is perhaps her most overtly structured collection in its sequential organization and use of traditional number symbolism. A sense of strict, systematic organization, however, is carefully balanced by the reflective, almost stream-of-consciousness quality of the actual poems, or "letters."

Many of the central images, symbols, and themes of Thibaudeau's poetry are evident in *Ten Letters*. The Martha figure, for example, seems to have her origins in *Ten Letters*, which includes historical women–Marianne Moore's mother, the speaker's mother and grandmother, the speaker herself–and mythological females, such as the "Liberty Lawn Lady," Mrs. Polyphemus, Ariadne, Penelope, and Dido. The female figure is, typically in Thibaudeau's writing, caught between two worlds or roles: the world of the domestic activities of wife and mother and the more poetic and cosmically creative world of the Martha figure, sensuous and powerful. The housewife "thinking on harp-like themes" is typified in "Letter Four":

> So must I record while thinking about how we
> are all exiles during
>
> exactly 110 minutes of interruptions varied
> and semi-tortuous,
>
> I have consumed
>
> 2 stale pieces second son birthday cake
> 1 cup instant coffee
>
> And given charitable offerings to gulls with
> aid of small hands
>
> And I have done motherly duties reading about
> St. Swithin's Day
>
> And bunking down various recalcitrants to the
> umpteenth.
>
> All the while thinking on harp-like themes.

It is important to note that what initiates and precedes the speaker's "recording" process are her reflections on "suffering dear Chinese poets / in exile." The artistic, the mundane, and the isolation of the artist are themes frequently integrated in Thibaudeau's writing.

The speaker's meditation on an artifact is consistently a poetic "catalyst" in Thibaudeau's writing. The artifacts, however, have tended to become less remote and more immediate and local than the Chinese paintings and Eskimo carvings in *Ten Letters*. In the two later collections—*My Granddaughters Are Combing Out Their Long Hair* and *The Martha Landscapes* (1984)—Thibaudeau frequently includes domestic artifacts or objects such as household tools, glass cupboards, quilts, heirloom silver spoons, copies of *Reader's Digest* and almanacs. There are subtle differences in the way in which the speaker's relationships with these objects is presented in *My Granddaughters Are Combing Out Their Long Hair* and *The Martha Landscapes*.

Objects in the 1977 collection tend to have a more sinister presence than those in *The Martha Landscapes*, reflecting the overall darker tone of the earlier volume. In "Nocturnal Visit to One Who Is a Chiropractor by Day," for example, the speaker describes a window box made to look like a lion in this way: "Leans head and mane on the topmost pane, / (I fear to rile it)." The win-

Front cover for the 1984 collection that includes Thibaudeau's poem for children "Throgmogle and Engestchin"; parodies of poems by Margaret Atwood, Al Purdy, Raymond Souster, and others; and the comic prose piece "Inwhich I Become Confused, the End of the World Being Imminent"

dow box is linked to a more generalized, threatening male presence in the poem that is portrayed through the imagery of sex and black magic: "('Voodoo Man, Voodoo Man, / Won't you cure me if you can?') / The Voodoo Man said, 'Lift the latch.'" Similarly, in "The Iron" the household object that gives the poem its title assumes a sinister and distinctly male life of its own; the victimization of the female speaker (the ironer) is fairly explicit.

Objects and artifacts are most often incorporated into a world of experience beyond the domestic, into a larger cycle. Dick Stingle has identified the organizing principle of modes and seasons in *My Granddaughters Are Combing Out Their Long Hair*. Thibaudeau's sense of inclusiveness, what Peggy Dragisic in an article in *Brick 5* calls her "tapestrial" or "big sea vision" emphasizing "the interconnectedness of all things," is shown in "White Bracelets," one of the most powerful poems in Thibaudeau's 1977 volume. This poem exhibits a familiar subject in Thibaudeau's writing–domestic tragedy–in this case, an attempted suicide. The poem's strength lies in its surprising inversion and ultimately in its affirmative vision. The speaker, whose wrists have healed into "white bracelets," is not left isolated by the incident but rather gains the realization that "we all have old scars"; she sees, in short, that suffering and isolation are part of a more inclusive human landscape. The white rings accent the movement outward from the "I" to a wider realm of experience. The combined fallibility and strength of the speaker in "White Bracelets" reflects Thibaudeau's "granddaughters" who are a paradoxical mixture of frailty and beauty, weakness and strength, "burnt out as falling stars" but still "singing them the old songs." They are survivors.

Although the poems in Thibaudeau's *The Martha Landscapes* are in some ways more documentary in intent and more local in scope, they are no less complex than her previous writing in terms of both theme and form. The art objects in *The Martha Landscapes* tend to be more integrated into everyday life. The activity of preserving, for example, offers a powerful metaphor for the themes of mutability, time, and the creative act. The delicate vines of Chinese art in Thibaudeau's *Ten Letters* are transformed into the more domestic, horticultural metaphor of "grafting or pruning," which aptly describes the poet's energies of adapting her own vision within the literary tradition and the cycles of nature.

The world of the more personal, immediate ancestral past is entered, in *The Martha Landscapes*, through remembrance and dream, as well as through artifact. "A Star Over the House Quilt," for example, provides a metaphor for art as a weaving together, a tapestry, to recall Dragisic's analysis, of the realms of the familiar (house) and the unknown (star). The grandmoth-

er's sugar shell reflects the merging of domestic concerns and the importance of remembrance. "'That spoon needs cleaning,'" the grandmother tells the speaker in "My Grandmother's Sugar Shell, Ontario Baroque." The speaker's remembering of her grandmother's voice leads to the poem's affirmation of the past and of the creative act.

Thibaudeau's *The Martha Landscapes* also exhibits a more distinctly playful tone and comic vision than her previous work. This collection includes the delightful child's poem "Throgmogle and Engestchin"; a series of parodies; and the comic, apocalyptic vision in the prose piece "Inwhich I Become Confused, the End of the Word Being Imminent." The "Super End of the World Special" at Eaton's department store reflects, in a superb comic scenario, the themes of quest and mortality.

It is the title poem of *The Martha Landscapes* that perhaps provides the strongest testimony in Thibaudeau's writing to the interconnectedness of people and places, to a cycle of life, death, and rebirth. Here Thibaudeau uses the figure of Martha as at once a separate being and an extension of the speaker's consciousness or identity. The death and separation of the speaker and her children as victims of a bear attack are balanced by the mythic journey of Martha, a woman capable of assuming numerous forms in various places. Martha's superhuman journey ends with her return to Canada and is paralleled by the rebirth of the speaker and a collective "we": "We let the fog lick us all over / now that we are born." This cycle of healing and rebirth as a collective experience and the framing of the fragile, mortal life with larger rejuvenating forces make the creative act, for Colleen Thibaudeau, meaningful and life-affirming.

Reference:
Brick 5 (Winter 1979).

Bertrand Vac
(Aimé Pelletier)
(20 August 1914-)

Jane Koustas
Redeemer College

BOOKS: *Louise Genest* (Montreal: Cercle du Livre de France, 1950);

Deux Portes . . . une adresse (Montreal: Cercle du Livre de France, 1952);

Saint-Pépin, P.Q. (Montreal: Cercle du Livre de France, 1955);

L'Assassin dans l'hôpital (Montreal: Cercle du Livre de France, 1956);

La Favorite et le conquérant (Montreal: Cercle du Livre de France, 1963);

Histoires galantes (Montreal: Cercle du Livre de France, 1965);

Mes Pensées "profondes" (Montreal: Cercle du Livre de France, 1967);

Le Carrefour des géants: Montréal, 1820-1885 (Montreal: Cercle du Livre de France, 1974);

Jean C. Lallemand raconte (Montreal: Louise Courteau, 1987);

Bizarres (Montreal: Guérin, 1988).

PLAY PRODUCTION: *Appelez-moi Amédée*, Montreal, Théâtre de l'Escale, Summer 1967.

courtesy of the author

Aimé Pelletier, who has written all of his works under the pseudonym Bertrand Vac, is a Montreal surgeon. Vac's literary career, which has spanned several decades, is marked by his constant attempt at various writing styles and different genres. The work of this three-time winner of the Prix du Cercle du Livre de France did, however, attract harsh criticism from the literary elite of the 1950s and 1960s, whom the author deliberately shunned. Shocked by Vac's bold subject matter and language, some critics openly disapproved when Vac received his literary awards, and Vac was not recognized as a major Quebec writer. However, there are contemporary critics who praise both his style and choice of subjects, crediting him as well with having introduced new literary forms to Quebec.

Vac was born Joseph-Omer-Aimé Pelletier on 20 August 1914 in Saint-Ambroise-de-Kildare (Joliette), Quebec, a small village about sixty-five miles north of Montreal. His parents were Arthur Pelletier, a physician, and Lumina Labbé Pelletier. First a student at the local school, Pelletier continued his studies at the Académie Saint-Viateur in Joliette (1921-1928) and graduated with a bachelor of arts degree from the Séminaire de Joliette in 1934. He completed medical studies at the Université de Montréal in 1940 and joined the Canadian Army Medical Corps in 1942, serving in London and then as a member of the field ambulance corps. Demobilized in 1946, he took additional medical training in

Paris, and in 1948 he returned to Montreal, accepting a position as a surgeon at the Hôpital Général de Verdun. He has never married.

His first novel, *Louise Genest* (1950), was awarded the Prix du Cercle du Livre de France. One of the few works of the 1950s dealing with the theme of the Canadian wilderness, the novel is set in Saint-Michel-des-Saints and the surrounding forest north of Joliette. Vac, an outdoorsman, based the story on an anecdote told to him by an Indian guide during a canoe trip.

The novel is the story of a woman married at seventeen to a rich but cruel and miserly alcoholic. Her life is made tolerable only by her son, Pierre. Stifled by village life, abused by her husband, Louise Genest transgresses territorial, cultural, and social boundaries when she leaves with Thomas Clarey, a Métis. However, the freedom and simplicity of life in the land of the "noble savage" cannot erase the guilt Louise suffers for having abandoned her son. When Louise learns that her husband, in order to punish her, has taken Pierre from school, she returns to the village only to be reminded of her husband's hatred and her adultery. Labeled "La Genest" and scorned in the village, Louise returns to the woods. She later learns that her son has been lost in the forest and sets out alone to find him. Having discovered only his rifle, she dies of exhaustion.

Like Germaine Guèvremont's *Le Survenant* (*The Outlander*, 1945), this novel deals with the theme of the secret and dangerous charm of the mysterious woodsman and with the suffocating nature of village life. Vac's novel focuses specifically on the consequences of Louise's succumbing to the lure of the wilds and her attraction to Thomas. The novel is a tool for social criticism, opposing highly codified and hypocritical village life to the freedom of a harmonious existence with nature.

Louise Genest met with a mixed reception from the critics, probably because of the novel's departure from popular literary trends and its "immoral" subject. It was heartily condemned by the abbé Emile Bégin, who saw Louise as a nymphomaniac casually ignoring her marital and maternal duties (*La Revue de l'Université Laval*, January 1951). For Clément Lockquell (*Culture*, December 1951) Louise was a lazy woman with no social conscience. Gilles Marcotte (*Le Devoir* 14 September 1950), focusing on the content and style, labeled the book "un assez mauvais roman de maigre substance psychologique et très mal écrit" (quite a poor novel of little psychological substance and

very badly written). Guy Sylvestre, however, admired Louise's courage (*La Revue Dominicaine*, November 1950), and on his radio program *Journal de Claude-Henri Grignon*, Grignon praised the novel's literary merit. The jury for the Cercle du Livre de France prize admired the novelist's use of the Canadian forest as background and claimed that *Louise Genest* brought honor to French-Canadian literature.

Vac was again awarded the Prix du Cercle du Livre de France for his second novel, *Deux Portes ... une adresse* (Two Doors ... One Address, 1952). The novel concerns Jacques Grenon, a Canadian army officer who must return to Montreal and to a seemingly meaningless life with his wife and two children after a grueling tour of duty in World War II France and an affair with a beautiful Frenchwoman, Françoise Clair.

Vac's account of the drudgery and horror of war is based on his own experience in the liberation of France. Grenon's life is centered on routine rather than heroic deeds and is made more difficult by letters from his wife which only remind him of the hollowness of their marriage. His feelings of alienation are magnified when he meets Françoise, whose interests go beyond the banalities and gossip which fill his wife's letters. Upon his imposed repatriation, Jacques feels spiritually dead and robbed of all initiative. Nevertheless he refuses an opportunity to return to France, clinging to his memories of Françoise and choosing to cope rather than to change.

In his preface to the first edition, R. P. A. Lamarche praises the novel as a realistic portrayal of a tragic and tormented era. Though the war experience and the problems of readaptation to civilian life were faced by many French Canadians, Vac's novel is one of the few dealing with this theme, and critics said little about this work.

In his third book, *Saint-Pépin, P.Q.* (1955), Vac describes the electoral campaign of Polydor Granger, an unlikely and unwilling small-town candidate to the Assemblée Législative. Pushed by his wife and opportunist friends, Polydor eventually wins the election in spite of a series of misadventures, including his unnecessary appendectomy and subsequent case of worms.

Satirical, caricatural, sometimes crude, *Saint-Pépin, P.Q.* was certain to shock Quebec critics and the public who, just emerging from the period in Quebec history now described as "la grande noirceur" (the great darkness), were unaccustomed to mockery of sacrosanct village life. Re-

LOUISE GENEST

Bertrand Vac

LE CERCLE DU LIVRE DE FRANCE

*Front cover for Vac's first novel and the first of his three
books to win the Prix du Cercle du Livre de France*

alizing the audacity of his project, Vac prefaced
the volume with an "Avertissement au lecteur"
(Notice to the Reader) in which, after denouncing hypocrites "à la Tartuffe" who hide their true
natures behind religion or use their faith to their
own interests, he states, "Même les situations les
plus grotesques de ce roman sont vécues; nous
n'avons qu'inteprété des scènes à peu près
quotidiennes de la vie de notre chère province"
(Even the most grotesque situations are true; we
have only interpreted scenes which occur daily in
our beloved province). This preface did little, however, to placate some critics, who condemned
Vac's use of slang, profanity, and bawdy stories.
Vac himself showed no remorse when he declared some ten years later that the public's judgment was better than that of those who were supposed to mold their opinion.

In 1956 Vac was awarded the Prix du
Roman Policier for *L'Assassin dans l'hôpital*. This
suspenseful thriller was adapted for television by
Radio-Canada the same year that it was published. Set in Ungava, the story concerns a
wealthy widow who knows the location of a rich
mining deposit. Hospitalized, she is cared for by
a nurse who is trying to discover the whereabouts
of the mine by administering truth serum to the
patient. The woman dies of an overdose before di-
vulging any information. Fearing the results of
the autopsy, the nurse murders the woman's doctor and must kill a third time to cover up the second death. Two private detectives painstakingly
untangle the threads of the mystery.

Like an experienced mystery novelist, Vac is
careful to let the tension mount slowly. He sur-
rounds the dying woman with plausible suspects
and gradually leads the reader to the conclusion
through a series of brief episodes. Recent critics,
Jean-Pierre Duquette and Jean-Paul Lamy, both
writing for the *Dictionnaire des œuvres littéraires du
Québec* in 1982, have recognized *L'Assassin dans
l'hôpital* as one of the first successful examples of
the detective novel in Quebec, though at the time
it was published critics said little about the work.

A painstakingly documented work, *La Favorite et le conquérant* (The Favorite and the Conqueror, 1963) represented yet another new direction for Vac and a departure from literary trends
of the period. Unlike other 1960s novels which
dealt primarily with Quebec, this work has an exotic subject and setting. Vac spent over ten years
and drew on more than three hundred sources
to create this vast narrative relating the sometimes crude and frequently violent adventures of
Tamerlane, a fourteenth-century Tartar chieftain,
ruler of Samarkand, and of his weak grandson,
Prince Khalil. Although the novel received little
recognition from reviewers, Claude Gingras, writing for *La Presse* (4 May 1963), praised the realistic setting, plot, and characters.

A third Prix du Cercle du Livre de France
was awarded to Vac in 1965 for *Histoires galantes*,
a collection of untitled short stories varying in
length from eight to thirty-six pages and centered on the theme of lighthearted sex; Vac,
tongue-in-cheek, recounts the adventures of se-
ducers and their prey. The stories, cynical,
comic, and ironic, are concisely written. In a few
words Vac introduces the characters, describes
the setting, and creates the atmosphere. The jury
for Prix du Cercle du Livre de France cited Vac
for his style, his effective use of dialogue, and his
subtle analyses, going so far as to claim, "C'est du
Maupassant." Others, however, could not accept

his "histoires lestes mais racontées sur un ton de rire" (naughty stories told in fun, as Jean-Ethier Blais described them in *Le Devoir*, 20 November 1965) and found the book scandalous.

In 1958 Vac took another new direction and wrote a play, *Appelez-moi Amédée* (Call Me Amédée). Though never published, the comedy was performed in 1967 by the Théâtre de l'Escale, on a ferryboat in the port of Montreal during Expo '67. Following the fair, the boat continued down the Saint Lawrence, making several stops, and up the Saguenay River to Chicoutimi. The play was thus seen by a large audience.

Vac's next work, *Mes Pensées "profondes"* (My "Profound" Thoughts, 1967), is a collection of maxims, aphorisms, and witty sayings. In *Le Carrefour des géants* (The Giants' Crossroads, 1974), subtitled *Montréal, 1820-1885*, Vac explores yet another literary form; this book is a social history of Montreal in which the author describes the growth of the city from a native's perspective. Vac paints a picture of Montreal, Montrealers, and their concerns and pastimes during a critical period from the decline of the fur trade to the city's rapid expansion with the opening of the railroad. The work was generally well received.

Vac's 1987 work, *Jean C. Lallemand raconte* (Jean C. Lallemand Recounts), is the biography of a prominent Montrealer who, as the cofounder of the Montreal Symphony Orchestra, made an enormous contribution to Quebec's cultural and social life. Based on numerous personal interviews and an extensive study of archives and Lallemand's personal correspondence, Vac's work portrays the life not only of Lallemand, who was born to wealthy parents in 1898, but also of a particular social and cultural elite, the residents of the once famous Golden Square Mile. Vac's account of Lallemand's almost fairy-tale existence is thus valuable as an illuminating biography of an important Montreal personality and as a social history of a bygone era.

Bizarres (1988), a collection of eight stories varying in length from ten to forty pages, is Vac's most recent publication. The collection includes "Nuits 1002 . . . 3, 4 et 5," originally written as part of *La Favorite et le conquérant* but not included in that volume. Critics were enthusiastic about Vac's latest contribution. Vac is currently completing a novel tentatively entitled "Les Volupteuses" (The Voluptuous Ones) which is based partially on a tragic love affair experienced by one of the author's acquaintances. Another book, "Le Choix de Bertrand Vac" (A Selection of Bertrand Vac), a collection of excerpts from previous works, as well as an account of a visit to China, awaits publication.

A brief overview of Vac's work suggests that in his attempt to experiment with literary forms and themes, he at times shocked the critics and the public. Though praised, he was frequently reproached by some who acknowledged his talent but were offended by his subject matter. In his article on the Quebec novel from 1939 to 1957 (in *Le Québécois et sa littérature*, edited by R. Dionne, 1984), Jacques Michon suggests reopening the file on the writers of this period, claiming that scholars have narrowed the perception of this literature to a few "representative" works. Such an undertaking is necessary in order to reevaluate the importance of Vac's contribution to Quebec literature.

Herman Voaden
(19 January 1903-   )

Sherrill E. Grace
University of British Columbia

BOOK: *Earth Song* (Toronto: Playwrights Co-op, 1976).

PLAY PRODUCTIONS: *Rocks: A Play of Northern Ontario*, Toronto, Central High School of Commerce, 22 April 1932;

Earth Song, Sarnia, Ontario, Sarnia Drama League, 16 December 1932;

Hill-Land: A Play of the Canadian North for a New Theatre, Toronto, Central High School of Commerce Play Workshop, 13 December 1934;

Murder Pattern: An Experiment Toward a Symphonic Theatre, Toronto, Central High School of Commerce Play Workshop, 30 January 1936;

Maria Chapdelaine: An Adaptation For a Symphonic Theatre, Toronto, Central High School of Commerce Play Workshop, 11 February 1938;

Ascend As the Sun, music by Godfrey Ridout, Toronto, Central High School of Commerce Play Workshop, 13 April 1942;

The Masque of the Red Death, adapted from Edgar Allan Poe's story, music by Ridout, Toronto, Central High School of Commerce, 19 February 1943;

Esther: A Dramatic Symphony, libretto by Voaden, music by Ridout, Toronto, Massey Hall, 29 April 1952;

The Prodigal Son: An Opera in Three Acts Based on Four Early America Prints, libretto by Voaden, score by Frederick Jacobi, Toronto, Recreation Commission of the Village of Forest Hill, 23 March 1954;

Emily Carr: A Stage Biography with Pictures, Kingston, Ontario, Queen's University, 6 August 1960.

OTHER: *Six Canadian Plays*, edited, with an introduction, by Voaden (Toronto: Copp Clark, 1930);

A Book of Plays for Schools and Community Drama Groups in Canada, edited, with a foreword, ep-

Herman Voaden (photograph copyright © by V. Tony Hauser)

ilogue, and two essays ("The Writing of One-Act Plays" and "Producing the Plays"), by Voaden (Toronto: Macmillan, 1935);

Four Good Plays to Read and Act, edited, with two essays ("To the Student" and "Theatre vs. Film and Radio"), by Voaden (Toronto & New York: Longmans, Green, 1944);

On Stage: Plays for School and Community, edited, with an introduction, by Voaden (Toronto: Macmillan, 1945); republished as *Nobody Waved Good-bye and Other Plays* (Toronto: Macmillan, 1966);

"Dramatic Art in Canadian Higher Education," in *The Humanities in Canada*, edited by Watson Kirkconnell and A. S. P. Woodhouse (Ottawa: Humanities Research Council of Canada, 1947), pp. 228-236;

"The Arts in Canada," in *Canada Overseas Reference Book*, edited by Robert Hamilton Coats (London: Todd, 1949), pp. 96-101;

Two Good Plays to Read and Act, edited, with an introduction, by Voaden (Toronto: Longmans, Green, 1953);

T. S. Eliot, *Murder in the Cathedral*, edited, with an introduction, by Voaden (Toronto: Kingswood House / London: Faber & Faber, 1959);

Four Plays of Our Time, edited, with a foreword and an introduction, by Voaden (Toronto: Macmillan, 1960);

Drama IV, edited, with a foreword and an introduction, by Voaden (Toronto: Macmillan, 1965);

Human Values in Drama, edited, with an introduction, by Voaden (Toronto: Macmillan, 1966);

William Shakespeare, *Julius Caesar*, edited, with an introduction, by Voaden (Toronto: Macmillan, 1966; New York: St. Martin's Press, 1966);

The Arts and Education, 2 volumes, edited by Voaden (Toronto: Canadian Conference of the Arts, 1967);

Look Both Ways: Theatre Experiences, edited by Voaden (Toronto: Macmillan, 1975);

Wilderness and *Murder Pattern*, in *Canada's Lost Plays*, volume 3, *The Developing Mosaic: English-Canadian Drama to Mid-century*, edited by Anton Wagner (Toronto: Canadian Theatre Review Publications, 1980), pp. 88-97 and 103-117;

Hill-Land, in *Major Plays of the Canadian Theatre, 1934-1984*, edited by Richard Perkyns (Toronto: Irwin, 1984), pp. 25-36.

PERIODICAL PUBLICATIONS: "A National Drama League: Its Relation to Little Theatre Activity and Play-writing in Canada," *Canadian Forum*, 9 (December 1928): 105-106;

"What Is Wrong With the Canadian Theatre?," *Globe* (Toronto), 22 June 1929, p. 22;

"Producing Methods Defined: Realism and Its Modern Successors Explained and Contra-Distinguished–'Symphonic Expressionism' as the Art of the Future," *Globe* (Toronto), 16 April 1932, p. 15;

"Canadian Plays and Experimental Stagecraft," *Globe* (Toronto), 23 April 1932, p. 18;

"Creed for a New Theatre: 'Symphonic Expressionism,' a Composite Blending of all Theatral Arts Explained in Detail as a Possible Stage Method for the Future," *Globe* (Toronto), 17 December 1932, p. 5;

"New Methods in Teaching Poetry," *School*, 21 (December 1932): 330-336;

"Dance of the Theatre: Impressions of the Dance in Four Countries," *Dancing Times*, 274 (July 1933): 333-335;

"An Experiment in the Teaching of Poetry," *English Journal*, 23 (April 1934): 309-313;

"Toward a New Theatre," *Globe* (Toronto), 8 December 1934, p. 19;

"An Experiment in Extensive Reading," by Voaden, G. K. D. Alderson, and G. H. Dickinson, *School*, 24 (December 1935): 229-301;

"Theatre Record, 1945," *Canadian Forum*, 25 (November 1945): 184-187;

"The Theatre in Canada: A National Theatre?," *Theatre Arts*, 30 (July 1946): 389-391;

"UNESCO and a World Theatre," *Theatre Arts*, 31 (July 1947): 23-26;

"The Arts and Unesco," *University of Toronto Quarterly*, 17 (January 1948): 161-167;

"*Murder Pattern* and the Critics," *Canadian Theatre Review*, 5 (Winter 1975): 61-62;

"Towards a Canadian Drama: a View From the Thirties," *Canadian Theatre Review*, 28 (Fall 1980): 10-17;

"A Letter From Voaden," *Theatre History in Canada*, 2, no. 2 (1981): 156-158;

"*Symphony: A Drama of Motion and Light for a New Theatre*," *Canadian Drama*, 8, no. 1 (1982): 74-83.

Herman Voaden's contribution to the artistic life of Canada has been enormous and multifaceted. Since the early 1920s he has served the arts, especially the theater, as teacher, editor, director, and playwright. During the 1940s, 1950s, and 1960s he participated in several strategic arts organizations, and in 1970 he was elected fellow of the Royal Society of Arts, followed by an appointment as member of the Order of Canada in 1974. He was awarded an LL.D. by St. Mary's University in 1988, and in 1989 he received the *diplôme d'honneur* from the Canadian Conference of the Arts. His alma mater, Queen's University, made him alumnus of the year for 1989.

Voaden, the third child of Dr. Arthur Voaden and Louisa Bale Voaden, was born in London, Ontario. After primary and secondary school education in London, he graduated from Queen's University, Kingston, Ontario, in 1923 with a degree in English and history. His passionate interest in the theater led him to return he didn't want to be safe about things.

(Her light follows the rhythm of the sentence, building to 2/8 on "safe" and falling to 1/8 on "about things". As the new sentence begins it builds to 2/8, and to 3/8 on "strong in me".)

And now his words are strong in me.

(The light builds to 4/8.) They are my words.

(Her light grows to 5/8 with her transfiguring vision. The violin theme leaps up with her faith.) I too shall see banners shaking before me--

(Her light builds to 6/8 on "great white" and to 7/8 on "blinding". The music builds with it.) A great white light blinding me--

(The light builds to full on "music ringing" and holds at 8/8 through the next three sentences, to "flashing northern lights".) music ringing in my ears.

I too shall hear the wilderness calling,

calling my life into a great adventure.

It will be my land.

Page from the typescript for Voaden's 1932 play Rocks *(by permission of the author)* there for a master's degree, which he received in 1926, having completed a thesis on the American playwright Eugene O'Neill. As well as directing and acting, Voaden had begun writing plays by 1927; when he became director of English at the Central High School of Commerce in Toronto in 1928, a position he held until his retirement in 1964, he was already formulating his avant-garde conception of "theatral" art which would become known in the 1930s as "symphonic expressionism." He was widely traveled and thoroughly conversant with the theories of Adolphe Appia and Gordon Craig, and with the most advanced experimental work of the European theater. In 1930-1931 he studied play writing with George Pierce Baker at Yale; Voaden's realistic one-act play *Wilderness* was written during this period, although it was not published until 1978 when it appeared in the magazine *Boréal*. (In 1980 it was included in Anton Wagner's anthology *Canada's Lost Plays*.) After his experience in New Haven, Voaden returned to Toronto to write and direct the "symphonic" plays which articulate his new vision for the theater.

Voaden's work, like his life, is inseparable from his nationalism. In the introductory manifesto to *Six Canadian Plays*, edited by Voaden in 1930, he called for a Canadian drama that would celebrate and express a uniquely northern experience and imagination, and this goal was further inspired by the Group of Seven painters, most notably by Lawren Harris. The first of his own productions to embody his evolving vision was the stunning *Rocks* (1932), which he directed for the stage at the Central High School of Commerce according to his symphonic expressionist principles by abstracting and stylizing *Wilderness*. A simple story of two women–mother and fiancée–who mourn the death in a blizzard of son and lover, *Rocks* employed sets recalling Harris's severe northern canvases and also made use of ritualized movement and speech, music, drumbeats, choral dancers, and a highly expressive orchestration of light. Voaden used light to represent the North and to symbolize the young woman's mystical acceptance of the land that has claimed her lover's life, and light would become the key element in his drama for conveying his deeply religious, idealistic, and metaphysical vision of life.

In *Earth Song* (produced in 1932 and published in 1976) Voaden used autobiographical experiences, most important his love for Violet Kilpatrick (16 December 1901-19 December 1984), whom he married in 1935, as the basis for a de-

tailed and lyrical dramatization of this philosophy. Through its synthesis of lyric speech, stylized dance and gesture, music and colored light, *Earth Song* celebrates the ritual progression of a contemporary Adam and Eve toward their "Godhood," but their goal is an ecstatic illumination that unites them, not with some transcendent spiritual order but with the earth, the cycles of the seasons, and each other. Because it requires Voaden's full "symphonic" method, *Earth Song* must be seen, heard, and experienced, rather than merely read, and the same is true for his subsequent plays.

Hill-Land (produced in 1934 and published in *Major Plays of the Canadian Theatre* [1984], edited by Richard Perkyns) dramatizes Voaden's hope for the emerging superman in his hero, Paul, who is able to transcend the death of his young wife through his life-affirming acceptance of a northern mysticism. *Murder Pattern* (produced in 1936, published in *Canadian Theatre Review* [Winter 1975], and included in *Canada's Lost Plays*) has a more substantial (and traditional) plot than any of the earlier plays, but like *Hill-Land* it ends in a death that marks a spiritually transfiguring vision of union with the land. Here Voaden recounts the story of an actual murder, but the beauty of the play stems from his orchestration of realistic, symbolic, and choral voices that elaborate and comment upon the dramatic action. The meaning of this symphonic expressionist play resides less in the sparse details of the story than in Voaden's successful orchestration of light, voice, and movement which together suggest the timelessness, lyric beauty, and profound faith in life that constitute his vision. *Ascend As the Sun* (produced in 1942) is, in many ways, reminiscent of Voaden's early play *Symphony* (published in *Canadian Drama* [1982] but never produced), and it recapitulates his central themes of spiritual affirmation and the evolution of the new man in the dramaturgy of his symphonic expressionist method. Recalling Strindberg's *To Damascus*, the hero, David, sets out on his life's journey beset by the terrifying forces of sexual and spiritual doubt; he resists the temptation to commit suicide and arrives at a transfiguring, ecstatic vision of life symbolized by the flood of light with which the play closes.

Ascend As the Sun was intended as part of a trilogy, but, appalled at the events of World War II, Voaden never completed this opus about the triumph of the human spirit. Instead, he redirected his energies into adaptations and collaborative activities. He adapted biblical verses for Canadian composer Godfrey Ridout's *Esther: A Dramatic Symphony*, which was performed in 1952 at Massey Hall, Toronto, by the Royal Conservatory Symphony Orchestra, and in 1954 he worked with the American composer Frederick Jacobi, providing the libretto for an opera entitled *The Prodigal Son*. His most recent completed play is the drama *Emily Carr*, a lyrical interpretation of this well-known Canadian painter's life using slide projections of her works; it was first produced at Queen's University in 1960 with Amelia Hall playing the part of Carr.

After World War II Voaden combined his teaching and editing with political and cultural activities. He ran as a candidate for the Cooperative Commonwealth Federation in four federal elections from 1945 to 1954; he prepared briefs on the arts in Canada for presentation to government committees and commissions; he served as first president of the Canadian Arts Council, 1945-1948, and as a member of the Canadian delegation to the 1946 UNESCO Conference in Paris. In 1949 Voaden helped to draft the recommendation which the Canadian Arts Council presented to the Royal Commission on National Development in the Arts, Letters, and Sciences (the Massey Commission), and it was these recommendations that led to the formation, in 1957, of the Canada Council. As associate director, then national director of the Canadian Conference of the Arts, 1966-1968, Voaden helped prepare a two-volume report on the arts and education in Canada, and from 1968 to 1970 he served as president of the Canadian Guild of Crafts.

Since 1976 Herman Voaden has begun to receive increasing attention from theater historians. Some of his important plays from the 1930s have been published, his "symphonic expressionist" method and religious vision are once more being discussed, and in March 1987 Heinar Pillar mounted a stunning revival of *Murder Pattern* at the George Brown Theatre in Toronto. Writing for the *Toronto Star*, 18 April 1942, theater critic Augustus Bridle described *Ascend As the Sun* as "the most dramatic event of its kind ever known" in the Canadian theater, and from the perspective of the late 1980s it seems clear that Voaden's vision of Canada and of the theater constitutes a contribution of major importance in this century. With Anton Wagner, he is currently preparing a definitive edition of his plays, "A Vision of Canada: Herman Voaden's Dramatic Works."

References:

Geraldine Anthony, "Herman Voaden," in her *Stage Voices: Twelve Canadian Playwrights Talk About Their Lives and Work* (Toronto: Doubleday, 1978), pp. 28-54;

Chad Evans, "Herman Voaden and the Symphonic Theatre," *Canadian Theatre Review*, 25 (Winter 1980): 37-43;

Alan Field, "Herman Voaden and the Test of Time," *Canadian Theatre Review*, 25 (Winter 1980): 91-95;

Sherrill Grace, "A Northern Modernism: 1920-1932: Canadian Painting and Literature," *Literary Criterion*, 19, no. 3-4 (1984): 105-124;

Grace, *Regression and Apocalypse: Studies in North American Literary Expressionism* (Toronto: University of Toronto Press, 1989);

Eva-Marie Kröller, "Literary Versions of Emily Carr," *Canadian Literature*, 109 (Summer 1986): 87-98;

Richard Perkyns, "Pioneers: two contrasting dramatic treatments (*Hill-Land* and *At My Heart's Core*)," *Canadian Drama*, 10, no. 1 (1984): 56-64;

Anton Wagner, " 'A Country of the Soul': Herman Voaden, Lowrie Warrener, and the Writing of *Symphony*," *Canadian Drama*, 9, no. 2 (1983): 203-219;

Wagner, "Herman Voaden's 'New Religion,' " *Theatre History in Canada*, 6, no. 2 (1985): 187-201.

Papers:

The major collection of Voaden materials, including letters, programs, manuscripts, posters, and notebooks, is at the Scott Library, York University, Toronto.

Bertram Warr

(7 December 1917-3 April 1943)

Keith Garebian

BOOK: *Acknowledgment to Life*, edited by Len Gasparini (Toronto: Ryerson, 1970).

When on 3 April 1943 he went down with his Halifax bomber during a Royal Air Force raid over Essen, Germany, Bertram Warr was twenty-five years old. The *Times Literary Supplement*, surprisingly, ran an obituary, which was as much a tribute to his pluck as it was to his poetry. Warr had published only one broadsheet of fourteen poems, *Yet A Little Onwards* (London: Favil, 1941), and only thirty-five other poems survive which are hardly enough to ensure him a lasting reputation.

As a poet Warr was often unsure of himself, struggling to handle themes without falling back on outworn conventions. The war poems are without the exhilaration of those of Rupert Brooke. They lack the irony and understatement of Robert Graves, the rich symbolic transmutations of Isaac Rosenberg, the vivid documentations of Edmund Blunden and Wilfred Owen, and the satirical finesse of Siegfried Sassoon. They are, however, faithful representations of the actuality of war and London life under duress, and their various free forms project a sincere, straightforward view. After his death, Warr's poems attracted the attention of Oscar Williams, Earle Birney, Lorne Pierce, A. J. M. Smith, Ralph Gustafson, and Alan Crawley–not purely on the basis of sentiment but because these eminent men felt that, had Warr survived, he could have been, as Birney put it, "a leading poet of his generation. . . ."

Warr's adolescence in Toronto was during the Depression. There was no money in the family to pay for his university education, so Warr worked as an office clerk after graduating from high school, taking an evening course in journalism from the University of Toronto. When he could no longer tolerate irksome office routine, he left the city in April 1938 for the Muskoka area of Ontario where he worked for the summer as a porter at a resort hotel. In September he went to Halifax with a friend, and the two of

them stowed away on a passenger liner on Christmas Eve. Discovered on board, they worked as stewards for the rest of the voyage and landed at Liverpool. A truck driver transported them to London where Warr worked at several menial jobs in order to finance his study at Birkbeck College, University of London, where he learned the poet's craft.

Although several of his collected poems in the posthumously published *Acknowledgment to Life* (1970) show no more than an impulse for poetry, the best ones indicate that Warr could leave aside the debts he probably owed to Eliot, Yeats, and Owen and express his own feelings in clever deployments of technique whose effects contribute to the meanings of the poems. As Len Gasparini, editor of *Acknowledgment to Life*, has pointed out, "The Deviator," for instance, reveals "Warr's ability to transform images through the symbolical scale of sound." The poem's strong variant assonance culminates in the final lines: "Saying there is no aloneness, there can be no dark cocoon, / With room for one, and an empty place, if love should come." "Death of an Elephant" has the phrase "pitiless as flood, submissive, too, as water," which prompted Robert Graves to write to Warr complimenting him on his ability to see "the same thing simultaneously in two conflicting aspects."

Even when Warr's verse is awkward, it holds surprises. Although the technique of "The Murder" is unpolished, the structure makes for an interesting parallel between the casual cruelty of a child's killing an insect and the condition of man's unimpressive struggle. At times Warr seems to have been influenced by Eliot's composed wit and poised irony; sometimes, in his naive romantic poems, he indulges either in Whitmanesque celebration of nature in vigorous copulation imagery ("Immaculate Conception") or in corrosive satire in which sex is treated as a base instinct ("Act of Love") and the poem title is an ironic comment.

However, Warr could be delicate even when experimenting with curious syntactical patterns

The Collected Poems of Bertram Warr
Acknowledgment To Life

Front cover for Warr's only book, published twenty-seven years after his death in a World War II bombing raid over Germany

and abstractions, turning seriousness into a dreamy moment of fulfillment "like the seed that whispers and is breathed upon" ("I Sit With Nothing In My Hands"). Warr never took flight from emotion. "On a Child with a Wooden Leg" reads like a forerunner of Raymond Souster's poetry in its terseness and images that convey pathos with free-verse directness: "In the evening after prayers, / Probably the parent observes / How incongruous, on the chair, / Is the single, folded sock; / And on the floor / The one shoe, / Dissatisfied, perhaps, in the incomplete life."

When Great Britain declared war against Germany, Warr did not want to return to Canada. He had already become a socialist after a period of religious skepticism that had impelled him to turn away from his Catholic upbringing. In "Psalm CLI" he expresses his bitter disillusionment with God. The title is a perverse irony in that with this poem Warr adds a new psalm to the 150 songs in the Bible, and this one cancels

all the hosannas. Warr's bitterness shows sardonically from the first lines: "Come you down here now to look at your world, / O little old man of the sky; / Thrust your crinkled old ear out from a cloud / And listen. Do you hear the cry?" Warr's poem is an inversion of sentiment and imagery of the final biblical psalm, and God is a weary old man with wavering senses and baffled perception. It is clear from this denunciation that Warr, affected by the desolation and emptiness he perceived in Britain and in all of the West, was exasperated with "god-suffering, man-weak" humanity.

Warr's socialism made him a proponent of the working classes, "the walkers on pavement, / who go grey-faced and given-up through the rain; / with twice turned collars crinkled, / and the patches bunched coarsely in crotches" ("Working Class"). Seeing England on the verge of ruin, the very houses forlorn and empty "like a lot of tarts / . . . with their legs cocked, showing the works" ("Stepney 1941"), the poet denounces the churchmen and politicians "with chaos in their pale old eyes"; cities will topple, he predicts, "dissolving and giving off gases," and the working classes will build on "the bleached bones" ("Working Class").

No doubt, his socialism was naive, the dream of an apocalypse in which the outworn and false in capitalist society will crumble so that the seed of Lenin's dream can be sown. But Warr's impulse toward social justice sharpened his yearning for a new age. His socialism caused him to see the war as a development in the universal class struggle, and rather than become a war resister, he chose to compromise with the will of the majority and participate in the next chapter of social history. In "An Unfinished Essay," included in *Acknowledgment to Life*, Warr calmly saw the inevitability of his own death in battle: "I shall not die by my own hand, but will be killed in the war. But this being killed will be only the completion of the death. The desire to die has been with me for some months." He had progressed through stages of despair and apathy: his desire to die was not an aspiration toward a higher and more satisfying state, but a resignation to timelessness. His resignation reached its epitome, perhaps, in "Acknowledgment to Life," in which he appears to have moved away from others into a monotonous "gnarled tightness" of life, becoming "as lonely as the universe." His solitary inner protest was an affecting youthful song in the midst of the "death convulsion of a system."

Robert Weaver
(6 January 1921-   )

Paul Matthew St. Pierre
Simon Fraser University

EDITED BOOKS: *Canadian Short Stories*, edited by Weaver and Helen James, with a preface by Weaver (Toronto: Oxford University Press, 1952);

Canadian Short Stories, edited, with an introduction, by Weaver (Toronto, London & New York: Oxford University Press, 1960);

Ten for Wednesday Night: A Collection of Short Stories Presented for Broadcast by "CBC Wednesday Night," edited, with an introduction, by Weaver (Toronto: McClelland & Stewart, 1961);

The First Five Years: A Selection from "The Tamarack Review," edited, with a preface, by Weaver (Toronto: Oxford University Press, 1962);

Canadian Short Stories, second series, edited, with an introduction, by Weaver (Toronto: Oxford University Press, 1968);

Poems for Voices, edited, with an introduction, by Weaver (Toronto: Canadian Broadcasting Corporation, 1970);

The Oxford Anthology of Canadian Literature, edited, with a preface, by Weaver and William Toye (Toronto: Oxford University Press, 1973; revised, 1981);

Canadian Short Stories, third series, edited, with a preface, by Weaver (Toronto: Oxford University Press, 1978);

Small Wonders: New Stories by Twelve Distinguished Canadian Authors, edited, with an introduction, by Weaver (Toronto: CBC Enterprises, 1982);

The "Anthology" Anthology: A Selection from 30 Years of CBC Radio's "Anthology," edited, with a preface, by Weaver (Toronto: Macmillan, 1984);

Canadian Short Stories, fourth series, edited, with a preface, by Weaver (Toronto: Oxford University Press, 1985);

The Oxford Book of Canadian Short Stories in English, edited, with an introduction, by Weaver and Margaret Atwood (Toronto & New York: Oxford University Press, 1986).

Robert Weaver (courtesy of Oxford University Press)

OTHER: Mavis Gallant, *The End of the World and Other Stories*, introduction by Weaver (Toronto: McClelland & Stewart, 1974);

"Hugh Garner," "Norman Levine," "Mystery and Crime," and "Short Stories in English," in *The Oxford Companion to Canadian Literature*, edited by William Toye (Toronto: Oxford University Press, 1983), pp. 290-291, 452-453, 540-542, 752-756.

PERIODICAL PUBLICATIONS: "John Sutherland and *Northern Review*," *Tamarack Review*, 2 (Winter 1957): 65-69;

"The World of the Just and the Unjust," *Tamarack Review*, 5 (Autumn 1957): 61-66;

"A Talk with Morley Callaghan," *Tamarack Review*, 7 (Spring 1958): 3-29;

"*Lady Chatterley* and All That," *Tamarack Review*, 21 (Autumn 1961): 49-57;

"The Role of the Canada Council," *Tamarack Review*, 24 (Summer 1962): 76-82;

"Editorial," *Tamarack Review*, 83/84 (Winter 1982): 3-4;

"In Tribute: Marian Engel," *Quill and Quire*, 51 (April 1985): 64.

Robert Weaver is one of the most prominent figures on the contemporary Canadian literary scene. Through his work compiling a series of standard short-fiction anthologies, founding and editing a literary periodical of consequence, and producing some ground-breaking literary programs on radio, Weaver has taught readers, writers, and critics alike how to refine their fictional sensibilities and evaluative criteria. As an editor he has introduced two generations of Canadians to their own literature and encouraged them to acclaim such established writers as Margaret Atwood and Mavis Gallant, to proclaim such emerging writers as Katherine Govier and Neil Bissoondath, and to reclaim such standard writers as Stephen Leacock and Charles G. D. Roberts. His efforts as an editor and anthologist have helped make the name *Weaver* synonymous with the Canadian short story.

Over the past two decades in particular, Weaver has provided Canadian writers with a forum for their short fiction and encouraged other editors to do the same. Through his long association with the Canadian Broadcasting Corporation (predating his inaugural short-story anthology of 1952), Weaver has fostered the development of the short story in Canada in two important ways: he has been instrumental in bringing published stories to radio and making them available again in print in his anthologies, and he has commissioned for radio broadcast stories which he later edited for publication. During the 1950s and 1960s especially, "publishing on the air" helped to create a new audience for short-story writers who often reached the Canadian public through British and American publishers.

Robert Leigh Weaver was born on 6 January 1921 in Niagara Falls, Ontario. His father, Walter, a medical doctor (who died when Robert was seven), and his mother, Jessie, a librarian, fostered in him an early respect for books and love for reading. He received his early schooling in Niagara Falls and completed his secondary educa-

tion in Toronto, where he, his sister, and his mother moved in 1936. After working briefly in a Toronto bank and after serving in the RCAF and the Canadian army during World War II, Weaver pursued his education at University College, University of Toronto, where he wrote for the newspaper, the *Varsity*, and cofounded the Modern Letters Club. During this time he also placed articles in *Canadian Forum*, the *New Republic*, and the *Nation*. After university graduation, and on the basis of these early publications, he took a position in November 1948 as a program organizer for the public-affairs division of CBC-Radio. Thus began his long and fruitful tenure with the Canadian Broadcasting Corporation.

The first radio program with which he was associated was the fifteen-minute weekly series *Canadian Short Stories*. Weaver's 1952 anthology of the same title, coedited with the show's producer, Helen James, features stories broadcast from 1946 to 1951 (notably by Ted Allan, Joyce Marshall, Hugh Garner, and Ethel Wilson). *Canadian Short Stories* was also the forerunner of Weaver's most celebrated radio program, *Anthology*, which began 19 October 1954 (with a short story by a little-known expatriate writer named Mordecai Richler) and ran for the next thirty years.

Anthology was a more comprehensive program than *Canadian Short Stories:* in addition to featuring a short-story reading each week, it addressed itself to other literary genres and the nonliterary arts, in poetry readings, interviews with authors, and panel discussions. For many years a thirty-minute program, it grew to an hour in 1968 and to two hours just before its end. By the time of his departure for early retirement in March 1985, Weaver had succeeded in entrenching *Anthology* in Canadian literary history. The program was less firmly grounded in the CBC, however, which canceled it in September 1985: *Anthology* and another show, *Booktime*, the last of the CBC's literary programs, were victims of federal government budget cuts to the arts.

Weaver was the originator of two other influential radio programs: *Critically Speaking*, a weekly arts magazine that ran through the 1950s and was restructured and retitled in the 1960s, and *Stories with John Drainie*, 1959-1965, which featured the celebrated Canadian actor reading an original short story each weekday afternoon. In the course of his work with these programs Weaver refined his critical voice toward sharp judgment and editorial stance toward scrupulous revision.

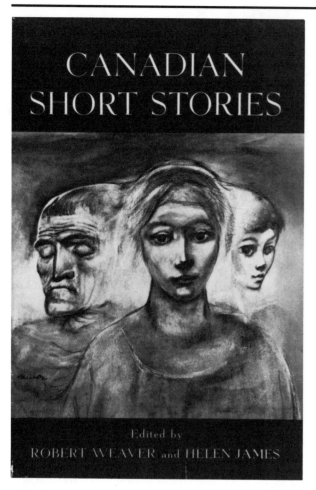

Dust jacket for an anthology of stories that were originally broadcast on CBC-Radio from 1946 to 1951. Most selections in the volume were read on the weekly program Canadian Short Stories, *for which Weaver served as editor. The producer was Helen James.*

Running concurrently with *Stories with John Drainie* and *Anthology* was *CBC Wednesday Night* (which had begun in 1948 and which was later called *Tuesday Night*), a program devoted mainly to drama, music, and documentaries, which Weaver elected to liven up with a shot of short fiction. Weaver's most important innovation was to invite writers to submit recent short stories for broadcast and for possible publication in book form. His intention was partly to respond to the resurgence of short fiction in Canada in the 1950s, but mainly to provide a common market for Canadian writers, readers, and listeners. One result of Weaver's "experiment" was his 1961 anthology, *Ten for Wednesday Night: A Collection of Short Stories Presented for Broadcast by "CBC Wednesday Night,"* a work which has assumed a special historical significance because of its showcasing of Weaver's literary discoveries Mordecai Richler and Alice

Munro alongside such established writers as Morley Callaghan, Hugh Garner, Ethel Wilson, and Gabrielle Roy.

Over the next twenty years Weaver would perform the same publishing experiment twice more. *Poems for Voices* (1970) comprises six lengthy radio poems (by Al Purdy, Margaret Atwood, John Newlove, Phyllis Gotlieb, Tom Marshall, and Alden Nowlan) which Weaver had commissioned for broadcast on *Anthology*. Weaver next commissioned twelve established and emerging writers to write new short stories to be read on *Anthology* and published later in book form. *Small Wonders: New Stories by Twelve Distinguished Canadian Authors* (1982) covers Canada, from Jack Hodgins's Vancouver Island to Alden Nowlan's New Brunswick, and acknowledges the growing internationalism of the Canadian short story, in works by American-born writers (Clark Blaise, Jane Rule, Kent Thompson) and stories with non-Canadian settings (the United States, France, Africa). As Weaver notes in his preface, "We are beginning to feel at ease in our place in the international literary community."

At the same time that he was working as a CBC editor and producer and compiling anthologies based on radio broadcasts, Weaver was moving into more conventional literary fields. He first departed from radio in autumn 1956 with the inaugural issue of the *Tamarack Review*, the respected journal of fiction, poetry, criticism, and review which he founded with some of his Toronto writer friends, among them William Toye (who from 1962 was Weaver's editor at Oxford University Press). With Toye's assistance Weaver edited *Tamarack Review* until its demise in 1982, in the process helping to form literary opinions in the most crucial quarter-century in Canadian literary history. *Tamarack Review* spotlighted early writing by Hugh Hood, Clark Blaise, and Dave Godfrey, as well as by Mordecai Richler and Alice Munro, but even more important it articulated some of Weaver's most important aesthetic positions, most notably his rejection of the idea of clearly delineated Canadian short-story traditions. Weaver's early efforts with *Tamarack Review* culminated in his editing of the retrospective *The First Five Years: A Selection from "The Tamarack Review"* (1962).

Building on the success of his 1952 volume edited with Helen James, Weaver has gone on to edit independently an ambitious series of anthologies entitled *Canadian Short Stories*, all published by Oxford University Press. The 1960 *Canadian*

Short Stories offers in its selections a brief history of the short-story form in Canada and concludes with works by several of the leading practitioners of the day. The second series (1968) features stories from the 1950s and 1960s; the third series (1978), stories from the 1960s and 1970s; and the fourth series (1985), stories from the 1980s. The four series together give a sense of the continuity of Canadian writing: for example, works by Alice Munro and Mavis Gallant appear in all four anthologies, and many other writers are represented more than once. Weaver is currently at work on the fifth series of *Canadian Short Stories.*

Two of Weaver's most ambitious projects are both collaborations: *The Oxford Anthology of Canadian Literature* (1973; revised, 1981), which he edited with William Toye, and *The Oxford Book of Canadian Short Stories in English* (1986), edited with Margaret Atwood. *The Oxford Anthology of Canadian Literature* covers four centuries of Canadian literature, ranging from the Jesuit *Relations* to Marshall McLuhan, from Marie de l'Incarnation to Pierre Vallières, and featuring such standard authors as Margaret Atwood, Earle Birney, Stephen Leacock, Margaret Laurence, and Northrop Frye. More an introductory textbook than a reference work, the anthology is noteworthy for its many excerpts from long works of fiction, verse, and criticism. Ten years after compiling *The Oxford Anthology*, Weaver contributed four articles to William Toye's *Oxford Companion to Canadian Literature* (1983): "Hugh Garner," "Norman Levine," "Mystery and Crime," and "Short Stories in English."

The Oxford Book of Canadian Short Stories in English is arguably Weaver's crowning achievement to date, emphasizing the delicate hand he has exercised in nurturing the short story over the last thirty years and in recognizing the best among the short stories of the last century. In her part of the anthology's introduction, Margaret Atwood acknowledges Weaver's profound influence on her career, and in his own part Weaver takes a little uncharacteristic pride in the fact that three stories from his 1952 anthology reappear in the present volume. Of the forty-one stories in *The Oxford Book of Canadian Short Stories in En-*

glish, most are by living authors, and more than a quarter are by writers under fifty years old: through their selections Weaver and Atwood seem to want to emphasize how recently the Canadian short story has come of age.

The Canadian literary community has repeatedly acknowledged its indebtedness to Weaver, whose books and radio programs for thirty years have virtually kept the short story alive as an outlet for literary publication in Canada. In 1979 Weaver was awarded the Molson Prize in recognition of his oeuvre and his influence. Since retiring from his position as a CBC producer in 1985, Weaver has continued to supervise the annual CBC-Radio Literary Competition which he started in 1978. In 1987 he was appointed fiction editor of *Saturday Night*, and in the June 1988 issue he featured Timothy Findley's new story "Almeyer's Mother" as the first in a monthly series of short fiction. Robert Weaver and Audrey Mackellan have been married for twenty-five years and have two children, David and Janice. The Weavers live in Toronto.

References:

John Bemrose, "Patron Saint of Prose," *Maclean's*, 98 (1 April 1985): 50b;

Doug Fetherling, "Anthology: The Secret Radio Programme that May Last Forever," *Saturday Night*, 94 (November 1979): 68-70;

Janet Hamilton, "Robert Weaver: The Best Friend a Short Story Ever Had," *Quill and Quire*, 54 (February 1988): 23;

Jeannine Locke, "Tiger of Canadian Culture Is a Pussycat," *Maclean's*, 82 (April 1969): 116-118;

D. Macfarlane, "Leave It to Weaver," *Today* (24 October 1981): 14-15;

W. H. New, "Canada: Story and History," in his *Dreams of Speech and Violence: The Art of the Short Story in Canada and New Zealand* (Toronto: University of Toronto Press, 1987), pp. 80-81.

Papers:

Robert Weaver's papers are at the Public Archives in Ottawa.

George Whalley

(25 July 1915-27 May 1983)

George Johnston
Carleton University

BOOKS: *Poems: 1939-1944* (Toronto: Ryerson, 1946);

No Man an Island (Toronto: Clarke, Irwin, 1948);

Poetic Process (London: Routledge & Kegan Paul, 1953);

Coleridge and Sara Hutchinson, and the Asra Poems (London: Routledge & Kegan Paul, 1955; Toronto: University of Toronto Press, 1955);

The Legend of John Hornby (London: John Murray, 1962; Toronto: Macmillan, 1962);

Studies in Literature and the Humanities, edited by Brian Crick and John Ferns (Montreal: McGill-Queen's University Press, 1985);

The Collected Poems of George Whalley, edited by George Johnston (Kingston, Ont.: Quarry, 1986).

OTHER: George Herbert Clarke, *Selected Poems*, edited by Whalley (Toronto: Ryerson, 1954);

Writing in Canada, edited by Whalley (Toronto: Macmillan, 1956);

A Place of Liberty: Essays on the Government of Canadian Universities, edited by Whalley (Toronto: Clarke, Irwin, 1964);

"Coleridge and Vico," in *Giambattista Vico: An International Symposium*, edited by Giorgio Tagliacozzo and Hayden V. White (Baltimore: Johns Hopkins University Press, 1969), pp. 225-244;

Death in the Barren Ground: The Diary of Edgar Christian, edited by Whalley (Ottawa: Oberon, 1980);

Marginalia, volume 12 of *The Collected Works of Samuel Taylor Coleridge*, 2 parts, edited by Whalley (London: Routledge & Kegan Paul / Princeton: Princeton University Press, 1980, 1985).

PERIODICAL PUBLICATIONS: "The Poet and his Reader," *Queen's Quarterly*, 54 (1947): 202-213;

George Whalley *(courtesy of William O'Neill*, Whig-Standard, *Kingston, Ontario)*

"The Dispersal of S. T. Coleridge's Books," anonymous, *Times Literary Supplement*, 28 October 1949, p. 704;

"Coleridge on Classical Prosody: An Unidentified Review of 1797," *Review of English Studies*, new series 2 (July 1951);

"In the Land of Feast and Famine: The Legend of John Hornby," *Cornhill*, no. 1011 (1957): 191-213;

"The Sinking of the Bismarck," *Atlantic Monthly*, 206 (July 1960): 60-64;

"Coleridge on the *Prometheus* of Aeschylus," *Proceedings of the Royal Society of Canada*, 54 (1961): II;

"On Translating Aristotle's *Poetics*," *University of Toronto Quarterly*, 39 (January 1970): 77-106.

George Whalley is best known as scholar, teacher, critic, and essayist of literary and public matters. His first two published books, however, and his latest, which appeared three years after his death, are of poetry, and he composed many radio productions on literary or biographical subjects. His biography of the Arctic adventurer John Hornby had considerable circulation in Canada and abroad and has been republished in paperback. He also wrote an influential book of poetic theory, *Poetic Process* (1953).

He was born on 25 July 1915 in Kingston, Ontario, son of the Very Reverend Arthur Francis Cecil Whalley and Dorothy Quirk Whalley. George Whalley studied at Bishop's University (B.A., 1935; M.A., 1948), at Oriel College, Oxford (B.A., 1939; M.A., 1945), and at King's College, London (Ph.D., 1950). He went to Oxford as Rhodes Scholar for Quebec. His studies there were interrupted by his five years' service with the Royal Canadian Navy Volunteer Reserve during World War II. He was promoted to the rank of lieutenant-commander in 1943. In the course of his naval service he was awarded the Royal Humane Society Bronze Medal for saving life at sea. He married Elizabeth Watts in 1944 in England, and their three children are Katharine, Christopher, and Emily. He taught, as lecturer and assistant professor of English, at Bishop's University from 1945 to 1948; he then joined the English department at Queen's University as professor and remained there until his retirement in 1980. He was twice head of the department. He was the recipient of four research fellowships and three honorary degrees. Whalley died of cancer in 1983.

His books of poetry *Poems: 1939-1944*, a chapbook (1946), and *No Man an Island* (1948) arose from his experiences as a naval officer. Many of the poems were written in action; others had to do with the life on leave in blacked-out and bombed London and the countryside of England. They are among the finer war poems and unusual in that they are drawn from naval experience. Here are lines from "Battle Pattern," his poem on the hunting and sinking of the German battleship *Bismarck*. He took part in this action as a sublieutenant on the tribal class destroyer *Tar-*

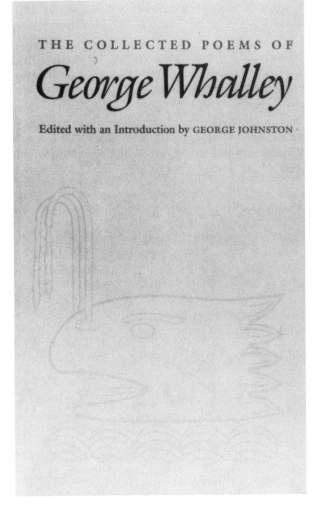

THE COLLECTED POEMS OF

George Whalley

Edited with an Introduction by GEORGE JOHNSTON

Front cover for Whalley's posthumously published collection, comprising all of the poems from his two earlier volumes and twenty-seven previously uncollected works

tar. The lines give his thoughts on the sailors aboard the maimed ship:

> At some moment the fact of doom
> had importuned its way into their minds
> like the sun insistently plucking at a late sleeper's
>   eyes:
> and the knowledge passed from eye to eye without
>   a word.

There are love poems in these collections, as well as meditations and descriptive poems. The mood of the time is strong in them all, and the language is clear and well handled, except for occasional touches of the conventionally poetic, which hardly appear in the action poems.

After the war his literary energies turned, for the most part, from poetry to prose. The posthumously published *Collected Poems of George*

Whalley (1986) prints twenty-seven later poems, virtually his entire postwar output, along with the whole of *No Man an Island*. Many of the later poems had been published in magazines, and some were still in manuscript. There is greater variety in their rhythms and verse patterns, and a more mature discrimination in choice of words, but the poignancy of the wartime poems is less often felt in them. Here is an untitled poem, however, that must be considered exceptional, if it is allegory, as it surely seems to be:

> Now that the dark sunburn
> has faded from the cheeks
> I am come to a winter land
> of rain and glistening streets
> and the soft persistent slash
> of rain at the window-glass.
> The leaves have dropped down
> under the rain and the wind's
> melancholy industry;
> and through the bare trees
> the rain drifts and slants
> in grey wisps from a grey
> sky. The leafless branches
> are silent athwart the wind,
> stripped of their summer warmth
> of sympathetic restlessness,
> their feeling ebbed and numb,
> motionless with misery.

There is a rhythmic and syntactic confidence in this that is beyond much of the poetry in the earlier book.

Whalley's next book after *No Man an Island* was *Poetic Process*, a thorough and sensitive exploration of what poetry is and how it is composed. In this book he turned to "the other harmony," and in it his achievement was marked by variety, purity of expression, moral stature, and sheer quantity. He was a perfectionist and wrote a prose that was quite his own, precise and elegant. There is an aesthetic as well as an intellectual pleasure to be had from reading it.

Poetic Process led Whalley into the study of Samuel Taylor Coleridge, as poet and as thinker, and this study became the central concern of his literary life. In 1955 he published a monograph on Coleridge, Sara Hutchinson, and the Wordsworth household at Dove Cottage, *Coleridge and Sara Hutchinson, and the Asra Poems*. He had already begun what was to be his largest and most absorbing work, his edition of Coleridge's marginalia for the Bollingen series *The Collected Works of Samuel Taylor Coleridge*, under the general editorship of Kathleen Coburn. Only the first volume,

which appeared in 1980, was published before he died. The organization of such an edition must be complex, and he had worked it out with painstaking ingenuity. His introduction and notes are written in his usual finely cadenced style. Before he died he had made two more volumes ready for publication and completed much of the preparatory work for the remaining two.

In 1953 he wrote *Death in the Barren Ground*, a radio play "for four voices and silence" based on the diary of Edgar Christian, who had died of starvation in a cabin by the Thelon River in northern Ontario. Whalley had been moved by reading this diary before the war and had intended writing something on it then. Response to this play led him to an interest in John Hornby, Edgar Christian's companion in death. Christian was a boy of sixteen, but Hornby was a veteran of the North, who had become a legendary figure. For nine years before the publication, in 1962, of *The Legend of John Hornby*, Whalley followed every clue that would lead to more knowledge of the man and his story. The book is written in his steady-paced prose; it is an absorbing story, well told, and is probably better known than any other of his many and varied writings. Here is a brief quotation:

> Conybeare, the hotel-keeper at Fort Smith, saw Hornby leave and long afterwards remembered vividly "this desperate man running away from civilisation, looking like death, making the tremendous trip in a little boat no better than a broken down packing case." Conybeare was not amphibious and perhaps exaggerates a little about the boat. But neither was Hornby amphibious, having always perversely refused to learn to swim. He went now into the North alone and with little provision. He loathed "civilisation" with an ineradicable hatred, and hated his own home almost as bitterly; he loved the unfenced land to the point of obsession. There was now nothing he could give to the country but his life. No temporal goal had any value for him or meaning: not wealth nor fame nor the oblique satisfaction of factual discovery.

In 1980 Whalley published an edition of Edgar Christian's diary titled, like the earlier radio play, *Death in the Barren Ground*.

A collection representing a small portion of Whalley's critical writings, *Studies in Literature and the Humanities*, edited by Brian Crick and John Ferns, was published posthumously in 1985. Another collection of his informal writings, which he prepared himself, awaits publication. There is still much material in the form of articles and radio scripts which one hopes may before long be collected. George Whalley had many gifts and a wide range of humane interests and many achievements as well, all of a high order of excellence, as poet, teacher, scholar, and writer of clear and elegant prose.

Reference:

Michael Moore, ed., *George Whalley: Remembrances* (Kingston, Ont.: Quarry, 1989).

Anne Wilkinson

(21 September 1910-10 May 1961)

Peter Stevens
University of Windsor

BOOKS: *Counterpoint to Sleep* (Montreal: First Statement, 1951);

The Hangman Ties the Holly (Toronto: Macmillan, 1955);

Lions in the Way: A Discursive History of the Oslers (Toronto: Macmillan, 1956; London: Macmillan, 1957);

Swann and Daphne (Toronto: Oxford University Press, 1960);

The Collected Poems of Anne Wilkinson, and A Prose Memoir, edited by A. J. M. Smith (Toronto: Macmillan, 1968; New York: St. Martin's Press, 1968).

Anne Wilkinson's poetry belongs to no specifically native Canadian tradition. Much of her work is teased out in metaphysical fashion, not only with something of the craggy paradoxes of John Donne but also with the witty elegance of Andrew Marvell. Grafted onto this style is a genuine simplicity which often carries echoes of nursery rhymes and fairy tales as well as the pared down structures of the poetry of Emily Dickinson and Elinor Wylie. While this kind of writing is unrelated to movements and developments in Canadian poetry, it is perhaps possible to see Wilkinson's poems as part of that stream in Canadian verse beginning in the 1920s, influenced by T. S. Eliot with some reference to Eliot's emphasis on the metaphysical poets. This particular strain surfaces in some other poets through the twentieth century, though they cannot be seen as a group. Such poets as Leo Ken-

nedy, James Wreford, and Jay Macpherson can be seen as writing within this mode. It can perhaps be traced to the early criticism of A. J. M. Smith, who did his graduate work on the metaphysical poets under Herbert Grierson at Edinburgh University. Smith, who indulged in this mode in his own poetry, became a friend of Wilkinson, and his critical essay on her poetry, which first appeared in the journal *Canadian Literature* (Autumn 1961) and was republished with some changes and additions as an introduction to *The Collected Poems of Anne Wilkinson* (1968), remains the primary piece of published criticism on her work.

Anne Cochran Boyd Gibbons, the daughter of George Sutton Gibbons and Mary Elizabeth Lammond Osler Gibbons, was born in Toronto on 21 September 1910. She was educated in a rather haphazard and informal manner in a variety of schools in Canada, Europe, and the United States. Through her mother she was connected to a well-known Canadian family, the Oslers, whose members include the distinguished physician, teacher, and historian of medicine Sir William Osler (1849-1919). She has written about the family members and their somewhat eccentric characters in *Lions in the Way* (1956), subtitled *A Discursive History of the Oslers*. She herself savored their eccentricities and enjoyed observing and participating in the same kind of quirks. She shows a witty appreciation of her odd schooling in "Four Corners of my World," a memoir first published in *Tamarack Review* (Summer 1961)

Anne Wilkinson (right) with Phyllis Webb and Morley Callaghan at the 1955 Canadian Writers Conference, Queen's University, Kingston, Ontario (Dewar / National Archives of Canada / PA-172304)

which appears as an appendix to the collected poetry.

On 23 July 1932 she married Frederik Robert Wilkinson, a surgeon. She became involved in the literary life developing in Toronto after World War II and, in the early 1950s, was a founding editor of *Tamarack Review*, which rapidly established itself as Canada's most prestigious literary magazine. Her own volumes of poetry were published about this time: *Counterpoint to Sleep* (1951) and *The Hangman Ties the Holly* (1955). These poems, together with others which had appeared in magazines and some still in manuscript, are included in *The Collected Poems of Anne Wilkinson*, edited by Smith. Wilkinson also published a modern fairy tale for children, *Swann and Daphne* (1960). She was the mother of three children, a daughter and two sons. Her marriage was dissolved in 1953. After a lengthy illness, Wilkinson died of cancer in 1961.

The titles of the two individual collections of poetry suggest something of the ambiguous and paradoxical nature of the themes of her poems, the ambivalences associated with the celebration of life within the embrace of death. That celebration of life she expresses as an idea of living to the fullest through sensuous immediacy but with a full knowledge of mortality. Such reverence for life within the context of death becomes more poignant in the last poems, informed by her own knowledge of impending death. Yet her language rarely loses touch with a lightness and delicacy of feeling, often wringing play out of paradox. This playful quality is evident in her use of near-parody in other poems and in nursery rhymes, as well as in her use of puns.

However, the poetry has a firmness of control that emphasizes its seriousness. Beneath the somewhat whimsical surface is both a stoic vision of life and a refusal to give in. She responds to the external world with all her senses, even as she recognizes that they will falter and decay. In such a poem as "Still Life" she writes of the body being metamorphosed to "rigid wood." But the wood is a living tree; the rigidity seems not to be mortal. The still life of the title is the poet's spirit which she would bend to the life of the tree: "Be still and let its green blood / Enter me." This

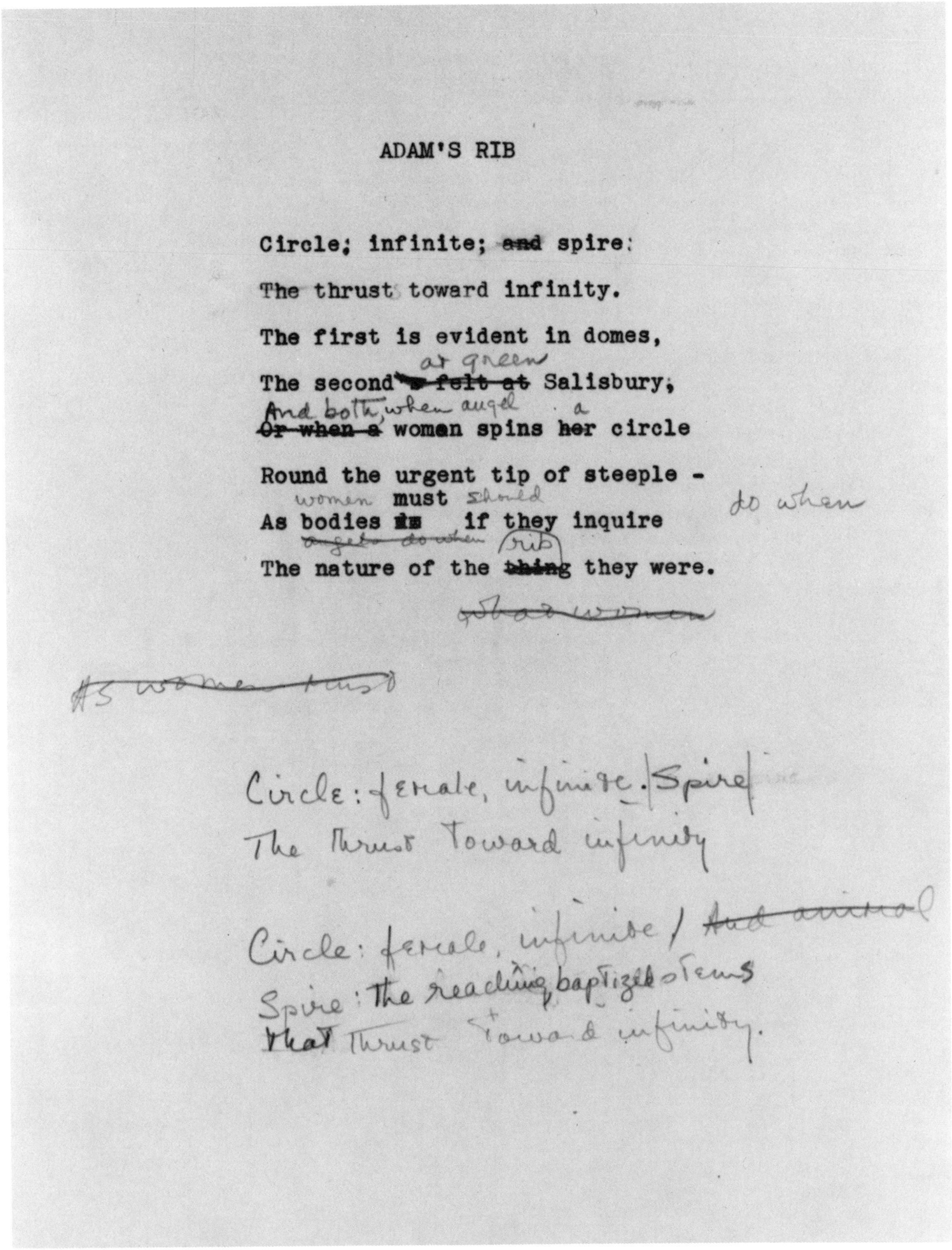

ADAM'S RIB

Circle; infinite; ~~and~~ spire:

The thrust toward infinity.

The first is evident in domes,

The second ~~felt at~~ *at green* Salisbury;

And both, when angel
~~Or when a~~ *a* woman spins her circle

Round the urgent tip of steeple –

women must ~~should~~
As bodies ~~is~~ if they inquire   *do when*

~~angel   do when~~ (rib)
The nature of the ~~thing~~ they were.

#5 woman must

Circle: female, infinite. Spire
The thrust toward infinity

Circle: female, infinite / And animal
Spire: the reaching, baptized stems
that thrust toward infinity.

Revised typescript for an unpublished poem by Wilkinson (Anne Wilkinson Papers, Thomas Fisher Rare Book Library, University of Toronto) poem strikes a central note of her work: the interrelation between man and nature which may find a kind of parallel in human love. But Wilkinson cannot resist the paradox of the involvement of physicality in love: bodily presences change and grow older through the continuing flow of time. Such a view is captured in one of her love poems, "In June and Gentle Oven," in which a mirage of the burgeoning summer is a metaphor for the blossoming of love. In the poem it is almost as if love in its fruition rises above time: the lovers "peel the skin of summer" so that they experience "the sap of June / aloof from seasons. . . ." However, the paradox of time remains; the complete last line reads: "aloof from seasons, flowing."

Wit and metaphoric exactness continue to inform the final poems, which approach pain and death with a seriousness that never becomes solemn, although on a few occasions, as in "Accustom the Grey Coils," a kind of nakedness of feeling obtrudes through the figurative grace. The sequence "A Sorrow of Stones" retains her use of formal metrics; the close of the poem echoes the whimsy and sentiment of Emily Dickinson: "I thought to lie like cream in a long black hearse / I had not calculated on this / Fall without end." A. J. M. Smith closes his critical essay on these poems by emphasizing the life-affirming qualities of the verse, suggesting that Anne Wilkinson is unique in Canadian poetry because she writes with "an accuracy, and an elegance that do not hide the intensity of the emotion."

Reference:

Robert Lecker, "Better Quick than Dead: Anne Wilkinson's Poetry," *Studies in Canadian Literature*, 3, no. 1 (1978): 35-46.

Papers:

Anne Wilkinson's papers are at the Thomas Fisher Rare Book Library, University of Toronto.

Adele Wiseman
(21 May 1928-   )

Ann Munton
University of British Columbia

BOOKS: *The Sacrifice* (Toronto: Macmillan, 1956; New York: Viking, 1956; London: Gollancz, 1956);
Crackpot (Toronto: McClelland & Stewart, 1974);
Old Woman at Play (Toronto: Clarke, Irwin, 1978);
Testimonial Dinner: A Play (Toronto: Privately printed, 1978);
Memoirs of a Book Molesting Childhood and Other Essays (Toronto: Oxford University Press, 1987).

OTHER: *Old Markets, New World*, sketches by Joe Rosenthal, text by Wiseman (Toronto: Macmillan, 1964).

PERIODICAL PUBLICATIONS: "Duel in the Kitchen," *Maclean's*, 74 (7 January 1961): 22-23, 74, 76-79;
"Montreal and French-Canadian Culture: What They Mean to English-Canadian Novelists," *Tamarack Review*, 40 (Summer 1966): 50;
"English Writing in Canada: The Future," *Proceedings and Transactions of the Royal Society of Canada*, fourth series, 5 (June 1967): 45-50;
"A Brief Anatomy of an Honest Attempt at a Pithy Statement about the Impact of the Manitoba Environment on My Development as an Artist," *Mosaic*, 3 (Spring 1970): 98-106;
"The Country of the Hungry Bird," *Journal of Canadian Fiction*, 31 / 32 (1981): 136-139;
"Excerpts from 'The Lovebound: A Tragi-Comedy,' " *Journal of Canadian Fiction*, 31 / 32 (1981): 140-147;
"Letter to Clara Thomas," *Canadian Woman Studies*, 8 (Fall 1987): 6-7.

Adele Wiseman, the daughter of Pesach (Peter) and Chaika (Clara) Rosenberg Waisman, was born in Winnipeg, Manitoba, on 21 May 1928. The third of four living children, Wiseman had an older sister, Marjm, an older brother, Harry, and a younger brother, Morris. A foster brother, Georg Feher, a Hungarian refugee,

Adele Wiseman (photograph by Arnaud Maggs)

joined the family after World War II. The times and her particular ethnicity shaped the writer who has become one of Canada's most sensitive delineators of the immigrant experience. Wiseman's Jewish consciousness was fed by the rich sense of biblical stories and *shtetl* lore from the European past that infused her home in North Winnipeg's immigrant neighborhood. Growing up during the Depression and during the war years, sensitive to the hardships of all Canadians but particularly of those new to the land, Wiseman learned firsthand the realities of Jewish persecution. "From early childhood," she wrote in *Memoirs of a Book Molesting Childhood and Other Essays* (1987), "I knew of 'that maniac' Hitler and his monstrous minions. He was the ongoing outgrowth of the pogroms my parents had survived, stories from real life that I am grateful they did not hide from us."

Her parents, skilled as tailor and dressmaker/dollmaker, provided Wiseman with creative mod-

343

els. While her writing is not directly autobiographical, her two novels and two plays boldly reflect her Jewishness, and her book about the creative process, *Old Woman at Play* (1978), opens up the subject by examining her mother and her work. The patterns of Wiseman's background and life–Bible lore, persecution in the Ukraine, immigration to the Canadian prairies, the Depression, the war, and the adaptation of successive generations of immigrants–form and re-form the patterns of her writing.

Wiseman's parents, poor Jews in the Ukraine, escaped persecution by fleeing to Canada. With their firstborn son already dead, Wiseman writes in *Old Woman at Play*, they "took their new hope, the six-week-old Marjm" and stole "across the Russian border." Making their way first across Europe, then the Atlantic, the Waismans continued halfway across Canada before settling in the north end of Winnipeg, already home to immigrants from many different countries. They lived on Burrows Avenue, but for six years during the worst of the Depression they moved into "the three-quarters-of-the-way-to-the-ceiling plasterboard compartments behind [their] shop, the 'Inkster Tailors.' " If they had escaped persecution in eastern Europe, they still had not escaped poverty. Before opening their own shop, Pesach Waisman "worked a ninety-six hour week in the factories, determined to conquer the new world for his children." After opening their own shop, Pesach and Chaika Waisman habitually worked well into the night, often going hungry themselves so that their children would have enough. But the necessities that the Waismans managed to provide for their daughter were greater than food, clothing, and shelter. They fed the young writer on stories as well. Pesach Waisman had wooed his wife in the Ukraine with stories, probably "the same stories," Wiseman writes, for "which we kids used to wait so ardently in the hope he might be home on time to tell us at bedtime." And even more, her mother "lassoed us daily and webbed us and gilded our lives with innumerable threads of prose . . . stories and persuasions and fantasies and cajolings and adjurations and just plain fast-talking that fogged up your brain with ideas, intoxicated you." For stories were in their blood. Sholem Aleichem and Hershl of Esterpol had come from the same neighborhood in the Ukraine, and Chelm, the town which inspired many humorous folk stories, was next door.

Although the young Wiseman read widely, she did not "write constantly." "I kept no diaries," she remarks in *Memoirs of a Book Molesting Childhood*, "did not try to imitate what I was reading." Her apprenticeship at this time consisted largely of a sensitizing to language. Wiseman pictures her young self as slightly clumsy and socially inadept, but neat in person and penmanship. She was antipathetic to rules, early learning the power of entertaining with stories. She also sought refuge in reading: "I belonged where I read, if nowhere else, through the very condition of my invisibility." But not all the books she read were comforting, because anti-Semitism could be found in books as well as in life, and this spurred Wiseman on in her own creativity to provide an alternate vision: "I knew very early that someone had to tell the other important stories, to provide the antidote to the poisonous errors, lest the whole glorious writing enterprise founder forever short of fulfilment."

Wiseman's formal schooling was a mixed experience. The Depression was in full force while she was in elementary school, and World War II was declared when she entered junior high school. She attended public school as well as the Jewish Peretz School after regular school hours, and then went to Saint John's Technical High School. Made unhappy by what she called "the rigidities of high school," Wiseman found university "a wonderfully liberating experience." She worked her way through the University of Manitoba from 1944 to 1949, graduating with an honors B.A. in English and psychology. The fact that she shared classes with returned soldiers "gave an extra dimension to my years of study," as she explained in *Memoirs of a Book Molesting Childhood*. She worked with Malcolm Ross and wrote for the university literary journal, winning the Chancellor's Prize for a short story. "I showed my earliest work to Malcolm," she notes, "and the great sensitivity and wonderful delicacy with which he handled one of my tentative stories in fact led me to the writing of my first novel." The other crucial connection Wiseman made in these years was with Margaret Laurence, who was to become over the years a friend who shared much, including the experiences of being a Canadian female writer.

After graduation Wiseman worked as a reader and tutor in the English department at the University of Manitoba and then moved to London, England, in 1950 to be a social worker at the Stepney Jewish Girls' Hospital. Moving

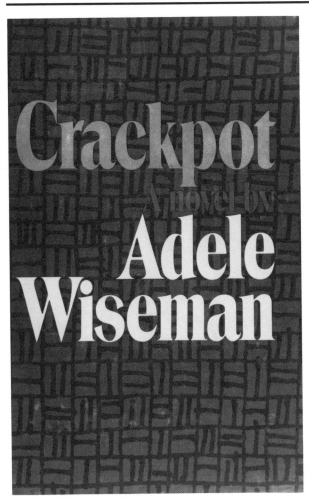

Dust jacket for Wiseman's 1974 novel, narrated by a prostitute named Hoda

Dmitry Stone. Their daughter, Tamara, was born in 1969. With her family, Wiseman moved that year to the City of York, near Toronto, where they have renovated a large, old home. Wiseman now writes full-time. Her second novel, *Crackpot*, was published in 1974; *Old Woman at Play* was published in 1978, and her second play, *Testimonial Dinner*, was published privately the same year. Wiseman received a Canada Council senior arts award to work on a third novel and was writer in residence at the University of Toronto in 1975 and 1976. In 1981 she traveled to China with a group of fellow Canadian writers.

Both of Wiseman's novels deal with Jewish immigration to Canada, the struggle to survive during the Depression and the war, and the tension between generations caught between the Old World and the New. Both novels condemn exploitation and persecution on the basis of race, class, or sex. Critics have described the development of Wiseman's novels as a progression from a tragic to a comic vision and associate it with a similar movement in Canadian literature as a whole. Wiseman herself, in a 1981 interview with Roslyn Belkin, describes her development as a move from myth to metaphor. It is also true that the movement from *The Sacrifice* to *Crackpot*, from tragic to comic vision, from myth to metaphor, is a movement from a traditional narrative with patriarchal bases to a feminist awareness of the world that involves the use of newer narrative techniques. This movement parallels Wiseman's own life journey, with her growing understanding of her mother's experiences as an immigrant and as a fellow woman artist being crucial.

Wiseman's particularly Jewish outlook comprehends suffering and marginalization–of the Jew, of the immigrant, and of women–as well as lessons learned from twentieth-century history: the inhumanity of people and the preciousness of life. For Wiseman, the artist's responsibility is to "use language not as a weapon with which to influence, tranquillize or control others, but as an instrument to create and explore analogous worlds and through them to try to comprehend himself and others"; "What the artist creates is consciousness."

The Sacrifice transforms biblical material and tells the story of a twentieth-century Abraham, desiring to be a patriarch and leading his wife, Sarah, and his only surviving son, Isaac, out of the pogroms of eastern Europe to a new world. But it is not the holy land that they reach, and God accepts the sacrifice of Isaac in the new

again in 1951, she taught at the Overseas School of Rome, returning to Winnipeg the next year. For three years she continued work on *The Sacrifice*, her first novel, supporting herself as a lab technician and as executive secretary of the Royal Winnipeg Ballet. *The Sacrifice* was published in 1956, winning the Governor General's Award for fiction and the Beta Sigma Phi Award. That year Wiseman returned to London to attend a writers' conference, remaining for a year to research her play "The Lovebound," unpublished except for an excerpt in the *Journal of Canadian Fiction* (1981). From 1957 to 1960 Wiseman lived in New York City on a Guggenheim fellowship; from 1961 to 1963 she again lived in London, writing children's stories. From 1964 to 1969 she was in Montreal, lecturing at Sir George Williams University and Macdonald College and serving as an assistant professor at McGill University. During this time she met and married marine biologist world. Abraham struggles to understand the ways of God and man but is ultimately driven to madness and murder (a parody of the sacrificial act). Like Hagar in Laurence's *The Stone Angel* (1964), Abraham has let pride obscure love. His grandson, Moses, restores continuity with the past by climbing the mountain to visit Abraham in his confinement. Abraham enjoins his grandson: "When a human being cries out to you, no matter who it is, don't judge him, don't harm him, or you turn away God Himself."

In *Crackpot* Wiseman, against a similar backdrop of pogroms and persecution, flight and resettlement, shifts her focus from the struggle of the first generation to that of the second, from the experiences of a patriarch to those of a female offspring. The narrative form and language are similarly altered. Whereas *The Sacrifice* is told by an omniscient narrator in a traditional pattern and with refined language, *Crackpot* is told from the point of view of Hoda, a self-educated but childlike prostitute. Patterns are important, with repetition and parallels among events and movements being crucial. As in *The Sacrifice*, wisdom comes after suffering, but in *Crackpot* there is, in Wiseman's words from *Old Woman at Play*, more "sly humour and self-mockery [in] the theme of essential human helplessness, the imperfect quality of all knowing."

Whereas *The Sacrifice* is patterned on a biblical story which provides a counterpoint throughout, *Crackpot* takes as its point of departure a creation metaphor from Cabalistic lore: "He stored the Divine Light in a Vessel, but the Vessel, unable to contain the Holy Radiance, burst, and its shards, permeated with sparks of the Divine, scattered through the Universe." Hoda's world is a fragmented one, and she, too, is fragmented ("Into how many pieces does one break and still bother to count the pieces?") when she is driven to incest in order to aid her son. But Hoda truly deals in love, and though she, like all those around her, is flawed, a "cracked pot," she finally acknowledges the "sparks of the Divine" among the suffering of the world and within herself and the possibility of wholeness.

Wiseman's plays also reflect the fragmentation of the Depression and World War II years. "The Lovebound" deals with the illegal emigration of Jews by ship from Germany immediately before the war and points out the complicity of other nations in the fate of the Jews who were repeatedly refused asylum. The play concentrates on the drama aboard one ship heading for Cuba,

Front cover for Wiseman's second play, which she describes in the introduction as "an attempt to express graphically my feeling not only of how much the past influences the present, but of the fact that it is alive and functioning in the present . . ."

where it is refused entry and forced to return to Germany. Wiseman explains: "What the play is really examining is the question of humanity, not only what happens to the victims but to those who cut them out of their place as fellow human beings." In both "The Lovebound" and *Testimonial Dinner* Wiseman tries "to define [her] Judaism" and the role of the Jew as "other" in society. In *Testimonial Dinner* she concentrates on the relationships among three generations of Jewish immigrants and links the dilemmas they face and have faced to a larger pattern within the history of Canada. As in *Crackpot* and *Old Woman at Play*, in the drama Wiseman experiments textually, blending history, memory, and imaginative leap. Louis Riel and Sir John A. Macdonald are characters and counterpoints to the struggle of the Jewish-Canadians to know themselves and their origins, the struggle between the visionary and the materialist views, between what is right and what is merely expedient. The theme of worlds coming together is worked out on several levels–events, symbols, and structure–while the interrelationship of past, present, and future is a theme that characterizes much of Wiseman's work.

Wiseman shares with Margaret Laurence an understanding of the need to come to terms with one's past and how the present and future must be read in relation to that past. She says of her play *Testimonial Dinner*, it "is an attempt to express graphically my feeling not only of how much the past influences the present, but of the fact that it is alive and functioning in the present, and active in determining the decisions which shape the future of the country and the individual destinies of our people." Laurence's character Morag, at the end of *The Diviners* (1974), studies the seeming paradox of the river which appears to flow in two directions at once and says: "*Look ahead into the past, and back into the future, until the silence.*" Wiseman's character Hoda, created about the same time as Morag, contemplates in a dream "the muddy waters" of life, her life, for the Indian name *Winnipeg* means "muddy waters," and her son David says of her, "*Backwards. . . . She occupies her past; she inhabits her life.*" In *Old Woman at Play* Wiseman contemplates her mother's past existence as an extension of her own and links it to her tomorrows. "Here I examined clues, discovered correspondences, and listened, hearing, in the shells of her past, the oceans of my future."

References:

Roslyn Belkin, "The Consciousness of a Jewish Artist: An Interview with Adele Wiseman," *Journal of Canadian Fiction*, 31 / 32 (1981): 148-176;

Russell Brown, "Beyond Sacrifice," *Journal of Canadian Fiction*, 16 (1976): 158-162;

Michael Greenstein, "Adele Wiseman," in *Canadian Writers and Their Works*, fiction series, volume 6, edited by Robert Lecker, Jack David, and Ellen Quigley (Toronto: ECW, 1985), pp. 239-270;

Greenstein, "Movement and Vision in *The Sacrifice*," *Canadian Literature*, 80 (Spring 1979): 23-36;

Margaret Laurence, Introduction to Wiseman's *Crackpot* (Toronto: New Canadian Library, 1978), pp. 3-8;

Patricia Morley, "Wiseman's Fiction: Out of Pain, Joy," *Etudes Canadiennes*, 4 (1978): 41-50;

Stanley Mullins, "Traditional Symbolism in Adele Wiseman's *The Sacrifice*," *Culture*, 19 (1958);

Helene Rosenthal, "Spiritual Ecology: Adele Wiseman's *The Sacrifice*," in *Writers of the Prairies*, edited by Donald Stephens (Vancouver: University of British Columbia Press, 1973), pp. 77-88;

K. H. Sherman, "*Crackpot*: A Lurianic Myth," *Waves*, 3 (1974): 5-10;

Donald Stephens, "Lilacs out of the Mosaic Land: Aspects of the Sacrificial Theme in Canada," *Dalhousie Review*, 48 (1969): 500-509.

George Woodcock

(8 May 1912-   )

Jack Robinson
Grant MacEwan Community College

BOOKS: *Six Poems* (London: E. Lahr, 1938);

Ballad of an Orphan Hand (London: E. Lahr, 1939);

The White Island (London: Fortune, 1940);

New Life to the Land: Anarchist Proposals for Agriculture (London: Freedom Press, 1942);

The Centre Cannot Hold (London: Routledge, 1943);

Railways and Society (London: Freedom Press, 1943);

Anarchy or Chaos? (London: Freedom Press, 1944);

Homes or Hovels: The Housing Problem and Its Solutions (London: Freedom Press, 1944);

Anarchism and Morality (London: Freedom Press, 1945);

What Is Anarchism? (London: Freedom Press, 1945);

William Godwin: A Biographical Study (London: Porcupine, 1946);

The Basis of Communal Living (London: Freedom Press, 1947);

Imagine the South (Pasadena: Untide Press, 1947);

The Incomparable Aphra: A Life of Mrs. Aphra Behn (London & New York: T. V. Boardman, 1948); republished as *Aphra Behn: The English Sappho* (Montreal: Black Rose, 1989);

The Writer and Politics (London: Porcupine, 1948);

The Paradox of Oscar Wilde (London & New York: T. V. Boardman, 1949; New York: Macmillan, 1950); republished as *Oscar Wilde: The Double Image* (Montreal: Black Rose, 1989);

The Anarchist Prince: A Biographical Study of Peter Kropotkin, by Woodcock and Ivan Avakumovic (London & New York: T. V. Boardman, 1950);

Ravens and Prophets: An Account of Journeys in British Columbia, Alberta and Southern Alaska (London: A. Wingate, 1952);

Pierre-Joseph Proudhon: A Biography (London: Routledge & Kegan Paul, 1956; New York: Macmillan, 1956);

To the City of the Dead: An Account of Travels in Mexico (London: Faber & Faber, 1957);

Incas and Other Men: Travels in the Andes (London: Faber & Faber, 1959);

George Woodcock (courtesy of the author)

Anarchism: A History of Libertarian Ideas and Movements (Cleveland: Meridian, 1962; Harmondsworth, U.K.: Penguin, 1962);

Faces of India: A Travel Narrative (London: Faber & Faber, 1964);

Asia, Gods and Cities: Aden to Tokyo (London: Faber & Faber, 1966);

Civil Disobedience (Toronto: Canadian Broadcasting Corporation, 1966);

The Greeks in India (London: Faber & Faber, 1966);

The Crystal Spirit: A Study of George Orwell (Boston: Little, Brown, 1966; London: Cape, 1967);

Kerala: A Portrait of the Malabar Coast (London: Faber & Faber, 1967);

Selected Poems (Toronto & Vancouver: Clarke, Irwin, 1967);

The Doukhobors, by Woodcock and Avakumovic (Toronto & New York: Oxford University Press, 1968; London: Faber & Faber, 1968);

The British in the Far East (London: Weidenfeld & Nicolson, 1969; New York: Atheneum, 1969);

Henry Walter Bates, Naturalist of the Amazons (London: Faber & Faber, 1969; New York: Barnes & Noble, 1969);

Hugh MacLennan (Toronto: Copp Clark, 1969);

The Hudson's Bay Company (New York: Crowell-Collier, 1970);

Canada and the Canadians (Toronto: Oxford University Press, 1970; London: Faber & Faber, 1970; Harrisburg: Stackpole, 1970; revised edition, London: Faber & Faber, 1973; Toronto: Macmillan, 1973);

Mordecai Richler (Toronto: McClelland & Stewart, 1970);

Odysseus Ever Returning: Essays on Canadian Writers and Writing (Toronto: McClelland & Stewart, 1970);

Mohandas Gandhi (New York: Viking, 1971); republished as *Gandhi* (London: Fontana, 1972);

Into Tibet: The Early British Explorers (New York: Barnes & Noble, 1971);

Dawn and the Darkest Hour: A Study of Aldous Huxley (London: Faber & Faber, 1972; New York: Viking, 1972);

Herbert Read: The Stream and the Source (London: Faber & Faber, 1972);

The Rejection of Politics, and Other Essays on Canada, Canadians, Anarchism and the World (Toronto: New Press, 1972);

Who Killed the British Empire? An Inquest (London: Cape, 1974; Toronto: Fitzhenry & Whiteside, 1974; New York: Quadrangle, 1974);

Amor De Cosmos, Journalist and Reformer (Toronto: Oxford University Press, 1975);

Gabriel Dumont: The Métis Chief and His Lost World (Edmonton: Hurtig, 1975);

Notes on Visitations: Poems, 1936-1975 (Toronto: Anansi, 1975);

Gabriel Dumont and the Northwest Rebellion (Toronto: Playwrights Co-op, 1976); republished as *Six Dry Cakes for the Hunted*, in *Two Plays* (1977);

Canadian Poets, 1960-1973: A List (Ottawa: Golden Dog, 1976);

South Sea Journey (London: Faber & Faber, 1976; Toronto: Fitzhenry & Whiteside, 1976);

Anima; or, Swann Grown Old: A Cycle of Poems (Coatsworth, Ont.: Black Moss, 1977);

Peoples of the Coast: The Indians of the Pacific Northwest (Edmonton: Hurtig, 1977; Bloomington: Indiana University Press, 1977);

Two Plays (Vancouver: Talonbooks, 1977)—comprises *Six Dry Cakes for the Hunted* and *The Island of Demons*;

Faces from History: Canadian Portraits and Profiles (Edmonton: Hurtig, 1978);

Gabriel Dumont (Don Mills, Ont.: Fitzhenry & Whiteside, 1978);

The Kestrel and Other Poems of Past and Present (Sunderland, U.K.: Coelfrith Press, 1978);

Thomas Merton, Monk and Poet: A Critical Study (Vancouver: Douglas & McIntyre, 1978; New York: Farrar, Straus & Giroux, 1978; Edinburgh: Canongale, 1978);

The Canadians (Toronto: Fitzhenry & Whiteside, 1979; Cambridge, Mass.: Harvard University Press, 1979; London: Athlone Press, 1980);

The Mountain Road (Fredericton: Fiddlehead, 1980);

A Picture History of British Columbia (Edmonton: Hurtig, 1980; Seattle: University of Washington Press, 1982);

The World of Canadian Writing: Critiques and Recollections (Vancouver: Douglas & McIntyre, 1980);

100 Great Canadians (Edmonton: Hurtig, 1980);

The Meeting of Time and Space: Regionalism in Canadian Literature (Edmonton: NeWest Institute for Western Canadian Studies, 1981);

Confederation Betrayed! (Madeira Park, B.C.: Harbour, 1981);

Ivan Eyre (Don Mills, Ont.: Fitzhenry & Whiteside, 1981);

The Benefactor (Lantzville, B.C.: Oolichan, 1982);

Letter to the Past (Toronto: Fitzhenry & Whiteside, 1982);

Collected Poems (Victoria, B.C.: Sono Nis, 1983);

Orwell's Message: 1984 and the Present (Madeira Park, B.C.: Harbour, 1984);

Patrick Lane and His Works (Downsview, Ont.: ECW, 1984);

Strange Bedfellows: The State and the Arts in Canada (Vancouver: Douglas & McIntyre, 1985);

The Walls of India (Toronto: Lester & Orpen Dennys, 1985);

Northern Spring (Vancouver: Douglas & McIntyre, 1987);

Beyond the Blue Mountains (Toronto: Fitzhenry & Whiteside, 1987);

Matt Cohen and His Works (Downsview, Ont.: ECW, 1988);

A Social History of Canada (Markham, Ont., London & New York: Penguin, 1988);

The Marvellous Century: A World Awakening (Toronto: Fitzhenry & Whiteside, 1988);

Caves in the Desert: Travels in China (Vancouver: Douglas & McIntyre, 1988);

Powers of Observation: Familiar Essays (Kingston, Ont.: Quarry, 1989);

The Century That Made Us: Canada 1814-1914 (Toronto: Oxford University Press, 1989).

RADIO: *El Dorado, Opening Night*, CBC, 9 March 1951;

The Magic Ass, adapted from Lucius Apuleius, *Four Classic Tales*, CBC, 25 April 1955;

Daphnis and Chloe, adapted from Longus, *Four Classic Tales*, CBC, 2 May 1955;

The Golden Fleece, adapted from Apollonius of Rhodes, *Four Classic Tales*, CBC, 9 May 1955;

Eros and Psyche, adapted from Apuleius, *Four Classic Tales*, CBC, 16 May 1955;

Riders to the Sea, adapted from J. M. Synge's play, *Vancouver Theatre*, CBC, 27 April 1959;

The Playboy of the Western World, adapted from Synge's play, *Sunday Night*, CBU, 3 May 1959;

The Shoemaker's Holiday, adapted from Thomas Dekker's play, *Wednesday Night*, CBC, 8 July 1959;

Venice Preserved, adapted from Thomas Otway's play, *Sunday Night*, CBU, 22 November 1959;

Phaedra, adapted from Jean Racine's play, *Sunday Night*, CBU, 28 February 1960;

The Bird of Stone, *Vancouver Theatre*, CBC, 14 March 1960;

The Island of Demons, sequel to *The Bird of Stone*, *Vancouver Theatre*, CBC, 21 March 1960;

The Crucifixion, scenes from the York Cycle, *Drama*, CBC, 15 April 1960;

Etiquette Through the Age, *Wednesday Night*, CBC, 29 June 1960;

Miracle Plays, *Wednesday Night*, CBC, 29 June 1960;

Maskerman, *Summer Stage*, CBC, 28 August 1960;

The Beaux Stratagem, adapted from George Farquhar's play, *Sunday Night*, CBU, 26 February 1961;

The Burning City, *Sunday Night*, CBU, 29 October 1961;

The Benefactor, *Wednesday Night*, CBC, 17 October 1962;

The Empire of Shadows, *Saturday Night*, CBC, 2 August 1964;

The Floor of the Night, *Midweek Theatre*, CBC, 21 July 1965;

Six Dry Cakes for the Hunted, *Bush and Salon*, CBC, 21 February 1975;

The Lion and the Tiger Cub, *Monday Evening*, CBC, 4 February 1976.

OTHER: *William Godwin: Selections from Political Justice*, edited by Woodcock (London: Freedom Press, 1943);

A Hundred Years of Revolution: 1848 and After, edited by Woodcock (London: Porcupine, 1948);

Oscar Wilde, *The Soul of Man Under Socialism*, introduction and notes by Woodcock (London: Porcupine, 1948);

The Letters of Charles Lamb, edited by Woodcock (London: Grey Walls Press, 1950);

A Choice of Critics: Selections from Canadian Literature, edited by Woodcock (Toronto: Oxford University Press, 1966);

Variations on the Human Theme, edited by Woodcock (Toronto: Ryerson, 1966);

William Cobbett, *Rural Rides*, edited by Woodcock (Harmondsworth, U.K.: Penguin, 1967);

George Meredith, *The Egoist*, edited by Woodcock (Harmondsworth, U.K.: Penguin, 1968);

The Sixties: Writers and Writing of the Decade, edited by Woodcock (Vancouver: University of British Columbia Publications Centre, 1969);

Charles Dickens, *A Tale of Two Cities*, edited by Woodcock (Harmondsworth, U.K.: Penguin, 1970);

Malcolm Lowry: The Man and his Work, edited by Woodcock (Vancouver: University of British Columbia Press, 1971);

Victoria, photographs by Ingeborg Woodcock, introduction by George Woodcock (Victoria, B.C.: Morriss, 1971);

Wyndham Lewis in Canada, edited by Woodcock (Vancouver: University of British Columbia Publications Centre, 1971);

Herman Melville, *Typee: A Peep at Polynesian Life*, edited by Woodcock (Harmondsworth, U.K.: Penguin, 1972);

Colony and Confederation: Early Canadian Poets and Their Background, edited by Woodcock

(Vancouver: University of British Columbia
Press, 1974);

*Poets and Critics: Essays from Canadian Literature,
1966-1974*, edited by Woodcock (Toronto:
Oxford University Press, 1974);

*The Canadian Novel in the Twentieth Century: Essays
from Canadian Literature*, edited by Woodcock (Toronto: McClelland & Stewart, 1975);

"Poetry," in *Literary History of Canada*, second edition, edited by Carl F. Klinck and others (Toronto & Buffalo: University of Toronto
Press, 1976), III: 284-317;

The Anarchist Reader, edited by Woodcock (London: Fontana, 1977; Atlantic Highlands,
N.J.: Humanities Press, 1977);

Thomas Hardy, *The Return of the Native*, edited
by Woodcock (Harmondsworth, U.K.: Penguin, 1978);

British Columbia: A Celebration, edited by Woodcock (Edmonton: Hurtig, 1983);

*A Place to Stand On: Essays by and about Margaret
Laurence*, edited by Woodcock (Edmonton:
NeWest, 1983);

Marcel Giraud, *The Métis in the Canadian West*, 2 volumes, translated, with an introduction, by
Woodcock (Edmonton: University of Alberta Press, 1986; Lincoln: University of Nebraska Press, 1986);

The Collected Works of Peter Kropotkin, 3 volumes to
date, introductions by Woodcock (Montreal:
Black Rose, 1989).

George Woodcock is one of Canada's foremost men of letters and the possessor of three distinct reputations. Canadians know him as a literary and social critic, radio dramatist, and editor
of the critical quarterly *Canadian Literature*, from
its inception in 1959 until his retirement in 1977.
In England, where he spent the first thirty-seven
years of his life, he is known as the biographer of
William Godwin, Aphra Behn, Oscar Wilde, and
of his contemporaries of the 1940s in London—
George Orwell, Herbert Read, and Aldous Huxley. He has also achieved international acclaim as
a historian of the anarchist movement and biographer of its central thinkers and as the author
of travelogues on South America and Asia. His
works have been translated into French, Swedish,
German, Italian, Spanish, Japanese, and Malaya-
lam.

Five months after his birth in Winnipeg on
8 May 1912, Woodcock's parents, Samuel and Margaret Lewis Woodcock, returned to England. Having come to Canada in 1907, they had failed to

make their fortune in farming. This land of lost
hopes remained the subject of their nostalgic
memories during Woodcock's boyhood, so that
when he came to live in Canada in 1949, it was
partly to discover the reality of this country and
partly to fulfill his parents' dream of an idyllic
wilderness existence. His childhood in rural
Shropshire and Cheshire and the Thames-side resort town of Marlow was darkened by news of Bol-
shevik atrocities and the horrors of World War I.
Woodcock completed his formal education by
graduating from grammar school in 1928, and
then, as he put it later, "the Depression closed
down over my youth." For eleven years he "clung
to the crumbling ledge of thirty shillings a week,"
commuting from Marlow to work as a railway
clerk in London, until in 1940 a small inheritance from his coal-mining grandfather, Samuel
Woodcock, allowed him to move to London and
freed him to write full-time. His two eloquent volumes of autobiography, *Letter to the Past* (1982)
and *Beyond the Blue Mountains* (1987), portray his
years in England and his life in Canada until
1972.

During these grim nine-to-five early years,
Woodcock launched his literary career. In the
late 1930s he became one of a group of poets
(Roy Fuller, D. S. Savage, Ruthven Todd, Keid-
rych Rhys) who contributed to Julian Symons's
Twentieth Century Verse. These writers were all
lower-middle-class autodidacts, and, though he
also contributed to Geoffrey Grigson's *New Verse*,
Woodcock felt more at ease within the *TCV*
group than among Grigson's upper-middle-
class university-educated poets (Charles Madge,
Kathleen Raine, Bernard Spencer, Francis
Scarfe). His feelings were based upon political orientation, for the *New Verse* poets carried forward
the Communist allegiances of the Auden-Spender-
Day Lewis generation, whereas Woodcock's political thinking led in a pacifist and libertarian direction during that era of Stalinist purges and
Russian betrayal of the loyalist cause in Spain.

Woodcock's poems of the time present what
he has called "private images of public ills." His
spare imagistic verses depict personal experiences as symbolic of the sense of doom caused by
economic depression, world war, fascism, geno-
cide, and mass movements of exiles. In his mythical poems he exposes the dangers of religious
myths, the social menace of hero worship, and
the blend of bravery and self-delusion embodied
by the social rebel and the agitator. The destruction of World War II prompted Woodcock to

hope, in his "Anarchist Elegies," that a better society would arise from the ashes of the old. Most revealing are his longer discursive poems in which he struggles to find a commitment to ideals within an atmosphere of despair and desolation.

When *New Verse* and *Twentieth Century Verse* ceased publication at the beginning of the war, Woodcock started *Now*. He had been a pacifist since before the Spanish civil war, and the new magazine combined this political bias with the literary goal of promoting "good writing and clear thought." In the summer and fall of 1941 Woodcock met Herbert Read and Marie Louise Berneri (the "darkly beautiful" daughter of the Italian anarchist Camillo Berneri, whom the Communists had assassinated in Barcelona in 1937) and, under their influence, converted to anarchism. *Now*, begun in April 1940, assumed an anarchist viewpoint in its seventh issue, in the autumn of 1941. Through Berneri, Woodcock became associated with Freedom Press, the anarchist publishing house that Peter Kropotkin had founded nearly sixty years before. In 1942 he began to write for the anarchist propaganda organ *War Commentary* (retitled *Freedom* after the war), later becoming one of its editors; he wrote several Freedom Press pamphlets on agriculture, railways, housing, utopian communities, and anarchist morality. In January 1943 *Now* came under the aegis of Freedom Press and in its last nine issues (which ran until 1947) doubled in size, with literary contributions by such writers as Read and Orwell.

Woodcock's friendship with Orwell began in 1942 and lasted until Woodcock departed for Canada. Orwell, a pragmatist and a liberal, showed what Woodcock called an "interested tolerance" toward anarchism and contributed not only articles but also funds to *Now*. Despite their political differences, the two men shared a belief that the freedoms of the individual are fundamental to a healthy society, and they labored together to protect civil liberties from postwar repression.

In the late 1940s Woodcock withdrew gradually from political activism. He was disgusted by the petty factionalism of party politics and argued that anarchist ideals must be scrutinized: his comrades disagreed. The literary life of bohemian London with its stimulating contacts with other writers also ceased to attract Woodcock, and he became disillusioned with the austerities of postwar England. On 10 February 1949 he married Ingeborg Linzer, an artist, and in April they voyaged to Canada. On 14 April, while their ship

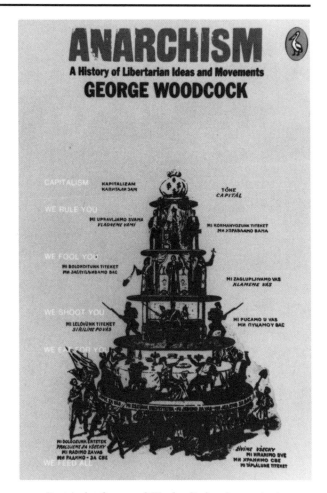

Dust jacket for one of Woodcock's best-known books

lay overnight in Halifax harbor, Berneri, who, in Woodcock's words in the preface to *Notes on Visitations: Poems, 1936-1975* (1975), "had embodied almost everything I stood for during the 1940s," died suddenly at the age of thirty-one. Within a year Orwell, too, was dead.

Though Woodcock's poetic voice was stilled for over two decades by Berneri's death and by the cultural shock of adapting to life in Canada, he had turned decisively to prose before leaving England, embarking upon a career as a biographer. Most of his works in the genre were what he has called "intellectual biographies," centering upon analyses of his subjects' ideas as expressed in their works, while relating these ideas to their lives. His *William Godwin: A Biographical Study* (1946) is a compelling portrait of the founder of modern anarchism, the man who was at first the lionized prophet of his revolutionary age and then the scapegoat for its failed idealism. In contrast, his *The Incomparable Aphra: A Life of Mrs. Aphra Behn* (1948; republished as *Aphra Behn: The En-*

glish Sappho, 1989) and *The Paradox of Oscar Wilde* (1949; republished as *Oscar Wilde: The Double Image,* 1989) are portraits of anarchist underdogs. Woodcock shows not only that Behn was the first Englishwoman to earn her living by writing but also that she espoused several quasi-libertarian principles, including the abolition of slavery. At the same time she was an ambitious royalist and a notorious libertine. Woodcock celebrates Behn for her anarchic spirit of boldly reveling in her own contradictions, though his effort to redeem Wilde from his reputation as sexual pariah makes *The Paradox of Oscar Wilde* a defensive work. Rather than accepting Wilde's untethered personality, he treats the poseur and aesthete too ponderously as an anarchist thinker.

In the 1950s Woodcock's *The Anarchist Prince: A Biographical Study of Peter Kropotkin* (cowritten with Ivan Avakumovic, 1950) and *Pierre-Joseph Proudhon: A Biography* (1956) expressed his growing critical detachment from anarchism. While his sympathy with the "sweet reasonableness" of Kropotkin and the "peasant radicalism" of Proudhon is obvious, he also excoriates the former's excessive optimism and the latter's tendency to couch his social theories and plans in "willful paradoxolatry."

It was with his 1966 study of Orwell, *The Crystal Spirit* (which won the Governor General's Award for nonfiction), that Woodcock reached his maturity as a biographer. In this appealing combination of one-part memoir and three-parts critical analysis, Woodcock balances a fondness for Orwell and a personal knowledge of his foibles with a sense of critical objectivity. The emphasis on ideas is suited to the subject (for Orwell admitted that he was a poor novelist), while Woodcock's emulation of Orwell's lucid "prose like a windowpane" is poignantly apposite. A subsequent book, *Orwell's Message: 1984 and the Present* (1984), further reflects on the relevance of Orwell's ideas to contemporary society.

Over the years between Orwell's death and the writing of *The Crystal Spirit,* Woodcock's retreat from anarchist dogmatism had made him more sympathetic with Orwell's moralistic and nondoctrinaire brand of socialism. His gradually developing portrait of Orwell as essentially a nineteenth-century liberal whose socialism was based upon the principles of brotherhood and decency is the best account of Orwell as a political thinker. Bernard Crick's lengthy authorized biography notwithstanding, Woodcock's view of Orwell as divided between the idealism of Don Quixote and the sensualism of Sancho Panza offers the most illuminating insights into Orwell's character and literary vision.

Later biographies include two further studies of literary figures of the 1930s and 1940s, *Dawn and the Darkest Hour: A Study of Aldous Huxley* and *Herbert Read: The Stream and the Source* (both published in 1972). As a young writer Woodcock had very much admired the "gleaming rationalism" of Huxley's social criticisms but felt betrayed when Huxley became a mystic. In *Dawn and the Darkest Hour* he argues that Huxley's forte is the pasquinade and that in striving to be a mystic Huxley went against his own nature and forsook the talents that had fed his best writing. Though Read had been his political mentor, Woodcock finds that the taciturn Yorkshireman compromised his roles as anarchist and poet in order to achieve the material security and social recognition represented by his acceptance of a knighthood. In these works Woodcock comes to terms with his own "lost leader" syndrome.

For their first few years in Canada, Woodcock and his wife faced harsh conditions. Attempting to realize a Tolstoyan ideal of rural self-sufficiency and an integration of intellectual and manual work, they built two houses in the wilderness near the village of Sooke on Vancouver Island. They gardened (no doubt drawing upon Woodcock's work as a market gardener and land reclaimer performed in lieu of military service because of his conscientious objection to the war), and Woodcock worked as a fruit picker and ditch digger until, after two years, misery forced them to abandon this way of life. The cultural scene was, in Woodcock's view, "as bleak as a Winnipeg winter." *Ravens and Prophets: An Account of Journeys in British Columbia, Alberta and Southern Alaska* (1952) reflects the confusion and regret of a man lost in the native land he did not yet understand. Eventually Woodcock obtained teaching posts at the University of Washington (in 1954-1955) and at the University of British Columbia (1956-1963). In the meantime, he became a radio dramatist and commentator, and later a television documentary scriptwriter and narrator, for the Canadian Broadcasting Corporation. He and his wife still live in Vancouver.

Woodcock's hundreds of radio talks concern the familiar subjects of his periodical writings of the 1940s: European literature, the social consciousness of various authors, artistic freedom, utopias (both literary and practical), trade unions, and anarchism. Though he admits that most of his radio plays are potboilers, there are among them several competent dramas which reflect the coherence and consistency of his thought. These neglected plays convey Woodcock's satirical view of property, the law, and human greed; his Wildean belief that charity is a humiliating stopgap measure which impedes real social change; his interest in the virtues of "primitive" versus "civilized" societies; his concern for the survival of minority peoples within a pluralist society; and his lament for the honorable man whose ideals are crushed by the exigencies of political power. The realistic prose dramas rely upon documentary veracity, while the symbolic verse plays contain characters which are ideas on legs and employ myth, fantasy, and the supernatural to suppress the demands of verisimilitude.

Throughout his difficult early years in Canada, Woodcock continued to write for *Freedom*, though he quarreled with his anarchist comrades in print and abandoned his old battle cry for a revolution of syndicalist unions. In his last article for the magazine, "Nurture the Positive Trends" (27 October 1956), he eschewed the "revolutionary illusion" and urged his fellow anarchists to "nurture the positive trends" toward freedom within a regional and pluralist society. From that time onward, Woodcock remained a "paper anarchist," a reformer and scholar rather than a revolutionary. In *Anarchism: A History of Libertarian Ideas and Movements* (1962) he stresses the anarchist morality of self-knowledge, self-discipline, mutual respect, and cooperation, denigrating those he considers myopic anarchists, such as the egoist Max Stirner, and Mikhail Bakunin's nihilist doppelgänger, Sergei Nechayev. He dispels the common misconception of anarchism as the theoretical justification for bombings and assassinations, the doctrine of misfits and brigands. At the same time, he criticizes its more idealistic tenets: the naive belief in the innate sociability of man, the reluctance to make social plans, and the constant gaze away from the present toward an ideal past or future. Anarchism is impracticable as the unitary philosophy of an entire society, Woodcock admits, but may serve as an ideal to inspire piecemeal social change and to protect group integrity and individual liberty in an age of centralization and uniformity. In *A Political Art: Essays and Images In Honour of George Woodcock* (1978) several of his friends from all periods of his career both praise and take issue with his stands on literature and politics.

Shortly after settling in Canada, Woodcock began to travel extensively and to write travelogues and social histories. *Ravens and Prophets* was followed by books on his journeys in Mexico (*To the City of the Dead*, 1957) and Peru (*Incas and Other Men*, 1959). In the 1960s several trips to the Far East resulted in the travelogues *Faces of India* (1964) and *Asia, Gods and Cities* (1966) and the social histories *The Greeks in India* (1966) and *Kerala: A Portrait of the Malabar Coast* (1967), on the southern Indian region. Then came two books on the British Empire: one a brilliant and richly detailed social history, *The British in the Far East* (1969), and the other a wide-ranging inquiry into the causes of the empire's demise, *Who Killed the British Empire? An Inquest* (1974). Another travelogue, *South Sea Journey* (1976), is based on his voyages in the South Sea Islands, which led also to a documentary television series. In *The Walls of India* (1985) he returns to India and reflects on his perceptions over the several years of his connections with the subcontinent. *Caves in the Desert* (1988) is an account of his 1987 visit to the People's Republic of China. The book describes Woodcock's travels in the north, looking particularly at ancient Buddhist sites along the Silk Road, at Xi'an (the ancient capital), at Datong, and at the edge of the Gobi Desert. *Caves in the Desert* won the 1989 Canadian Authors Association Award for Nonfiction.

All of these travel books are "personal testaments," depicting Woodcock's emotional and intellectual engagement in the drama of reacting to new places and people. He often gains entry to experiences normally closed to outsiders, whether a Samoan feast or an audience with the Dalai Lama. The five-volume chronicle of his twenty years of travels to India records the ebb and flow of an enchantment, beginning with an innocent wonder at the land's complex charm (recorded in *Faces of India*) and ending in suggestions of terrible, irrevocable divisions (presented in *The Walls of India*). Woodcock's exasperation with the subcontinent's social problems has twice prompted direct action. After a visit to northern India in 1961, he and his wife founded the Tibetan Refugee Aid Society to help Tibetans who had fled from Communist oppression in their homeland. For more than eighteen years the society raised and distributed three million dollars through volunteer labor. The Woodcocks have subsequently founded a second support organization, CIVA (Canada-India Village Aid), which assists hospital and dam-building projects in rural India. The pro-

ceeds from *The Walls of India*, among other enterprises, help finance this organization.

Like Woodcock's biographies, most of the
travel works are distinguished by a literary grace-
fulness, comprising a breadth of literary allusion,
an adept use of symbolic scenes and incidents, eloquent and sometimes poetic prose, metaphorical
chapter headings, and a whimsically observant
sense of humor. Woodcock's commitment to social melioration is evinced by his relentless criticisms of racial prejudice, religious intolerance,
economic disparities, and the inequities of imperialism. Ideas are also paramount in his quests for
the national myths of various countries, his speculations about the interrelations between religious
and cultural myths and the origins and movements of peoples, and in his general historical
overviews.

Woodcock's Canadian social histories are informed by his stance as a nonacademic historian
who addresses the public at large. He disparages
the "strictly academic gatherers and arrangers of
facts," as he described them in "The Servants of
Clio: Notes on Creighton and Groulx" (*Canadian
Literature*, Winter 1979), favoring the controversial historians "whose grand coordinating visions
help to shape the way a people or a period will regard itself by giving it a plausible past." Woodcock celebrates Donald Creighton's mythical kind
of history, his deliberately literary style, and his
imaginative insight into "character and circumstance," though he disagrees with Creighton's conservative centralist assumptions. Creighton's virtues, according to Woodcock, affirm the stature
of historical writing as a creative endeavor.

Woodcock's vision of Canada is expounded
in four social histories of the country, *Canada and
the Canadians* (1970), *The Canadians* (1979), *A Social History of Canada* (1988), and *The Century That
Made Us: Canada 1814-1914* (1989), which combine historical analysis with journalistic impres-
sionism, as well as in *Confederation Betrayed!*
(1981) and *Strange Bedfellows: The State and the
Arts in Canada* (1985), in which he attacks Prime
Minister Pierre Elliott Trudeau's centralism and
the interference of a centralist state in regional
publishing and especially broadcasting. It is a pro-
gressivist vision, portraying in Canadian history
the march of progress toward the regional and
pluralist present. As an anarchist, Woodcock argues that Canada's relatively decentralized social
structure enhances local communal life and in-
creases the freedom of individuals and groups.
He sees the country as a "political continuum"

*Dust jacket for Woodcock's study of the Métis leader who was
Louis Riel's companion in the Northwest Rebellion of 1885*

rather than a nation-state and hopes that the
loose federation of regions and peoples will become merely a collection of cantons. In various
pockets of Canadian society, such as the cultures
of the Métis, the Doukhobors, and Inuit, Woodcock discovers anarchist inclinations. His maxim
for Canadian pluralism (and for that of India,
Asia, and the South Sea Islands) is "unity in diversity."

The weaknesses of Woodcock's decentralist
vision of Canada were publicly elucidated when
his radio talk on the "Anti-Nation" was published
in the *Canadian Forum* and then made the basis of
a symposium which occupied an entire issue of
the magazine and became a book, *Nationalism or
Local Control*, edited by Viv Nelles and Abraham
Rotstein in 1973. The contributors pointed out
that the proposal of the division of Canada into
cantons ignores the need for a national bulwark

against American imperialism and neglects the consideration that local control may be no more humane or efficient than a national bureaucracy. It implies, moreover, a problematic limitation of technological development and an incumbent lowering of the standard of living. Its biographical emphasis portrays the past as a drama of individual beliefs and actions, disregarding the clash of groups and the sway of impersonal economic and social forces.

However, Woodcock's myth of Canada does provide a plausible account of the Canadian past. It entails, moreover, a challenge to the conventional historical account of the deeds of great men. Woodcock goes some distance toward fulfilling George Grant's plea for a record of the lives of "the losers of history" in his studies *The Doukhobors* (cowritten with Ivan Avakumovic, 1968), *Gabriel Dumont: The Métis Chief and His Lost World* (1975), and *Peoples of the Coast: The Indians of the Pacific Northwest* (1977). He asserts that the disappearance of these peoples represents an indictment of Canadian democracy. These three volumes are accomplished works which have done much to increase the appreciation of Canada's cultural mosaic. *The Doukhobors* dispels several prejudices and misconceptions about the controversial Russian sect, and Woodcock also refrains from idealizing the Doukhobors as peasant anarchists, as Tolstoy and Kropotkin did in the early years of this century. *Peoples of the Coast* is a groundbreaking omnibus study of several diverse tribes whose advanced arts have enriched British Columbian culture immensely. *Gabriel Dumont: The Métis Chief and His Lost World*, which earned Woodcock his second University of British Columbia Medal for Popular Biography, is a highly imaginative narration based largely upon hearsay and conjecture, featuring an array of villains and symbolic incidents and a thematic tension between Louis Riel, the conventional tragic hero of the Northwest Rebellion of 1885, and his little-known Métis companion, Gabriel Dumont. Woodcock argues that Riel is an unhealthy hero, an ineffectual visionary who represents only "our consciousness of deprivation and alienation from meaningful existence," whereas Dumont, the multilingual and eminently capable man of action, is the authentic leader of a doomed people during the bygone era of the buffalo hunt; as such, he symbolizes both one particular failure and the ongoing challenge of Canadian pluralism.

As in the international travelogues, Woodcock's personal presence is very much a part of

Dust jacket for Woodcock's 1975 poetry collection. As he comments in the preface, the volume is "intended to explain the kind of double background out of which my work has emerged: the England of the Thirties and Forties, complicated in my case by the presence of Canada. . . ."

the drama of his Canadian social histories: he is a part of the action, attending a Doukhobor *sobranie* or simple political-religious community meeting in one instance and a Salish spirit dance in another. Also similar is the persistence of his social criticisms. In *Canada and the Canadians* he presented his centennial portrait of the country, focusing not on glowing depictions of great accomplishments, but on the ways in which economic disparities are shaped by regional and racial power blocs. In *100 Great Canadians* (1980) he included not only the canonized heroes and artists of Canada's "founding peoples" (a nomenclature he rejects because it relegates all but the English and French either to oblivion or to the demeaning category of "native peoples," which implies a stature equal to that of the flora and fauna) but also Métis and Inuit leaders, women's rights activists, mountain men, and bush pilots.

Woodcock's primarily thematic criticism of Canadian literature reflects his self-defined role as a "public critic." Paralleling his attitude as a social historian, he deplores the dogmatism and lack of imagination of most academic criticism, especially the narrow textual approach of the New Critics. The practical critic of an emergent literature must not view the literary text in vacuo, Woodcock insists, but in its intentional, biographical, social, and historical contexts. He believes that good criticism is a matter of "empathetic understanding" and concurs with Herbert Read in eschewing the academic allegiance to universal critical standards. Dismissing the romantic notion of a hierarchy of literary forms, he supports Wilde's contention that criticism must be not merely ancillary to literature but "creative" in its own right.

This eclectic and empathetic kind of criticism has saved Woodcock from the attempts to impose thematic patterns upon Canadian literature presented by Margaret Atwood, D. G. Jones, Frank Davey, and others. In a 1955 manifesto of the duties of the Canadian critic he advised that definitions of the literary tradition should be mitigated by an awareness of the unique sensibility of each author and of the influences of older literatures upon our own. Only in isolated and tentative comments has he intimated that his view of Canadian literature conforms to his vision of its regional and pluralist culture.

Woodcock's best criticisms are his portraits of Canadian writers which make use of his knowledge of broader literary currents. Irving Layton, he argues cogently, is a romantic clown and social rebel whose refusal to edit his muse results in a plethora of throwaway poems and doggerel verse. He perceives that Morley Callaghan is not "a naturalistic writer to be discussed in terms of psychological probability," as Edmund Wilson thought, but a "writer of parables in the moralist tradition" associated with the *récits* of André Gide and Albert Camus. Woodcock shows that A. J. M. Smith's poems reflect "a latter-day classicism enriched by the discoveries of the symbolists and imagists." He also demonstrates that the heroines of Margaret Laurence's Manawaka novels have characters reflecting the ancient humors, and that the novels are dominated respectively by imagery of earth, air, fire, and water. These and other important contributions to Canadian criticism are contained in his three volumes of essays, *Odysseus Ever Returning* (1970), *The World of Canadian Writing* (1980), and *Northern Spring* (1987), and in his monographs *Hugh MacLennan* (1969), *Mordecai*

Richler (1970), *Patrick Lane and His Works* (1984), and *Matt Cohen and His Works* (1988). In addition, Woodcock has edited several critical anthologies on Canadian writers and writing, including *A Place to Stand On: Essays by and about Margaret Laurence* (1983).

In his self-proclaimed role of "field practitioner" of literary criticism, Woodcock has sought to exemplify for the Canadian public how a man of "empathetic imagination" uses and appreciates literature. He has stated his admiration for the structuralist edifice of critic Northrop Frye but has refused to study literature as a self-enclosed system of any kind, insisting that works must be placed in their biographical and social contexts. Hence, he has repeatedly declared his willingness to commit what the American New Critics called the biographical, intentional, and affective fallacies. In general, his criticism has reflected the virtues of an unconstricted Edwardian exercise of taste, including a penchant for frank evaluation, though at times he has succumbed to the "mutual kindliness" shown by Canadian authors and critics and attributable to the smallness of their literary world.

As editor of *Canadian Literature* from 1959 to 1977 Woodcock performed the vital service of providing a meeting place for writers and their audiences at a time when one was much needed. In his maiden editorial he declared: "We welcome the reflections of writers on their own craft with as much interest as the analyses of the critics." Denigrating the "rather academic ferment" of critical anthologies culled from the magazine's pages, he preferred to see the eighteen years of issues that he edited as "a sensitive chronicle, a kind of ongoing history" of "the extraordinary changes which have taken place in writing and in the ambience in which writers work." In accordance with this view, many of Woodcock's articles have been impressionistic surveys of new developments in literature and the literary milieu. *Taking It to the Letter* (1981), a collection of correspondence, records the emerging literary friendships that developed while he supervised the journal; *Beyond the Blue Mountains* also reflects on his years as editor of the journal.

In addition to a Governor General's Award and two U.B.C. medals for biography, Woodcock has received the Molson Prize (1973), the National Magazine Award (1979), and five honorary doctoral degrees; he has declined the Order of Canada because it is an honor conferred by the state rather than by his fellow writers. His most recent books include *The Marvellous Century: A World Awakening* (1988), a social history on the fifth century B.C., and *Powers of Observation* (1989), a collection of thirty-five very brief essays on a variety of topics, written in the 1980s for the periodical *City & Country Home*. Among his current projects are a second book on China and a translation of Proust. Whatever works George Woodcock has yet to offer will no doubt continue to reflect values and predilections formed by the polemical spirit of the 1930s and 1940s in England. The emphasis upon ideas has marked his views of literature, criticism, and history, and the common thread running throughout his labyrinthine oeuvre has been his humane, critical, and reformist version of anarchism. He will doubtless maintain his cosmopolitan interests and social criticisms and remain wary of the shortcomings of academe, writing for the public at large with easy erudition, whimsical humor, irony, ardent idealism, and remarkable versatility.

Letters:

Taking It to the Letter (Montreal: Quadrant, 1981);

Letters from Sooke: A Correspondence between Sir Herbert Read and George Woodcock (Victoria, B.C.: Victoria Book Arts Club, 1982);

The Purdy-Woodcock Letters, edited by George Galt (Toronto: ECW, 1988).

References:

Doug Fetherling, Introduction to *A George Woodcock Reader*, edited by Fetherling (Toronto: Deneau & Greenberg, 1980);

Peter Hughes, *George Woodcock* (Toronto: McClelland & Stewart, 1974);

Viv Nelles and Abraham Rotstein, eds., *Nationalism or Local Control: Responses to George Woodcock* (Toronto: New Press, 1973);

W. H. New, ed., *A Political Art: Essays and Images In Honour of George Woodcock* (Vancouver: University of British Columbia Press, 1978).

Papers:

Most of George Woodcock's papers are held by the Douglas Library, Queen's University. The University of British Columbia Library has manuscripts for his radio broadcasts of the 1950s.

James Wreford
(James Wreford Watson)

(8 February 1915-   )

Jeanette Lynes
Mount Allison University

SELECTED BOOKS: *Of Time and the Lover* (Toronto: McClelland & Stewart, 1950);

General Geography, as J. Wreford Watson (Toronto: Copp Clark, 1957);

North America, Its Countries and Regions, as Watson (London: Longmans, 1963; revised edition, New York: Praeger, 1967; London: Longmans, 1968);

A Geography of Bermuda, by Watson, John Oliver, and C. H. Foggo (London: Collins, 1965);

Canada, Its Problems and Prospects, as Watson (Don Mills, Ont.: Longmans, 1968);

A Social Geography of the United States (London & New York: Longmans, 1979);

Countryside Canada (Fredericton: Fiddlehead, 1979).

OTHER: *Unit of Five,* edited by Ronald Hambleton, includes poetry by Wreford (Toronto: Ryerson, 1944);

Geographical Essays in Memory of Alan E. Ogilvie, edited by Watson and Ronald Miller (London: Nelson, 1959);

The British Isles: A Systematic Geography, edited by Watson and J. B. Sissons (London: Nelson, 1964);

The American Environment: Perceptions and Policies, edited by Watson and Timothy O'Riordan (London & New York: Wiley, 1976).

James Wreford Watson is a distinguished cartographer and social geographer. He also writes poetry, short fiction, and critical reviews. His literary work, written under the name of James Wreford, has been included in anthologies—most notably Ronald Hambleton's *Unit of Five* (1944)—and published in magazines in Great Britain, Canada, and the United States. His first collection of verse, *Of Time and the Lover,* appeared in 1950, and in 1979 his second, *Countryside Canada,* was published.

Front cover for Watson's 1979 poetry collection, his third publication under the name James Wreford

Watson, the son of James Watson, a clergyman, and Evelyn Russell Watson, was born on 8 February 1915 in Shensi, China. He studied in China and Scotland, receiving an M.A. from the University of Edinburgh in 1936. Watson married Jessie Black, a professor of education at Edinburgh, in 1939, and the couple moved to Canada the same year. They have two children, Margaret and James. In 1945 Watson received a Ph.D.

from the University of Toronto. Since 1954 he has resided in Edinburgh.

Watson's career as a geographical researcher and professor of geography has been a long and productive one. He has lectured in geography at the University of Sheffield (1937-1939), at McMaster University, Hamilton, Ontario (1939-1949), and at the University of Edinburgh (1954-1975). He was chief geographer and director of geographical survey for the Canadian government from 1949 to 1954 and director of the Centre of Canadian Studies in Edinburgh from 1975 to 1982. Watson is a fellow of the Royal Societies of Canada and Edinburgh, a member of the Royal Geographical Society, the American Geographical Society, the Association of American Geographers, the Canadian Association of Geographers, and the British Association of American Studies.

Although his work was published in numerous literary periodicals, Watson's place in Canadian poetry rests primarily on two publications: thirteen of his poems included in Ronald Hambleton's important anthology *Unit of Five* and *Of Time and the Lover*, which won a Governor General's Award for 1950.

The six years that elapsed between *Unit of Five* and *Of Time and the Lover* affected little change in Watson's poetic vision and technique. The poems in *Unit of Five* clearly display his technical skill–particularly in the use of the quatrain–and his preoccupation with themes of love, mortality, sin, and redemption. These earlier poems also reveal the weak aspects of Watson's verse: its sometimes obscure quality, its tendency to overuse figurative language, and its penchant for didacticism. Another aspect of Watson's poetic style is the frequent use of questions, which becomes ponderous at times.

Watson's poetry can be classified as Christian pastoral elegy in that many of his poems portray man existing in a fallen world, a moral wilderness marked by conflict, dubious technological development, industrialization, and greed. The poet seeks for himself and mankind a way out of the moral and spiritual wasteland of the modern world. He seeks, in short, redemption, renewed life, and hope. Redemption brings with it the possibility of immortality. In Watson's vision, faith in salvation and love–both sexual and religious love, as Northrop Frye notes–provides the keys to solving modern man's moral and spiritual malaise.

The tone of the speaker in Watson's poems is elegiac–lamenting man's falling away from the green world or state of wholeness and trust in divine authority–and stoic in an Arnoldian vein that advocates a stance of moral balance and alertness and discourages impulsiveness. Watson's speaker points out the strength that may be gained through suffering in "In Snows of Deep December" from *Of Time and the Lover*:

> Yet in the rigid answer
> Of this last, first estate,
> we'll find a steady pattern
> where light and dark equate,
>
> where balance hope and hunger
> love and the pain of love;
> and we may from this winter
> a greater season prove.

Watson's poetic voice is one of control and balance in which despair and a sense of loss are tempered by an inherent belief in the triumph of goodness and truth over wickedness and the certainty of a final redemption or deliverance through Christ.

One of the most unique aspects of Watson's poetry is his use of climatological, geological, and geographical images and metaphors to describe moral conditions within the "map" of human experience. He delineates in his poems a kind of moral geography. The navigational instruments of fallen man, Watson writes in such poems as "Lay Your Brave if Broken Heart," from *Unit of Five*, are limited and fallible: "How shall he hold the heights / or prove his ancient power / whose very map and compass are / the mortal hour?" The map is sometimes a metaphor for a surface or illusory, superficial kind of control, as in "The Warm Front and the Cold." Climatic zones, cloud types, rock and land formations form an integral part of Watson's moral landscape. In *Of Time and the Lover* the north symbolizes "a fixed point in the stress / of time and circumstance." More often, however, the north or wintry zone is associated with a world of despair and alienation. The wearing away of the land–sometimes through human exploitation and sometimes through the forces of time–is a metaphor for the malaise of the modern world, the "erosion and landslip of the times."

Watson's poems sometimes make reference to specific aspects of the modern world, such as industrialization and war, that have contributed to man's fallen state. In "Northland," for example, the "ageless earth" symbolizes God; the north, or "child of the granite shoulder," represents Christ; and man's "plundering" of the landscape with "railways and mines" for profit represents human sin and violation of the divine covenant. Certainly World War II, in Watson's thirteen-part long poem "Of Time and the Lover," is an important aspect of the social and moral chaos characterizing the modern world. But Watson is not primarily a social poet, and he tends to use such subjects as technology and war as illustrations of an abstract conflict between good and evil rather than to treat them as specific issues.

Watson's Christian pastoral elegies point toward apocalypse and judgment. On the day of deliverance and revelation, land forms that demarcate, divide, and create boundaries will dissolve, as Watson writes in "Northland," describing the judgment day in geological terms as "the day that the glaciers descend." In fact, one of the most powerful sequences in Watson's poetry occurs in the final lines of "Of Time and the Lover," in which the poet describes his particular version of geological apocalypse and ultimate liberation:

> And though I go where thunders go
> from gun to gun, and lightnings play
> between electric planes, and glow
> cities that furnace night and day,
> to where the storms in crimson pour
> the pent-up cumulus of war,
>
> yet still the singing in the heart
> swifter than flying feet will fly,
> till longitudes no longer part
> and continents together lie,
> and I can run, and all the way,
> the whole night long, be running into day.

The ending of "Of Time and the Lover" is the strongest part of the poem. In fact, Dorothy Livesay, in her review of Watson's collection, suggested that his compositional strategy consisted of "getting hold of a strong last line and building the poem around it." Reviewers of *Of Time and the Lover* agreed upon Watson's technical skill.

Livesay compared his work to the Canadian poet L. A. MacKay, also "a classicist." Al Purdy and Northrop Frye noted the influence of A. E. Housman on Watson, and Frye, in his poetry survey of "Letters in Canada: 1950," argued that Watson's Canadian predecessor is Archibald Lampman, pointing out their shared concerns with nature and "the city at the end of things." Purdy criticized the obscurity of Watson's poems but praised their "faultless" technique and what he perceives as the greater spontaneity of the love poems as opposed to the more intellectual verse. Purdy called Watson "a happy blend of lyric poet and clear-thinking intellectual." The least favorable reception of Watson's *Of Time and the Lover* came from Livesay, who pointed out, in her review in *Contemporary Verse*, its derivative qualities. Certainly Watson's purpose as a poet was not one of experimentation but he did, as Livesay also recognized, write with a cohesive vision and considerable technical skill.

After a gap of twenty-nine years, Watson's second book of poetry, *Countryside Canada*, appeared. The poems in this volume do not represent any significant change in technique, but they reveal, again, the intellectual at work with words. As though rediscovering his country, Watson here responds through poetry to a series of places, from Newfoundland to the Yukon. Through place—the term that the professional geographer uses to construct and interpret the world—the geographer-poet attempts to demonstrate the strength of his culture and his own personal roots in it. As Michael O. Nowlan put it in a review for *Atlantic Canada* (May 1980), the poet's "style and diction are powerful in describing the vastness of Canada. Moreover, these poems are not for the mystic or strict poetry lover; they are utterances of realistic detail and sense." Watson, as Nowlan observes, writes with "geographer's mind and poet's eye."

Supplementary Reading List

Atlantic Provinces Literature Colloquium. Saint John, New Brunswick: Atlantic Canada Institute, 1977.

Atwood, Margaret. *Survival: A Thematic Guide to Canadian Literature*. Toronto: Anansi, 1972.

Avis, Walter, and others. *A Concise Dictionary of Canadianisms*. Toronto: Gage, 1973.

Bailey, A. G. *Culture and Nationality: Essays*. Toronto: McClelland & Stewart, 1972.

Baillargeon, Samuel. *Littérature canadienne-française*, third edition, revised. Montreal & Paris: Fides, 1960.

Bélisle, Louis-Alexandre. *Dictionnaire général de la langue française au Canada*. Quebec: Bélisle, 1957.

Bélisle. *Dictionnaire nord-américaine de la langue française*. Montreal: Beauchemin, 1979.

Beraud, Jean. *350 Ans de théâtre au Canada français*. Montreal: Cercle du Livre de France, 1958.

Berger, Carl. *The Writing of Canadian History: Aspects of English-Canadian Historical Writing*. Toronto: Oxford University Press, 1976.

Bessette, Gérard. *Une Littérature en ébullition*. Montreal: Editions du Jour, 1968.

Bhabha, Homi. "Representation and the Colonial Text: A Critical Exploration of Some Forms of Mimeticism," in *The Theory of Reading*, edited by Frank Gloversmith. Brighton, Sussex: Harvester, 1984, pp. 93-122.

Blais, Jacques. *De l'ordre et de l'aventure. La Poésie au Québec de 1934 à 1944*. Quebec: Presses de l'Université Laval, 1975.

Blodgett, E. D. *Configuration: Essays on the Canadian Literatures*. Toronto: ECW, 1982.

Bonenfant, Joseph, and others, eds. *A l'ombre de DesRochers: Le Mouvement littéraire des Cantons de l'est 1925-1950*. Sherbrooke, Quebec: Editions de l'Université de Sherbrooke, 1985.

Bonheim, Helmut. *The Narrative Modes: Techniques of the Short Story*. Cambridge: Brewer, 1982.

Brown, E. K. *Responses and Evaluations: Essays on Canada*. Toronto: McClelland & Stewart, 1977.

Brunet, Berthelot. *Histoire de la littérature canadienne-française*. Montreal: L'Arbre, 1946.

Cameron, Donald. *Conversations with Canadian Novelists*, 2 volumes. Toronto: Macmillan, 1973.

The Canadian Encyclopedia, second edition, 4 volumes. Edmonton: Hurtig, 1985.

Canadian Literature Index, quarterly index to book and periodical publications, with annual cumulations, edited by Janet Fraser. Toronto: ECW, 1985- .

Capone, Giovanna. *Canada: il villaggio della terra*. Bologna: Pàtron Editore, 1978.

Cappon, Paul, ed. *In Our House: Social Perspectives on Canadian Literature*. Toronto: McClelland & Stewart, 1978.

Caron, Anne. *Le Père Emile Legault et le théâtre au Québec*. Montreal: Fides, 1978.

Chaudhury, Uta. *Der Frankokanadische Roman de la terre: eine Entwicklungsstudie*. Bern & Frankfurt am Main: Herbert Lang & Peter Lang, 1976.

Cloutier-Wojciechowska, Cécile, and Réjean Robidoux, eds. *Solitude rompue*. Ottawa: Editions de l'Université d'Ottawa, 1986.

Codignola, Luca, ed. *Canadiana*. Venice: Marsilio, 1978.

Collet, Paulette. *L'Hiver dans le roman canadien français*. Quebec: Laval, 1965.

Collin, W. E. *The White Savannahs*. 1936; republished, Toronto & Buffalo: University of Toronto Press, 1975.

Colombo, John Robert. *Colombo's Canadian Quotations*. Edmonton: Hurtig, 1974.

Colombo, comp. *Colombo's Canadian References*. Toronto, Oxford & New York: Oxford University Press, 1976.

Colombo and others, comps. *CDN SF & F: A Bibliography of Science Fiction and Fantasy*. Toronto: Hounslow, 1979.

Craig, Terrence. *Racial Attitudes in English-Canadian Fiction, 1905-1980*. Waterloo: Wilfrid Laurier University Press, 1987.

Cude, Wilfred. *A Due Sense of Differences: An Evaluative Approach to Canadian Literature*. Lanham, Md.: University Press of America, 1980.

Daymond, Douglas. *Towards a Canadian Literature*, volume 2. Ottawa: Tecumseh, 1985.

Daymond, and Leslie Monkman, eds. *Canadian Novelists and the Novel*. Ottawa: Borealis, 1981.

De Leon, Lisa. *Writers of Newfoundland and Labrador*. St. John's: Jesperson, 1985.

Dooley, D. J. *Moral Vision in the Canadian Novel*. Toronto: Clarke, Irwin, 1981.

Ducrocq-Poirier, Madeleine. *Le Roman canadien de langue française de 1860 à 1958*. Paris: Nizet, 1978.

Duffy, Dennis. *Gardens, Covenants, Exiles: Loyalism in the Literature of Upper Canada/Ontario*. Toronto: University of Toronto Press, 1982.

Duhamel, Roger. *Manuel de littérature canadienne-française*. Montreal: Editions du Renouveau Pédagogique, 1967.

Eggleston, Wilfrid. *The Frontier and Canadian Letters*. 1957; republished, Toronto: McClelland & Stewart, 1977.

Egoff, Sheila. *The Republic of Childhood: A Critical Guide to Canadian Children's Literature in English*, second edition. Toronto: Oxford University Press, 1975.

Fairbanks, Carol. *Prairie Women: Images in American and Canadian Fiction*. New Haven & London: Yale University Press, 1986.

Falardeau, Jean-Charles. *Imaginaire social et littérature*. Montreal: Hurtubise HMH, 1974.

Frick, N. Alice. *Image in the Mind: CBC Radio Drama, 1944-1954*. Toronto: Canadian Stage and Arts Publications, 1987.

Frye, Northrop. *The Bush Garden: Essays on the Canadian Imagination*. Toronto: Anansi, 1971.

Frye. *Divisions on a Ground*. Toronto: Anansi, 1982.

Frye. *The Modern Century*. Toronto: Oxford University Press, 1967.

Gagnon, Serge. *Quebec and Its Historians*, 2 volumes, translated by Jane Brierly. Montreal: Harvest House, 1982, 1985.

Gauvin, Lise, and Laurent Mailhot. *Guide culturel de Québec*. Montreal: Boréal Express, 1982.

Gnarowski, Michael. *A Concise Bibliography of English-Canadian Literature*, revised edition. Toronto: McClelland & Stewart, 1978.

Grandpré, Pierre de. *Histoire de la littérature française de Québec*, volume 2, 1900-1945. Montreal: Beauchemin, 1967.

Gross, Konrad, and Wolfgang Klooss, eds. *English Literature of the Dominions*. Würzburg: Verlag Königshausen & Neumann, 1981.

Guillaume, Pierre, Jean-Michel Lacroix, and Pierre Spriet, eds. *Canada et canadiens*. Bordeaux: Presses Universitaires de Bordeaux, 1984.

Hall, Roger, and Gordon Dodds. *Canada: A History in Photographs*. Edmonton: Hurtig, 1981.

Hancock, Geoff. *Canadian Writers at Work: Interviews*. Toronto: Oxford University Press, 1987.

Harper, J. Russell. *Painting in Canada: A History*. Toronto: University of Toronto Press, 1970.

Harrison, Dick. *Unnamed Country: The Struggle for a Canadian Prairie Fiction*. Edmonton: University of Alberta Press, 1977.

Harrison, ed. *Crossing Frontiers*. Edmonton: University of Alberta Press, 1979.

Heath, Jeffrey M., ed. *Profiles in Canadian Literature*, volumes 1-4. Toronto & Charlottetown: Dundurn, 1980-1982.

Innis, Mary Quayle, ed. *The Clear Spirit: Twenty Canadian Women and Their Times*. Toronto: University of Toronto Press, 1966.

Johnson, Harry G. *The Canadian Quandary: Economic Problems and Policies.* Toronto: McClelland & Stewart, 1977.

Jones, D. G. *Butterfly on Rock.* Toronto: University of Toronto Press, 1970.

Jones, Joseph. *Terranglia.* New York: Twayne, 1965.

Kallmann, Helmut, and others. *The Encyclopedia of Music in Canada.* Toronto: University of Toronto Press, 1981.

Keefer, Janice Kulyk. *Under Eastern Eyes: A Critical Reading of Maritime Fiction.* Toronto: University of Toronto Press, 1987.

Keith, W. J. *Canadian Literature in English.* London & New York: Longman, 1985.

Keith, and B. -Z. Shek, eds. *The Arts in Canada: The Last Fifty Years.* Toronto, Buffalo & London: University of Toronto Press, 1980.

Keitner, Wendy, ed. *"Surveying the Territory"* and *"Staking Claims,"* Canadian issues of *Literary Criterion*, 19, 3-4 (1984) and 20, 1 (1985).

Klinck, Carl F., ed. *Literary History of Canada*, 3 volumes, second edition. Toronto: University of Toronto Press, 1976.

Kline, Marcia B. *Beyond the Land Itself: Views of Nature in Canada and the United States.* Cambridge: Harvard University Press, 1970.

Laflamme, Jean, and Rémi Tourangeau. *L'Eglise et le théâtre au Québec.* Montreal: Fides, 1979.

Lafortune, Monique. *Le Roman québécois.* Quebec: Mondia, 1985.

Lecker, Robert, and Jack David, eds. *The Annotated Bibliography of Canada's Major Authors*, 6 volumes, ongoing. Downsview, Ontario: ECW, 1979- .

Lecker and David, eds. *Canadian Writers and Their Works*, 6 volumes, ongoing. Toronto: ECW, 1983- .

Léger, Jules. *Le Canada français et son expression littéraire.* Paris: Nizet & Bastard, 1938.

Legris, Renée, and Pierre Pagé. *Répertoire des dramatiques québécoises à la télévision.* Montreal: Fides, 1977.

Lemieux, Louise. *Pleins feux sur la littérature de jeunesse au Canada français.* Montreal: Leméac, 1972.

Lemire, Maurice. *Les Grands Thèmes nationalistes du roman historique canadien-français.* Quebec: Presses de l'Université Laval, 1970.

"Letters in Canada." Annual review, *University of Toronto Quarterly*, 1936- .

Lewis, Paula Gilbert, ed. *Traditionalism, Nationalism, and Feminism: Women Writers of Quebec.* Westport, Conn. & London: Greenwood Press, 1985.

Lochhead, Douglas, comp. *Bibliography of Canadian Bibliographies*, second edition, revised and enlarged. Toronto: University of Toronto Press, 1972.

MacDermott, Doireann, ed. *Autobiographical and Biographical Writing in the Commonwealth.* Sabadell, Spain: Editorial AUSA, 1984.

Mailhot, Laurent. *La Littérature québécoise.* Paris: Presses Universitaires de France, 1974.

Major, Jean-Louis. *Le Jeu en étoile: Etudes et essais.* Ottawa: Editions de l'Université d'Ottawa, 1978.

Mandel, Eli, ed. *Contexts of Canadian Criticism.* Chicago & London: University of Chicago Press, 1971.

Marcotte, Gilles. *Une Littérature qui se fait. Essais critiques sur la littérature canadienne-française,* second edition. Montreal: HMH, 1968.

Marcotte. *Le Roman à l'imparfait: essai sur le roman québécois d'aujourd'hui.* Montreal: La Presse, 1976.

Marshall, Tom. *Harsh and Lovely Land: Major Canadian Poets and the Making of a Canadian Tradition.* Vancouver: University of British Columbia Press, 1979.

Mathews, Robin. *Canadian Literature: Surrender or Revolution.* Toronto: Steel Rail, 1978.

Maugey, Axel. *Poésie et Société au Québec (1937-1970).* Quebec: Presses de l'Université Laval, 1972.

May, Cedric. *Breaking the Silence: The Literature of Quebec.* Birmingham, U.K.: University of Birmingham, 1981.

McConnell, R. E. *Our Own Voice: Canadian English and How It Is Studied.* Toronto: Gage, 1979.

McCourt, E. A. *The Canadian West in Fiction.* Toronto: Ryerson, 1949.

McGregor, Gaile. *The Wacousta Syndrome: Explorations in the Canadian Langscape.* Toronto, Buffalo & London: University of Toronto Press, 1985.

McKillop, A. B., ed. *Contexts of Canada's Past: Selected Essays of W. L. Morton.* Toronto: Macmillan, 1980.

McLeod, A. L., ed. *The Commonwealth Pen: An Introduction to the Literature of the British Commonwealth.* Ithaca: Cornell University Press, 1961.

Moisan, Clément. *L'Age de la littérature canadienne.* Montreal: Edition HMH, 1969.

Monkman, Leslie. *A Native Heritage: Images of the Indian in English-Canadian Literature.* Toronto: University of Toronto Press, 1981.

Moritz, Albert and Theresa. *The Oxford Illustrated Literary Guide to Canada.* Toronto: Oxford University Press, 1987.

Moss, John. *Patterns of Isolation in English Canadian Fiction.* Toronto: McClelland & Stewart, 1974.

Moss. *A Reader's Guide to the Canadian Novel.* Toronto: McClelland & Stewart, 1981.

Moss. *Sex and Violence in the Canadian Novel.* Toronto: McClelland & Stewart, 1977.

Moss, ed. *Future Indicative: Literary Theory and Canadian Literature.* Ottawa: University of Ottawa Press, 1987.

Moss, ed. *Modern Times: A Critical Anthology.* Toronto: NC Press, 1982.

Narasimhaiah, C. D., ed. *Awakened Conscience.* New Delhi: Sterling, 1978.

New, W. H. *Among Worlds: An Introduction to Modern Commonwealth and South African Fiction.* Erin, Ontario: Press Porcépic, 1975.

New. *Articulating West.* Toronto: New Press, 1972.

New. *Dreams of Speech and Violence: The Art of the Short Story in Canada and New Zealand.* Toronto: University of Toronto Press, 1987.

New. *A History of Canadian Literature.* London: Macmillan, 1989.

New, comp. *Critical Writings on Commonwealth Literatures: A Selective Bibliography to 1970, With a List of Theses and Dissertations.* University Park: Pennsylvania State University Press, 1975.

New, ed. *Dramatists in Canada: Selected Essays.* Vancouver: University of British Columbia Press, 1972.

New, ed. *A Political Art.* Vancouver: University of British Columbia Press, 1978.

Nicholson, Colin, and Peter Easingwood, eds. *Canadian Story and History, 1885-1985.* Edinburgh: Edinburgh University Centre of Canadian Studies, 1985.

Northey, Margot. *The Haunted Wilderness: The Gothic and Grotesque in Canadian Fiction.* Toronto & Buffalo: University of Toronto Press, 1976.

OKanada. Ottawa: Canada Council, 1982.

O'Leary, Dostaler. *Le Roman canadien-français.* Montreal: Cercle du Livre de France, 1954.

Pacey, Desmond. *Creative Writing in Canada,* second edition, revised. Toronto: Ryerson, 1961.

Pacey. *Essays in Canadian Criticism 1938-1968.* Toronto: Ryerson, 1969.

Pache, Walter. *Einführung in die Kanadistik.* Darmstadt: Wissenschaftliche Buchgesellschaft, 1981.

Paradis, Suzanne. *Femme fictive, femme réelle: Le Personnage féminin dans le roman féminin canadien-français, 1884-1966.* Quebec: Garneau, 1966.

Park, Julian, ed. *The Culture of Contemporary Canada.* Ithaca: Cornell University Press, 1957.

Paul-Crouzet, Jeanne. *Poésie au Canada.* Paris: Didier, 1946.

Petrone, Penny, ed. *First People, First Voices.* Toronto: University of Toronto Press, 1983.

Pierce, Lorne. *An Outline of Canadian Literature.* Toronto: Ryerson, 1927.

Press, John, ed. *Commonwealth Literature: Unity and Diversity in a Common Culture.* London: Heinemann Educational, 1965.

Racine, Claude. *L'Anticléricalisme dans le roman québécois, 1940-1965.* Montreal: Hurtubise HMH, 1972.

Rashley, R. E. *Poetry in Canada: The First Three Steps.* Toronto: Ryerson, 1958.

Reid, Dennis. *A Concise History of Canadian Painting.* Toronto, Oxford & New York: Oxford University Press, 1973.

Rhodenizer, V. B. *A Handbook of Canadian Literature.* Ottawa: Graphic, 1930.

Ricou, Laurence R. *Everyday Magic: Child Languages in Canadian Literature.* Vancouver: University of British Columbia Press, 1987.

Ricou. *Vertical Man/Horizontal World.* Vancouver: University of British Columbia Press, 1973.

Riedel, Walter E. *Das Literarische Kanadabild.* Bonn: Bouvier, 1980.

Riedel. *The Old World and the New: Literary Perspectives of German-speaking Canadians.* Toronto: University of Toronto Press, 1984.

Riemenschneider, Dieter, ed. *The History and Historiography of Commonwealth Literature.* Tübingen: Gunter Narr Verlag, 1983.

Rièse, Laure. *L'Ame de la poésie canadienne-française.* Toronto: Macmillan, 1955.

Robidoux, Réjean, and André Renaud. *Le Roman canadien-français du vingtième siècle.* Ottawa: Editions de l'Université d'Ottawa, 1966.

Ross, Malcolm. *The Impossible Sum of Our Traditions: Reflections on Canadian Literature.* Toronto: McClelland & Stewart, 1986.

Ross, ed. *The Arts in Canada.* Toronto: Macmillan, 1958.

Ross, ed. *Our Sense of Identity: A Book of Canadian Essays.* Toronto: Ryerson, 1954.

Roy, Camille. *Manuel d'histoire de la littérature canadienne de langue française,* tenth edition. Montreal: Beauchemin, 1945.

Ryan, Toby Gordon. *Stage Left: Canadian Theatre in the Thirties: A Memoir.* Toronto: CTR, 1981.

Sarkonak, Ralph, ed. "The Language of Difference: Writing in QUEBEC(ois)," special issue of *Yale French Studies,* no. 65 (1983).

Schoeck, Richard J., ed. "Canada," special issue of *Review of National Literature,* 7 (1976).

Servais-Maquoi, Mireille. *Le Roman de la terre au Québec.* Quebec: Presses de l'Université Laval, 1974.

Shek, Ben-Zion. *Aspects of Social Realism in the French-Canadian Novel.* Montreal: Harvest House, 1977.

Sirois, Antoine. *Montréal dans le roman canadien.* Montreal: Didier, 1970.

Smith, A. J. M. *On Poetry and Poets.* Toronto: McClelland & Stewart, 1977.

Smith. *Towards a View of Canadian Letters.* Vancouver: University of British Columbia Press, 1973.

Smith, ed. *Masks of Fiction: Canadian Critics on Canadian Prose.* Toronto: McClelland & Stewart, 1961.

Smith, ed. *Masks of Poetry.* Toronto: McClelland & Stewart, 1962.

Staines, David, ed. *The Canadian Imagination.* Cambridge: Harvard University Press, 1977.

Stephens, Donald G., ed. *Writers of the Prairies.* Vancouver: University of British Columbia Press, 1973.

Stevenson, Lionel. *Appraisals of Canadian Literature.* Toronto: Macmillan, 1926.

Story, G. M., and others, eds. *Dictionary of Newfoundland English.* Toronto: University of Toronto Press, 1982.

Stouck, David. *Major Canadian Authors.* Lincoln: University of Nebraska Press, 1984.

Stratford, Philip. *Bibliography of Canadian Books in Translation: French to English and English to French. Bibliographie de livres canadiens traduits de l'anglais au français et du français à l'anglais.* Ottawa: CCRH, 1977.

Stuart, E. Ross. *The History of Prairie Theatre: The Development of Theatre in Alberta, Manitoba, and Saskatchewan.* Toronto: Simon & Pierre, 1984.

Stuewe, Paul. *Clearing the Ground: English Canadian Literature After Survival.* Toronto: Proper Tales, 1984.

Sutherland, Ronald. *The New Hero: Essays in Comparative Quebec/Canadian Literature.* Toronto: Macmillan, 1977.

Sutherland. *Second Image.* Toronto: New Press, 1971.

Tallman, Warren. *Godawful Streets of Man,* special issue of *Open Letter,* 3, no. 6 (1976-1977).

Taylor, Charles. *Six Journeys: A Canadian Pattern.* Toronto: Anansi, 1977.

Thomas, Clara. *Our Nature—Our Voices: A Guidebook to English-Canadian Literature.* Toronto: New Press, 1972.

Tougas, Gérard. *Histoire de la littérature canadienne-française.* Paris: Presses Universitaires de France, 1960. Translated by Alta Lind Cook as *History of French-Canadian Literature.* Toronto: Ryerson, 1966.

Toye, William, ed. *The Oxford Companion to Canadian Literature.* Toronto: Oxford University Press, 1983.

Trudel, Marcel. *L'influence de Voltaire au Canada,* 2 volumes. Montreal: Fides, 1945.

Turnbull, Jane-M. *Essential traits of French-Canadian poetry.* Toronto: Macmillan, 1938.

Urbas, Jeannette. *From "Thirty Acres" to Modern Times; The Story of French-Canadian Literature.* Toronto & New York: McGraw-Hill Ryerson, 1976.

Véronneau, Pierre, ed. *Histoire du cinéma du Québec,* 2 volumes. Quebec: Musée du cinéma, 1979.

Viatte, Auguste. *Histoire littéraire de l'Amérique française des origines à 1950.* Quebec: Presses Universitaires Laval, 1954.

Wagner, Anton, ed. *The Brock Bibliography of Published Canadian Plays in English 1766-1978.* Toronto: Playwrights, 1980.

Walsh, William. *A Manifold Voice: Studies in Commonwealth Literature.* London: Chatto & Windus, 1970.

Wardhaugh, Ronald. *Language & Nationhood: The Canadian Experience.* Vancouver: New Star, 1983.

Warwick, Jack. *The Long Journey: Literary Themes of French Canada.* Toronto: University of Toronto Press, 1968.

Waterston, Elizabeth. *Survey: A Short History of Canadian Literature.* Toronto: Methuen, 1973.

Watters, R. E. *A Check List of Canadian Literature and Background Material 1628-1950,* revised edition. Toronto: University of Toronto Press, 1972.

Wilson, Edmund. *O Canada: An American's Notes on Canadian Culture.* New York: Farrar, Straus & Giroux, 1965.

Woodcock, George. *Canada and the Canadians.* Toronto: Oxford University Press, 1970.

Woodcock. *Northern Spring.* Vancouver: Douglas & McIntyre, 1987.

Woodcock. *Odysseus Ever Returning: Essays on Canadian Writers and Writing.* Toronto: McClelland & Stewart, 1970.

Woodcock. *The World of Canadian Writing.* Vancouver: Douglas & McIntyre, 1980; Seattle: University of Washington Press, 1980.

Woodcock, ed. *The Canadian Novel in the Twentieth Century.* Toronto: McClelland & Stewart, 1975.

Woodcock, ed. *A Choice of Critics.* Toronto: Oxford University Press, 1966.

Woodcock, ed. *Poets and Critics.* Toronto, Oxford & New York: Oxford University Press, 1974.

Wyczynski, Paul, and others. *Archives des lettres canadiennes.* Montreal: Fides. No. 2 (*Ecole littéraire de Montréal,* 1972); no. 3 (*Roman,* 1971); no. 4 (*Poésie,* 1969); no. 5 (*Théâtre,* 1976).

Contributors

Alexandre L. Amprimoz...*Brock University*
Neil Besner..*University of Winnipeg*
Russell Brown................................*University of Toronto, Scarborough Campus*
Roger Chamberland..*Université Laval*
William Christian ....*University of Guelph*
Fred Cogswell..*University of New Brunswick*
Frank Davey..*York University*
Anne de Fabry..*King's College*
Paul Denham ....*University of Saskatchewan*
Sandra Djwa ....*Simon Fraser University*
D. J. Dooley ....*St. Michael's College, University of Toronto*
Gwladys Downes..*University of Victoria*
Margery Fee ....*Queen's University at Kingston*
Louise H. Forsyth...*University of Western Ontario*
Wynne Francis ....*Concordia University*
Keith Garebian..*Mississauga, Ontario*
Richard Giguère ....*Université de Sherbrooke*
Susan Gingell..*University of Saskatchewan*
Jill Tomasson Goodwin..*University of Waterloo*
Sherrill E. Grace ....*University of British Columbia*
Gerry Gross...*Concordia University*
Ralph Gustafson...*North Hatley, Quebec*
John E. Hare ....*University of Ottawa*
Susan Jackel..*University of Alberta*
Chris Johnson ....*University of Manitoba*
George Johnston ....*Carleton University*
J. Kieran Kealy ....*University of British Columbia*
Jane Koustas...*Redeemer College*
Jeanette Lynes ....*Mount Allison University*
Louis K. MacKendrick ....*University of Windsor*
T. D. MacLulich ....*Victoria, British Columbia*
Lorraine McMullen...*University of Ottawa*
Grazia Merler ....*Simon Fraser University*
Allison Mitcham...*University of Moncton*
Ann Munton ....*University of British Columbia*
Ira Bruce Nadel ....*University of British Columbia*
W. H. New ....*University of British Columbia*
Barbara Opala...*Concordia University*
Barbara Pell..*Trinity Western University*
Laurie Ricou ....*University of British Columbia*
John Ripley..*McGill University*
Wendy Robbins ....*University of New Brunswick*
Jack Robinson..*Grant MacEwan Community College*
Hans R. Runte..*Dalhousie University*
Antoine Sirois ....*Université de Sherbrooke*
Peter Stevens..*University of Windsor*

Paul Matthew St. Pierre ....*Simon Fraser University*
Walter E. Swayze ....*University of Winnipeg*
Lee Briscoe Thompson ....*University of Vermont*
Jean Vigneault ....*Université de Sherbrooke*
Jerry Wasserman ....*University of British Columbia*
Elizabeth Waterston ....*University of Guelph*
Lorraine Weir ....*University of British Columbia*
George Woodcock ....*Vancouver, British Columbia*

Cumulative Index

Dictionary of Literary Biography, Volumes 1-88
Dictionary of Literary Biography Yearbook, 1980-1988
Dictionary of Literary Biography Documentary Series, Volumes 1-6

Cumulative Index

DLB before number: *Dictionary of Literary Biography,* Volumes 1-88
Y before number: *Dictionary of Literary Biography Yearbook,* 1980-1988
DS before number: *Dictionary of Literary Biography Documentary Series,* Volumes 1-6

A

B

F

G

Giono, Jean 1895-1970................................DLB-72

Giovanni, Nikki 1943-......................DLB-5, 41

Gipson, Lawrence Henry 1880-1971.................DLB-17

Giraudoux, Jean 1882-1944................................DLB-65

Gissing, George 1857-1903................................DLB-18

Gladstone, William Ewart 1809-1898................DLB-57

Glaeser, Ernst 1902-1963................................DLB-69

Glanville, Brian 1931-................................DLB-15

Glapthorne, Henry 1610-1643?........................DLB-58

Glasgow, Ellen 1873-1945................................DLB-9, 12

Glaspell, Susan 1876-1948........................DLB-7, 9, 78

Glass, Montague 1877-1934................................DLB-11

Glassco, John 1909-1981................................DLB-68

Glauser, Friedrich 1896-1938................................DLB-56

F. Gleason's Publishing Hall................................DLB-49

Glück, Louise 1943-................................DLB-5

Godbout, Jacques 1933-................................DLB-53

Goddard, Morrill 1865-1937................................DLB-25

Goddard, William 1740-1817................................DLB-43

Godey, Louis A. 1804-1878................................DLB-73

Godey and McMichael................................DLB-49

Godfrey, Dave 1938-................................DLB-60

Godfrey, Thomas 1736-1763................................DLB-31

Godine, David R., Publisher................................DLB-46

Godkin, E. L. 1831-1902................................DLB-79

Godwin, Gail 1937-................................DLB-6

Godwin, Parke 1816-1904................................DLB-3, 64

Godwin, William 1756-1836................................DLB-39

Goes, Albrecht 1908-................................DLB-69

Goffe, Thomas circa 1592-1629................................DLB-58

Goffstein, M. B. 1940-................................DLB-61

Gogarty, Oliver St. John 1878-1957............DLB-15, 19

Goines, Donald 1937-1974................................DLB-33

Gold, Herbert 1924-................................DLB-2; Y-81

Gold, Michael 1893-1967................................DLB-9, 28

Goldberg, Dick 1947-................................DLB-7

Golding, William 1911-................................DLB-15

Goldman, William 1931-................................DLB-44

Goldsmith, Oliver 1730 or 1731-1774................DLB-39

Goldsmith Publishing Company................................DLB-46

Gomme, Laurence James
 [publishing house]................................DLB-46

González-T., César A. 1931-................................DLB-82

The Goodman Theatre................................DLB-7

Goodrich, Frances 1891-1984 and
 Hackett, Albert 1900-................................DLB-26

Goodrich, S. G. [publishing house]................DLB-49

Goodrich, Samuel Griswold 1793-1860 ...DLB-1, 42, 73

Goodspeed, C. E., and Company................................DLB-49

Goodwin, Stephen 1943-................................Y-82

Gookin, Daniel 1612-1687................................DLB-24

Gordon, Caroline 1895-1981................DLB-4, 9; Y-81

Gordon, Giles 1940-................................DLB-14

Gordon, Mary 1949-................................DLB-6; Y-81

Gordone, Charles 1925-................................DLB-7

Gorey, Edward 1925-................................DLB-61

Gosse, Edmund 1849-1928................................DLB-57

Gotlieb, Phyllis 1926-................................DLB-88

Gould, Wallace 1882-1940................................DLB-54

Goyen, William 1915-1983................................DLB-2; Y-83

Gracq, Julien 1910-................................DLB-83

Grady, Henry W. 1850-1889................................DLB-23

Graf, Oskar Maria 1894-1967................................DLB-56

Graham, George Rex 1813-1894................................DLB-73

Graham, Gwethalyn 1913-1965................................DLB-88

Graham, Lorenz 1902-................................DLB-76

Graham, Shirley 1896-1977................................DLB-76

Graham, W. S. 1918-................................DLB-20

Graham, William H. [publishing house]............DLB-49

Graham, Winston 1910-................................DLB-77

Grahame, Kenneth 1859-1932................................DLB-34

Gramatky, Hardie 1907-1979................................DLB-22

Granich, Irwin (see Gold, Michael)

Grant, George 1918-1988................................DLB-88

Grant, Harry J. 1881-1963................................DLB-29

Grant, James Edward 1905-1966................................DLB-26

Grass, Günter 1927-................................DLB-75

Grasty, Charles H. 1863-1924................................DLB-25

Grau, Shirley Ann 1929-................................DLB-2

Graves, John 1920-................................Y-83

Graves, Richard 1715-1804................................DLB-39

Graves, Robert 1895-1985................................DLB-20; Y-85

H

Cumulative Index

N

P

Q